POETRY
for Students

Advisors

Jayne M. Burton: Language Arts Teacher, Samuel V. Champion High School, Boerne, Texas. B.A. from Christopher Newport University. Member of National Council of Teachers of English and Sigma Tau Delta International English Honor Society; Chapter President of Delta Kappa Gamma International Society for Key Women Educators.

Kate Hamill: English Teacher, Catonsville High School, Catonsville, Maryland. B.A. from Pomona College; M.A. from University of Virginia; MSEd from University of Maryland.

Mary Beth Maggio: Language Arts Teacher, Schaumburg District No. 54, Schaumburg, Illinois. B.A. from Illinois State University; M.A. from Northern Illinois University.

Thomas Shilts: Youth Librarian, Capital Area District Library, Okemos, Michigan. M.S.L.S. from Clarion University of Pennsylvania; M.A. from University of North Dakota.

Amy Spade Silverman: Taught at independent schools in California, Michigan, Texas, and New York. B.A. from University of Michigan; M.F.A. from University of Houston. Member of National Council of Teachers of English, Teachers and Writers, and NCTE Opinion Panel. Exam Reader, Advanced Placement Literature and Composition. Poet, published in *North American Review*, *Nimrod*, and *Michigan Quarterly Review*, among other publications.

Mary Turner: English and AP Literature and Composition Teacher. B.S. from East Texas University; MEd from Western Kentucky University.

Laura Jean Waters: Certified School Library Media Specialist, Wilton High School, Wilton, Connecticut. B.A. from Fordham University; M.A. from Fairfield University.

POETRY
for Students

**Presenting Analysis, Context, and Criticism
on Commonly Studied Poetry**

VOLUME 38

Sara Constantakis, Project Editor

Foreword by David J. Kelly

GALE
CENGAGE Learning

Detroit • New York • San Francisco • New Haven, Conn • Waterville, Maine • London

GALE
CENGAGE Learning

Poetry for Students, Volume 38

Project Editor: Sara Constantakis

Rights Acquisition and Management: Margaret Chamberlain-Gaston, Sara Crane

Composition: Evi Abou-El-Seoud

Manufacturing: Rhonda Dover

Imaging: John Watkins

Product Design: Pamela A. E. Galbreath, Jennifer Wahi

Content Conversion: Katrina Coach

Product Manager: Meggin Condino

© 2011 Gale, Cengage Learning

ALL RIGHTS RESERVED. No part of this work covered by the copyright herein may be reproduced, transmitted, stored, or used in any form or by any means graphic, electronic, or mechanical, including but not limited to photocopying, recording, scanning, digitizing, taping, Web distribution, information networks, or information storage and retrieval systems, except as permitted under Section 107 or 108 of the 1976 United States Copyright Act, without the prior written permission of the publisher.

Since this page cannot legibly accommodate all copyright notices, the acknowledgments constitute an extension of the copyright notice.

For product information and technology assistance, contact us at
Gale Customer Support, 1-800-877-4253.
For permission to use material from this text or product,
submit all requests online at **www.cengage.com/permissions.**
Further permissions questions can be emailed to
permissionrequest@cengage.com

While every effort has been made to ensure the reliability of the information presented in this publication, Gale, a part of Cengage Learning, does not guarantee the accuracy of the data contained herein. Gale accepts no payment for listing; and inclusion in the publication of any organization, agency, institution, publication, service, or individual does not imply endorsement of the editors or publisher. Errors brought to the attention of the publisher and verified to the satisfaction of the publisher will be corrected in future editions.

Gale
27500 Drake Rd.
Farmington Hills, MI, 48331-3535

ISBN-13: 978-1-4144-6705-4
ISBN-10: 1-4144-6705-2

ISSN 1094-7019

This title is also available as an e-book.
ISBN-13: 978-1-4144-7389-5
ISBN-10: 1-4144-7389-3
Contact your Gale, a part of Cengage Learning sales representative for ordering information.

Table of Contents

Just a Few Lines on a Page

I have often thought that poets have the easiest job in the world. A poem, after all, is just a few lines on a page, usually not even extending margin to margin—how long would that take to write, about five minutes? Maybe ten at the most, if you wanted it to rhyme or have a repeating meter. Why, I could start in the morning and produce a book of poetry by dinnertime. But we all know that it isn't that easy. Anyone can come up with enough words, but the poet's job is about writing the *right* ones. The right words will change lives, making people see the world somewhat differently than they saw it just a few minutes earlier. The right words can make a reader who relies on the dictionary for meanings take a greater responsibility for his or her own personal understanding. A poem that is put on the page correctly can bear any amount of analysis, probing, defining, explaining, and interrogating, and something about it will still feel new the next time you read it.

It would be fine with me if I could talk about poetry without using the word "magical," because that word is overused these days to imply "a really good time," often with a certain sweetness about it, and a lot of poetry is neither of these. But if you stop and think about magic—whether it brings to mind sorcery, witchcraft, or bunnies pulled from top hats—it always seems to involve stretching reality to produce a result greater than the sum of its parts and pulling unexpected results out of thin air. This book provides ample cases where a few simple words conjure up whole worlds. We do not actually travel to different times and different cultures, but the poems get into our minds, they find what little we know about the places they are talking about, and then they make that little bit blossom into a bouquet of someone else's life. Poets make us think we are following simple, specific events, but then they leave ideas in our heads that cannot be found on the printed page. Abracadabra.

Sometimes when you finish a poem it doesn't feel as if it has left any supernatural effect on you, like it did not have any more to say beyond the actual words that it used. This happens to everybody, but most often to inexperienced readers: regardless of what is often said about young people's infinite capacity to be amazed, you have to understand what usually does happen, and what could have happened instead, if you are going to be moved by what someone has accomplished. In those cases in which you finish a poem with a "So what?" attitude, the information provided in *Poetry for Students* comes in handy. Readers can feel assured that the poems included here actually are potent magic, not just because a few (or a hundred or ten thousand) professors of literature say they are: they're significant because they can withstand close inspection and still amaze the very same people who have just finished taking them apart and seeing how they work. Turn them inside out, and they will still be able to come alive, again and again. *Poetry for Students* gives readers of any age good practice in feeling the ways poems relate to both the reality of the time and place the poet lived in and the reality of our emotions. Practice is just another word for being a student. The information given here helps you understand the way to read poetry; what to look for, what to expect.

With all of this in mind, I really don't think I would actually like to have a poet's job at all. There are too many skills involved, including precision, honesty, taste, courage, linguistics, passion, compassion, and the ability to keep all sorts of people entertained at once. And that is just what they do with one hand, while the other hand pulls some sort of trick that most of us will never fully understand. I can't even pack all that I need for a weekend into one suitcase, so what would be my chances of stuffing so much life into a few lines? With all that *Poetry for Students* tells us about each poem, I am impressed that any poet can finish three or four poems a year. Read the inside stories of these poems, and you won't be able to approach any poem in the same way you did before.

David J. Kelly
College of Lake County

Introduction

Purpose of the Book

The purpose of *Poetry for Students* (*PfS*) is to provide readers with a guide to understanding, enjoying, and studying poems by giving them easy access to information about the work. Part of Gale's "For Students" Literature line, *PfS* is specifically designed to meet the curricular needs of high school and undergraduate college students and their teachers, as well as the interests of general readers and researchers considering specific poems. While each volume contains entries on "classic" poems frequently studied in classrooms, there are also entries containing hard-to-find information on contemporary poems, including works by multicultural, international, and women poets.

The information covered in each entry includes an introduction to the poem and the poem's author; the actual poem text (if possible); a poem summary, to help readers unravel and understand the meaning of the poem; analysis of important themes in the poem; and an explanation of important literary techniques and movements as they are demonstrated in the poem.

In addition to this material, which helps the readers analyze the poem itself, students are also provided with important information on the literary and historical background informing each work. This includes a historical context essay, a box comparing the time or place the poem was written to modern Western culture, a critical overview essay, and excerpts from critical essays on the poem. A unique feature of *PfS* is a specially commissioned critical essay on each poem, targeted toward the student reader.

To further help today's student in studying and enjoying each poem, information on audio recordings and other media adaptations is provided (if available), as well as reading suggestions for works of fiction and nonfiction on similar themes and topics. Classroom aids include ideas for research papers and lists of critical and reference sources that provide additional material on the poem.

Selection Criteria

The titles for each volume of *PfS* are selected by surveying numerous sources on notable literary works and analyzing course curricula for various schools, school districts, and states. Some of the sources surveyed include: high school and undergraduate literature anthologies and textbooks; lists of award-winners, and recommended titles, including the Young Adult Library Services Association (YALSA) list of best books for young adults.

Input solicited from our expert advisory board—consisting of educators and librarians—guides us to maintain a mix of "classic" and contemporary literary works, a mix of challenging and engaging works (including genre titles that are commonly studied) appropriate for different age levels, and a mix of international, multicultural and women authors. These advisors also consult on each volume's entry list, advising on which titles are most studied, most appropriate, and meet the broadest interests across secondary (grades 7–12) curricula and undergraduate literature studies.

How Each Entry Is Organized

Each entry, or chapter, in *PfS* focuses on one poem. Each entry heading lists the full name of the poem, the author's name, and the date of the poem's publication. The following elements are contained in each entry:

Introduction: a brief overview of the poem which provides information about its first appearance, its literary standing, any controversies surrounding the work, and major conflicts or themes within the work.

Author Biography: this section includes basic facts about the poet's life, and focuses on events and times in the author's life that inspired the poem in question.

Poem Text: when permission has been granted, the poem is reprinted, allowing for quick reference when reading the explication of the following section.

Poem Summary: a description of the major events in the poem. Summaries are broken down with subheads that indicate the lines being discussed.

Themes: a thorough overview of how the major topics, themes, and issues are addressed within the poem. Each theme discussed appears in a separate subhead.

Style: this section addresses important style elements of the poem, such as form, meter, and rhyme scheme; important literary devices used, such as imagery, foreshadowing, and symbolism; and, if applicable, genres to which the work might have belonged, such as Gothicism or Romanticism. Literary terms are explained within the entry, but can also be found in the Glossary.

Historical Context: this section outlines the social, political, and cultural climate in which the author lived and the poem was created. This section may include descriptions of related historical events, pertinent aspects of daily life in the culture, and the artistic and literary sensibilities of the time in which the work was written. If the poem is a historical work, information regarding the time in which the poem is set is also included. Each section is broken down with helpful subheads.

Critical Overview: this section provides background on the critical reputation of the poem, including bannings or any other public controversies surrounding the work. For older works, this section includes a history of how the poem was first received and how perceptions of it may have changed over the years; for more recent poems, direct quotes from early reviews may also be included.

Criticism: an essay commissioned by *PfS* which specifically deals with the poem and is written specifically for the student audience, as well as excerpts from previously published criticism on the work (if available).

Sources: an alphabetical list of critical material quoted in the entry, with full bibliographical information.

Further Reading: an alphabetical list of other critical sources which may prove useful for the student. Includes full bibliographical information and a brief annotation.

Suggested Search Terms: a list of search terms and phrases to jumpstart students' further information seeking. Terms include not just titles and author names but also terms and topics related to the historical and literary context of the works.

In addition, each entry contains the following highlighted sections, set apart from the main text as sidebars:

Media Adaptations: if available, a list of audio recordings as well as any film or television adaptations of the poem, including source information.

Topics for Further Study: a list of potential study questions or research topics dealing with the poem. This section includes questions related to other disciplines the student may be studying, such as American history, world history, science, math, government, business, geography, economics, psychology, etc.

Compare & Contrast: an "at-a-glance" comparison of the cultural and historical differences between the author's time and culture and late twentieth century or early twenty-first century Western culture. This box includes pertinent parallels between the major scientific, political, and cultural movements of the time or place the poem was written, the time or place the poem was set (if a historical work), and modern Western culture. Works written after 1990 may not have this box.

What Do I Read Next?: a list of works that might give a reader points of entry into a classic work (e.g., YA or multicultural titles) and/ or complement the featured poem or serve as a contrast to it. This includes works by the same author and others, works from various genres, YA works, and works from various cultures and eras.

Other Features

PfS includes "Just a Few Lines on a Page," a foreword by David J. Kelly, an adjunct professor of English, College of Lake County, Illinois. This essay provides a straightforward, unpretentious explanation of why poetry should be marveled at and how *PfS* can help teachers show students how to enrich their own reading experiences.

A Cumulative Author/Title Index lists the authors and titles covered in each volume of the *PfS* series.

A Cumulative Nationality/Ethnicity Index breaks down the authors and titles covered in each volume of the *PfS* series by nationality and ethnicity.

A Subject/Theme Index, specific to each volume, provides easy reference for users who may be studying a particular subject or theme rather than a single work. Significant subjects from events to broad themes are included.

A Cumulative Index of First Lines (beginning in Vol. 10) provides easy reference for users who may be familiar with the first line of a poem but may not remember the actual title.

A Cumulative Index of Last Lines (beginning in Vol. 10) provides easy reference for users who may be familiar with the last line of a poem but may not remember the actual title.

Each entry may include illustrations, including photo of the author and other graphics related to the poem.

Citing Poetry for Students

When writing papers, students who quote directly from any volume of *PfS* may use the following general forms. These examples are based on MLA style; teachers may request that students adhere to a different style, so the following examples may be adapted as needed.

When citing text from *PfS* that is not attributed to a particular author (i.e., the Themes, Style, Historical Context sections, etc.), the following format should be used in the bibliography section:

"Angle of Geese." *Poetry for Students*. Ed. Marie Napierkowski and Mary Ruby. Vol. 2. Detroit: Gale, 1998. 8–9.

When quoting the specially commissioned essay from *PfS* (usually the first piece under the "Criticism" subhead), the following format should be used:

Velie, Alan. Critical Essay on "Angle of Geese." *Poetry for Students*. Ed. Marie Napierkowski and Mary Ruby. Vol. 2. Detroit: Gale, 1998. 7–10.

When quoting a journal or newspaper essay that is reprinted in a volume of *PfS,* the following form may be used:

Luscher, Robert M. "An Emersonian Context of Dickinson's 'The Soul Selects Her Own Society'." *ESQ: A Journal of American Renaissance* 30.2 (1984): 111–16. Excerpted and reprinted in *Poetry for Students*. Ed. Marie Napierkowski and Mary Ruby. Vol. 1. Detroit: Gale, 1998. 266–69.

When quoting material reprinted from a book that appears in a volume of *PfS,* the following form may be used:

Mootry, Maria K. "'Tell It Slant': Disguise and Discovery as Revisionist Poetic Discourse in 'The Bean Eaters'." *A Life Distilled: Gwendolyn Brooks, Her Poetry and Fiction*. Ed. Maria K. Mootry and Gary Smith. Urbana: University of Illinois Press, 1987. 177–80, 191. Excerpted and reprinted in *Poetry for Students*. Ed. Marie Napierkowski and Mary Ruby. Vol. 2. Detroit: Gale, 1998. 22–24.

We Welcome Your Suggestions

The editorial staff of *Poetry for Students* welcomes your comments and ideas. Readers who wish to suggest poems to appear in future volumes, or who have other suggestions, are cordially invited to contact the editor. You may contact the editor via E-mail at: **ForStudentsEditors@cengage.com.** Or write to the editor at:

Editor, *Poetry for Students*
Gale
27500 Drake Road
Farmington Hills, MI 48331-3535

Literary Chronology

c. 620 BCE: Sappho is born in Mytilene, Greece.

c. 580 BCE: Sappho's "Fragment 16" is written.

c. 560 BCE: Sappho dies in Mytilene, Greece.

1770: William Wordsworth is born on April 7 in Cockermouth, Cumberland, England.

1807: William Wordsworth's "The World Is Too Much with Us" is published in *Poems in Two Volumes*.

1821: Charles Baudelaire is born on April 9 in Paris, France.

1850: William Wordsworth dies on April 23 at Rydal Mount, Rydal, Westmoreland, England.

1857: Charles Baudelaire's "Invitation to a Voyage" is published in *The Flowers of Evil*.

1867: Charles Baudelaire dies of the after-effects of a stroke and life-long drug addiction on August 31 in Paris, France.

1874: Gertrude Stein is born on February 3 in Allegheny, Pennsylvania.

1887: Marianne Moore is born on November 15 in Kirkwood, Missouri.

1898: Federico García Lorca is born on June 5 in Andalusia, Spain.

1902: Langston Hughes is born James Langston Hughes on February 1 in Joplin, Missouri.

1902: Nazim Hikmet is born on January 15 in Salonikan in the Ottoman Empire.

1913: May Swenson is born on May 28 in Logan, Utah (some sources cite 1919).

1914: Octavio Paz is born on March 31 in Mexico City, Mexico.

1918: Alexander Solzhenitsyn is born on December 11 in Kislovodsk, Russia.

1923: Marianne Moore's "Marriage" is published.

1925: Langston Hughes's "Weary Blues" is published in *Opportunity* magazine.

1925: Maxine Kumin is born on June 6 in Philadelphia, Pennsylvania.

1926: Frank O'Hara is born on March 27 in Baltimore, Maryland.

1928: Maya Angelou is born on April 4 in St. Louis, Missouri.

1931: Federico García Lorca's "The Guitar" is published in Spanish in *Poema del cante jondo*. It is published in English in *Poem of the Deep Song*.

1933: Nazim Hikmet's "Letter to My Wife" is written while he was in prison.

1936: Dahlia Ravikovitch is born on November 17 in Ramat Gan, Palestine.

1936: Federico Garcí Lorca is executed on August 18 or 19 in Granada, Spain.

1946: Bei Dao is born Zhao Zenkai on August 2 in Beijing, China.

1946: Gertrude Stein dies of complications from stomach cancer on July 27 in Paris, France.

1949: Octavio Paz's "Dos Cuerpos" is published in Spanish in *Libertad bajo palabra*. It is published in English in 1959.

1952: Marianne Moore is awarded the Pulitzer Prize for Poetry.

1956: Gertrude Stein's "Stanza LXXXIII" is published in *Stanzas in Meditation*. It was written in 1932.

1961: Maxine Kumin's "400-Meter Freestyle" is published in *Halfway*.

1963: Nazim Hikmet dies of a heart attack on June 3 in Moscow, Russia.

1964: Alexander Solzhenitsyn's "A Storm in the Mountains" is published in Russian in the journal *Grani*. It is published in English in 1971 in *Stories and Prose Poems*.

1964: Frank O'Hara's "Poem (Lana Turner Has Collapsed)" is published in *Lunch Poems*.

1966: Frank O'Hara dies after being hit by a car on July 25 in Long Island, New York.

1967: Langston Hughes dies following prostrate surgery on May 22 in the Harlem neighborhood of New York, New York.

1967: May Swenson's "Fable For When There's No Way Out" is published in *Half Sun Half Sleep*..

1969: Dahlia Ravikovitch's "Pride" is published in Hebrew in *The Third Book*. It is later translated into English.

1970: Alexander Solzhenitsyn is awarded the Nobel Prize in Literature.

1972: Marianne Moore dies on February 5 in New York, New York.

1978: Maya Angelou's "Still I Rise" is published in *And Still I Rise*.

1989: May Swenson dies of a heart attack on December 4 in Ocean View, Delaware.

1990: Bei Dao's "All" is published in *The August Sleepwalker*.

1990: Octavio Paz is awarded the Nobel Prize in Literature.

1998: Octavio Paz dies of cancer on April 19 in Mexico City, Mexico.

2005: Dahlia Ravikovitch dies on August 21 in Tel Aviv, Israel.

2008: Alexander Solzhenitsyn dies of heart failure on August 3 in Moscow, Russia.

Acknowledgments

The editors wish to thank the copyright holders of the excerpted criticism included in this volume and the permissions managers of many book and magazine publishing companies for assisting us in securing reproduction rights. We are also grateful to the staffs of the Detroit Public Library, the Library of Congress, the University of Detroit Mercy Library, Wayne State University Purdy/ Kresge Library Complex, and the University of Michigan Libraries for making their resources available to us. Following is a list of the copyright holders who have granted us permission to reproduce material in this volume of *PFS*. Every effort has been made to trace copyright, but if omissions have been made, please let us know.

COPYRIGHTED EXCERPTS IN *PfS*, VOLUME 38, WERE REPRODUCED FROM THE FOLLOWING PERIODICALS:

American Poetry Review, v. 23, September-October 1994; v. 29, March/April 2000. Copyright © 1994, 2000 by *The American Poetry Review*. Reproduced by permission.—*Callaloo*, v. 19, Winter 1996. Copyright © 1996 by Johns Hopkins University Press. Reproduced by permission.—*Canadian Review of American Studies*, v. 21, 1990. Copyright © 1990 by *Canadian Review of American Studies*. Reproduced by permission.—*Contemporary Literature*, v. 32, Summer 1991. Copyright © 1991 by The University of Wisconsin Press. Reproduced by permission.—*Criticism*, v. 48, Summer 2006.

Copyright © 2006 by Wayne State University Press. Reproduced by permission.—*Iowa Review*, Summer/Fall 1975. Copyright © 1975 by *The Iowa Review*. Reproduced by permission.—*Middle East*, April 2002. Copyright © 2002 by Al Bawaba, Ltd. Reproduced by permission.—*Modern Language Quarterly*, v. 66, December 2005. Copyright © 2005 by Duke University Press. Reproduced by permission.—*Nation*, v. 22, April 27, 1876. Copyright © 1876 by *The Nation*. Reproduced by permission.—*positions: East Asia Cultures Critique*, v. 15, 2007. Copyright © 2001 by University of Oklahoma and by Duke University Press. Re-produced by permission.—*Journal of Modern Literature*, v. 5, September 1976; v. 30, Summer 2007; v. 31, Fall 2007; v. 33, Winter 2010. Copyright © 1976, 2007, 2010 by Indiana University Press. All reproduced by permission.—*Parnassus*, v. 16, 1990. Copyright © 1990 by *Parnassus*. Reproduced by permission.—*Philological Quarterly*, v. 83, Spring 2004. Copyright © 2004 by *Philological Quarterly*. Reproduced by permission.—*Publishers Weekly*, v. 241, October 31, 1994. Copyright © 1994 by *Publishers Weekly*. Reproduced by permission.—*Raritan*, v. 12, no. 2, Fall 1992. Copyright © 1992 by *Raritan*. Reproduced by permission.—*Review of English Studies*, v. 177, February 1994. Copyright © 1994 by permission of Oxford University Press.—*South Atlantic Review*, v. 56, January 1991. Copyright © 1991 by Georgia State University. Reproduced by permission.—*Spectator*, no. 1784, September 6, 1862. Copyright © 1862 by *The Spectator*. Reproduced by permission.—*The Hudson Review*, Vol. XXVII, Autumn 1974. Copyright © 1974 by *The Hudson Review*. Reproduced by permission.—*Twentieth Century Literature*, v. 45, Winter 1999. Copyright © 1999 by *Twentieth Century Literature*. Reproduced by permission.—*World Literature Today*, v. 82, no. 6, November-December 2008. Copyright © University of Oklahoma 2008. Reproduced by permission.—*World Literature Today*, v. 75, Summer-Autumn 2001. Copyright © University of Oklahoma 2001. Reproduced by permission.—**World Literature Today**, v. 63, Winter 1989; v. 64, Spring 1990; v. 65, Winter 1991; v. 69, Autumn 1995 Copyright © 1989, 1990, 1991, 1995 by *World Literature Today*. All reproduced by permission.

COPYRIGHTED EXCERPTS IN *PfS*, VOLUME 38, WERE REPRODUCED FROM THE FOLLOWING BOOKS:

Balmer, Josephine. From "Sappho," in **Classical Women Poets**. Translated by Josephine Balmer. Bloodaxe Books, 1996. Copyright © by Josephine Balmer 1996. Reproduced by permission.—Dao, Bei. From "All," in **The August Sleepwalker**. Translated by Bonnie S. McDougall. New Direction Books, 1988. Copyright © 1988 by Bei Dao. Reproduced by permission.—Hagen, Lyman B. From "Poetry: Something About Everything," in **Heart of a Woman, Mind of a Writer, and Soul of a Poet: A Critical Analysis of the Writings of Maya Angelou**, University Press of America, 1997. Copyright © 1997 by Rowman & Littlefield. Reproduced by permission.—Hikmet, Nazim. From "Letter to My Wife," in **Poems of Nazim Hikmet**. Translated by Randy Blasing and Mutlu Konuk. Persea Books, 2002. Copyright © 1994, 2002 by Randy Blasing and Mutlu Konuk. Reproduced by permission.—Newton, Candelas. From "Lesser-Known Poetry," in **Understanding Federico García Lorca**. University of South Carolina Press, 1995. Copyright © 1995 by University of South Carolina Press. Reproduced by permission.—Octavio Paz, "Two Bodies," by Octavio Paz, translated by Muriel Rukeyser, from **Selected Poems**. Copyright © 1973 by Octavio Paz and Muriel Rukeyser. Reproduced by permission of New Directions Publishing Corp.—Sappho. From "Fragment 16," in **Greek Lyric**. Translated by David M. Campbell. Harvard University Press, 1982. Copyright © 1982 by Harvard University Press. Reproduced by permission.—Stone, Rob. From "Weeping Blood: 'Poema del Cante Jondo'," in **The Flamenco Tradition in the Works of Federico García Lorca and Carlos Saura: The Wounded Throat**, Edwin Mellen Press, 2004. Copyright © 2004 by The Edwin Mellen Press. Reprinted by permission.—Swenson, May. From "Fable for When There is No Way Out," in **Half Sun, Half Sleep: New Poems**. Copyright © 1967 by May Swenson. Reproduced by permission of The Literary Estate of May Swenson. All rights reserved.—Symons, Arthur. From "An Excerpt from 'Charles Baudelaire: A Study'," in **Charles Baudelaire: A Study**. Elkin Mathews, 1920. Elkin Mathews, 1920. Copyright © 1920 by Elkin Matthews. Reproduced by permission.

Contributors

Bryan Aubrey: Aubrey holds a Ph.D. in English. Entries on "Letter to My Wife," "Pride," and "The World Is Too Much with Us." Original essays on "Letter to My Wife," "Pride," and "The World Is Too Much with Us."

Cynthia Gower Betts: Betts is a novelist, playwright, and freelance writer. Entry on "Still I Rise." Original essay on "Still I Rise."

Kristy Blackmon: Blackmon holds a bachelor's degree in English from Southern Methodist University. Entry on "Two Bodies." Original essay on "Two Bodies."

Rita Brown: Brown is an English professor. Entry on "The Weary Blues." Original essay on "The Weary Blues."

Catherine Dominic: Dominic is a novelist and a freelance writer and editor. Entries on "Stanza LXXXIII" and "A Storm in the Mountains." Original essays on "Stanza LXXXIII" and "A Storm in the Mountains."

Charlotte M. Freeman: Freeman is a freelance writer and former academic who lives in Montana. Entry on "All." Original essay on "All."

Joyce Hart: Hart is a freelance writer and the author of more than thirty nonfiction books for students. Entry on "400-Meter Freestyle." Original essay on "400-Meter Freestyle."

Diane Andrews Henningfeld: Henningfeld is a professor of literature who writes widely for educational publications. Entry on "The Guitar." Original essay on "The Guitar."

David Kelly: Kelly is a college instructor of creative writing and literature. Entry on "Poem (Lana Turner Has Collapsed)." Original essay on "Poem (Lana Turner Has Collapsed)."

April Dawn Paris: Paris is a freelance writer with a bachelor of arts degree in classics and a minor in English. Entry on "Marriage." Original essay on "Marriage."

Rachel Porter: Porter is a freelance writer and editor who holds a bachelor of arts degree in English literature. Entry on "Fable for When There's No Way Out." Original essay on "Fable for When There's No Way Out."

Bradley A. Skeen: Skeen is a classics professor. Entries on "Invitation to the Voyage" and "Fragment 16." Original essays on "Invitation to the Voyage" and "Fragment 16."

400-Meter Freestyle

Pulitzer Prize-winning poet Maxine Kumin's poem "400-Meter Freestyle" closely follows the movements of an accomplished swimmer competing in a swim meet. The poem is very visual, an effect achieved not only through Kumin's poetic verbal expressions but also through the layout of the words on the page.

As readers imagine the scene that Kumin's poem creates, they also see the unusual pattern of the words: at the end of a line, the words represent a quick turn by flowing down the edge of the page. The lines of words mimic the physical route of the swimmer, who is first moving down the lanes of the pool and then quickly turning underwater at each end of the pool. The combination of Kumin's carefully chosen, descriptive words and the clever placement of those words on the page creates a strong impression for the reader. It is easy to imagine oneself in the grandstand, watching this race, from the sound of the starter gun to the final tally of the clock.

"400-Meter Freestyle" was first published in 1961 in Kumin's first published collection, *Halfway*. The poem has since been republished in her highly praised 1997 collection of new and old poems, *Selected Poems, 1960–1990*. This particular poem is often used in classrooms as a good example of concrete poetry.

MAXINE KUMIN

1961

Maxine Kumin (*AP Images*)

AUTHOR BIOGRAPHY

Kumin was born in Philadelphia, Pennsylvania, on June 6, 1925, the youngest of four children born to Peter and Doll Winokur. She attended Radcliffe College in Cambridge, Massachusetts, where she studied literature and history and graduated with a master's degree in 1948. Although she had been exposed to literature in college, her interest in poetry was sparked later while attending a workshop taught by John Holmes. It was in this adult-education class that Kumin not only began to write but also met the poet Anne Sexton, who would become a collaborator and a lifelong friend.

In 1961, Kumin published her first poetry collection, *Halfway*, which contains "400-Meter Freestyle." This decade proved fruitful for the young author, who published another poetry collection, *The Privilege* (1965); two novels, *Through Dooms of Love* (1965) and *The Passions of Uxport* (1968); and sixteen children's books.

Besides writing, Kumin has spent much of her life as a teacher, working at some of the best colleges and universities in the country, including Princeton, Columbia, Tufts, Brandeis, and the Massachusetts Institute of Technology. She was also selected as the poetry consultant to the Library of Congress from 1981 to 1982. From 1989 until 1994, Kumin was the poet laureate for the state of New Hampshire. In 1995, she served as the chancellor for the Academy of American Poets.

Kumin has won numerous awards, including the 1973 Pulitzer Prize for Poetry for her collection *Up Country:Poems of New England*. She has also won the Poets' Prize, the Aiken Taylor Award for modern poetry, the American Academy of Arts and Letters Award, and the Sarah Josepha Hale Award.

She married Victor Kumin, an engineering consultant, in 1946. In 1976, Kumin, along with her husband and their three children, moved to a 200-acre farm in New Hampshire. It is this rural setting, where Kumin and her husband have remained ever since, that has inspired much of her later writing, which often reflects on the abundance of nature that surrounds her farm.

In 1998, at age seventy-three, Kumin suffered a severe injury while tending to horses, one of her favorite hobbies. Not only did she survive the accident, but after healing, she continued to teach and to write. An account of her accident and subsequent healing process is found in her memoir, *Inside the Halo and Beyond: The Anatomy of a Recovery* (2000).

In the first decade of the twenty-first century, Kumin, still a prolific writer, published two more children's books, *Mites to Mastodons: A Book of Animal Poems, Small and Large* (2006) and *What Color Is Caesar* (2010), as well as several more collections of poetry, including *The Long Marriage* (2001), *Jack and Other New Poems* (2005), and *Still to Mow* (2007). She has also written two books of essays, *Always Beginning: Essays on a Life in Poetry* (2000) and *Roots of Things* (2010).

POEM SUMMARY

Lines 1–29

Kumin's poem "400-Meter Freestyle" has possibly become popular as much for its form as for its content. The poem is written in what is called a concrete style, meaning that the layout of the words on the page reflects the content of the poem. In the case of "400-Meter Freestyle," the lines are connected alternately at the end of one line and then at the beginning of the next to mimic the movement of a competitive swimmer's actions in a pool. Thus, like a swimmer making turns at either end of the pool, the visual image of the poem makes similar turns. Though the style is expressive, the reading of the poem can, at first, be somewhat confusing, and readers might have to work at making sense of it. For instance, the word at the end of the first line is physically connected to the end of the second line. However, the proper reading of the poem requires that one read the curving, vertical end of the first line and then jump back to the beginning of the second line. The process is not difficult; it merely takes a little time to get used to the pattern.

The poem begins as if the race has just begun. Readers can imagine that just before the poem begins, a line of swimmers had been waiting for the starting gun to go off. The setting of the poem is obviously at a competitive swimming meet. The speaker of the poem could either be in the audience at the meet or be watching the competition on television. Either way, the action starts at the sound of the starting gun. As soon as the gun goes off, the speaker zeroes in on one specific male swimmer. This man dives aggressively but gracefully, destroying the tranquillity of the water, which had been completely still. As the swimming begins, the speaker marvels at both the strength and the agility of the man's fast strokes. The man is obviously determined to waste no time in getting a leading edge over his competitors. Every stroke is perfect.

As if watching the fast actions of the swimmer in slow motion, the speaker of this poem sees the swimmer pull on the water with each stroke, catching the water in his cupped hands and pulling against the water with the long extension of his arms in order to propel his body forward. This is a practiced swimmer, the speaker notes, who has obviously learned the secrets of his sport, generating speed in the water. He knows how to take advantage of the water to move himself across the pool at a high speed without sapping all his strength.

It is obvious to the speaker that the swimmer has not only trained hard for this event but also learned everything he needs to know about how to trim seconds off his time. His body is strong and efficient; his muscles make no unnecessary movement, waste no energy. Every time this athlete exerts a muscle, it is for a specific reason. Every movement in the water appears to be focused on only one thing: winning. From his wrists to his ankles, every body part knows what to do and when to do it. Even his mouth, through which he must breathe, catches an inhalation and almost simultaneously spits out the water that tries to make its way down his throat. As if this man has spent most of his life preparing for this moment, no movement is wasted, no energy is expelled except to take him to his ultimate goal, that of being the first to reach the end of this race.

Lines 30–61

In the second half of the poem, the speaker continues to study the swimmer. She notices more intricate details about this athlete. For instance, she is surprised by how white the bottoms of his feet are as they pedal their way through the water and propel his body from one end of the pool to the other. When the swimmer reaches one wall of the pool, the speaker is stunned at how gracefully he dives under the water, how he twists his body, with his feet being the last part of his body to disappear. Under the surface of the water, the swimmer turns and pushes against the lower part of the wall of the pool, projecting his body forward in a different direction, back to the other end of the pool. This underwater turn takes place almost as if it is one motion rather than a continuum of specific actions. In a 400-meter freestyle event, the swimmer must complete eight lengths of a 50-meter pool. This means that the swimmer must complete seven of these turns. After each turn, the swimmer reappears at the surface, and his strong stroking of the water returns. To more perfectly mimic the swimmer's motions, Kumin has written the poem so that each half has eight horizontal lines, as if she too were swimming eight lengths.

As the poem continues, the speaker observes the swimmer more closely, wondering whether he is tiring yet. All that she sees, though, is the continuation of his strong movements. He looks little different in the middle of the race from how he looked in the beginning. He remains steady, and his arms and feet are constantly pushing the water in the same quick rhythm. His body moves as if in a trance, knowing what to do without him having to tell it what comes next. Even his breathing appears mechanical or is well practiced. The swimmer does not look as if he ever runs out of breath, as he never has to take long gasps. His lungs are patient, and he takes well-paced short breaths. The only part of his body, according to the speaker, that might be complaining is his heart, which might be crying out in pain. The heart must be pumping blood furiously through the swimmer's body, fueling his muscles and his lungs. The speed at which the swimmer moves must be tiring his heart as he lunges forward, plowing through the water in his last laps.

As the end of the race comes into view, the man's heart, lungs, muscles, arms, and legs push all their remaining energy into their movements as they surge toward the finish line. When the race is complete, the speaker looks at the race clock, which records the swimmer's time: about four minutes, twenty-five seconds. Though the speaker announces the time in the poem, there is no comment about the results of the race. The speaker does not say whether this swimmer's time has won him the race, but a little research reveals that the swimmer's time is of Olympic standards.

THEMES

Discipline

One of the main underlying themes in Kumin's poem "400-Meter Freestyle" is the discipline and training that are necessary in order for an athlete to reach his or her peak performance level. The way the speaker describes the swimmer, with his carefully polished skills, which are easily recognized as he moves across the water, makes it apparent that this athlete has put a lot of discipline into his preparation. The speaker notices the way his body moves as if it were a machine. The various parts of his body are smoothly coordinated. His arms and hands pull against the water as his legs and feet paddle him forward.

From the speaker's description and recognition of the swimmer's effort, readers might conclude that the speaker knows something about swimming and the discipline that it takes to get one's body in shape for the excruciating exertion that is required to take part in a competition at this level. There is a tone of empathy in her descriptions, which subtly acknowledges her awareness of the swimmer's efforts.

The time given at the end of the poem suggests that the race the swimmer is involved in is at a highly competitive level, probably even the Olympics. This places the intensity of the required discipline at a very high degree.

Sports

The background of Kumin's poem is a sporting event. Though there is no mention of the crowd, the noise, or the excitement, or even any notice of the other competitors, readers who have ever attended, watched, or taken part in a sport can imagine these elements as they read the poem.

Sporting events are filled with excitement. The athletes involved in the competition are nervous as they think about all the training they have gone through in order to get to this competition. They must be wondering how their training is going to pay off on this day. The audience, too, is excited. People have come from all around to witness this sporting event. They have probably followed the contests that have led to this particular competition. They have chosen the athletes they believe will do best and will root for them, hoping they will win. Sporting events encourage a level of excitement, as well as the noise of the crowd, as individuals root for their favorite athlete or team, yelling out the participants' names to encourage them to go faster, play harder.

In all sports, especially those that involve racing, the start of the event is highly anticipated. In swimming, the start is announced by the sound of the starting gun. In this poem, the anticipation of this sound is short-lived because the poem begins as the gun goes off. However, the speaker stretches this highly anticipated moment by having the sound of the gun reverberate in the dives of the athletes into the water.

Through sporting events, athletes tend to inspire their audience. Viewers recognize the grace and power that the athletes have cultivated through their consistent and intense training. Sports can be entertaining for both the participants and the athletes, but more importantly, both athletes and audience are inspired to reach for their goals and perform at their peak.

Strength

Strength is both a goal and a by-product of an athlete's training. All types of sports demand that an athlete develop certain strengths and skills for his or her particular sport.

In swimming, upper-body strength is crucial. The arm and shoulder muscles are the primary parts of the body that are used to move the swimmer through the water. Leg muscles are also built up to supplement the strength of the upper body.

TOPICS FOR FURTHER STUDY

- Choose a subject or an object that interests you and write a poem about it. Use the concrete style as the form of your poem, which means you need to place the lines of your poem so they form an image that corresponds to your poem. For instance, if you write about an apple, the lines of your poem could create the image of an apple. Go online and do a Web search for examples of concrete poems. Do not feel limited to objects. You might write about a tornado, for example, or some other weather event. You could use the image of a broken heart to write about a failed romance. Finish your project as a poster for display in the classroom.

- Research a different style of poem, other than concrete poems. Write a clear definition of the style and find samples of it. Include a short history for the style and research poets who use or used each form. Place your findings on a Web page and provide links to more detailed information. Invite your classmates to view your work.

- Choose a concrete poem from a print or online source. As you read the poem to the class, have friends (whom you have prepped) help you act out the poem. Do not tell the rest of the class the subject of the poem. When you are finished presenting the poem, ask the rest of the class to guess what it was about.

- Find a video of a 400-meter swim race on YouTube. Act as narrator of the film by reciting Kumin's poem while the race is played on video. Memorize the lines of the poem and practice your recitation with the video, trying to match the poem to the swimmer's movements.

- Write a concrete poem, but rather than choosing any ordinary object to write about, find an object that is specific to your heritage: something with religious, cultural, or historical significance. If you are unsure what symbol to choose, talk to your parents or grandparents, asking them to help you. From the information you gain from them, create your poem and then read it to your class.

- Read the young-adult collection of concrete poems *A Poke in the I*, edited by Paul B. Janeczko (2005). In this collection you will find Monica Kulling's "Tennis Anyone?" How is Kulling's concrete poem similar to Kumin's "400-Meter Freestyle"? How do these poems differ? Compare the effects of the concrete form in the two poems. Evaluate which poet does the better job and explain why in a short essay.

Lungs must also be strong, as swimmers must not only supply their muscles with great amounts of oxygen, as runners do, but must also regulate their breathing because they are working while immersed in water.

Throughout Kumin's poem, the speaker reflects on the swimmer's strength. That strength is one of the main focuses of the speaker's attention. His strength is displayed, for example, in his arms as he pulls himself through the water. This strength is visualized not only through his motions but through the visible curves and flexing of his muscles. Though there is a moment when the speaker questions the reliability of the swimmer's endurance, he quickly proves that his strength will not fail him as he pushes toward the finish line.

Beauty

Beauty is a minor theme, but it is one that flows through the poem. The descriptions that the speaker uses in describing not just the swimmer and his movements but also the water suggest beauty. Though the word *beauty* is never used, the descriptions the speaker provides are embedded with elements that indicate physical beauty.

Full-size competitive swimming pool (Vatikaki /
Shutterstock.com)

The water is as perfect as glass before the swimmers enter the pool. As the swimmers dive in, the speaker then focuses on the special way this one swimmer cups the water with his hands and moves through the water as if he has a magical power. She sees the rippling of his muscles, a body of statuesque form. His mouth is mentioned: a perfect siphon that feeds oxygen to his lungs and banishes the water from his throat. The bottoms of his feet astonish the speaker with their white color. Then, as he completes his underwater turns, the speaker praises him for his beautiful, rhythmic grace.

STYLE

Visual Poetry

Visual poetry is both a poem of words and phrases as well as a visual expression that offers an image, on the paper, of the poem's topic. For example, in a visual poem, if the writer mentions a falling leaf, the few words that mention this image may be printed in a way that suggests that the letters of those words are falling down the page.

In a more substantially visual poem, a style referred to as concrete poetry, the full form of the poem becomes a visual representation of the subject of the poem. For example, a poem about a bird would take on the visual form of a bird, or a concrete poem about a tree would be printed on the page in the shape of a tree. In Kumin's poem about competitive swimming, the form is created by the swimmer's path. The lines of words on the page cross back and forth, turning at alternate ends of the page as a swimmer would turn at each end of the pool. This image of lines reinforces the words of the poem. Readers are brought into the poem not only through the verbal description that the poet offers but also through the image that the lines of the poem present. This helps readers to imagine they are sitting in the audience, watching the swimming meet.

Tone

The tone of Kumin's poem is light and playful. Though there may be a deeper meaning in the words and ideas of this poem, "400-Meter Freestyle" is also simply a poem about swimming and the delight in watching an athlete's skill and grace. This accessibility is true of most concrete poetry. Concrete poems place the emphasis on the shape of the poem and are often about topics that can be taken rather lightly.

With "400-Meter Freestyle," the poem's words, along with its concrete form, convey what one might see at a swim meet. Though the subject of this poem, the swimmer, must take his sport seriously if he wants to win, the poem does not mention the swimmer's inner experience. Instead, the poem is written from the point of view of an observer. The speaker is obviously someone who enjoys and appreciates the sport. The speaker conveys that he or she is aware of the effort and discipline that is necessary to be as graceful and as powerful as is the swimmer that is being observed. However, sitting in the audience watching the event provides more fun than the serious work that the athlete must endure. The intent of the poem is to display light-hearted excitement rather than to explore the deeper challenges that might be required of the swimmer. Though the speaker infers the discipline and

COMPARE & CONTRAST

- **1960s:** At the 1960 Summer Olympics in Rome, the United States men's swim team finishes in first place with fifteen medals. Nine of them are gold.

  Today: The United States claims ten gold, two silver, and five bronze medals in the men's swimming events in the 2008 Summer Olympics in China.

- **1960s:** On August 17, 1962, Murray Rose breaks another world record, swimming the 400-meter freestyle in a Chicago meet in 4 minutes, 13.4 seconds.

  Today: At the 2009 World Swimming Championships, German Paul Biedermann

  sets a new world record in the 400-meter freestyle with a time of 3 minutes, 40.07 seconds.

- **1960s:** In 1964, Australian Dawn Fraser wins Olympic gold in the women's 100-meter freestyle. She becomes one of two women to win individual gold medals in three Olympics (1956, 1960, and 1964) for the same event.

  Today: U.S. swimmer Michael Phelps wins eight gold medals in the 2008 Summer Olympics, breaking the record for the most gold medals won by an individual in a single Olympics.

---

training that the swimmer obviously has gone through, there is no mention of how deeply challenged the swimmer might have been to accomplish this feat. The swimmer is, instead, observed from a distance and is celebrated for his success.

Single-Syllable Words

Most of the words in Kumin's poem are composed of single syllables. This use of single-syllable words provides two elements to the poem. The first is the beat or rhythm. The single-syllable words flow out of the mouth easily and in a steady beat. They require a sound and then a pause, one after the other. Single syllables are also quick to say, so there is a repetitive and quick beat, mirroring the excitement of someone watching a competitive event. If readers imagine a radio or television sports announcer keeping track of what is happening at a swimming meet, the sound of the announcer's voice can have the same quick and repetitive beat.

The second reason for using these single-syllable words is to mimic the physical characteristics of the swimmer in this poem. The swimmer's arms keep up a quick, repetitive movement, as do his legs and feet as they kick through the water. The swimmer's breaths are short and fast as he

tries to keep up a rhythmic breathing pattern. The poem also refers to the swimmer's heart, which must be pounding to a similar beating rhythm, as short and as quick as single syllables.

Poetic Devices

Throughout this poem, Kumin makes use of poetic devices. Poetic devices, such as alliteration (using two or more words near each other with the same initial consonant) and simile (the comparison of two things that are dissimilar), enhance the language of a poem. For instance, Kumin describes the surface of the water in the pool as glass. First, this provides the reader with an image of how still the water is. The stillness also suggests that no other swimmers are in the water yet; tension is building as the athletes line up on their starting podiums and wait for the gun to start the race. Finally, the image of glass emphasizes not just the sound but also the breaking of the tension, so that when the swimmers dive into the still water, it sounds as if they are breaking through a plate of glass.

There are also several instances of alliteration in this poem. In the first line, two words begin with a hard *c*, as the starting gun goes off and the swimmers create loud splashes as they dive into the pool. Later, an *m* sound complements the description of the smooth mechanics of the swimmer's mouth. Since sounding out the letter *m* places an emphasis on the reader's lips, someone reading this poem aloud will echo the movement of the swimmer's mouth as he manipulates air into his lungs and siphons out the water that flows across his lips.

HISTORICAL CONTEXT

Murray Rose

Murray Rose was born in 1939. At the age of seventeen, he won three of his eventual four gold medals in swimming at the Olympics. Though Rose was born in Scotland, his family moved to Australia when he was very young, and he swam for Australia in the Olympics. The 400-meter and 1500-meter freestyle were his best events. At the time, Rose was the youngest athlete to win three gold medals in an Olympic event.

Rose competed in both the 1956 (Melbourne, Australia) and 1960 (Rome, Italy) Olympics. In Rome, Rose won his fourth gold medal, which was in the 400-meter freestyle event, as well as a silver and a bronze medal for the 1500-meter freestyle and the 200-meter freestyle relay, respectively.

The young athlete was very popular in his day because of his youth and accomplishments, as well as his good looks and his special diet: vegetarianism (which was much less common than it is today). Among the vegetables that he ate, Rose included seaweed, which gained him the nickname "The Seaweed Streak."

When it was time for college, Rose moved to the United States and attended the University of Southern California, where he continued his training. Though living in the United States, Rose competed in the 1960 Olympics on the Australian team, defending his title. In his lifetime, Rose set fifteen world records, and he remains, to this day, one of Australia's swimming legends.

Probably not coincidentally, Rose broke the world record for the 400-meter freestyle in 1958 with a time of 4 minutes, 25.9 seconds—the time that Kumin lists for the swimmer in her poem.

Olympic Swimming

Olympic swimming events first appeared in the 1896 competitions in Athens, Greece. These events were open only to men and consisted of the 100-, 500-, and 1200-meter freestyle races. At this time, swimming races were conducted in open water, such as lakes, rivers, or the ocean. It was not until 1908 that a swimming pool was used for Olympic swimming events.

Some of the more unusual swimming events in early Olympic games included an underwater swim, a swimming obstacle race, and the plunge. The plunge consisted of having the swimmers take a standing dive and then remain motionless underwater for at least one minute or until their bodies naturally rose back to the surface.

Women entered the Olympics for the first time in 1912. Sarah Durack, from Australia, was the first woman to win a gold medal in swimming, for the 100-meter freestyle in 1912.

Olympic swimmers who have made the headlines include Johnny Weissmuller, who won his five gold medals in 1924 and 1928. Weissmuller was best known, though, for his movie roles: he played Tarzan in twelve films. In 1936, twelve-year-old Inge Sorensen won a bronze medal in the 200-meter breaststroke. This preteen wonder from Denmark became the youngest medalist ever in an individual event. Mark Spitz was the swimmer to watch in the 1970s as he won seven gold medals, breaking the standing world records in all seven events. Another star from Australia was Ian Thorpe, who in 2000, at seventeen years of age, won four medals and broke his own world record in the 400-meter freestyle. His time was 3 minutes, 40.59 seconds. Thorpe was the hero of Michael Phelps as he was growing up and training for his own Olympic run. Phelps beat Spitz's record for the most gold medals won in a single Olympics, winning eight of them in 2008.

Concrete Poetry

"400-Meter Freestyle" is an example of concrete poetry, a poem whose form on the printed page takes on an image that reflects the subject of the poem. This type of shaped writing is also referred to as visual poetry, which has a long history.

Ready for competition (Chad McDermott / Shutterstock.com)

Though the term "concrete poetry" is rather modern, having been coined in the 1950s, when samples of this type of poetry were exhibited in Brazil, the idea of visual poetry is much older. For example, Lewis Carroll's *Alice's Adventures in Wonderland* (1865) contains a poem in the shape of a mouse's tail.

The American poet e. e. cummings (1894–1962) is often referred to as a visual poet. His visual poems, or pattern poems, formed shapes, but these shapes did not necessarily take their form from the subject of the piece. In "O sweet spontaneous earth," the poem's broken lines and misplaced punctuation create a ragged edge on the page. Another example of a pattern poem comes from famed poet Dylan Thomas (1914–1953). Thomas wrote "Vision and Prayer" in the shape of a diamond.

As the twentieth century progressed, concrete poetry took a more specific form, one related to the title, theme, or subject of the poem. In Eugen Gomringer's (1925–) "Silencio," the layout of the words on the page includes a central black space, meant to reflect the feeling of silence. Robert Yehling's (1959–) poem "Uplifting" moves across the page in the form of a horizontal V shape, as if the words are about to be uplifted.

CRITICAL OVERVIEW

Kumin is often praised for her down-to-earth poetry about people and nature. Critics have commented favorably on her 1997 collection of poetry in which this poem was reprinted. Judy Clarence, in a review of *Selected Poems, 1960–1990* for *Library Journal*, refers to Kumin as "one of the very best poets writing today." In this collection, Clarence says, "the reader can move slowly, meanderingly, deliciously through the stages of Kumin's poetic life." In another review of the same collection, Dulcy Brainard, writing for *Publishers Weekly*, refers to Kumin's "perceptive, distinctive voice." Brainard ends the review by stating that the "evolution and inherent integrity" of her work, which is "wise, generous and passionate, is deftly captured in this forceful selection."

In his review of the collection, Ben Howard, writing for *Poetry*, finds that Kumin "has shown not only constancy but remarkable consistency." Howard adds: "She has held fast to her dominant themes, her inductive methods, and her darkly ironic outlook"; her "earthy realism, her generous receptivity" are important elements of her work. Readers may not find depth in Kumin's poems, but this is not to be lamented, for Kumin offers something else. "Her adroit and passionate language," Howard concludes, "offers sustenance of another kind."

Richard Tillinghast, in the *New York Times Book Review*, found Kumin's collection to be a reminder of why many people read poetry. Tillinghast writes, "Her poems bracingly remind us of several enduring virtues valued by anyone who reads verse for pleasure." He also praises the poet for being versatile. Kumin, unlike some other contemporary poets, has not, over the years, found a comfortable form and gotten stuck in it. Tillinghast finds that "she has the versatility to build an orderly, measured structure in rhyme and meter, or to adopt the easier virtues of free verse for a more transient, informal effect."

Writing for *World Literature Today*, B. A. St. Andrews states that "one hears neither disenchantment nor romanticism" in Kumin's poetry, adding, "rather, her creative landscape is a solid, sacred place where the rituals of life, love, and death are performed purely."

In a review of Kumin's 1980 collection of essays *To Make a Prairie* in the *Boston Globe*, Christina Robb compared Kumin's work to that of poet Robert Frost. "She has Frost's intelligence," Robb states, but unlike Frost, Kumin has "a gift for loving." In Robb's view, Kumin "insists on making something more than pretty images in her poetry" and has "a warmth and a tone of commonness."

CRITICISM

Joyce Hart

Hart is a freelance writer and the author of more than thirty nonfiction books for students. In the following essay, she explores the absences in Kumin's poem "400-Meter Freestyle."

At first glance, Kumin's poem "400-Meter Freestyle" appears to have a full range of intricate details about a swimmer competing in a sporting event, everything from the gun that rings out at the beginning of the race to the clock that registers the duration of the race at the end. The poem mentions the swimmer's rippled muscles, the way he synchronizes his arms and legs, even the shocking whiteness of the soles of his feet. However, on reflecting on the poem, readers might also begin to notice the absences in Kumin's poem. Where are the other swimmers, for example? Where are the spectators? Where are the sounds and smells? Where, in fact, is the swimmer? Though readers see the parts of the swimmer, such as his feet, his hands, his legs, his arms, and his mouth, there is no mention of the swimmer in his entirety. He is never seen as a whole person. The poem contains another important vacancy as well. Where is the speaker?

Kumin chooses to begin this poem with the starting gun. She omits the vision, easily imagined, of the swimmers lined up on their starting podiums, shaking their arms and legs to rid themselves of muscle and psychological tension. Because of this omission, readers do not witness the swimmers preparing for their plunge into the water as the starter raises the gun, preparing to sound out the signal for the race to begin. As a matter of fact, readers are given no sight of the other swimmers even when they are in the pool. There is no sense of where they are in relation to

WHAT DO I READ NEXT?

- Kumin's 2007 collection of poems *Still to Mow* deals with common things in the poet's life, topics such as how it feels to grow old, what her Jewish American childhood was life, the war in Iraq, and being a soccer mom in the 1960s.

- *The Roots of Things* is Kumin's 2007 collection of essays covering topics such as personal identity, raising horses, life at Radcliffe College in the 1940s, living in the country, and writing poetry. She also comments on several others, including Jane Kenyon (a poet) and Carol Houck Smith (a famous editor).

- For a closer look at other poems written around the same period as "400-Meter Freestyle," read Kumin's poetry collection *Bringing Together: Uncollected Early Poems, 1958–1988*, published in 2003. A look at the friendship between Kumin and Anne Sexton is offered in verse in this collection.

- *Roots and Flowers: Poets Write about Their Families* (2001), edited by Liz Rosenberg, offers young-adult readers a message from Kumin about her great-grandfather. Poets also included are Donald Hall, Stanley Kunitz, Maria Mazziotti Gillan, and others.

- Rita Dove, like Kumin, served as the U.S. poet laureate and won a Pulitzer Prize. In *Sonata Mulattica* (2010), Dove writes in a narrative poetic style to tell the story of George Augustus Polgreen Bridgetower (1780–1860), a violin prodigy who studied with famed composer Joseph Haydn (1732–1809). What makes this story even more interesting is that Bridgetower was the grandson of an African prince.

- *War Dances* (2010) offers Sherman Alexie's Native American perspective on life. In this book are poems, short stories, and essays on topics concerning various questions about life, including the complexities of fatherhood.

THROUGH THE POEM'S ABSENCES, KUMIN
PUSHES READERS INTO THIS POEM, ENCOURAGING
THEM TO ENLIVEN THE COMMENTARY BY FILLING IN
ALL THE EMPTY SPACES."

the one man who earns the poem's full focus. Readers do not know whether this athlete is in first place or last or somewhere in the middle of the group. There may as well be no group. Only the lone male swimmer exists.

There is no audience. No one but the speaker seems to be watching this contest, and the speaker is all but invisible. There are no shouts. No one is calling out any of the swimmers' names to encourage them on. There are, in fact, no noises at all, not even the sound of the starting gun. There are no smells, such as the familiar chlorine smell of a swimming pool. All the senses, except for sight, are absent from this poem. Readers must use their imaginations to bring the sounds and smells into the poem. One possible reason for these absences is that the speaker is watching the race from home, on her television set. That would explain the absence of smells and perhaps sounds, if the sound is muted. The other swimmers, though, would still be in full view on the television screen. The swimmer on whom the poem focuses would still have competitors.

Perhaps this is a one-man heat, in which the swimmer is in the pool by himself, racing against the clock. However, where is the swimmer? Where is the sum of his body? The speaker of this poem watches the swimmer only in parts. Readers are made aware of the swimmer's artful hands as they carefully scoop at the water to propel him forward. The swimmer's arms are rippled with tense muscles. His legs kick at the water in scissor-like motion, assisting his arms, providing more power to his projection across the pool. His feet flap as they paddle against the watery mass, as a duck gains speed to lift its feathered body into eventual flight. The speaker also notices the swimmer's mouth as the swimmer twists his head far enough out of the water to take a quick, short breath. Before inhaling, that same

mouth spits out the water that it has captured while submerged. But where is the hair or the swimming cap that has been carefully placed on the top of the swimmer's head? What about the his eyes, for instance—does he wear swimming goggles? The swimmer's lungs and heart are mentioned, but not his chest or back.

Though various parts of the swimmer's body are mentioned—are in fact admired for their well-practiced movements and honed skills—one may ask, where is the swimmer as a whole? Where is the man? As he dives into the water at the beginning of the poem, his body is surely outstretched and visible before he disappears under the water, but the speaker makes no comments about this. Even as he moves across the length of the pool, more than mere parts of him could easily be recognized. His psychology is just as much a blank spot as his physical being. If the speaker can imagine the swimmer's lungs and heart, could she not also envision what he is thinking about or feeling emotionally? Do athletes clear their minds of all thoughts like a yogi? Do they practice visualization and imagine their strokes or envision themselves winning? Are they concentrating on the time of world records in hopes of breaking them? None of this is mentioned or speculated upon. Instead, the speaker refers to the swimmer's actions as being mechanical. She praises him for his ability to be machine-like, making his moves without having to think about them because he is so perfectly practiced. This seems to be the speaker's overall view of the man and the reason she envisions him by his various parts. The swimmer, as conveyed in this poem, is not a man: he is a well-oiled, precision-inspired machine.

For all these questions about the swimmer, readers are left without answers. All they see from the poem's offerings are the separate parts—two legs, two arms, two feet, two hands, and one mouth—of one man's body, racing in a vacuum only against the abstraction of time.

Then there is the speaker. The question in connection to the speaker is not so much who she is—we may, for convenience, consider the speaker female, like the author—but rather where she is. Readers can get so caught up in the speaker's descriptions and actions of the swimmer that they do not pay much attention to the physical or emotional aspects of the speaker. The speaker, in this poem, is almost like a sports

Freestyle swimmers racing (Andrey Yurlov / Shutterstock.com)

announcer, but her announcements lack certain elements. She does offer commentary through her descriptions of the swimmer's physical motions. She even guesses at the strain being put on the swimmer's heart, as well as the patience of his lungs as they wait for a burst of oxygen with the next inhalation. However, she shows no attachment to the race or to the swimmer. She observes him as one who might observe a well-made automobile or a cleverly constructed computer. She praises the swimmer for his obvious intensive training as one might praise the compatibility of well-meshed gears in a car's transmission. She comments on the sleekness of the swimmer's moves as one might appreciate the clever applications of a new laptop computer.

Like the gun at the beginning of the poem and the clock at the end—like the swimmer himself—the speaker of this poem is a representation of something abstract. Both the speaker and the swimmer are functions: things that exist for the purpose of this poem but that are not wholly alive. Like the absent audience and the missing competitors, the speaker does not appear to be a

part of this sporting event. She hovers somewhere over the swimming pool like a ghost. She has no feelings that are expressed. Like the swimmer, whom she describes as parts of a body, the speaker is merely a pair of eyes. If she is more than that, it is merely because the reader supplies the rest. Just as the reader assumes that the arms, legs, feet, and hands of the swimmer are attached to a human torso, so too must the reader assume that the speaker is a person who is not only watching the swim meet but also feeling the excitement and intensity that sporting competitions supply. Just as readers must fill in the absent noises of the audience, smells of the pool, and presence of the other swimmers on the starting podiums and in the pool, so too must they create the humanness of the speaker.

These absences were all created purposefully, through the poet's craft. The careful absences force the reader to dive into this poem, just as the swimmer dives into the pool. By making readers plunge themselves into the poem, the poet makes readers become a part of the poem. Through the poem's absences, Kumin pushes readers into this poem, encouraging them to enliven the commentary by filling in all the empty spaces.

Source: Joyce Hart, Critical Essay on "400-Meter Freestyle," in *Poetry for Students*, Gale, Cengage Learning, 2011.

SOURCES

"Biography," in *Maxine Kumin Home Page*, http://www.maxinekumin.com (accessed September 9, 2010).

Brainard, Dulcy, Review of *Selected Poems, 1960–1990*, in *Publishers Weekly*, April 28, 1997, Vol. 244, No. 17, p. 70.

Clarence, Judy, Review of *Selected Poems, 1960–1990*, in *Library Journal*, June 15, 1997, Vol. 122, No. 11, p. 74.

"Current Exhibits, World Records, Men—400m Free," in *International Swimming Hall of Fame*, http://www.ishof.org/exhibits/world_records/400free_men.htm (accessed September 5, 2010).

Espinosa, Cesar, *Corrosive Signs: Essays on Experimental Poetry (Visual, Concrete, Alternative)*, Maisonneuve Press, 1990.

Howard, Ben, Review of *Selected Poems, 1960–1990*, in *Poetry*, June 1998, Vol. 172, No. 3, p. 165.

Kumin, Maxine, "400-Meter Freestyle," in *Maxine Kumin: Selected Poems, 1960-1990*, W. W. Norton, 1997, pp. 21-22.

"Maxine Kumin [1925–]," in *Modern American Poetry*, http://www.english.illinois.edu/maps/poets/g_l/kumin/kumin.htm (accessed September 9, 2010).

Robb, Christina, Review of *To Make a Prairie*, in *Boston Globe*, February 1, 1980, p. 1.

St. Andrews, B. A., Review of *Selected Poems, 1960–1990*, in *World Literature Today*, Summer 1998, Vol. 72, No. 3, p. 623.

"Sport: Scoreboard, Jan. 21, 1957," in *Time Online*, http://www.time.com/time/magazine/article/0,9171,865674,00.html (accessed September 5, 2010).

"Stories about USMS Swimmers," in *U.S. Masters Swimming*, http://www.usms.org/hist/sto/index.php?ID=187&srt= (accessed August 5, 2010).

Tillinghast, Richard, Review of *Selected Poems, 1960–1990*, in *New York Times Book Review*, August 3, 1997, p. 10.

FURTHER READING

Bodden, Valerie, *Concrete Poetry*, Saunders, 2010.
    Written for young-adult readers, this book guides the student through an introduction to and basic history of some of the best concrete poetry that has been published over the years.

Bohn, Willard, *Modern Visual Poetry*, University of Delaware Press, 2000.
    Bohn offers a history and examples of visual poetry, including a section on concrete poetry. Both well-known and little-known poets' works are offered, as well as discussion about the form of visual poetry and what direction it might take in the future.

Braham, Jeanne, *The Light within the Light: Portraits of Donald Hall, Richard Wilbur, Maxine Kumin, and Stanley Kunitz*, David R. Godine, 2007.
    In this book, readers learn about the lives and works of some of the best American poets. Critics often describe the poets who are included as those most heavily influenced by Robert Frost's work. Using interviews with the poets, as well as examining their work, Braham brings insights into the poets' artistic achievements.

Grosholz, Emily, ed., *Telling the Barn Swallow: Poets on the Poetry of Maxine Kumin*, University Press of New England, 1997.
    In this collection of essays, poets such as Alicia Ostriker, Henry Taylor, and Wendell Berry reflect on the writings of Kumin. Topics that are discussed include the poets who have influence Kumin's writing, her thematic patterns, and the form of her poetry. Also included are poems written to Kumin or written about her and her work.

Mullen, P. H., *Gold in the Water: The True Story of Ordinary Men and Their Extraordinary Dream of Olympic Glory*, St. Martin's Griffin, 2003.
    Covering the victories and the defeats and how both of these affect the athletes who experience them, Mullen takes readers inside the lives of some of the young men who have dedicated themselves to making it to the Olympics. The book offers a look at the training that is required, the emotional roller-coaster ride that the athletes experience, their injuries, and the excitement of winning.

Tibballs, Geoff, *The Olympics' Strangest Moments: Extraordinary but True Stories from the History of the Olympic Games*, Anova Books, 2008.
    Tibballs recounts some of the more bizarre and controversial moments of the Olympic Games from the beginning of the modern games in 1896 to the return to Athens in 2004. From one athlete who was dubbed the slowest swimmer ever to compete to the unfortunate athlete who lost a gold medal after being helped over the finish line, the events captured in this book have the potential to make readers laugh and cry.

SUGGESTED SEARCH TERMS

Maxine Kumin

Maxine Kumin AND bibliography

Maxine Kumin AND 400-Meter Freestyle

400-meter freestyle AND Olympics

Maxine Kumin AND poetry

concrete poetry

concrete poetry AND Maxine Kumin

swimming AND 400-meter AND Olympics

Olympic records AND swimming

All

BEI DAO
1990

Although Bei Dao has been publishing poetry in his native China since the 1970s, it was 1990 before his poem "All" was published in English. "All" appeared in *The August Sleepwalker*, translated by Bonnie S. McDougall and released by New Directions simultaneously with Bei Dao's short-story collection *Waves*. Since the early 1970s, he has been known for his imaginative and avant-garde poetry as well as for his political activism. He was a member of the Democracy Wall movement of the late 1970s, and his most famous poem, "The Answer," which was written during that period, became an anthem of dissent during the 1989 Tiananmen Square demonstrations. Although Bei Dao strenuously disavows that he was a leader of any movement, particularly a political movement, it was in part because his poetry was used as political anthem that he was exiled in 1989 and has never been allowed to return to China. In the intervening years, Bei Dao has continued to write; seven collections of poetry, one collection of short stories, and two collections of essays have been published in English translation. "All" is one of Bei Dao's early poems, written sometime between 1970 and 1989. (The poems in *The August Sleepwalker* are not identified by date.) Like many of Bei Dao's poems, "All" relies on highly personal imagery, which is in part why the Chinese government viewed it as a politically subversive poem. In a political system in which all thoughts,

Bei Dao (© Alberto Paredes / Alamy)

feelings, and needs of the individual were supposed to be subordinated to the state, Bei Dao's insistence in his work on the legitimacy of the individual experience marked him as both artistically and politically progressive.

AUTHOR BIOGRAPHY

Bei Dao was born Zhao Zhenkai on August 2, 1949, in Beijing, mere months before the People's Republic of China came into being. His was a prominent family, and he went to the best schools. In the 1960s, like many students, Bei Dao joined the Red Guards—a student movement in China's Cultural Revolution—and participated in Mao Zedong's civil war against anyone declared a member of the liberal bourgeoisie. Bei Dao became disillusioned with the violent tactics of the Red Guards and was banished to the countryside, where he spent eleven years employed as a construction worker. During the Cultural Revolution,

all literature on subjects other than Marxism and Mao's thoughts were banned. In an interview with Siobahn LaPiana for the *Journal of the International Institute*, Bei Dao explained, "Not only did I go into houses to look for things, I also organized the stealing of books from the libraries, because the libraries were all closed at that time." While in the countryside, Bei Dao organized a group of friends who met every two weeks. In the same interview, he told LaPiana, "We got together for reading, studying and writing. We would exchange our writings among ourselves. This was very important to me. One of the great motives for this secret writing was the tremendous pressure we were all experiencing, both political pressure and societal pressure. We were feeling very depressed. It all had to be done in secret."

In the late 1970s, after Mao's death, Bei Dao was allowed to return to Beijing, where, along with his fellow poet Mang Ke, he founded *Jintian* (Today), China's first unofficial literary magazine. It was Mang Ke who gave the poet his pen name, Bei Dao, which means "Northern Island"—a reference both to his origins in the northern city of Beijing and to his rather remote and cool personality. *Jintian*, which was often published as large broadsides pasted to empty walls in the capital, became increasingly popular, and Bei Dao and his fellow poets Mang Ke, Duo Duo, Gu Cheng, Yang Lian, Shu Ting, and others who became known as the Menglongshi, or "Misty Poets," also became hugely popular, especially among the young. Although their poetry was not overtly political, they were artistically groundbreaking. In a nation where all language had been subverted to overtly political aims, that these poets described subjective experience and extolled the inner lives of individuals was both exciting and subversive.

Although Bei Dao disavows being a leader of the democracy movement, his poetry became central both to the Democracy Wall protests of 1976 and to the students who led the 1989 protests in Tiananmen Square. Bei Dao was in Berlin during the 1989 uprising and watched from afar as students chanted lines from his poem "The Answer" at the soldiers in Tiananmen Square. Bei Dao has lived in exile ever since, and it was not until 1996 that his wife and daughter were allowed to join him. During his years of exile, he has taught at many American universities, and although he has been allowed to return to Hong Kong, where he teaches at the Chinese University of Hong Kong, he still has not been allowed to return to China. Bei Dao's many awards include the Aragana Poetry Prize from the International Festival of Poetry in Casablanca, Morocco, a Guggenheim Fellowship, the Swedish PEN Tucholsky Prize, and the Jeanette Schocken Literary Prize in Germany.

POEM TEXT

> All is fate
> all is cloud
> all is a beginning without an end
> all is a search that dies at birth
> all joy lacks smiles   5
> all sorrow lacks tears
> all language is repetition
> all contact a first encounter
> all love is in the heart
> all past is in a dream   10
> all hope comes with footnotes
> all faith comes with groans
> all explosions have a momentary lull
> all deaths have a lingering echo

POEM SUMMARY

Bei Dao's poem "All" is written in one single stanza of fourteen lines, each of which posits a metaphoric statement about the nature of totality. Although not divided into couplets, the poem uses parallel structure to create a series of seven paired lines. There are no transitions between the lines to link them to one another; the links are created solely by juxtaposition and parallel structure.

Lines 1–2

The first two lines each contain three words and are the most direct metaphors in the poem. The first line declares that everything is fate and therefore predetermined and outside the control of the individual human being. Fate is a version of destiny and has, through the centuries in both Western and Chinese thought, been considered an eternal force that operates on human beings and upon which they have no ability to act. The second line declares that everything is cloud, the implication being that the nature of the world is shrouded in mist, obscured, difficult to envision or comprehend. This could be a reference to the Menglongshi or "Misty Poets" school, of which Bei Dao is a founder, or to the criticisms of the

original Menglongshi group. Unlike the clear poetics sanctioned by the Chinese government, which declared that poetry was supposed to uplift the masses by extolling the virtues of the theories of Lenin, Marx, and Chairman Mao by which the nation was ruled, the poems by the Menglongshi are obscure, unclear, or misty. These are the qualities of a cloud, and by stating that the nature of the all is like a cloud, the poet seems to be positing that the nature of reality is perhaps not as clear as one would like it to be.

Lines 3–4

The second two lines are more complex and take as their topic beginnings and endings, birth and death. Bei Dao is famous for his use of both cryptic statements and paradox, and in this couple, both are found. In the third line, Bei Dao states that the nature of the all is a beginning, that everything is always beginning, and that there is no end. The paradox here is that the use of the word "beginning" implies an ongoing line in time of which the beginning is the start, and the end is the end. But Bei Dao is stating that all of life is a beginning, that everyone is always beginning, and that there is no end. Line four, which is much more enigmatic, states that the nature of being is searching and that the search somehow ends at birth. The paradox here is that birth, which is a beginning, is described as the end of something, a search. These two lines seek to ask the reader to think about the nature of the universe and the roles of beginnings and endings, birth and death.

Lines 5–6

The third set of two lines tackles the meaning of happiness and sorrow, and again the reader is presented with two paradoxical statements. In line 5, Bei Dao declares that the state of joy is one that is devoid of smiles. This seems contradictory, for when one is happy, one naturally smiles. So what is it about a state of joy that would preclude smiling? The standard definition of joy includes concepts like happiness, bliss, gladness, delight, and a state of well-being and satisfaction. The reader is pushed to question whether a joy that appears without smiles could truly be joy. Similarly, in the following line, Bei Dao posits a sorrow that is devoid of tears. Both of the emotional states described in these lines are characterized by a lack of their central quality and hence represent two more paradoxes with which the poet asks the reader to wrestle.

Lines 7–8

The fourth set of lines once again retreats further from the clarity of universal definition and closer to the misty world of individual perception. The reader is told that language, which is absolutely essential to the poet, is only repetition. Language is not meaningful but is just an echo, something repeated back from one person to another in the same way that some birds can learn to speak. A parrot might be able to repeat a word, but one cannot say that the parrot is really communicating, for it is impossible to claim that the bird has learned to use language with any awareness of what it is saying. Language, the poet seems to be saying, is as empty and hollow as the emotions described in the pair of lines that precede this one. However, while language may be simply a series of empty repetitions, the poet declares that all contact between people is a new encounter. While this could be a good thing, since novelty is exciting, it can also be read as another example of the emptiness of the world the poet describes. A world in which people are always encountering one another for the first time is one in which people have no history together and do not know one another. That this line can be read, paradoxically, as representing both an exciting new possibility and a frightening example of emptiness forces the reader to contemplate the possibility that the all can be more than one thing at the same time.

Lines 9–10

The fifth set of coupled lines appears to be a set of clichés. That love exists in the heart and that the past seems a dream are both platitudes of the sort that one might find in a greeting card, not metaphorical insights that one would expect from a poet such as Bei Dao. Are these lines sincere, or are they here to challenge the reader to think for him- or herself? Coming from a society in which the government did not hesitate to tell the people what to believe, one cannot help but wonder if Bei Dao is doing something similar with this poem. The poem is a relentless series of statements claiming to define the nature of ultimate reality, and each set of statements seems to be pointing out the hollow nature of such statements. Finally comes a statement about the ultimate human longing, the longing for love, and one is told simply that it is in the heart. As for the past, it is like a dream, something that does not really exist, something one might well have made up. The two qualities that bind people to one another, love and shared experience, are, in the universe of

this poem, as disappointing and hollow as all the other certainties the poet has discussed.

Lines 11–12

The sixth set of coupled lines tackles hope and faith, the qualities that sustain people through hard times. Hope, we are told, is always conditional, it comes with parenthetical remarks, notes that somehow mediate the state. To hope is to be optimistic, to live in the expectation that a given situation will have a positive outcome even in the light of present uncertainty, while faith, the subject of the second line in this couple, is like hope, to live in the expectation of a good outcome, but to do so in the face of opposition or despair. Although the poem posits that hope is mediated somehow by qualifications, it claims that faith is accompanied by the sound of pain and sorrow. Again, we are presented with a paradox, to have faith means to live in the expectation of a good outcome, and yet in the process of doing so we are told that this state is experienced through pain and sorrow.

Lines 13–14

The final set of coupled lines not only brings about the end of the poem but also carries images of the end of human life. It is as though the poem itself, concerned as it is with the nature of life, can only end in death. The poet reminds us that during an explosion, there is a moment when all seems to hold still, when the sound waves have not yet caught up to the concussion, and when in the midst of cataclysm, there is a moment of quiet. Again, this paradoxical image of quiet in the midst of violent action asks one to reexamine one's assumptions about the world. Finally, the poem ends with death and the idea that all deaths, not just our own or those of our loved ones, carry on into the world.

Like many of Bei Dao's poems, "All" comprises a series of paradoxical statements, largely unlinked by logical transition. In "All," the statements seem to be linked in pairs, as evidenced by parallel word structure and paradoxical imagery.

THEMES

Totalitarianism

Totalitarianism is a political system in which the individual is completely subordinated to the control of the state. Totalitarian regimes enforce their views through the use of extensive surveillance by

TOPICS FOR FURTHER STUDY

- Select a poem by a classical Chinese poet such as Du Fu, Wang Wei, Han Shan, Po Chü-i, or Li Po, and write an essay in which you compare and contrast it with "All." Research the aesthetic goals of classical Chinese poetry, and compare and contrast the ways in which Bei Dao's contemporary poem adheres to these goals and diverges from the poem you chose.

- Each line in "All" contains an abstract concept that the poet posits as definitional. Team up with a partner and research online images. Find one illustration that you feel visually represents each of the assertions being made in the lines of the poem and use an online photo program like iPhoto to create a slide show. Then, using a program like Garage-Band, create a podcast of your slide show in which you narrate each slide with the line of poetry it represents.

- Read Marianne Satrapi's young-adult graphic novel *Persepolis: The Story of a Childhood*. While Satrapi's book is set in a different place and time than "All," both writers sought to communicate what it is like to live under a repressive political regime. Compare the lives of both writers, and write a short story or poem in which they somehow encounter one another. Feel free to use graphics, as in the Satrapi novel, to illustrate how these two authors might have recognized one another as young people rebelling against similar constraints.

- Bei Dao has lived in exile since 1989. For the first seven years of that exile, he had only fleeting visits with his daughter and his wife, and his marriage ultimately did not survive the ordeal. Team up with several classmates and write a short play in which you dramatize the experience of being exiled. Where is your protagonist when he or she is exiled? Why does the government declare that this person can never return home? What loved ones does your character leave behind? Your play should have at least three scenes. When it is complete, perform it for your class.

- During the Democracy Wall protests of 1976, Bei Dao, Mang Ke, and the other contributors to the underground literary magazine *Jintian* often published their work by printing it on poster-sized broadsides that they plastered on walls around Beijing. Because Chinese is an ideographic language, it lends itself particularly well to graphic display. Working in small groups, create a poster (using traditional poster board or an online program such as Glogster) of "All" that you feel represents the poem in a graphic manner and that would attract the attention of busy passersby on a city street. When you are finished, each group should display their poster, and the class should discuss which version they feel is most effective and why.

- During the Chairman Mao era of Chinese history, ordinary language was very specifically subordinated to the political aims of the ruling party. In an interview for *Agni* magazine, Bei Dao stated that "for creative writers the goal has been to create a *new language* that would put some distance between them as members of the *literati* and the government in power." People are all confronted every day with language that has been subverted to other purposes, whether by the government, by popular culture and advertising, or by religions and the military. Working in small groups, and using the Internet, newspapers, and magazines for sources, collect ten examples of phrases that exemplify this manipulation of language. Write a poem that explores the ways that these phrases have been used to express something other than their ordinary meaning.

secret police, often reinforced by the systematic use of spies and informers. Every level of social interaction in a totalitarian society, from the workplace to the family, is undermined by spying in order to subordinate the citizenry to the absolute control of a single party and a single leader. Totalitarianism originated in Germany in the 1930s and 1940s and found its full expression under Hitler's Nazi regime. Following closely were the regimes of Benito Mussolini in Italy, Joseph Stalin in Russia, and Mao Zedong in China. True totalitarianism is a modern phenomena, relying as it does on technologies of surveillance and the systematic erosion of family and community bonds. In the absence of these bonds, individuals can be more easily manipulated by propaganda to do the will of their leaders.

Bei Dao is almost exactly as old as the People's Republic of China, a nation that came into being as a revolutionary experiment seeking economic freedom for all, including the peasant classes who had been desperately poor throughout the nation's five-thousand-year history. However noble the initial goals of the revolution, by the time Bei Dao reached young adulthood, a cult of personality had grown up around Chairman Mao. Following the lead of Stalin in Russia and the long Chinese history of autocratic rulers who were treated as demigods, Mao set himself up as the "Great Leader." His image and sayings were ubiquitous, in every classroom and office, on every postage stamp, and on banners in every city. The famous *Little Red Book* of Mao's thoughts and sayings was carried by more than two billion Chinese citizens, and its contents were considered a belief system that covered all situations. The Cultural Revolution was an expression of this totalitarianism, one in which the leader urged the masses to enforce his definitions of moral and political purity, and much of Bei Dao's poetry is written as a response to the way the state sought to infiltrate all levels of language and the violent means by which they enforced that infiltration. In "All," the concept of totalitarianism is expressed through a string of similes, each of which claims to define the entirety, the whole, and to assign a singular meaning to which everyone must subscribe. In this way, the poem mimics the oppressiveness of a totalitarian regime.

Individualism

While the poetry of Bei Dao and the other Misty Poets has been criticized for being obscure and indistinct (both elements of the Chinese word

misty), Bei Dao has, throughout his career, defended his poetry as fulfilling the true role of the artist in society, to express the inner imagination of the individual and to rescue language from those forces that seek to drain it of its meaning. For Bei Dao, these forces can be the state, which for most of his life has sought total control of language and meaning, or, as he has discovered in the decades that he has lived in the West, the corrosive effect of being defined as a "dissident" poet. In an interview with Stephen Ratiner for *Agni* magazine, Bei Dao stated, "I don't see myself as a representative of such-and-such a trend or political opinion. I see myself as an individual who is trying to create a new form of language, a new mode of expression."

"All" exemplifies this tension between those who seek to control language through definition and those who seek to claim a space for individual meaning. On one level the poem mimics the voice of the repressive regime, proclaiming in fourteen different ways that it knows the nature of entirety, asserting that the poet, like the state, has the right to define the true nature of those experiences that form the core of human life: sorrow, joy, language, love, hope, faith, contact, and death. However, the metaphors Bei Dao uses, which seem nonsensical in some cases and merely obscure in others, serve to demonstrate that the language of artistic expression remains individual. What defines the all for Bei Dao might not define the all for someone else, and it is in this gap that freedom lies. In "All" as in many of Bei Dao's poems, the poet seems to be trying to both define and escape definition at the same time. The problem with definition is that it necessarily limits the possibilities of the individual, and for Bei Dao, this is not exclusively a problem of the totalitarian Chinese state; it is one he has experienced in his years in the West as well. In the same interview with Ratiner, Bei Dao explained that at each writer's conference and poetry festival that he attends in the West, he is asked exactly the same questions, about his pseudonym, about his famous poem "The Answer" and Tiananmen Square, and about being an exile. He told Ratiner, "You're slotted into an 'image,' into a sort of representative 'story angle' and you can never leave it. You're stuck there for the rest of your life." In much the same way that his poem "All" seeks to undermine the concept of totalization, Bei Dao continues to seek new language in which he can give true expression to his individual imagination.

Cloud in the sky (Panom | Shutterstock.com)

STYLE

Translation

Poetry depends for its meaning and effect not only on the literal meanings of the words on the page but also on formal qualities like sound, rhyme, rhythm, and allusion, each of which can be very difficult or even impossible to render in translation. Historically, many translators have considered literary quality nearly impossible to duplicate and so have concentrated on faithful rendition of the literal meaning. Bonnie McDougall, who has translated not only Bei Dao's poetry but also the poetry of many other Chinese writers, disagrees. In her essay "Problems and Possibilities of Translating Contemporary Chinese Literature," published in the *Australian Journal of Chinese Affairs*, she notes,

> Poetry translation above all requires special consideration in regard to language and form. In recent years it has become commonplace to claim that in translating a poem the translator should produce a form corresponding as much as possible to the form of the original. While this may seem self-evidently desirable, it represents by no means the only or even the best approach to literary translation.

McDougall's approach is to analyze how the original poem attempts to either conform to or rebel against the formal or stylistic conventions of the culture in which it was written. In the case of Bei Dao, she noticed that the poems in the collection that became *The August Sleepwalker* fall into several categories: rhymed poems written in the kind of stanzas typical of Western poetry, short lyric poems without stanza divisions that may or may not contain rhymes (she cites "All" as her example of this type of poem), and long sectional poems comprised of many short sections linked together. Chinese, like many non-English languages, contains a wealth of rhyme, and while in Bei Dao's stanzaic poems, the rhyme provides a deliberate emphasis and cadence to the lines, in his non-stanzaic lyrics, the rhyme does not seem to be an integral element of the overall effect rendered by the original poem. In these cases, McDougall notes,

> In the translation of Bei Dao's poetry . . . it seemed to me . . . to be quite inappropriate to employ rhyme in accordance with the poet's own practice. It is well-known that rhyme in Chinese verse, compared with English verse, is

relatively easy to achieve, and even the modern Chinese poets of this century have generally continued to employ rhyme in a fairly relaxed and casual way. Its absence, therefore, creates a strikingly modern effect that is not echoed in the lack of rhyme in modern English verse.

Short non-stanzaic poems like "All" still left McDougall with the problem of how to denote their modern quality—to convey that these poems were more closely related to the work of Western poets like Federico García Lorca and Paul Celan than they were to the classical Chinese lyrics of Du Fu and Han Shan, which they superficially resembled. Her solution was to indicate the modern quality of the poems through lack of capitalization. In her article, she explains,

> The choice between capital or lower-case letters at the beginning of each line of verse . . . play[s] a similar function in contemporary English poetry to the use of rhymed or unrhymed verse in contemporary Chinese poetry. . . . The absence of capitals creates the same "modern" effect as the absence of rhyme in Chinese.

She comments that since Chinese is an ideographic language that does not use capitalization at all, any translator will have to make a decision about how to capitalize the English translation. For McDougall, the decision to use capitalization to indicate in English a specific quality in the original Chinese was a strategic one. Each of these decisions is typical of those that any translator faces when trying to decide how to faithfully render not only the linguistic content of a poem in another language but also the artistic and literary nature of that poem in a language that may not share the poetic conventions of the original.

Metaphor

Metaphor is one of the central stylistic hallmarks of poetry, for most poems seek to use figurative language in order to evoke new ways of thinking, whether that shift is in the way one thinks about a particular subject or in the nature of language itself. The work of the poet is to expand the ordinary meanings of words and expressions in order to illuminate new ways of thinking or feeling. There are two primary forms of metaphor: comparative metaphors, which rely on the formula *A is B*, and substitution metaphors, in which the poet uses term *A* in place of term *B*. The first type of metaphor is the one that Bei Dao relies upon in "All," and this comparative metaphor can be seen as a sort of condensed simile in which the "like" or "as" is not stated. Both of these metaphoric structures imply that the poet is saying something other than what he or she means and that in order to understand the true meaning of a poem, the reader must puzzle out the true meaning. Modern critics, however, have dismissed this interpretation of the role of metaphor as old-fashioned and have posited instead that by creating metaphors, the poet is expanding the reader's understanding beyond the boundaries of ordinary thought. That is, by working with language in a metaphoric manner, the poet creates new ways of imagining language and the world. Because much of Bei Dao's work has involved exposing the ways that the totalitarian regime of Chairman Mao degraded language and emptied it of meaning, it is safe to claim that his work subscribes to this expansionist approach to language and metaphor.

HISTORICAL CONTEXT

The Cultural Revolution

The Cultural Revolution began in 1966 and ushered in a decade of violence and chaotic upheaval in China. In the early 1960s, more practical and less ideological officials who sought to modernize China posed a threat that Mao Zedong was unable to fend off from within the Communist Party. In order to defeat those he felt threatened his control of the party and the state, Mao unleashed the forces of unemployed young workers and discontented students. Free for the first time from the rigid constraints of the educational and party-controlled workforce, these "Red Guards," as they named themselves, were easily led and went on a rampage of destruction. They denounced anyone they were led to believe represented the "liberal bourgeoisie" that Mao wanted purged—turning first on teachers in the schools, often beating them savagely and parading them through the streets wearing tall dunce caps, and sometimes turning even on their own parents. Anyone with education, or who possessed books or artwork, or who worked as a professional was in danger. Bei Dao himself was a member of the Red Guards, and although he later denounced the movement, sickened by the violence and rampant manipulation of young people by the state, it was the books he stole from libraries and private homes that provided his education not only in Chinese poetry but in world poetry as well. During the eleven years of exile to the countryside that was his punishment for trying to leave the Red Guards, Bei Dao formed an underground group of fellow students for the purposes of writing and self-education. While the most violent phase of the

COMPARE
&
CONTRAST

- **1970s:** Bei Dao and Mang Ke found the underground magazine *Jintian* and publish poetry by the group soon to be known as the Menglongshi, or "Misty Poets." Because of scarce resources and government censorship, they publish many editions by printing them on large posters and plastering them on walls around the capital. Although subscriptions steadily increase and copies are sent to many corners of China, *Jintian* is shut down by the police in 1980.

  1990s: Bei Dao revives *Jintian*, publishing the magazine from exile in Sweden. Although funding is always a challenge, the magazine remains in print to the present day, serving as a forum for modern Chinese poetry.

  Today: Bei Dao is still forbidden to return to the People's Republic of China, although he teaches at the Chinese University in Hong Kong. He continues to be more famous outside of China than he is inside the country, where his poetry is still suppressed.

- **1970s:** The work of the Menglongshi is declared subversive because it insists that individual perceptions, feelings, and artistic expression cannot be dictated by the state. As a group, their artistic mission is to reclaim language from the debased state in which it resides after the Cultural Revolution.

  1990s: After Bei Dao's poem "The Answer," which was written during the Democracy Wall demonstrations of the 1970s, becomes the anthem of rioting students during the Tianan-

men Square massacre of 1989, Bei Dao and three other members of the Menglongshi are exiled.

  Today: Efforts of the Chinese government to silence Bei Dao have failed. His poems have been translated into more than twenty-five languages, and he is repeatedly nominated for the Nobel Prize in Literature.

- **1970s:** While the most violent aspects of the Cultural Revolution ended with the Party Conference in 1969, the cultural and political repressions of the Cultural Revolution continue until Mao Zedong's death in 1976.

  1990s: After Mao's death, Deng Xiaoping takes leadership of the Chinese Communist Party and introduces the "socialist market economy," a series of reforms that open the country to foreign investment and limited private competition. Deng continues to crack down on artistic freedom and political dissent. He leads the country until his death in 1997.

  Today: Following the reforms set in place by Deng Xiaoping, China is now the second-largest economy in the world, right behind the United States of America. It is the world's fastest-growing economy, and where Mao sought to export revolution, the current People's Republic of China deploys its huge reserves of cash to build relationships of "soft power" (achieving goals through attraction rather than coercion) around the world. While per-capita income has risen, artistic and political dissent continue to be repressed.

Cultural Revolution came to an end with the Ninth Party Congress in 1969, the Cultural Revolution lingered on until Mao's death in 1976.

Democracy Movements of 1976–1978 and 1989

In the wake of the Cultural Revolution and the death of Mao, a period of political uncertainty

ensued between 1976 and 1978. During this period, young writers like Bei Dao, who had been publishing underground via mimeographs and hand copies, began to surface. In the autumn of 1978, large-character posters, a traditional form of Chinese dissent, began to appear on a wall near the Xidan intersection in Beijing, giving the Democracy Wall movement its name. It was at this time that Bei Dao and Mang Ke began publishing *Jintian*, which appeared both as a traditional bound magazine and in the form of large-character posters. The Democracy Wall movement continued throughout the winter of 1978–1979, as people gathered to discuss the effects of the Cultural Revolution, to publicly criticize Mao's mistakes, and to demand democratic reforms. Although Deng Xiaoping had supported the democracy protesters who gathered in Tiananmen Square in 1976, it became clear when he cracked down on the Democracy Wall movement in 1978 that his earlier support was less for democratic reform than it was in opposition to the "Gang of Four," powerful leaders in the party whom he sought to depose. It was during this time that Bei Dao wrote what is probably his most famous poem: "The Answer," with its anthem-like refrain. In the spring of 1979, the Democracy Wall movement was crushed by Deng, who jailed many dissenters, including Wei Jingshen, who also posted work on the wall and who remains incarcerated.

By the late 1980s, economic reform was well under way in China. Outside investment was becoming common, agricultural communes were being dismantled, and once again, students and intellectuals came to Tiananmen Square to demonstrate for democratic reform. They were seeking freedom of speech and of the press, increased funding for education, economic growth unhindered by political corruption, and a move toward democracy. The movement began as an expression of mourning for the death of Hu Yaobang, one of the few high-ranking party members who supported reform. Protests grew in intensity, and students took to chanting Bei Dao's poem "The Answer" at television cameras, soldiers, and party officials. As Greer Mansfield noted in his *Trope* magazine profile of Bei Dao, Wuer Kaixi, one of the student leaders of the 1989 uprising, said that he got his political ideas "from reading the poetry of Bei Dao." When the tanks finally rolled in on June 6, 1989, to disperse the protesters, Bei Dao was in Germany; he has never been allowed to return. In addition to the hundreds of deaths, many of the student protesters were jailed, although a few, including Wuer Kaixi, managed to escape the country. Televised internationally in real time, the student protests provided a rare glimpse into the internal divisions that still roil the nation.

Economic Growth in the Twenty-first Century

In 2010, China surpassed Japan and became the world's second-largest economy, behind the United

Moment of explosion (*Markus Gann / Shutterstock.com*)

States. Spurred by reforms in the 1980s that opened China to private enterprise, as followed by efforts in the 1990s to dismantle state-held businesses that were monopolistic, the economy of China has become the fastest growing in the world. However, as business has grown, the government has grown right along with it and still holds monopolies on many sectors of the economy, including telecommunications, airlines, and transportation. While China has opened the door to capitalist investment, it continues to maintain that it is a socialist system. As reported in the *New York Times*, Prime Minister Wen Jiabo reaffirmed this in an address given in March 2010, when he stated, "The Socialist system's advantages . . . enable us to make decisions efficiently, organize effectively and concentrate resources to accomplish large undertakings." While China's economy is booming and per-capita income has risen steadily over the past two decades, democratic reform has stalled. Although Chinese leaders often give lip service to the idea that China is moving toward democracy, the ongoing imprisonment of political activists and the enduring exile of artists like Bei Dao belies these assurances. In an unusually candid interview with the English-language *China Daily* in March 2010, Li Fei, a high-ranking party official, as quoted by Edward Wong in a *New York Times* article, stated bluntly that "different countries have different election rules and a socialist China won't follow Western election campaigns."

CRITICAL OVERVIEW

Bei Dao's poem "All" first appeared in English as part of his collection *The August Sleepwalker*. Although the poem was not reviewed individually, the collection did attract significant critical acclaim. *The August Sleepwalker* was one of the first works to appear in English by any member of the Menglongshi, or "Misty Poets." This group came to prominence in the mid-1970s during the tumultuous years surrounding the death of Chairman Mao. Mao's death opened a small period in which the Chinese people were encouraged to express their political opinions, and the artists of the Menglongshi school took advantage of this opportunity to start China's first underground literary magazine, *Jintian*.

It was the Chinese scholar and translator Bonnie McDougall who first brought Bei Dao's poetry to the West. In the early 1980s, she began publishing translations of his poetry in academic publications, and in 1990, New Directions published translations of two collections: poetry in *The August Sleepwalker* and short stories in *Waves*.

Bei Dao's work has most often been reviewed autobiographically and politically. That is, his work has been seen, even in English translation, as the expression of someone who experienced very specific political and social oppression and whose poetry speaks to that oppression. Gregory Lee, for example, reviewing *The August Sleepwalker* for *China Quarterly*, notes that "what this book amply reaffirms is Bei Dao's status as a pioneer in the post-Cultural Revolution literary world, and as a champion of defiance against the Marxist-Leninist cultural orthodoxy." On the other hand, W. J. F. Jenner, writing for the *Australian Journal of Chinese Affairs*, claims that it is precisely Bei Dao's position in time and history that is the limiting factor in his work. In his review of *The August Sleepwalker*, Jenner claims,

> The language available to Bei Dao is too weak to carry much of a burden. This is not the poet's fault: it was bad luck to be born into a period when the resources of China's literary tradition were out of reach, and the culture was left with a written code that while purporting to reflect living speech could in fact only be used to its full effect by people soaked in the concise but daunting written code of the past.

Other reviewers of Bei Dao's work have stuck closer to the poems themselves and were not solely influenced by the poet's dramatic autobiography. John Cayley, writing in the *Bulletin of the School of*

Oriental and African Studies, published at the University of London, notes that despite the backlash inside of China from a younger generation of poets, rereading the poet's work

> confirms an achievement fully acknowledged . . . in his own culture. He is never quite sentimental, his work is personal and deeply felt, sometimes lost in Buddhist speculation but as often engaged in contemporary history. He can be humorous and satirical . . . and, after seducing the reader with a seedy, lyrical rhapsody, he can pull him up sharp with a concrete, contemporary image.

Michelle Yeh, in *World Literature Today*, agrees, noting that *The August Sleepwalker* is "not just a representative work by an important Chinese poet . . . it is probably one of the most concise and penetrating introductions to Chinese poetry of the last decade." She praises the publication of the collection as

> a new beginning in contemporary Chinese poetry, a watershed that assumes several meanings. First, it is a revival and a continuation of the best of the May Fourth literary tradition, which asserts esthetic consciousness and upholds artistic integrity. Second, it is a courageous revolt against the subjugation of literature to political ends that has unfortunately always existed in post-1949 China. Third, despite differences in styles, it has inspired a new generation of poets who have the same courage and imagination to treat poetry as art and to go beyond their predecessors in their exploration of the language and the literary form.

Yeh finishes her glowing review by noting that "both for his poetic vision and his pivotal position Bei Dao will remain one of the most important figures of twentieth-century Chinese poetry."

CRITICISM

Charlotte M. Freeman
Freeman is a freelance writer and former academic who lives in Montana. In the following essay, she examines the way Bei Dao uses paradox in his poem "All."

Bei Dao's poem "All" relies on paradox, a form of metaphor, to explode the notion that the nature of reality is singular, unitary, and can be known, in part as a reaction to the totalitarian regime under which Bei Dao was raised, a regime that declared that words have only a single meaning—the one dictated by the state. The poem is a single stanza of

WHAT DO I READ NEXT?

- *Blue House* (2000) is Bei Dao's first book of essays translated into English. This deceptively simple collection gives a portrait of the poet in exile, a man without a home who drifts from one academic position to another. Written with the same lucid eye, attention to physical detail, and tenderness toward the people he loves as his poetry, this volume portrays the life of a man wrenched from his home against his will and his determination to keep writing.

- In *Waves* (1990), Bei Dao turns to fiction to describe what life was like in the years just after the Cultural Revolution. In six stories and a novella, Bei Dao describes not only the hopelessness and despair of life in a society gone mad but also the passion, anger, and hope that sustain his characters as they strive to remake their lives in the aftermath. The beauty of these stories lies not only in the language but in the ways that Bei Dao's characters resist their fates.

- Gene Luen Yang's prizewinning graphic novel for young adults *American Born Chinese* (2008) is the story of Jin Wang, a lonely Taiwanese American boy navigating the challenges of middle school in San Francisco. The novel filters Jin Wang's feelings of being born in the wrong body through the story of the Chinese folk hero the Monkey King and through the figure of Chin-kee, an amalgamation of every ugly Chinese American stereotype. This lively and emotionally affecting book was the first graphic novel nominated for the American Book Award.

- Moying Li was only twelve years old when the Cultural Revolution swept across China.

In *Snow Falling in Spring: Coming of Age in China during the Cultural Revolution* (2010), written for a young-adult audience, she tells the story of that traumatic time.

- The noted anthologist Tony Barnstone and the Chinese poet-scholar Chou Ping have edited *The Anchor Book of Chinese Poetry: From Ancient to Contemporary, the Full 3000-Year Tradition* (2005). This comprehensive volume covers as much of the massive history of Chinese poetry as one is likely to find in English and does a masterful job of putting the poets and their eras in context.

- In *The Search for Modern China* (1999), Jonathan Spence covers the last four centuries of Chinese history. With a narrative style that brings events to life, Spence covers the British attempts to subdue the Chinese with opium, the brutal Japanese occupation of World War II, the rise of Mao, and the devolution of the nation into chaos during the Cultural Revolution. Including more than two hundred illustrations and a generous glossary, this is an excellent single-volume guide to the period.

- Paul Celan's *Selections* (2005), edited by Pierre Joris, is an excellent introduction to the work of a poet who was a central influence on Bei Dao. The book is an anthology of not only the poetry of Celan—whose given name was Paul Antschel—but also numerous commentaries by critics and philosophers, as well as letters from the poet to his wife and colleagues, making this edition an excellent introduction to Celan's artistic projects, work, and life.

---

fourteen lines comprising seven sets of paired lines. These are not couplets in the Western sense of the word, because they are not end rhymed; however, their parallel structure and linked content point to a series of subunits within the

singular poem. Written before Bei Dao was exiled from China, the poem expresses the longing of the poet for artistic freedom, for escape from the control of the state, and for a world in which self-determination is possible.

" FOR READERS ACCUSTOMED TO PARSING A POEM IN SEARCH OF A SINGLE, UNIFIED MEANING, BEI DAO CAN BE FRUSTRATING."

In "Paradoxy and Meaning in Bei Dao's Poetry," published in *Positions: East Asia Cultures Critique*, Dian Li notes that in the West, [Bei Dao] "is a reminder of China's repression and intolerance, a poetic enigma whose well-translated elliptical syntax and cryptic imagery represent a complex interior response to a hostile exterior world." These are qualities readily visible in "All," for it is a poem that relies on syntactical juxtaposition rather than logical transition for much of its power; it contains cryptic imagery; and it is almost entirely concerned with defining the nature of the exterior world from within the interior understanding of the poet. "All" relies for its power on one of Bei Dao's signature poetic lines, the statement. The entire poem is a series of statements devoid of interpretation, and their power derives from the manner in which they pile upon one another, beginning with abstraction and ending in concrete images of violence and death.

Although Bei Dao's poetry has been criticized, as Dian Li notes, for the manner in which his "enigmatic style, fractured syntax, and disjunctive imagery have conspired to resist reading even by expert readers," he goes on to argue that this is because the poet is committed to paradox, a poetic practice that, if it "produces meanings at all, they are always multiple, undifferentiated, and indeterminate." The production of multiple, undifferentiated, and indeterminate meanings can be seen as the only sane response when one has grown up, as Bei Dao did, in a totalitarian regime where language was wholly subordinated to the interests of state control. The China of Bei Dao's childhood was one where, as he told Stephen Ratiner of *Agni* magazine in 1991, the government was the sole source of meaning, and as such, had infiltrated every aspect of normal life. Bei Dao recounted,

> In the late stages of the Cultural Revolution . . . all our word-groups became fixed by the Party. . . . Take the word "sun" or the word "red." "Sun" really means "the leader," and "red" means "the Party." I had a friend from middle school who

was asked, "What color do you like?" His response was, "I like blue." And this boy was censured for having the wrong political attitude, for being politically incorrect.

Bei Dao has made it his life's work to resist this colonization of language, and his poetry is largely concerned with trying to explode our commonplace understanding of words. Paradox is one of his most powerful tools for accomplishing this.

We see this in action in "All" in the way that Bei Dao's imagery builds in complexity. The first line is relatively simple; the idea that fate is a ruling principle in the universe is a common one both in China and in the West. However, complication ensues with the second line, when he compares the nature of the universe to a cloud. We have not quite entered the world of paradox yet, however, for while a cloud is a specific weather event, one can see how a comparison to the nature of the universe makes sense. A cloud is mysterious and unknowable, high up the mountainside, which it usually obscures. The nature of the universe is mysterious and unknowable and is often obscured by many things, including our imperfect understanding and our inability to clearly describe something that is so difficult to comprehend.

It is in the second set of coupled lines that Bei Dao introduces paradox into the poem, when he claims that everything is a continual beginning, and those beginnings have no end. This is an old philosophical conundrum, both in the West and in the East. In the West the concept is best expressed in the Greek philosopher Heraclitus's observation that one can never step in the same river twice: water continues to flow, so each time one puts one's foot in the river, one is stepping into different water than before. This metaphor for the relentless march of time is analogous to the Chinese Daoist belief that the universe is like water, characterized by change and flow. However, the line with which this one is paired is indeed paradoxical, for in it, the poet claims that the nature of life is a search, and that the search expires when we are born. How can birth be a death? The two concepts are opposites, and here the poet marries them to one another in a typically paradoxical statement. This statement begins a series of paradoxes, one more strange than the last. In short order, Bei Dao claims both that joy is devoid of happiness and that sorrow is devoid of tears, thereby building definitions of joy and sorrow that eliminate a central quality of each term.

Although the explicit subject of the poem is the nature of the universe, and the poem seeks to describe the ineffable force that runs through everything, one could argue that in doing so, the poem also seeks to explore the nature of those central experiences that make us fully human—birth and death, sorrow and joy, beginnings and endings, love and language, and above all, contact. These are the central concerns of the experience of human life, and they are also the intimate human experiences into which the Chinese government of Bei Dao's youth sought to inject itself. In a world where all meaning is externally dictated, then, as the poet notes, all language can become simple repetition, drained of its meaning, series of slogans parroted back by a colonized people. In a world in which the state claims that the relationship of the individual to the state must trump all others, then, as in Bei Dao's experience in the Cultural Revolution, children will turn against parents, students will riot against their teachers, and the educated classes will destroy the cultural heritage of their own nation.

Bei Dao has a well-deserved reputation for gloominess, and readers can see why in these images; and yet "All" is not a poem drained of all hope. The poem is filled with bleak imagery, posing the ideas that love only exists in the innermost confines of the heart, where it must be guarded like a secret, that the past seems like a dream, and that all contact with one's fellow citizens is as if meeting a stranger for the first time. However, it is in the gaps between definitions that the poet poses a space of freedom. Each of the paradoxes from which the poem is built contains a small open space. Because they are paradoxical, they cannot impose meaning in the way that Chairman Mao's propagandists and watchdogs of ideological purity imposed meaning. If the nature of the universe is both a beginning and an ending, then it cannot be reduced to either term. It exists somewhere in between the two terms, leaving a space in which the reader is free to interpret for himself.

That freedom exists, even in a totalitarian society, in these tiny gaps is brought home by the final two lines of the poem. In every explosion, there is a lull, a moment where time seems to hold still. In everyday life, this is caused by the lag between what we can see, an explosion, and the time it takes the sound waves to catch up with our sight. Bei Dao follows this with the final image of the poem, that every death (the natural outcome of an explosion) leaves behind it an

Sometimes there is sadness without tears (*Rudyanto Wjaya | Shutterstock.com*)

echo. Just as the momentary lull in the explosion is the result of the activity of sound waves, so Bei Dao also uses the imagery of sound to assert that every life leaves a trace behind. In a society dedicated to subsuming the individual to the collective, this assertion that the individual continues to matter is more revolutionary than it might appear to us in the West. Like the lull, the echo represents an open space, a moment in which sound pauses, in which we wait to hear what will come next. One could argue that it is precisely these open spaces, these moments in which we wait, in which interpretation has not yet closed off the possibilities of meaning, that Bei Dao seeks through his use of paradox, juxtaposition, and parallel structure.

For readers accustomed to parsing a poem in search of a single, unified meaning, Bei Dao can be frustrating. He is utterly disinterested in the sort of poem that builds incrementally to a single climax, exploring a concept and finally coming to some conclusion about the nature of that concept. For

Bei Dao, that smacks of the kind of imposition of meaning by which the Communist leadership exerted its iron grip not only over the people but also over their imaginations. Bei Dao seeks something different, a poetry of gaps and omissions, a poetry that, like the cloud in the second line, perhaps obscures but also leaves room for a reader's imagination to interpret for himself what meanings might be inspired by the images the poet presents.

Source: Charlotte M. Freeman, Critical Essay on "All," in *Poetry for Students*, Gale, Cengage Learning, 2011.

Daniel Simon

In the following essay, Simon asserts that although "Bei Dao's poetry is often linked to the public spectacle of 'protest' literature, it is better to think of his dedication to the form, rather, as an alternate world spoken into existence by the 'still, small voice' of the imagination."

As the twenty-second Puterbaugh fellow in a forty-year tradition, Bei Dao joins the ranks of Octavio Paz, Edouard Glissant, and Czeslaw Milosz in being known not only—although principally—as a poet, but also for his contributions as a fiction writer and essayist. Bei Dao's ties to *World Literature Today* include his nomination by Eliot Weinberger, in 1996, for the Neustadt International Prize for Literature, and his own nomination of Gary Snyder, in turn, for the 2004 Neustadt award. As part of the week-long celebration of his life and work at the University of Oklahoma in April 2008, the Puterbaugh Conference on World Literature included Bei Dao reading his poems to a packed auditorium on the OU campus in addition to lively discussions of Chinese culture, literature, language, and politics by Peter Gries, Mark Frazier, Ming Chao Gui, Yunte Huang, Ning Yu, Dian Li, Yibing Huang, and Jonathan Stalling.

Although Bei Dao's poetry is often linked to the public spectacle of "protest" literature, it is better to think of his dedication to the form, rather, as an alternate world spoken into existence by the "still, small voice" of the imagination. My favorite vision of Bei Dao is of him at work for eleven years, during the early 1970s, as a concrete mixer and ironworker, a trade that he describes in a text called "Shifu" (meaning "master" or "teacher" in Chinese) in the essay collection *Midnight's Gate*. In that essay, he describes standing over an anvil hammering iron with the master, Yan Shifu. As the apprentice, Bei Dao must wield the heavier hammer, a "fourteen-pound sledge" that he synchronizes with the master's smaller hammer, alternating blows

"light and heavy, quick and slow, the sounds rising and falling." After a full day of hammering iron, Bei Dao would go back to his room and read into the night, the vision of the hot metal sparks still dancing like stars in his eyes.

As dim as those sparks from thirty years ago may be today, Bei Dao's craft of poetry remains a very workmanlike, tactile trade. In the first poem in the collection called *Forms of Distance*, Bei Dao writes: "It's been a perfectly normal year / my sledgehammer sits idle, and yet / borrowing the light of the future / I glimpse that metric standard in platinum / here on the anvil." And in a poem from his 1991 collection *Old Snow*, he writes: "The new century's tongue is beaten by four hammers in turn."

Later, in a 1998 interview, Bei Dao insisted that "a poet must establish his world through his poems—a sincere and unique world, a world of justice and humanity." The world of Bei Dao's poems, a testament of fire and an object of that making we call poetry, holds justice and humanity as ideals, even as the jagged edge of reality—what he calls the "stray bullets of ideology" or the "shattered mirror" of history—punctures any false hope in a politics of utopia or easy redemption. Much like Wallace Stevens's poet-as-noble-rider, Bei Dao insists on the creative freedom of the imagination, which must press back against the pressures of reality, "a violence from within that protects us from a violence without," in Stevens's phrase.

As his translator David Hinton notes, "Bei Dao's poems are constructed from splinters of civilization frittering itself away in a ruins of the spirit; and at the same time, in the private space they create, the poems open forms of distance from those ruins." Bei Dao reaffirms life's ascent "in search of a language," "a million scintillating suns" reflected in the shattered mirror, the "East's imagination" like a sun "hanging in the air" above the forger's kiln, a butterfly fluttering "among the huge dark words of history." Truly, the apprentice has now become the master.

Source: Daniel Simon, "China's Harmonious Blacksmith," in *World Literature Today*, Vol. 82, No. 6, November/ December 2008, p. 3.

Claudia Pozzana

In the following excerpt, Pozzana discusses Bei Dao's poetry and states that a "world" for Bei Dao is a category internal to poetry, elaborated at a distance from philosophy.

> WHAT MAKES THE SENSIBILITY OF POETRY TOWARD LOVE EVEN MORE INTENSE IS PROBABLY THE TORSION THAT THE LOVING SCENE IMPARTS ON THE LANGUAGE, CREATING AN IMBALANCE BETWEEN THE EXORBITANT POWER OF LANGUAGE AS A TOTALITY OF SIGNIFIERS, AND THE ESSENTIALITY, MAYBE THE INDIGENCE, OF THE DECLARATION 'I LOVE YOU.'"

"A poet," writes Bei Dao, "must establish his world through his poems—a sincere and unique world, a world of justice and humanity." But what is a world? Though this is a philosophical question, it is posed by Bei Dao with an intrinsically poetic rationality and recalls what has been a recurrent theme in both ancient and modern Chinese poetry: that "to create worlds" is a basic requirement of poetic subjectivity. A "world" for Bei Dao is a category internal to poetry, elaborated at a distance from philosophy. "Justice and humanity" are similarly construed and, far from designating the substance of "man," they are rather stakes for poetry to delineate with an independent mode of thinking.

The world of Bei Dao is populated by various figures, among them a "Northern island": *Bei* means "north" and *Dao*, "island." This pseudonym was invented by the poet Mang Ke, Bei Dao's friend and cofounder with him in 1978 of *Jintian* (*Today*), the independent review that opened a new space of intellectual possibility for poetry and literature in China. The pseudonym identified the main quality that makes Bei Dao an emblematic figure in contemporary Chinese poetry: a subjective persistence in conditions of the greatest isolation and desertification, even at the risk of becoming a submerged island. The following lines from "Boat Ticket," one of Bei Dao's early poems, sketch a sort of self-portrait:

the island that rises from the ebbing tide
solitary as the heart
lacks the soft shadow of bushes
and chimney smoke

CONTEMPORARY POETIC CONFIGURATION

Bei Dao displays a persistent insularity and a quiet stubbornness, qualities that are shared by various other personalities that comprise what can be called a contemporary Chinese poetic configuration. The establishment of *Jintian* was the foundational event of this configuration, as it made available to readers a vast underground poetry that had had, until then, no outlet in the established publishing apparatus. At the time of its founding, young poets faced not only an iniquitous lack of freedom in publishing, but also an intellectual crisis concerning issues of Chinese cultural consistency. Despite the vigilance of the repressive apparatus, these poets displayed a rare capacity for self-organization and public intervention, supported by a remarkable level of literary scholarship that was, in most cases, acquired through nonacademic curricula. *Jintian* exposed a major discontinuity in the realm of artistic and poetic thinking by revealing a subjective capacity at the edge of a void or, more precisely, the courage to approach this void as the opening of new possibilities for thought.

In the late seventies, the question of "thinking" in the Chinese mother tongue was overwhelmed by the chasm opened by the Cultural Revolution. In that chasm, the group of *Jintian* poets exposed the saturation of an entire network of cultural conditions for thinking in poetry and the arts, whereas in the artistic and literary discourses grounded in "revolutionary culture" those young poets could see only anemic simulacra of thought, refractory to any artistic invention.

Although it persisted in official discourse after the seventies, the framework of a didactic vision of arts that was typical of socialism had collapsed, inexorably discredited by the effects of the Cultural Revolution. This vision had been meant to raise mass aesthetic consciousness and social morality, but in fact it shaped consensual opinions about state policies. This cultural condition for the arts having been exhausted, the first issue at stake in the late seventies was the urgent need for an independent intellectual space for poetry: a space to be invented in conditions of greatest indigence for cultural references, established models, and general theories.

In the last two decades, the problem of such an independent space for poetry has undergone various refinements and nonlinear reshapings. Current periodizations of the contemporary

Chinese poetic scene—those separating *menglong* and *post-menglong*—make sense only as processes of invention and reinvention of that intellectual space and not as cultural labels of alternative poetic sects in reciprocal competition. In the words of Mo Mo, a poet of the so-called *post-menglong* generation: "As for the spiritual condition and the cultural framework, the critical situation that the poets [in the nineties] should face is the same as that of Mang Ke and Bei Dao [in the late seventies]."

WORLD

Though insular, the world of Bei Dao is characterized by an infinite vastness apt to agitate every fixed and firm place: "How big is the world" exclaims a verse of "Cold Hope," a poem that, while written before 1978, anticipates some constituent elements of Bei Dao's developing style of abstraction. The cold hope is the intellectual operator that, in the world created by the poem, permits a division between a desire for truth and an impending nihilism. The infinite variety of things—earth, sun, sea, night, sky, dreams—is not distinguished from annihilation: "the earth is flying away" and "the drawn back horizon" collapses with a cry, the sun "falls in the abyss," an "insane slaughter," perhaps unstoppable, of "frail reeds" is completed, and perhaps we have lost "the sun and the earth / and ourselves."

The music that such multiplicity intones— "what is this noise / that seems coming from the sky?" (section 7)—turns into "serious funeral music," a solemn *"ouverture"* of temporal finitude, inducing a belief in death (section 13):

> Sounds of bells announcing the time
>
> This solemn *ouverture*
> leads me to believe in death

A few verses earlier, this annihilating faith had claimed that "Newton is dead" (section 8). This is obviously an untruth, since Newton cannot but be an immortal not only for science, but also for poetry. As Álvaro de Campos wrote, "the binomial of Newton is as beautiful as the Venus of Milo." The poem continues in an alarming succession of figurations of morbid dispersion, until the nihilist drift is suddenly diverted by an unexpected desire for truth (section 16):

> I would want that every man alive
> laugh truly
> cry frankly

From this desire—that for better or for worse, in joy and in sorrow, there are truths for everyone—the poem moves from belief in death to disbelief in it and its signs (section 20):

> Sounds of bells announcing the time
> this solemn *ouverture*
> what does it mean?

In the final verses, despite the burdensome legacy of earth, a positive figure of subjectivity appears:

> Hope
> The inheritance of this earth
> Seems so heavy
>
> Calm
> Cold

This calibrated abstraction of his verses reveals that the world of Bei Dao is, essentially, a world of thought. What he shares with other authors of the Chinese contemporary poetic configuration is the vision of poetry as a singular form of rationality: an intellectual space that makes it possible to create independent paths. The poetic world of Bei Dao creates itself through a net of distances that define his own intellectual singularity.

Every poet develops her or his own way of knowing and thinking in poetry that is discontinuous with other modes of knowing and thinking: it is unique. This uniqueness, or intellectual singularity, depends on the capacity of the poet to create her or his own world and categories through specific poetic operations. Moreover, to create its own categories, poetry cannot but be in continuous dialogue with and vis–vis the multiplicity of possible modes of thought and logics. It is the availability of poetry to virtually every mode of rationality that requires subtle forms of intellectual distance.

In Bei Dao's verses there are at least three series of distances that deserve close reflection and which concern the main entities to which his poetry as "thought" relates. The first is language itself—that is the core matter of poetry. The second concerns relationships with other singular rationalities, namely love and politics. A third distance is established from the sphere of knowledge that is particular to philological-literary fields.

LANGUAGE

Bei Dao's poetry starts with a disbelief that essentially questions language. This starting gesture estranges poetic rationality from the high opinion that language has of itself: every language represents itself as a totality of signifiers and imposes a belief in this representation on speakers of that language. The verses of "Answer," the poem that made Bei Dao famous, declare instead:

> I tell you, world
> I—do—not—believe!
> . . . .
> I do not believe the sky is blue
> I do not believe the echo of thunders
> I do not believe the dreams are false
> I do not believe the death is without judgment

It was in the precarious negation of this chain of signifiers that those "do-not-believe" proclamations became a sort of manifesto of the *Jintian* review that opened the new Chinese poetic constellation. Though some younger Chinese poets have seen only their heroic overtones, in fact these verses deliberately disavow the communicative obviousness of language and aim to open new possibilities for the relationship between poetry and the Chinese language, revealing the latter as an entity suspended between "five thousand years pictograms" and "the fixed gaze in the eyes of the men of the future." The Chinese language, far from being the icon of cultural substance, was declared a topography of possible inventions for poetry and thought. Furthermore, any illusory pretense of a social and pedagogical function of poetry, or of any *cultural* production of language, was considered expired. As the poem "Language" concludes:

> Many languages
> fly through the world
> but the production of language
> can neither increase nor decrease
> the silent pain of humanity

This meditation on language, recurrent in the verses of Bei Dao, constitutes a wide horizon of questions that have also been explored by other contemporary Chinese poets. By the end of the seventies, these poets were focused on an "issue of language" in China. They dealt with an increase in intrinsically poetic reflections as a political "matter" of the subjective difficulties of "Chineseness," beyond any simulacra of community that pervaded their contemporary cultural scene.

Since the 1989 disaster in Tian'anmen Square, Bei Dao, like other Chinese poets, has being living in exile. Consequently, the issue of a relationship with the Chinese language registers a particular personal distance for him. The exile, however, is not only negative. For example, in "Old Snow" the fact that the relationship between language and poetic writing is displaced may be favorable to poetic inspiration. The "foreigner's small room" is often visited by the "old snow"—an image of poetic thinking that revitalizes "an ancient language."

The exiled poet takes an indifferent attitude toward his native language, regarding any cultural substance. "I speak Chinese to the mirror" reads the first verse of "A Local Accent." Language as a mirror returns an image of a communitarian identity to the speaker but, for Bei Dao, "the homeland is a local accent." The communitarian illusion that one belongs to a language or culture hides the fact that language and culture belong to anyone: that they belong to the poet, and not vice versa. As Bei Dao recently asserted: "To be in exile allows a distance: between me and my culture, between the present and the past." This distance is even more manifest in notions of Chinese or Western culture: "I do not think to belong to either of the two. It is a kind of freedom not to be obliged towards any culture."

POLITICS

Bei Dao was initially considered to be an overly politicized poet. However, his poems clearly evidence an intrinsic tension with political matters. "Poetry," stated Bei Dao in a recent interview, "does not work directly in political situations. It operates in deeper ways to open the imagination and to change our way of thinking and speaking." Beyond his image as a dissident, the key point of his relationship with politics is a poetical reflection on language as a national political issue. With this perspective, he not only establishes a distance from, but also a subjective relationship with, politics and its substantives.

In the poem "Void," for example, a series of relevant political themes such as indigence, freedom, and victory are rethought in the light of the category of *void*—indeed a high category in classical Chinese thought:

> Indigence is a void freedom is a void
> in the orbits of the marmorean statue
> victory is a void

What is at stake is the unnamable limit between language and poetry: for is not the void of signifiers, the discontinuity intrinsic in language, one of the main worries of every poet?

> desperation is a void
> on the bottom of a friend's glass
> betrayal is a void
> on the photo of a loved one

disgust is a void
in that long-awaited letter
time is a void

Only after these more personal specifications does the poem return in the final verses to a "political" reference—the void of "history":

history is a void
a genealogical registry that continues
only the dead can obtain recognition

The fact is that *history* has been, in the political culture of the twentieth century, virtually synonymous with *politics*. The void in question in this poem points to the contemporary intellectual exhaustion of historical visions of politics. It also concerns, to be sure, history as a keyword in the Chinese cultural tradition. In an interview with his French translator Chantal Chen-Andro, Bei Dao asserts: "The Chinese life is intrinsically linked with history. It must carry the burden of history. The word 'History' in my poems may have an ironic connotation. The poet must try to resolve the problem of this burden. It is a word that circulates in China between intellectuals. A word repeated too often.... We must get away from this position. Objective history does not exist, it is only something that is always being repeated."

LOVE

In that same interview, when asked about the many distances and empty spaces in his poems, Bei Dao answered that "the distance is, first of all, between life and poetry . . . life is something different from poetry.... And furthermore, a 'colder' attitude is needed. To retract from these ardors, these impulses. To create a distance from *pathos*. If one experiences love, he cannot talk about it in this way, it is ridicule. To talk about it directly is too simple."

Nevertheless, a love scene often appears in Bei Dao's verses and exemplifies how the distance from pathos is constructed. In the poem "Comet," a crisis is explicitly underway from the first verses:

Come back, or go away forever
Do not remain so at the door
like a stone statue
with the look that does not expect any answer
discuss everything that is between us

A stereotypical scene: the choice looks decisive, compared with the intolerable indecision of the beloved. But in the central strophe any reference to this alternative disappears:

In effects difficult to imagine
it is not the darkness, but the dawn;

will the light of one lamp endure?
Perhaps a comet will rise
that drags dust of ruins
and names of the defeated
making them shine, ignite, incinerate

The main difficulty at this point is contemplating a recommencement, but there remains the possibility that the fascinating and destructive figure of a comet will appear on the horizon. In the third and last strophe, the initial alternative reappears, but is radically unbalanced:

Come back, we will build our home again
or leave forever, like a comet
shiny and icy like frost,
that rejects the darkness dusk submerging itself
    within,
crossing the white corridor that links one night to
    the other
in an echoing valley
you sing alone

Every poem of love is based on the difficulty of love. In this case, the distance from pathos that for Bei Dao must qualify love poetry is created by a poetic meditation on a typical argument of love—"come back or leave forever." Ultimately, its subjective fallacy is revealed: the choice seems to be drastic but its pathos is empty. If the beloved were to come back, the poem would be exhausted at the first verse of the third strophe, on the scene of domestic repair. Instead, the chance for intense love verses is ignited only by the possibility of the beloved's ultimate departure.

In these verses, a subjective singularity comes progressively into focus, after being denied in the first strophe and subordinated to a false alternative. In the last seven verses, three frames occur in fast succession: in the first, the loved one, going away, would become a "shiny and icy" comet whose fascination seems to be the result of its contradictory indecision toward the dusk. In the second, toward the antepenultimate verse, the subjective existence of the beloved is recognized not only in the darkness of the night, but also in the luminous corridor of the days. Finally, in the last two verses, the singularity of his song is emphasized by the echoes of the valley.

Subjecting the amorous scene to such scrutiny exposes language as the privileged land on which the plot unfolds and, at the same time, meditates on the distance between the rationality of poetry and love. The poem is an unceasing expression of an embarrassed separation regarding love

itself—surely not for a lack of emotional partici-
pation, but because of the heterogeneity between
the inner thought of love and the inner thought of
poetry. The distance between the two singular
rationalities is unavoidable. However, this very
distance is a sensitive matter for poetry because a
special proximity is also at stake. If poetry is so
often attracted by love, it is because the amorous
scene is articulated in declarations whose primary
matter—the language—is *the same* as that with
which the poetry engages in hand-to-hand com-
bat. It is for similar reasons that poetry also estab-
lishes, through its enunciations and declarations, a
"relationship at a distance" with politics.

What makes the sensibility of poetry toward
love even more intense is probably the torsion
that the loving scene imparts on the language,
creating an imbalance between the exorbitant
power of language as a totality of signifiers,
and the essentiality, maybe the indigence, of the
declaration "I love you." The language is forced
to undress all of its communicative functions to
traverse the uneasiness of the scene. Bei Dao
calls this crossing "the step," as in the poem
"This Step," indicating not only "the distance
between us," but also the intrinsic imbalance of
amorous rationality: "death is only a step away"
and "hatred is only a step away." Or, as
described in "Absence": "love and hatred bite
the same apple."

In "Elegy," the tension between poetry and
love increases around the coexistence of love and
death, whose *trait-d'union* is the widow. In the
first strophe, she appears as a figure of the
mourning ritual, and, in the second, as both an
object of desire and a desiring subject:

> The widow offers her broken tears
> to an idol, she waits for the milk from the breast
> that pack of small wolves just born
> jumping, one by one, the line between life and death

While, in the first verses, the widow mourns
the spouse, surrounded by a horde of feeders
who long for her breast, in the second strophe,
the same breast slips into the symbolic order of
desire and she sensually advances, available for
an extraordinary love and making grain grow
from marble:

> you come towards me, erect, the small hard breasts
> we meet on the fields
> the grain on the granite grows madly
> you are that widow, the disappeared
> is me, magnificent desire of a life
> we lie together, bathed in sweat
> the bed goes adrift on the river of dawn

In the emotion of the encounter, she is iden-
tified as the same figure of the first strophe, "the
widow." In lying beside her, the "magnificent
desire of a life" can be realized, but only by imag-
ining occupying the place of the disappeared:
"you are that widow, the disappeared / is me."
The figure of the mother-widow appears like the
joint between eros and thanatos: the title "Elegy"
emphasizes that the meditation on the twofold
registry of mourning and desire in the love scene
is firmly grounded in poetic rationality. . . .

Source: Claudia Pozzana, "Distances of Poetry: An
Introduction to Bei Dao," in *positions: East Asia Cultures
Critique*, Vol. 15, No. 1, 2007, pp. 91–111.

Dian Li

*In the following excerpt, Li examines the elements
of paradox in Dao's poetry.*

. . . Arguably the most eminent Chinese poet
today, Bei Dao lives and writes in two worlds. In
China, he is a memory, a literary giant of the
1980s whose pathbreaking writings influenced a
generation and sparked the democracy move-
ment that helped accelerate the country's reform
and openness. In the West, he is a reminder of
China's repression and intolerance, a poetic
enigma whose well-translated elliptical syntax
and cryptic imagery represent a complex interior
response to a hostile exterior world. Such differ-
ent reactions toward Bei Dao underscore the
transformation of the poet himself—from an
uncompromising young rebel in pre-1989
China to a mellowing and meditative poetic
voice in exile in the West.

Born in Beijing in 1949 (the year of birth for
the People's Republic of China), Bei Dao's life
for the most part has intertwined with the poli-
tics of China. Mao's crusade of sending the city
youth to the countryside (the rustication cam-
paign known as *zhishi qingnian shangshan xiax-
iang*) caught Bei Dao right after his high school
graduation, and he was sent to work as a con-
struction worker in a Beijing suburb, where he
started to write perhaps to fight boredom and a
feeling of despair. By the end of the 1970s, China
had just awakened from the nightmare of its
Cultural Revolution, and the oppressive Maoist
ideology had lost much of its credibility. After
years of overfeeding on the formulaic propaganda
of socialist literature, the public, especially young
readers, were ready for an alternative. Thus Bei
Dao's personal pulse became that of a generation.

WRITING IS ALWAYS A PUBLIC ACT BECAUSE
THE LANGUAGE ONE USES IS IN THE PUBLIC DOMAIN.
IN THEORY AT LEAST, THERE IS NO WRITING THAT
CANNOT BE DECIPHERED, AND TO USE WRITING TO
KEEP ONE'S SECRET THEN IS AT BEST A SELF-
DELUSIONAL ACT."

Although, understandably, his writings paralleled the official poetry in their style of grandiosity and sloganizing, they could not be more different in message. The significance of a simple statement such as "I—do—not—believe!" can only be grasped by those who must believe nothing else but Mao. The central concern of Bei Dao's poetry at this time was a plea for the restoration of personal space and life's ordinariness against a general deprivation of humanity in China for the past decade. "I am no hero," he writes. "In an age without heroes / I just want to be a man." Being a man means, Bei Dao repeatedly clarifies, living a life of dignity and fulfillment without political consequences. Such apolitical ideas were given a political reading by both the student protesters of the 1980s and the Chinese government. When Bei Dao's influence spread from small circles of friends to many college campuses, the literary establishment launched a campaign against him and a like-minded group of young poets, maliciously labeling their works "Misty Poetry," a label that Bei Dao would later gleefully embrace. The official hostility made Bei Dao famous but it ultimately led to his forced exile in 1989 following the Tian'anmen Square student protest.

"The exile of the word has begun," Bei Dao announced upon his arrival in Europe in the spring of 1989, immediately becoming the symbol of China's abortive democracy movement. He revived his short-lived journal *Jintian* (*Today*) and made it an important forum for the community of exiled Chinese writers and artists. By now, Bei Dao's writing career in exile is longer than it was in China, and he has a much larger body of work to match, all of which has been translated into over thirty languages. At present, maintaining a principal residence in the United States, Bei Dao continues to be a citizen of the world, giving readings and lectures in places as far away as Latin America and Africa. The recent "lenience" by the Chinese government to allow him family visits in Beijing does little to change Bei Dao's status as an exiled poet. As tragic as exile has been to his family life, Bei Dao has relished the unexpected freedom and the opportunity to work "the word" to attain the realm of pure poetry, a poetry of linguistic exactitude and aesthetic bliss. In terms of style and technique, he has become a bold experimentalist in truncated word combinations and disjointed images. He has also reinvigorated his efforts to draw on classical Chinese poetry as well as his favorite Western poets such as Paul Celan and César Vallejo. Removed from familiar sensations and relationships, Bei Dao seizes the singularity of his life in exile and contextualizes his heightened sense of subjectivity in everything that is happening—be it an accidental mosquito bite, a Bach concert, or a phone call home. In this mundaneness of life, however, an opponent always lurks, invisible and in some cases unnamable, working to undermine life's promise and fragment the self. It can be argued that exile is only an occasion for Bei Dao's profound sense of alienation and pessimism and that he also is reiterating a truth about modern life in general, a truth that is more powerful and long-lasting than a single political ideology. It is also evident that exile has reinforced Bei Dao's belief in paradoxy as a strategy for meaning that was derived from his oppositional poetics in China.

Throughout his career, however, Bei Dao has been beset with the complaint of readability. The label of Misty Poet is his legacy in China and continues to define him abroad. In recent times, a growing number of critics—for reasons very different from those of his official Chinese critics in earlier times—have expressed frustration with Bei Dao's poetry: how his enigmatic style, fractured syntax, and disjunctive imagery have conspired to resist reading even by expert readers. For example, Michael Duke, an esteemed scholar of contemporary Chinese literature, has declared that Bei Dao's poetry "as a whole did not make any sense." The Taiwan writer and critic Lee Kuei-shien offers a similar reaction: "The more I read the less sense he makes to me. The knots of so many contradictions are beyond unraveling, and the more I try to interpret, the greater the apparent disarray." If the "sense" that the two critics wish to make is a traditional thematic unity and interpretative certainty, Bei Dao's poetry is bound to cause disappointment. The impression that Bei Dao is not committed to "meaning," this essay will argue, is because he is committed to paradox. If paradox produces meanings at all, they are always multiple, undifferentiated, and indeterminate. The unending display of paradoxes, whose power comes from an imaginative reordering of things and events, forms a key aspect of Bei Dao's poetic world.

THROUGH THE PRISM OF PARADOX

Paradox, as commonly understood, is a play on logic; it first invokes contradictions and then subverts them by the power of reason to finally dissolve them altogether. In the end, logic survives a serious challenge but ultimately prevails. At least this is how two contemporary rhetoricians, Jeanne Fahnestock and Marie Secor, characterize the strategy of paradox in literary criticism. Identified as one of the six fundamental topoi in rhetoric, the paradox topos is used by critics to "show how contradictory elements can be unified via creative interpretation." If "all good literature commonly expresses a paradoxical view of life" and "the techniques of literature are in themselves interestingly paradoxical," as Harvey Birenbaum writes in his joyful book *The Happy Critic*, then we would have to consider finding and solving paradoxes a centerpiece in the puzzle of literary interpretation. Obviously, this proposal, which is of great interest to my reading of Bei Dao, is premised on the belief that all paradoxes are solvable and it is from the process of such a solution that meanings are derived. The question is what constitutes the solution of a paradox. Does it function to negate or reaffirm the paradox that it helps to explain? To answer this question, we need to first take a short detour into the philosophical discourse of paradox in China and the West.

The idea of paradox proper in the Chinese tradition comes from the philosopher Gongsun Long's (ca. third century BC) famous proposition *baima fei ma*, which is the conclusion of his mind-boggling disputation about the relationship between whole and part. Translated literally, *baima fei ma* becomes "a white horse is not a horse." However, this conventional translation, as the Chinese scholar Chen Jianzhong points out, is derived from a misunderstanding of the word *fei*, which, in classical Chinese philosophical texts, expresses negativity in many more

forms than the familiar "not to be." Using examples from Gongsun Long's other writings, as well as from writings by Gongsun Long's contemporaries, Chen decides that *fei* in this particular context should mean "is different from" and then goes on to rerender *baima fei ma* as "a white horse is different from a horse." This new interpretation of Gongsun Long, of course, does not take paradoxy out of his argument, but it does repair Gongsun Long's reputation as a mere sophist and places him in the forefront of the Chinese epistemological tradition, which valorizes incongruity and contradiction as a path to knowledge and a way of understanding the world. That paradoxy is more than an exercise of sophistry and that it is an indispensable instrument to truth are evident in the Western tradition as well. In Plato's *Parmenides*, which is generally considered the chief source for paradox in literature and rhetoric in the West, Plato has the sage Parmenides and a young Socrates engage in an astonishing dialectical contest. They argue simultaneously the opposite sides of a question and play with antithetical pairs such as likeness and unlikeness, being and nonbeing endlessly. The purpose is to find a way to access truth, and truth is shown to reside in a paradoxical state, which means, as pointed out in Charles D. Presberg's reading of Plato, that truth exists "not so much between as beyond extremes, each of which is both enlightening and deficient, both partially true and partially false."

The idea of truth in paradoxy comes through in a spectacular fashion in the following classical tale, known to every educated Chinese person. Once upon a time, a blacksmith comes to the marketplace to sell the weapons he has made. Holding up a spear, he declares to the assembled crowd: "This is the sharpest spear you will ever find. It will pierce through any shield." Then he lifts a shield and says, "This is the sturdiest shield in the world. Nothing can pierce it." Someone in the crowd asks, "What if I use your spear to pierce your shield?" The blacksmith cannot muster an answer. Needless to say, paradoxy is practiced by both the blacksmith and the spectator, perhaps without their self-knowledge, but what is the solution to the hapless blacksmith's contradictory claims? A pragmatic person might say, let us test the spears against the shields as suggested by the spectator and we can do it hundreds of times so that we will reach a statistical truth as to which is more powerful. This approach fits the billing of "creative interpretation" advocated by Fahnestock and Secor, which may indeed resolve the blacksmith's contradictions. The Chinese reader throughout history, however, has shown little interest in such a scientific method. He identifies with the wise spectator but is content to let the blacksmith keep his puzzle. He embraces the paradox as a whole and takes no sides in the power of the spear or the shield, for the meaning of the paradox lies precisely in the symbiotic relationship between the spear and the shield: there is no absolute power when comparing the two, and the function of one depends upon the other, like yin and yang, like everything else in the world.

It is little wonder that the blacksmith's dilemma has become an all-time favorite in the Chinese collective memory. The cosmic view that is derived from a proper reading of the paradox is now a familiar one to those who have studied Chinese culture: everything has its opposite and the world is full of contradictions; change happens constantly to alter the constitution of the opposites but never annihilates one position or the other. The name of this cosmic view is, of course, Daoism in the tradition of Lao-Zhuang. According to the late scholar of classical Chinese literature, James J. Y. Liu, paradoxy is central to the cosmology of Daoism. Both Lao Zi and Zhuang Zi employ the paradox of language as a strategy of persuasion and a way of articulating the presence of the Dao, which exists beyond but can only be comprehended within the means of language. Many of the parables and metaphors pervasive in their writings invariably express the idea that language is always inadequate but necessary for describing reality. For example, having asserted that the Dao cannot be named in the very beginning of "Dao De Jing," Lao Zi nevertheless goes on to name it, with an admitted hesitation:

> I do not know its name;
> I style it "Tao" [Dao];
> And, in the absence of a better word, call it "The Great."

In the same vein, Zhuang Zi writes: "The Dao has never had boundaries, and the words have never had constancy. The great Dao is not called by name; great eloquence does not speak." Zhuang Zi not only upholds the "provisionality" of language but also goes further than Lao Zi in minimizing the value of language so as to deny the distinction between speaking and silence. At the end of chapter 25 in *Zhuang Zi yinde*, he writes: "If speech is adequate, then one can speak all day and fully describe the Dao; if speech is not adequate, then one can speak all day and merely fully describe things. The

ultimate of the Dao and of things cannot be adequately carried either by speech or by silence. Neither to speak nor to be silent is the way to discuss the ultimate." The leap from "either/or" to "neither/nor," as James J. Y. Liu argues, represents a significant development in Zhuang Zi's thinking through paradoxy. What appears to be a repudiation of binary oppositions by Zhuang Zi is in fact an admission of all paradoxes. This is to say that opposites are not to be united or reconciled but should be accepted as they are, alone and together. If Zhuang Zi's paradoxical thinking points toward mysticism, that is because he believes that truth itself—with the Dao as its ultimate signifier—is mysteriously elusive, with access to it depending not on analysis or scientism but on embodiment and conviction, so that one needs to take on the role of an aesthetician but not that of a logician, for an aesthetician is a connoisseur of paradox and a logician its detractor.

How much of this collective memory is alive with Bei Dao? It is always risky to guess one individual's scope of reception to his culture, but one should not underestimate the power of "cultural sedimentation," as the respected contemporary Chinese philosopher Li Zehou has admonished us. "Writing is a way to keep a secret," Bei Dao declares, using his favorite form of sentence-structure—the statement—and this is one of the many Bei Dao statements that have taken his audiences by surprise. There is no easy way to argue away the contradictions apparent in the statement. All writers want to be read, and Bei Dao is no exception. Writing is always a public act because the language one uses is in the public domain. In theory at least, there is no writing that cannot be deciphered, and to use writing to keep one's secret then is at best a self-delusional act. Still, it would be futile to argue logically against Bei Dao because he has already precluded the power of logic in his revelation about writing and the self. The key word here is "secret," a loaded signifier of cosmic dimensions that points to the mosaic of his inner contradictions—contradictions that are not for him to keep but for him to share and that can only be expressed in writing paradoxically. A paradox begets another paradox, which may be the best way to describe Bei Dao's view of writing.

To see the world through the prism of paradox is clearly evident in Bei Dao's following remarks: "There are many principles in the world, and many of these principles contradict each other. Tolerance for the existence of another's principle is the basis for your own existence." It is interesting to note that Bei Dao uses the word "principles" without rendering a value judgment, yet they "contradict" one another, as do the spear and the shield. Tolerance, a nonprinciple acting like the highest principle of all, is the distance that keeps the contradictions in check, or in other words, it is like a Daoist belief that prevents the spear and the shield from testing each other for the absolute domination of one over another. It should not be surprising that Bei Dao's words translate the Chinese blacksmith's tale so well if we remember that paradox in the Chinese context thrives on irreconcilable opposites and unending contradictions.

It may be time now for us to follow Bei Dao into his poetry where he has kept his secrets to share with us. In the following readings of Bei Dao's poems, I will try to describe the poet's construction of meanings between opposites and his reliance on split imagery, both strategies of paradoxy that are as much about the revelation as about the reveiling of a skeptical mind. . . .

Source: Dian Li, "Paradox and Meaning in Bei Dao's Poetry," in *positions: East Asia Cultures Critique*, Vol. 15, No. 1, 2007, pp. 113–36.

Jeffery Twitchell-Waas

In the following review, Twitchell-Waas argues that Dao's poetry is "likely to strike Western readers as either irritatingly amorphous or as an apt expression of exile and linguistic alienation."

The development of Bei Dao's poetry over the past two decades has in a sense lived up to the accusation of "obscure" or "misty" (menglong) with which Chinese officialdom denounced him and his fellow poets in the early 1980s. The label stuck, and the Misty Poets became renowned as marking the first decisive break with Maoist literature. For Western readers, while the early work that provoked the charge hardly appears especially obscure, Bei Dao's recent poetry has become increasingly hermetic. *Unlock* is the fourth collection by Bei Dao to appear since he was forced into permanent exile in 1989—all handsomely produced in bilingual editions by New Directions. (Another volume, *The August Sleepwalker*, translates a comprehensive selection of his early verse.)

As the best-known post-Maoist poet, both inside and outside China, Bei Dao has experienced a reception of his work determined to a considerable degree by his early adoption as a spokesperson for a dissatisfied younger generation in China and his inevitable labeling and marketing as a dissident writer in the West. The hermeticism of his recent poetry is continuous with his earlier work in that it is an assertion of subjectivity against those social pressures that would deny individuality, which presumably now includes the expectations of his Western audience. By his own admission, Bei Dao has been strongly drawn to a number of Western poets of agonized exile and linguistic estrangement, such as Tsvetaeva, Vallejo, and Celan.

For those familiar with Bei Dao's other volumes that have appeared over the course of the 1990s (see e.g. WLT 66:3, p. 578, and 72:1, p. 202), *Unlock* does not offer any striking new developments. We find here the usual carefully constructed short lyrical poems that deliberately undermine surface coherence to suggest more oblique meanings. Given the complex of pressures that would attempt to determine the poet's identity, these poems can be understood as efforts to construct a private space, a space that is constantly threatening to collapse into mere characters on the page. As with a number of exiled Chinese poets, Bei Dao's poetry tends toward an elusive fluidity, momentarily coalescing in striking images, for which Bei Dao has always been noted, only to segue surrealistically into non sequiturs. The translators have valiantly attempted to replicate the syntactical looseness whereby a following line can be read simultaneously as both discrete from its preceding line and continuing it in a redirected trajectory.

Bei Dao's poetry has always been relatively disembodied—unsituated in a definite space and time—and this tendency has now reached the point where there are virtually no concrete indicators of the poet's specific culture or setting. Or, more precisely, the siting of his poetry is largely within language itself, the compulsive groping within the traumatized Chinese of the mainland for renewed possibilities, which often depend on subtle shifts and contrasts of tone and register. Inevitably, translation will tend to result in an even more abstract version. Such poetry is likely to strike Western readers as either irritatingly amorphous or as an apt expression of exile and linguistic alienation.

Source: Jeffery Twitchell-Waas, Review of *Unlock*, in *World Literature Today*, Vol. 75, Summer/Autumn 2001, pp. 106–108.

SOURCES

Bei Dao, "All," in *The August Sleepwalker*, translated by Bonnie McDougall, New Directions, 1990, p. 35.

"Bei Dao," in *Poets.org: From the Academy of American Poets*, http://www.poets.org/poet.php/prmPID/774 (accessed August 16, 2010).

"A Brief History of the Misty Poets," in *Poets.org: From the Academy of American Poets*, http://www.poets.org/viewmedia.php/prmMID/5663 (accessed September 10, 2010).

Cayley, John, Review of *The August Sleepwalker*, in *Bulletin of the School of Oriental and African Studies*, University of London, Vol. 53, No. 3, 1990, pp. 558–59.

Fenby, Jonathan, *Modern China: The Fall and Rise of a Great Power, 1850 to the Present*, Ecco Press, 2008, pp. 22–23, 441, 451.

Jenner, W. J. F., Review of *The August Sleepwalker*, in *Australian Journal of Chinese Affairs*, Contemporary Chia Center, Australian National University, No. 23, January 1990, pp. 193–95.

LaPiana, Siobahn, "An Interview with Visiting Artist Bei Dao, Poet in Exile," in *Journal of the International Institute*, University of Michigan, Vol. 2, No. 1, Fall 1994, http://hdl.handle.net 2027/spo.4750978.0002.102 (accessed September 10, 2010).

Lee, Gregory, Review of *The August Sleepwalker*, in *China Quarterly*, No. 121, March 1990, pp. 149–51.

Li, Dian, "Paradoxy and Meaning in Bei Dao's Poetry," in *Positions: East Asia Cultures Critique*, Duke University Press, Spring 2001, Vol. 15, No. 1, pp. 113–36.

Liu, Binyan, "The Chinese Government's Opposition to Reform," in *The Tiananmen Square Massacre*, edited by Kelly Barth, Greenhaven Press, 2003, pp. 10–13, 24.

Mansfield, Greer, "Unlocking Bei Dao," in *Trope*, February 2010, http://tropemag.com/Books/Unlocking_Bei_Dao.htm (accessed August 16, 2010).

McDougall, Bonnie, Introduction to *The August Sleepwalker*, New Directions, 1990, pp. 9–14.

———, *Fictional Authors, Imaginary Audiences: Modern Chinese Literature in the Twentieth Century*, Chinese University Press, 2003, pp. 172–75.

———, "Problems and Possibilities of Translating Contemporary Chinese Literature," in *Australian Journal of Chinese Affairs*, Contemporary China Center, Australian National University, 1991, Vol. 25, pp. 37–67.

Preminger, Alex, and T. V. F. Brogan, eds., "Metaphor" and "Translation," in *New Princeton Encyclopedia of Poetry and Poetics*, Princeton University Press, 1993, pp. 760–61, 1303.

Ratiner, Steven, "Reclaiming the World: A Conversation with Bei Dao," in *Agni Magazine Online*, Vol. 54, 2001, http://www.bu.edu/agni/interviews/print/2001/ratiner-beidao.html (accessed August 16, 2010).

Wines, Michael, "China Fortifies State Business," in *New York Times*, August 29, 2010, http://www.nytimes.com/2010/08/30/world/asia/30china.html (accessed September 4, 2010).

Wong, Edward, "Official in China Says Western-Style Democracy Won't Take Root There," in *New York Times*, March 20, 2010, http://www.nytimes.com/2010/03/21/world/asia/21china.html (accessed September 4, 2010).

Wright, Edmund, "Cultural Revolution," "Gang of Four," and "Totalitarianism," in *Oxford Dictionary of World History*, Oxford University Press, 2006, pp. 164, 239, 641.

Yeh, Michelle, Review of *The August Sleepwalker*, in *World Literature Today*, Vol. 64, No. 1, Winter 1990, pp. 191–92.

FURTHER READING

Bei Dao, *The Rose of Time: New and Selected Poems*, translated by Yanbing Chen, et al., New Directions, 2010.

This bilingual volume presents poems from each of Bei Dao's books that have been published in English—*The August Sleepwalker*, *Old Snow*, *Forms of Distance*, *Landscape Over Zero*, and *Unlock*—as well as fifteen new poems. Each poem is presented on facing pages with its original Chinese version, and the book includes a preface by the poet and an afterword by Weinberger, a highly respected literary critic and translator. Of this volume, Greer Mansfield of *Trope* magazine states that "this is a book you should travel wearying distances for, fight fierce sea creatures for (if you find that you need to), and then love, cherish, read, and read again. Then buy again in several copies to send to all your friends."

Bei Dao, *Midnight's Gate: Essays*, translated by Matthew Fryslie, New Directions, 2005.

In this collection of essays and meditations, Bei Dao describes the experience of exile. Like his poetry, his essays rely on allusive language and elliptical narrative structure to recount experiences as diverse as the destruction of Palestine, a baseball game in Sacramento, California, and a conflagration in New York. In this volume, Bei Dao also writes about his eleven years as a concrete mixer and ironworker during his internal Chinese exile, as well as his travels among writing programs and poetry workshops around the world.

Celan, Paul, *Selected Poems and Prose of Paul Celan*, edited by John Feltsiner, W. W. Norton, 2001.

Bei Dao has spoken in several interviews about the effect Paul Celan's work has had on his own, as well as his affinity for Celan's position as an exile who chose to write in the language shared by his parents and his oppressors. Celan is known as well for the dense imagistic poetic style in which he sought to express the inexpressible. Although multilingual, Celan, who made much of his living as a translator, wrote almost exclusively in German, the language of the concentration camps in which he spent the years 1942–1944 and in which his parents perished.

Finkel, Donald, ed., *A Splintered Mirror: Chinese Poetry from the Democracy Movement*, translated by Donald Finkel and Carolyn Kizer, North Point Press, 1991.

One of the only anthologies in English to cover the Menglongshi poets as a group, this collection gives an overview of the many poetic approaches this group took to the political and linguistic repression they faced. While some of the poetry might seem obscure to Western readers, this collection's value lies in the overview it gives of this artistic and political moment in Chinese history.

Lee, Li-Young, *Behind My Eyes*, W. W. Norton, 2007.

Like Bei Dao, Li-Young Lee comes from a high-ranking Chinese family. His father was a personal physician to Mao Zedong before relocating the family to Indonesia, where he helped found Gamaliel University. In the late 1950s, the family fled anti-Chinese violence and spent several years living in Hong Kong and Japan before moving to the United States in 1964. Lee was educated in American universities and began publishing poetry in the early 1990s. Influenced by both his father's Christian ministry and his studies of classical Chinese poets like Du Fu and Han Shan, Lee's work is suffused with tenderness and a concise poetic style.

Watson, Burton, *The Columbia Book of Chinese Poetry from Early Times to the Thirteenth Century*, Columbia University Press, 1984.

This anthology contains over four hundred poems by ninety-six of China's great classical poets. Each of the great poets is represented by a chapter containing a generous selection of iconic poems, while minor poets are grouped by time period and poetic school. Watson is one of the most respected translators of ancient Chinese, and many of her translations have come to be considered the standard English version against which all others are judged.

SUGGESTED SEARCH TERMS

Bei Dao

Menglongshi AND Misty Poets

Democracy AND Wall

Cultural Revolution

Jintian AND Today

Bei Dao AND Misty Poets

Mao Zedong AND Cultural Revolution

Chinese Revolution

Tiananmen Square massacre

classical Chinese poetry

exile AND poetry

Fable for When There's No Way Out

"Fable for When There's No Way Out," by May Swenson, was published in her 1967 collection *Half Sun Half Sleep*. It is one of Swenson's better known and most frequently taught poems. In the poem, a baby bird struggles to break out of his shell. After struggling to the point of frustration and nearly to the point of giving up and accepting death, the bird unexpectedly finds a surprising means of freeing himself. "Fable for When There's No Way Out" was written at the height of Swenson's career, although it stands apart from her body of work in many ways. Unlike many of her other poems, it is both a narrative and a fable, meaning that it tells a story and teaches a lesson. However, like many of her poems, it centers around the opposition of extremes, in this case the forces of reason and emotion. It also includes themes of determination and survival. Although it was written after the modern period, its psychological component and nontraditional style characterize it as a modernist poem.

MAY SWENSON

1967

AUTHOR BIOGRAPHY

Swenson was born Anna Thilda May Swenson to Margaret and Dan Arthur Swenson on May 28, 1913 (some sources cite 1919), in Logan, Utah, the first of ten children in a large Mormon family. Her parents were both Swedish immigrants, with

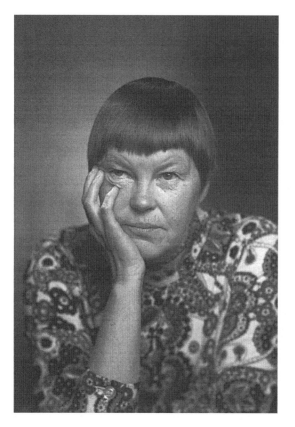

May Swenson (© Oscar White / Corbis)

her father working as a professor of mechanical engineering at Utah State Agricultural College. Swedish was the language regularly spoken in Swenson's household; English was her second language. She was interested in writing from a young age and kept journals while she was growing up. In high school, she won a twenty-five-dollar prize for her short story "Christmas Day," which was published in the school newspaper.

Swenson began attending Utah State Agricultural College in 1930. It was there that she published her first poem, "The Scribbler," in the campus literary magazine. In 1934 she received her bachelor's degree in English, with a minor in art. She spent the following year working as a reporter in Utah, but in 1935, she moved to New York, where she remained for most of her adult life. In New York City she worked in several different fields, including jobs as a stenographer, ghost-writer, secretary, and manuscript reader, while also writing her own poetry. In 1950, she met the poet Elizabeth Bishop, with whom she would maintain a lifelong friendship and correspondence. From 1959 to 1966, she worked as an editor for New Directions Press.

Swenson's first volume of poetry, *Another Animal*, was published in 1954. She published several other collections, including *A Cage of Spines* (1958) and *To Mix with Time: New and Selected Poems* (1963), before leaving New Directions Press in 1966 to devote herself to writing full time. During the late 1960s and early 1970s, she taught at and served as poet-in-residence for several universities, including Bryn Mawr, the University of North Carolina, the University of California at Riverside, Purdue University, and Utah State University, while still continuing to publish original work. In 1967 she published the volume *Half Sun Half Sleep*, which includes the poem "Fable for When There's No Way Out."

Swenson's work has a reputation for being varied and experimental. In addition to her ten volumes of poetry, she has also published three collections of poetry for children, a collection of essays, and a one-act play, as well as translations of Swedish poets' work. Her poetry, which has been compared to the work of e. e. cummings, is often vividly imaginative and suggestively erotic. Swenson was a lesbian, and although she did not go out of her way to advertise herself as such, she did once allow a poem of hers to be published in a collection of lesbian poetry.

Swenson has received numerous awards, honors, and honorary degrees for her work, including a MacArthur Fellowship, which she completed in 1987. She served as chancellor of the American Academy of Poets from 1980 until her death. Swenson died of a heart attack on December 4, 1989, in Ocean View, Delaware. She is buried in Logan, Utah.

POEM TEXT

Grown too big for his skin,
and it grown hard,

without a sea and atmosphere—
he's drunk it all up—

his strength's inside him now,   5
but there's no room to stretch.

He pecks at the top
but his beak's too soft;

though instinct and ambition shoves,
he can't get through.   10

Barely old enough to bleed
and already bruised!

In a case this tough
what's the use

if you break your head   15
instead of the lid?

Despair tempts him
to just go limp:

Maybe the cell's
already a tomb,   20

and beginning end
in this round room.

Still, stupidly he pecks
and pecks, as if from under

his own skull—   25
yet makes no crack . . .

No crack until
he finally cracks,

and kicks and stomps.
What a thrill   30

and shock to feel
his little gaff poke

through the floor!
A way he hadn't known or meant.

Rage works if reason won't.   35
When locked up, bear down.

POEM SUMMARY

"Fable for When There's No Way Out" is a narrative poem, which means that it has a definable plot. It contains eighteen stanzas, each of two lines. In the poem's thirty-six lines, an omniscient narrator details the struggle of a baby bird trying to break out of his shell. Although the poem is divided into short stanzas, which are composed of relatively short sentences, the stanzas can be grouped into five different movements, each of which represent a different stage of the baby bird's struggle.

Stanzas 1–3
In the first movement, stanzas 1 through 3, the action of the poem is ambiguous to the reader. Although the pronoun "his" is used in the first line, the reader has no idea who the male character is or whether he is human. The poem immediately thrusts the reader into a state of confusion, because the first three stanzas are nonsensical until coupled with the understanding that the poem is about a baby bird trying to break free. Before this realization, the first three stanzas seem vague and perhaps metaphorical; after this realization, the meaning of these stanzas begins to fall into place. The skin mentioned in line 1 is the bird's shell, the water and air are the embryonic fluid within the shell, and the fact that the bird cannot spread out indicates that it is time for him to hatch.

Stanzas 4–8
In the fourth stanza, it is mentioned that the male character pecks and has a beak. It suddenly becomes clear that the character in question must be a bird of some sort. With this knowledge, the first three stanzas can be reevaluated to gain additional meaning. Each stanza in the second movement, the movement of aspiration and struggle, is indicative of the bird's struggle to get out and his inability to crack his shell. In stanzas 4 and 5, the reader learns that although the bird instinctively knows that he needs to break out, he does not seem to be strong enough. Stanza 6 reveals that he is becoming injured as he strives to break free. Stanzas 7 and 8 comprise a rhetorical question that represents the bird's emotions as he tries and fails to break the shell while attaining self-inflicted wounds. The bird asks himself, What is the point of trying to break out if I die in the process?

Stanzas 9–11
Stanzas 9 through 11 constitute the movement of despair. They describe the hopelessness that the bird feels after the initial fight to break out. In stanza 9, he considers giving up, which would mean certain death, as the narrator points out in stanzas 10 and 11.

Stanzas 12–13
In stanzas 12 and 13, despite his discouragement, the bird continues, without success, to peck at his shell. This movement of the poem is the movement of endurance. These two stanzas also contain powerful and complicated imagery. The narrator compares the bird's shell to the skull of his own head. This phrasing invokes the circular image of the bird trying to get out of his own body or trying to break out of himself, which is, in a sense, what he is doing. This imagery highlights a prominent theme of the poem: the struggle between mind and body.

Stanzas 14–17
The fifth movement, stanzas 14 through 17, is the movement of success. The crack occurs in stanza 14, and the realization of the crack occurs in stanza 15. The bird is simultaneously surprised and overjoyed to have finally broken through. Surprisingly, in his desperate flailing to get out,

he broke through the shell in the exact opposite way that he had been aiming to: with his foot, through the floor of the shell, rather than with his beak through the top. The narrator reveals that the bird was not even aware that this way of breaking free was an option and that his breaking through the shell with his foot was unintentional.

Stanza 18

The last movement of the poem, which is contained in the last stanza, presents the moral or lesson of the fable that is the poem. The lesson is that sometimes, pure emotion, such as rage, can lead to a solution that could not be arrived at by simply thinking a problem through. It was not the baby bird's determination nor his logic that led him to break free of the shell, but rather the unbridled flailing that was brought on by his mounting frustration. The bird's entire struggle was completely necessary in order for him to succeed, for without it, he never would have become infuriated enough to move in such a violent way, to break the shell with his foot.

THEMES

Rationality

Many critics have noted that Swenson's poetry often contains oppositions of extremes. In "Fable for When There's No Way Out," calm, logical reason is contrasted with desperate, unbridled rage, quite explicitly in the thirty-fifth line of the poem. While the two terms are contrasted in line 35, as concepts they are folded into the entire poem and, in addition to being opposed, work in conjunction with one another. Often, the lack of fulfillment of one's reasonable or rational impulses leads to an emotional response, and conversely, when an emotional response does not lead to a productive conclusion, one searches for a reasonable answer. Thus is the interplay of these two forces in the poem. The bird's rational impulses tell him he must poke the shell with his beak in order to break it, yet his beak is not strong enough to make the slightest crack. Despite constant failure, he continues, reasonably, to peck, as the unsavory alternative to breaking out of the shell is eminent death. As he pecks and pecks and remains trapped, his anger begins to rise, and his emotions take hold of him. It is only through his consuming frustration that he accidentally finds a way out that he did not even realize was possible.

TOPICS FOR FURTHER STUDY

- "Fable for When There's No Way Out" is a fable poem, meaning that it is centered around animals and demonstrates a lesson through a story. Come up with a lesson you would like to teach your classmates, and write a fable poem that demonstrates that lesson. Lead a class discussion to see whether your classmates have understood your lesson after you present your poem.

- Using the Internet, research the modernist period in poetry. Look through the book *Reflections on a Gift of Watermelon Pickle* (1967), a collection of modern poetry for young adults edited by Stephen Dunning and others, and choose a poem from the collection. Compare and contrast it to "Fable for When There's No Way Out." What elements do the poems share? How do they vary? What characteristics does each poem possess that are in keeping with the tenets of modernist poetry? Using a computer program, create a chart that demonstrates your findings.

- Nearly all cultures have their own folktales and fables, and some popular fables exist in several cultures, in slightly different versions. Pick a culture that interests you, and research a popular fable from that culture. Create a digital multimedia presentation in which you explain the history, plot, and moral of the fable to your classmates.

- "Fable for When There's No Way Out" is a narrative poem, but it is also lyrical and meditative at moments. Examine Swenson's volume *Half Sun Half Sleep*. Do you think "Fable for When There's No Way Out" is consistent with the other poems of this collection, or do you think it stands out? Explain your reasoning in a paper in which you contextualize the poem within the collection of its publication.

Thus, it would have been impossible for the bird to reason his way out; his becoming enraged was necessary for him to break free. However, the

Chicken breaking free of its shell *(Ljupoco Smokovski /*
Shutterstock.com)

bird's reasonable impulse was also necessary for him to gain freedom. Were it not for the constant denial of his efforts, he would have never become upset enough to accidentally break through his shell. Thus, these two forces are not entirely opposed but rather work in collaboration. The irony of the poem is that hatching baby birds are rarely regarded as reasonable or able to feel rage, and to consider them so is to personify the bird. Often in Swenson's poems, and certainly in this one, she imposes a human perspective on a natural occurrence.

Determination

In addition to the bird's emotional responses, determination is a factor that helps him succeed and serves as a theme of the poem. The bird's determination is largely derived from his survival instinct, yet, because the poem is a fable, it is meant to be understood on a larger scale. The message is that there is always another way to accomplish a task, and if you are determined and diligent you will find a means to reach your goal. Although for a moment the bird is overwhelmed with despair, he determinedly keeps going and breaks through in a way he had not even intended.

The bird's determination is what ultimately causes him to become so frustrated that he is led to an unexpected reward: he succeeds.

Survival

Survival is also a major theme of the poem, for although it may initially seem like an innocent morality tale, it is fairly dark in subject matter. In stanzas 9 through 11, the bird is tempted to give up all together, let his body go weak, and waste away to death. His egg, which had once provided him nourishment and afforded his growth, would then become his casket. Although this is something that does occur in nature, it could also be projected onto a human situation. People frequently become discouraged to the point of hopelessness, yet the poem teaches the lesson that if you want to survive badly enough, success is possibler.

STYLE

Narrative Poem

"Fable for When There's No Way Out" is a narrative poem, which means that it is a poem that tells a story. Unlike some lyric poems, which convey the private thoughts and emotions of the speaker, a narrative poem always has a plot that can be summarized. In "Fable for When There's No Way Out," first a baby bird tries to break out of his shell, then he becomes discouraged, and yet he continues to peck, until finally he finds an unexpected way out of his shell. Some narrative poems are as short as a few lines, while others are as long as a book. They can have a traditional meter and rhyme scheme, or they can be prosaic. There are many different genres of narrative poetry. "Fable for When There's No Way Out" is a short, free-verse narrative poem.

Fable

A fable is a short tale, composed in prose or verse, that demonstrates a specific moral. The moral is usually stated in an epigram at the end of the story. Fables almost always feature animals as the main characters. Because it satisfies all of these conditions, "Fable for When There's No Way Out" is quite literally a fable. The first seventeen stanzas of the poem tell a story, and the last stanza, an epigram of sorts, states the lesson. Swenson went through a period in which she wrote many fables and experimented with retelling classic fables, although the majority of this work was never published.

Auditory Devices

Swenson's poems are often identifiable by their fluid musicality, and "Fable for When There's No Way Out" is no exception. The poem is free verse, meaning that it has no regular rhythm or rhyme scheme, and it is also entirely void of perfect rhyme (a rhyme in which the final accented vowels of words, as well as all following sounds are congruent). Rather, the poem is regulated by the placement of "half rhymes," words that have similar sounds but are not perfect rhymes. Half rhyme is the result of assonance and consonance, two auditory devices that are prevalent in the poem. Assonance is the repetition of similar vowel sounds, while consonance is the repetition of similar consonant sounds. Assonance is usually more noticeable than consonance, but not always. In prose, half rhymes can occur accidentally, but in poetry, like all auditory devices, they are usually intentional. The placement of half rhyme in "Fable for When There's No Way Out" is quite purposeful.

The first section (stanzas 1–3) of the poem, which establishes the setting, is entirely void of half rhyme. The fact that this section is also void of action, paired with the lack of half rhyme, makes the section read more slowly than other parts of the poem.

However, the next section (stanzas 4–8) is heavy with half rhyme. Stanza 4 contains assonance, with the short *o* sound in *top* and *soft*. Stanzas 5–7 contain assonance of the long *u* sound in *through*, *bruised*, and *used*, as well as consonance of the *b* and *d* sounds in *bleed* and *bruised*. Stanza 8 also contains consonance of the *d* in *head* and *lid*. The abundance of assonance in this section has the effect of speeding up the reading pace and heightening the level of excitement. When sounds are repeated, the poem naturally reads faster and seems more dramatic. The auditory effects in this section reflect the action of the section. It is only fitting that as the bird is desperately pecking to get out, the poem should contain heightened drama and quicker lines.

In the third section (stanzas 9–11), as the baby bird becomes dispirited, the poem decreases in pace. Assonance occurs at the end of the section with the long *u* sound in *tomb* and *room*, which highlights the gravity of the bird's situation; if he

does not find a way out, he will die before he is even hatched.

The fourth section (stanzas 12 and 13), in which the bird begins pecking again, is also largely devoid of action and half rhyme, yet the momentum slowly builds again between this section and the next (stanzas 14–17) with the repetition of the word *crack* in lines 26–28. *Crack* is an onomatopoetic word, which means that the word itself sounds similar to the action it describes. By repeating the word *crack* in three consecutive lines at the climax of the poem, the reader can almost hear the baby bird breaking through his shell. Following the climax, the assonance immediately resumes with the short *i* sound in the word *thrill* and the similar sound in *feel*. However, line 34, the last line of this section, breaks the quick flow of the short lines and half rhyme with a relatively long line that is entirely devoid of rhyme. This is because the action of the poem ends in line 33, and line 34 is the narrator's reflection on the bird's success.

The last two lines of the poem, although certainly rhythmic, are also bereft of half rhyme. They stand apart from the rest of the poem as the lesson, or moral, of the story of the poem, which is highlighted by the patterned consonance of the *r* and *w* sounds within line 35. They emphasize the fact that the bird could not get out of his shell until his enraged flailing led him to accidentally break through with his foot.

HISTORICAL CONTEXT

Modernist Poetry

Although modernist poetry was at its peak during the 1920s and 1930s and is assessed as having ended at the close of World War II in 1945, many poets, Swenson among them, were still emulating the modernist style well into the 1960s. Modernism, which was a movement away from Victorianism and the realistic Georgianism, spanned all genres of literature, including poetry. Many poets began shifting their style toward modernism in the wake of World War I as a means of expressing the sometimes horrific unpredictability of modern life. Swenson's good friend Marianne Moore was a noted modern poet, along with Ezra Pound, Gertrude Stein, Virginia Woolf, and others. Modernist writers strayed from literary traditions and conventions and were experimental in their works. They also, for the first time, sometimes included a psychological

COMPARE
&
CONTRAST

- **1960s:** In 1962, the environmental movement is drawn into the public sphere with the publication of Rachel Carson's *Silent Spring*.

  Today: Environmentalism is a well-known worldwide concern. In 2009, a climate-change summit, with participants from all over the world, is hosted in Copenhagen, Denmark.

- **1960s:** In 1965, artist Alan Sonfist proposes his influential piece "Time Landscape," which becomes a hallmark of the land art movement. Land art, or earth art, is a movement that emerges in the 1960s fusing art and nature. Rather than impose a sculpture on a landscape, the land artist uses the landscape to form the sculpture.

Today: Art dealing with nature is still a popular concept. In 2010, the Nature Consortium of Seattle, Washington, hosts the Arts in Nature Festival.

- **1960s:** In 1960, influential poet and critic Karl Shapiro publishes *In Defense of Ignorance*, an attack of the tenets of modern poetry.

  Today: Because of increasing variance in an ever-expanding field, trends in contemporary poetry are becoming increasingly difficult to pinpoint, because the field is ever expanding. David Leman and Amy Gerstler's anthology *The Best American Poetry of 2010* includes a vast array of poets, of all different genres.

component in their work. Although many modern writers viewed the world as disjointed, they believed in art as a restorative, uniting force. The use of symbolism, myth, stream of consciousness, and imagery increased during the modern period. A subset of modernism was imagism, which was a style characterized by sharp language and ample imagery. Although not directly associated with this movement, Swenson was often commended for her use of poetic imagery. "Fable for When There's No Way Out" fits many of the criteria of an imagist poem in that it presents a subject clearly and directly without straying from it, its rhythm is musical rather than metric, and it is composed in free verse. The majority of Swenson's work satisfies the specifications for modernist poetry.

Environmentalism

Like that of several poets writing in the 1960s, much of Swenson's work (roughly three-fourths of it) deals with nature in some capacity. This is unsurprising, considering that this decade was the time in which the environmental movement began to grow significantly and the newly popular concept of environmentalism was frequently

discussed in the media. The movement was sparked in 1962 with the publication of Rachel Carson's nonfiction opus *Silent Spring*, which chronicles the horrors of DDT, a pesticide that had negative impacts on the environment and wildlife, particularly birds. Around this time, environmental advocacy groups such as Greenpeace started springing up rapidly. Ecological awareness, organic gardening, and recycling centers also became prevalent in the 1960s. There was a trend toward spending more time outside and an increase in outdoor recreational activity. The newfound popularity of the environmental movement was partially a result of rising standards of living, partially influenced by an increase of citizens who had completed higher education, and largely a result of several environmental disasters that took place during the decade: in 1965, New York City experienced a power blackout and garbage strikes, and 1969 saw both the burning of the Cuyahoga River in Cleveland, Ohio, and the Santa Barbara oil spill. All in all, social attitudes were shifting in favor of environmentalism, and this trend was reflected in the art and poetry of the day.

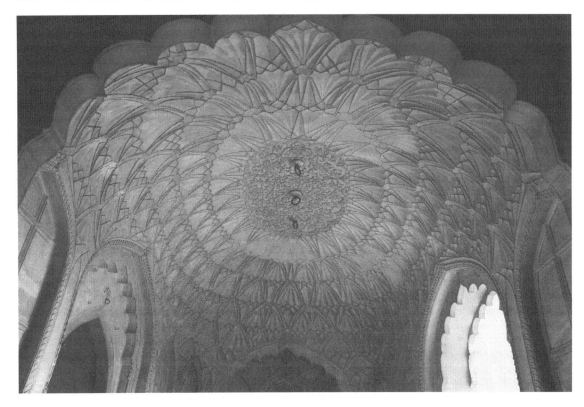

Round tomb room *(Rudolf Tepfenhart / Shutterstock.com)*

CRITICAL OVERVIEW

Given the breadth and influence of Swenson's work, it has received surprisingly little critical attention. The first book of criticism solely dedicated to Swenson's work, *Body My House*, edited by Paul Crumbley and Patricia M Gantt, was not published until 2006. However, several essays regarding her poetry were published prior to that. In a 1995 essay, "Poet's Eye View," in the *Women's Review of Books*, Priscilla Long reviewed the 1994 compilation of Swenson's nature poetry, *Nature: Poems Old and New*, which includes "Fable for When There's No Way Out." In the review, Long points out the acoustic qualities of Swenson's poetry:

> Swenson was an unrelenting lyrical poet, a master of the poetic line in which similar sounds accumulate and resonate so that the poem exists, beyond its meanings, as a rattle or a music box or, in moments of greatness, a symphony.

Long claims that this gift for lyricism perhaps stems from "Swenson's formidable powers of observation." Long also comments on Swenson's gift for nature poetry and notes that roughly three-quarters of her work deals with natural imagery. Of her nature poetry, Long opines,

> Swenson's vision of the natural world establishes how much we are part of it, whether we like it or know it or not. . . . In the world of Swenson's poetry, we look at these plants, these animals, with an eye that sees them on their own terms.

In her 2005 essay "May Swenson's Performative Poetics," published in *Marianne Moore, Elizabeth Bishop, and May Swenson: The Feminist Poetics of Self-Restraint*, Kirstin Hotelling Zona reinforces many of Long's claims regarding Swenson's work. According to Zona, "Swenson thrived on the unlikely observation." Zona, like many other critics, also asserts that Swenson was somewhat fixated on oppositions and extremes. "Swenson insists on the interdependence of extremes, revealing connections where oppositions normally endure," she writes. Zona also comments on Swenson's powerful, often sensual imagery, as well as her reluctance to label things or to identify them.

In her 1994 essay "Life's Miracles: The Poetry of May Swenson," published in the *American Poetry Review*, Grace Schulman also points out Swenson's reluctance to label things: "The poet's unnaming allows her to rename, in an effort to see things outside the context of common parlance." Schulman also focuses on the poet's penchant for inquiry, stating, "Questions are the wellsprings of May Swenson's art." In "May Swenson's Art of Wonder," published in 2010 in *First Love and Other Adventures*, Schulman says of Swenson, "Early and late, her intellectual probing is accompanied by passionate identification with objects, with technology, and, especially, with nature." Like Zona, Schulman points out Swenson's tendency to fixate on oppositions, or as she puts it, divisions:

> The title of her 1967 volume, *Half Sun Half Sleep*, announces that division of what May Swenson once called "the primitive bipolar suspension in which my poems often begin to form." Her theme of division is conveyed by many of her shaped poems, or those which contain visual as well as textual metaphors.

Although criticism of Swenson's work has not been abundant, it has been consistent. Nearly all critics of Swenson's poetry draw attention to her greatest strengths: her lyrical tone, close observation, sensual imagery, and insistent questioning.

CRITICISM

Rachel Porter

Porter is a freelance writer and editor who holds a bachelor of arts in English literature. In the following essay, she argues that "Fable for When There's No Way Out" is deceptively irresolute and mirrors reality more than it provides an allegorical lesson.

"Fable for When There's No Way Out" seems to be a straightforward narrative fable poem that easily resolves itself in the clearly stated lesson, or moral, that constitutes the last stanza. However, there are several indicators, including a disjointed, somewhat paradoxical conclusion and a prevalence of oppositional forces, that the poem may actually not resolve all of the tensions that it presents. Upon in-depth examination, "Fable for When There's No Way Out" proves itself to be less an ideal fable and more a realistic portrait of life.

A first reading of the poem provides the reader with a satisfying conclusion. The tension

'FABLE FOR WHEN THERE'S NO WAY OUT' PLAYFULLY AND SELF-CONSCIOUSLY UNDERMINES AND INADVERTENTLY REINFORCES ITS OWN MORAL LESSON. THE POEM AS A WHOLE APPEARS TO BE LESS AN IMPARTMENT OF ADVICE AND MORE A TESTAMENT TO THE IMPOSSIBILITY OF PREDICTING LIFE'S EVENTS."

is resolved, the story has a happy ending, and there is a logical lesson to be derived from the tale that the poem tells. The poem does not contain any unexpected surprises and is structured as a standard narrative. The problem of the poem is set forth by the first three stanzas, which introduce the reader to the setting of the poem and the character of the baby bird. Rising action occurs as the bird attempts to break out of his shell. The tension mounts as his attempts are continually thwarted and he begins to feel hopeless and then further mounts as he resumes the cause. The climax occurs when, after constant struggle, the bird finally manages to break through. The denouement and conclusion occur when the poem's narrator gives commentary on the bird's reaction and provides the moral lesson to complete the story. The struggle is resolved, and the lesson is learned.

However, upon further examination there seems to be some lingering tension at the end of the work. In fact, the last stanza is disjointed from the poem in several ways. Whereas the cadence of the stanzas that build toward the end (stanzas 14–17) smoothly conveys rising action, climax, and falling action, the last stanza abruptly breaks away from the story with a harsh, sharp, declarative statement. Moreover, the half rhyme that had been present for the entire poem, excepting the first three stanzas, completely dissolves, giving the impression that the poem has come full circle, and indeed it has. Considering the fragility of the young bird, whose beak was not even strong enough to crack his shell, the fact that he has managed to move on to the next phase of life implies that he will likely repeat a slightly different version of the struggle depicted in the poem countless times. Because struggle is inevitable in the life

WHAT DO I READ NEXT?

- *Nature: Poems Old and New* is a compilation of Swenson's work that was published in 2000, eleven years after her death. This collection includes poems, all somewhat related to nature, that have been previously published in Swenson's books as well as that have only been published in magazines and journals.

- *Elizabeth Bishop: Poems, Prose and Letters* is a collection of Bishop's work, edited by Robert Giroux and Lloyd Schwartz and published in 2008. Bishop was a lifelong friend of Swenson's, and many connections have been made between the two authors' poetry. Swenson and Bishop maintained steady correspondence for several decades. This book offers an overview of Bishop's work.

- *The Wicked Sisters: Women Poets, Literary History, and Discord*, published in 1992 by Betsey Erkkila, is a study of the poets Emily Dickinson, Marianne Moore, Elizabeth Bishop, Adrienne Rich, and Gwendolyn Brooks. Through these poets, the author examines the struggles that women have had within literary circles over many decades. This book is a valuable aid for contextualizing Swenson's work, which has often been regarded as feminist.

- *Selected Poems*, by Gwendolyn Brooks, is a 2006 anthology of Brooks's most exemplary poetry. Brooks is not only one of the most well-known modern poets, one who was writing and publishing poetry at the same time as Swenson, but also a significant icon of the Black Arts movement, which was gaining steam in New York City at the pinnacle of Swenson's career.

- *Painterly Abstraction in Modernist American Poetry: The Contemporaneity of Modernism*, by Charles Altieri, examines the reactions of the modernist poet to the modernist art movement. This 2009 work argues that the modernist poets, such as Swenson, actually aimed to resist the tendencies of their contemporary culture through abstraction.

- *Modern American Poetry: Echoes and Shadows*, edited by Sheila Griffin Llanas, was published in 2009. This work is a collection of poems by many of Swenson's fellow modernists, such as Robert Frost, William Carlos Williams, and e. e. cummings. Llanas also provides critical commentary concerning styles and techniques for each of the poems.

- *American Sports Poems*, edited by Swenson and R. R. Knudson, is a collection of 158 poems from a diverse group of poets targeted for young-adult readers. In addition to four poems by Swenson, the 1995 compilation includes poems by Elizabeth Bishop, Ernest Hemingway, Ogden Nash, and Eugene O'Neill, among the famous poets represented.

of any creature, the poem is actually self-consciously anything but conclusive. The bird's triumphant ending, breaking out of his shell, actually constitutes the beginning of his life in the outside world. Likewise, the moral at the end implies imminent struggle in the life of the reader, as it imparts advice on how to deal with it. The plot of the poem itself, the hatching of a baby bird, is actually one of the most iconic and recognizable symbols for beginning. Thus, the poem does not give the impression of a complete narrative but rather one that ends in an ellipsis.

Residual tension also results from the fact that although the ending of the poem implies that in certain situations rage is superior to reason, in this case, the two opposing forces were both necessary to achieve the successful conclusion at the end. If the bird was entirely devoid of reason, which in this situation is loosely synonymous with the rational will to survive, he would not have become frustrated enough to move so violently as to accidentally crack his shell. Likewise, had the bird been entirely levelheaded and calm, he never would have become frustrated and heated enough to break out. In fact, the resolution of the story was the result of a delicate balance between oppositional forces, none of which are superior or inferior to each other, and all of which are interdependent. The bird has grown stronger every day, yet he is still too weak to break his shell with his beak. His instinct is to survive, yet he is also gripped with overwhelming despair that causes him to consider death. It is the tension between all of these factors that adds drama and excitement to the poem and makes the poem a narrative. Without any one of these elements, the poem would be a lyric concerning a strong, heroic baby bird destined for success, or a weakling who never made it out of his shell, rather than a narrative concerning a creature with realistic faults and strengths. These tensions do not simply resolve at the end of the poem, because they will follow the bird throughout his life.

Upon examination, the lesson in the last stanza of the poem is fairly puzzling and paradoxical. It advocates harnessing rage as a productive force when reason fails, yet rage is not typically an emotion considered to be at easy disposal. Rage is the involuntary feeling of violent anger that usually arises from some sort of frustration. In the eighteenth stanza, the narrator recommends using the negative force of rage to achieve a positive outcome, yet in the poem, the bird reaches his solution completely inadvertently, not purposefully. Because extreme emotions almost always result from a lack of control, calmly recommending them in the moral of a fable seems counterintuitive. Indeed, nearly everything about this poem is indicative of accident and a lack of control, bordering on eroticism. Diction choices, particularly tactile words such as *hard, soft, stretch,* and *limp,* coupled with the imagery of the bird frantically struggling to break through a barrier, in addition to the rhythm of the poem, which starts slow, speeds up, slows down, and then speeds up again, seem to signify something similar to a sexual awakening. Prescribing a practical, moral lesson for situations that are emotional, fleshy, and perhaps erotic is completely incongruous because a necessary condition for those types of situations is lack of control. In situations where the advice of the poem might be useful, collected, rational thought would be necessary in order to employ it.

The fact that the poem is surprisingly irresolute, conflicted, and paradoxical is reflected in its form. Just as the meaning of the poem is confusing, hazy, and nontraditional, so too is its structure.

Man peering out of broken wall (*Rudyanto Wjaya | Shutterstock.com*)

The poem is neatly divided into eighteen stanzas, each of two lines, and unlike many of Swenson's other poems, it does not employ experimental typography. At first glance, it appears to be a fairly traditional poem. However, none of the stanzas have a steady metric pattern, consistent syllable count, or perfect rhyme. Yet the poem does contain ample use of half rhyme, making some sections cohesive and the overall auditory effect of the poem somewhat lyrical, albeit a lyrical sound that is wildly inconsistent. The poem, then, both is and is not lyrical and rhythmic, just as it has a moral, albeit a moral that is somewhat undermined by the poem that precedes it. The assonance and consonance create a sense of fluidity, but the many inconsistencies resist fluidity and prevent the poem from seeming cohesive. The poem has enough "poetic" qualities for it to lend itself to an imposed poetic reading, yet the structure of the poem is also indicative of tension, anxiety, and irresolution.

"Fable for When There's No Way Out" playfully and self-consciously undermines and inadvertently reinforces its own moral lesson. The poem as a whole appears to be less an impartment of advice and more a testament to the impossibility of predicting life's events. By taking an unpredictable and delicate situation that is dependent on a plethora of balancing factors, such as the birth of a baby bird, and forcing that situation into the mold of a fable, Swenson proves that there are some parts of life that simply refuse to conform to logic. Thus, the advice the poem gives, that rage can be more effective than reason, may in fact be true, yet it loses its potency when presented as advice. Ultimately, "Fable for When There's No Way Out" is a testament to the fact that sometimes a solution can be found even when things seem utterly and desperately hopeless.

Source: Rachel Porter, Critical Essay on "Fable for When There's No Way Out," in *Poetry for Students*, Gale, Cengage Learning, 2011.

Grace Schulman

In the following essay, Schulman explores Swenson's treatment of the themes of life, love, and death in her poetry.

The voice of May Swenson combines the directness of intimate speech and the urgency of prayer:

> Body my house
> my horse my hound
> what will I do
> when you are fallen
>
> Where will I sleep
> How will I ride
> What will I hunt
>
> Where can I go
> without my mount. . .

The magic of that lament, "Question," from *Another Animal* (1954), is in its contrasts: while the details are specific, the central situation is a mystery that terrifies with each new speculation. Here as elsewhere in her poems, Swenson dwells on the living body with an immediacy that heightens the dread of its loss. Other gestures that recur in Swenson's poetry are the insistent, unanswerable questions, "what will I do." "How will I ride," "What will I hunt," "Where can I go," all of them precise, all ironic, because futile. Here they are enhanced by obsessive rhyme ("house," "horse," "hound," "hunt," "mount"). Their futility is emphasized by the absence of punctuation, and again by its sudden presence, in the final line.

> THE IMPACT OF HER POEMS LIES IN THEIR URGENT SPEECH AND INCANTATORY RHYTHMS, THEIR MUSIC OF CHARMS, SPELLS, CURSES, RITUAL DANCES. NEVER DOES THE TYPOGRAPHY, HOWEVER INTRICATE, SUPERSEDE THE CADENCE. AS IN PRIMITIVE POETRY, WORD AND APPEARANCE ARE FUSED FOR A TOTAL EFFECT."

They are meditations. Admirable too, is the voice that is neither androgynous nor gendered, but one that encompasses both sexes in its fluid boundaries and essentially human dimension: "What will I hunt," the male speaker's question, modulates here, with no abrupt tonal change, to a woman's query, "With cloud for shift / how will I hide?"

Questions are the wellsprings of May Swenson's art. She inquires about simple things, such as "What is the worm doing / making its hole," and about principles such as "What / is it about, / the universe, / the universe about us stretching out?" or, considering the moon landing, "Dare we land upon a dream?" In her speculations and her close observations, she fulfills Marianne Moore's formula for the working artist: "Curiosity, observation, and a great deal of joy in the thing." In subject matter a poet who, like Donne, takes all of knowledge as her province, she is as comfortable with animals and flowers as she is with antimatter, electronic sound, and DNA. Some of her chosen forms incorporate questions, such as her ballad, "The Centaur": "*Where have you been?*" "*Been riding.*" Another is the ancient riddle, a form that enables her to concentrate on the object without naming it. "The Surface," for example, has affinities to Dickinson's riddles, and to her wit: "First I saw the surface, / then I saw it flow, / then I saw the underneath," the poet begins, and gradually unravels the answer, the image of an eye. Swenson riddles in a quest to find a higher reality obscured by conventional names, and to fathom what is deepest within the self. By rejecting ready-made definitions—those designations that enlighten—Swenson sees in the dark. She derides the ordinary labeling of things with its consequent reduction of greatness:

They said there was a Thing
that could not Change
They could not Find
it so they Named
it God...
("God")

The poet's unnaming allows her to rename, in an effort to see things outside the context of common parlance. Continually the search is for a deeper meaning, the essence of the thing observed. In "Evolution," the first poem of her first book, she exclaims:

beautiful each Shape
to see
wonderful each Thing
to name
here a stone
there a tree
here a river
there a Flame...

May Swenson was born in 1913 in Logan, Utah, of a Mormon family, and educated at Utah State University. She was a New Yorker from 1936, and lived in Sea Cliff, New York, for twenty-three years before her death in Ocean View, Delaware, in 1989. In her lifetime, she published eleven books over three decades, nine of them poetry collections, from *Another Animal* (1954) to *In Other Words* (1987). Honored as she was during her lifetime, her books included only four hundred and fifty of the nine hundred poems she composed. Since her death, as new poems and new books continue to appear, it becomes apparent not only that he output is larger than readers have supposed, but that her stature is major.

Nature (1994), the newest of the posthumous books, contains some early poems, hitherto unpublished, whose dominant tone is awe: "Remain aghast at life," the poet resolves in "Earth Your Dancing Place," composed as early as 1936:

Enter each day
as upon a stage
lighted and waiting
for your step...

Wonder prevails in "Manyone Flying" (1975), another of the poems that appear posthumously in *Nature*. Here, the poet, in the guise of a high flying bird, considers the divisions between the individual and humanity:

Out on the edge,
my maneuverings, my wings, think

they are free. Flock, where do we
fly? Are we Ones? Or One, only?
if only One, not lonely... being Manyone...
but Who are We? And Why?

The liveliest of the posthumous books, *The Love Poems of May Swenson* (1991), contains poems that illuminate the work as a whole. Here, the poet who continually questions existence finds love at the source of the quest: existence depends on the other. The bridge between self and other is basic to the polarities, found throughout her work, of life and death, wildness and restraint, past and present, sun and moon, stone and flame. Although out of the fifty-five poems, *The Love Poems* contains only thirteen hitherto unpublished, as well as some familiar poems in altered forms, their publication—as well as their arrangement here—reveal the force of that important theme. And as the love poems occupy the full span of her career, having been composed between 1938 and 1987, so does the theme.

Before elaborating on that large concern, I want to comment on the poetry's marvelous erotic power. Heightened sensations recall the Song of Songs: "thy breasts shall be as clusters of the vine" (King James Version 7:8). All the more credible for risking sentimentality without approaching it, Swenson conveys physical intimacies and shares sensual delights, as, for example, the "dark wild honey,"

Thick transparent amber
you brought home,
the sweet that burns.

The poet cries out in passion: "Burn radiant sex born scorpion need." She writes of joy: "A rain of diamonds / in the mind ("Love Is"); of pain: "Now heart, take up your desert; / this spring is cursed" ("Wild Water," 1938); and of yearning: "my body is a sharpened dart / of longing / coming toward you always," in "The Equilibrist," composed in the forties. As for her lustiness, I cannot describe it better than did Edward Hirsch, who wrote in a review of *Love Poems*: "The birds, and especially the bees, have never been so slyly deployed."

Vivid, moving, the love poems take in the intricacies of human nature, the natural world, geography, and invention. They are poems of intense love between women, written at a time when that genre was rare in poetry. I say love between women with qualifications, because of the poetry's aesthetic complexity. Swenson's tone embraces the full human drama. Her metaphors often are male, or animal, or flower. Nevertheless, the sexual love she dramatizes so brilliantly is Sapphic. This is subtly and beautifully apparent in the imagery of four poems that did not appear during Swenson's lifetime:

> I exist in your verdant garden
>
> I unfurled in your rich soil
> ("You Are")
>
> We are released
> and flow into each other's cup
> Our two frail vials pierced
> drink each other up
> ("In Love Made Visible," 1946)
>
> To feel your breast
> rise with my sigh
>
> To hold you mirrored
> in my eye
>
> Neither wanting more
> Neither asking why
> ("Neither Wanting More," 1944)
>
> I open to your dew,
> beginning in the spring again. . .
> ("Annual," 1959).

Sexy poems dominate this book, either by shining out in their own light or by illuminating others. In *Love Poems*, many titles are familiar to Swenson's readers, such as "August Night" and "Another Animal." Those familiar poems are strengthened by the context of the newly-published pieces. For example, "The School of Desire" (from *A Cage of Spines*, 1958) is a symphonic reiteration—the theme stated in full force—of the wildness and freedom that are more reflective in the more recently surfaced poems such as "In Love Made Visible." In a biography published in 1993, *The Wonderful Pen of May Swenson*, R. R. Knudson observed, "For May, power was fear pushed back." So, too, many of the love poems, like primitive chants, derive their power from the expression of inner wildness as well as the immense effort to order it. "The School of Desire" captures the poet's energies at their strongest:

> Unloosed, unharnessed, turned back to the wild by
>   love,
> the ring you cantered round with forelock curled,
> the geometric music of this world
> dissolved and in its place,
> alien as snow to tropic tigers, amphitheatric space
> you will know the desert's freedom, wind and sun
> rough-currying your mane, the plenitude
> of strong caresses on your body nude.

And yet, while the poems capture the physical ecstasy of consummated love, they also evoke the elusiveness of a world beyond the physical. In the grand design of an Elizabethan sonneteer, she writes of mutability: desire changes, the moment it is given form, to flame up and die. Love, a reaction against the process of temporal decay, can enable flesh-bound companions at least to intuit spiritual value.

> In love are we set free
> Objective bone
> and flesh no longer insulate us
> to ourselves alone. . .
> ("In Love Made Visible")

As I've said, *The Love Poems* highlights Swenson's manner of incessant inquiry. Early and late, her intellectual probing is accompanied by passionate identification with objects, with technology, and, especially, with nature: the lion's yearning, the lamb's way, the deer's eye; recumbent stones, thighs of trees, horses whose colors are "like leaves or stones / or wealthy textures / liquors of light."

On the other hand, when human love is at stake, human sensibility replaces the unity with animals, as in the poem "Evolution":

> an Evolution strange
> two Tongues touch
> exchange
> a Feast unknown
> to stone
> or tree or beast. . .

In the love poems, particularly those that appeared recently, the persistent questions of Swenson's world are put aside as the lover lies content without searching for data: "Because I don't know you / I love you," admits the speaker of an early poem. Fulfillment is

> To hold you mirrored
> in my eye
>
> Neither wanting more
> Neither asking why. . .

Although the love poems do not question overtly, they exhibit a more essential phase of the poet's constant quest. Swenson's earliest efforts on any theme probe the reality of being, and the utter dependence of being upon its opposite is dominant here, especially in the early, posthumously-published work: "As you are Sun to me / O I am moon to you," cries the lover in "Facing." "They are like flame and ice / the elemental You and Me," begins "The Indivisible Incompatibles," a poem written in the 1940s. The lovers are "Not twin / but opposite / as my two hands are opposite," according to "Symmetrical Companion," another early poem, from 1948, that has for an ending, "Come release me / Without you I do not yet exist." Even more directly, the lover asserts:

I dwell
in you
and so
I know
I am

no one
can be sure
by himself
of his own being. . .

And, more firmly, "because you believe I exist I exist" ("You Are").

Here the passion is metaphorical, though the details are concrete. The lovers of her poems, steamy though they are, represent parts of a divided self. Their union, that blessed state in which opposites are conjoined, reveals essential being. Mooring in one's otherness allays unanswerable queries about life and death. Furthermore, the process of finding a hidden part of the self reveals a remote world beyond the tangible: "In love are we made visible. . . In love are we set free."

The title of her 1967 volume, *Half Sun Half Sleep*, announces that division of what May Swenson once called, "the primitive bipolar suspension in which my poems often begin to form." Her theme of division is conveyed by many of her shaped poems, or those which contain visual as well as textual metaphors.

Actually, the poet's primary effects are her cadences. The impact of her poems lies in their urgent speech and incantatory rhythms, their music of charms, spells, curses, ritual dances. Never does the typography, however intricate, supersede the cadence. As in primitive poetry, word and appearance are fused for a total effect.

As if to demonstrate subtly that the shaped poems have an auditory life of their own, May Swenson chose to read aloud many of her typographical poems in 1976 on a Caedmon recording, which could not, of course, exhibit the visual pattern to her listeners. One of the poems she read was "The Lightning," which she referred to as a pivotal poem in *Half Sun Half Sleep*. Of its typographical device, the visual metaphor, she commented: "As seen on the page, there is a streak of white space that runs diagonally through the body of the poem

and this even splits some of the words." The poem celebrates speech, and the white streak creates meditative pauses in lines, indicating the gap between word and event, between experience and its realization in the poem:

"The Lightning"
The lightning waked me. It slid unde r
my eyelid. A black book flipped ope n
to an illuminated page. Then insta ntly
shut. Words of destiny were being ut-
tered in the distance. If only I could
make them out!. . . Next day, as I lay
in the sun, a symbol for concei ving the
universe was scratched on my e yeball.
But quickly its point eclipse d, and
softened, in the scabbard of my brain.
My cat speaks one word: Fo ur vowels
and a consonant. He rece ives with the
hairs of his body the wh ispers of the
stars. The kinglet spe aks by flashing
into view a ruby feath er on his head.
He is held by a threa d to the eye of
the sun and cannot fall into error.
Any flower is a per fect ear, or else it
is a thousand lips . . . When will I grope
clear of the entr ails of intellect?

Swenson spoke, too, of a poem whose title is, antithetically, "Untitled," commenting on an earlier version she read on the recording. She described the visual metaphor created by the typographical appearance on the page, noting that "two black crooked lines pass through the text as if to x it out. The bipolar words 'you,' 'me,' are in the center as if entangled where the two black lines cross." Here, the spaces are between words, and they designate a meditative, almost painful effort at speech. "I will be earth you be the flower. . . ," the poem begins, and the voice rises in passionate intensity as the lovers flail, boat and sea, earth and flood, desert and salt.

Utterance is the theme, too, of "Fountains of Aix," a poem from the 1963 collection, *To Mix With Time*. In it, the word "water" is split fifteen times from its lines, and poured, in effect, down the side of one stanza:

A goddess is driving a chariot through water.
Her reins and whips are tight white water.
Bronze hoofs of horses wrangle with water.

The streak of space separates the fountain's sculptures from the water spouting from their mouths. Here are dolphins and lions and bulls, and "faces with mossy lips unlocked," all uttering water, "their eyes mad / or patient or blind or astonished." She builds a metaphor of the fluidity of utterance, and thence of poetry. Swenson's pauses emphasize her wonder: In "Fire Island," from *Iconographs* (1970), the poet contemplates the miracle of beholding light and dark—milky foam, black sky—of solitude and the group—walkers on the beach and "other watchers"—while the two ends of the narrow island are splayed out in type above and below, creating pauses between the letters of the words "Fire" and "sight."

Typographical pauses appear throughout Swenson's writing career. Some are part of an intricate pattern, as in "The Fountains of Aix" and "The Lightning." Many occur in poems of two columns, and of those, some are read down the page, some across the page and still others across *and* down. Early and late, those patterned spaces between the words indicate opposites, ironies, reversals, paradoxes, ambiguities. For example, in a poem whose title conveys a moment in time, "While Sitting in the Tuileries and Facing the Slanting Sun," the poet ironically associates, and then divides by space, a swaddled infant in Giotto's fresco, "Birth of the Virgin," and a mummy in the Vatican Museum:

> There is a Person
> of flesh that is a rocking Box
> There is a Box
> of wood that is a painted Person. . .

In "Bleeding," from *Iconographs*, a space through the center is a jagged, running wound, effecting caesuras of hesitation in a dialogue between the knife and the cut. The force grows along with the grim realization that bleeding is precisely feeling, in this devastating relationship:

> I feel I have to bleed to feel I think said the cut.
> I don't I don't have to feel said the knife drying now
> becoming shiny.

Like the polarized images found throughout Swenson's work, the contrasts created by her typographical separations have their roots in the love poems. There are the two columns of "Evolution" and "Facing" (both to be read down the page, rather than across), each indicating another animal, the lover who is an aspect of the self. Like all the love poems, these two praise opposite beings—flame and ice, sun and moon—who move forward to their destiny.

The love poems, with their high energy and "desert freedom," contain, as do the poems of Shakespeare and Sir Philip Sidney, the irony that vitality can emphasize its very opposite, the certainty of life's decline. From early on, May Swenson sings of life in death's shadow, as in "Question," quoted above, and in poems that

have the word "Death" in their titles: "Deaths," "Death Invited," "The Shape of Death."

Did Swenson suffer great personal loss? Her biographer, R. R. Knudson, writes that the death of a beloved grandfather prompted May, as a child, to question the finality of loss. Then, as a teenager, May questioned Mormonism, and, in fact, normative religions with their conventional notions of God. It seems that later she was deeply saddened by the atrocities of World War II. Young May's lover, the Czech poet, Anca Vrboska, lost her family to the Nazi death camps. While Vrboska wrote of Auschwitz directly, Swenson internalized, objectified, searched, as always, for the essence of death:

> I will lie down in Autumn
> let birds be flying
>
> swept into a hollow
> by the wind
> I'll wait for dying
>
> I will lie inert unseen
> my hair same-colored
> with grass and leaves. . .
> ("I Will Lie Down")

Later still, in those poems whose titles say "death," Swenson plays on the Elizabethan paradox that tragic implications are perceived in the midst of life's personal, intimate experience. All are poems that embody contrasts, either in their divided shape on the page, or in their imagery, or both. A fascinating early example is "Death, Great Smoothener":

> Death,
> great smoothener,
> maker of order,
> arrester, unraveler, sifter and changer
> death, great hoarder;
> student, stranger, drifter, traveler,
> flyer and nester all caught at your border;
>
> death,
> great halter;
> blackener and frightener,
> reducer, dissolver,
> seizer and welder of younger with elder,
> waker with sleeper
>
> death, great keeper
> of all that must alter;
> death,
> great heightener,
> leaper, evolver,
> greater smoothener,
>
> great whitener!

The poem's sheer energy cries of life even as it speaks to death. It has the sound of a pagan incantation, with its frightening direct address presented in clusters of heavy stresses. Swenson achieves her falling rhythm here, as in "Question," with reversed iambs, and depicts death in lists of epithets, enforced by rhyme: "order," "hoarder," "border." In contrast to the chant rhythm, the typographical shape on the page is that of an ornate Christian cross. The resonant epithets echo, for me, Caedmon's hymn, the legendary first song of our first English poet, a song of thanksgiving:

> Nu sculon herigean heofonrices weard
> metodes meahte and his modgethanc
> weorc wuldorodur swa he wundra gehwos
>
> now shall we praise heaven's keeper
> the maker's might and his mind thought
> father of the world as of all wonder. . .

Poetically, their techniques are alike: to sing of God. Caedmon takes epithets for the Anglo-Saxon warlords, such as ruler and father, and qualifies them with Christian adjectives such as . . . "eternal." Swenson chants death in life, and engraves a pagan rhythm in a Christian cross.

The poetry of May Swenson celebrates life's miracles even with death in view: the wonder of speech ("Fountains of Aix"); the grandeur of God ("God"); the radiance of sight ("Fire Island"). In each of these three poems, typographical divisions—white streaks down the middle of the text—make for breath-catching pauses that enhance the excited tone. The ambiguities and paradoxes of Swenson's poetry result from basic contradiction between our illusion of permanence and an underlying certainty of fatality. This contradiction is articulated explicitly in one of the love poems, "The Shape of Death," as it was printed, in *Iconographs*, with a white streak down the middle of the text:

> What does love look like? We know the shape of
>   death.
> Death is a cloud, immense and awesome. At first a
> lid is lifted from the eye of light. There is a
> clap of sound. A white blossom belches from the
> jaw of fright.

Then, in sharp contrast to those positive assertions about death, love is presented in a series of questions: "What is its / color and its alchemy?" "Can it be sown and harvested?" The resounding theme of Swenson's poems is there, in her concluding statement. Like life, love, though fatally transient, is "not alien—it is near—our very skin, a sheath to keep us pure of fear."

Source: Grace Schulman, "Life's Miracles: The Poetry of May Swenson," in *American Poetry Review*, Vol. 23, No. 5, September/October 1994, pp. 9–13.

Mona Van Duyn

In the following essay, Van Duyn offers a tribute to Swenson, reflecting on both Swenson's personal attributes and on her poetry.

May Swenson twice warmly introduced me from the reading platform, but I never had the privilege of introducing her. When I was invited to write a "blurb" for her last book, my eager pen moved on and on, writing, I knew, too long a response to be useful; passages were, however, taken from that tribute and printed on the book, along with praise from some of her many other admirers. I will begin by repeating those relatively condensed feelings of mine about her work, with the already printed parts indicated by quotation marks:

> "May Swenson's is an art that comes as close as I know to what I like to think must have been the serious fun, the gorgeous mix of play and purpose of Creation itself. One almost feels that nothing has gone before it; no visions of earlier perfections impinge on its originality; it is a First Thing."

Under the spell of her work, poems of more apparent high finish seem false—their glaze would not have let show the grainy, the gritty detail; the big and little pits; the funny, the quirky, the cranky; the gratuitous streakings of the earth itself out of which the poems were shaped. Focused almost always on a reality outside herself, her camera records it for our viewing, and, in "Double Exposure" like that produced by the human lovers who simultaneously snap pictures of each other in her poem of that name, her ground in return has pictured for us the poet's face at camera. "Drawn up into" her own absolutely unmistakable "squint," her lens of hard-headed affectionate wonder is aimed *into* the light by a mind that has always taken its own advice to "make your own moves."

> "What would the rest of us who truly love the world, but whose self-absorption will not usually permit so clear a sight of it, do without her poetry?"

And now we must do without any more of it than we already have.

I first met May, whose poetry I loved, so many years ago that I cannot guess at the date, when, in the early days of readings, she was invited to Washington University (St. Louis). In those bygone days the poet was put up in the guest room of someone congenial (ours, almost always) and fed by that host; the payment was a pittance. May had given few readings (I none, I think), and the rows of chairs in the reading room were arranged in a semi-circle which curved round behind the podium. I sat on one of the ends, front row, and could see May's knees shaking so wildly all during her performance that I wondered how they could hold her upright. Her voice was, throughout, courageously and amazingly controlled, as if the knees were living a terrified life of their own which had nothing to do with the mind, face, and voice. How I admired her! Later, of course, along with the rest of us, she became a calm performer.

At home with us, she and my husband (Jarvis Thurston) discovered a warm connection which kept them excitedly chattering for hours. They had both grown up in Mormon families in Utah, May in Logan, Jarvis in Ogden; May came from a large family of eight or nine children, my husband had only one sister by a mother who was his father's fifth wife (the wives were not simultaneous—each of them had died before a remarriage), but he lived in a small community filled with his grown-up half-brothers and half-sisters. Both he and May had "escaped" from Mormonism, physically and emotionally. While she rested before returning, May read a book of my poems and enthusiastically praised it. When she left St. Louis, Jarvis and I knew we had found a friend, one whom we did not often see in person, but who had permanently lodged herself in our affections.

Still, we did meet from time to time, at Bread Loaf, New York, or St. Louis, and kept in erratic touch by mail. For one reason or another, Jarvis and I never got out to the Sea Cliff house with the inadequate or nonexistent heating system which there was never enough money to repair. May was one of the most unmaterialistic people I know. Nunlike, she warmed and fed herself primarily with writing. A croissant, a paté, the goodies I bought for her lunch when she came to see us in a borrowed apartment in Manhattan, seemed gustatory wonders to her. Some genius in the mysterious award-making machine of the MacArthur Foundation gave her a MacArthur in time for her and Zan to go to New Zealand, feel its warmth, and see its animals. The first taste of travel pleasures came in the nick of time.

Her poems were often playful, as Marianne Moore's were often playful—in rhyming, in

tone, in shape. Different as they are from each other, unique as is each poet's voice, it is as if the most minute detail of the visible world flowered for both of them with a brightness that lit up the dark personal feelings; or that the rich, exciting passage of discovery through external Creation continually brought to them both "good tidings of comfort and joy." Zan tells me that May particularly loved my poem "Letters from a Father," which contains a litany of birds, seen toward the morose and self-hating end of the father's life with the kind of love with which May saw them (and all nonhuman creatures) *all* her life. In my poem "the world," through the birds which come to a new bird feeder, slowly "woos its children back for an evening kiss."

That round, lined face, framed by an undeviating Dutch bob, its characteristic expression seeming to say, "I am precisely who I am; take me or leave me," will stay with us as long as we can keep our own memories. She was a wonderful woman, a wonderful poet.

Source: Mona Van Duyn, "Important Witness to the World," in *Parnassus*, Vol. 16, No. 1, 1990, pp. 154–56.

SOURCES

"The Birth of Environmentalism," in *Making the Modern World*, http://www.makingthemodernworld.org.uk/stories/the_age_of_ambivalence/02.ST.06/ (accessed September 12, 2010).

Crumbley, Paul, and Patricia M. Gantt, eds., "May Swenson Chronology," in *Body My House: May Swenson's Work and Life*, Utah State University Press, 2006, pp. 8–10.

"Cuyahoga River Fire," in *Ohio History Central*, July 1, 2005, http://www.ohiohistorycentral.org/entry.php?rec = 1642 (accessed October 15, 2010).

"Finding-Aid for the May Swenson Papers," in *Washington University in St. Louis Web site*, http://library.wustl.edu/units/spec/manuscripts/mlc/brooke/findingaidshtml/wtu00111.html (accessed September 8, 2010).

Long, Priscilla, "Poet's Eye View," in *Women's Review of Books*, Vol. 12, No. 4, January 1995, pp. 8–9.

"May Swenson," in *Poets.org*, http://www.poets.org/poet.php/prmPID/168 (accessed September 4, 2010).

Murfin, Ross, and Supriya M. Ray, "Modern Period (in English and American Literature)," in *The Bedford Glossary of Critical and Literary Terms*, Bedford/St. Martins, 2003, pp. 269–71.

Schulman, Grace, "Life's Miracles: The Poetry of May Swenson," in *American Poetry Review*, Vol. 23, No. 5, September 1994, pp. 9–13.

———, "May Swenson's Art of Wonder," in *First Loves and Other Adventures*, University of Michigan Press, 2010, pp. 40–52.

Silveira, Stacy J., "The American Environmental Movement: Surviving through Diversity," in *Boston College Website*, http://www.bc.edu/bc_org/avp/law/lwsch/journals/bcealr/28_2-3/07_TXT.htm (accessed September 12, 2010).

Swenson, May, "Fable for When There's No Way Out," in *Half Sun, Half Sleep: New Poems*, Charles Scribner's Sons, 1967, p. 46.

Zona, Kirstin Hotelling, "May Swenson's Performative Poetics," in *Marianne Moore, Elizabeth Bishop, and May Swenson: The Feminist Poetics of Self-Restraint*, University of Michigan Press, 2005, pp. 121–50.

FURTHER READING

Crumbley, Paul, and Patricia M. Gantt, eds., *Body My House: May Swenson's Life and Work*, Utah State University Press, 2006.

Crumbley and Gantt's *Body My House* is the first and only current collection of critical essays devoted exclusively to the work of Swenson. The essays included in this collection cover the entire range of Swenson's work, and the book also includes biographical information on the author.

Davis, Alex, and Lee M. Jenkins, eds., *The Cambridge Companion to Modernist Poetry*, Cambridge University Press, 2007.

Swenson's work was sometimes considered to be modernist, and it is frequently compared to the work of other modernist poets such as Ezra Pound and Gertrude Stein. This book provides a comprehensive examination of modernist poetry, including information on its history, development, major authors, and critical reception.

Knudson, R. R., *May Swenson: A Poet's Life in Photos*, Utah State University Press, 1997.

This work includes over one hundred and sixty photographs of Swenson, along with bibliographic information and excerpts from her poetry and letters, to provide a holistic portrait of the poet. This work was compiled by Knudson, Swenson's companion for over twenty years.

Parisi, Joseph, and Kathleen Welton, eds., *100 Essential Modern Poems by Women*, Ivan R. Dee, 2008.

Several of Swenson's poems are included in this collection by Parisi and Welton, along with those of many of her female contemporaries. This book provides a means to contextualize Swenson's work with that of her peers.

SUGGESTED SEARCH TERMS

May Swenson

May Swenson AND Fable for When There's No Way Out

May Swenson AND Half Sun Half Sleep

May Swenson AND modern poetry

May Swenson AND narrative poem

modern poetry AND women

modern poetry AND nature

modern poetry AND Half Sun Half Sleep

May Swenson AND nature poetry

May Swenson AND Elizabeth Bishop

Fragment 16

SAPPHO

C. 580 BCE

Sappho is one of the greatest poets ever to write, and she is the earliest female writer of whom history has any knowledge. Coming at the very beginning of the Western literary tradition, Sappho's influence is impossible to overestimate. She is the kind of poet that other great poets, from her contemporary Alcaeus to the American Ezra Pound, claim as their favorite poet. The philosopher Plato called her the tenth Muse. Her works are uniquely clear, simple, and compelling in their beauty. Nevertheless, Sappho's poems are known only from quotations by other authors in antiquity or through damaged manuscripts found by archaeologists in Egypt a century ago. For this reason, there exist only two complete poems; but fragment 16 is almost complete, and its full sense can be rendered in translation. The main theme of almost all Sappho's poetry is the universal human experience of love. Fragment 16 concerns the destructive power of desire that can drive its victims to acts of violence and madness, suggesting that the frenzy of warfare is the only thing that can be compared to love.

Sappho's works were translated into English in 1958 by Pound's disciple Mary Barnard. Since then, her translation has become the most popular version of Sappho's work, and it is the source of much information about Sappho. Barnard titled her translation of this fragment "To an Army Wife in Sardis," despite the fact that it is addressed only to the reader, does not explicitly concern anyone married to a soldier, and does not

Sappho (The Library of Congress)

mention Sardis. The construction of that title seems to collapse together several ideas from the poem into a new orientation that Sappho herself may never have envisioned. Included here are a prose-poem translation by David M. Campbell and a five-stanza verse translation by Aaron Poochigian, given the similar title "To an Army Wife (Troy)."

AUTHOR BIOGRAPHY

There are two sources of information about the life of Sappho: her own writings, from which deductions about her life can be made, and what was written about her life by other authors in antiquity. Some of those other authors were working hundreds of years later, and they may or may not have had access to the facts. Sappho was often used as a character by writers of comedies, and those fictional stories seem to have entered the biographical tradition at many points as if they were facts. However, it is worth noting that Sappho was a favorite of the comic poets precisely because they could expect everyone in

the audience to have read her poetry. Anything that can be said about her life is tentative. Indeed, there is a growing body of scholarship on her, including Yopie Prins's *Victorian Sappho*, which deals with how each generation in the nineteenth and twentieth centuries imposed its own ideas on Sappho's biography.

With caution in mind, it is possible to make some reasonable inferences about Sappho's life. She lived most of her life in the Greek city of Mytilene on the island of Lesbos, off the coast of Asia Minor (modern Turkey). She was born into an aristocratic family, probably not later than 610 BCE. Sappho's family seems to have been exiled from Mytilene for a few years about 600 BCE, to live in Sicily but later return.

Her mother, as well as her daughter, are said to have been named Cleius. The meaning of Sappho's own name is probably related to the crystalline qualities of sapphire. The fact that she had a daughter and yet had a respected place in society as a writer of public poetry indicates that she was married, but there is no reliable information about her husband.

Greek women were often responsible for devising and enacting the religious rituals that pertained to women in particular, and this was the focus of Sappho's life as a poet. Like many Greek women, she composed hymns sung at weddings (*epithalamia*) and at religious festivals celebrated by women. She composed not only the words but also the music and choreography that accompanied the performance (although no traces of these nonliterary elements survive). It may be taken for granted that all of Sappho's poems were accompanied by music. The hymns she wrote for public performance would have been performed by a group of aristocratic Mytilenean *parthenoi* girls between the ages of puberty and marriage (perhaps twelve to fifteen or sixteen years old). She would have been in charge of instructing them in singing and dancing. No doubt this had a socializing and cultivating effect on the girls, but it is going too far to describe Sappho as running a girls' finishing school, as was once commonly done. Greek women who had similar responsibilities (Anagora—possibly Anaktoria—of Miletus, Gongyla of Colophon, and Eunica of Salamis are the names supplied by tradition), came from other Greek cities to study with her to perfect their own poetry and dramaturgy (arranging dramatic elements for the stage). Sappho also wrote poetry centered around her private life and probably performed it within her circle of personal friends, and she wrote other poems that seem entirely personal in nature and that do not have an obvious audience. Fragment 16 falls into this category.

Fragment 58 was recently completed by new textual discoveries and is one of Sappho's two surviving complete poems. In it, the poet laments that she is now too old to dance and contemplates the slow approach of death. If these sentiments reflect Sappho's own life, then she lived to old age. The often-repeated story that Sappho killed herself by leaping from a cliff after an unhappy love affair was invented by the comic poet Menander and cannot be taken as historical truth.

POEM TEXT

Some say a host of cavalry, others of infantry, and others of ships, is the most beautiful thing on the black earth, but I say it is whatsoever a person loves. It is perfectly easy to make this understood by everyone: for she who far surpassed mankind in beauty, Helen, left her most noble husband and went sailing off to Troy with no thought at all for her child or dear parents, but (love) led her astray . . . lightly . . . (and she?) has reminded me now of Anactoria who is not here; I would rather see her lovely walk and the bright sparkle of her face than the Lydians' chariots and armed infantry . . . impossible to happen . . . mankind . . . but to pray to share . . . unexpectedly.

POEM SUMMARY

Stanza 1

The first line introduces a priamel, or misdirection, that suggests several false candidates for the most beautiful thing on earth before introducing the poet's true opinion. The priamel is a widespread poetic technique used to introduce anything that is going to be discussed in superlative terms. The supposed objects of beauty in this case are bodies of armed men organized into infantry, cavalry, or fleet, the three modes of ancient warfare. That the life of a soldier is a thing to be desired and praised above all else was one of the core assumptions of the ancient Greek aristocratic society in which Sappho lived. In particular, it was enshrined in the poetic tradition beginning with the *Iliad* of Homer, the earliest and greatest Greek poem,

which tells the story of ten days' fighting during the Trojan War.

The second line establishes that indeed a judgment is being made about the greatest beauty on earth. This decision recalls the judgment of Paris, the Trojan prince who was asked by the goddesses Hera, Aphrodite, and Athena to decide which of them was the most beautiful. This is another reference to the epic cycle of the Trojan War. The true answer to the question of what is most beautiful is then presented: it is whatever one desires most. The Greek term here for desire is *erân*, meaning not *to love* but *to lust after*.

Stanza 2

The narrative voice of the poem, which is not necessarily identical to Sappho the poet, promises to explain in simple terms that her answer to the question of what is most beautiful is the correct one. Her explanation takes the form of an example: Helen of Troy. Helen herself is deemed the most beautiful woman who ever lived, and it seems that this status makes her uniquely suited to demonstrate what is the most beautiful as a category. Physical beauty cannot be separated from moral goodness in the Greek language, so Sappho points out a paradox by establishing that the best and most beautiful woman abandoned everything that women like Sappho and her audience are supposed to think best, beginning with leaving the best of husbands (Menelaus, the king of Sparta). This might well suggest that for Sappho, desire is a more powerful force than love.

Stanza 3

Helen abandoned her home in Sparta, leaving not only her husband but also her parents and her child. The parents' love (*phileîn*) for their daughter, Helen, contrasts with the desire that is the main concern of the poem. According to the poetic tradition, Helen's father (at least her human foster father) was Tyndarius, and her mother was Leda. This is the Leda who was seduced by Zeus in the form of a swan, so that Helen's true father was the king of the Greek gods. Leda laid a clutch of five swans' eggs, hatching Helen and her sister Clytemnestra, and her two brothers, the heroes Castor and Pollux. The fifth egg remained unhatched in a temple in Sparta with a prophecy that it would hatch when Sparta was in need of a savior. Helen's daughter was named Hermione.

The poet says that Helen was led astray by desire. Then, because of the imperfect preservation of the single manuscript source for the poem, there is a gap where the last line of this stanza and the first two lines of the next have been obliterated. The implication is that Helen was compelled to leave her home by desire for the man who led her away. Though he is not, as far as scholars can tell, mentioned by name in the poem, this man is Paris, whose bribe for picking Aphrodite as the winner in the beauty contest between the goddesses was possession of Helen, the most beautiful of mortal women. It may be that Helen, despite transgressing the standards of behavior for a Greek woman, can still be described as the most beautiful—and therefore the best—because the invasive force of desire left her not responsible for her actions; she was compelled by the goddess Aphrodite.

Stanza 4

The remnant of this stanza turns to a woman or girl named Anaktoria, who is now far removed from Sappho, although no hint of the circumstances is given. However, it is possible that Anaktoria is in a position that mirrors that of Helen, who was led away from her husband by her lover Paris. Similarly, it seems that perhaps Anaktoria was led away from her lover Sappho by her husband after their wedding.

Stanza 5

Anaktoria is parallel to Helen in another way. To Sappho, Anaktoria is the most beautiful sight in the world, because she is the thing that Sappho desires most. She shares with Helen the quality of being the most beautiful thing in the world to someone. Sappho dwells on watching Anaktoria's body as she walks or perhaps dances, which contrasts with the bodies of troops that were suggested as possible candidates for the most desired thing in the first stanza. Sappho also describes the beauty of Anaktoria's flirtatious expression and her smile. The poet comments again on the superiority of Anaktoria's beauty to that of Lydian war chariots and soldiers, the symbols of wealth and empire.

THEMES

Warrior-Heroes

The beginning of fragment 16 introduces the idea that many people find military formations

or displays the most beautiful thing in the world. This idea is offered as misdirection, in contrast to the poet's opinion, but it is an important suggestion nevertheless. However, it has more deeply Greek meanings as well. Greeks considered that the normal state of a city was war, to be interrupted by brief periods of peace now and again. Accordingly, the highest virtues that Greek men could aspire to were martial—having to do with war. This was carried to the greatest extreme in Sparta, where every element of public and private life was subordinated to the profession of war, but life as a warrior was an ideal shared by all Greek aristocrats. Indeed, in the generation before Sappho, her city of Mytilene had become the main military power on Lesbos by defeating the other Greek city-states on the island. A good comparison is fragment Z34 by Sappho's contemporary Alcaeus, a meditation on the pride he takes in his own armor. In terms of poetry also, the Homeric tradition was the model against which all later Greek writing had to be measured, and the *Iliad* is chiefly concerned with military matters. Sappho is suggesting that some may think the aristocratic life of a warrior is the best thing in life and the finest subject for poetry, but no, Sappho says: that position is held by the most private feelings of desire. Sappho may even be suggesting that for men, war is the finest thing, but for women it must be the private world of feeling. In that case, Sappho is suggesting that the greatest war and the greatest poems—that is, most admired by men—both began with a woman's private desires, in Helen's betrayal of her family.

At the end of the poem, Sappho returns to the military display that fails to be as beautiful as the beauty of the woman she desires. Now, though, she is no longer talking about Greek militarism but Lydian militarism. The Greeks considered the Lydians to be a barbarian people, culturally inferior to themselves, but they acknowledged, at the beginning of the sixth century BCE, that Lydia was at the same time dramatically more wealthy and more militarily powerful than any Greek state. Sappho's home of Lesbos was a small island off the coast of Asia Minor, but the Lydians ruled a vast empire that controlled most of Asia Minor, including all the Greek cities on the mainland. Moreover, Lydia had vast natural resources of gold and silver and had recently invented coinage. Sappho's contemporary Alcaeus fought as a mercenary for the Lydians. Therefore, Lydia here stands not only

TOPICS FOR FURTHER STUDY

- Prepare a handout with a number of lesser-known English poems or parts of poems, no more than ten or fifteen lines each. One or several poems can be used. Prepare each sheet by tearing it into a dozen or so small pieces, making sure that there is printed text on each torn fragment. For each torn sheet, throw away half of the fragments. Organize your classmates into groups of about four students and give each group the remains of one poem to try to reconstruct. The first step is to fit the poem back together like the pieces of a jigsaw puzzle. Next, take a fresh sheet of paper and copy out all the letters, leaving space for the gaps left by the missing pieces; place a dot under letters that are cut in half or otherwise cannot be read with certainty. Each group should count or estimate how many letters, spaces, and punctuation marks are in each line of the poem. Finally, have the groups write down any educated guesses about what letters or words they think ought to fill in the gaps. (This can be turned into a larger writing assignment if the students write down the reasons they thought certain letters or words ought to be restored in the gaps.) After the groups have worked over their fragments as much as they can, show them an intact copy of their poem. (If desired, the poems can be copied out by hand, in all capital letters, without spaces between words or punctuation marks,

to better simulate the way Greek manuscripts were written.)

- Using Google Books, search for terms such as *Sappho*, *Sapphic*, and *Lesbian* by decade, for example, limiting the first search to 1861–1870, then 1871–1880, and so on until about 1920. Noting the highest-ranked hits, describe how the words are used in each decade and how usage changes over time. Present your results systematically in a paper, describing your method, your findings, and your conclusions, or construct a digital time line that illustrates the changes.

- Read the sections dealing with Helen of Troy in the work of Alcaeus (fragment 42) and in Homer's *Iliad*, which is commonly read by young-adult audiences. How is Helen presented by Homer, Alcaeus, and Sappho? Write a brief paper comparing the approaches.

- Read fragment 26 by Sappho and a free-verse poem of another culture from the young-adult poetry anthology *Truth and Lies: An Anthology of Poems*, by Patrice Vecchione. As you analyze the two poems, try to determine what truth and what lies are hiding in the verse. Write a comparative essay that illustrates your findings.

- Compose a song you might like to have performed at your wedding, drawing on themes from Greek mythology.

as a pinnacle of military power with its war chariots (a weapon unknown in the Greek world) but as the symbol of a wealthy, decadent Orient. However, even all the display that Lydia is capable of does not compare to the beauty of Anaktoria seen through Sappho's desire. Although Anaktoria is certainly removed from Sappho by distance and may well be now living in a different city, there is no suggestion in the poem that she is living in the Lydian capital of Sardis, despite the title given by the translator Barnard.

Lust

English uses the word *love* to mean a wide range of feelings that ancient Greek rendered as separate, more specific words. *Philein* meant the kind of affection that one might feel for a parent, for a child, or for a spouse. *Erân*, however, meant physical desire. Sappho, of course, uses these and other words that are often translated as *love* in their separate senses. In fragment 16, Sappho discusses the power of *erân*, not *philein*. It is interesting that, to begin, Sappho compares desire

Ancient Greek horseman (*Panos Karapanagiotis | Shutterstock.com*)

with the feelings one has upon watching a martial parade. This suggests, with unusually penetrating insight, that feelings one might have at such a spectacle may not be limited to pride or patriotism but may also include desire for the soldiers.

For Sappho, as for the ancient Greeks in general, desire was seen as something that came from outside the self, as if one were being possessed by the goddess Aphrodite (an idea expressed in fragment 1). Desire is something that one does not want to experience but that overcomes the will and makes people feel things and act in ways that they would consciously reject if they could; experiencing desire is like being under a spell. The normal Greek idiom for the satisfaction of desire is to say that desire is *cast out*. Experiencing desire is like having an illness, with symptoms of fever and shivering (fragment 31). In fragment 15, Sappho settles on Helen of Troy as the archetype, or representative, of the person driven by desire. Helen abandoned her parents, her husband, and her daughter, the people whom she ought to have loved, because she was driven by an overpowering desire for her lover Paris. Homer makes clear in the *Iliad* that in fact Helen hated Paris, but

Aphrodite filled Helen with a desire she could not fight against.

Now, the narrator of this poem finds herself afflicted with desire. She cannot think of Helen and Paris without being reminded that she feels desire for Anaktoria in the same way that Helen did for Paris. By mentioning Anaktoria just after describing how Helen abandoned her family, the poem raises the possibility that the poet also has a family that she might abandon for Anaktoria's sake. The way that Anaktoria walks and the smile on her face fill the speaker with desire, so that she thinks her more beautiful than an army arrayed for battle. Love and war are both destructive forces, however beautiful and attractive they may be.

STYLE

Lyric Poetry

Fragment 16 is a lyric poem, meaning that it is meant to be sung to the accompaniment of a lyre. There remains, however, no trace of the music Sappho wrote to accompany it. More specifically, it is written in sapphics, a kind of four-line stanza in which each of the first three lines has eleven syllables (arranged, like all Greek poetry, in a pattern of syllables with long and short vowels, in contrast with English poetry, which is an arrangement of stressed and unstressed syllables), followed by a fourth line of five syllables. Some ancient sources say that Sappho invented this meter, others suggest that Alcaeus invented it and Sappho perfected it, but it may well have been a traditional meter local to Lesbos. The first book of the Alexandrian edition of Sappho was devoted to sapphics and was comprised of poems that amounted to 330 stanzas. In modern arrangement, the first forty-eight fragments of Sappho are in this meter. Sapphics have frequently been imitated by lyric poets of all periods in tribute to Sappho, from the ancient Roman poet Catullus to the American beat poet Allen Ginsberg. The nineteenth-century English poet Algernon Charles Swinburne wrote an especially fine poem, titled "Sapphics," in this meter.

Priamel

A priamel is a device in which a poem begins with a subject that is presented as a foil (a contrast) for the true subject that will be introduced later. Sappho's fragment 16 is often cited as an especially artful example of this device. In this case, military displays are presented as the height of beauty, only to have that idea dismissed in favor of the idea that whatever one desires is the height of beauty. Sappho has in mind the emphasis on military matters in Homer's *Iliad*. One could also argue that she is contrasting the spheres of interest of men and women—war and love—though ultimately she is concerned with her own private feelings as opposed to what concerns the world at large.

HISTORICAL CONTEXT

Preservation

Printing in the West was invented hundreds of years after the flourishing of Greek civilization, so the publication and preservation of texts was far different from anything encountered today. All reading matter had to be written out by hand (that is, in manuscript), either by private individuals or by professional scribes whose business was to copy entire books. The body of Sappho's poetry began with her own handwritten versions

of her texts. Copies of these must have been made for use in instructing her chorus of *parthenoi* in their performance and also circulated to friends. The Mytilenean poet Alcaeus, her contemporary, for instance, knew of Sappho's work and wrote admiringly of it. The similarity and novelty of the work of these two poets in writing about matters of intense personal concern in short lyric poems like fragment 16 suggest that they could have commonly shared their work and influenced each other's artistic direction. Sappho's female friends and students may also have received copies of her poetry. Certainly, Sappho's songs were performed in foreign cities like Athens in her lifetime, suggesting a wide and rapid spread of her works, aided in part by professional performers. No systematic edition of Sappho's poems was made until the Hellenistic period (the third and second centuries BCE), when scholars working at the Library of Alexandria (which was later destroyed) gathered all of her works that were known at that time into a collection of nine books or scrolls (each up to thirty pages long) arranged by the individual meters of the poems. All modern knowledge of Sappho's poetry is based on that edition.

All that historians have of her poetry amounts to probably less than 5 percent of what she wrote. No intact copy of the Alexandrian edition of Sappho's works exists, but fragments of it have been preserved in two ways. First, Sappho was widely read and admired throughout antiquity, and many later scholars and poets quoted her works. Modern scholars have combed over all the surviving ancient literature to gather any quotations of Sappho, even the briefest ones. The longest such fragment is fragment 1, a hymn to Aphrodite that was quoted in its entirety by the Roman-era historian Dionysius of Halicarnassus. The other main source is the Greek city of Oxyrhynchus in the Egyptian desert. Archaeologists began excavating there in the late nineteenth century and found that the extremely dry conditions had preserved a large proportion of all of the books that had ever been thrown away into the town's garbage dump. Eventually, millions of partial pages and scraps of paper were recovered, only a small part of which have been edited and published. This proved to be an incredibly valuable source of lost Greek literature, especially of Sappho's work. Several individual pages of her poems have been discovered that were probably part of small anthologies that were excerpted from the Alexandrian edition. For example,

COMPARE
&
CONTRAST

- **580s BCE:** Women maintain their position within society only by remaining secluded within their own homes and having contact outside of their families only under the most carefully chaperoned circumstances.

  Today: Women are free to have careers working outside the home and social lives with friends outside of family members as they please.

- **580s BCE:** Homosexuality in the modern sense of definitive preference for adults of the same sex is virtually unknown, while pederasty (mentoring-like relationships between older

men and adolescent boys) is viewed as a vital form of social integration and mentoring.

  Today: Homosexuality is a divisive political issue, and homosexuality and heterosexuality are often perceived as absolute and mutually exclusive orientations.

- **580s BCE:** The primary form of public poetry is newly composed hymns; most poetry is sung.

  Today: Professional poetry is located in the university or published in books and is rarely liturgical or meant to be performed as song.

---

fragment 58 was found at Oxyrhynchus and identified as a poem of Sappho's in 1922, but unfortunately the page was torn in half vertically, leaving only the line-endings intact. Only in 2005 did Martin L. West realize that another Oxyrhynchus fragment joins up with it to complete the text, supplying one of only two complete Sappho poems. Fragment 16 also comes from Oxyrhynchus and, after fragments 1 and 58, is the most completely preserved of Sappho's poems, having only some damage in the fourth stanza. It is impossible to tell whether some fragmentary lines farther down the page belong to the poem, but the better-preserved text is complete in itself even if it might be part of a larger conception.

Although there is no evidence for it, the statement is frequently made that the Christian scholars of the Byzantine Empire systematically eradicated Sappho's works because they objected to the nature of her subject matter. It is true that many Greek authors, such as the Greek philosopher Porphyry of Tyre, did have their books burned by Christian emperors and Church councils, but Sappho was never singled out for this treatment. The truth is that her works vanished from the Byzantine educational curriculum because her dialect became too archaic and obscure to be read easily. At some

point in the middle of the Byzantine period (around the year 1000 CE), the Alexandrian edition of Sappho ceased to be copied, to become rare and forgotten when Byzantine scholars fled the impending Turkish conquest of Constantinople in the years before 1453. It was these scholars who brought their libraries to Italy, saving the bulk of the Greek literature still preserved. Sappho, however, was already missing from among their books.

The Trojan War

The Trojan War was the subject of the cycle of Homeric poetry, including the *Iliad*, the *Odyssey*, and many other less-well-known poems, and it was one of the most important reference points in establishing Greek identity. The *Iliad* provides a context for aristocratic martial virtue by which Greek men measured themselves, and that forms the background for the opening of Sappho's poem. The events that led up to the war are more clearly alluded to in the second and third stanzas. The goddess Eris (strife) threw a golden apple bearing the inscription "To the fairest" into the assembly of the gods, and it was claimed by Aphrodite, Hera, and Athena. They chose the Trojan prince Paris to judge which of them was the most beautiful. Each goddess offered him a bribe. Aphrodite's bribe succeeded: she promised

Roman infantry *(William Aftard McCarthy / Shutterstock.com)*

to give Paris the most beautiful mortal woman for his wife. This was Helen of Sparta, who was already married to king Menelaus and had a daughter, Hermione, with him. Paris went to Sparta on the premise of a diplomatic mission and kidnapped Helen, carrying her off to become Helen of Troy. When every prince in Greece had contested for Helen's hand, they had sworn an oath to guarantee her marriage to the eventual successful suitor (Menelaus), so each was obliged to lead his own army in the grand expedition to Troy to take Helen back, producing the Trojan War. Aphrodite filled Helen with desire for Paris that she could not resist; this desire led her to abandon her family and thus help trigger an unimaginably destructive war.

CRITICAL OVERVIEW

The older view of Sappho in relationship to her social framework may be exemplified by Denys Page's comments in his work *Sappho and*

Alcaeus. Page was one of the outstanding text critics of the twentieth century, and his work is still fundamental to the texts of Sappho. However, in regard to Sappho's sexuality, which is of central importance to understanding the meaning of her poems, he shies away and claims that "the question is not one which can be discussed at all on the basis of reliable evidence," meaning that the only reliable evidence would be something that is not found in any Greek lyric poet of Sappho's era: a graphic description of a sexual encounter, something Page does not require to accept, for instance, that Alcaeus was attracted to women. The difference is explained in Page's further statement that "there is no evidence in the fragments of Sappho for any impropriety in the conduct of herself or her companions." While Page appears to be striving for a neutral presentation of fact against what he viewed as distasteful sensationalism, he clouds his own judgment by assuming that the restrictions of his own morality could be applied to someone who lived twenty-six hundred years ago in an almost completely alien culture. He is the one who would view sex between women as an impropriety, not necessarily Sappho. Thus, he is almost deciding the issue before he properly asks his question.

Views like this were no longer possible in serious scholarship after K. J. Dover addressed the matter in his book *Greek Homosexuality*:

> So long as we think of the world as divided into homosexuals and heterosexuals and regard the commission of a homosexual act, or even the entertaining of a homosexual desire, as an irrevocable step across a frontier which divides the normal, healthy, sane, natural and good from the abnormal, morbid, insane, unnatural and evil, we shall not get very far in understanding the Greek attitudes to homosexuality.

Glen W. Most, in a 1981 article in *Classical Quarterly*, notes that over time consensus had been achieved in understanding what Sappho's fragment 16 says, and he offers an interpretation of what the poem means. Homer describes Helen in ways that would lead the reader to think she was beautiful, but he never uses that word to describe her. Most scholars note the particularity of the Greek word for beautiful (*kalos*), that it also means good in every sense, including the moral sense. Most suggests that since Sappho used this word to describe Helen, she considered her blameless for her actions, as she was compelled by a desire that was outside of her control. A 2010 article by Eric Dodson-Robinson in *Arethusa* links fragment 16 more closely than ever before to traditional poetry, arguing that the judgment about what is most beautiful (military display or the desired person), is an echo of the judgment of Paris theme and that the poem serves in some way to comment on Sappho's own composition of traditional wedding poetry.

William H. Race, in his 1989 article in the *Classical Journal*, suggests that Sappho's poetry is radically different from Alcaeus's in taking her own inner person as its true subject, and he argues this on the basis of a comparison between Sappho's fragment 16 (rather than one of her more obviously personal poems, such as fragment 31) because of its close thematic parallels with Alcaeus's poetry, such as his fragment 42. This idea has been explored extensively in later work on Sappho. Eva Stehle, in *Performance and Gender in Ancient Greece*, moves beyond simply reading Sappho as a poet of the inner life to conceiving her, in her most personal poems, such as fragments 1 and 16, as a poet writing

for a reading audience, against the more commonly held opinion that Greek poetry in the sixth century could not be separated from a context in performance and singing.

CRITICISM

Bradley A. Skeen

Skeen is a classicist. In the following essay, he explores the social and historical context of Sappho's erotic poetry.

Thanks to cultural discussions begun by the nineteenth-century decadent poets Theophile Gautier and Algernon Charles Swinburne, the terms *Sapphic* and *lesbian* are inextricably linked with female homosexuality. As a consequence, the primary image of Sappho in popular culture today is as an icon of homosexuality. However, involving any figure from antiquity in modern cultural constructs does nothing to help understand that figure either historically or aesthetically. Rather, a poet like Sappho becomes completely hidden underneath a caricature that actively prevents any real understanding or interpretation. It is true that much of Sappho's poetry, including fragment 16, concerns her desire for other women, but ripping this solitary fact out of context and pretending that it exists in a modern context tells us nothing about Sappho and cannot be a firm foundation for argument that pertains to modern times, because the recontextualization is obscuring and falsifying.

It is, however, profitable to look at homoerotic desire in Sappho's social and historical context precisely because her poetry functions within that context. Knowing about Sappho's world provides the best hope of hearing Sappho's own voice. Objective study of Greek society, especially Greek private life, is a relatively recent phenomenon compared with the study of Greek political and military history. In particular, the study of homoerotic desire in the Greek world in a detached and objective way, not intended to function in a modern political context, begins with Kenneth J. Dover's magisterial study *Greek Homosexuality*, written in 1978. Since then, the study of sexuality in antiquity has become one of the most vital fields of studies in the classics, since the evidence on the matter had never been properly evaluated before.

The Greek city-states considered citizenship a jealously guarded commodity and took steps to ensure that the right of citizenship remained within

WHAT DO I READ NEXT?

- Marguerite Johnson's *Sappho* (2007) is an introduction to the author, her poetry, and her times. It is intended for a general audience.

- In *The Complete Poems of Sappho* (2009), editor Willis Barnstone takes a moderate course of translation by trying to remain faithful to the words of the fragments, filling in words or phrases only when the meaning is clearly obvious. The book contains a notes section and a section of ancient testimony about Sappho.

- "A Sappho of Green Springs," a short story first published in 1891 by Bret Harte (Mark Twain's first editor from his days as a journalist in California), is an established classic frequently found on young-adult reading lists. It concerns a talented female poet living in rural California. The story is interesting because the term *Sappho* refers here only to her abilities as a poet, being written in complete innocence of the modern associations of Sappho and lesbianism then being forged in European literature.

- *Sappho's Immortal Daughters* (1995), by Margaret Wilson, provides close readings of Sappho's poetry and biographical testimonies. It is notable chiefly for its explanation

of the difficulties scholars face in dealing with fragments of ancient texts. It illustrates the problems clearly and simply by using as examples well-known English poems and presenting them (with graphic diagrams) in the same fragmentary condition as poems like Sappho's and attempting to reconstruct them by the same techniques that are used to edit fragments of Greek literature.

- Jane Snyder's *The Woman and the Lyre: Women Writers in Classical Greece and Rome* (1989) provides a survey of known women writers from classical antiquity, including Sappho.

- *The Archaeology of Greece* (1996), by William R. Biers, is an introduction to the treasures of the Greek world, explaining the social context of the archaeological findings. The book contains pictures as well.

- *Classical Chinese Poetry: An Anthology* (2008), compiled and translated by the poet David Hinton, covers three thousand years of ancient Chinese poetry by focusing on a smaller number of poets and more works by each of them to allow a better feeling of voice.

civic control. The only class of people who were automatically entitled to citizenship were the legitimate offspring of married citizen couples. Marriages were solemnized only within the two families of the bride and groom, but the city took notice of the marriage when its adult children were admitted into the citizen body. The city asserted an interest in the legitimacy of children produced within marriage. For this reason, adultery was a capital crime in most Greek cities, since it could result in noncitizens being falsely enrolled as citizens if there were unrecognized illegitimate births. However, the city, and society in general, took no interest in proscribing sexual behavior beyond that

single issue. As a consequence, Greek men of the aristocratic and citizen classes had far greater freedom of action in sexual matters than their female counterparts.

Greek women lived secluded lives within the household. Greek homes were segregated by sex. In one compound within the house lived the male head of the family, male children over seven years of age, and any male slaves or servants, usually sleeping and eating together, rather like a military mess. There were similar arrangements for the female members of the household in the other compound of the house. Young male children lived in the women's quarters. While the

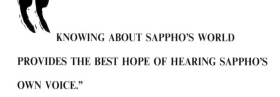

men would often go outside of the house to work, the only work allowed to aristocratic women was in spinning wool and making clothes, which were done inside the house. Female slaves or servants would take care of other chores that required leaving, such as fetching water from public fountains. Only the head of the household or married sons who lived at home could enter the women's quarters for what might be termed conjugal visits. Because of this pattern of life, married couples could conceivably go for long periods without seeing each other, even while living in the same household, though, obviously, contact and the intimacy of emotional bonds could be as close as the husband wished. The wife was unable to take the initiative in such matters. Because of the cloistering of women within the household, courting between men and women was almost unknown.

Virtually the only way that men might even see marriageable but unmarried women was during their attendance at religious festivals. A common setting of the Greek novels of the later Hellenistic period entailed couples who fell in love at first sight at such a festival. Indeed, one of the functions of the public performances of the choruses of unmarried girls (*parthenoi*) that Sappho oversaw was to introduce them to the public as potential brides. In general, however, marriages were arranged by the parents of the prospective bride and groom on the basis of what was economically or politically advantageous for the family as a whole. For this reason, marriages were often between close blood relatives: cousins, or in many cities, including Athens, even between half-siblings. In other cases, couples might never have seen each other before their wedding day. The typical age of marriage for girls was between one and four years after menarche, roughly twelve to sixteen years old. Men, on the other hand, rarely married before they had completed their compulsory military service (ages eighteen to nineteen) and

ideally not before they were able to establish their own independent household, so it would be rare for a groom not to be at least ten years older than his bride. Given the high rate of death in childbirth, men would have two, three, or more wives in their lifetimes, and in each case would probably seek out a previously unmarried girl possibly decades younger than himself. It can be seen already that there is a disconnect between Greek and modern American social customs and practices. The very relationships that were considered the most normative and ideal in Greece, between men in their mid- to late twenties and fourteen- or fifteen-year-old girls, are illegal in America, and a man who expresses sexual interest in a girl of that age would be considered criminally deviant. Even before going further, it is clear that a historical or critical investigation that singles out female homosexuality in ancient Greece in an attempt to impose values from a different culture on it will never be able to understand its subject within its larger frame of reference, which is particular to Greek culture. Every culture's arrangements about sexuality are unique and determined by a historical process, so it is not helpful to treat any particular social concept as universal.

It is also true, however, that human beings are social animals and enjoy courting. There is no reason to think that many Greek married couples did not become intensely emotionally bonded, but other options were available, especially to Greek men. So long as it did not entail adultery in the sense of confusing the parentage of children of female citizens, Greek men were free to seek out almost any relationship they wanted with women. The relationship between Pericles, the leader of Athens during the Peloponnesian War, and Aspasia is only the most famous example of the kind of relationships that were possible between male citizens and noncitizen women. He met her when she was working as an entertainer at a party he attended, courted her, and formed a romantic bond. He undertook to establish her in her own household. This relationship is far closer to the paradigm of marriages growing out of dating relationships that is the modern American norm than was Greek marriage. Yet from the viewpoint of Greek society, Aspasia had a legal status that was little different from a prostitute because she was not sheltered within an aristocratic household. Sappho wrote a poem (fragment 202) teasing her brother Charaxus for indulging in a similar affair. More strictly defined prostitution was legal in Greek society and was not considered a shameful institution for the men who used brothels. By the same token, Greek men had unlimited access to their own slaves of both sexes. The context in which Pericles met Aspasia was the symposium, an after-dinner party that was the centerpiece of social life among Greek aristocrats. The dinner guests and partygoers were exclusively male; the only women allowed were entertainers and prostitutes. Aristocratic boys, though, between the ages of puberty and adulthood (usually taken as the beginning of military service around age eighteen), were also present. The closest approach to modern dating relationships in ancient Greece, based on flirting and courting, with a fine balance between pursuit based on desire and continence based on the chastity of the pursued, took place in the setting of the symposium between adult men (the *erastes*, or desirer) and young men in their mid- to late teens (the *eromenos*, or desired). This kind of relationship, not one between two adult men (which did occur but was actually frowned upon as ridiculous by the consensus of Greek society), is what is typically meant by Greek homosexuality. The older man was meant to help educate the boy he pursued and to provide him with the military equipment he would need on reaching adulthood, as well as other gifts. The greatest gift was entry into the social networks of elite Greek society facilitated within the framework of these romantic relationships, as much as by the family. It is clear, from comparison with ethnographic evidence from other cultures around the world, that these relationships had, in earlier stages of Greek history, been a kind of initiation of boys into the community of adult male citizens. This kind of relationship, between an adult man and a youth, is generally called pederasty.

The sexual prospects open to aristocratic Greek women were far more limited than those available to their husbands. Although women, including Sappho, admired the beauty of young men, in line with the social norms established among men, any relationship with a man of any age would have been considered adulterous and therefore forbidden. Taking the male world as a model, however, it is easy to suggest that relationships between women may have been commonplace. However, evidence for this, as for anything connected with women's private lives in Greece, is harder to come by. A generation

before Sappho, the male poet Alcman composed choral songs to be sung by groups of unmarried girls in Sparta (fragment 1, *Partheneion*), generically almost identical to Sappho's public poetry. The lyrics that he wrote make fairly plain that the girls in the chorus, or at least girls of their age and class, had erotic relations with adult women. Of course, Sparta is an exception in the Greek world. The strict military discipline that governed the city kept male Spartan citizens living in barracks for about the first twenty years of their adult lives, with visits allowed to wives only a few times a year. On the other hand, it is possible to read many of Sappho's poems as referring to her desires for girls who might have been her own students in the chorus of *parthenoi* that she oversaw. One way of reading fragment 31, for instance, is to interpret Sappho as consumed with feelings of desire and jealousy at the wedding of a girl who had been her lover or at least whom she strongly desired. The same may be true in fragment 16, where Anaktoria is lost to Sappho because she is far away. This need not mean that she has gone to a foreign city, merely that she has gone to a place that is inaccessible, namely, into the home of her husband. If that is the case, then Helen's flight from her family because of desire would become a mirror image of what Sappho is experiencing: Anaktoria running away from Sappho's desire into the seclusion of her new family. However, this must remain speculation. Sappho does not even supply the age of Anaktoria.

The biographical tradition is little help in this matter because it tended to satirize Sappho's romantic life, following the extensive treatment of Sappho by the comic poets. *If* Sappho's lovers are younger than her, and *if* she has a role in educating them, then it is tempting to see her engaged in a perhaps widespread practice in Greek society parallel to Greek pederasty that may also have had antecedents in old initiation rites. However, there is no definite evidence than can support such a claim. As a consequence, the nature of Sappho's homoerotic relationships remains a hotly disputed topic among scholars. It is nevertheless clear that Sappho does represent herself in relationships with, or at least in pursuit of, many women, and that these affairs engage the most powerful and intimate emotions of her inner life. In her own view, they are refined and beautiful feelings, and there is no reason to think her audience would have interpreted them differently. The official religious cults of her city entrusted her to write their hymns, a remarkable honor that confirms that Sappho was in no sense socially marginalized. While the larger typology of Greek sexual life can help to find an interpretative framework for Sappho's poems and the desires they highlight, the fragmentary nature of Sappho's poetry and our relative ignorance of women's lives in ancient Greece still make any conclusions that can be reached about Sappho highly tentative.

Source: Bradley A. Skeen, Critical Essay on "Fragment 16," in *Poetry for Students*, Gale, Cengage Learning, 2011.

Josephine Balmer

In the following excerpt, Balmer examines how Sappho's life and poetry were intrinsically related.

Sappho, the most revered of all classical women poets, lived in the city of Mytilene on Lesbos, an island off the coast of Asia Minor, around 600 BC. About two hundred fragments of her lyric poems survive, although little is known of her life. However, a few of her poems refer to the struggle for power between aristocratic factions in Mytilene, suggesting she was a member of the wealthy ruling-class. Apart from this her poetry, as Joan DeJean has recently noted, relegates men to a peripheral role, and is concerned almost exclusively with women—their family relationships, their religious festivals and female deities, particularly Aphrodite, and most of all, their intense emotional relationships.

Such relationships have obsessed studies of her work throughout the ages, from the salacious gossip of Greek comic playwrights to Victorian gentleman scholars. This century, Freudians, feminists and philologists have all argued about her sexuality, poring over her fragmentary poems as if they were a biographical tract. In 1913, one German scholar postulated that Sappho was the 'headmistress' of a school of girls on Lesbos, dedicated to the cult of Aphrodite, and her most intense declaration of sensual desire (No. 2), was a wedding-hymn for a favourite 'pupil.' In 1979 the feminist scholar Judith Hallett also claimed that Sappho held a 'formal' position on Lesbos, with her poetry acting as 'a sensual consciousness-raiser' for segregated young girls 'on the threshold of marriage and maturity.' The debate over her sexuality still rages, with some scholars convinced of Sappho's lesbianism, others concentrating on a more emotional sensuality.

More productive is the study of Sappho's poetic concerns, examining how she establishes an alternative world in which a set of female values are asserted in direct opposition to those of male culture. In No. 4, for example, she asks the question 'what is the loveliest sight on earth?' and after rejecting armies, cavalries or fleets—the male forces of war—she answers it, 'whatever you desire,' using the example of Helen's desertion of Menelaus for Paris of Troy to prove the point. But whereas in Homer's *Iliad*, Helen is a passive figure stolen away like an inanimate object to live in misery and regret in Troy until reclaimed by the Greeks as a prize of war, Sappho's Helen acts of her own free will, motivated only by desire. In a direct echo of a passage from Homer, where Helen weeps as she remembers the home and family she has left behind, Sappho has her Helen care nothing for her husband, child or parents, transforming her from a puppet of kings into a decisive woman, forsaking her traditional role as daughter, wife and mother for the demands of her own sexuality.

Over and over again in Sappho's poetry she rewrites male literary tradition, replacing it with a parallel female value-system. In Hesiod's epic poetry, for example, marriage is depicted as an evil, with women a burden, 'a bane to mortal men.' In Sappho's wedding songs, she reasserts both the qualities of the bride, and the good-fortune of the groom, who relishes, rather than fears, his change of status. Similarly, a recent study by Eva Stigers has shown how Sappho subverts erotic male poetry, overturning its emphasis on domination and submission to find metaphors based on 'female biology and psychology'; where Anacreon characterises his male lover as a charioteer, holding the reins to his soul, for example, Sappho portrays her beloved, Atthis, as a tiny child. Important here, too, is Sappho's constant expression of memory and loss, whether for the past pleasure of Anactoria's 'radiant, sparkling face' (No. 4) or the luxuries of her youth (No. 3), asserting the value of individual women and establishing a collective history.

But most of all, Sappho transformed the lyric genre, a new form of personal literary expression replacing—as well as subverting—Homer's epic poems. Ancient commentators record that Sappho invented many analogies which later became commonplace: the moon as 'silver,' for example, a reflection of the growing use of coinage, or love as 'bittersweet.' To jaded modern palates, the freshness of such poetry, its directness and vigour, can easily be overlooked. Yet its intensity burned throughout antiquity, still influencing poetic declarations of emotion over five hundred years later when the Latin male poet Catullus imitated her work.

But Sappho's poetry also spoke for her community, for the women she addresses in her poems, who listened and composed alongside her. To the later classical women poets, too, her poems were a source of inspiration, borrowed, imitated and honoured in their own work, links in a chain which stretched from Nossis and Erinna in the third century BC to Julia Balbilla in the second AD—and beyond to H. D., May Sarton, and Adrienne Rich in our own.

Source: Josephine Balmer, "Sappho," in *Classical Women Poets*, translated by Josephine Balmer, Bloodaxe Books, 1996, pp. 23–25.

SOURCES

Alcman, "1. Maiden Song," in *Greek Lyrics*, 2nd ed., translated by Richmond Lattimore, University of Chicago Press, 1960, pp. 33–35.

Dodson-Robinson, Eric, "Helen's 'Judgement of Paris' and Greek Marriage Ritual in Sappho," in *Arethusa*, Vol. 43, No. 1, 2010, pp. 1–20.

Dover, K. J., *Greek Homosexuality*, rev. ed., MJF Books, 1997.

Lardinois, André, "Lesbian Sappho and Sappho of Lesbos," in *From Sappho to de Sade: Moments in the History of Sexuality*, edited by Jan Bremmer, Routledge, 1989, pp. 15–35.

Most, Glen W., "Sappho Fr. 16. 6-71L-P," in *Classical Quarterly*, Vol. 31, No. 1, 1981, pp. 11–17.

Page, Denys, *Sappho and Alcaeus: An Introduction to the Study of Ancient Lesbian Poetry*, Clarendon Press, 1955.

Prins, Yopie, *Victorian Sappho*, Princeton University Press, 1999.

Race, William H., "Sappho Fr. 16 L.-P. and Alkaios Fr. 42 L-P. Romantic and Classical Strains in Lesbian Lyric," in *Classical Journal*, Vol. 85, No. 1, 1989, pp. 16–33.

Sappho, "Fragment 16," in *Greek Lyric*, translated by David A. Campbell, Harvard University Press, 1982, p. 67.

———, *Sappho*, translated by Mary Barnard, foreword by Dudley Fitts, University of California Press, 1996, p. 41.

———, "To an Army Wife (Troy)," in *Sappho: Stung with Love; Poems and Fragments*, translated by Aaron Poochigian, Penguin, 2009, p. 58.

Stehle, Eva, *Performance and Gender in Ancient Greece: Nondramatic Poetry in Its Setting*, Princeton University Press, 1997.

West, Martin L., "The New Sappho," in *Die Zeitschrift für Papyrologie und Epigraphik*, Vol. 151, 2005, pp. 1–9.

FURTHER READING

Burnett, Anne Pippin, *Three Archaic Poets: Archilochus, Alcaeus, Sappho*, Harvard University Press, 1983.
    Burnett analyzes Sappho in comparison with these two other lyric poets of her time.

Campbell, David A., trans., *Greek Lyric: Sappho and Alcaeus*, Loeb Classical Library, 1982.
    This volume is the only translation into English of all Sappho's fragments, no matter how brief, as well as the reports of her life. In addition to the English translation, this edition also prints the original Greek text of Sappho's poems. The volume also contains the fragments of Alcaeus's work.

Jong, Erica, *Sappho's Leap*, W. W. Norton, 2003.
    Best-selling novelist Jong based this book on the biographical tradition of Sappho.

Reynolds, Margaret, *The Sappho History*, Palgrave, 2003.
    Reynolds presents a history of Sappho's reception by poets and historians in later ages.

Sappho, *If Not, Winter: Fragments of Sappho*, translated by Anne Carson, Alfred A. Knopf, 2002.
    Carson's book presents one of the most recent translations of Sappho by a poet rather than a classicist, together with the original Greek text in a bilingual edition.

West, Martin L., *Ancient Greek Music*, Clarendon, 1992.
    West discusses the role of musical performance in ancient Greek life and surveys the scant evidence for Greek musical performance and notation.

SUGGESTED SEARCH TERMS

Sappho

Alcaeus

Corinna

pederasty

decadent movement

Lesbos

Sapphic stanza

epithalamion OR epithalamia

Alcman

Helen of Troy

translation AND Sappho

The Guitar

Of all twentieth-century Spanish poets, few strike such emotional chords with readers as Federico García Lorca. The Academy of American Poets describes Lorca as "possibly the most important Spanish poet and dramatist of the twentieth century." His brilliant and innovative poetry captured the hearts of his fellow Spaniards during his own lifetime, and his fame as a poet, artist, musician, and dramatist has only grown in the years since his death at the young age of thirty-eight. The circumstances of his tragic death at the hands of fascist Nationalist militia in 1936 sometimes overshadows his poetry in the minds of readers. His work is nonetheless worthy of both study and admiration. In particular, his early poetry, rooted in the folk traditions and music of his native Andalusia, continues to intrigue and delight readers and critics alike.

FEDERICO GARCÍA LORCA

1931

In 1921, Lorca set out to write a volume of poetry that would explore the music known as *cante jondo*, or "deep song," a type of flamenco music played by the Gypsies of Andalusia. Lorca viewed authentic flamenco as an expression from the heart and soul of a stigmatized people. He strove not to imitate the *cante jondo* but rather to use it as inspiration for his poetry. The volume *Poem of the Deep Song* is subdivided into suites, or sequences of poems, devoted to different forms of deep song. The opening sequence, "Poem of the Gypsy *Siguiriya*," includes seven poems, the second of which is "The Guitar," a poem that expresses the anguish and pain of life through the metaphor of a musical instrument.

Federico García Lorca (Getty Images)

Although Lorca wrote nearly all of the poems included in this collection in November 1921, the book itself was not published until 1931. "The Guitar" is also included in *Federico García Lorca: Collected Poems*, edited by Christopher Maurer, published in a revised bilingual edition in 2002. For students studying in both English and Spanish, the facing-page translations in this book are particularly useful.

AUTHOR BIOGRAPHY

Lorca was born on June 5, 1898, in a village not far from Granada, Spain. His father, Federico García Rodríguez, was a landowner and agriculturist. His mother, Vicenta Lorca Romero, was a primary-school teacher. Lorca and his mother were very close, and he developed his love of music from her.

The family lived in the countryside on a fertile plain known as the *vega*. Lorca enjoyed a rural childhood that fostered his connection with and appreciation for nature. In 1909, the family moved to Granada to ensure secondary education for Lorca. As a young man, Lorca was interested in literature, art, and music and felt deeply connected to Andalusia, the part of Spain where he lived. Rob Stone, writing in *Anales de la literatura española contemporánea*, notes, "[Lorca's] childhood in Granada was spent exploring a landscape that was dominated by Arabic monuments such as the Alhambra and populated by the performers and protagonists of flamenco song." Religion would be another influence on the young poet; however, though Lorca was raised Catholic, he rejected the church while still in his teens.

While in Granada, Lorca associated himself with other young people holding similar interests and founded a literary discussion group called Rinconcillo. His writing career began with the publication of *Impresiones y viajes* published in 1919 and later translated into English as *Impressions and Landscapes* (1987).

In 1919, Lorca moved to Madrid and became active in theater, meanwhile maintaining his interest in poetry and the music of Andalusia. Over the next ten years, Lorca spent part of his time in Madrid, living at the Residencia de Estudiantes, and summers in Granada. When composer Manuel de Falla moved to Granada around this time, he and Lorca became good friends, sharing interests in folk music and flamenco.

Lorca's first collection of poems, *Libro de poemas* (Book of Poems), was published in 1921. While the volume showed some promise, Lorca quickly turned away from its style and themes. Instead, he began producing short-lined lyric poems, organized together in suites. In 1921, in anticipation of a *cante jondo* festival and competition organized by Falla and himself, Lorca wrote the verses (including "The Guitar") that eventually constituted the volume *Poema del cante jondo* (*Poem of the Deep Song*), which was not published until 1931. During the same period, he also composed the poems of another volume, *Canciones* (Songs).

In the following years, Lorca pursued his interest in Gypsy culture and music and produced what was destined to be his most popular work, *Romancero gitano*, in 1928; this volume was translated into English as *Gypsy Ballads* and published in 1951. He also entered into a serious, complicated relationship with painter Salvador Dalí during the 1920s, a relationship that ended abruptly in 1928 and threw Lorca into an emotional crisis.

His family, aware of his growing depression, sent him to New York in 1929, where he took courses in English and wrote the essays that make up the book *Poeta in Nueva York* (published as *Poet in New York* in a bilingual edition in 1940). He left New York in 1930, traveling to Cuba. While in Cuba, he began to work on a play, and theater became his consuming interest for several years. He returned to Spain later in 1930.

In 1931, the Second Spanish Republic came to power. Lorca and his family were supporters of the Republicans. Shortly thereafter, Lorca wrote and produced his play *Bodas de sangre*

(Blood Wedding), his first dramatic financial success.

After a trip to Argentina, Lorca began once again writing poetry as well as drama. He returned to Spain in 1934, a time of political unrest as liberal left-wing factions (sometimes collectively called the Republicans) squared off against right-wing fascists (known as the Nationalists). In 1936, fascist military leader General Francisco Franco attempted to seize power, and Spain was thrust into civil war. Lorca, now back in Granada, was arrested by soldiers associated with Franco shortly after his brother-in-law, the Socialist mayor of Granada, was murdered by Nationalist forces. Lorca is believed to have been murdered on August 18 or 19, 1936. He was buried in an unmarked grave.

Over the course of his short life, Lorca wrote over forty volumes of poetry, essays, and plays. His work has been translated into many languages, and readers all over the world know and love his poems. Although his tragic end sometimes overshadows the critical assessment of his poetry and drama, Lorca continues to be considered the foremost literary figure of his generation and perhaps of twentieth-century Spain.

POEM SUMMARY

Lines 1–6

"The Guitar" is a short lyric poem of twenty-seven lines. It is the second poem in the sequence "Poem of the Gypsy *Siguiriya*," included in *Poem of the Deep Song*. The *siguiriya* is one of the most important types of flamenco, an Andalusian style of music and dance. The *siguiriya* is a somber, solemn dance following a twelve-beat measure, and the song that accompanies the dance is dramatic and powerful. The music for the *siguiriya* is always played on a guitar.

The first poem of the sequence is called "Landscape," and it serves to set the scene for the poems that follow, in much the same way as a stage is set before the beginning of a flamenco dance. Then, the guitar begins playing. Thus, the placement of "The Guitar" as the second poem in the sequence has significance.

The first two lines of the poem form one sentence, a sentence that anthropomorphizes the guitar by telling the reader that it is crying. Thus, Lorca is comparing the music of the guitar

to the sound of crying. These two lines repeat as the third sentence in the poem in lines 5 and 6.

It is important to remember that this poem was originally written in Spanish, and so any discussion of the sounds of the poem must take into account both the original poem and its translation. For example, in the original Spanish, the repeating lines have a total of twelve syllables. Because these are the lines that open the poem, the twelve syllables are significant in that they mirror the twelve-beat measure of the *siguiriya*. Lines 3 and 4, enclosed by the repeating lines, provide an image of broken drinking cups, contributing to the overall sorrowful tone set in the opening lines.

Lines 7–16

Lines 7 and 8 form the fourth sentence in the poem, while lines 9 and 10 form the fifth sentence. The two sentences carry similar meanings; indeed, lines 8 and 10 contain identical words. This section of the poem states that the guitar cannot be made quiet. In other words, the crying of the guitar will happen no matter what the player, the singer, the dancer, or the audience attempts to do. The lines echo each other.

Lines 11–14 form the sixth sentence of the poem. These lines describe the crying of the guitar, comparing it to sounds in nature such as rain and the breeze. The crying never ceases, never changes. In addition, Lorca writes that the crying is like a gale blowing over barren lands covered with snow. These lines not only emphasize the mournful sadness of the sound of the guitar but also connect the poem and the *siguiriya* to a cold, uncaring natural world.

Lines 15 and 16 repeat lines 9 and 10, offering yet one more refrain, emphasizing that the crying cannot be stopped. This section of the poem serves to underscore the meaninglessness of human existence, as exemplified by the crying guitar.

Lines 17–24

Lines 17 and 18 form the next sentence. Lorca writes that the guitar is crying for places and things far away. The implication is that these are things impossible to obtain, although desired. Accordingly, the crying of the guitar may be caused by an unceasing desire for that which cannot be gained.

In lines 19 and 20, the next sentence in the poem, Lorca compares the crying for that which cannot be obtained to the desert crying for flowers. Lines 21–24 form the longest sentence in the poem, and the images of death and uselessness pile up in this section. The guitar cries as if it is a directionless spear, moving through the air without a goal; as if it is the end of a day that had no beginning; and as if it is a bird that has died on the limb of a tree. These lines underscore the themes of anxiety, death, and existential anguish.

Lines 25–27

Line 25 is an exclamation, a direct address to the guitar, ending with an exclamation point. It is as if the speaker cannot bear the pain that the crying of the guitar gives him. It is a wail of grief and sadness. The last two lines of the poem form the final sentence, which may have several meanings. These lines say that the soul has been injured to death by five sharp weapons. On the one hand, the number five recalls the five wounds of Christ in medieval Catholic iconography. In turn, Our Virgin of Sorrows (Virgen de las Angustias) is the patron saint of Granada, Lorca's birthplace and an important location in Andalusia and for flamenco, and is often pictured with a sword piercing her heart. Although Lorca professed to be an atheist and broke ties with the Catholic Church at a young age, according to Stone in "Misticismo y lujuria: The Sacred and the Profane in *Poema del cante jondo*," the iconography of the Catholic Church would have been pervasive throughout Granada and the countryside. Finally, the lines can be interpreted as the soul of the guitar, or the listener, being put to death at the hands of the guitarist, his five fingers serving as cutting blades.

THEMES

Suffering

William Berrien, in an obituary for Lorca appearing in *Books Abroad* in 1937, notes that the themes of *Poem of the Deep Song* include "passion, suffering, [and] death." "The Guitar" demonstrates through imagery and theme the extraordinary suffering inherent in the human condition. Lorca, through the device of anthropomorphism, humanizes the guitar. Thus, the guitar engages in human actions and feels human emotions. For example, the guitar cries in its suffering. Like a suffering human being, the guitar cries for things that are far away, things that it cannot have. Because the guitar cannot have these things, the suffering is not

only painful, it is also unending. The crying goes on without stop, and the crying is amplified by the forces of nature, such as the water and the wind. The suffering, therefore, is pervasive: human beings, things, and nature all suffer together in the pain of existence.

Unlike Christian theology, which points to an end to suffering through Jesus, the worldview of the guitar is one of suffering that even transcends death. In poems that use Christian symbolism and motifs, for example, a bird in a tree might point to grace, forgiveness, redemption, and new life. In the world of the Romany and by extension in Lorca's world, the bird in the tree is not symbolic of new life but rather is dead. Likewise, the final image in the poem is of a heart pierced to death by sharp instruments, a potent symbol of the painful death of body and soul.

Music

As Edward F. Stanton notes in his article "García Lorca and the Guitar," the poet was surrounded by Andalusian music and folklore throughout his childhood. The family home often hosted flamenco sessions, and thus from a young age, Lorca was fascinated by both music and the guitar. Stanton points out that "the guitar is a recurrent motif in Lorca's work." In *Poem of the Deep Song*, Lorca includes three poems with this motif.

Lorca's task in this brief poem is to somehow find language that is able to touch the reader's mind, senses, and heart in the same way that music does. Thus, not only is music the subject of the poem, it is also the vehicle that delivers the meaning of the poem. This is a difficult task; when the reader is alone with the poem, reading is a silent activity. Evoking music in silent reading requires great skill with the poetic devices of assonance (repetition of vowel sounds), alliteration (repetition of sounds at the beginning of words), and rhythm.

Beyond the stylistic devices and the structural necessities of such a poem, however, music also functions as a theme. "The Guitar" is filled with descriptions of the instrument's wailing or crying. Obviously, a musical instrument cannot literally cry. Nonetheless, the music arising from the guitar sounds sad and anguished, filled with suffering, to its listeners. In this poem, Lorca demonstrates how music itself can reveal an entire worldview, a worldview of an outcast, oppressed people. In addition, the music of the poem reveals Lorca's fascination with existential anguish, the pain of

TOPICS FOR FURTHER STUDY

- Watch the documentary film *Gypsy Heart: The Heart and Soul of Flamenco*, featuring Omayra Omaya, directed by Jocelyn Ajami, and released on DVD in 2005. Take notes while you watch the film, and use your notes as you compose a review of the film, connecting what you have learned about flamenco with what you have learned about Lorca.

- With a small group of classmates, plan a reading of Lorca's poetry from *Poem of the Deep Song*. Locate these poems either in a book in your library or as digital files online. Prepare for your reading by finding MP3 files of suitable flamenco guitar music to play in the background. Decorate your classroom with photos and artwork you find of Andalusia and Granada. Present the poems in both Spanish and English if possible.

- Research the Romany (also called Romani or Roma) people. Who are they and where did they come from? Why are they called Gypsies, and why has this become a pejorative term? How have the Romany been mistreated and marginalized throughout history? What was Lorca's connection with the Romany of Andalusia? Write a well-organized, documented research essay, citing your sources. Illustrate your essay with photos and artwork found online, provide background music for the reader when you post your essay to your class Web site, and invite your classmates to comment on your conclusions.

- Do an online search to locate *The Cricket Sings: Poems and Songs for Children* (1981), written by Lorca, translated into English by Will Kirkland, and illustrated by Maria Horvath. Obtain a copy of the book at your library or through your library's interlibrary loan system. With a small group, prepare a presentation for young children based on these poems. With your teacher, locate an elementary classroom where you can present your program.

- Read the novel *The Flamenco Academy*, by Sarah Bird, published in 2007, featuring young-adult protagonist Cyndi Rae Hrncr, a girl of Czech heritage who moves to New Mexico, where she becomes passionately involved in flamenco music and dancing. Demonstrate your ability to articulate new information in a clear manner by preparing and delivering a book review for your class, connecting the novel to the poem "The Guitar."

- With a small group of your classmates, create a Web site on the subject of the Generation of '27, a group of influential Spanish poets, including Lorca, who achieved fame in the 1920s. Include pages containing biographies of each of the important poets, samples of their work, and digital recordings of their poems.

- In 1922, Lorca and his friend the composer Manuel de Falla organized and sponsored a conference on the traditional form of Andalusian music known as *cante jondo*, or deep song. Lorca prepared and delivered several lectures on the topic. Demonstrate your own ability to manage and share your independent learning: identify something you feel passionate about, locate a classmate who shares your interest, and develop a lecture to offer your classmates so that they can learn about your interest.

- With a small group of students, research the Spanish Civil War and the days leading up to the death of Lorca. Acting as investigative reporters and using video technology available on your computer, record a simulated newscast about Lorca's disappearance and ultimate death.

- Write an essay in which you compare and contrast Lorca's flamenco-inspired poetry with the jazz-inspired poetry selected and edited by Sascha Feinstein and Yusef Komunyakaa in *The Jazz Poetry Anthology*, published in 1991.

Spanish guitar resting on old wall (*Jose AS Reyes / Shutterstock.com*)

being alive. Thematically, then, the music serves to underscore human suffering as well as the ultimate purposelessness of life.

Nihilism

Nihilism is a term coined in the early nineteenth century from the Latin root *nihil*, meaning "nothing." In its most radical form, nihilism includes the beliefs that nothing has any value and that life is purposeless. Further, nothing can be known or communicated, and there is neither morality nor justice in existence. Nihilism leads to extreme pessimism or, on the other hand, to hedonism, the belief that the pursuit of pleasure is the only purpose of life. Stone notes in several articles that deep song is essentially nihilistic. Likewise, Christof Jung, in his chapter "Cante Flamenco" in *Flamenco: Gypsy Dance and Music from Andalusia*, writes, "a sense of nihilism evokes a deep fatalism; death is one of the principal themes of cante jondo."

"The Guitar" demonstrates the nihilistic theme that runs through flamenco as well as through Lorca's poetry. Not only does the guitar cry disconsolately, but further the things for which it yearns are unobtainable. The images throughout the poem point to uselessness, meaninglessness, and death.

STYLE

Repetition

Lorca's poetry is noted for its musical qualities. One of the ways that he achieves these qualities in poems such as "The Guitar" is through the use of repetition. He repeats certain sounds, words, phrases, lines, and ideas.

In a musical ballad, for example, the poet might use a refrain to connect the varying lyrics. The old Scottish song "The Broom of the Cowdenknowes" illustrates the device. After a stanza that moves the meaning of the ballad ahead, a repeating refrain begins with the words, "Oh, the broom, the bonnie bonnie broom..." The refrain musically connects each of the verses to each other.

In "The Guitar," Lorca repeats Spanish sounds produced by letters such as *ll*, a combination that sounds in English like the letter *y* in the word *yellow*. Lorca also repeats particular phrases. For example, in each of lines 8, 10, and 16, he uses the same three words. He also repeats whole sentences: lines 1 and 2 compose a complete sentence of five words, which is then repeated in lines 5 and 6. Finally, Lorca repeats particular words throughout the poem. Forms of the word *weep*, for example, are used seven times. The result of so much repetition is a poem that is at once musical and tightly organized, although it does not have regular rhyme or rhythm.

Assonance

Assonance is similarity in vowel sounds within different words. Assonance is similar to rhyme; however, two rhyming words will have the same consonant and vowel sounds. For example, the word *beach* rhymes with the word *reach*, while the word *beach* is assonant with the word *leak*. Along with alliteration, the repetition of the beginning sounds of words, assonance serves to hold a poem together.

Lorca uses assonance effectively in "The Guitar," although in translation this feature is somewhat lost. Spanish is very amenable to the use of assonance since so many words end in either the letter *a* or the letter *o*. In addition, in this poem, the word for *weep* in Spanish is assonant with the Spanish word for *guitar*. Such similarities in sound link the words tightly and help create the overall tone, mood, and lyrical quality of Lorca's work.

Images

The poet Pedro Salinas wrote in a speech delivered in 1942 and later published in *MLN* that "Federico was not an intellectual: he saw everything in images, and in the projection of fantasy." Although the word *image* generally refers to a visual picture, images in poetry can appeal to any of the senses. Lorca fully exploits the potential of the image in his poem "The Guitar." He creates a unifying auditory image through his repetition of words depicting the crying of the guitar. This sound echoes throughout the entire poem.

In addition, Lorca creates tactile images in the lines describing the breaking of the glasses in the morning and in the reference to land covered by snow. The reader can feel these images on his or her skin, just as the warm dirt of the south in line 19 can also be felt through the sense of touch. Lorca creates an olfactory image in line 20 with a reference to a sweet-smelling flower.

The poem's most striking images are visual. The images are of barren, dead, broken objects and scenes. He writes of unrelieved darkness and death by using images such as a tree with a dead bird. The poem ends with the most striking image of all, one that figures in Catholic iconography and also in songs of unrequited love, the pierced heart. In this instance, Lorca uses his image as both metaphor and symbol. Image, then, is one of the primary literary stylistic devices used by Lorca to create a poem that is at once the sound of a guitar and singing and the thematic equivalent of a meaningless, empty universe.

HISTORICAL CONTEXT

Flamenco and the Cante Jondo Festival

Critics have long noted the influence of flamenco music on Lorca's poetry. Although the word *flamenco* is well known around the world, few understand its history. *Cante jondo* is "the oldest and purest version of the flamenco tradition," according to Mary Etta Hobbs in her 2004 dissertation, "An Investigation of the Traditional *Cante Jondo* as the Inspiration for the Song Cycle *Five Poems of García Lorca* by Elisenda Fábregas." She notes further, "surprisingly to many Westerners, these are not songs of celebration but of intense grief."

Flamenco's roots are buried deep in the musical traditions of Andalusia's earliest settlers; after the eight century, the influx of Arab people and their music, as well as that of Jewish and African peoples, contributed to the mix. The Romany people migrated from India and spread through Europe, reaching Spain about the mid-fifteenth century, bringing their own musical traditions. About the same time, Christian forces took control of Spain in the Reconquest, forcing Muslims, Jews, and Romany to assimilate or leave. Consequently, these groups became outcasts and were persecuted. The music known as "deep song" grew out of this potent stew.

In the nineteenth century, deep song became increasingly popular among the public despite the outcast nature of its performers. As an increasing number of non-Romany began to perform flamenco, the character of the music changed. There was great concern among some musicians and writers that deep song would become an inauthentic art form. Lorca was among these.

Thus, one of the most important historical events with regard to the composition of "The Guitar" was the first-ever El Concurso del Cante Jondo, a festival and competition organized by

COMPARE & CONTRAST

- **1920s:** The Romany people exist as outsiders throughout Europe, and many live in Andalusia, Lorca's home.

  1930s: During the Nazi occupation of much of Europe, the Romany are rounded up, beaten, and later sterilized and sent to concentration camps.

  Today: The Romany are ethnic minorities in many European countries and still suffer from discrimination.

- **1920s:** King Alfonso XIII and dictator Miguel Primo de Rivera rule a Spain beset by poverty and class conflicts.

  1930s: The Second Spanish Republic, elected by the people, comes to power, as Alfonso XIII abdicates. By 1936, fascist forces under Francisco Franco clash with Republican forces, with Franco the ultimate victor. Franco rules until his death in 1975.

  Today: Spain is a parliamentary monarchy under King Juan Carlos and governed by an elected parliament. Spain is a full member of the European Union.

- **1920s:** Flamenco is a traditional form of music performed by the Romany people of Andalusia, Spain, and enjoys a resurgence of popularity during this decade.

  1930s: Flamenco goes through a period of commercialization and hybridization; during the Spanish Civil War and World War II, it appears that flamenco may slide into oblivion.

  Today: Flamenco enjoys a return to its roots and widespread popularity with new festivals and contests. Young singers and dancers are learning the traditional forms of the art.

Lorca and his friend, composer Manuel de Falla, and held in Granada on June 13 and 14, 1922. According to the Academy of American Poets, "Spain's most famous 'deep song' singers and guitarists participated."

The motivation behind the festival was Falla and Lorca's desire to encourage the performance of deep song and to prevent the over-commercialization of flamenco. In addition, the organizers hoped to find new, talented deep song singers, known as *cantaors*. Lorca delivered a now-famous lecture on deep song that not only traces the historical roots of the form but also provides a blueprint of his plan for the poetry included in *Poem of the Deep Song*.

The Second Republic and the Spanish Civil War

Although the events of the Spanish Civil War occurred after Lorca wrote "The Guitar," the publication of the poem coincided with early events leading to the uprising and war. The Spanish Civil War affected Lorca's entire generation. The poets, artists, and musicians of his era were all deeply marked by the events of the 1930s; for Lorca, these events cost him his life.

Spain was plagued for many years by the repressive regime of dictator Miguel Primo de Rivera and King Alfonso XIII. In 1929, the worldwide economic situation affected the value of the Spanish peseta, leading to unrest. The king attempted to distance himself from Primo de Rivera, but he acted too late. In 1930, a coalition led by Spaniards attempting to establish a republic deposed the king, who subsequently abdicated and left Spain. In April 1931, the Republicans won municipal elections and established a provisional government. Lorca and his family were closely tied to many Republicans. For a brief period of time, the downtrodden and poor outcasts of Spanish society hoped for a brighter future.

However, the Republican government was not stable, and over the next five years, socialists,

Beautiful white camellias (crystalfoto | Shutterstock.com)

communists, right-wing Republicans, left-wing Republicans, the military, and other factions vied for power. Cary Nelson, in "The Spanish Civil War: An Overview," reports, "When a progressive Popular Front government was elected in February 1936, with the promise of realistic land reform one of its key planks, conservative forces immediately gathered to plan resistance." The military, the Catholic Church, and capitalists all feared the reforms planned by the Popular Front.

Meanwhile, the forces of fascism were rising around the world, reacting violently against democratically elected governments. In Germany, Italy, and Japan, strong fascist military leaders took control of their countries. In Spain, the military, under their fascist leader Francisco Franco, rebelled against the Popular Front government on July 18, 1936, plunging the country into a long and bloody civil war. Adolf Hitler and Benito Mussolini both supplied men and arms to Franco, escalating the rebellion into full-scale war.

Lorca, who had been in Madrid, chose to go to Granada on July 14, 1936, so he was there with his family at the time of the military uprising. As

an artist and a family member of the socialist mayor of Granada, Lorca was vulnerable to attack from the right. On August 16, 1936, the mayor was murdered by fascist militia. On the same day, Lorca was arrested. His last hours remain cloaked in mystery, but it is believed he was executed on August 18 or 19.

The Spanish Civil War resulted in victory for Franco, who ruled Spain from 1939 to 1975. Many artists and writers memorialized the civil war and the Republican cause, with works such as *Homage to Catalonia* (1938), by George Orwell, and *Guernica* (1937), a horrifying painting by Pablo Picasso.

CRITICAL OVERVIEW

Although he lived to be only thirty-eight years old, Lorca's reputation as a poet, dramatist, and essayist was already well established at the time of his death. His fame has not diminished in the intervening years. Writing in the *Dictionary of*

Literary Biography, Andrew Anderson summarizes Lorca's critical and popular stature, noting,

> Federico García Lorca's reputation rests equally on his poetry and his plays. He is widely regarded as Spain's most distinguished twentieth-century writer, his work has been translated into at least twenty-five languages, and his name is as familiar to the general reader as those of novelists Miguel de Cervantes and Benito Pérez Galdós.

As early as 1937, American critics appreciated both Lorca's talent and his untimely death. William Berrien, in *Books Abroad*, notes,

> to the student of Spanish literature, the death of García Lorca will mean the loss of the leading poet of his generation at the very moment when his work had attained its surest form and deepest inspiration and his vision was steadily broadening.

Lorca's poetry appeals to readers for a variety of reasons. In a *Dublin Magazine* review of Lorca's poetry, for example, Edward C. Riley lauds Lorca's visual imagery. He also asserts, "Like all the great Spanish poets he exploits to the full the musical qualities of the language."

Other critics have noted the strong influence of nature on Lorca's work. In "Nature and Symbol in the Poetry of Federico García Lorca," Gustavo Correa argues that Lorca "was a poet of Nature." He further asserts that in the poems of *Deep Song*,

> the air vibrations at night and in the dawn are the same vibrations of the guitar strings, which, in turn, put in motion the foliage of the trees and the hair and skirts of the gypsy girls.... Grief and dark premonitions permeate the landscape.

Likewise, Rob Stone, in his essay "Weeping Blood: *Poema del cante jondo*," notes,

> The guitar had become a key element in the performance of flamenco by Lorca's time. Its plaintive sound is evocative of the mood of the cante and the player's flourish underpins the cry of the cantador. In 'La guitarra,' the anthropomorphised instrument becomes the voice of Nature expressing universal anguish.

Further, Stanton in his essay "García Lorca and the Guitar," appearing in *Hispania* in 1975, focuses specifically on the guitar, writing, "The guitar is a recurrent motif in Lorca's work." Stanton also argues that the guitar cries for the existential anguish of life: "The motive for this wailing lies in a futile yearning for what cannot be—the yearning of hot southern sand for flowers and fertility."

Perhaps Lorca's career is best described by Christopher Maurer in his introduction to *Federico García Lorca: Collected Poems* (2002):

> In the thirteen plays and nine books of verse he was able to complete between 1917 and 1936—an amazingly short career—he spoke unforgettably of all that most interests us: the otherness of nature, the demons of personal identity and artistic creation, sex, childhood, and death.

CRITICISM

Diane Andrews Henningfeld

Henningfeld is a professor of literature who writes widely for educational publications. In the following essay, she demonstrates the ways that Lorca incorporates the aesthetics, structures, and traditions of cante jondo, *or deep song, in "The Guitar."*

From an early age, Federico García Lorca was fascinated by Romany culture and music, especially flamenco. Most people have seen at some time a representation of flamenco: women swirling in ruffled skirts, clicking castanets, and dancing to the music of a guitar. However, this popular version of flamenco has little connection with the *cante jondo*, or deep song, that riveted Lorca for so many years. Deep song is authentic flamenco, growing out of the pain and suffering of the Romany people, an ethnic group often called Gypsies who originally migrated from India across Europe and who endured oppression and discrimination wherever they traveled. As Rob Stone writes in his article "Misticismo y lujuria: The Sacred and the Profane in *Poema del cante jondo*,"

> Flamenco is the song of a race in flux. The quintessential moment of the *cante* sees the performer suspended in the realization of hopelessness, floating in a hostile cosmos, an unloved orphan of a storm that will inevitably return for him. He is as alone as it is possible to be—he is the *portavoz* [spokesperson] for a persecuted, nomadic race.

Therefore, to fully understand a poem such as "The Guitar," one of the first poems included in Lorca's volume *Poema del cante jondo*, or *Poem of the Deep Song*, it is important to be familiar with the aesthetics, structures, and traditions of deep song and flamenco. Lorca incorporates these elements into "The Guitar," attempting to recreate in language the emotional and cognitive content of the music of deep song.

WHAT DO I READ NEXT?

- Just as the aesthetic of flamenco inspired Lorca's poetry, the jazz aesthetic has had a similar influence on the poets whose work is collected in the volume *Jazz Poems*, edited by Kevin Young and published in 2006. Poems by Langston Hughes, Gwendolyn Brooks, Yusef Komunyakaa, Rita Dove, Ntozake Shange, and others are included.

- Paul Preston's *The Spanish Civil War: Reaction, Revolution, and Revenge* (revised and expanded version) is the benchmark history of the 1936 war that caused the death of Lorca. Published in 2007, the book traces Francisco Franco's rise to power.

- Carol Hess writes about the life of musician Manual de Falla, Lorca's friend and collaborator, in her book *Sacred Passions: The Life and Music of Manual de Falla* (2008).

- Michael Leapman discusses the lives of young people victimized by the Nazis and other fascists during World War II in his young-adult history *Witnesses to War* (2000). In the chapter titled "The Gypsy at Auschwitz," he details the oppression and cruelty endured by the Romany.

- *Gypsies and Flamenco: The Emergence of the Art of Flamenco in Andalusia* (2003), by Bernard Leblon, traces the influence of the Romany on the dance and music of Andalusia.

- *For Whom the Bell Tolls* (1940) is Ernest Hemingway's classic novel set during the Spanish Civil War.

- Federico Bonaddio's *A Companion to Federico García Lorca* (2007) offers both criticism and analysis of Lorca's poetry, theater, and music. The book offers students a deeper look into the work of one of Spain's most important writers.

- Translated by Greg Simon and Steven F. White, *Poet in New York: A Bilingual Edition* (1998), by Lorca, offers a bleak picture of the city, written during the poet's nine-month stay in the United States in 1929–1930.

IN 'THE GUITAR' LORCA CREATES A LYRIC THAT EXPRESSES THE ANGUISH OF HUMAN EXISTENCE, AN EXISTENCE AT ONCE MELODIOUS AND MONOTONOUS, FULL OF DESIRE AND SUFFERING, AN EXISTENCE, ULTIMATELY, DEVOID OF MEANING."

Aesthetics is the set of principles that underlie and guide an artist or artistic creation. As a traditional art form, flamenco follows a number of highly stylized aesthetic features, including its division into a number of different genres as well as the organization of the performance. Edward F. Stanton notes in his article "The Poetry of Federico García Lorca and 'Cante Jondo'" that Lorca organizes his book in divisions, each "based on a corresponding flamenco genre—*siguiriya gitana, soleá, petenera.*"

It should be noted that organizing his book in this way was innovative as well as experimental. In the introduction to *Federico García Lorca: Collected Poems*, editor and translator Christopher Maurer explains that during the 1920s, Lorca was fully engaged in "the possibilities, almost unexplored until then in Spanish poetry, of a new form: the sequence of short related poems." Maurer goes on to argue that Lorca borrowed this organizational structure from music. Given Lorca's deep interest in and fascination with flamenco, it seems a natural conclusion that he would use the generic divisions of flamenco to organize a volume of poems.

Of particular interest for the poem "The Guitar" is the flamenco genre known as *siguiriya gitana*. The first subdivision of *Poem of the Deep Song* is titled "Poema de la siguiriya gitana," or "Poem of the Gypsy *Siguiriya*." The *siguiriya* is perhaps the deepest, most intense, and most anguished of all flamenco forms. As Lorca writes in his essay "Deep Song,"

> Gypsy *siguiriya* had always evoked (I am an incurable lyricist) an endless road, a road without crossroads, ending at the pulsing fountain of the child Poetry. The road where the first bird died and the first arrow grew rusty.

These are the same images Lorca includes in "The Guitar." The *siguiriya* then, is a style of flamenco that is somber, sad, and filled with anguish. Everything in the performance works together to produce a tone of suffering and a sense of hopelessness.

In addition to structuring his book around the genres of flamenco, Lorca also carefully arranged the poems within each subdivision. In the case of "Poem of the Gypsy *Siguiriya*," the individual poems within the sequence mirror the performance of this kind of flamenco. The first poem in the sequence, for example, is called "Paisaje," or "Landscape." In this poem, Lorca sets the scene and introduces key images such as trees and birds. The setting is the Andalusian countryside, the home of the Spanish Romany, and the home of flamenco. Lorca places "The Guitar" immediately after "Landscape." Once the stage has been set, flamenco performances often begin with soft guitar music. According to Stanton,

> The position of ["The Guitar"] at the beginning of the book is very proper, since the first timid strummings of the guitar usually create the atmosphere for the performance of *cante jondo*, enticing and drawing the initial notes from the singer.

Lorca also drew on the phrasing of deep song in his composition of "The Guitar." In a flamenco performance, a singer known as the *cantaor* creates the song as he sings it, according to Mike Marqusee's article "Flamenco's Humane Roots," in the London *Guardian* of February 5, 2010. He adds,

> The *cantaor* can dwell at length on a single phrase, probing and elongating it, then complete the rest of the verse in a rush of tumbling syllables.... It's an immensely suspenseful music, building to serial climaxes, hesitating, holding back, plunging forward.

In "The Guitar," Lorca begins slowly, using short phrases and sentences. His repetition of certain phrases mimics the *cantaor's* dwelling on a certain passage of music. As the poem continues, it picks up speed as Lorca piles on images and sounds. By lines 21–24, he reaches the longest sentence in the poem. The slow beginning followed by the rush of images creates suspense only released by his exclamation in line 25.

Likewise, the rhythms and sounds of flamenco find expression in "The Guitar." These rhythms may not be very obvious in an English translation but are quite evident in Spanish. For example, the first and third lines of the poem each have two accented syllables in the original Spanish, while the second and fourth lines have one. Following this, lines 7–10 set up another pattern, with just one accented syllable per line. These short lines, with their sharp accents and repetitions, mimic the stylized hand clapping of the flamenco. In line 19, a new pattern emerges, now that the singer and guitar are in full voice. Each of these lines has three accented syllables; the effect of the additional stresses is to move the poem along rapidly. Finally, in line 25, Lorca addresses the guitar directly in a four-syllable line, beginning with a stressed syllable. This line is as loud as a gunshot, as a clap of thunder. Lorca constructs the final two lines of the poem with two unaccented syllables followed by an accented one, so that the lines in Spanish sound as *da da DEE da da DEE da | da DEE da da DEE da*. This rhythm signals the ending of the poem, the quiet after the outburst.

In addition to rhythmic considerations, Lorca also uses sound devices to bring a musical quality to the work. Stanton argues, "The strong pattern of assonance, the refrain-like repetitions, and the parallel constructions imitate a monotonous drone." Again, the assonance, or the repetition of vowel sounds, is not as evident in the English translation as it is in the original Spanish. However, readers of the English translation should note that in Lorca's language, the sounds of the words he chooses are both assonant and alliterative. The repetition of similar sounds is reminiscent of the *cantaor's* embellishment of particular sounds and words. Lorca also chooses to repeat certain phrases and words, again adding a musical quality to the poem.

Thus, while Lorca does not try to rewrite old folk lyrics, he does attempt to recreate in language the music of the deep song. That he did so early in his career seems to have had a profound effect on the rest of his brief life. As Maurer asserts,

> Lorca's encounter with *cante jondo* was of incalculable importance to him. It helped him face a variety of aesthetic problems and define his relation to "traditional" art, and it made him meditate for the first time on Granada's (and thus his own) place in Western culture.

In "The Guitar" Lorca creates a lyric that expresses the anguish of human existence, an existence at once melodious and monotonous, full of desire and suffering, an existence, ultimately, devoid of meaning. In the wailing of

Windy winter scene (leonid_tit | Shutterstock.com)

the guitar, the reader can hear the sound of Romany voices and feel the pain of the Romany worldview.

Source: Diane Andrews Henningfeld, Critical Essay on "The Guitar," in *Poetry for Students*, Gale, Cengage Learning, 2011.

Rob Stone

In the following excerpt, Stone identifies mythology and "flamenco deep song" as being both the context and framework for García Lorca's Poem of the Deep Song.

Flamenco deep song offered Lorca the key to a philosophy that was anathema to the Catholic Church, for the Church dominated Spain with a dogma and moral code that outlawed behaviour prompted by instincts that were contrary to social decorum and its rigid adherence to rules of gender and patriarchy. However, the philosophy which Lorca identified in the lyrics and performance system of deep song inspired and allowed for the poetic expression of his own existential anguish and sexual confusion to such an extent that, in spite of its adherence to the essentially nihilist philosophy of deep song, the triumph of his

Poema del cante jondo is that it constituted an act of Creation; for by delineating the mythological world of flamenco, Lorca effectively redefined the world in which he and the Gypsies lived. This analysis of the appropriation by Lorca of flamenco deep song in the genesis and writing of *Poema del cante jondo* reveals how its complex semiological system combining performance, form and content was to provide the true context and origin of the philosophy, themes and images that would influence him throughout his entire career as playwrite and poet. . . .

SOLITUDE AND DEATH

Just as solitude comes after grief, so after the *siguiriya* comes the *soleá*—one of the few examples from *Poema del cante jondo* to imitate the structure of the *cante* which inspired it. Here, the humanised *cante* recognises that its cry—its *duende*—is carried on the wind (the vehicle of *duende*) and, because of this, it sees the connection between inherent solitude and death; for it had left the balcony open until dawn, the time when death traditionally comes for prisoners, soldiers, etc. The *soleá* is female, dressed in the

> THIS CENTRE IS WITHIN MAN AND MAY BE
> TANGIBLY REPRESENTED BY THE ACTION OF THE
> HEART, WHETHER PHYSICAL (BLOOD IN, BLOOD OUT)
> OR EMOTIONAL (LOVE IN, LOVE OUT). CHOICES OF
> THE HEART ARE WHAT LEAD MAN TO HIS DESTINY."

black of mourning, and is the most philosophical of the *cantes*, going beyond the cry of the *siguiriya* to deliver an equally sad but reasoned aesthetic of existence. The final cry of the poem is an attempt at catharsis which echoes the anguish of the *siguiriya*. The *soleá* recognises the cyclical nature of life in the mythological world of flamenco and sees mourning as the stimulus for procreation in the sense that death (and a fear of it) accentuate the desire for new life.

The wind, which comes like flamenco from the east, also brings with it the common symbols of the mythology of flamenco and induces inevitable consequences in 'Encrucijada':

Viento del Este,
un farol
y el puñal
en el corazón.
(I:309)

It is perhaps ironic that, rather than provide solace, hope or meaning, the deified wind constantly confounds the suffering of the human protagonists in the landscape of flamenco by its own circumscribed role in the spiritual wasteland—a barren, desolate landscape which may also be interpreted as Lorca himself. To this end, in 'Puñal' the relationship between man and landscape is rendered in terms of the metaphor which equates a knife in the heart with the blade of a plough in the earth:

El puñal,
entra en el corazón,
como la reja del arado
en el yermo.
(I:308)

It is relevant to relate this imagery to the observation recounted in the first chapter of the young poet who followed a plough and discovered the Roman mosaic. In the poetic consciousness of Lorca, man and Nature are part of the same

mythological system: as the plough reveals the ancient mosaic, so the knife in man's heart reveals his mythological role. In 'Baladilla de los tres ríos' the wind makes contact with the river and the friction between these two opposing elements creates a third element—"un fuego fatuo de gritos" (I:296)—a fire which consumes the human element, the cries of whom are recognisably those of the *cante* flamenco.

In many cultures, the elements of fire, air, earth and water were originally objects of adoration and so the first deities were the personification of these elements. Their likenesses were sculpted in stone or marble, such as the Minerva of the Parthenon or the statue of Apollo in Rome and scholarly poets such as Homer, Virgil and Ovid brought these statues to life in their epic poems, thereby populating the ancient lands of Greece and Rome with fabulous heroes and villains, gods and goddesses. In a letter to Adolfo Salazar in 1922 Lorca describes his identical intentions in the writing of *Poema del cante jondo*: "Saco a relucir en él a los cantaores viejos y a toda la fauna y flora fantásticas que llena estas sublimes canciones. [. . .] El poema empieza con un crepúsculo inmóvil y por él desfilan la siguiriya, la soleá, la saeta, y la petenera. El poema está lleno de gitanos, de velones, de fraguas, tiene hasta alusiones a Zoroastro" (VI:784). The allusion to Zoroaster, whose dualistic religion was founded on the comparable concept of a struggle of the forces of light and creation against evil and darkness, is a testament to the scale of Lorca's endeavour. The protagonists of the landscape of flamenco are the performers, personified styles and dramatis personae of *cante* flamenco. Thus, for example, the *soleá* is a female in mourning and the *siguiriya* represents human anguish in the presence of death in the same way that the statue of the *Venus de Medici* in the Florence Museum is the perfect representation of female beauty. In addition, the umbrella title of the collection denotes a singular '*Poema*' which makes clear Lorca's intention that, by design, *Poema del cante jondo* is, though fragmented, an epic poem.

In attributing the original 'legends' of the *cante* to anonymous authors, Lorca wrote "no son de nadie, están flotando en el viento como vilanos de otro y cada generación los viste de un color distinto, para abandonarlos a las futuras" (VI:219). The wind carries symbols, legends and *duende*—the various elements of *cante* flamenco—

but it may also bring sand and fire and provoke drought, which are contributing factors to the hostility of the landscape. Human life in the mythological world of flamenco would appear to have a very precarious existence, and it is for this reason that the first explicit attempt at locating the Gypsies in the hostile landscape of *Poema del cante jondo* finds them wailing in their traditional refuge of 'La cueva':

> De la cueva salen
> largos sollozos
> [. . .]
> El gitano evoca
> países remotos.
> (I:313)

If, in 'El grito,' the Gypsies had lit candles within—"(Las gentes de las cuevas / asoman sus velones.)" (I:300)—here their wailing accompanies the *llanto* of the guitar and the combined sound is *cante* flamenco.

The guitar had become a key element in the performance of flamenco by Lorca's time. Its plaintive, melancholic sound is evocative of the mood of the *cante* and the player's flourish underpins the cry of the *cantaor*. In 'La guitarra,' the anthropomorphised instrument becomes a voice of Nature expressing universal anguish:

> Llora monótona
> como llora el agua
> como llora el viento
> sobre la nevada.
> (I:299)

It is a weeping voice, allied with the weeping of anthropomorphised water and the deified wind. Its weeping is a "flecha sin blanco" (I:299), which evokes the parallel mythological imagery of Cupid's arrows and utilises the concept to signify the frustrated love common to the *cante* flamenco and Lorca himself. To this end, the conclusion of the poem presents an extended metaphor which transforms the guitar into a heart pierced by the five fingers of the player:

> ¡Oh guitarra!
> Corazón malherido
> por cinco espadas.
> (I:299)

The guitar becomes in turn Lorca's own heart and its expressive sound parallels his own anguish. In 'Encrucijada,' the player of the instrument is identified as the ubiquitous wind, thus confirming Lorca's place in the hostile landscape of flamenco in the sense that he too is an instrument of *duende*:

> La calle
> tiene un temblor
> de cuerda,
> en tensión,
> un temblor
> de enorme moscardón.
> (I:309)

As the trembling air signifies the nearness of death, so the buzz of the guitar string prepares us for the cry of the *cantaor*: both of which signify the presence of *duende*. The metaphor of the anthropomorphised guitar is extended in 'Muerte de la Petenera' where its strum accompanies the *cantaor* at the moment of death:

> Largas sombras afiladas
> vienen del turbio horizonte,
> y el bordón de una guitarra
> se rompe.
> *Cien jacas caracolean.*
> *Sus jinetes están muertos.*

In 'Las seis cuerdas,' the metaphorically transformed guitar has the power to condition and exploit the subconsciousness of the poet/*cantaor* and his audience, thus stimulating repressed emotions and fears: "La guitarra / hace llorar a los sueños" (I:330). The sound of the guitar is unambiguously the weeping of lost souls who are trapped behind its strings just as the Gypsies are trapped in their caves:

> El sollozo de las almas
> perdidas
> se escapa por su boca
> redonda.
> (I:330)

A hand, that of the wind, strums the strings across the sound hole of the guitar and their vibrations spin a giant web across the mouth of the Gypsy cave—here *aljibe*, meaning subterranean prison in addition to well of sighs:

> Y como la tarántula,
> teje una gran estrella
> para cazar suspiros,
> que flotan en su negro
> aljibe de madera.
> (I:330)

The anguish of existence in the philosophy of flamenco is inescapable. The sighs of these imprisoned souls are those of the humans who are trapped in the uncongenial landscape: the Gypsies in their caves, and Lorca in his private sexual torment, whose cries are the poems of *Poema del cante jondo*. Indeed, although the apparent victim of the antagonistic universe of flamenco is the Gypsy race, its primary victim, as represented in *Poema del cante jondo*, is Lorca himself. In 'Pueblo' the description of the titular village stems directly from Lorca's experience and observation of the Gypsy area of Granada. "Sobre el monte pelado / un calvario" (I:307), for example, suggests a metaphorical allusion to the description of the Albayzín as it appears in *Impresiones y paisajes*: "Son las calles estrechas, dramáticas, escaleras rarísimas y desvencijadas, tentáculos ondulantes que se retuercen caprichosa y fatigadamente [. . .] son extraños senderos de miedo y de fuerte inquietud" (VI:145). It is therefore significant that Lorca should conclude this poem with a personal cry of despair based on his own experience of the town—"¡Oh pueblo perdido / en la Andalucía del llanto!" (I:307)—and it is at this moment in *Poema del cante jondo* when Lorca abandons a pretence of objectivity and himself enters the mythological landscape of flamenco, thus making explicit his symbiosis with the prevailing philosophy of the *cante*.

First person subjectivity is emphasised in 'Encrucijada', where the 'yo' stands alone, and where the consequence of the action of 'Puñal' in the setting of 'Pueblo' provokes the anguish of the attending poet:

Por todas partes
yo
veo el puñal
en el corazón.
(I:310).

The 'Encrucijada' of the title is the choice which any existential philosophy proposes: to accept or fight against one's condition. The crossroad is a universal symbol: two roads which intersect create a centre. This centre is within man and may be tangibly represented by the action of the heart, whether physical (blood in, blood out) or emotional (love in, love out). Choices of the heart are what lead man to his destiny. Man encounters his fate at a crossroads and some, such as Oedipus, will meet death, whereas Lorca takes both options by splitting himself in two. This is the private creation and public diffusion of *Poema del cante jondo* and this is also where Lorca's private and public personas divide; for in the coincidence of the *Concurso* and *Poema del cante jondo* the public/private conflict which typified the history of flamenco was personified in the enthusiastic public conformity and anguished private persona of the poet.

The poems 'La Lola' and 'Amparo' offer portraits of similarly contrasting female archetypes under the collective heading of 'Dos muchachas' and they attest to the conflict within Lorca by delineating the dual nature of the poet and accentuating his feminine side. Lola is a stereotype in a clichéd Andalusian setting. She washes nappies while dreaming of love and waits like a Gypsy Cinderella for the young bullfighters to come. This is the superficial image of Andalusia as celebrated in the opera *Carmen* and in the music of Glinka and others. Lorca encapsulates the cliché within a melodramatic chorus:

¡Ay, amor,
bajo el naranjo en flor!
(I:338)

Lola's—and so Lorca's—clichéd alter ego is Amparo, a lonely, frustrated spinster who sits embroidering in her shadowed patio. If, as Lorca attests, "la mujer en el cante jondo se llama Pena . . ." (I:220), then this is her portrait and her chorus:

¡Qué sola estás en tu casa
vestida de blanco!
(I:339)

There is a sharp irony at work in these poems: the name Lola is derived from Dolores, meaning pain, while Amparo derives from the verb 'amparar' and suggests protection. The climax of 'Amparo' shows the poet choosing the protection of contextualised, meaningful suffering in favour of the unbearable banality of an ordinary, ignorant life. Between the public and the private, the superficial and the *jondo*, in his work and in his life, Lorca recognised the inevitable division he had to make as a poet in order to maintain his celebrity without sacrificing his creativity, and he personifies this duality in these two opposing portraits of Spanish sensibility. The *encrucijada* of Lorca's *camino* as a poet is contained in the climax of this poem:

Amparo,
¡y qué difícil decirte:
yo te amo!
(I:339) . . .

Source: Rob Stone, "Weeping Blood: *Poema del cante jondo*," in *The Flamenco Tradition in the Works of Federico García Lorca and Carlos Saura: The Wounded Throat*, Edwin Mellen Press, 2004, pp. 33–64.

Candelas Newton

In the following excerpt, Newton discusses García Lorca's lesser-known poems, including his autobiographical poems, free verse, musical, and "darklove" sonnets.

This chapter will discuss Lorca's lesser-known poetry collections, the familiarity of which is gradually increasing as all aspects of Lorca's work continue to attract critical attention. Lorca's youthful *Book of Poems* (1921), which was overshadowed for decades by the author's more mature works, is available in Ian Gibson's 1982 critical edition. In this work can be seen the origin of some of Lorca's major themes and images. *Songs* (1927) and *Suites* (written between 1921 and 1923), thematically related, though less structurally fixed than *Poem of the Deep Song* (1931), appear as a distinct cycle of Lorca's production, particularly after more precise boundaries between these two collections were established by a 1983 publication of a compilation of the suites. A number of odes, also dating from the 1920s, reflect Lorca's experimentation with artistic form and poetic images in the Gongorine and avant-garde styles. Lorca's poetry of the 1930s—in particular, *Diván del Tamarit* (*The Divan at Tamarit*, 1940), which has already been the subject of a number of critical works, and *Sonetos [del Amor oscuro]* (*Sonnets [of Dark Love]*), first published in authorized form in 1984 to a great deal of interest even outside of academic circles—is very much open to further readings, as are his plays from that same period.

EARLY WORKS

Lorca's contact with avant-garde groups in Madrid in the early 1920s and the admiration he and his generation shared for Góngora are reflected in his collections from the 1920s in a greater concern for artistic form and emphasis on the image. The aesthetics of the imagination, as the metaphoric transformation of reality, prevail in these works. Their innovative character culminates in *The Gypsy Ballads*, a collection situated at a crossroads in Lorca's aesthetic development (see chapter 1 of the present study). The mythic character of *The Gypsy Ballads* allows the exploration into realms outside logical representation. This exploration is fully pursued in Lorca's later works through the aesthetics of the inspiration.

BOOK OF POEMS

The somewhat autobiographical *Book of Poems* in many ways serves as a mirror of Lorca's childhood and adolescence in the Granadine vega. These poems express Lorca's nostalgia for the union with nature and the religious faith he enjoyed in his childhood, the crisis brought about by temporal awareness and sexual awakening, and

the subsequent alienation and loss of faith. "Encrucijada (Julio de 1920)" ("Crossroads [July 1920]," *CP* [*Collected Poems*] 58–61) illustrates the young author's critical stance toward his life and poetry:

> Oh, what sorrow to have
> poems off in the distance
> of passion, and a brain
> all stained with ink!
> Oh, what sorrow not to have
> the happy man's fantastical
> shirt—a tanned skin,
> the sun's carpet.
> (Flocks of letters
> wheel round my eyes.)
> Oh, what sorrow the ancient
> sorrow of poetry,
> this sticky sorrow
> so far from clean water!
> Oh, sorrow of sorrowing
> to sip at the vein of lyric!
> Oh, sorrow of blind fountains
> and mills without flour!
> Oh, what sorrow to have
> no sorrow, to spend life
> on the colorless grass
> of the hesitant lane!
> Oh, the deepest sorrow:
> the sorrow of joy, a plow
> cutting furrows for us
> where weeping bears fruit!
> (The cold moon rises
> on a paper mountain.)
> Oh, sorrow of truth!
> Oh, sorrow of the lie!

The repeated apostrophe (the addressing of a person or a personified thing rhetorically) calls attention to the subjectivity of the poetic speaker articulating his sorrow, a typically Romantic stance. However, the speaker's sorrow and feelings of alienation from nature are expressed through the confrontation with poetic language. The apostrophes point to the speaker's presence in the poem as an artist struggling with language, caught in the crossroads of different artistic traditions. "Passion" (as opposed to reason), "the happy man's fantastical shirt," a "tanned skin" (images of his fusion with the sun and nature), and "clean water" nostalgically allude to a direct contact with the world and to a lost language that was able to transparently reflect it. Instead, the speaker now confronts a language in which the ink (representing the materiality of the words) impedes linking directly with the referent, and in which words can no longer be made to reproduce mimetically the plenitude of nature. The alphabet is no longer the instrument used to create worlds by naming them, but rather its flocks of letters obscure the direct perception of the world through the eyes. The recognition of the autonomy of poetic language parallels the speaker's awareness of his estrangement from nature.

Poetic self-consciousness increases with the references to the "ancient sorrow of poetry" and "the vein of lyric" which characterize poetry as a discourse traditionally associated with the expression of feelings. The emotional content of poetry becomes "sticky" because the repetition of sentimental formulas and clichés clouds the sincerity of the emotion. The speaker realizes that experience cannot be transparently expressed in disregard of language as the means of representation. Unlike the childhood state, to which this early book is a nostalgic farewell, the speaker is forced to accept the existence of external things as different from himself. The distance from nature's language of vitality provokes the images of dryness and lack of productivity ("Oh, sorrow of blind fountains / and mills without flour"). No matter how artificial sorrow may become in the poetic text, its complete absence would mean the "colorless grass" and "hesitant lane" of a life without passion. Sorrow is ingrained in joy and therefore is the root of all feelings ("The sorrow of joy, a plow / cutting furrows for us / where weeping bears fruit"). Later in Lorca's poetry, this sorrow will become the Gypsy *pena* (pain) of *Deep Song* (see chapter 1 of the present study). The "paper mountain" at the end of the poem reverses the image of the rising sun. It suggests premonition and fatality, which are associated with the moon in Lorca's writings. The "paper mountain" the poet is accumulating in his attempts to write refers also to the act of writing itself. The aesthetic crossroads is an ethical one as well: "Oh, sorrow of truth! / Oh, sorrow of the lie!" Confronting the truth or falsity of language necessitates wrestling with the truth or falsity of personal beliefs, a question found at the core of this early collection of poetry.

Beginning with this early collection, the moon imbues Lorca's writings with the foreboding, premonition, and fatalism that is traditionally associated with that symbol. As evident in "Crossroads," poetic writing is marked by a nostalgia for an original fusion with nature that time has dispersed. This accounts for the recurring themes of pain and sorrow in many compositions and for the reiterated tone of loss, frustration, and unfulfillment in Lorca's poetry. . .

Source: Candelas Newton, "Lesser-Known Poetry," in *Understanding Federico García Lorca*, University of South Carolina Press, 1995, pp. 83–113.

SOURCES

Anderson, Andrew A., "Federico García Lorca," in *Dictionary of Literary Biography*, Vol. 108, *Twentieth-Century Spanish Poets, First Series*, edited by Michael L. Perna, Gale Research, 1991.

Berrien, William, "Spain Loses a Great Poet," in *Books Abroad*, Vol. 11, No. 2, Spring 1937, pp. 159–61.

Bryant, Tony, "Flamenco," in *Andalucia.com*, October 14, 2009, http://my.andalucia.com/articles/flamenco-passionate-and-seductive-art-form (accessed August 15, 2010).

Correa, Gustavo, "Nature and Symbol in the Poetry of Federico García Lorca," in *Lorca's Legacy: Essays on Lorca's Life, Poetry, and Theatre*, edited by Francesca Colecchia and Manuel Duran, Peter Lang, 1991, pp. 85–94.

"Federico García Lorca," in *Academy of American Poets*, http://www.poets.org/poet.php/prmPID/163 (accessed August 5, 2010).

García Lorca, Federico, "Deep Song," in *In Search of Duende*, edited by Christopher Maurer, translated by Christopher Maurer and Norman Thomas di Giovanni, New Directions, 1998, pp. 4–23.

———, "La guitarra/The Guitar," in *Federico García Lorca: Collected Poems*, rev. ed., edited and translated by Christoper Maurer, Farrar, Straus and Giroux, 2002, pp. 98–101.

Hancock, Ian, "A Brief Romani Holocaust Chronology," in *Open Society Institute*, 1991, http://www.osi.hu/rpp/holocaust.html (accessed October 6, 2010).

Hobbs, Mary Etta, "An Investigation of the Traditional *Cante Jondo* as the Inspiration for the Song Cycle *Five Poems of García Lorca* by Elisenda Fábregas," PhD dissertation, University of North Texas, 2004, p. 1.

Jung, Christof, "Cante Flamenco," in *Flamenco: Gypsy Dance and Music from Andalusia*, edited by Claus Schreiner and Reinhard G. Pauly, Hal Leonard, 1996, pp. 57–66.

Marqusee, Mike, "Flamenco's Human Roots," in *Guardian* (London, England), February 5, 2010, http://www.guardian.co.uk/commentisfree/2010/feb/05/flamenco-spain-roots (accessed October 6, 2010).

Maurer, Christopher, Introduction to *Federico García Lorca: Collected Poems*, rev. ed., edited by Christopher Maurer, Farrar, Straus and Giroux, 2002, pp. xi–lxiv.

Nelson, Cary, "The Spanish Civil War: An Overview," in *Modern American Poetry*, http://www.english.illinois.edu/maps/scw/overview.htm (accessed October 6, 2010).

Riley, Edward C., "Considerations on the Poetry of García Lorca," in *Dublin Magazine*, Vol. 27, No. 1, January/March 1952, pp. 14–22.

Salinas, Pedro, "Federico García Lorca," in *MLN*, Vol. 87, No. 2, March 1972, pp. 169–77.

Stanton, Edward F., "García Lorca and the Guitar," in *Hispania*, Vol. 58, No. 1, March 1975, pp. 52–58.

———, "The Poetry of Federico García Lorca and 'Cante Jondo,'" in *South Atlantic Bulletin*, Vol. 39, No. 4, November 1974, pp. 94–103.

———, *The Tragic Myth: Lorca and Cante Jondo*, University Press of Kentucky, 1978, p. 38.

Stone, Rob, "Misticismo y lujuria: The Sacred and the Profane in *Poema del cante jondo*," in *Anales de la literatura española contemporánea*, Vol. 24, No. 1–2, 1999, pp. 213–26.

———, "Weeping Blood: *Poema del cante jondo*," in *The Flamenco Tradition in the Works of Federico García Lorca and Carlos Saura: The Wounded Throat*, Mellen Press, 2004.

FURTHER READING

Charnon-Deutsch, Lou, *The Spanish Gypsy: The History of a European Obsession*, Pennsylvania State University Press, 2004.
    Charnon-Deutsch traces the history of the Romany in Spain from the Middle Ages to the present day, including discussions of music, dance, and the visual arts created by and inspired by Spanish Romany.

García Lorca, Federico, *Selected Letters*, edited and translated by David Gershator, Marion Boyars, 1984.
    This book is a collection of Lorca's letters, dating from 1918 to 1936, closing with a note stating his intention to go to Granada, where he met his death. Gershator notes that through Lorca's letters, the reader sees "an uninten-

tional self portrait, at times a much more intimate portrait than any biographer could achieve."

Gibson, Ian, *Federico García Lorca: A Life*, Faber and Faber, 1990.
    Gibson's book is a biography of Lorca, tracing his family and young life, his literary achievements, and his mysterious death.

Hancock, Ian, *We Are the Romani People*, University of Hertfordshire Press, 2002.
    Hancock, a Romany himself, offers an illustrated introduction to Romany life. It includes an overview of their history, information about their food and culture, and an explanation of the struggles they face in contemporary society.

SUGGESTED SEARCH TERMS

Federico García Lorca

The Guitar

La guitarra

Poem of the Deep Song

Poema del cante jondo

flamenco AND Lorca

Gypsies

Gypsies AND Lorca

Andalusia AND Lorca

Spanish Civil War

Romany OR Romani

Granada

Invitation to the Voyage

CHARLES BAUDELAIRE

1857

Charles Baudelaire is one of the best-known French poets of the nineteenth century and perhaps the most influential French writer of his generation. His work helped transform the literary period of romanticism into the newer movements of decadence and symbolism. Devoted to ideals of pleasure, indulgence, and melancholy, he died at the age of forty-six, broken by sensual indulgence.

Baudelaire's great work *The Flowers of Evil* was published in 1857, a book collection of lyric poems. The reaction to the work was notable: Baudelaire was tried and convicted for obscenity by the French government. The work shocked the French reading public and was considered obscene in its depiction of lesbianism. Its rejection of bourgeois (middle-class) morality, however, was perhaps more deeply shocking. Six poems were condemned and were not published again in France until 1949.

"Invitation to the Voyage," not among the condemned pieces, is one of the poems from *The Flowers of Evil*. It is a hymn to transcendent beauty that the poet creates within his own soul, separate from and almost incommunicable to the world. In an exploration of his interior world, Baudelaire proves himself a master of human psychology as much as of poetic art. Here he has as much in common with the later psychological work of Sigmund Freud as with the literary movements of symbolism and decadence.

Charles Baudelaire (The Library of Congress)

AUTHOR BIOGRAPHY

Baudelaire was born in Paris, France, on April 9, 1821. His father, François, a civil servant, died six years later. Baudelaire's mother remarried Jacques Aupinck, an army officer who made a second career as an ambassador in the French foreign service. Baudelaire's intense feelings of alienation in adulthood are often traced to the emotional distance from his mother that he suffered while she was courting her second husband. Baudelaire was educated at a first-rate boarding school in Lyons, France, and earned a law degree in Paris, but he had no particular interest in pursuing any professional career that his stepfather's patronage could have guaranteed for him, or even, as yet, in writing professionally. It was probably during this time that he contracted syphilis and started to abuse laudanum (an opiate drug). His stepfather sent Baudelaire on a trip to India in the hope that it would set him on some definite path, but that plan did not meet with much success.

On his return to France, Baudelaire received his inheritance from his father's estate, and he began to spend it at a rapid rate, making friends with the artistic avant-garde of Paris, those who were interested in new and experimental art forms. He became close friends with the photographer Félix Nadar and the painter Édouard Manet. He also became acquainted with Théophile Gautier, a poet and critic with whom he had very close artistic interactions. Baudelaire's mother saw to it that his money was put into a trust so that he could not squander it all at once, and she then broke off all contact with her son for many years. Baudelaire published his first writing in 1845, a review of the Salon, an annual show of new works by painters in the French Academy. His first major accomplishment as a writer was translating works of Edgar Allan Poe, which he would publish in periodic volumes for the rest of his life. Baudelaire's championing of Poe, as well as the high quality of his translation, made the American poet exceptionally important in nineteenth-century French literature. Baudelaire also began to see Poe as his artistic role model. In 1857, Baudelaire published *The Flowers of Evil*, a collection of poems including "Invitation to the Voyage." This was the work that established him as an early important figure in the symbolist and decadent movements. In 1860, Baudelaire was one of the few French people to react enthusiastically to the music of Richard Wagner when it was performed in Paris for the first time, and his critical discussion of Wagner is still important.

In 1866, worn out by disease and addiction, Baudelaire suffered a stroke that left him paralyzed and confined to a sanatorium (a rest home for care of the ill). He died on August 31, 1867, at the young age of forty-six. In 1869, Baudelaire's sister published two works by her brother: a revised edition of *The Flowers of Evils*, with some new poems added, and *Paris Spleen*, an entirely new work on the same themes as *The Flowers of Evil* with many of the individual prose poems bearing the same titles as poems in the original work, including "Invitation to the Voyage."

POEM SUMMARY

"Invitation to the Voyage" is poem number 53 in *The Flowers of Evil*. Although it certainly stands alone, a larger context for the poem is to be had by reading the poem within its whole sequence.

Stanzas 1–2

The narrative voice or speaker of the poem—who can for convenience be called the poet, bearing in mind that he is a character within the poem and

MEDIA ADAPTATIONS

- "Invitation to the Voyage" was set to music by the French songwriter Léo Férré in 1957. There are video clips available online of Férré performing the song, and it was recorded by Eileen Mager on the 2003 audio CD *Classic French Songs.*

not necessarily identical with Baudelaire himself—addresses an indistinct object. The speaker calls the addressee of the poem his sister and his daughter, but that very paradox suggests that she is actually neither of those. He invites her to come away to some vaguely defined place—described only as *there*—where the two of them will love each other for the rest of their lives. This place is stormy, with rain blocking out the sun, and it resembles the addressee's eyes, which shine through their tears like the sun shining through clouds. Her eyes, moreover, are mysterious and treacherous.

There are more mysteries here than are contained in the addressee's eyes. To begin with: who is she? By calling her his daughter and his sister, the poet makes clear that she can be neither. The simplest way of reading the poem would make her the poet's lover. Her identity seems to be dissolved in the acid of the poet's imagination, resolved into whatever it is the poet loves, in whatever way that he loves. She is not, then, a woman at all, but part of the world that the poet's imagination creates in the fantasy of the poem. The reader can perhaps get closer to her true identity with the help of Baudelaire's hero Poe. In his poem "Ulalume," Poe uses *sister* as a designation for his psyche or soul. In many respects, it makes the most sense to treat the addressee of Baudelaire's poem as the poet's own soul or poetic self. Who else but his own soul could share the images evoked in the poet's imagination? And indeed, the poem is a sort of guided tour though an extended daydream created by the poet. This interpretation makes sense of a line in the poem in which the world itself, or at least the land to which they will travel, looks like the beloved: the world that is created in the poet's imagination naturally resembles his own soul. The

imagination makes a link between the world and the soul: it is like a mirror in which the soul and the conscious self can see each other. That Baudelaire should consider his own soul storm-tossed, treacherous, and tearful will come as no surprise to the reader of *The Flowers of Evil* as a whole, which, in part at least, is a catalog of uncontrollable, destructive passions.

After describing the stormy landscape of his soul, Baudelaire introduces a refrain that is repeated after each of the three major stanzas of "Invitation to the Voyage." In this case, the text presents a contrast, looking at the meteorological and emotional disturbance of the first stanza and claiming that everything in that other place is beautiful and calm. The refrain is like an incantation that Baudelaire hopes to use to transform his inner turmoil into peace and beauty.

Stanzas 3–4

The poetic voice now describes the sensuous beauty of his and his beloved's (that is, his own soul's) meeting place. The emphasis is on delicacy. The place described is a house or suite of rooms filled not only with the perfume of fresh-cut flowers but with the more rare and esoteric scent of amber. Amber, which is fossilized pine resin, is a clear golden crystal. Ordinarily amber has no scent, but when it is warmed to body temperature by being held, it gives off a delicate perfume that is the distillation of the scent of pine. The sense of sight, though less important than smell in Baudelaire's imaginative world, is also appealed to by the gleaming dark wood of the furniture, the many mirrors, and the height of the painted or coffered ceilings. The character of the room is Oriental, giving everything an exotic air that adds another layer of richness to the beauty of the place. It is significant that the luxurious retreat is a set of rooms rather than a garden, a seashore, or some other place of natural beauty. On one level, Baudelaire is embracing the human above the natural, which is a characteristic of decadent literature rather than romantic literature, though Baudelaire's poetry has characteristics of both movements. On another level, it is a further emphasis on the inner focus of the poem. In poetic figures, dreams, and other symbolic systems, the compartmentalized rooms of a house frequently stand for the structure of the body or even the mind. There could be no more ideal location for the meeting between Baudelaire and his own soul. Indeed, the only action of the third stanza is the anticipation of this house revealing its secrets to the soul (now named explicitly) in its own language.

The repeated refrain now seems like a reasonable description of the well-ordered house in which Baudelaire imagines his soul to be placed. By coming to that place, he has imposed the order and beauty that he wants on the earlier chaos.

Stanzas 5–6

The fifth stanza moves from the house or apartment to the city around it. This city is also a place of delicate and sensuous beauty, a world bathed in the subtle shades of gold contained within the sunset. There is much about the town that suggests Venice, a port that makes a link between East and West and that is built on canals, but it is decidedly not Venice since it seems to look to the sunset over the water (while Venice is on the eastern coast of Italy). Perhaps its conception has something to do with Baudelaire's trip to India. The main feature of the city is the ships in its harbor, which bring in cargo from across the sea, no doubt from the exotic Orient, as suggested in the third stanza. The poet tells his soul that the riches in these ships will grant the soul whatever it desires. Finally, sleep descends over the world, and at last the order and luxury of the final refrain bring to a conclusion the poem's voyage.

THEMES

Romanticism

In German and English literature, romanticism is the name usually given to the period between about 1790 and 1830, whose major writers included Johann Wolfgang von Goethe, Heinrich Heine, Samuel Taylor Coleridge, William Wordsworth, Percy Bysshe Shelley, George Gordon Byron, and John Keats. The somewhat more diffuse movement known as romanticism in France was not as limited in time and lacked the same ideological uniformity and rigor that characterized the German and English movements. A basic idea shared by all types of romanticism is a sense that the modern world is broken. History is seen as a succession of stages, each of which reacts with its predecessor to create a new age that perfects and transcends the last age. In its strictest form, romanticism held that antiquity, characterized by personal integration and meaning (expressed in the virtues of ancient art and literature), gave rise to the modern world, which was characterized by social disintegration and the rise of dominant individual identities (characterized by the

scientific and industrial revolutions). Romanticism's goal was to reconcile these two opposites to create a future with the virtues of both and the faults of neither. However, romanticism, precisely because it was enmeshed in modern individuality, was aware above all that no such reconciliation was likely to, or perhaps ever could, take place. This sense of failure and incompleteness is illustrated in such famous works as Keats's "Ode to a Nightingale," in which the poet's soul soars upward toward a vision of the utopian future or higher world but remains blind and crashes back down in failure and death. Another example is Goethe's "The Sorcerer's Apprentice," in which modernity is seen as an unstoppable process running out of control, with ever-increasing potential for destruction. Karl Marx's political philosophy of Communism shares a similar view of history, based on the work of the romantic philosopher Georg Wilhelm Friedrich Hegel, interpreting it as a series of dialectical resolutions of different economic modes. (A dialectic is a method of argument in which two opposing viewpoints—thesis and antithesis—are synthesized, or merged.) In Marx's view, history was destined to end in a worker's paradise whereby the nineteenth-century bourgeois-dominated industrial economy would give way to worker-controlled industry.

In France, romanticism, typified by the works of Victor Hugo, tended to be more superficial and to rely on the outward trappings of past ages or natural settings rather than philosophical analysis. At the same time, the sense of loss associated with modernity took the more concrete form of longing for a past world and social order—the *ancien régime*—that had been destroyed by the French Revolution. This backward-looking view appears, for example, in historical novels such as Hugo's *The Hunchback of Notre Dame* or Alexandre Dumas's *The Three Musketeers*. Hugo recognized Baudelaire's strong new romantic voice in *The Flowers of Evil*, a work that had much in common with the German origins of romanticism. For all his flouting of bourgeois respectability and prosperity, Baudelaire was a careful craftsman as a poet, and as much a student of his literary ancestors as he was an inventor of new poetry. While Baudelaire's poetry laid the foundations of many forms that would be used in later literary movements, such as decadence and symbolism, it is equally inspired by the older poetry of romanticism.

It is rare for any poet to present a coherent vision of the romantic dialectic in a single poem.

TOPICS FOR FURTHER STUDY

- In "Invitation to the Voyage," Baudelaire describes a wide range of luxury goods and artworks, and he implies still more in the form of exotic imports from the Orient. Use a search engine such as Google, including searches specifically for images, to find illustrations of the items mentioned in the poem. Go further and research luxury items that were exported from India and China to Europe in the nineteenth century, such as porcelain, silk, and antiquities. Prepare a digital multimedia presentation that discusses the country of origin, the means of production, and the reception of various Eastern cultural products in Europe.

- Write a paper comparing and contrasting the treatment of similar themes in "Invitation to the Voyage" in *The Flowers of Evil* and in the prose poem of the same title in *Paris Spleen*.

- Read more extensively in *The Flowers of Evil* and in *Songs of Life Hope*, by the Nicaraguan symbolist poet Ruben Dario. Give a talk to your class comparing the themes in the two collections. Use PowerPoint or a video editing program to illustrate the themes and words of the poems chosen from both collections.

- Make a list of themes from your favorite young-adult novel or short story, perhaps something you have recently read in class. Write a brief symbolist poem on the same themes. You might find it helpful to consult a guide to poetic composition written for young adults, such as Nancy Bogen's award-winning primer from 2007, *Be a Poet!*

- Felicien Rops and Odelon Redon were symbolist artists who were directly influenced by Baudelaire. Create a digital multimedia presentation showing connections between themes in *The Flowers of Evil* and some of their paintings and drawings.

- The American poet and short-story author Edgar Allen Poe had tremendous influence on French literature, largely through Baudelaire's translations. Write a paper exploring symbolist and decadent themes in some of Poe's poems, such as "Ulalume" or "The Raven," which are commonly read by young-adult audiences.

By its very nature, romanticism viewed modernity as so many splintered fragments, so a romantic poem is more typically situated in one stage of the romantic process. This is true of "Invitation to the Voyage"; however, this poem is unusual in being set within the romantic synthesis, when the resolution of opposites has produced a new and perfect future. In the first stanza of the poem, the poet addresses storm-tossed nature, and in the next stanza, the reader sees that nature revealed as the poet's own soul. By uniting in love, the poet and his soul bring forth a new world of beauty and harmony (the third stanza) in which opposites are reconciled (the fifth stanza). In this paradise, East and West come together, and trade brings the goods of foreign lands to the new place created by the union of the two. The self and the other become united. However, the poem ends in sleep, suggesting that in the hereafter, some new dialectic may rise up to even greater heights in the next age.

One model for the romantic dialectic is the Christian sequence of the creation of humans in Eden and the fall of humans into sin, followed by the reconciliation and new dispensation of grace in the incarnation of Jesus. Accordingly, Karen Harrington, in her article in *Understanding "Les Fleurs du Mal,"* describes the paradise that Baudelaire establishes in the poem as a "retrieval of the Edenic paradise." This is all strictly romantic, if uncharacteristically optimistic for romanticism (and for Baudelaire, for that matter). However, Baudelaire's poetry also has a vital difference from its romantic precedents: the progress achieved in the poem is entirely personal. It is a vision achieved within the self. The world and the age are not reconciled, but only the poet and his own soul.

Bouquet of the rarest blooms (*Jaren Jai Wicklund | Shutterstock.com*)

The romantic vision of the world had become entirely collapsed into an individual, so Baudelaire offers an internal solution to the romantic problem. If the most important principle of modernity is individuality, and if that stands in the way of synthesis with the naive, undifferentiated identity of the past, then he is satisfied to have the synthesis take place within the self alone. What is reconciled is the duality of human nature. This is a step away from romanticism and toward decadence.

Exoticism

A reader's first impulse might be to discuss the theme of beauty in "Invitation to the Voyage," but it quickly becomes apparent that for Baudelaire, beauty is not enough. It is not enough to have cut flowers; they must be not common roses but the most exotic flowers. Perfume is not enough; he must have the scent of amber, which can only be conjured by the ritual of heating the stone in the hand, something that seemed like a form of magic to the ancients. The beauty of the room is not enough; it has to be reflected and replicated by a profusion of mirrors. All the beauty to be had in France is not enough; Baudelaire must import the beautiful from the mysterious Orient and all the foreign nations of the world. In each case, Baudelaire requires that beauty take the most exotic and rarefied form imaginable. His aesthetic embraces a hypersensuousness that is remarkable for being impossible to satisfy. The ideal world he creates pointedly has the effect of blaming the real world for its mundane insufficiency.

STYLE

Decadence

Decadence literally means a falling away from some perceived height of perfection. Often it means the substitution of the selfish pursuit of pleasure for the working toward the achievement of some goal. In these senses, it was used as a term of condemnation against the generation of French writers and artists who flourished at the end of the nineteenth century. They proudly took up the slur, though, and began using it to describe their movement, calling themselves decadents. Baudelaire somewhat preceded other French poets in calling his own work

COMPARE
&
CONTRAST

- **1850s:** France is a dictatorship that tightly controls and censors art and literature.

  Today: France is a republic where any form of artistic expression may be freely published.

- **1850s:** The world of Bohemian artists that is set up in opposition to the conventions of mainstream society seems bizarre and threatening, filled with poverty, disease, drug addiction, and political radicalism. Stereotypical views of the Paris Bohemian scene can be found in Giacomo Puccini's opera *La Bohème* or George du Maurier's novel *Trilby*.

Today: The artistic counterculture is commonplace in every type of media. It is celebrated rather than condemned in the adaptation of *La Bohème* as the musical *Rent*.

- **1850s:** Poetry is the dominant art form in France. Contemporary poetry is widely read by most educated French people.

  Today: A common perception is that modern poetry is limited to a small audience of university intellectuals and has little popularity among the general public. It is rarely reviewed by the mainstream press.

decadent. The later generation looked back to Baudelaire and to Poe as their inspirations. Baudelaire's decadent tendencies are well displayed in "Invitation to the Voyage." He rejects the romantic worship of nature and celebrates the beauty of man-made things, such as a house and a city. Where he does acknowledge natural beauty, it is in the sunset, a symbol of decline and ending. The only beauty that interests him is obscure and rarefied; indeed, it seems that Baudelaire finds appealing those very qualities of being exquisite and rare, rather than any beauty in the objects or scenes themselves. The ideal that he creates is, on the other hand, private and isolated from the world, a complete turning inward. He wants to luxuriate in private pleasures and joys, turning his back on the world.

Symbolism

In 1886, the Greco-French poet Jean Moréas wrote *The Symbolist Manifesto* to answer criticism of modern French art as decadent and to distinguish what he thought of as the symbolist school from the decadents. Like the decadents, though, he looked to Baudelaire as the originator of his own moment. The difference between decadence and symbolism is more one of emphasis than a true division of literature into separate genres, and many figures, like Baudelaire, can be genuinely said to belong to either, depending upon the

perspective from which they are considered. Symbolism looked to religious mythology and mysticism for inspiration and wished to encapsulate its artistic expression in forms as meaningful, powerful, and beautiful as the most moving elements of religion. Symbolism's goal was to communicate with the reader or the viewer (since symbolism was more an artistic than a literary movement) through symbols that would affect, even mesmerize, but would above all merely communicate, without plainly stating an idea. In fact, plain, open communication seemed vulgar in comparison. Baudelaire certainly embraces the symbolist program in "Invitation to the Voyage." This poem is a forest of symbols drawn from philosophy, theology, and psychology. It enters into a conversation with the reader, demanding an effort of interpretation comparable to the creative effort of the poet.

HISTORICAL CONTEXT

Second French Empire

As a cultural entity, the Second Empire in France corresponds to the Victorian era in the English world. It represented the ascendancy of the bourgeoisie, the middle class of entrepreneurs and civil servants. In 1848, the French monarchy, which had been imposed by France's foreign conquerors

Luxurious 19th-century boudoir *(Antonin Vodak / Shutterstock.com)*

after the Napoleonic wars, collapsed, and a new regime, known as the Second Republic, came to power. The nature of the new government was at first uncertain. There were revolutions all over Europe in 1848, which was also the date of the publication of Marx's *Communist Manifesto*. Some French people hoped for a radical reform of society, and this interested Baudelaire, who became active as a journalist during this period of uncertainty. In the end, however, power was placed in the hands of the bourgeoisie. This change of power from the aristocracy to the middle class was a result of the expanding wealth being created by the Industrial Revolution. The social tone of the new bourgeois culture was intensely conservative and devoted to the idea of keeping up a show of respectability. Open displays of sexuality, political radicalism, and the seeking of pleasure for its own sake were rejected as undisciplined and self-indulgent. The favored virtues were self-reliance, industry, and the amassing of personal wealth. Louis-Napoleon (also known as Napoleon III), nephew of the first emperor of France, was elected president of the new republic. In 1851, he staged a coup d'état

and became dictator. The next year, his position was confirmed by a national referendum, and Louis-Napoleon ruled in what became known as the Second Empire, but the character of French society did not perceptibly change.

Resistance to the bourgeois lifestyle among young French intellectuals and artists came to be called Bohemian, both because the poor students who made up the movement lived in the Bohemian, or Gypsy, quarter of Paris and because the Gypsies were taken as a model community that was self-sufficient and unconcerned about the approval of society at large. Baudelaire naturally gravitated to this counterculture, and he passionately lived out its objections to bourgeois conventions. He refused to be married but took mistresses; he refused to work as a lawyer or at another career, instead writing poetry that could never have sustained him financially. He wrote *The Flowers of Evil*, which bourgeois society inevitably judged obscene and censored. "Invitation to the Voyage" inherently mocks bourgeois culture by admiring beauty for the pleasure it gives rather than as a display of wealth and status.

Orientalism

According to the theory of Orientalism developed by the postmodernist critic Edward Said, European and American literature uses the Orient, or really any alien culture, as a screen on which to project elements of Western culture that are disfavored and to be rejected from the Western self-image. Thus, the Orient is exotic and foreign because it is alien, but more particularly, it is weak instead of strong, effeminate instead of masculine, luxury loving rather than disciplined, magical rather than religious. The actual character of Asian or African cultures is irrelevant to this process; they are obliterated under the weight of stereotypes that Europeans wish to deny in themselves. It is hardly surprising, then, that Baudelaire, who himself had been to India, constructs his world of ideal beauty in "Invitation to the Voyage" out of elements of Orientalist myth. Because Baudelaire rejected the conventions of bourgeois society, he purposefully picks up the cast-offs of that culture and celebrates the laziness, sensuousness, and love of luxury that it rejected. Bourgeois culture was seen as pretending that these undesirable traits did not exist in the West but could be found only in the East. Baudelaire assembles an imaginative merchant fleet to gather all the elements of Oriental decadence to his soul.

CRITICAL OVERVIEW

When *The Flowers of Evil* was published in 1857, it was well received by established members of France's literary world such as Théophile Gautier and Victor Hugo. It was recognized as something entirely new and entirely modern. An even more decisive reaction, however, was Baudelaire's prosecution for obscenity over the book. French society could not as yet accept a work that so thoroughly celebrated the individual over society.

Two important modern readings of "Invitation to the Voyage" are made by Leo Bersani in *Baudelaire and Freud* and by Harrington in her article on the poem in the 1997 book *Understanding "Les Fleurs du Mal."* Bersani recognizes that the poem is entirely about the interior condition of the poet. It slips back and forth between reality and imagination in a way that leaves the reader breathless and confused. The poem's elusive character mocks reality and never allows the reader to make a definite connection to it: "the poem is a

tease, and with his teasing, shifting tone and his mobile attention the poet protects both his own and the woman's indeterminacy of being."

Harrington agrees that "Invitation to the Voyage" is a dream or flight from reality to a place within. Seen in a theological framework, the voyage of the poem's title is a journey back to a place and time before the fall in the Garden of Eden. She agrees with Bersani that the role of the woman in the poem is merely to awaken the poet's desires, but the speaker seems to find on his own the emotional calm that Harrington sees as the goal of the poem.

CRITICISM

Bradley A. Skeen

Skeen is a classicist. In the following essay, he explores Baudelaire's "Invitation to the Voyage" in light of Freudian psychoanalysis.

Baudelaire's "Invitation to the Voyage" is not an easy poem to understand. Its language is symbolic or allegorical and therefore requires effort beyond ordinary reading to disentangle and interpret. For instance, the title of the poem talks about a voyage, or, better, a journey. However, a cursory reading finds no journey ever mentioned in the poem. There is talk about merchant ships in a harbor, but they do not seem to be connected to any journey that could be the one mentioned in the title. So what does it mean? The poet invites his addressee to live with him and love with him forever, and one may suppose that this is the journey that is meant: the journey of life. Other symbols are also clear because they are commonplace. The stormy skies that the poet sees in the addressee's eyes are, of course, stormy emotions of rage and passion, a common figure of speech. However, much of the poem does not yield to such superficial interpretation. Indeed, it would be a difficult task to discover every possible meaning that is contained in the poem's symbols, and not necessarily any would prove entirely useful, since there is a reason to read the poem in its own allusive form rather than an essay explaining the poem. Nor is it at all certain that even Baudelaire himself could fully explain the poem, since, as the ancient Greek philosopher Plato observed, the poet is often powerless to explain his own poetry. For Plato this served as the start of a theory concerning the divine inspiration of art, but today, one might simply say that the poet is not consciously

WHAT DO I READ NEXT?

- Henri Murger's *Bohemians of the Latin Quarter*, a hybrid of a novel and a collection of short stories, was published in book form in 1851, though parts of it had been published in newspapers as early as 1845. It is a thinly fictionalized account of life in the counterculture artists' community in Paris. Rarely read today, it is the basis of the 1896 opera *La Bohème*, by Puccini, and the 1897 opera of the same name by Ruggero Leoncavallo. An English translation is available at http://www.gutenberg.org/ebooks/18445.

- *Paris Spleen* is a collection of prose poems written by Baudelaire and published posthumously in 1869. In this work, he revisits the same themes and subjects he originally developed in *The Flowers of Evil*.

- In 1997, Pamela Prince and Jane Handel edited a monograph devoted entirely to "Invitation to the Voyage," which prints a bilingual text (in French and the English translation) of that poem alone. The work, *L'Invitation au Voyage/Invitation to the Voyage: A Poem from "The Flowers of Evil,"* is illustrated with photographs by Baudelaire's friend Nadar and other contemporary photographers.

- Kenneth Cornell's 1951 book *The Symbolist Movement* is the standard English language introduction to symbolism.

- Oscar Wilde's fairy tales are the pieces of symbolist literature aimed at a young-adult audience. They are reprinted in numerous modern editions and include such stories as "The Star-Child," "The Selfish Giant," and "The Happy Prince." Signet Classics issued a reprint edition of *Complete Fairy Tales of Oscar Wilde* in 2008.

- In the fifteenth century, the emperor of China commissioned the construction of the largest sailing vessels ever built. Called the treasure ships, these large fleets made repeated voyages as far away as Africa. The purpose of these voyages was to collect tribute to the emperor from the local populations of the lands visited, of which the emperor believed he was the rightful ruler. This interest in exotic and rare goods that could be brought back from across the sea is a mirror image of the desire expressed in "Invitation to the Voyage," where the poet experiences the exotic beauty of goods brought to Europe from China. Ray Conloque's 2007 *Shen and the Treasure Fleet* is a young-adult novel based on the first voyage of these ships.

aware of the meaning of his own work. But what does that very odd expression itself mean?

In the 1890s, Sigmund Freud was in the process of creating the modern science of psychoanalysis. He was seeing patients who seemed to have mental or emotional disturbances that baffled ordinary medical doctors. His patients were often depressed, or wanted nothing to do with their families, or would almost faint with fear whenever they saw a horse (at a time when horses were as common in the street as cars are now): they were experiencing mental and emotional problems. What Freud found was that his patients both knew and did not know what was causing

their affliction. They would never tell him openly what was wrong but would let it slip in any number of ways, most notably in their dreams, which would reenact the cause of their difficulties as a little drama, veiled in symbols that let them tell the story without knowing they were telling it. To cure his patients, Freud had to slowly talk them around to discovering the truth for themselves; if he just told them the truth flat out, they denied it. What Freud discovered was that the mind is divided into a conscious part, of which one is constantly aware, and an unconscious part, which contains all of the instinctual drives and all the information that the conscious mind would rather not be aware of.

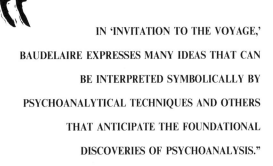

In between, there was a mechanism that Freud likened to the censorship of the bourgeois state. The real censors that controlled information in nineteenth-century Austria-Hungary or France would do things like ban newspaper stories that criticized the government or stop the publication of books that contained supposedly obscene material, as they did with *The Flowers of Evil*. The censor within the mind would likewise let unobjectionable material pass from the unconscious to the conscious, material such as hunger or the memory of something that made one laugh in kindergarten. However, other material the censor would hold back, not letting the conscious mind know anything that it considered objectionable or unpleasant. The censor would, however, let the forbidden material pass in the form of a symbol, as if it was not able to understand what the symbol meant. Real-world censorship often operates the same way, as when, during the Nazi occupation of France in World War II, Jean Anouilh was able to publish his *Antigone* because the censor did not recognize it as a symbolic attack on Nazi tyranny. Freud discovered that the mind creates its own symbolic language and that understanding this language was useful for more than interpreting his patient's dreams.

Freud often admitted that what he discovered had been known to creative artists and writers for centuries. Psychoanalysis analyzes ideas, language, and dreams as symbols that express ideas that are both important and unacceptable to the patient. When decoded, these symbols can reveal aspects of a patient's history or unconscious mind that might have led to neurosis or to a level of anxiety that called out for treatment. A more fundamental implication of Freud's discovery is the insight that as the human mind evolved to create and master

language, it also developed the capacity to communicate ideas in the language of symbols, which exists both above and below the level of ordinary language. The symbolic forms used by the mind are partially common to all humans (especially in areas important in our evolutionary history, such as reproduction or avoiding predators), partially reliant on cultural convention (as when everyone in the West knows what the symbol of a cross means), and partially invented by the individual based on his or her own talent and experience. It is here that everyone comes closest to the poet or author, and Freud soon realized that psychoanalysis could become a powerful tool of literary criticism because of the similarity between the symbolism of the unconscious mind and the symbolism of art. Thus, with the insights that Freud gleaned from therapeutic analysis, it is often possible to interpret seemingly impenetrable symbolism in literature.

In "Invitation to the Voyage," Baudelaire expresses many ideas that can be interpreted symbolically by psychoanalytical techniques and others that anticipate the foundational discoveries of psychoanalysis. The poet is consumed by love; it is the whole meaning of his life. This foreshadows Freud's theory of libido. Because of the nature of evolution, the most important drive in all animals is to reproduce themselves, and human beings are no different. Thus, the whole human personality, according to Freud, is driven by this instinct. Humans, because of their intellectual sophistication, are able to channel it into other areas of life and divert the energies and interests (libido) that arise from reproduction to other activities that fulfill the reproductive need symbolically, such as in hard work that accomplishes something, artistic creativity, or the building up of civilization itself.

In the same way, the poet in "Invitation to the Voyage" is able to build up the whole world of his poem from love. It is also interesting, from this viewpoint, that the object of the poet's love is unclear and the reader cannot tell whether it is his sister, his daughter, his lover, or his own self. Freud would call this state undifferentiated. Even the youngest child possess all the libido that an adult does, but that energy does not become focused on reproduction until biological maturity is reached. In infancy, this love is given first to whoever provides the baby with the food and care it needs to survive, and then to the child's parents and family through various stages of development; the love is expressed in symbolic terms that allow the basic instinct to be redirected. Baudelaire, in the beginning of his poem, is celebrating the unique intensity of this undifferentiated love that can still be recalled by adults. Baudelaire was unusually aware of the fact that romantic love is a development of the love expressed in childhood. He was able to write in a letter to his mother, as quoted by Barbara Johnson in *Mother Tongues*: "There was in my childhood a period of passionate love for you." Bourgeois culture was scandalized when Freud suggested that love within the family arises from the same psychic origins as romantic love, and it was just as scandalized fifty years earlier when Baudelaire made the same suggestion in "Invitation to the Voyage," collapsing the various kinds of love into their original state.

The second major stanza turns to the description of a house, namely, the structure that will be the dwelling of Baudelaire and his soul. In one sense, this must necessarily be the body—Baudelaire's own body. Because the body indeed seems to the mind as a vessel containing it, the body is often referred to as a home for the soul. The illusion and metaphor of indwelling in the body is so strong that Freud is able to list the body symbolized as a house among his examples of nearly universal dream and literary symbols in *The Interpretation of Dreams*: "The human body as a whole is pictured as a house by the phantasy of the dream, and each individual organ of the body as part of the house." Still, it hardly seems likely that Baudelaire could have associated the perfection and beauty of the house in his poem with his own body. One may go a little further than Freud was able to in 1900 and suggest that the house stands here for the mind itself, with all its individual parts and divisions that Freud was only just then discovering. That conception much better explains the otherworldly perfection of this house.

Other symbols, such as the aforementioned journey of life and storm of emotions, are of this same commonplace kind. The same is also true of the general symbolic scheme of the first stanza. There, the addressee of the poem—the poet's beloved, or his own soul, or any of the many ways this figure can be conceptualized—is equated with the entire world. The landscape looks like the addressee, and the storm clouds that are in the sky are also in her eyes. The very common comparison between a human figure, especially a female figure, and the world or the landscape is, in Freud's view, a remnant from infancy and even earlier phases of development, when the baby is actually contained within the body of its mother. Later, it is commonly said that the mother, as primary caregiver, is the

baby's whole world. This symbolism is so pervasive that it has given rise to the idea that a human being is a sort of scale model of the universe, with direct and real correspondences between the miniature and the larger parts. This idea is mythological, but as myth so often does, it expresses something that is psychologically true.

The third major stanza turns to the port above which the house stands, with its ships loaded with exotic trade goods. It does not take much imagination to see that this commerce itself can stand for the exchange of information between the unconscious and conscious minds. This is particularly true since the stanza ends in sleep, when the dreams that will come will permit a heightened exchange between the levels of consciousness.

Perhaps most interesting of all, however, is the end of the second major stanza, in which the soul is described as having its own secret language. This is Baudelaire, as it were, acknowledging that this psychoanalytical interpretation is on the right track. He is very clearly anticipating Freud's discoveries. Baudelaire is indeed conscious that he is using poetry and its symbolic language to reveal secrets of his own inner mind that cannot quite be put plainly into words, whether or not he himself knows their meanings. In the end, though, this treatment is very superficial. Acknowledging the greatness of Freud's achievement, it is obvious that the real meaning behind the poem could only come in discussion between the critic and the poet, to tease out what personal worlds of meaning storms and amber and the Orient had for Baudelaire. As Plato said long ago, real learning can come only through dialogue.

Source: Bradley A. Skeen, Critical Essay on "Invitation to the Voyage," in *Poetry for Students* Gale, Cengage Learning, 2011.

Arthur Symons

In the following excerpt, Symons terms The Flowers of Evil *the "most curious, subtle, fascinating, and extraordinary creation of an entire world."*

Baudelaire's genius is satanical; he has in a sense the vision of Satan. He sees in the past the lusts of the Borgias, the sins and vices of the Renaissance; the rare virtues that flourish like flowers and weeds, in brothels and in garrets. He sees the vanity of the world with finer modern tastes than Solomon; for his imagination is abnormal, and divinely normal. In this age of infamous shames he has no shame. His flesh endures, his intellect is flawless. He chooses his own pleasures

Tools for the voyage (*Triff | Shutterstock.com*)

delicately, sensitively, as he gathers his exotic *Fleurs du Mal*, in itself a world, neither a *Divina Commedia* nor *Une Comédie Humaine*, but a world of his own fashioning.

His vividly imaginative passion, with his instincts of inspiration, are aided by a determined will, a self-reserve, an intensity of conception, an implacable insolence, an accurate sense of the exact value of every word. In the Biblical sense he might have said of his own verse: "It is bone of my bone, and flesh of my flesh." The work, as the man, is subtle, strange, complex, morbid, enigmatical, refined, paradoxical, spiritual, animal.

Fascinated by sin, he is never the dupe of his emotions; he sees sin as the Original Sin; he studies sin as he studies evil, with a stern logic; he finds in horror a kind of attractiveness, as Poe had found it; rarely in hideous things, save when his sense of what I call a moralist makes him moralize, as in his terrible poem *Une Charogne*. He has pity for misery, hate for progress. He is analytic, he is a learned casuist. . . .

His soul swims on music played on no human instrument, but on strings that the Devil pulls, to which certain living puppets dance in grotesque fashion, to unheard-of rhythms, to the sound of violins strummed on by evil spirits in Witches' Sabbats. Some swing in the air, as hanged dead people on gallows, and, as their bones rattle in the wind, one sees Judas Iscariot, risen out of Hell for an instant's gratification, as he grimaces on these grimacing visages.

Les Fleurs du Mal is the most curious, subtle, fascinating, and extraordinary creation of an entire world ever fashioned in modern ages. Baudelaire paints vice and degradation of the utmost depth, with cynicism and with pity, as in [*Une Charogne*], where the cult of the corpse is the sensuality of asceticism, or the asceticism of sensuality: the mania of fakirs; material by passion, Christian by perversity.

Les Fleurs du Mal are grown in Parisian soil, exotics that have the strange, secretive, haunting touch and taint of the earth's or of the body's corruption. In his sense of beauty there is a certain revolt, a spiritual malady, which may bring with it the heated air of an alcove or the intoxicating atmosphere of the East. Never since Villon has the flesh of woman been more adored and abhorred.

> BAUDELAIRE BRINGS EVERY COMPLICATION OF TASTE, THE EXASPERATION OF PERFUMES, THE IRRITANT OF CRUELTY, THE VERY ODOURS AND COLOURS OF CORRUPTION TO THE CREATION AND ADORNMENT OF A SORT OF RELIGION, IN WHICH AN ETERNAL MASS IS SERVED BEFORE A VEILED ALTAR."

Certain of these Flowers of Evil are poisonous; some are grown in the hotbeds of Hell; some have the perfume of a serpentine girl's skin; some the odour of woman's flesh. Certain spirits are intoxicated by these accursed flowers, to save themselves from the too much horror of their vices, from the worse torture of their violated virtues. And a cruel imagination has fashioned these naked images of the Seven Deadly Sins, eternally regretful of their first fall; that smile not even in Hell, in whose flames they writhe. One conceives them there and between the sun and the earth; in the air, carried by the winds; aware of their infernal inheritance. They surge like demons out of the Middle Ages; they are incapable of imagining God's justice.

Baudelaire dramatizes these living images of his spirit and of his imagination, these fabulous creatures of his inspiration, these macabre ghosts, in a fashion utterly different from that of other tragedians—Shakespeare, and Aristophanes in his satirical Tragedies, his lyrical Comedies; yet in the same sense of being the writer where beauty marries unvirginally the sons of ancient Chaos.

In these pages swarm (in his words) all the corruptions and all the scepticisms; ignoble criminals without convictions, detestable hags that gamble, the cats that are like men's mistresses; Harpagon; the exquisite, barbarous, divine, implacable, mysterious Madonna of the Spanish style; the old men; the drunkards, the assassins, the lovers (their deaths and lives); the owls; the vampires whose kisses raise from the grave the corpse of its own self; the Irremediable that assails its origin: Conscience in Evil! There is an almost Christ-like poem on his Passion, *Le Reniement de Saint-Pierre*, an almost Satanic denunciation of God in *Abel and Cain*, and with them the Evil Monk, an enigmatical symbol of Baudelaire's soul, of his work, of all that his eyes love and hate. Certain of these creatures play in travesties, dance in ballets. For all the Arts are transformed, transfigured, transplanted out of their natural forms to pass in magnificent state across the stage: the stage with the abyss of Hell in front of it.

It is Baudelaire who, in Hell as in earth, finds a certain Satan in such modern hearts as his; that even modern art has an essentially demoniacal tendency; that the infernal pact of man increases daily, as if the Devil whispered in his ear certain sardonic secrets.

Yet, tainted as the style is from time to time, never was the man himself tainted: he who in modern verse gave first of all an unknown taste to sensations; he who painted vice in all its shame; whose most savorous verses are perfumed as-with subtle aromas; whose women are bestial, rouged, sterile, bodies without souls; whose *Litanies de Satan* have that cold irony which he alone possessed in its extremity, in these so-called impious lines which reveal, under whatever disguise, his belief in a mathematical superiority established by God from all eternity, and whose least infraction is punished by certain chastisements, in this world as in the next.

Has Baudelaire *l'amour du mal pour le mal* [an evil love of evil]? In a certain sense, yes; in a certain sense, no. He believes in evil as in Satan and God— the primitive forces that govern worlds: the eternal enemies. He sees the germs of evil everywhere, few of the seeds of virtue. He sees pass before him the world's drama: he is one of the actors, he plays his parts cynically, ironically. He speaks in rhythmic cadences.

But, above all, he watches the dancers; these also are elemental; and the tragic fact is that the dancers dance for their living. For their living, for their pleasure, for the pleasure of pleasing others. So passes the fantastic part of their existence, from the savage who dances silent dances—for, indeed, all dancers are silent—but without music, to the dancer who dances for us on the stage, who turns always to the sound of music. There is an equal magic in the dance and in song; both have their varied rhythms; both, to use an image, the rhythmic beating of our hearts.

The greatest French poet after Villon, the most disreputable and the most creative poet in French literature, the greatest artist in French verse, and, after Verlaine, the most passionate, perverse, lyrical, visionary, and intoxicating of modern poets, comes Baudelaire, infinitely more perverse, morbid, exotic than these other poets. In his verse there is a deliberate science of sensual perversity, which has something almost monachal in its accentuation of vice with horror, in its passionate devotion to passions. Baudelaire brings every complication of taste, the exasperation of perfumes, the irritant of cruelty, the very odours and colours of corruption to the creation and adornment of a sort of religion, in which an eternal mass is served before a veiled altar. There is no confession, no absolution, not a prayer is permitted which is not set down in the ritual.

There is something Oriental in Baudelaire's genius; a nostalgia that never left him after he had seen the East: there where one finds hot midnights, feverish days, strange sensations; for only the East, when one has lived in it, can excite one's vision to a point of ardent ecstasy. He is the first modern poet who gave to a calculated scheme of versification a kind of secret and sacred joy. He is before all things the artist, always sure of his form. And his rarefied imagination aided him enormously not only in the perfecting of his verse and prose, but in making him create the criticism of modern art.

Next after Villon, Baudelaire is the poet of Paris. Like a damned soul (to use one of his imaginary images) he wanders at nights. . . . [A] kind of intense curiosity, of excitement, in his frequentation of [Parisian] streets, comes over him, like one who has taken opium . . . .

He is the first who ever related things in the modulated tone of the confessional and never assumed an inspired air. The first also who brings into modern literature the chagrin that bites at our existence like serpents. He admits to his diabolical taste, not quite exceptional in him; one finds it in Petronius, Rabelais, Balzac. In spite of his magnificent *Litanies de Satan*, he is no more of the satanical school than Byron. Yet both have the same sardonic irony, the delight of mystification, of deliberately irritating solemn people's convictions. Both, who died tragically young, had their hours of sadness, when one doubts and denies everything; passionately regretting youth, turning away, in sinister moods, in solitude, from that too intense self-knowledge that, like a mirror, shows the wrinkles on our cheeks.

Source: Arthur Symons, excerpt from *Charles Baudelaire: A Study*, Elkin Mathews, 1920, p. 116.

Henry James

In the following excerpt, James calls The Flowers of Evil *a "sincere book" but finds little else to praise.*

'Les Fleurs du Mal' is evidently a sincere book—so far as anything for a man of Baudelaire's temper and culture could be sincere. Sincerity seems to us to belong to a range of qualities with which Baudelaire and his friends were but scantily conversant. His great quality was an inordinate cultivation of the sense of the picturesque, and his care was for how things looked, and whether some kind of imaginative amusement was not to be got out of them, much more than for what they meant and whither they led, and what was their use in human life at large. . . . Baudelaire had a certain groping sense of the moral complexities of life, and if the best that he succeeds in doing is to drag them down into the very turbid element in which he himself plashes and flounders, and there present them to us much besmirched and bespattered, this was not a want of goodwill in him, but rather a dulness and permanent immaturity of vision. For American readers, furthermore, Baudelaire is compromised by his having made himself the apostle of our own Edgar Poe. . . . With all due respect to the very original genius of the author of the 'Tales of Mystery,' it seems to us that to take him with more than a certain degree of seriousness is to lack seriousness one's self. An enthusiasm for Poe is the mark of a decidedly primitive stage of reflection. Baudelaire thought him a profound philosopher, the neglect of whose golden utterances stamped his native land with infamy. Nevertheless, Poe was vastly the greater charlatan of the two, as well as the greater genius.

'Les Fleurs du Mal' was a very happy title for Baudelaire's verses, but it is not altogether a just one. Scattered flowers incontestably do bloom in the quaking swamps of evil, and the poet who does not mind encountering bad odors in his pursuit of sweet ones is quite at liberty to go in search of them. But Baudelaire has, as a general thing, not plucked the flowers—he has plucked the evil-smelling weeds (we take it that he did not use the word flowers in a purely ironical sense), and he has often taken up mere cupfuls of mud and bog-water. He had said to himself that it was a great shame that the realm of evil and unclean things should be fenced off from the domain of poetry; that it was full of subjects, of chances and effects; that it had its light and shade, its logic and its mystery; and that there was the making of some capital verses in it. So he leaped the barrier, and was soon immersed in it up to his neck. Baudelaire's imagination was of a melancholy and sinister kind, and, to a considerable extent, this plunging into darkness and dirt was doubtless very spontaneous and disinterested. But he strikes us on the whole as passionless, and this, in view of the unquestionable pluck and acuteness of his fancy, is a great pity. He knew evil not by experience, not as something within himself, but by contemplation and curiosity, as something outside of himself, by which his own intellectual agility was not in the least discomposed, rather, indeed (as we say his fancy was of a dusky cast), agreeably flattered and stimulated. In the former case, Baudelaire, with his other gifts, might have been a great poet. But, as it is, evil for him begins outside and not inside, and consists primarily of a great deal of lurid landscape and unclean furniture. . . .

A good way to embrace Baudelaire at a glance is to say that he was, in his treatment of evil, exactly what Hawthorne was not—Hawthorne, who felt the thing at its source, deep in the human consciousness. Baudelaire's infinitely slighter volume of genius apart, he was a sort of Hawthorne reversed. . . . [In Baudelaire's] pages we never know with what we are dealing. We encounter an inextricable confusion of sad emotions and vile things, and we are at a loss to know whether the subject pretends to appeal to our conscience or—we were going to say—to our olfactories. "*Le Mal?*" we exclaim; "you do yourself too much honor. This is not Evil; it is not the wrong; it is simply the nasty!" Our impatience is of the same order as that which we should feel if a poet, pretending to pluck "the flowers of good," should come and present us, as specimens, a rhapsody on plum-cake and on cologne-water. Independently of the question of his subjects, the charm of Baudelaire's verse is often of a very high order. He belongs to the class of geniuses in whom we ourselves find but a limited pleasure—the laborious, deliberate, economical writers, those who fumble a long time in their pockets before they bring out their hand with a coin in the palm. But the coin, when Baudelaire at last produced it, was often of a high value. He had an extraordinary verbal instinct and an exquisite felicity of epithet. . . . Baudelaire is extremely remarkable in his talent for suggesting associations. His epithets seem to have come out of old cupboards and pockets; they have a kind of magical mustiness. Moreover, his natural sense of the superficial picturesqueness of the miserable and the unclean was extremely acute; there may be a difference of opinion as to the advantage of possessing

such a sense; but whatever it is worth, Baudelaire had it in a high degree.

Baudelaire repudiated with indignation the charge that he was what is called a realist, and he was doubtless right in doing so. He had too much fancy to adhere strictly to the real; he always embroiders and elaborates and endeavors to impart that touch of strangeness and mystery which is the very *raison d'etre* of poetry. Baudelaire was a poet, and for a poet to be a realist is of course nonsense. The idea which Baudelaire imported into his theme was, as a general thing, an intensification of its repulsiveness, but it was at any rate ingenious. . . . Occasionally he treats agreeable subjects, and his least sympathetic critics must make a point of admitting that his most successful poem is also his most wholesome and most touching: we allude to "Les Petites Vieilles"—a really masterly production. But if it represents the author's maximum, it is a note which he very rarely struck.

[On the whole, Baudelaire] was the victim of a grotesque illusion. He tried to make fine verses on ignoble subjects, and in our opinion he signally failed. He gives, as a poet, a perpetual impression of discomfort and pain. He went in search of corruption, and the ill-conditioned jade proved a thankless muse. . . . What the poet wished, doubtless, was to seem to be always in the poetic attitude; what the reader sees is a gentleman in a painful-looking posture, staring very hard at a mass of things from which we more intelligently avert our heads.

Source: Henry James, "Charles Baudelaire," in *Nation*, Vol. 22, No. 565, April 27, 1876, pp. 279–81.

Algernon Charles Swinburne

In the following excerpt, Swinburne brings Baudelaire to the attention of English-speaking readers in the nineteenth century.

[M. Baudelaire] has more delicate power of verse than almost any man living, after Victor Hugo, Browning, and (in his lyrics) Tennyson. The sound of his metres suggests colour and perfume. His perfect workmanship makes every subject admirable and respectable. Throughout the chief part of [the *Fleurs du Mal*], he has chosen to dwell mainly upon sad and strange things—the weariness of pain and the bitterness of pleasure—the perverse happiness and wayward sorrows of exceptional people. It has the languid lurid beauty of close and threatening weather—a heavy heated temperature, with dangerous hothouse scents in it; thick shadow of cloud about it, and fire of molten light. It is quite clear of all whining and windy lamentation; there is nothing of the blubbering and shrieking style long since exploded. The writer delights in problems, and has a natural leaning to obscure and sorrowful things. Failure and sorrow, next to physical beauty and perfection of sound or scent, seem to have an infinite attraction for him. In some points he resembles Keats, or still more his chosen favourite among modern poets, Edgar Poe; at times, too, his manner of thought has a relish of Marlowe, and even the sincerer side of Byron. From Théophile Gautier, to whom the book is dedicated, he has caught the habit of a faultless and studious simplicity; but, indeed, it seems merely natural to him always to use the right word and the right rhyme. How supremely musical and flexible a perfect artist in writing can make the French language, any chance page of the book is enough to prove; every description, the slightest and shortest even, has a special mark on it of the writer's keen and peculiar power. The style is sensuous and weighty; the sights seen are steeped most often in sad light and sullen colour. As instances of M. Baudelaire's strength and beauty of manner, one might take especially the poems headed *Le Masque, Pärfum Exotique, La Chevelure, Les Sept Vieillards, Les Petites Vieilles, Ilrumes et Pluies....*

[The sonnet titled *Causerie* is a complete] specimen of the author's power. The way in which the sound and sense are suddenly broken off and shifted, four lines from the end, is wonderful for effect and success. M. Baudelaire's mastery of the sonnet form is worth remarking as a test of his natural bias towards such forms of verse as are most nearly capable of perfection.... Not the luxuries of pleasure in their simple first form, but the sharp and cruel enjoyments of pain, the acrid relish of suffering felt or inflicted, the sides on which nature looks unnatural, go to make up the stuff and substance of this poetry. Very good material they make, too; but evidently such things are unfit for rapid or careless treatment. The main charm of the book is, upon the whole, that nothing is wrongly given, nothing capable of being re-written or improved on its own ground. Concede the starting point, and you cannot have a better runner.

Thus, even of the loathsomest bodily putrescence and decay he can make some noble use....

Another of this poet's noblest sonnets is that *A une Passante*, comparable with a similar one of Keats, "Time's sea hath been five years at its slow ebb," but superior for directness of point and forcible reality. Here for once the beauty of a poem is rather passionate than sensuous....

There is noticeable also in M. Baudelaire's work a quality of *drawing* which recalls the exquisite power in the same way of great French artists now living. His studies are admirable for truth and grace; his figure-painting has the ease and strength, the trained skill, and beautiful gentle justice of manner, which come out in such pictures as the *Source* of Ingres....

It may be worth while to say something of the moral and meaning of many among these poems. Certain critics, who will insist on going into this matter, each man as deep as his small leaden plummet will reach, have discovered what they call a paganism on the spiritual side of the author's tone of thought. Stripped of its coating of jargon, this may mean that the poet spoken of endeavours to look at most things with the eye of an old-world poet; that he aims at regaining the clear and simple view of writers content to believe in the beauty of material subjects. To us, if this were the meaning of these people, we must say it seems a foolish one; for there is not one of these poems that could have been written in a time when it was not the fashion to dig for moral motives and conscious reasons. Poe, for example, has written poems without any moral meaning at all; there is not one poem of the *Fleurs du Mal* which has not a distinct and vivid background of morality to it. Only this moral side of the book is not thrust forward in the foolish and repulsive manner of a half-taught artist; the background, as we called it, is not out of drawing....

[Those] who will look for them may find moralities in plenty behind every poem of M. Baudelaire's; such poems especially as *Une Martyre*. Like a mediaeval preacher, when he has drawn the heathen love, he puts sin on its right hand and death on its left.

[We] may note a few others in which [a] singular strength of finished writing is most evident. Such are, for instance, *Le Cygne, Le Poison, Tristesses de la Lune, Remord Posthume, Le Flacon, Ciel Brouillé, Une Mendiante Rousse* (a simpler study than usual, of great beauty in all ways, noticeable for its revival of the old fashion of unmixed masculine rhymes), *Le Balcon, Allegorie, L'Amour et le Crâne,* and the two splendid sonnets marked xxvii. and xlii. We cite these headings in no sort of order, merely as they catch one's eye in revising the list of contents and recall the poems classed there. Each of them we regard as worth a separate study, but the *Litanies de Satan*, as in a way the key-note to this whole complicated tune of poems, we had set aside for the last. . . .

Here it seems as if all failure and sorrow on earth, and all the cast-out things of the world—ruined bodies and souls diseased—made their appeal, in default of help, to Him in whom all sorrow and all failure were incarnate. As a poem, it is one of the noblest lyrics ever written; the sound of it between wailing and triumph, as it were the blast blown by the trumpets of a brave army in irretrievable defeat. . . .

[*Litanies de Satan* is not] more finished than the rest; every verse has the vibration in it of naturally sound and pure metal. It is a study of metrical cadence throughout, of wonderful force and variety. . . . We know that in time it must make its way. . . .

Source: Algernon Charles Swinburne, "Charles Baudelaire: *Les Fleurs du Mal*," in *Spectator*, No. 1784, September 6, 1862, pp. 998–1000.

SOURCES

Abrams, M. H., *The Mirror and the Lamp: Romantic Theory and the Critical Tradition*, Oxford University Press, 1953.

Baudelaire, Charles, "Invitation to the Voyage," in *The Flowers of Evil and Paris Spleen*, translated by William H. Crosby, BOA Editions, 1991, pp. 106–109.

Bersani, Leo, *Baudelaire and Freud*, University of California Press, 1977.

Bowra, C. M., *The Romantic Imagination*, Oxford University Press, 1961.

Freud, Sigmund, *The Future of an Illusion*, translated by James Strachey, W. W. Norton, 1961.

———, *The Interpretation of Dreams*, 3rd ed., translated by A. A. Brill, MacMillan, 1913, http://books.google.com/books?id=OSYJAAAAIAAJ&pg=PR3#v=onepage&q&f=false (accessed September 20, 2010).

Gay, Peter, *The Bourgeois Experience: Victoria to Freud*, Oxford University Press, 1985.

Gioia, Dana, "Can Poetry Matter?" in *Dana Gioia Home Page*, http://www.danagioia.net/essays/ecpm.htm (accessed October 18, 2010).

Harrington, Karen, "L'invitation au voyage," in *Understanding "Les Fleurs du Mal": Critical Readings*, edited by William J. Thompson, Vanderbilt University Press, 1997, pp. 109–121.

Johnson, Barbara, *Mother Tongues: Sexuality, Trials, Motherhoods, Translation*, Harvard University Press, 2003, p. 82.

Lloyd, Rosemary, *Charles Baudelaire*, Reaktion, 2008.

Moréas, Jean, "The Symbolist Manifesto," in *European Literature from Romanticism to Post-Modernism: A Reader in Aesthetic Practice*, edited by Martin Travers, Continuum International, 2006, pp. 147–49.

Poe, Edgar Allan, "Ulalume," in *The Works of Edgar Allan Poe*, Vol. 2, edited by John Henry Ingram, W. J. Widdleton, 1876, pp. 20–23, http://books.google.com/books?id=4cFEAAAAYAAJ&dq=ulalume%20inauthor%3Apoe&pg=PA20#v=onepage&q=ulalume%20inauthor:poe&f=false (accessed September 20, 2010).

Said, Edward, *Orientalism*, Pantheon, 1978.

Siegel, Jerrold, *Bohemian Paris: Culture, Politics, and the Patterns of Bourgeois Life, 1830–1930*, Johns Hopkins University Press, 1999.

Weir, David, *Decadence and the Making of Modernism*, University of Massachusetts Press, 1995.

FURTHER READING

Baudelaire, Charles, *Intimate Journals*, translated by Charles Isherwood, Random House, 1930.
 Written in his final years and published after his death, the essays in this volume intertwine Baudelaire's political, philosophical, and aesthetic ideas with his personal experience.

Gautier, Théophile, *Short Works of Théophile Gautier*, translated by Lafcadio Hearn, BiblioLife, 2008.
 Gautier was Baudelaire's closest colleague as a poet. This translation by Hearn contains a selection of Gautier's works, including "King Candaules," "Clarimonde," and "The Mummy's Foot."

Hemmings, F. W. J., *Baudelaire the Damned: A Biography*, Scribner, 1982.
 Hemmings compiled a standard biography of Baudelaire.

Lloyd, Rosemary, *Baudelaire's World*, Cornell University Press, 2002.
 Lloyd's work is more of a critical appraisal of Baudelaire's work in all genres than a biography. It concentrates on the influence of earlier writers on Baudelaire.

Porter, Laurence M., *Approaches to Teaching Baudelaire's "Flowers of Evil,"* Modern Language Association of America, 2000.
 The essays in this volume suggest strategies for teaching Baudelaire's poetry to students at various levels in different educational contexts.

SUGGESTED SEARCH TERMS

Charles Baudelaire

Les Fleurs du Mal AND The Flowers of Evil

L'invitation au voyage AND Invitation to the Voyage

decadent movement

symbolists

Baudelaire AND Invitation to the Voyage

Baudelaire AND romanticism

Baudelaire AND French literature

The Flowers of Evil AND Baudelaire

Letter to My Wife

NAZIM HIKMET

1933

"Letter to My Wife" is a free-verse poem by Nazim Hikmet, the most famous Turkish poet of the twentieth century. The poem was written in 1933, while Hikmet was incarcerated in the Bursa prison in Turkey. Hikmet was known for his Communist beliefs, and in March 1933, the book he had published the previous year, *Gece gelen telegraf* (A Telegram Received at Night), was banned. He was arrested two weeks later, charged with spreading Communist propaganda. He received a six-month sentence but was also sentenced to one year's imprisonment on another charge of defaming a prominent Turkish individual in one of his poems. During his imprisonment, he was charged with yet another, much more serious offense. Along with twenty-three others, he was accused of being a member of a Communist organization that was plotting to overthrow the government. The prosecutor sought the death penalty, and Hikmet alludes to his possible execution in the poem. He was released in August 1934 in a general amnesty, having spent sixteen months in prison. The woman to whom the letter is addressed was Piraye Orfi. Although Hikmet refers to her as his wife they were not yet married; they had been living together at the time of his arrest and would marry in 1935.

"Letter to My Wife" is typical of Hikmet's work in that it breaks with Turkish tradition by employing free verse and unusual typography; it is one of many poems Hikmet wrote during the various periods in his life when he was imprisoned.

Nazim Hikmet (AP Images)

Some of these other poems were also inspired by Piraye Orfi. "Letter to My Wife" is available in *Poems of Nazim Hikmet,* translated from the Turkish by Randy Blasing and Mutlu Konuk, published by Persea Books in 2002. It can also be found online at the Web site PoemHunter.com and (in a translation by Fuat Engin) on the online Nazim Hikmet Home Page.

AUTHOR BIOGRAPHY

Hikmet was born in Salonika, now in Greece but then part of the Ottoman Empire, on January 15, 1902. Hikmet's father, Hikmet Bey, was a government official, and the entire family, going back several generations, was part of the Ottoman ruling class. Hikmet grew up in turbulent times. The family moved to Istanbul, and in 1914 the Ottomans entered World War I on the German side. Hikmet, barely a teenager, began writing patriotic poetry. Later in the decade he attended the Turkish naval academy, but he was discharged in 1919. Having no wish to remain in Istanbul, which was under Allied occupation after the war, he traveled in 1921 to Anatolia, in the eastern part of the country, where he worked as a schoolteacher in the small town of Bolu.

In 1922, Hikmet visited Russia, where he attended the University of the Workers of the East in Moscow. The Russian Revolution had taken place only five years earlier, and Hikmet became an enthusiastic supporter of Communism. He returned to Turkey in 1924, where he was soon arrested for working at a progressive magazine.

He escaped to Russia in 1926, where he met the poet Vladimir Mayakovsky, who was to prove a marked influence on Hikmet's work. Under a general amnesty, Hikmet returned to Turkey in 1928.

By the late 1920s, Hikmet had established a formidable reputation as an innovative poet. He published nine books of poetry between 1929 and 1936; he also wrote plays and novels and worked as a journalist, translator, and screenwriter.

Hikmet was arrested in 1933 and convicted for alleged subversive activities. It was while he was in prison that he wrote "Letter to My Wife." The addressee was Piraye Orfi, who would become Hikmet's third wife in 1935. Hikmet was released from prison in 1934. However, he was arrested again in 1938 and sentenced to twenty-eight years in prison for publishing work that allegedly incited the Turkish armed forces to rebel. Hikmet continued to write while imprisoned, and his poems circulated in manuscript form. None of his books were published in Turkey from 1936 until after his death.

Hikmet remained in prison throughout the 1940s. During this time he wrote what is regarded as his masterpiece, the epic poem *Human Landscapes* (published in 1966–1967 and in English translation in 1982). In September 1949, an international committee made up of prominent artists and intellectuals, including French philosopher Jean-Paul Sartre, was formed in Paris to campaign for Hikmet's release. As the campaign intensified, Hikmet went on a hunger strike in prison. He was released in July 1950 as part of a general amnesty. In the same year, Hikmet was awarded the International Peace Prize.

After his release, Hikmet lived with his cousin, Münevver Andaç, having divorced his wife in 1949. Despite his release he was still not safe in his own country, and in 1951 he traveled again to Moscow, where he lived the remainder of his life in exile. During the 1950s he traveled extensively in Europe, Asia, and Africa. Having been stripped of his Turkish citizenship, he acquired Polish citizenship in 1959. Hikmet died of a heart attack on June 3, 1963, at his home in Moscow.

POEM TEXT

My one and only!
Your last letter says:
"My head is throbbing,

my heart is stunned!"
You say: 5
"If they hang you,
         if I lose you,
                  I'll die!"
You'll live, my dear—
my memory will vanish like black smoke
         in the wind.   10
Of course you'll live, red-haired lady of my
         heart:
in the twentieth century
                  grief lasts
                           at most a year.
Death—   15
a body swinging from a rope.
My heart
         can't accept such a death.
But
you can bet   20
         if some poor gypsy's hairy black
                  spidery hand
                           slips a noose
                                    around my neck,
they'll look in vain for fear   25
                  in Nazim's
                           blue eyes!
In the twilight of my last morning
I
will see my friends and you,   30
and I'll go
to my grave
         regretting nothing but an unfinished
    song. . .

My wife!
Good-hearted,   35
golden,
eyes sweeter than honey—my bee!
Why did I write you
                  they want to hang me?
The trial has hardly begun,   40
and they don't just pluck a man's head
                           like a turnip.
Look, forget all this.
If you have any money,
                  buy me some flannel underwear: 45
my sciatica is acting up again.
And don't forget,
a prisoner's wife
                  must always think good thoughts.

POEM SUMMARY

Stanza 1

In the poem "Letter to My Wife," a date and place appears immediately under the title of the poem. This indicates that the poem was written on November 11, 1933, in Bursa Prison.

MEDIA ADAPTATIONS

- *A Tribute to the Poetry of Nazim Hikmet*, by the Abidin Ensemble, is a setting of ten poems by Hikmet, sung in the original Turkish. It was released by Magda on audio CD in 2006.

The poem itself is in the form of a letter sent by a prisoner to his wife. In the first line, the poet expresses his devotion to and affection for his wife. In the next line, he refers to a letter he has received from her, and in lines 3 and 4, he quotes from that letter. His wife wrote about how distressed she was to hear about his situation. This situation is revealed in the next quotation from the wife's letter, in lines 6–8. It appears that the prisoner is in danger of being executed. His wife says in her letter that she herself will die if that happens.

In line 9, the poet tries to reassure her. He says that she will not die if he is executed. She will continue to live, and she will soon forget him. He refers to her in an affectionate way that reveals his love for her, but then he comments in a general way about the times in which they live: grief does not last long for anyone.

Stanza 2

In stanza 2, the poet describes death by hanging, but he says that he cannot really believe with his heart that such a fate awaits him. He refuses to accept such a notion. However, in lines 19–27, he states that should such an execution take place—and he imagines the hand of the executioner putting the noose around his neck—any witnesses present will not see any fear in his eyes. He continues (beginning with line 28), by saying that as time expires on his last morning he will see his wife and friends. He probably means that he will see them in his mind's eye. He says he will go to his death with no regrets, except for the fact that there were still things he wanted to do with his life.

Stanza 3

In stanza 3, he addresses his wife directly and compliments her. He praises her qualities of heart, and her eyes, which draw him like a bee is drawn to honey. In lines 38–42, the poet reveals why his wife wrote to him, concerned that he might be executed. It was he who told her about the possibility of this execution, he says, and now he seems to regret that he ever mentioned it to her. He says that the trial has only just begun and implies that not only do such trials take time but also a sentence of hanging is not rendered without serious deliberation.

In the next line (line 43), the poet tells his wife to forget such matters. He switches the topic to more mundane, everyday things. He tells her that if she can afford it, she should buy him some flannel underwear; he thinks it might alleviate his sciatica (pain from an inflamed nerve). He finishes the letter by telling his wife that she should be positive and cheerful in her thoughts.

THEMES

Love

One theme of "Letter to My Wife" is love between a man and his wife. The couple in the poem are deeply concerned about each other. They have written to each other more than once since the man's imprisonment. The husband has confided his worst fears to his wife, and she has responded with fear and distress about his possible fate. She feels she cannot go on living without him. In the letter that constitutes the poem, the writer more than once expresses his love for his wife. This is apparent in the first line, in which he refers to the unique, and presumably indispensable, relationship he has with her. It is also noticeable in the term of affection he uses about her in line 11. In stanza 3 he pays her many compliments and makes clear that he is in love with her. He regrets saying something in his previous letter that caused her to worry. The love presented is an ideal kind of marital love, in which each person is concerned for the welfare of the other. If the husband is in a desperate situation, the love he feels for his wife helps him to survive and to face whatever lies ahead.

Courage

The theme of courage appears mostly in the second stanza. The poet first creates a vivid image of a hanging, in line 16, and then elaborates on it in lines 19–24. He imagines the moment the noose is placed around his neck, assuring his wife that he will show no fear. Although in lines 17 and 18 he points out that he is not resigned to such a death, by the end of the stanza he is saying that should death come to him in such a manner, he will have no regrets about his conduct in life or about whatever he did that led to his death sentence.

Optimism

Although the situation in which the poet finds himself could hardly be called encouraging or hopeful, he shows that he can maintain an optimistic attitude. He reassures his wife that she will be quite able to live without him. He writes in an optimistic tone throughout, and his final piece of advice to his wife is that as the wife of an imprisoned man she must maintain positive rather than negative thoughts about the situation.

Grief

Although the poem is primarily personal, about a man on trial for his life who is writing a message to his wife, there is one line in which the poet makes reference to the wider situation in which they both live. Whereas she has told him she would feel unimaginable grief should he die, he tells her this is not so. She will quickly forget him, as grief in the twentieth century does not last for more than a year. This is an enigmatic comment, but Hikmet may be alluding to the violence of the twentieth century, even though he was writing when only one-third of the century had passed. He may be referring to the huge loss of life in World War I, in which about sixteen million people died. This was still strongly in people's memories in the 1930s. Perhaps he is saying that untimely or violent death is so common that people are almost getting used to it.

Imprisonment

The letter, in the form of a poem, is written from the speaker's prison cell. The reality is that he is in confinement and is being put through the judicial system of his country. His trial has just begun, and he faces possible execution. However, he says nothing about whatever charge has been brought against him, nothing of whether he is innocent or guilty. He does not speculate on whether he will receive a fair trial. What the letter-poem strongly suggests is that the fact of imprisonment does not have to determine how a man feels. Inner qualities, such as courage, love, and optimism, as well as cheerfulness, are more important than restrictions

TOPICS FOR FURTHER STUDY

- Write a free-verse poem addressed to an absent relative or friend, imagining that you are in a difficult situation somewhere and need to contact, and reassure, someone you love. Read some of Hikmet's poems to his wife for inspiration. There is no need to stick to a real situation you have been in; feel free to use your imagination.

- As a global ideology, Communism is now largely a spent force, but during much of the twentieth century, millions of people in China, the Soviet Union, North Korea, Cuba, and Eastern Europe lived under Communist regimes. Research the history of twentieth-century Communism in the Soviet Union. Bear in mind that Hikmet, a man who was committed to freedom and social justice, remained a Communist all his life and lived his last thirteen years in Russia. With a group of students, make a class presentation, using PowerPoint or similar digital presentation technology, that describes the goals and theory of Communism and the extent to which the Soviet Union lived up to those goals. What were the main differences between what Communism promised in theory and what it delivered in practice? Include charts and graphs in your presentation.

- *The Honorable Prison*, by Lyli Becerra de Jenkins (1988), is a young-adult novel that uses as its background political repression in

South America. An entire family is imprisoned because the father writes magazine articles attacking the military government. Read the novel and write an essay in which you compare the story of the family with that of Hikmet in Turkey.

- What are human rights? Read the Universal Declaration of Human Rights, adopted by the United Nations in 1948, while Hikmet was imprisoned. Then go to PEN American Center's "Writers in Peril" Web page (www.pen.org/viewmedia.php/prmMID/773/prmID/172) for an account of the recent treatment in Turkey of the publisher, Ragip Zarakolu. Write an entry in your Web log that points out that human rights for writers, journalists, and publishers remain an issue in Turkey, sixty years after Hikmet was released. What parallels do you see between Hikmet's experiences with the Turkish authorities and the current treatment of Zarakolu?

- Read some other poems by Hikmet that are addressed to his wife. Examples include "Hymn to Life," "Letters from a Man in Solitary," and "I Want to Die Before You," available at www.poemhunter.com. Choose one poem you like, and write an essay in which you compare and contrast it with "Letter to My Wife." In what senses do the poems resemble each other? How do they differ?

---

imposed on a man from without. He is still in charge of how he feels about what is happening to him, even though he may have no power to influence the outcome.

STYLE

Free Verse

The poem is written in free verse. Free verse does not observe any traditional poetic form; it does

not depend on rhyme or meter (the rhythm of a poem's syllables). Instead, the poet uses other means to create the effects desired. A feature of much free verse, which is highly noticeable in this poem, is variation in the lengths of the lines. Five of the lines consist of only one word, and in two of these cases (lines 19 and 29), the line break comes where one might least expect it. Seven lines consist of only two words. In contrast, many of the lines are much longer. The longest is line 10, which contains thirteen syllables, amounting to six poetic feet. (A foot consists of

Letter to my wife (Dewayne Flowers | Shutterstock.com)

two or three syllables, with one or more being stressed and the others unstressed.)

In the way the poem appears on the page, it does not employ the traditional straight left-hand margin but instead opts for variety in the placement of the lines. A notable example occurs in lines 20–24, where each line begins further to the right than the previous line. Some lines begin immediately below where the previous lines end; examples include lines 17 and 18, lines 32 and 33, and lines 38 and 39, as well as the final two lines of the poem. By using this technique, the poet gains maximum variety in how the poem appears on the printed page.

Imagery, Simile, and Metaphor

The poet employs figurative language on a number of occasions. When he tells his wife that her grief for him, should he be executed, will not last long, he uses a simile, comparing memory to smoke that disappears in the wind. A simile occurs when one object or abstract quality is compared to another dissimilar thing using *like* or *as* in a way that brings out a resemblance between the two.

The poet uses the metaphor of a bee to describe his relationship with his wife. The metaphor works because bees are drawn to honey, and the poet, seeking words to describe the attraction he feels toward his wife, states that her eyes are sweeter than honey. He means that her eyes are the honey to his bee. (The poet seems to be referring to his wife as the bee, but the metaphor works better if he himself is the metaphorical bee.) Elsewhere, the poet uses strong visual images, such as that of the body of a hanged man and the hangman placing the noose around the condemned man's neck.

Diction

Mixed in with the poetic imagery is a more conversational tone and the use of colloquial diction. This is especially apparent in the second half of the final stanza, when the poet tells his wife to forget the difficult topic of his possible execution and concentrate on some mundane matters instead.

HISTORICAL CONTEXT

Turkish History, 1914–1940

The Ottoman Empire entered World War I in 1914 on the side of the Central Powers, or Triple Alliance (Germany, Austria-Hungary, and the Ottoman Empire). After the victory of the Allied powers (principally Great Britain, France, and Russia), the Ottoman Empire was partitioned. This was accomplished by the Treaty of Sèvres in 1920, which Turkey was forced to sign. Under the treaty, Greece was given territorial gains at Turkey's expense. Istanbul (then Constantinople) was occupied by the Allies. Turkish dissatisfaction at the terms of the treaty produced a nationalist independence movement led by Mustafa Kemal (later known as Kemal Atatürk). In the resulting war of independence, which lasted from 1919 to 1922, Turkey drove the Greeks from Izmir (also known as Smyrna) and secured favorable terms from the Allies in the Treaty of Lausanne in 1923. Turkey regained Eastern Thrace from Greece, and Britain agreed to withdraw from Istanbul. On October 23, 1923, Turkey proclaimed itself a republic, and Kemal became its first president.

For the remainder of the decade, Kemal embarked on an ambitious program of reform aimed at transforming Turkey into a secular rather than Islamic state. He reformed the education system, replacing religious with secular schools, and replaced Islamic law with a secular civil code. He also extended political rights to women and moved the capital city from Istanbul to Ankara.

In the first few years of the new republic, there was a certain amount of political freedom and freedom of the press. It was at this time, after his return from Moscow in 1924, that Hikmet was contributing to *Aydinlik*, the official Turkish Communist Party magazine in Istanbul. However, in 1925, the political situation in Turkey began to change as a result of a rebellion by Kurds in Turkey's eastern provinces who wanted to reassert the influence of Islamic law in Turkey, in opposition to Kemal's secular government. The revolt was put down within two months, and its leader was executed. Using the rebellion as a pretext, the government began to repress its political opponents. Kemal banned the opposition Progressive Republican Party

and closed down five newspapers in Istanbul. Newspaper editors, including editors and staff of *Aydinlik*, were arrested, and some were put on trial, accused of undermining the government. Nearly fifty members of the Communist Party and other left-wing organizations were also arrested. Hikmet fled to Izmir to avoid arrest but was sentenced in his absence to fifteen years in prison. In September 1925 he escaped to Moscow. In 1926, following a conspiracy to assassinate Kemal, there was more extensive repression in Turkey, and a number of people were executed in public.

The events of 1925 set the entire tone for Hikmet's future relations with the Turkish state. Although he had, naturally enough, supported the Turkish cause in the war of independence, he had become disillusioned with Kemal's movement as early as 1921. This occurred after the murder of Mustafa Suphi, a prominent Communist leader, and up to fifteen members of the Turkish Communist Party as they crossed the Black Sea on a diplomatic mission. According to Hikmet's biographers, Saime Göksu and Edward Timms, in *Romantic Communist: The Life and Work of Nazim Hikmet*, the full details of the crime were never brought to light, but Hikmet blamed the Kemal government for dragging its heels in prosecuting one of the principal suspects, Yahya Kahya, who was later tried but acquitted. The murder of Suphi, according to Göksu and Timms, "made a profound impression on Nazim [Hikmet], hastening his disillusionment with the Kemalist regime, and Mustafa Suphi became one of his heroes."

By the late 1920s, Kemal had solidified his hold on power; his control of the National Assembly could not be challenged. According to historians A. J. Grant and Harold Temperley in their book *Europe in the Nineteenth and Twentieth Centuries, 1789–1950*, Kemal Atatürk was "ruthless in his suppression of all opposition, particularly in the early days of his régime. His methods were undoubtedly those of a dictator." (The Turkish leader added the honorific name Atatürk, meaning "Father of the Turks," in 1934.) Grant and Temperley quote a comment made by Atatürk himself in 1932:

> Let the people leave politics alone for the present. Let them interest themselves in agriculture and commerce. For ten or fifteen years more I must rule. After that perhaps I may be able to let them speak openly.

COMPARE
&
CONTRAST

- **1930s:** Turkey is a sovereign state under the strong, if dictatorial, leadership of Kemal Atatürk. It is the first time in two hundred years that Turkey has not been subject to interference by other nations. Turning his back on Turkey's Islamic tradition, Atatürk pursues a policy of secularization and Westernization.

  Today: Turkey is a multiparty parliamentary democracy. Almost all Turkey's citizens are Muslim, but its government is secular, and the nation continues to identify with the West. In 2005, Turkey applies to join the European Union, and negotiations continue as of 2010. Turkey is also a member of the North Atlantic Treaty Organization, the Western military alliance, and maintains close relations with the United States.

- **1930s:** As they did in the 1920s, the Kurds in Turkey rebel against the Turkish government. Revolts in 1930 and 1937 are suppressed by the Turkish army. Kurdish areas are put under martial law; hundreds of thousands of Kurds are deported or killed.

  Today: Like their predecessors in the 1930s, recent Turkish governments have had to deal with a militant Kurdish separatist movement. The insurgency ended in 1999 but resumed in 2004. In an incident in 2010, Kurdish militants belonging to the Kurdistan Workers Party, or PKK, kill six Turkish soldiers near the border with Iraq. The PKK campaigns for an independent Kurdistan state. It is regarded as a terrorist organization by the United States. There are nearly twelve million Kurds in Turkey, which amounts to about 18 percent of the population.

- **1930s:** Hikmet employs modern politics as a theme in poetry and introduces free verse for the first time in Turkish poetry. This is in contrast to traditional Turkish folk poetry, which observes a formal meter.

  Today: Prominent Turkish poets include Sabit Ince (b. 1945), Enis Batur (b. 1952), Haydar Ergulen (b. 1956), Lale Müldür (b. 1956), Ahmet Yalçnkaya (b. 1963), and Mehmet Erte (b. 1978).

Göksu and Timms emphasize that although Turkey at this time was a dictatorship, many left-wing intellectuals embraced some of Atatürk's reforms, which included changes in language. The traditional Arabic characters were replaced with the Latin alphabet. Hikmet, however, refused to compromise his political beliefs and as a Communist continued to oppose the Westernizing policies of the Atatürk government.

Atatürk was not to be granted his desire for ten or fifteen more years of rule. He died in November 1938, a few months after Hikmet was sentenced to twenty-eight years in prison, in spite of his direct personal appeal to the president for clemency. Several other Communist activists also received long sentences in Turkey in the late 1930s. This was in keeping with developments elsewhere in Europe at the time, including the triumph of fascism in Italy and Spain and that of National Socialism in Germany. Although when World War II broke out in 1939, Turkey declared its neutrality, the passing of a National Defense Law in 1940, which gave the government emergency powers, offered Turkey's political prisoners little hope for clemency.

CRITICAL OVERVIEW

Hikmet established himself as an innovative poet of radical views during the late 1920s and 1930s. In Turkey, he was an extremely popular poet. His biographers Göksu and Timms point out that he was the first Turkish poet to introduce

Hikmet fears a gypsy will hang him (boumen&japet / Shutterstock.com)

"the language of modern politics" into poetry. They further comment that "the impact of these revolutionary new themes is reinforced by a new poetic style shot through with irony and dissonance, disrupting the melodious rhythms of Ottoman diction with the rugged irregularity of its lines." However, because of his persecution, no poetry by Hikmet was published in Turkey from 1936 until after his death. During this time he was published extensively abroad, in Bulgaria, Greece, Germany, Italy, and the Soviet Union. After his death, his work began to be published again in Turkey; during the 1960s and 1970s, almost all of his works were either reprinted or published for the first time there. Unfortunately, military coups in Turkey in 1971 and again in 1980 resulted in more repressive policies, and Hikmet's poetry was again banned. In subsequent decades, however, he once more emerged as a revered figure. Göksu and Timms describe him as "a kind of Turkish national poet" and comment that "it is not simply Nazim's

personal courage but the imaginative power of his writings that gives his work its enduring value."

Hikmet's work first became available to English-speaking readers in the 1960s. His *Selected Poems*, translated by Taner Baybars, was published in London in 1967, and other translations followed during the 1970s and 1980s. In 2002, to mark the one-hundredth anniversary of Hikmet's birth, *Poems of Nazim Hikmet*, a translation of his work by Randy Blasing and Mutlu Konuk, first published in 1994, was expanded and reissued. In the foreword to that volume, American poet Carolyn Forché, noting how much time Hikmet spent in prison or exile, comments that he "is one of the twentieth century's strongest voices of the carceral imagination and exilic being." Forché also notes that Hikmet "is in love with life in its fecundity, complexity, beauty, and horror; to live, for him, is a *solemn duty* and he excoriates himself for fleeting moments of self-pity." A contributor to *Publishers Weekly* comments that the translations in this volume capture the "power and originality of the work. . . . As Hikmet grew, he delivered a richness and humanity unparalleled in its freedom from bitterness."

It was testimony to the esteem in which Hikmet's work is held that another English translation of his poetry was published in that same centenary year. This was *Beyond the Walls: Selected Poems*, translated by Richard McKane and others. In a review for *Booklist*, Ray Olson comments, "Hikmet is best . . . when he is singing the beauties of Turkey, the Turks, his wives . . . and his friends."

CRITICISM

Bryan Aubrey

Aubrey holds a Ph.D. in English. In the following essay, he discusses Hikmet's "Letter to My Wife" in the context of Hikmet's life and the many other poems he wrote to Piraye Orfi.

Nazim Hikmet was nineteen years old when he made the decision, in 1921, to join the Turkish Communist Party. He knew at the time that this was a dangerous direction to take. It could have cost him his freedom and possibly even his life, but Hikmet was a man who had the courage of his convictions, and he remained a committed Communist for his entire life. The more than

WHAT DO I READ NEXT?

- Hikmet wrote his greatest work in prison during the 1940s, but it was not published until the 1960s. It is available in English as *Human Landscapes from My Country: An Epic Novel in Verse*, translated by Randy Blasing and Mutlu Konuk (2009). This book presents the lives of ordinary Turkish people from all walks of life and social classes. Hikmet has empathy for them in their joys, sorrows, and heroism. The novel also clearly reveals the suffering and trials that Hikmet himself endured during his imprisonment.

- "To Althea, from Prison" is a love poem published in 1649 by Sir Richard Lovelace (1618–1657), a seventeenth-century English poet. Lovelace fought on the Royalist side in the English Civil War and was imprisoned. He wrote the poem in 1642 during his imprisonment. The identity of Althea, the woman to whom the poem is addressed, is unknown. The poem can be found in Lovelace's *Lucasta Poems* (2010).

- "The Prisoner of Chillon" is a verse narrative by English romantic poet George Gordon Byron (1788–1827). Written in 1816, it is one of Lord Byron's most popular poems. It is narrated by the sole prisoner in a castle dungeon in Chillon, in Geneva, Switzerland. Byron visited the castle and was inspired to write the poem after being told the story on which the poem is based: in the sixteenth century, a monk named François Bonivard, the sole survivor of a family that had been martyred, was imprisoned in the dungeon for four years. The poem can be found in Byron's *Selected Poems*, edited by Susan J. Wolfson and Peter J. Manning (2006).

- *First Annual Nazim Hikmet Poetry Festival: A Chapbook of Talks and Poetry* (2009) contains readings and talks from the first-annual Nazim Hikmet Poetry Festival, which was held in April 2009 in North Carolina. The book includes commentary by the North Carolina poet laureate Katherine Stripling Byer and articles on Hikmet's life and poetry by Greg Dawes and Erdag Goknar. Also included are ten poems from the poetry competition, by Judy Light Ayyildiz, Katherine Barnes, Jeffery Beam, David Need, Pamela Richardson, Christopher Salerno, Tony Tost, Chris Vitiello, Guney Acipayamli, and Mimi Herman.

- In *Lost Childhood: My Life in a Japanese Prison Camp during World War II* (2008), Annelex Hofstra Layson tells of the three and a half years she spent as a child in Japanese prison camps during World War II. She was only four years old in 1942 when the Japanese invaded the island of Java in the Dutch East Indies (now Indonesia). She and her family were sent to prison camps. In this young-adult memoir, written sixty years after the events it relates, Layson tells of the horrors that she and other prisoners endured. The book is aimed at young readers with the goal of giving hope to those who have been affected by war and to inspire young people to work for peace.

- *The Courage to Stand Alone: Letters from Prison and Other Writings* (1997), by Wei Jingsheng, is a collection of letters by an imprisoned Chinese dissident who is an advocate for democracy. Wei was arrested in 1978, and he wrote these letters during the first fifteen years of his imprisonment. They present Wei's views on a range of subjects, including human rights. The letters, edited and translated by Kristina M. Torgeson, are addressed to family members as well as government officials. Wei was released in 1993 but then quickly jailed again until 1997, when he was released and deported to the United States. These letters show that the harsh conditions he endured in prison did not break his spirit.

thirteen years he spent in prison did not cause him to rethink his core beliefs. Even in Russia in the 1950s and 1960s, when the repressive, totalitarian nature of the Soviet Union was readily apparent, Hikmet remained in the Communist fold. This did not stop him, however, from raising his voice against some of the injustices he saw around him. The great Russian poet Yevgeny Yevtushenko, who knew Hikmet in the 1950s, wrote in his preface to *Romantic Communist: The Life and Work of Nazim Hikmet*, by Saime Göksu and Edward Timms, "[Hikmet] spoke out boldly on any topic, criticised the authorities, and defended talented people who were being persecuted."

It is clear from Yevtushenko's account that in Russia, Hikmet remained true to the ideals he had adopted as a young man in Turkey. Readers in the United States, where the words *Communist* and *Communism* have always had a bad odor, may need to make a leap of imagination to understand that in the early 1920s, to many idealistic young men in the poorer parts of Europe, as well as to intellectuals, Communism represented the prospect of a bright new dawn for the human race. It held out the hope of a society in which justice, fairness, and prosperity were open to all. A parallel to this belief might be found in the enthusiasm with which young poets in England and elsewhere greeted the French Revolution in 1789, which seemed to promise a great new era of justice and freedom. So it was for many of the politically minded in the early 1920s, before the Communist system in Russia had solidified, under Joseph Stalin (1878–1953), into a rigid, totalitarian government that brooked no opposition. When Hikmet first arrived in Moscow in 1921, the excitement of

new beginnings was in the air, and all branches of the arts—film, poetry, dance, art, theater— were flourishing. As Yevtushenko describes it, "Nazim found himself amidst the convulsive post-revolutionary artistic renaissance that made haste to flower, sensing instinctively the tragic brevity of its blossoming."

While in Russia, Hikmet studied the writings of Karl Marx (1818–1883) and Friedrich Engels (1820–1895), both important Communist thinkers, but he appears never to have concerned himself greatly with abstract doctrines and theories. He was more interested in dramatizing his political causes through poetry and theater. The young man who returned to his homeland and walked the streets of Istanbul in the 1920s was constantly questioning established opinions; he was a passionate man of the arts possessed of deep emotions and enthusiasms, a lover of life, literature, and women, as well as social justice.

With his good looks and charismatic manner, Hikmet did not have difficulty attracting female company. He first met Piraye Orfi, who was to become the addressee of his "Letter to My Wife," in 1928 or 1929. As Saime Göksu and Edward Timms explain in their biography of the poet, Orfi was a friend of Hikmet's sister, Samiye. She came from a wealthy family and was married with two children, but she had separated from her husband. One of the most noticeable things about Orfi was her red hair, to which Hikmet would draw attention in his poems. According to Göksu and Timms, Orfi was "rather reserved and formal with a strong personality and a progressive outlook." Although she had not had a university education, she was a highly intelligent woman, and Hikmet soon came to value her artistic judgments. For over a year beginning in 1932, they lived together in a large old villa near Istanbul, along with Hikmet's sister and brother-in-law and five members of Orfi's family, including one of her sons. Their happiness was interrupted in 1933 by Hikmet's arrest and imprisonment, which would place a long shadow over their relationship for the next seventeen years.

In November 1933, when Hikmet wrote "Letter to My Wife," he was on trial and facing a possible death sentence, and his grisly images of a hanging in the poem suggest that he took such a possibility very seriously. The actual conditions of his imprisonment at this time, however, were not too severe. Along with thirty-five other political

Hikmet explains the trial to his wife (*Mark Payne / Shutterstock.com*)

prisoners, he was kept apart from the general prison population, and the men organized themselves along the lines of their Communist principles: food rations were shared equally, and those who had food sent to them by relatives and friends shared what they received. Hikmet organized an educational program and continued to write poetry. Released in 1934, he married Orfi the following year, and it seems that for a few years they knew happiness together. The poem "Hymn to Life," written in 1937, is a sensual celebration of the love he felt for his red-haired wife. Life took a darker turn for their relationship, however, when Hikmet was arrested and jailed again in 1938. He was to endure twelve years in prison, and over the next decade he would address many of his poems to his wife. It appears that she was his inspiration, helping him to maintain his spirits and his optimism. The memory of her gave him the will to go on.

For a period of months in 1938, Hikmet was kept in solitary confinement. In his poem "Letters from a Man in Solitary," which was written at that time, he addresses his wife with endearments and tells her that he has carved her name on the band of his wristwatch using his fingernail. In

"On Death Again," a poem written a year later, he confesses to her that he is once again brooding on death, and he wonders which of them will die first, and where. He knows they may be far apart when it happens. He consoles himself with the knowledge that they have loved each other and have fought in the cause of the people.

In the early 1940s the poems to Orfi, written in Hikmet's characteristic free-verse, conversational style, continued to come. "Letter from Chankiri Prison," written at various times during 1940, is full of warm memories of Orfi and reminiscences; they would read poetry together; he has a photograph of her, and he asks her not to forget him. In "Letter from My Wife," he turns the tables and writes an imaginary love letter from Orfi to him, in which she envisions that in death their ashes will mingle in the earth, and perhaps one day a wild flower will spring up with two stems. Most notable of all the Orfi poems, perhaps, are "9–10 p.m. Poems," a collection of thirty-two short poems, each one dated at some point between late September and mid-December 1945. These are searingly honest poems, almost all of them addressed directly to Orfi, and it is impossible not to be moved by them. Hikmet presents himself in all his human contradictions and in the ebb and flow of different moods. Sometimes he admits to self-pity, but more often he rises above it, ready to greet the freshness of life in each moment. In the richness of their imagery and the tenderness and depth of feeling they record, these poems may remind readers of Pablo Neruda's *Cien soneto de amor* (One Hundred Love Sonnets), which the Chilean poet wrote to his wife and published in 1960.

The story of Hikmet and Orfi, however, did not have a happy ending. Although more love poems flowed from Hikmet's pen in the late 1940s, they were not for Orfi. Instead, Hikmet's attention turned to a younger woman, Münevver Andaç, whom he had first met in 1935. She visited him in prison in 1948, and Hikmet found himself so drawn to her that he conveyed to Orfi that their marriage could not continue. The reader who comes upon the poem Hikmet wrote in 1950, "After Getting Out of Prison," and is unaware of Hikmet's life story at this point can be forgiven for thinking that the wife who lies by Hikmet's side and is pregnant with their child is Orfi, but in fact the poet is referring to Andaç.

Although Hikmet's relationship with Orfi did not survive the strains of his long imprisonment, the many poems he wrote to his red-haired wife remain—a permanent testament in art to feelings that sometimes prove all too transient in life.

Source: Bryan Aubrey, Critical Essay on "Letter to My Wife," in *Poetry for Students*, Gale, Cengage Learning, 2011.

Mutlu Konuk Blasing

In the following excerpt, Blasing compares Hikmet and Ezra Pound in terms of modernist poetry.

POETRY AND THE STATE

This is Ezra Pound in Washington, D.C., in 1945: "If I ain't worth more alive than dead, that's that. If a man isn't willing to take some risk for his opinions, either his opinions are no good or he's no good" (qtd. in O'Connor 5). One takes a risk in speaking one's opinions, and Pound casts such risk-taking as a moral test of the value of one's opinions *and* of one's character. Not usually shy of asserting that he's speaking truth, Pound here settles for "opinions": the moral good is not a function of Truth. The question is: where does

ONE DOES NOT ANALYZE A POLITICS BY ITS POETICS. AESTHETICS AND POLITICS HAVE TO BE KEPT DISTINCT SO THAT WE CAN JUDGE THEIR SEPARATE OPERATIONS."

poetry belong in this configuration of character, political opinions, and the risk of speech that would test the moral value of both?

Pound made this statement while awaiting trial on charges of treason for his Radio Rome broadcasts in support of Mussolini—and Hitler—during the war. He had first been held in an Army Disciplinary Training Center (DTC) outside Pisa from May to November 1945, then flown to the US. An insanity plea kept his case from coming to trial, but at the price of a twelve-and-a-half-year stay at St. Elizabeths federal mental hospital in Washington.

Nazim Hikmet, who invented modern poetry in Turkish, also took a risk for his opinions, went through two military trials—unprecedented for a civilian—behind closed doors, and was sentenced to twenty-eight years in prison. The charge against him was inciting army and navy cadets to revolt, based on the "evidence" that his books—perfectly legal and freely sold in bookstores at the time of the trials in 1938—were discovered in some cadets' lockers. His thirteen-year stretch in prison for voicing his communist opinions overlaps with Pound's incarceration in Pisa and then at St. Elizabeths between 1945 and 1958. So also do the two poets' stories overlap.

Both poets considered themselves true patriots; both were ultimately charged with treason; and free speech was the issue in both cases. Pound's Radio Rome broadcasts are largely incoherent ravings about bankers and finance capital—"international wandering Loan Capital" (March 15, 1942)—metonymically collapsed into virulent anti-Semitism and mixed with invectives against Roosevelt and Churchill. "There's an idea afloat here that I have betrayed this country," Pound said in Washington; "If that damned fool idea is still in anybody's head, I want to wipe it out.... What I want to know is whether anybody heard my broadcasts and, if so, how they could have any earthly idea of what I was talking about" (qtd. in Torrey 178–79). How indeed?

Pound's anti-Semitism is absolutely indefensible, but his insistence as an American citizen on his constitutional right to free speech is defensible. Also, as Richard Sieburth puts it, the speeches are "morally unconscionable but technically not treasonable" (xi). Of course, the American Army was no more imperiled by Pound's speeches than the Turkish Army had been by Nazim's books when military courts sentenced him to twenty-eight years. I bring up Pound alongside Nazim, because the *Pisan Cantos* were written largely at the DTC, in the company of common criminals—thieves, rapists, and murderers, as well as the AWOL and the deserters who made up the majority. Pound was the only civilian at the DTC, a camp housing some 3,600 inmates. In this, the only integrated camp in the Mediterranean Theatre, most of the prisoners were black (Sieburth xii–xiii, xix), and Pound incorporated the prisoners' language into his text, performing such amazing feats as moving from "saeculorum Athenae / *glaux, glaukopis,* / olivi / that which gleams and then does not gleam" to "everyone of them g.d.m.f. generals / c.s. all of 'em fascists" in twelve lines (74: 438–39). He invented a new textual space in Canto 74, where a black prisoner judging the generals to be fascists in a string of bleeped words is heard in Pound's textual utopia of gods and goddesses, their monumentality reaffirmed with their Latin epithets and their attendant train of Greek script. This new kind of openness to extra-textual history is generally read as marking the postmodern turn of the *Cantos*, redirecting the course of American poetry after 1950.

Nazim invented a new language in prison. His epic, *Human Landscapes from My Country*, written in Bursa Prison, hosts the life stories of his fellow inmates and a variety of other stories, regional idioms and folk sayings he heard from the prisoners. He takes the measure of these various materials and the ongoing "live" talk among diverse characters in his poetic lines, where we also hear the conversations of just about everyone concerned with the course of WWII, including prisoners and guards airing their views of Hitler, and Nazim's protagonist—who is not a poet—lecturing on Karl Marx and his economic theories. Nazim's poem has more than 300 live characters on stage—or screen, for movies provided one model for the poem, along with *War and Peace*, which he translated for the Ministry of Education while in prison,

and, surprisingly, William Langland's "Piers Plowman," which he came across in a history of English literature.

In confinement, the poets were left alone with their resources as poets, even as those resources were put to the test when they were exposed to people and lives with which they would not otherwise have had contact. I am not arguing that prison is good for poets; I am calling attention to how serving time in prison served these two poets and how it reshaped their poetry to give us works that were hugely influential in the course of the history of poetry in their languages—and beyond. During the war, Pound wrote only two cantos—the so-called Italian cantos, 72 and 73, celebrating fascism (Torrey 171). In the six months he spent at the DTC, he drafted the Pisan cantos. Olga Rudge's response was: "I felt it the best thing they could have done for the *Cantos*, to shut you up for a while." Although some passages that ended up in the *Pisan Cantos* were conceived before Pisa, the *Cantos* changed course with the insertion of Pound's current experience. While the form of the poem, Pound explained, had its "inner shape," "the life of the D.T.C. passing OUTSIDE the scheme cannot but impinge, or break into the main flow" (O. Pound 177). Neither was Nazim writing much poetry after 1936, which, according to Hikmet Kıvılcımlı, put him in such a paranoid state of panic (92) that a rash act on his part—in effect informing the police about an army cadet seeking him out—ended up putting the army on his trail. But once in prison, he wrote his best work.

Moreover, Pound owes his influence on American poetry in part to his holding court at St. Elizabeths for years, "educating" a younger generation of poets. Similarly, Nazim would not have the status he has both in and outside Turkey if prison had not sequestered him from the polemics and petty quarrels of the Istanbul literary scene and exposed him to the masses, now no longer a theoretical abstraction. He was already a famous poet when he went to prison, but he became a public figure in a different sense—an embodiment not only of a radical political vision of justice, but also of all that was wrong with the new Turkish Republic and how it conducted itself, inventing *ex post facto* civil laws to keep Nazim in prison. Pound also became a public figure in a similar "different" sense, as he came to serve as the locus of ideological debates—both political and cultural—at the time. Ironically, their governments' attempts to curb the poets' power in effect granted them a public presence—a more than poetic presence—that they would not have had otherwise.

When Nazim's writing was banned from publication and he was consigned to the company of a prison audience of mostly peasants, he had to re-imagine his poetry, as he had to re-conceive his audience. And like Pound, Nazim also turned prison into an academy, teaching basic literacy, French, philosophy, literature, painting, political thought and current events. Inmates in Bursa Prison remember regular classes he taught on dialectical materialism (Göksu and Timms 263). But prisons at the time were also the center of intellectual life in Turkey, and he educated a generation of Turkish artists and writers, some of whom were incarcerated for reading his books. Exuberant, assertive, egocentric yet generous, Nazim—like Pound—had a presence that attracted all who knew him.

Remarkably, for years neither poet made a concentrated effort to get out; incarceration became a sad kind of patronage. Pound was very comfortable at St. Elizabeths; not only did he not try to get out, but he even resisted others' efforts to free him. For example, he rejected, in 1955, one plan for his release by demanding "complete exoneration and a conversion of official America to the views he expressed on Rome Radio." A frustrated T. S. Eliot concluded: "Pound does not want to accept freedom on any terms that are possible" (Torrey 256). Nazim eventually went on a hunger strike—but only after enduring twelve years of prison with the knowledge that no case whatsoever had been made against him. Was he doing some kind of penance?

Although Nazim did not engage in any communist activities or propaganda, or attempt to force his views on anyone, his writings caused far more collateral damage than Pound's. Nazim's lawyer, Mehmet Ali Sebük, who finally engineered his release, writes: "Hundreds, thousands of young men lost their freedom for reading and praising his work" (58). This responsibility, of which Nazim could not have been unaware, might go toward answering the question he posed to Sebük after thirteen years inside: "How is it that I stood for this injustice?" (81). As Sebük says, "They had put him in a coffin and watched and waited for him to die" (265). And he took it for thirteen years.

Ideologically worlds apart, Pound and Nazim understood their poetry as a political project. For both, poetry was the highest art; they had the loftiest conception of their art. At the same time, they held the broadest understanding of the form and function of poetry and wrote epics that host the history that includes them. Nazim's poem has a further turn, for he incorporates his "Epic of the Independence War," a separate story of heroic episodes in the war against the occupying Allied armies, into the larger epic of *Human Landscapes*. In Book II, a waiter reads aloud the "Epic of the Independence War" to the dining car staff on the Istanbul-Ankara Express, from a hand-copied manuscript attributed only to "a poet in prison." The anonymity and the fact that both the "Epic" within *Human Landscapes* and *Human Landscapes* itself circulated in manuscript form invoke the tradition of epic poems circulating communal knowledge orally through changing reciters and scribes and accruing historical layers as they are transmitted, copied and recopied, cited and recited. Nazim positions the epic as a collective cultural product, rather than as a story that transpires in the "wilds of one man's mind," and he is not present in the poem—neither as an "ego scriptor" nor as an epic hero. Nazim's collective audience is not all in his head, or in his conversations with poets past. The difference between *Human Landscapes* and the *Cantos* lies not only in their poetic content but in how or where poetry is located: in one man's mind or in the social fabric.

Putting the two poets side by side forces us to question the relationship between the new poetry and radical politics—whether fascist or communist—in the early twentieth century. We have to either bracket political content to focus on "modernist" poetic forms, or bracket forms to address political content. With both poets in focus, we cannot stabilize the relationship between formal practices and political values. Nor can we lose sight of either politics or poetry, because the consequences of their politics affected the forms of their poetry. If politics is seen as the ground, formal practices that marked the poets' historical importance in their different languages and literatures lose their significance—if not their relevance altogether. If form is the ground, politics wobbles and becomes harmless, which it certainly was not. We have to keep the politics and the poetry separate and acknowledge the power each holds in its own right, as well as over each other. We have to think of the ground-figure relations in each case on a model somewhat like Yeatsian interpenetrating gyres—"One gyre within the other always"—as antinomies: "Dying each other's life, living each other's death" (300). In Yeats's model, as one vortex widens its circle, the other, moving in the opposite direction, narrows to a point. This model of interpenetrating vortices also works with our readings. Depending on what we place in ascendancy, we commit ourselves to a position on the cultural status of poetry—whether it matters at all in the public realm or, conversely, whether political arguments matter at all in the poetic realm.

Both poets were impelled to address economic injustice, but a major difference between them is that they took different routes to arrive at their politics and their modern poetics. Pound's modernism was formulated as an aesthetic agenda in the early teens—with his Imagist housecleaning of the last remnants of the nineteenth century and his Vorticist projection of a modern alternative—which then developed into a political and economic agenda. He writes in "Murder by Capital" (1933): "What drives, or what can drive a man interested almost exclusively in the arts, into social theory or into a study of the . . . economic aspects of the present? What causes the ferocity and the bad manners of revolutionaries?" (228). He has no "personal grievance" against the system—"I have grown, if not fat under the existing order, at least dangerously near it." "Why, then," he asks, "have I blood lust? I have blood lust because of what I have seen done to, and attempted against, the arts in my time"; his concern is "what specific wrong has the present order done to writers and artists *as such*, not as an economic class or category, but specifically *as artists*? And why should some of them be 'driven' to all sorts of excessive opinion, or 'into the arms of' groups who are highly unlikely to be of use to them?" (229, 228).

The "excessive opinion" he has in mind here is what drives "our Bolshevik friends," but his statement would apply equally to himself. The specific wrong is the "continuous sin against the best art of [the] time": "A publishing system," "tolerated almost without a murmur," in effect "erect[ed] barriers against the best writing." And the root of this "sin" is economic: "The lack of printed and exchangeable slips of paper corresponding to extant goods is at the root of bad taste"; "with a decent fiscal system the few hundred people who want work of first intensity could at any rate have it, whether it were supposed to leaven the mass or not" (229). The best books would then be printed, the best music performed, and so on, at the time they were produced; if "serious art," though "unpopular at its birth," reached public circulation, it would trickle down to improve mass "taste."

Similarly, in this essay he is interested in the "unemployment problem" as "distinct from all questions of general social justice, economic justice, etc.":

> The unemployment problem I have been faced with for a quarter of a century, is not or has not been the unemployment of nine million or five million . . . it has been the problem of the unemployment of Gaudier-Brzeska, T. S. Eliot, Wyndham Lewis the painter, E. P. the present writer, and of twenty or thirty musicians, and fifty or more other makers in stone, in paint, in verbal composition. (230)

For Pound, the poet has "a definite reason for being interested in economics" on grounds that are clearly distinguished from "questions of the relations" of capitalism and art to the "great public or the mass":

> The effects of capitalism on art and letters, apart from all questions of the relations of either capitalism, art, or letters, to the great public or the mass, have been: (1) the non-employment of the best artists and writers; (2) the erection of an enormous and horrible bureaucracy of letters, supposed to act as curators, etc., which bureaucracy has almost uninterruptedly sabotaged intellectual life, obscuring the memory of the best work of the past and doing its villainous utmost to impede the work of contemporary creators. (232)

Art, artistic bureaucracies, economic power, capitalism, the bourgeois public, the working masses, and "excessive opinions" of various stripes are all ingredients in the brew that was modernism or avant-gardism. And these ingredients combined differently in the case of each poet. All modernist poets had to steer their way to some clear position on the purpose and function of their poetic work at a most turbulent historical juncture of many crisscrossing paths and choices of roads to take.

Nazim also led a campaign against the literary and cultural establishments and their stranglehold on the new arts. His movement, "Smashing the Idols," in 1929–30, yielded a series of sustained invectives against the poets left over from Ottoman days. Nazim's poetic movement was necessarily politicized, but not only because he was a communist. He attacked the establishment, speaking as a modern poet voicing the social realities of the new Turkish Republic. But in return, he was cast as a betrayer of the nation. He was caught in an asynchrony of political and cultural histories: the poets of the former Ottoman Empire did not disappear with the empire; instead, they retained their hegemony over the literary scene. There was no "cultural revolution" in Turkey, and "Turkishness"—a concept being forged during the transition to a nation state—meant different things to different camps.

Nazim's point of origin for his campaign was not just a concern for the state of the arts. He also had no personal grievance against the system; he came from aristocracy, though not from money, for which he had nothing but contempt. His point of origin was 1921, when he escaped Istanbul—then under Allied occupation—and traveled through Anatolia, the Turkish heartland stricken with poverty, plagued by disease, and currently at war with the occupying Allied armies. He continued east into revolutionary Russia, traveled through the famine country, and ended up in Moscow. All this was traumatic for a nineteen-year-old poet from a privileged social background.

In a 1957 poem written in exile, Nazim recalls his first arrival in Moscow:

> This city is my city.
> I came here at nineteen,
>   arriving at Kiev Station
>   three hours late.
> . . . .
> The year was 1922.
> Ah, those were the days.
> My heart leaping like a fish in water,
> the gloom gone to my head like wine,
> I'd come from Anatolia via Batum
> with just one question for Comrade Lenin.... (*Poems*)

"I had a question for him," he writes later, in 1961:

> "Comrade Lenin, tell me, as quickly as possible, what you did in Russia and how. I want to do the same thing in Turkey." But I was told it would take a long time to learn the secret; "for now, study at the University." And everywhere I went, factories, theaters, I looked for the answer. The answer I sought was how a revolution could be made in Turkey. I knocked on every door. But only one opened up the secret for me: the Meyerhold Theater. (qtd. in Fevralski 87)

Here he is talking not about the revolution in the streets but of a revolution on the stage. Vsevolod Meyerhold's radically innovative work established him as a pioneer in modern theatre, but how could the Meyerhold Theater answer the would-be revolutionary's question to Lenin?

Nazim's historical experience, the hunger he witnessed on his journey from Istanbul to Moscow, had forced not only a political but a poetic crisis. He needed a new art form. He had no precedent in Turkish poetry for divagating beyond the parameters of Ottoman court poetry written in quantitative meters, and oral folk poetry composed in syllabics. These forms—and the diction that came with them—in effect restricted the historical visibility/audibility of experiences that did not fall within the limits of their generic lyric *topoi*—love, loss, time, death—and of the vocabulary that addressed such universal topics in the two traditional meters. The pre-existing forms came with their politics: the generic rules and political ideologies reinforced each other to withstand encroachments from "outside" poetic discourse. The two kinds of poetry of two different socio-economic classes—a privileged class and a dispossessed class at a great remove from the center of Ottoman court power—in effect conspired to protect a poetic domain, if a domain strictly divided within itself. Nazim broke down those barriers, crossing formal and political borders without a passport—which became a habit with him.

Nazim's friend at the time and, much later, his biographer, Vala Nureddin (Va-Nu) remembers Nazim's frustration in trying to write about the Russian famine. One day, however, Nazim triumphantly burst into their room in Moscow (in the building that used to be the Bank of Holland) and flung a sheaf of papers on the rococo table—a table he likened to the carcass of an extinct animal—and announced "the end of meter and rhyme." "These pages had the first free verse lines in Turkish literature," Va-Nu writes (270). The poem was "The Eyes of the Hungry" (1922):

> *Not a few*
>   not five or ten
>   **30.000.000**
>   **30.000.000!**
> . . . .
> **Some only**
>   **bones**
>   **knocking knees**
>   **dragging**
>   **swollen**
>   **bellies!**

Some only
    skin . . . skin!
Only
    their eyes
      are alive!*(835 Satir 24–25)*

Nazim's free-verse revolution was triggered by a social shock; he turned a social experience into a formal poetic resolve. His concern was actual poverty and hunger—not the sins of capitalism against the arts.

The modernisms of Pound and Nazim, although comparable in their stances toward the literary and cultural establishments in their different contexts, cross in a kind of chiastic structure of different genetic paths and comparable generic positions that also points to one of the difficulties of defining modernism, let alone an international modernism. In Nazim's case, social, political and economic questions end up with an artistic agenda; Pound starts with art and ends with a political-economic agenda. The Meyerhold Theater answers Nazim's political question; Mussolini answers Pound's aesthetic question: "Mussolini has told his people that poetry is a necessity *to the state*" (Torrey 138). Their crossing paths make for different kinds of modernism, one focusing on the special power of art to raise social and political awareness and accountability, the other on the claim of "contemporary creators"—an aristocracy dispossessed by the market system—to recognition of their special power. In a statement to the press upon his second return to Turkey in 1928—a statement comparable to Pound's "Murder by Capital"—Nazim offers this explanation:

> I came to clear my name of the charges against me in trials in my absence. I do not belong to any organization. I am interested only, and especially, in the implications of Marxism and communism for literature.
>
> There is a literary school in Russia known as the "left wing." This is usually understood as Futurist. But the "left wing" is Constructivist. I belong to that school and I want to spread its thought. (*Konuşmalar 7*)

While Pound could be said to politicize his aesthetic values and commitments, Nazim seems to aestheticize his political commitment. Pound follows the political imperatives of his art; Nazim follows the aesthetic imperatives of his politics. When we have both poets in focus, Walter Benjamin's chiastic structure in his 1936 essay "The Work of Art in the Age of Mechanical Reproduction" does not apply. At the end of his essay,

Benjamin cites a long passage from Marinetti's celebration of the beauties of war, and ends with a cryptic and puzzling statement:

> Mankind, which in Homer's time was an object of contemplation for the Olympian gods, now is one for itself. Its self-alienation has reached such a degree that it can experience its own destruction as an aesthetic pleasure of the first order. This is the situation of politics which Fascism is rendering aesthetic. Communism responds by politicizing art. (242)

Benjamin's distinction between rendering politics aesthetic and making art political and his aligning these strategies—which are difficult to distinguish on formal grounds—with fascism and communism, do not help us in the case of poetry. But by invoking Marinetti—indeed, to clinch his point—he necessarily places poetry in the context of his discussion of visual mass media. Both Nazim and Pound insisted that their art was political, and while the poets' political thought certainly diverged, the formal effects of this divergence are not clear. And the difference between a Marinetti and a Mayakovsky in their poetic practices—again, allowing for different literary-historical and cultural contexts—is no clearer.

"The logical result of fascism is the introduction of aesthetics into political life," Benjamin writes, and "all efforts to render politics aesthetic culminate in one thing: war" (241). In 1935, Nazim published a pamphlet on German fascism and racism, where he, too, wrote that the end of fascism was war—but without a detour into aesthetics. What confuses Benjamin's position is the "introduction of aesthetics" into *his* political discourse. Benjamin's inserting aesthetics into what was a fairly clear political divide by 1936—fascism vs. communism, which is his starting point—is a kind of aestheticizing of politics at the meta-level of theory. Politics and aesthetics are two different practices with different histories. Why then the need to establish some stable correlation—or even collusion—between them? Such attempts at correlation invariably collapse poetry into politics, for this is a one-way street. One does not analyze a politics by its poetics. Aesthetics and politics have to be kept distinct so that we can judge their separate operations. A theoretical need to conflate the two serves the interests of political content. . . .

Source: Mutlu Konuk Blasing, "Nazim Hikmet and Ezra Pound: To Confess Wrong without Losing Rightness," in *Journal of Modern Literature*, Vol. 33, No. 2, Winter 2010, pp. 1–23.

HUMAN LANDSCAPES FROM MY COUNTRY IS

A MODERNIST WORK EMANATING FROM THE

PARTICULAR CONTEXT OF A DEVELOPING COUNTRY.

IT CONFRONTED BUT ALSO CONSTITUTED

MODERNITY IN A PLACE WHERE MODERNITY HAD

BECOME A NATIONAL POLITICAL PROJECT."

Marian Aguiar

In the following excerpt, Aguiar examines the role played by modernism within a global context of development, using Hikmet's poetry as examples.

For many places in the world the most immediate relationship with the modern has been through modernization projects. The internationalization of modernist studies beyond Europe demands that critics grapple with this history of development. This is an area well traveled by social science, but literary studies may offer a new perspective on one of the key issues at stake in this history: the fraught cultural affiliations of modernity. We may explore these conflicted relationships by looking at the work of Turkish poet Nâzim Hikmet (1902–1963), whose poetry revealed the bifurcated world inside one of the most famous national modernization projects.

This paper will offer a look back from current theoretical discussions on modernity to a mid-twentieth century context in which Turkey was connected to both Western European and Soviet influences. In 1930s and '40s Turkey I find two contrasting views in the context of global modernization: that of the national campaign and that of the modernist literary writer encountering development. In both rhetorical contexts, in different ways, modernity became emblemized by technological materials. By looking back specifically at the way the railways as a "synonym for ultra-modernity" (Hobsbawm 111) were imagined, I locate the literary writer within and outside of a modernity as it was cast in terms of development projects.

Modernity's master narrative was never whole, in the sense that the evolving philosophical conception of the modern consistently posited its own negation as the backbone of its very existence. An early notion simply designated a transition between antiquity and the new, but the term underwent a significant shift in meaning during the period of Enlightenment. Modernity became a mode of relating to contemporary reality. In this mode, the present is continually interrogated by self-conscious subjectivity, creating a forward-driving paradigm that rejected both the immediate past and, perhaps more importantly, the present (Habermas 16).

Modernity's allure lies in its distinct temporality, for it conceives of the "now" as a moment of possibility. This is modernity's promise, its beguiling narrative of transformation. The imminent temporality is closely related to the project of modernization. Modernity's time of "now" is both prophetic and anticipatory of change not yet realized, providing a mode for social transformation within global contexts that include development, colonization, and nationalism. The imperative to change is the conceptual core of modernity, placing it always at odds with the present as well as the past. Modernity engages in a permanent critique—it is a utopian concept. It is for this reason that modernity has become a locus for change across the world. Historically, modernity has been a mode for transformation compatible with different ideological commitments and various cultural identities.

This understanding, perhaps best articulated by Michel Foucault, calls forth the ethics of modernity as "a mode of relating to contemporary reality; a way, too, of acting and behaving that at one and the same time marks a relation of belonging and presents itself as a task" (39). In other words, this modernity-as-attitude is not simply a consciousness, for it simultaneously embodies a subjectivity (mode), an ethical and political responsibility (*ethos*), a set of material practices (way of acting and behaving), and a project (task). Thus, modernity not only heralds change, it bears responsibility for that change.

Reading these processes together, one may see the outlines of a modernity bound to express conflict and resistance. Twentieth-century nationalists, keen to model their country's development on powerful western countries, were attracted to post-Enlightenment knowledge frameworks. These leaders often based their plans for development on the scientific rationalism that had formed a guiding principle for colonial and imperial projects (Prakash). As decolonizing leaders appropriated ideology mired in imperial history, they found themselves faced with a question of cultural ownership. In locations struggling to maintain autonomy through the process of development, the question became: "Who owns modernity?"

In the historical context of early- to mid-twentieth century Turkey, political and philosophical debates had long raised questions about the cultural affiliations of modernity, especially about its religious identity. Beginning in the Ottoman period, modernization projects, driven by international investment, prompted contention over foreign influence, as public debates questioned the place of Islam in a development model based on Europe. For many, the boundaries of Turkish modernization remained clear: as early twentieth-century sociologist Ziya Gokalp put it: "only the material civilization of Europe should be taken and not its non-material aspects" (qtd. in Kadioğlu 183). These modernizers wanted to borrow "advanced" technology, invite certain financial investments from the West, but leave behind European cultural and spiritual affiliations. The problem they faced was that of determining which concepts would interfere with Islamic and Turkish identity. Such a detachment of the material from the spiritual was not simple to achieve in either conceptual or practical terms. This difficulty was manifested not only in public debate, but also in poetry, which, as I will argue in what follows, was an alternative site for the articulation of a modern national identity that sustained important cultural elements from the past. This poetic vision was offered in response to the "modernity-as-project" (Kasaba 24) that dominated the political landscape carved out by Mustafa Kemal.

Mustafa Kemal (Atatürk), who led the Republic of Turkey as President from 1923 to 1938, saw modernity as both secular and antithetical to parts of Turkey's cultural past. Kemal wanted to "inscribe a firm signature of science and reason" by transforming the individual Turk into a modern rational subject (Bozdoğan 26). The leader purged many non-secular elements in Turkish society, abolished state religion and religious courts, banned the fez (an Ottoman symbol of reform), altered the calendar, and changed the writing system from Arabic characters to a Latin alphabet. The last was perhaps the most remarkable change, generating a break with a philosophic and literary tradition rooted in Arabic learning. As Feroz Ahmad eloquently

puts it, "At a stroke, even the literate people were cut off from their past. Overnight, virtually the entire nation was made illiterate" (qtd. in Kadioğlu 186). Kemal's rigid separation of secular and spiritual elements opted for "a general state of amnesia which would lead to a process of estrangement of the people from some of their own cultural practices" (Kadioğlu 186). Kemal attacked history, using modernizing measures to sever the present from a cultural past.

With Kemal's policies, Turkey became a model for national modernization, influencing secularizing development programs in such countries as India. The Republic of Turkey witnessed material and cultural changes in some form at all levels of society following the reforms, as institutional, ritual, symbolic, and aesthetic aspects of modernity entered national consciousness (Bozdoğan 5). Nevertheless, many aspects of Turkish society remained the same, with landowners and a military and bureaucratic elite maintaining power over a large peasant society. Rather than a linear process of modernization towards a militantly secular, ethnically homogeneous republic, the Turkish experience, as Resat Kesaba has explained, "appeared to be culminating in economic backwardness and social flux, with Muslim and secularist, Turk and Kurd, reason and faith, rural and urban—in short, the old and the new—existing side by side and contending with, but more typically strengthening, each other" (17).

It is not simply historical perspective that offers this complex view of Turkey's modernity, however. Nâzim Hikmet envisioned this heterogeneous space in his modernist work *Human Landscapes from My Country*, written in the 1940s and published only in fragments during the poet's lifetime (Konuk, "Introduction" ix; *Romantic Communist* 234). Hikmet was Kemal's contemporary, a poet and journalist of national and international renown, whose imprisonment ultimately led to a popular campaign for his release—a hunger strike by well-known Turkish poets Orhan Veli, Melih Cevdet Anday and Oktay Rifat, as well as an outpouring of international support led by writers such as Bertolt Brecht, Pablo Neruda, Jean-Paul Sartre, and Luis Aragon. According to some reports, the poet enjoyed the personal respect of the politician, and as a young man he had been active in Mustafa Kemal's bid to end the foreign occupation that followed World War I (*Romantic Communist* 15). In fact, in 1921, Hikmet was introduced to the future president of Turkey at a historic moment when the country balanced between the epoch of the Ottoman dynasty and the advent of the modern republic. A short time later, Hikmet enlisted in Kemal's armed forces and was sent to teach in a remote town, where he would be part of a nationalist program to bring secular values to even the most traditional areas (*Romantic Communist* 23).

Yet in the years that followed, the political paths of the modernizing reformer and the communist diverged, and Hikmet was in and out of prison or exile during this president's administration (*Romantic Communist* 62). The poet was sentenced to a twenty-eight year sentence in 1938, the same year Mustafa Kemal died. The military ostensibly brought the charges, but many saw the government as ultimately responsible (*Romantic Communist* 144). Hikmet was charged with inciting the army to revolt, a sentence handed down after evidence was presented that a small group of soldiers were studying his 1936 historical poem, "The Epic of Sheikh Bedreddin." He was freed only in 1950 after the new regime of Celal Bayar brought in an amnesty bill that reduced the sentences of long-term prisoners (*Romantic Communist* 216).

Several years into the 1938 prison sentence, Hikmet resolved to write an epic of the everyday person. The poet began *Human Landscapes from My Country*, a work in Turkish, an encyclopedia of vignettes representing the lives of the ordinary people who made up Turkey in the 1940s (Konuk, "Introduction" xii); the book evolved into a manuscript of 60,000 lines of verse (17,000 survived confiscation and exile to Russia), with revisions and new perspectives overlaid upon the original work until the late 1950s (*Romantic Communist* 217). In *Human Landscapes from My Country* Hikmet used the epic form, the form Ezra Pound dubbed "a poem including history," structuring the work around the motif of the journey and presenting the narrative in episodic movements (Konuk, "Introduction" xii). His work offered both the historical sweep of an epic and the nation-building imagery associated with the genre. He was inspired, in part, by a Turkish work that described William Langland's *Piers Ploughman*, a work that offered a cross-section of society through its characters. Hikmet wrote of his new work: "I am going to try to portray the people of my country in various historical times, using the most representative types" (qtd. in Göksu and Timms 219). Kemal had demanded selective cultural amnesia as the cost for modernity; Hikmet

revealed how those pasts continued to thrive inside the transforming spaces of Turkey.

Hikmet is considered one of Turkey's greatest writers and has been the subject of a number of biographical and critical works in his native tongue. Although he is revered internationally by fellow poets, no major critical study and very little criticism has appeared in English. Two early critics, Saime Göksu and Edward Timms, published the first and only biography in English in 1999. Göksu and Timms also published early criticism, placing Hikmet within the Avant-Garde tradition as a political poet ("Poetry and Politics in Kemalist Turkey"). Mutlu Konuk Blasing and Randy Blasing provided introductions as well as books of translations, focusing on the lyricism of Hikmet's work. In *Human Landscapes from My Country*, Konuk Blasing asserts, Hikmet developed a new poetic idiom by using techniques such as rhyme and repetition to "correspond to the rhythms of peasant life and speech" (Konuk Blasing, "Translating Poetry" 45). According to Konuk, "Hikmet regarded his language as a historical synthesis of oral poetry—which, designed to be sung, relied heavily on such mnemonic devices as rhyme, meter, and repetition—and its antithesis, the printed prose novel designed to be read silently in private" (Konuk, "Introduction" xiv).

Hikmet's epic may be called modernist on several grounds. On a formal level, his poetics shared elements with both Eastern and Western modernist movements. He was directly influenced by Russian Futurist celebration of mechanization and has often been compared to Vladimir Mayakovsky. With his stream of consciousness narrative, invocation of myth and shifting perspective, Hikmet's style resonated with the formal innovations of British modernists. Like other modernist writers, Hikmet's prosody departed from past traditions of narrative and verse in his own cultural context. Saime Göksu and Edward Timms discuss Hikmet's use of a "modernistic technique of montage" as an aesthetic technique (*Romantic Communist* 236–237). Furthermore, the form the poet chose for the epic was experimental; he became one of a select few in that era to break away from the confines of traditional Ottoman poetry into free verse. Perhaps Hikmet was trying to correct the nihilism of futurism and tie it to a proletarian revolution through the technique of the epic.

Blasing and Konuk Blasing's translation of Hikmet's work provided the source for the following analysis of *Human Landscapes from My*

Country, and thus my reading is necessarily shaped by their interpretation of the poet's language, style and even political commentary. Describing the challenges of translating a poetic text, Konuk Blasing outlined some of the difficulties translating Hikmet's poetry as a work in which language and content are steeped in national context. Many of his formal innovations cannot cross languages intact; for example, Hikmet used the rhyme schemes of older forms of Turkish poetry to satirically comment upon earlier traditions. Konuk Blasing describes how the translator replants in a new linguistic and national context a "seed" that contains and informs new elements of meaning, forms, words, etc. ("Translating Poetry" 44). A translated work is, in other words, a layered work.

An exploration of that layering dictates the material treated and the approach taken in the following account of the poem's meanings. I have turned to *Human Landscapes from My County* as a striking example of a modernist work defined in cultural terms. Given that the field of representation extends beyond the literary to a broader field of representation (described by Raymond Williams as a "structure of feeling" [*Marxism and Literature* 132]), an approach that synthesizes different levels of culture becomes necessary. Hikmet's writing placed him into a discursive formation of modernist writing understood in terms of a trans-national movement of formal innovation. Yet he may also be called a modernist in other senses. Like other modernist writers from both the West and the East, his work was dominated by what has been termed "the sense of the modern as intervening and transformative in an international and revolutionary climate shaped by cataclysmic war and massive political and social upheaval" (Kolocotroni, Goldman, and Taxidou xix). Hikmet provided a "cultural, ideological, reflective, and . . . theory-forming response to modernization" (Soja 29). Social geographer Edward Soja characterizes modernism as both subjectivity and strategy in close relation with the social and economic changes of modernization. *Human Landscapes from My Country* is a modernist work emanating from the particular context of a developing country. It confronted but also constituted modernity in a place where modernity had become a national political project. As such, the poem and its consideration are important contributions to a modernist studies expanded to a global perspective....

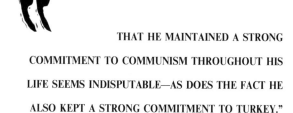

THAT HE MAINTAINED A STRONG COMMITMENT TO COMMUNISM THROUGHOUT HIS LIFE SEEMS INDISPUTABLE—AS DOES THE FACT HE ALSO KEPT A STRONG COMMITMENT TO TURKEY."

Source: Marian Aguiar, "Nazim Hikmet's Modernism of Development," in *Journal of Modern Literature*, Vol. 30, No. 4, Summer 2007, pp. 105–21.

Jon Gorvett

In the following essay, Gorvett comments on the centennial of Hikmet's birth.

"Will my funeral start out from my courtyard? How will you get me down from the third floor? The coffin won't fit in the elevator, and the stairs are awfully narrow." . . . Nazim Hikmet, "My Funeral," Moscow, April 1963.

A burial can be a tricky business, as Nazim Hikmet's words illustrate. As time passes, dealing with a hero from the 'losing' side can pose many problems—particularly when words are what the hero is famous for, and those words form such powerful, lyrical poetry.

A hundred years ago this winter, one of the world's greatest modern poets, Nazim Hikmet, was born in the then-Ottoman city of Thessalonika. His life—much of it spent on the run, in prison, in fear of assassination, or, finally, in exile—is being celebrated this year at a series of events around the globe. In January, one of these events was held at the Royal Festival Hall in London. There, a packed house witnessed a recital of some of Hikmet's best-known work in English, followed by a rapturous performance of the same in Turkish, sang and danced, as much as it was spoken, by Genco Erkal, one of Hekmit's greatest interpreters.

In Turkey, hardly a week has gone by without some recital, discussion or comment being made on Hikmet's life and works. However, amongst all this celebration, the sound from those narrow stairs, as the pall-bearers try to squeeze the coffin down, has become increasingly disturbing—with shouting and even the sounds of a struggle rising above the otherwise decorous hymns of mourning.

"We are facing a ruthless attack," claims poet Ahmet Telli. "They are trying to incorporate Nazim into a view of the world which he was totally opposed to . . . they are trying to turn this commemoration into an official ceremony."

Nazim Hikmet was a member of the Turkish Communist Party, and remained a committed Marxist all his life—despite expulsion from the party for a period after the war, and the fact it was illegal to be a member. By the time he was 31, he was facing 61 years and six months in a Turkish prison, having already spent most of his 20s in and out of jail and in and out of the country. In Moscow in the 1920s, the then-capital of the revolution, he had met Mayakovsky and the other Russian futurists and begun writing poetry that also broke the rules—rejecting the formalistic, aristocratic traditional forms in favour of blank verse and a concious attempt to "take the poetry out of poetry." Thus his poems read simply, but with a fierce musicality, a thumping rhythm that carries authentically strong feelings as well as political messages.

"When the aesthetic structure of Nazim Hikmet's poetry is examined," says poet Sukran Kurdakul, "even those who disagree with everything he stands for politically must acknowledge that he was a great poet."

And those who disagree with everything he stands for are many—though their responses to him have often been a little confused. Principal among his opposers in recent years has been the rightist National Action Party (MHP), which now forms the second largest bloc in the ruling coalition government. They have consistently labelled Hikmet a traitor to the national cause and blocked any attempt to officially rehabilitate him. In the 1970s, militants from this group, known as the 'Grey Wolves,' were responsible for the killing of dozens of communists in the dirty war that led up to the 1980 coup. Despite this, their leader at the time, Alpaslan Turkes, concluded his closing speech at an MHP congress once with a nationalist-sounding quote—which turned out to be from a poem by Nazim Hikmet.

Skip forward to 1999, and still more strange bedfellows. At the closing session of the Organisation for Security and Co-operation in Europe (OSCE) conference in Istanbul, the highest representative of the Turkish state, then-President, Suleyman Demirel, finished off his address to the principal leaders of the capitalist world with a few lines of verse—which were, once again, part of a poem by Hikmet.

This is even more ironic when the last stages of Hikmet's life are looked at. When the poet was finally released from prison in 1950—thanks in part to a worldwide campaign for his release led by Pablo Picasso, Simone de Beauvoir, Jean-Paul Sartre and Paul Robeson—he was forced to flee the country after several attempts on his life (most likely by the forerunners of the Grey Wolves). He returned to Moscow, where he died of a heart attack in 1963. In the meantime, the Turkish state, which Demirel later represented in its highest office, stripped him of his Turkish citizenship and denounced him as a traitor.

Surely this was a testimony to the power of his work, if not also to the way in which it could be used for purposes Hikmet himself would have choked on. As a final example, with the 100th birthday party about to start, Demirel's successor, President Ahmet Necdet Sezer, attended a concert in Ankara at the end of 2001 at which a much-acclaimed work entitled 'Nazim' by the composer Fazil Say was performed. Genco Erkal also recited some of Hikmet's poems in his inimitable style. The audience applauded the work, then applauded President Sezer.

"It occurs to me that Nazim and the government have made peace tonight," Erkal then told reporters.

But many would argue that that is far from the case.

"The people who today are acting as if they own Nazim Hikmet are the same as those who declared him a traitor in the past," says Murat Tokmak, General Secretary of the leftist workers' union, DISK.

The Nazim Hikmet Foundation, which has organised many of the international commemorations, also has reservations. Demet Elkatip, a Foundation spokeswoman, points to the frequent campaigns her group has launched to restore Hikmet's Turkish citizenship.

"Signatures were collected and the issue was put to a vote in parliament twice, in 1995 and again in 2000," she says. "Both times the motion was defeated."

This anniversary also comes at a time when Turkey is attempting to amend some of the more repressive elements of its constitution—under the terms of which many other poets and writers have found themselves thrown into prison. Yet, while some may feel Nazim has made peace with the government, others point to cases such as the recent trial of publisher Fatih Tas, facing jail for printing US writer Noam Chomsky's work in Turkey, as further evidence that the government still has not made progress in dealing with these issues.

Back on the stairs then, the coffin seems jammed, and the argument continues: traitor, national hero, international revolutionary—or, the fate of many such troublesome geniuses, acceptable romantic. That he maintained a strong commitment to communism throughout his life seems indisputable—as does the fact he also kept a strong commitment to Turkey. His poems are shot through with a sense of place, often given a tragic twist by his very absence from his homeland: "Nazim Hikmet is a whole," says writer Zeynep Oral, "with his communism, his love, his poems and his longing. Taking one part of this whole and leaning everything on it is wrong."

The debate seems likely to continue though, with Nazim Hikmet's legacy being closely fought for. Despite the 40 years since his death, his verses still refuse to lie down.

> "I love my country . . . I love my country . . . I swung in its lofty trees, I lay in its prisons. Nothing relieves my depression Like the songs and tobacco of my country. . . . and then my working, honest, brave people. Ready to accept with the joy of a wondering child, everything progressive, lovely, good, half hungry, half full, half slave . . ."

Nazim Hikmet, I Love My Country

Source: Jon Gorvett, "Hero or Traitor?" in *Middle East*, April 2002, pp. 42–43.

SOURCES

Arsu, Sebnem, "Turkey: Kurdish Separatists Kill 6 Soldiers, Military Says," in *New York Times*, July 20, 2010, http://www.nytimes.com/2010/07/21/world/europe/21briefs-TURKEY.html (accessed September 12, 2010).

Forché, Carolyn, "Foreword," in *Poems of Nazim Hikmet*, translated by Randy Blasing and Mutlu Konuk, rev. ed., Persea Books, 2002, p. x.

Göksu, Saime, and Edward Timms, *Romantic Communist: The Life and Work of Nazim Hikmet*, St. Martin's Press, 1999, pp. 31, 59, 76, 138.

Grant, A. J., and Harold Temperley, *Europe in the Nineteenth and Twentieth Centuries, 1789–1950*, 6th ed., Longmans, 1969, p. 449.

Hikmet, Nazim, "Letter to My Wife," in *Poems of Nazim Hikmet*, translated by Randy Blasing and Mutlu Konuk, rev. ed., Persea Books, 2002, pp. 38–39.

Olson, Ray, Review of *Beyond the Walls: Selected Poems*, in *Booklist*, Vol. 98, No. 22, August 2002, p. 1913.

Olson, Robert, "The Kurdish Rebellions of Sheikh Said (1925), Mt. Ararat (1930), and Dersim (1937–8): Their Impact on the Development of the Turkish Air Force and on Kurdish and Turkish Nationalism," in *Die Welt des Islams*, Vol. 40, No. 1, 2000, pp. 67–94.

"Poets from Turkey," in *Turkey: Poetry International Web*, http://turkey.poetryinternational.org.poetryinternationalweb.org/piw_cms/cms/cms_module/index.php?obj_id=11619 (accessed September 10, 2010).

Review of *Poems of Nazim Hikmet*, in *Publishers Weekly*, Vol. 241, No. 13, March 28, 1994, p. 90.

Uysal, Ahmet, "Kurdish Separatism Is a Threat to the Future of the Middle East," in *Today's Zamen*, July 2, 2010, http://www.todayszaman.com/tz-web/detaylar.do?load=detay&link=214854 (accessed September 10, 2010).

Yevtushenko, Yevgeny, "Preface," in *Romantic Communist: The Life and Work of Nazim Hikmet*, by Saime Göksu and Edward Timms, St. Martin's Press, pp. xvi, xxii.

FURTHER READING

Kemal, Orhan, and Bengisu Rona, *In Jail with Nazim Hikmet*, Saqi Books, 2011.
> This is an account of the friendship between Hikmet and another of Turkey's most prominent literary figures, Kemal Orhan. The young Kemal was an admirer of Hikmet's poetry. Like Hikmet, he was a communist, and he was imprisoned from 1940 to 1943 on charges similar to those leveled against Hikmet. In prison the two men shared a cell, and Hikmet proved to be a lasting influence on the younger man. Rona translates Kemal's memoir about his prison years and also includes some of Kemal's prison notes and some of Hikmet's letters from prison.

Kinzer, Stephen, *Crescent and Star: Turkey between Two Worlds*, rev. ed., Farrar, Straus and Giroux, 2008.
> This is an engaging introduction to modern Turkey by a former *New York Times* Istanbul bureau chief. Kinzer describes some of the problems Turkish society faces, but he is optimistic about the future growth of democracy there.

Mango, Andrew, *Atatürk: The Biography of the Founder of Modern Turkey*, Overlook TP, 2002.
> This is a comprehensive biography of the man who presided over the development of the modern Turkish state during the 1920s and 1930s, a period when Hikmet was imprisoned more than once. The book gives insight not only into Atatürk but also into the times in which he lived.

Pamuk, Orhan, *Istanbul: Memories and the City*, Vintage, 2006.

Pamuk, Turkey's best-known novelist, wrote this memoir about growing up in this ancient city. Pamuk was born in 1952, and the memoir ends during his adolescence, so this is a portrait of Istanbul in the 1950s and 1960s—only a few decades after Hikmet lived there.

SUGGESTED SEARCH TERMS

Nazim Hikmet

Letter to My Wife

Kemal Atatürk

free verse

human rights AND Turkey

Ottoman Empire

Communism

political prisoners

prison poetry

Nazim Hikmet AND free speech

Nazim Hikmet AND prison poetry

Marriage

MARIANNE MOORE

1923

Marianne Moore's poem "Marriage" is her longest work. "Marriage" is an example of modernism, meaning that it breaks with traditional Western poetry in both style and subject matter. Published in 1923, "Marriage" explores traditional gender roles and the relationships between men and women. In this poem, Moore studies the dynamics of a traditional marriage, as well as its role in culture and society. While this is not an overtly feminist work, in it Moore does argue that the institution of marriage results in a loss of freedom and independence for women, which reflects the patriarchal attitudes and overwhelming pressure to marry that women faced at the time. It is interesting that "Marriage" is Moore's longest poem because she never married, choosing instead to remain single. The poem is available in *The Poems of Marianne Moore*, published in 2003 and edited by Grace Schulman.

AUTHOR BIOGRAPHY

Moore was born in Kirkwood, Missouri, in 1887. She never had a relationship with her father, who had a nervous breakdown before she was born. Moore, her mother, and her brother lived with her grandfather, a Presbyterian minister, in Carlisle, Pennsylvania, until she was seven. After the death of her grandfather, Moore's family stayed with other relatives. Her mother eventually

Marianne Moore *(The Library of Congress)*

Hilda Doolittle (who wrote poetry under the name H.D.) encouraged her to submit her work to the literary journal *Egotist*. Reviews of Moore's work were mixed. Some critics argued that her writing style could not be classified as poetry; among these was Harriet Monroe, the editor of the journal *Poetry*, although she did publish Moore's work. Moore wrote her early poetry, including "Marriage," in the newer free-verse style. Her poetry was recognized and praised by other modernist poets, such as Ezra Pound, T. S. Eliot, William Carlos Williams, and Doolittle. She was greatly influenced by Pound and often shared her poems with him before they were published.

Moore's first volume of work, *Poems*, was published in 1921 without her knowledge. Doolittle and another friend collected and submitted Moore's poetry while she was working as an assistant at a New York public library. During this time, Moore's poetry also appeared in the journals *Dial*, *Egotist*, and *Poetry*, alongside the works of other great modern poets of the day. Moore took over as editor of *Dial* in 1925. She continued to write on and off throughout her life. Over time, Moore's work was publicly acknowledged. When her *Collected Poems* was published in 1951, she was awarded the Pulitzer Prize for Poetry as well as the National Book Award. Moore died in 1972.

supported the family by teaching. The family remained close. Moore's mother, Mary, and brother, Warner, both had a profound impact on her personal life and her literary career.

In 1905, Moore began attending Bryn Mawr College. Although she had the desire to write, she did not have the required grades to major in English. The courses she did take, however, influenced her concise writing style. Schulman describes Moore's education in *Marianne Moore: The Poetry of Engagement*: "Moore majored in economics and history, minoring in biology and spending much of her time in biological laboratories." According to a 1960 interview with Donald Hall later published in Charles Tomlinson's *Marianne Moore: A Collection of Critical Essays*, she credited aspects of her poetic style to her work in the biology labs.

After graduating in 1909, Moore taught at the U.S. Indian School in Carlisle. She eventually moved to New York City, and her school friend

POEM SUMMARY

Lines 1–20

William Carlos Williams explains that Moore "despised connectives" in his article in *Marianne Moore: A Collection of Critical Essays*. In "Marriage," Moore moves rapidly from one point or description to the next. She does, however, argue in a precise order as she examines the roles of men and women in marriage.

In the first twenty lines, Moore describes the role of marriage in society. Lines 1 and 2 define marriage in business terms. The terminology suggests that marriage is a construct of society rather than a relationship between two people. She makes that claim in lines 3–5 that marriage does not require people to change what they believe, but the way she words line 4 makes clear that she is being sarcastic.

Moore presents the irony of marriage in lines 6–8. The private relationship is now a very public institution. It is no longer between two people.

MEDIA ADAPTATIONS

- Redwood Audiobooks has a link dedicated to the poems of Marianne Moore at http://listentogenius.com/author.php/295/258 that features "Marriage," along with other poems. The selections are narrated by Kimberly Schraf.

She goes on in lines 9 and 10 to question what Adam and Eve would think about the evolution of marriage. She uses militaristic language to describe her observations of marriage in lines 11–15. In lines 14 and 15, she defines traditional marriage in a quotation by Sir Francis Bacon.

Following this unflattering description of marriage, Moore asserts in lines 16 and 17 that avoiding marriage is difficult and almost criminal. The next three lines reinforce Moore's confusion regarding why people marry. Lines 18 and 19 mock the inability of psychology, a relatively new science at the time, to explain marriage. She ends the section still skeptical of psychology in line 20.

Lines 21–60
Moore examines marriage throughout time, and she begins with the biblical first couple, Adam and Eve. Eve appears to be alone when she is first examined in the poem, as Moore describes her beauty in lines 21–25. She continues the description of Eve in lines 25–30. Here, in lines 25–28, she lists the exact activities of a woman reported in *Scientific American*. This illustrates just how peculiar Moore's society considered talented and accomplished women to be. Lines 31–34 are the first conversation between Adam and Eve, and they illustrate the irony of being together and independent. Moore portrays the beauty and danger of love in lines 35–41. Eve succumbs to this passion and loses her freedom. Line 42 is attributed to George Shock.

The Garden of Eden is outlined in lines 43–60. Eve is doomed, as is Eden, which Moore describes as a "flawed experiment" in lines 43

and 44, and lines 46 and 47 reinforce the idea that Eden, like marriage, cannot succeed. The following quotation used to depict Eden in lines 48–55 is from Richard Baxter's *The Saints at Everlasting Rest*. This section concludes with the first sin in lines 56–60. In Genesis, Adam and Eve eat the forbidden fruit, typically pictured as an apple, after being deceived by the snake. For this they are driven out of Eden. To many theologians in Moore's time, Eve shoulders more of the blame because she is the first to eat the fruit. Moore describes the injustice of the situation in line 60.

Lines 61–129
Moore explores Adam and his relationship with Eve in this section. Adam is beautiful, but his beauty is troubling, according to lines 61 and 62. She describes Adam's perceived power in lines 63 and 64, sarcastically using language that the Christian establishment typically used to describe God's power. The images in lines 65 and 66 are unusual for describing a man. Women are often compared to cats in literature, while "colubrine" means snakelike. The quotation is from a literary review in the *New Republic*. Adam, and in a way marriage, is a monster, according to line 67. The Persian miniature is a small painting that pictures marriage. The picture Moore describes in lines 68–73 sounds lovely, but it is of a paddock or a corral.

Adam is defined as an orator in this section. He lives for words and prophesies in lines 74–77. The quotation in lines 83 and 84 is from an essay about the orator Edmund Burke, and it serves to warn the reader of Adam's state of mind. Lines 85–88 indicate that Adam disregards Eve as a person with a mind of her own. Immediately after pointing out Adam's fault, Moore allows him to go on speaking as an orator in lines 89 and 90. Lines 91–97 are another quotation from the Puritan theologian Richard Baxter. Once Adam is married to Eve, his mindset becomes apparent in lines 98–100. Lines 101 and 102 are translations from the Anatole France children's story "À travers champs" (Across Fields). Adam wants to be an idol to Eve, but being one does not give him any real security.

The nightingale in lines 103–114 represents Eve and their marriage. What bothers Adam specifically is its silence in lines 105 and 106 because it is the opposite of his orations. Line 108 is from the poem "The Nightingale," and the quotation that follows is from *Feminine Influence on the Poets*, by Thomas Edward. According to lines 114 and 115, the nightingale unsettles Adam, but the apple still draws him. Lines 116–123 explore the conflict between Adam's passion and his desire to remain in control. Lines 116 and 117 and lines 121–123 are again attributed to Baxter. Adam's attitude as a confident orator and philosopher is lost because of his marriage, according to lines 124–129. The description of marriage in line 125 comes from William Godwin, who supported ending the legal institution of marriage.

Lines 130–144

This section specifically studies weddings. It begins in line 130 by invoking the Greek god of marriage, Hymen. He is compared to the Roman god of love, Cupid, in line 131. Hymen is the god invoked in ancient Greek marriage hymns. In the view of the poet, the god is not helpful and loses his significance when compared to the god of love in lines 132–134. Moore again refers to marriage as a doomed experiment in lines 135 and 136.

She goes on to describe the beauty of the ceremony in lines 137–140. The flowers named in lines 139 and 140 and the ceremony are not all that comes with a wedding. The hopper in line 143 probably refers to a storage container, and line 144 warns that marriage contains the same destructive traps that Adam and Eve found.

Lines 145–192

Moore invokes famous names as examples of suffering in marriage. Lines 146–152 are quoted from Anthony Trollope's *Barchester Towers* and mention the myth of Hercules. The story of Hercules would have been familiar to Moore's original readers. In this instance, Hercules is searching for golden apples of the Hesperides. In his home life, however, he is driven mad and kills his first wife and children. His second wife accidentally kills him when he chooses to marry a younger woman.

Moore again calls marriage an experiment in lines 154 and 155, before explaining the natural conflict that occurs in marriage in lines 156 and 157. The conflict, however, comes from the desire to love, as she explains in line 158. A quotation from a medieval teacher, Robert of Sorbonne, sums up the idea that truth must be tested in lines 159–161. Moore uses feline imagery in lines 162–164 to pave the way for the next mythological guest.

The goddess Diana is the only unmarried individual listed in "Marriage." She is the virgin huntress of the Romans. Diana is sometimes conflated with the goddess of the crossroads, Hecate, which explains her dark appearance in lines 165–167. Whatever her incarnation, this deity remains single. Lines 166 and 167 are from the apocryphal book (not included in the Bible) Ecclesiasticus. Diana's hand in the next line resembles Adam's feet in line 84. Diana shows the way to independence in lines 169–173. This independence, however, comes at the price of being alone.

Artist C. Bertram Hartman's description of married couples in lines 174–177 is not very pleasant. They look like people with a chronic disease. Moore blames the Western mindset for misery in marriages. *Occidental* is a term for the West and its culture. Lines 178 and 179 refer to the British and American distaste, at the time, for displaying emotions publicly. The irony is that as people try to maintain self-control, they lose themselves.

The following lines invoke the story of Esther. Line 180 is a quotation from *The Expositor's Bible*. In the book of Esther, Ahasuerus is advised to send away his queen, Vashti, because she refuses an order. He looks for a new bride among the beautiful women in his kingdom and discovers Esther. The banquet in lines 180–185 is a reference to a banquet Esther throws for Ahasuerus and Haman. Haman plots to destroy all Jews in the land. At the banquet, Esther reveals that she is Jewish and begs for her life and the lives of her people, and Haman is executed. Line 182 is taken from William Shakespeare's fantasy play *The Tempest*.

Lines 186–189 are quoted from the Romanian-French writer la Comtesse de Noailles's *Femina*. This quotation introduces the danger associated with the inequality in marriage in lines 190–192. Men may misuse their power. Moore's wording in line 192 hints at the potential for domestic violence.

Lines 193–243

Here, Moore illustrates the conflict between married couples in the 1920s. She presents an argument between a man and woman referred to by pronouns. The dialogue shows that both parties are unsuited for marriage, and they make their complaints using different quotations. Lines 193–198 begin with the man's complaints about the woman's appearance. "The Rape of the Lock," by Mary Frances Nearing (a satiric poem to which Moore contributed), is quoted in lines 193–195. Lines 197 and 198 are from *The Syrian Christ*, by A. Mitram Rhibany.

The woman responds in lines 199–203 by accusing the man of greed. This section is a quotation from Miss M. Carey Thomas, the president of Moore's college. The complete quotation is included in Moore's notes. He continues to complain in lines 204–218, in an unflattering tirade that compares her to death and finds only her appearance pleasing, according to line 212. Lines 206 and 207 are from Amos 3:12, and line 210 is attributed to Ezra Pound. The man ends by calling the woman childish in lines 215–218.

She argues his lack of worth in lines 219–227. She calls him a nomad (a wanderer) in line 220. Lines 221 and 222 echo Charles Reed and remind the reader that this relationship is for life. She questions what can be done in line 223 and ends by insulting his friends in lines 224–227. He, like Adam, must monopolize the conversation and has the last word by insulting her friends in lines 228 and 229.

Moore reminds readers in lines 230–232 of the inequality in marriage by quoting Edmund Burke. She analyzes the problem and blames the egotism of both the husband and wife. His self-importance is described in lines 233–235; her vanity and selfishness are illustrated in subsequent lines, 236–241. In the end, couples whom society would consider to be well married are truly poor because of their unending conflict.

Lines 244–288

The poet expresses frustration with the married couples in this final section. She wonders if there is a way to help them in line 244, but goes on to call them "condemned savages" in lines 245 and 246. She asserts that visionaries do not waste their time trying to make others better in lines 247–249. Here she ends the question but leaves the reader with the knowledge that trying to help this couple would be useless.

Moore uses the term *petrine* in line 250, which is a reference to the apostle Peter. While he is known as the leader of the early Christian church, Peter also denied knowing Christ before the crucifixion. The story of a woman leaving her husband, which Moore describes in lines 251 and 252, is from Simon Puget and was published in the *English Review*.

Men are established orators in the poem; lines 253 and 254 show the orator taking a less

powerful role because of love, although the poem had previously argued that this cannot be true in reality. Moore sums up the idea of love by quoting *The Original Fables of La Fontaine* in lines 255–257. She outlines her observations of love in lines 258–261. The struggle is not over the idea of unity; it is simply one individual fighting another.

In lines 261–264, Moore compares the curved or "cycloid" path of marriage to the story of Columbus and the egg. In this legend, Christopher Columbus says he can make an egg stand on its end. He then cracks the bottom of the egg and sets it down to prove that there is an answer to every question.

Line 265 describes Euroclydon as charitable or generous. Euroclydon is the wind that shipwrecked the apostle Paul. The wind is not interested in the affairs around him in lines 266–268. The first break in the poem comes at line 269. The speech from Euroclydon in lines 269–275 uses the pronoun "I" and might speak for Moore herself. The speaker explains that it is not possible for him or her to be unhappy and ignore it. There is another line break, and the speaker goes on to share wisdom on the subject of marriage in lines 276–284. The answer to the question, in the form of a quotation from Daniel Webster, is set apart in lines 285 and 286, indicating that freedom and togetherness can be combined. The final two lines of the poem (287–288), however, seem to contradict this answer. The fact that the word *book* is capitalized indicates that it is probably the Bible, from which Moore's society derived its ideas of the proper roles in marriage. The final line is a masculine pose, further indicating the inequality in marriage.

THEMES

Marriage

Before the twentieth century, American and British literature typically portrays marriage positively. It is a goal or a reward in many books and poems. In the 1920s, however, women's rights became a significant topic, thanks to the campaign for women's suffrage. Writers such as Moore explored the potential imbalance of power between husbands and wives in marriage. Moore classifies marriage as an institution in the first line of the poem. In some ways, Moore presents marriage as a type of bondage that some people, particularly women, can never escape.

TOPICS FOR FURTHER STUDY

- Reread lines 25–28 of "Marriage." This is a description of a woman from *Scientific American*. Research the accomplishments of women over the past century. How have society's attitudes in the United States toward women changed? How have opportunities, expectations, and visions of and for women changed? Write a paper contrasting the woman mentioned in Moore's poem with some examples of accomplished women—that is, those with well-rounded sets of life and social skills—of the twenty-first century.

- Create Twitter, Facebook, or blog accounts for two characters mentioned in "Marriage" who have opposing views, such as Adam and Eve or Diana and Cupid. Research your two characters and create messages between them concerning marriage and independence. Pair up with a classmate, and each of you choose and write one of the views.

- Read the young-adult novel *Koyal Dark, Mango Sweet* by Kashmira Sheth. Consider Jeeta's dilemma and write a short story in which Marianne Moore and Jeeta meet. What type of advice would they give each other?

- Write your own poem about marriage responding to Moore's ideas. Situate your poem within the context of a digital multimedia presentation using art and music. Write an essay explaining why and how your poem compares with the themes and style of Moore's poem.

"Marriage" addresses the first marriage, that of Adam and Eve, early in the text. The description of Eve before she meets Adam is almost feminist. By herself, Eve is beautiful, talented, and intelligent. Adam enters her world, and they soon eat the forbidden fruit. Eve is blamed, even though Adam is also guilty. Moore describes Adam as beautiful but monstrous and snakelike. Eve's independence is lost once she marries.

Adam forgets that she has a mind, and he desires to be an idol to his wife. Later marriages echo the same imbalance seen in Adam and Eve's. Their relationship is a foreshadowing of a future where husbands have more power than their wives.

Women are not free from Moore's criticisms. Toward the end of the poem, she examines the relationships of her own time period in the modern man and woman. Moore paints both men and women as being too self-involved. Neither one is willing to sacrifice for the other. The dialogue between them is hostile, and the beautiful, intelligent version of Eve seems lost forever.

Although the poem is a critique of the institution of marriage, Moore never directly calls for an end to the institution. After painting an appalling picture of marriage, she concludes that the men and women she describes are not against the idea of unity and marriage, but they are against each other. She never offers a solution to the conflicts between husbands and wives, but the characters in her poem make the idea of broader peaceful resolution less than hopeful.

Freedom

Freedom is a common theme in Moore's work. Women seem to lose more freedom in marriage than men, according to Moore. This imbalance is due to the legal restrictions most women faced in the early twentieth century, as well as the overwhelming pressure on women to marry. The patriarchal (that is, favoring men) legal system of the 1920s left women with little recourse to escape abusive or unhappy relationships.

Moore alludes in her poem to the power that men have. Given the potential unhappiness associated with marriage, Moore questions why people marry. Obligation is one reason that she gives for giving up personal freedom; love is another. Regardless of the reason for marriage, the result is the same. Eve marries Adam out of love but loses her independence. The modern woman may marry out of obligation, but she gives up her freedom when she does.

Moore shows the loss of independence that comes with being married, but she also reveals a way to keep one's independence: remain single. She admits that avoiding marriage is not easy and calls upon potentially criminal cleverness. The poem invokes different literary characters as examples of marriage. Each one seems to give credibility to the idea that marriage equals a loss of freedom.

Symbols of the institution of marriage (Mardre | Shutterstock.com)

Moore deviates from stories of married figures when Diana emerges. In Roman mythology, Diana is the virgin goddess of the hunt, and she appears in the poem to show the way to independence and how to avoid bondage. She is alone, and her choice to never marry grants her independence. The description of Diana is a quotation from the religious text Ecclesiasticus, describing an evil woman. The source of the quotation is included in the notes to the poem. The idea that remaining single may be perceived as criminal or morally degenerate is the price to be paid for refusing to live up to the expectations of society, but staying single does provide a certain freedom.

The final four lines of the poem address the question of whether a married individual can be free. The first two lines are a quotation from Daniel Webster that hints at the idea that it is possible to be free or independent in marriage. However, Webster is male. Throughout the poem, men are responsible for women's loss of freedom and independence, so this quotation still undercuts the idea that women can remain free in marriage.

STYLE

Collage
Collages appear in both art and literature. In literary terms, a collage is made by placing quotations or sound devices in a poem or story. The quotations do not necessarily need to relate directly to the subject of the poem or story. "Marriage" is an excellent example of a collage. Moore weaves together quotations and descriptions from other poets, journals, dictionaries, and essays throughout the poem to make her point. Collage is a technique that many modernist poets embraced. Collages also appear in the works of Moore's friends and contemporaries T. S. Eliot and Ezra Pound.

Dialectic

To put it simply, a dialectic is a debate. Dialectics typically examine problems or issues. "Marriage" explores the problems associated with marriage as well as the different motivations and desires that cause people to get married. The poem presents the opposing ideas between what people desire in marriage and Moore's observations of marriage itself. Williams describes the poem as "an anthology of transit. It is a pleasure that can be held firm only by moving rapidly from one thing to the next." The poem indeed moves fluidly from one point or example to the next; in the end the matter is unresolved, but it is argued well.

Free Verse

"Marriage" is a free-verse poem, as are many of Moore's earlier works. *Free verse* is a loose term that means a poem is not organized into a traditional format, such as a sonnet or a villanelle, that uses strict patterns of rhyme or rhythm. The first 268 lines of "Marriage" are grouped to form one long stanza, while the final 20 lines are visually separated from the rest of the poem to emphasize their importance. Free verse was used in many modernist poems of the early twentieth century. "Marriage" is an unrhymed poem, meaning that the final words in the lines do not necessarily rhyme with each other. The rhythm is occasionally iambic, such as at lines 98–100. An iamb is a set of two syllables, the first unaccented and the second accented, and it is the most common poetic meter in English. However, in general, what sporadic rhythm can be found seems governed by the individual lines rather than imposed.

HISTORICAL CONTEXT

Women's Rights

"Marriage" was written in 1923. This was only three years after the Nineteenth Amendment, which guaranteed women the right to vote, was ratified to end a half-century struggle. Most suffragists were originally also abolitionists who fought to end slavery. The fight for women's suffrage and equal rights officially began in 1848 at a convention in Seneca Falls, New York. Early champions of women's rights included Susan B. Anthony, Lucretia Mott, and Elizabeth Cady Stanton.

Besides the right to vote, many suffragists fought for the rights to property, education, and employment. Many married women in the late nineteenth century and early twentieth century could not legally separate their property from their husbands' property, and cases of spousal abuse were rarely punished. This is why Moore hints several times in "Marriage" at the power men have over women. Women had little legal recourse to protect their property or their safety. Gradually, legal acts protecting women's rights were adopted in different states. For example, the Married Women's Property Act, which allowed women to legally keep their property separate, was introduced to the New York Constitutional Convention. It was finally passed in 1848—twelve years after it was introduced.

The right to vote did not guarantee equality, and many people, even women, rejected the idea of women's rights. Equality was not universally embraced, and society still held women to different standards than men. Moore's poem reflects the changing attitudes towards women and marriage. The continuing changes in society may explain why the poet was unable to answer her own question of whether or not someone can be both married and independent.

World War I

World War I began in Europe in 1914. America did not become involved until 1917 after German U-boats sank multiple American commercial shipping vessels. The war officially ended in 1918, but it had a profound impact on people throughout the 1920s. The horrors of trench warfare and new weapons and machinery (tanks, land mines, machine guns) made it possible to cause severe injury and mass death from a distance. This forever changed warfare. Many soldiers never emotionally or physically recovered from the horrors that they witnessed.

Throughout the war and shortly thereafter, some Americans began to reject the values of contemporary society. They lost their ideals because the war caused devastation and loss of life on such a great scale. Some writers born at the turn of the century moved to or lived in Europe and explored themes of loss and despair. Writers such as Hemingway were described as part of the "Lost Generation." Moore, however, held a unique point of view compared with many of her contemporaries, and she was never part of the Lost Generation. She remained a modernist who explored the changes around her with curiosity and optimism rather than fear and disillusionment. As Linda Leavell explains in the article "When Marianne

COMPARE & CONTRAST

- **1920s:** Women gain the constitutional right to vote with the ratification of the Nineteenth Amendment, but they still do not have guaranteed equal rights under the law.

   Today: Despite the failure of the Equal Rights Amendment to gain ratification, for the most part, women have the same opportunities as men and hold public office and run major corporations.

- **1920s:** World War I, called the Great War at the time, causes devastation in Europe. New technology is responsible for the considerable loss of life in the war, and the subsequent disillusionment explored by writers in the 1920s is a result of the war's costs. Writers such as Ernest Hemingway and T. S. Eliot explore themes of loss and death.

   Today: International conflicts and wars are still occurring, but new smart-bomb technology has made it easier for militaries to pinpoint the enemy and destroy targets without killing as many civilians. Writers such as Khaled Hosseini still explore conflict and its effect on society.

- **1920s:** Women face changing roles and expectations as they are allowed more freedom and independence. Married women, however, are still expected to follow traditional roles.

   Today: Nontraditional marriages are becoming more common. Wives may make more money than their husbands, and more men are choosing to stay at home with their children.

Moore Buys Pictures," published in *American Literary History*, "Rather than lamenting the loss of traditional values in an increasingly diverse world, Moore witnesses truth in the diversity itself."

"Marriage" was written in a time of change. Besides the changes to women's rights, society was changing its morals. Moore illustrates this in her poem as she describes modern marriage. "Marriage" explores the conflicts between the sexes, both on a personal level and in society. Moore leaves the question of marriage unanswered; perhaps she hoped that in the future it might be a partnership of equals.

CRITICAL OVERVIEW

Critical views of "Marriage" have evolved since its publication in 1923. Early criticisms, mostly written by her peers, such as Williams in *Marianne Moore: A Collection of Critical Essays*, were favorable and praised her modern style. In his 1925 essay, Williams praises the fact that Moore does not use abstract symbolism even though the poem explores the complexities of personal relationships. Many modern poets showed a distaste for abstractions, but for Moore, Williams says, "an apple remains an apple whether it be in Eden or the fruit bowl where it curls." Williams does indicate that because Moore "despised connectives" it takes some effort on the part of the reader to understand her poems. This difficulty, however, is a trait that he admired.

Later criticism of Moore and "Marriage" was mixed. Some feminist critics saw her work as groundbreaking, while others feel that she suppresses sexuality in her work and does not reflect true feminism. She was criticized in 1957 for expressing the idea that mothers should not have careers. Critic David Bergman, in his 1983 article "Marianne Moore and the Problem of 'Marriage,'" explains that "though her stylistic rebellion is never explicitly feminist, her attack on the authority of the past is a clear indictment of the patriarchy." As a product of her time, Moore does not share all the sentiments of later feminists, yet this is no reason to ignore the feminist qualities of her work.

Tempting apple (*Aldis Kotlers / Shutterstock.com*)

Critics have also clashed over the quality of Moore's style. The precision that has won her praise among her peers is sometimes considered unemotional. Schulman argues the opposite in her book *Marianne Moore: The Poetry of Engagement*. She believes that "because it is headed for such dangerous territory, [Moore's] examination of human feeling is balanced by an equally strong desire to regulate it." She illustrates this in her discussion of the poem "Marriage," stating that "the jocular tone, cheerfully and self-protectively covering the violence that has been perceived, only deepens the wonder of that mystery."

CRITICISM

April Dawn Paris

Paris is a freelance writer with a bachelor of arts in classics and a minor in English. In this essay, she considers "Marriage" as a commentary on society.

Marianne Moore's poem "Marriage" is a commentary on society. She points out the irony of a private relationship becoming a public institution in the first twenty lines. Randall Jarrell comments in the critical essay "Her Shield," published in *Marianne Moore: A Collection of Critical Essays*, that "Marriage" is "the most ironic poem, surely, written by man or woman." The quotations that Moore uses in this collage come from a variety of sources, both ones that support the idea of marriage and ones that argue to end it. Marriage, as she sees it, has little chance of success not only because of the character flaws of the individuals involved but also because of its function as a social institution.

As an institution, marriage is embraced by society, despite the pain it is known to cause, particularly to women. David Bergman defines society's view of marriage in the early twentieth century in his article printed in *American Literature* titled "Marianne Moore and the Problem of

WHAT DO I READ NEXT?

- *Marianne Moore: Selected Letters*, published in 1997, is a collection of letters to and from her friends and family. The book provides insight into Moore's writing process and beliefs. The editor, Bonnie Costello, provides valuable background information to help readers better understand decades of Moore's correspondence.

- Wendelin Van Draanen's young-adult novel *Flipped*, published in 2001, is a fictional story that shows how the complex relationships between men and women begin in childhood. The conflict between Bryce and Juli is based on personal feelings, misunderstanding, and societal pressures.

- *Secret Keeper*, by Mitali Perkins (2009), takes place in India in the 1970s. This is the story of a teenage girl who longs for freedom but is limited by society. *Secret Keeper* illustrates that issues concerning family, society, and women's rights are important in every culture.

- *Century of Struggle: The Woman's Rights Movement in the United States*, by Eleanor Flexner and Ellen Fitzpatrick, was published in 1996. The history concludes in 1920, but it provides a valuable perspective about women in the early twentieth century and the changing political and social climate in which Moore lived.

- Edited by Joseph Parisi and Kathleen Welton in 2008, *100 Essential Modern Poems by Women* contains biographies as well as selected poems of many female poets in the early twentieth century. This volume shows the diverse way these female authors express themselves.

- *Forces in Modern & Postmodern Poetry* (2007), written by Albert Spaulding Cook and edited by Peter Baker, explores and compares the styles of different modern poets. It is an important text for understanding the diverse forms that modern poetry can take.

- Ezra Pound's *Selected Poems*, a 1957 collection, is an excellent example of the modern poetry and free verse written by the friend and mentor of Marianne Moore.

- *The Sun Also Rises*, originally published by Ernest Hemingway in 1926, explores social issues, gender issues, marriage, and relationships. Jake Barnes and Brett Ashley both lead complicated lives after falling in love during the war.

'Marriage.'" In his opinion, people tend to ignore the warnings that marriage could make them unhappy because "true believers are proud of their suffering; they are happy to be martyrs to conventionality." The poem paints a brief and gloomy account of marriage, as Moore conjures up literary figures who suffered because of it. Rather than seeing the unhappiness of other married couples as a warning, people disregard the dangers associated with marriage and get married in order to fulfill their obligations to society.

After providing a brief report on marriage in the 1920s, Moore studies the relationship between Adam and Eve. As the first married couple, Adam and Eve are not bound by the conventions of society until they create one. They begin their marriage out of love and passion rather than obligation. Moore describes the scene in lines 35–41. Their passion, however, is dangerous, according to lines 39–41. The marriage between Adam and Eve cannot be saved by passion. Each one has different expectations of their marriage. While the author implies that the couple might never be happy if left alone, there is an obvious shift in their relationship after the snake interferes.

In Moore's poem, Eve's mistake of speaking with the serpent and eating the apple is due to her being polite, in line 57. Eve feels an obligation to speak with the snake. This desire to be polite is Eve's undoing. Paradise is lost and can never be recovered. Furthermore, the marriage between Adam and Eve cannot be one of unity because Eve takes the blame for their disobedience. Their marriage is not one of equals. One act of perceived decorum literally changes Eve's world. Adam becomes the moral authority over his wife, who is described as the primary flaw in lines 42 and 43. Moore's description of Adam in lines 61–67, however, does not build confidence in his ability to fulfill the role of the moral authority.

Adam speaks as an orator, but he does not listen. In line 85, he forgets about his wife's feelings and opinions. He continues speaking in the next line and never realizes his mistake. Adam enjoys the authoritarian role. In fact, his delight in lines 101 and 102 is in being an idol to his wife. This earliest society distorts the relationship between husband and wife, and Moore argues that it remains distorted. Despite Adam's moral flaws, future societies come to embrace the hierarchy in marriage that is established by Adam and Eve. The poem provides evidence of this continued inequality by reminding readers of other couples, such as Ahasuerus and Vashti, and the role that society played in their relationships.

Adam appears in more than one of the author's poems. The actions of the first man and woman help establish the troubling moral conventions of future societies. Linda Leavell explains this in her critique published in *American Literary History*, "When Marianne Moore Buys Pictures." The poet believes that society causes confusion, speaking of "the days of spiritual oneness: the days before society, even a society of

two, could create civilization, language, art, and the other 'refinement[s]' that make truth murky." Moore asserts that as time progresses, marriage loses its ability to create unity because it is an institution of society, not a relationship of equals. The trappings of weddings described in lines 138–141 may be beautiful, but they are also dangerous. The ceremony of marriage, in her opinion, is insignificant, according to lines 130–134. It is a meaningless ritual of society that leads to misery and a loss of freedom.

Using another biblical story, Moore illustrates one way that society influences marriage. The story of Esther and her banquet in line 180 would have been familiar to Moore's original audience. The king, Ahasuerus, is married before first meeting Esther. According to the first chapter of the book of Esther, the king becomes drunk and demands that his wife, Vashti, come to banquet. When she refuses to do as he commands, Ahasuerus becomes enraged. His advisors warn him that allowing Vashti to go unpunished will ultimately undermine the authority that husbands traditionally have over their wives.

The fear that Vashti's actions would become an example that other women might follow reveals that she is seen as a threat to society. Rather than resolving the conflict between the king and queen, the advisors tell the king to dissolve his marriage and find a new bride. In order to safeguard the institution of marriage, society dictates ending one. The king is then advised to choose a new bride from among the most beautiful women in his kingdom. His new bride, Esther, is able to save her people because the king observes the judgment of society and ends his first marriage. In a way, the outcome justifies his decision to punish Vashti. According to Moore, society continues to wreak havoc in the relationships of married couples thousands of years in the future. She illustrates this point with a couple from her own time period.

The nameless, bickering married couple that Moore describes in lines 193–229 do not argue with each other specifically. Rather, he and she mimic what society has taught them. Several of his arguments are based on religious texts, *The Syrian Christ* and the book of Amos. He also quotes from the parody "The Rape of the Lock," as well as from the modern poet Ezra Pound. Her arguments, on the other hand, are not from religious texts. She quotes author Charles Reade, who never married, and the president of

Blooming lotus flower *(juliengrondin | Shutterstock.com)*

Bryn Mawr, M. Carey Thomas. Moore, a graduate of Bryn Mawr, would be familiar with Thomas's beliefs about society and how it dictates the specific roles of men, women, and marriage.

Again, Bergman's "Marianne Moore and the Problem of 'Marriage'" provides enlightenment. According to him, Thomas "believed that women were the equals—not superiors—of men, and needed merely the removal of barriers in order to show their true aptitude." Society, however, is what imposes these barriers. Moore and her readers are aware of the roles that society and social custom play in sexual stereotypes and marriage. Married couples are products of this society, and as long as society interferes in their relationships, their marriages cannot be truly successful.

As products of the culture in which they are born, the unnamed man and woman do not have a great chance at happiness together. Society makes them both selfish, as Moore explains in

lines 230–234. Each one acts according to the rights and obligations that are acceptable to society. Neither, however, has any understanding of selflessness, as each one ignores the needs of the other. His first love is himself, as the poet shows in lines 233–235. His love for his wife cannot match his own selfishness, which means that he will place his needs above hers. His self-entitled attitude is reinforced by society's acceptance of unequal roles in marriage.

Her selfishness is inspired by her vanity. Moore shows a woman obsessed with her appearance in lines 236 and 237. This echoes his argument about a woman's appearance in lines 193–195, when he discusses the fear of having an unattractive wife by quoting "The Rape of the Lock." A woman's physical appearance, Moore implies, provides value to her husband and herself. Society reinforces this idea and creates a world that encourages women to be vain and conceited.

The couple that Moore shows her readers could be anyone in her social circle. They abide by social rules, and outwardly they seem to behave correctly, according to line 243. The truth, however, is very different. The poem refers to this socially acceptable couple as savage in line 245. Their attempt to be noble and do the right thing fails miserably. In an effort to be civilized by getting married, it becomes impossible for them to behave like civilized people.

"Marriage" is a commentary on the social institution, but the poet reserves judgment on the feelings behind that institution. As Henry Gifford explains in his critical essay "Two Philologists," published in *Marianne Moore: A Collection of Critical Essays*, "the institution or enterprise, the obligation, are weighted against the private feelings." She makes clear that as long as society dictates the roles and responsibilities of married couples, their relationships will be difficult. She does not, however, take away hope that society can change, and perhaps marriage can change along with it.

Source: April Dawn Paris, Critical Essay on "Marriage," in *Poetry for Students*, Gale, Cengage Learning, 2011.

Linda Leavell

In the following excerpt, Leavell states that "Marriage" presents an impassioned indictment of all loveless marriages but allows for those rare marriages that exemplify the paradox of "liberty and union, now and forever."

Marianne Moore's earliest critics occasionally praised but more often disparaged the seeming absence of emotion in her work. In early reviews Ezra Pound praised her "arid clarity," and H. D. said her poems gave the effect of "light flashed from a very fine steel blade." But when her first book, *Poems*, appeared in 1921, most critics concurred: Miss Moore's considerable wit did not compensate for the deficit of emotion. Harriet Monroe called the poems "stiff but static studies of a highly evolved intellect," products of a "grim and haughty humor."

It might be argued that Bryher and H. D., who assembled and published *Poems* without Moore's consent, inadvertently omitted those poems in which Pound had earlier detected "traces of emotion." But so strongly did Moore believe her critics had misjudged her work that she henceforth defended the presence of "gusto" in her own writing and of profound feeling wherever it might pass (as in Henry James) as the opposite. "The

> GIVEN THAT MOORE HERSELF NEVER MARRIED AND APPARENTLY NEVER FELL IN LOVE, READERS HAVE LONG PUZZLED OVER THE INSPIRATION FOR 'MARRIAGE.'"

deepest feeling always shows itself in silence," she warned, "not in silence, but restraint" (*Becoming* 124). In "Novices," the first poem she published after reading reviews of her book, not only are the suave, young sophisticates "blind to the right word, [and] deaf to satire," but they also dismiss as boring "the detailless perspective of the sea." Little do they suspect what lurks beneath that placid surface, a power that Moore equates with "the spontaneous unforced passion of the Hebrew language— / an abyss of verbs full of reverberation and tempestuous energy" (*Becoming* 113–14). The theme of undetected but stormy passion would inform most of the poems that Moore wrote over the next few years, including her two longest ones, "Marriage" and "An Octopus." Early notes for these poems and for "Silence," quoted above, appear interspersed in the same notebook (Notebook 1251/17, *RML*). "An Octopus" describes a "deceptively reserved and flat" glacier system atop a volcano; the poem takes a jab at the Greeks, who (in contrast to the Hebrews) prefer smooth surfaces and distrust complexities they cannot comprehend (*Becoming* 125–32).

Given that Moore herself never married and apparently never fell in love, readers have long puzzled over the inspiration for "Marriage." Why would the least autobiographical member of her famously impersonal generation devote her longest poem to such a subject? "Marriage" is now often read as a reproach to Moore's friends Bryher and Robert McAlmon, who married hastily and without love in February 1921. But that is only the most publicized of the marriages to which she objected. Far more offensive to her personally were the conjugal arrangements of another close friend, Scofield Thayer, who while living apart from his wife proposed marriage to Moore in April 1921. Although William Carlos Williams's *Autobiography* mentions the possibility of such a proposal (163–64), Moore herself never mentions it, and no one has paid serious attention to the rumor. Letters in the Moore archive, however, and especially those written by the poet's mother, reveal not only the evolution of Moore's friendship with Thayer but also the very day the proposal took place.

... When he returned to New York in the fall of 1923, he was greeted with the appearance of Moore's "Marriage," published in a small series of pamphlets called *Manikin*. Monroe Wheeler, who published the series, had become close to Marianne and Mary during Thayer's absence. Wheeler invited Moore to write something for *Manikin*, and in January 1923 she promised him "Marriage," a long poem for which she had begun taking notes the previous summer. She worked earnestly on the poem over the next four months and gave it to Wheeler in April. It appeared in late September just as Thayer returned from Europe. "Scofield turned white at sight of *Manikin*," Marianne was told, "and said 'Why does this poem appear in book form before anyone has had a chance to bring it out?'" (MWM to JWM, 28 Oct. 1923, *RML*).

If Marianne took pleasure in "stabbing" Thayer by offering her George Moore essay to Broom, how much greater the pleasure of answering Thayer's marriage proposal and allowing Monroe Wheeler to publish it with one brutal stroke. Before even reading the poem, Thayer would have recognized the stab since he knew that Marianne had willingly sacrificed about $180 that the *Dial* would have paid her for the poem (Schulze 459). Hearing that Thayer "turned white" when he saw *Manikin* provided the vicarious satisfaction of watching him "struggle for life—but with little noise." Two lines from "Marriage"— "the crumbs from a lion's meal, / a couple of shins and the bit of an ear"—in this context seem directly aimed at Thayer. This quotation from the book of *Amos* appears early in the notebook where Moore drafted ideas for "Marriage." The notebook also includes references to Bluebeard and acacias, suggesting she had in mind her earlier poem about a tyrannical husband. The reiteration in the notebook of the line—"men have power / and sometimes one is made to feel it"—suggests that the feeling figured prominently in the poem's conception (Notebook 1251/17, *RML*).

"I am so thankful," Mary confided to Warner after "Marriage" appeared, "that a really strong buffer has interposed itself between Scofield—and

Rat; I mean Glenway [Wescott] and Monroe [Wheeler]. They are a safe and giving pair; the most poisonous could not hate them or question their nobility, yet they have so much poise and dignity that no one would presume to brush them off. And when Scofield went away [to Europe], he felt he could preempt Rat utterly.... He knew Alfred Kreymborg had done all of Rat's publishing, & that Dr. Williams was an adherent, but he waggled by them, as a great poppa dog. Now he finds a pair that are all in all to each other, that not only affect Rat but are accepted by Rat as congenial" (28 Oct. 1923, *RML*).

Moore recognized the power imbalance in her friendship with Thayer, which surely contributed even at first to her feeling "scared." Not only did he have more power over her literary career than anyone else, but she also learned to accept his invitations to expensive restaurants without, as she wrote, "sullying friendship by reciprocal givings." Moreover, she liked Thayer. But her anxiety over dressing for tea at the Benedick shows that she did not altogether trust him. In dressing for tea, she both wanted to meet Thayer's high aesthetic standards and also to present herself, not as a bohemian woman, but as a professional writer, an elegant and calm "mountain of ice." When Thayer proposed, he violated not only his marriage vows but also the tenuous balance of their friendship. He became the Bluebeard she had feared all along.

Besides Thayer's proposal, a possible stimulus for "Marriage" is an exhibit of Bibles at the main branch of the New York Public Library and in particular an illustration of Adam and Eve. Moore described the illustration to Warner just before she promised the poem to Wheeler and two months later wrote that she was "still worrying over 'Marriage' which I am writing for Mr. Wheeler—(on Adam and Eve.)" "I am hoping in this to give a good [deal] of offense to [those who] promote the oriental view and to those who advocate the if at first you don't succeed try try again, phase of the matter" (postscript to MWM to JWM, 18 March 1923, *RML*). She had accused George Moore of sharing "the oriental conception that to be inescapably associated with woman, is degradation." Evidence of this is his sympathy with the Old Testament view of woman as an evil temptress (*Complete Prose* 66). The notes to "Marriage" in Observations refer to the "Oriental" concept that "silence on the part of women ... is as poetry set to music" (*Becoming* 146).

Another likely stimulus is E. E. Cummings's "Puella Mea," which had appeared in the *Dial* just as Moore and Thayer were becoming friendly with one another. Marianne thought the poem placed Cummings "on a position of unassailable eminence" (MM to Yvor Winters, 25 Apr. 1922, *RML*), and Mary called it an "exquisite poem very long." But Ezra Pound and others whose opinion Thayer valued "tried hard to cast mud." Hoping that Marianne would share his admiration for his friend's poem, Thayer arranged for her to sit next to Cummings at a party, but because she could not praise it unequivocally, she did not mention it. "What do you think of Cummings's poem?" Thayer asked outright as he walked her home from the party.

"Marvelous imagery," said Marianne. "One feels Spenser's *Epithalamion* in its presence, and Boccaccio."

"Ah! I'm delighted," replied Thayer. "Ezra Pound says Cummings has no promise, no real genius."

"I fear that is sour grapes," said Marianne. "It is the very thing that Ezra Pound would like to do himself;—but after all the heights the poem reaches it leaves one feeling antagonistic."

"No! How so? in what respect? Particularize!"

"O no—that is not necessary—do you not feel it yourself?"

"Why no!"

"Ah?" asked Marianne. "Well that is the way it affects me." Then she said goodnight and went inside.

"Ought I to have said right out," Marianne asked Mary just afterward, "that it was only a cheap low charlatan that would defile his beautiful thing with the word 'lascivious,' as if he dared not risk being thought heavenly minded?" For Mary the phrase "her slim lascivious arms" "opened the gates of hell for just one little bit" on Cummings's "picture of a heaven-tinted earth" (MWM to JWM, 1 Feb. 1921, *RML*). For Marianne such language was not only offensive but also disrespectful. Cummings's first book disappointed her, she said later, because not one poem was "complimentary to women when so much of it is about woman" (MM to Yvor Winters, 30 Oct. 1924, *RML*).

The antithesis of Cummings's "Puella Mea," Marianne Moore's "Marriage" is a mock epithalamium employing the conventional dialogue between groom and bride, in this case Adam and Eve. "I wonder what Adam and Eve / think of it by this time," the poet muses. Unlike in Genesis and *Paradise Lost*, Eve appears first, and her ability to "write simultaneously / in three languages / . . . and talk in the meantime" rivals Adam's traditional power to name. Both characters are appallingly self-centered. "He loves himself so much, / he can permit himself / no rival in that love. / She loves herself so much, / she cannot see herself enough." There is no doubt, however, what the poet thinks of "that invaluable accident / exonerating Adam." Protesting the "oriental view," she makes both sexes bear responsibility for the "savage" state into which marriage has fallen. As in conventional epithalamia, Hymen is invoked to lead the marriage procession. But he appears as "Unhelpful Hymen! / a kind of overgrown cupid / reduced to insignificance" by the advertising and commercial fanfare that accompany modern marriage. As is the case throughout the poem, no culture has got it right, neither high nor low, ancient nor modern, classical nor biblical, oriental nor occidental. . . .

Source: Linda Leavell, "Frightening Disinterestedness: The Personal Circumstances of Marianne Moore's 'Marriage,'" in *Journal of Modern Literature*, Vol. 31, No. 1, Fall 2007, pp. 64–79.

Heather Cass White

In the following excerpt, White argues that "Marriage," perhaps Moore's most difficult poem, represents the high point of her work in free verse.

. . . "Marriage," Moore's longest and perhaps most difficult poem, represents the high point of her work in free verse. During the years from 1921 to 1925, when she was publishing primarily in the *Dial*, Moore's poems turn from eccentric syllable grids and elaborate rhyme schemes to free verse in which quotation plays a newly important role. "Marriage" is the most formally self-reflective of these poems. Read as an experiment in pushing certain of her stylistic innovations to their limits, it has much to say about the skepticism with which Moore regarded her fascination with unsociably complicated forms. From its opening lines onward, "Marriage" poses its subject as a problem, a set of alternatives to be tested and explored, whether by disputation or conversation, as the case may turn out. Part of the difficulty of "Marriage" lies in its rapid, unmarked stylistic shifts. To the eye the poem is a long column of free verse, unpunctuated by stanzas, syllable grids, or rhymes. Within that uniformity, however, lies a bewildering array of stylistic modes. As I will argue, a consideration of how these modes do and do not harmonize will show one way that Moore found to write in the complicated registers of conversation. The first 15 lines introduce possibilities for thinking and talking about marriage that the rest of the poem will follow:

> Marriage
> This institution,
> perhaps one should say enterprise
> out of respect for which
> one says one need not change one's mind
> about a thing one has believed in,
> requiring public promises of one's intention
> to fulfill a private obligation:
> I wonder what Adam and Eve
> think of it by this time,
> this firegilt steel
> alive with goldenness;
> how bright it shows—
> 'of circular traditions and impostures,
> committing many spoils,'
> requiring all one's criminal ingenuity
> to avoid! (*Selected Poems* 72)

While posing the definitional problems of marriage (institution or enterprise?) that will become the subject of the poem, these first lines also lay out the various stylistic tools with which the poem will consider "opposites / opposed each to the other, not to unity." In wondering "what Adam and Eve think of it by this time," they begin by introducing a mythical, allusive framework for marriage, a thread that will run through the poem as it uses images of Eden and its inhabitants to discuss the allurements and dangers of marriage. Immediately after these lines, the poem turns from literate, ironical allusiveness to vivid metaphors of the poet's own devising: "this firegilt steel / alive with goldenness; / how bright it shows." The reference to Adam and Eve suggests to the reader that this poem has a history in a much older story, and that the poet's relationship to that story is likely to be both witty and serious. The quick shift to a descriptive metaphor for a wedding ring, however, changes the poem's register; suddenly the poet is working in a contemplative and lyrical vein, albeit one still tempered by a certain skepticism: the ring glittering in this poem is not in fact gold, but gilt steel.

The next four lines display two of Moore's most familiar stylistic devices: quotation and epigram. By way of amplifying her own metaphor for the wedding ring, she quotes Francis Bacon: "of circular traditions and impostures, / committing many spoils." The manner in which the poet adduces this quotation is logically audacious. It does not in fact refer to marriage at all, but by virtue of

the word circular, a link to the ring implicit in the preceding lines, Moore is able to treat it as though it does. With this verbal sleight-of-hand in mind, Moore writes of "Marriage," in the notes at the end of the *Complete Poems*, that it is made of "statements that took my fancy which I tried to arrange plausibly." While this description drastically understates the force of the poem, it does mark one of its persistent methods: the assemblage of independent verbal objects against the organizing backdrop of the idea of marriage.

The section ends with one final stylistic shift, into epigram, as the poet exclaims of marriage that it requires "all one's criminal ingenuity / to avoid!" The dramatic suspension of the enjambment in these lines, a brief suspension that lends force to their wit, is a device Moore uses sparingly, as in "The Labors of Hercules" when she notes "it is one thing to change one's mind, / another to eradicate it" (*Selected Poems*). Her more usual mode is aphorism: "distaste which takes no credit to itself is best," "It is not what I eat that is / my natural meat," "The gleaning is more than the vintage." In "Marriage," however, Moore interlaces her tendency to moral formulations with humor, as in the lines about "criminal ingenuity," and a kind of doubt, which turns what might elsewhere have been instructive aphorism into something more cutting. For example, she says of Adam that "he loves himself so much, / he can permit himself / no rival in that love" and says "there is in woman / a quality of mind / which as an instinctive manifestation / is unsafe" and calls marriage itself "Unhelpful Hymen! / a kind of overgrown cupid."

If the poem "Marriage" has a motto, it might well be the 19th line: "we are still in doubt." As an exposition and as an experiment in style, the poem asks the same question: is the "striking grasp of opposites / opposed each to the other, not to unity," an "amalgamation which can never be more / than an interesting impossibility"? Expositionally, it wonders about the possibility of amalgamating in marriage public and private, institution and enterprise, man and woman, individual and community. Stylistically it combines "experiment," "fine art," "ritual," and "recreation" in conjoining its disparate tools: allusion, metaphor, citation, and epigrammatic commentary. This combination is itself an uneasy marriage, which verges frequently on unintelligibility as competing modes work side by side. Like the idea of marriage that the poem investigates, the poem itself keeps asking whether the "disputation" by which it must prove itself is a fight that will tear it apart or a conversation that will bind it together, in however uneasy a peace.

In this sense, the question of how "plausibly" the poet manages to arrange her different poetic materials is of the essence. Like a good conversationalist, she should be able to inflect each change in tone, image, idea, and method so that the whole to which they contribute has a discernible shape that does not distort any one of its elements. The possibility of achieving such a balance is an issue that concerns Moore from some of her earliest poems onward. "Marriage" poses the problem of complexity that must not become murkiness, either formally or thematically. Formally, as we have seen, it moves in undemarcated, rapid-fire transitions between stylistic methods, principally allusion, metaphor, citation, and epigram, challenging the reader and the poet to find the "hidden principle" by which they may be understood to belong to the same poem. Thematically, it concerns the confusion that results when Adam and Eve talk to each other, implicitly asking if their conversations can be understood to constitute the "unity" of marriage. More specifically, it asks what efficacy "politeness" can have in making conversationalists out of these opposed people, who stand in unequal relations to the social structures of the world they inhabit. . . .

Source: Heather Cass White, "Morals, Manners, and 'Marriage': Marianne Moore's Art of Conversation," in *Twentieth Century Literature*, Vol. 45, No. 4, Winter 1999, p. 488.

SOURCES

Bergman, David, "Marianne Moore and the Problem of 'Marriage,'" in *American Literature*, Vol. 60, No. 2, May 1988, pp. 241–54.

"Charles Reade," in *Encyclopedia Britannica*, http://www.britannica.com/EBchecked/topic/492817/Charles-Reade (accessed October 12, 2010).

Cogan, Jacob, and Lori Ginzberg, "1846 Petition for Women's Suffrage, New York State Constitutional Convention," in *Signs*, Vol. 22, No. 2, Winter 1997, pp. 427–39.

"Definition: Euroclydon," in *Webster's Online Dictionary*, http://www.websters-online-dictionary.org/definitions/Euroclydon?cx = partner-pub-0939450753529744%3Av0qd01-tdlq&cof = FORID%3A9&ie = UTF-8&q = Euroclydon&sa = Search#922 (accessed October 12, 2010).

Gifford, Henry, "Two Philologists," in *Marianne Moore: A Collection of Critical Essays*, edited by Charles Tomlinson, Prentice-Hall, 1969, pp. 172–78.

Hall, Donald, "The Art of Poetry: Marianne Moore," in *Marianne Moore: A Collection of Critical Essays*, edited by Charles Tomlinson, Prentice-Hall, 1969, pp. 20–45; originally published in *Paris Review*, 1960.

Jarrell, Randall, "Her Shield," in *Marianne Moore: A Collection of Critical Essays*, edited by Charles Tomlinson, Prentice-Hall, 1969, pp. 115–24.

Leavell, Linda, "When Marianne Moore Buys Pictures," in *American Literary History*, Vol. 5, No. 2, Summer 1993, pp. 250–71.

———, "Marianne Moore, Her Family, and Their Language," in *Proceedings of the American Philological Society*, Vol. 147, No. 2, June 2003, pp. 140–49.

Moore, Marianne, "Marriage," in *The Poems of Marianne Moore*, edited by Grace Schulman, Viking Penguin, 2003, pp. 155–62.

Schulman, Grace, *Marianne Moore: The Poetry of Engagement*, University of Illinois Press, 1986.

Williams, William Carlos, "Marianne Moore (1925)," in *Marianne Moore: A Collection of Critical Essays*, edited by Charles Tomlinson, Prentice-Hall, 1969, pp. 52–59.

FURTHER READING

Eliot, T. S., *Selected Poems*, Harcourt, 1936.
    T. S. Eliot was a modernist poet with a close connection to Moore. Eliot presents a masculine point of view in his poems that is useful to compare and contrast with Moore's.

McMillen, Sally, *Seneca Falls and the Origins of the Women's Rights Movement*, Oxford University Press, 2009.
    McMillen explores the reforms and changes of the women's movement. She shows the connection between reforms affecting both race and gender.

Molesworth, Charles, *Marianne Moore: A Literary Life*, Atheneum Books, 1990.
    Molesworth provides a general overview of Moore's life. He does not have permission to quote directly from her letters and private documents, but these are the sources he used to create this helpful biography.

Perkins, David, *A History of Modern Poetry*, Volume II: *Modernism and After*, Belknap Press of Harvard University Press, 1987.
    Perkins explores the poetry of the twentieth century. This volume examines poets around the globe and provides a broad view of modern and postmodern poetry.

SUGGESTED SEARCH TERMS

Marianne Moore

Marianne Moore AND Marriage

modernist poetry

modernist poetry AND Marriage

women AND modernist poetry

women's rights AND 1920s

Marianne Moore AND criticism

free verse AND poetry

modernist poetry AND free verse

women's suffrage AND America

Poem (Lana Turner Has Collapsed)

FRANK O'HARA

1964

Frank O'Hara wrote "Poem (Lana Turner Has Collapsed)" as a lighthearted response to a headline in the *New York Post* that caught his eye. In the poem, he plays two conflicting attitudes off of each other for comic effect. One personality that comes out in this poem is that of the beleaguered urban dweller who is late for meeting someone and is faced with bad weather. O'Hara contrasts this personal inconvenience with the nation's fascination with celebrities, even though they live their lives with no knowledge of the problems of the people who follow them in the news. By discussing what turned out to be a minor incident in the life of movie star Lana Turner, the poet conveys a panic about the fate of a celebrity he will never know.

O'Hara, who was one of the rare openly gay writers in the early 1960s, uses this poem to poke fun at the camp approach that many urban gay men had toward celebrities, particularly female movie stars. When he wrote this, Judy Garland and Joan Crawford, as well as Turner, were considered gay icons. The gay community's reverence for glamorous actresses was always accompanied by a sense of ironic amusement, an attitude that O'Hara clearly conveys in this poem.

This poem was originally published in O'Hara's 1964 collection *Lunch Poems*, so named because most of them were written during his lunch hour while working in New York. It is one of his most frequently anthologized poems and is also available in *The Collected Poems of Frank O'Hara*, published in 1995.

Frank O'Hara (Getty Images)

AUTHOR BIOGRAPHY

O'Hara was born in Baltimore, Maryland, in 1926. He grew up believing his birth date to be June 27, although later records showed that his parents had changed documents to make him appear to be born well after their marriage. He was the first child of Russell O'Hara, an English instructor, and Katherine Broderick O'Hara. The year after the boy's birth, the family moved to Grafton, a suburb of Worcester, Massachusetts, where O'Hara attended school. He joined the navy near the end of World War II, serving as a sonar man on the USS *Nicholas*, a destroyer, from 1944 to 1946.

After his discharge from the navy, O'Hara attended Harvard. He initially majored in classical piano, which had been his interest throughout his childhood. Early on, however, he became interested in writing and changed his major to English literature. He graduated from Harvard in 1950 and the following year earned a master of arts degree in comparative literature from the University of Michigan. That year he also won the Hopwood Award, an important poetry prize, for his manuscript *A Byzantine Place: 50 Poems and a Noh Play.*

In 1951, O'Hara moved to New York, the city with which he would be associated for the rest of his life. He took a job manning the information desk at the Museum of Modern Art. In 1952 his first poetry collection, *A City Winter and Other Poems* was published. He left the museum in 1953 to work as an associate editor for *Art News* but returned to the museum three years later to work as an assistant to the director of the international program. By 1960, he was regarded as an important young poet and was given significant attention in the anthology *The New American Poetry, 1945–60.* That same year his play *Awake in Spain* was produced, and he was appointed assistant curator of painting and sculpture exhibitions by the museum. He also published numerous pieces of art criticism. Over the next few years, O'Hara became recognized as one of the central figures in what would be called the New York School of Poetry.

O'Hara died suddenly in 1966 when, vacationing on Fire Island, Long Island, he was run over by a dune buggy while waiting on the beach for a taxi to take him home after a party in the early morning hours. He was forty years old.

POEM SUMMARY

Line 1

"Poem (Lana Turner Has Collapsed)" starts out with an exclamation. The news about Lana Turner is apparently sketchy, because the poet knows nothing more about her situation than her collapse. Nothing is said about what might have caused her to collapse or her condition afterward. The uncertainty is part of the problem, serving to heighten the narrator's fears about her safety.

By the time this poem was written in 1963, Lana Turner had passed her peak as a movie star. She was in her forties, and fans that had looked at her as a glamorous beauty were moving on to newer actresses. Still, her scandalous personal life kept her in the news, making her an object of fascination for certain fans, such as the poet.

Lines 2–6

After beginning with the poet's shock about Lana Turner, the poem immediately shifts to a personal level. The poet describes where he was when he found out the shocking but vague news about Turner. Specifically, he focuses on the inclement weather. The rain or snow he describes seems to

MEDIA ADAPTATIONS

- This poem has been adapted to song in the classical mode by soprano Melanie Helton on her 2008 audio CD *And Flowers Pick Themselves*, on the Blue Griffin label.

- Readers can hear Frank O'Hara himself read "Poem (Lana Turner Has Collapsed)" before an audience by visiting the Frank O'Hara Web site (www.frankohara.org). The poems were read by O'Hara at a poetry reading at the Lockwood Memorial Library, State University of New York, Buffalo, on September 25, 1964.

- O'Hara also can be heard reading this poem on *Poetry Speaks: Great Poets Read Their Works, from Tennyson to Plath*, a book and three-CD collection narrated by Charles Osgood. It was released by Sourcebook Mediafusion in 2001.

be a major inconvenience, or at least the most significant inconvenience in his life at the time.

In line 4, the poem introduces another person, using the second-person pronoun. At first, this person seems to be racing along the street with the poet and having a conversation with him about whether the precipitation falling from the sky would properly be characterized as rain or snow or hail. Soon, though, in line 8, the poet makes clear that the person referred to is not present after all. The discussion about whether it is hailing or not must have occurred before the person was walking along the street, possibly on the telephone.

The poet self-consciously refers to hail twice in lines 4 and 5 to draw attention to what a strange, uncommon event hail is. He notes that falling hail strikes people on the head, hard. The implication is that his head is not being struck with much force, so what he is feeling must therefore be snow.

After the brief internal argument with the other person about whether it is snow or hail falling from the sky, line 6 brings the poem back to the story of the poet's day, with the narrative entering back into the present stream of events.

Lines 7–9

In lines 7 and 8, the poet explains his situation: he was racing through the city to be with the other person when the cloudburst occurred. As is often the case in the city, especially when it rains or snows, traffic was at a standstill, a situation that is compared to the weather in the way that it hinders the poet's plans. The snow and the traffic frustrate the poet, keeping him from reaching the other person on time. It is one of those instances in which a person, selfishly feeling the difficulty of life, is vulnerable to a greater disaster that will help put the small annoyances in perspective.

Lines 10–11

In the center of the poem, the narrative returns to the present tense, which was used in the first line. The poet takes readers back to the suddenness of the moment when he learned the shocking news about Lana Turner. The news is made even more shocking the second time around because it is announced in line 11 with capital letters, in addition to the exclamation mark that was also used in line 1. Repeating the exact words from line 1 in this way shows readers that the poem is quoting a newspaper headline that is meant to convey shock and horror, although the poet is clearly mocking the headline's overinflated sense of urgency.

Lines 12–13

The poet compares Lana Turner's life to his own. Hollywood became the capital of the film industry because of its consistently warm, sunny weather. He knows that the snow giving him trouble is not what caused Turner to fall. In line 13, he exaggerates to emphasize his point, making the false claim that the entire state of California is never subject to rain. Although it is not true, this statement is telling. It shows the poet to be desperate in his need to believe that Lana Turner could not be troubled by the small, everyday things that make his own life difficult.

Lines 14–16

The comparison between the poet's life and Turner's life continues, as he strains to make sense of her collapse. He assumes that she might have overindulged at a party, which is the assumption that people frequently have when they hear about stars who suddenly have trouble functioning. Without saying that Turner probably collapsed at a party, he at least implies as much by suddenly bringing up his own behavior at parties. Although he cannot relate to the idea of partying to the point of collapsing, he clearly makes that logical jump, pushing Lana Turner's story into the stock narrative for failing movie stars.

Line 17

When the poet uses the first-person-plural pronoun, he is referring to her fans across the world who wish her well, even if, as he has just done, they are willing to make unfounded assumptions about her. He also seems to be indicating the community of gay men in the 1960s who idolized glamorous movie stars like Turner and Judy Garland. The poem takes on an effeminate voice with the soft, breathless interjection that starts the line and his choice of the strong emotional word to describe the devotion of her fans.

The end of the final line shows the mixed emotions evident throughout the poem. After expressing love for the actress, the poet gives her a direct command: it does not sound like the kind of gentle request that an adoring fan would make, but instead this sharpness indicates the speaker's fear. He is faced with a situation so terrible that he does not want to believe it is true, and so he dispenses with politeness and demands that the horrible thought of Lana Turner's mortality be immediately waved away.

THEMES

Modern Life

In this poem, O'Hara shows some of the obstacles that can make modern life a struggle. He describes being delayed in his quest to show up at the appointed time because of the weather. There is nothing particularly modern about weather, which has been thwarting the plans of humans throughout all of history; but the poem comes nearer to the troubles of modern times when it describes how the speaker is stuck in traffic, which has traditionally been an urban problem but is spreading to wider areas farther from big cities as the population increases.

What marks this as a particularly modern poem is the role that mass media plays in it. The news suddenly appears to a person walking down the street when he looks over and sees the headline of a newspaper, which has presumably been printed

and distributed to the newsstand or vending box within the past few hours. The media age that made Lana Turner a star in the 1930s and 1940s allows her fans frequent updates about her life. As O'Hara implies in this poem, the information overload of the late twentieth century combines with the traffic congestion of the industrial age and the struggle against weather that has always been part of the human condition to make life frustrating for the modern human.

Obsession

This poem shows the obsession that its speaker has with movie star Lana Turner. He describes being focused on meeting his friend at an appointed time, a mission that is suddenly complicated by an abrupt change in the weather. Showing up on time seems difficult enough, but then he is distracted with the news of Turner's collapse. Because Turner means so much to him, this news takes precedence over everything else going on.

Although people usually think that an obsession is a negative thing, O'Hara presents it as a benefit here. The poet's troubles are relatively minor, and the news of the actress's sudden illness allows him to shift the focus from his current situation to hers. The panic about racing through the city and being delayed by the sudden storm pales, by comparison, when he thinks about what might be happening to Turner. He is not actually close to her, however, so his life will not really be affected by her collapse. In the perspective of this poem, celebrity watching is just a handy distraction to keep the small problems of everyday life from growing to overwhelming proportions.

Drug Abuse

This poem does not explicitly mention drug or alcohol use or abuse, but the topic is an almost unavoidable conclusion for readers who are following O'Hara's sequence of thought. His reaction to Lana Turner's collapse leads him first of all to apply his immediate circumstances to hers: because he is racing through snow and rain, he wonders if there is snow or rain involved in her crisis but decides that they would not be a factor since she lives in Hollywood. Following that, he assumes that she must have collapsed at a party. He looks at his own extreme behavior at parties and compares it with Turner's. He has behaved foolishly, disgracefully at parties, in ways that are apparently specific to parties, which strongly implies alcohol

TOPICS FOR FURTHER STUDY

- Several of the films Lana Turner made in the early 1960s, including *Imitation of Life* and *Peyton Place*, were helped at the box office by the publicity surrounding her turbulent public life. Pick a review of a film by an actor who has been in trouble lately, and analyze it for clues that the reviewer is responding to the actor, not the role. Rewrite the review in an unbiased way, without talking about the actor's life.

- The narrator seems to be speaking with his friend in one part of the poem but is racing to meet his friend a few lines later, indicating that the discussion about hail was just in his imagination. Propose an imaginary dialogue with a friend as you do some other task during the day. In the evening, write it down, shaping your words into a poem that reflects the themes and style of "Poem (Lana Turner Has Collapsed)."

- Recently, the ABC-TV award-winning series *Mad Men* has popularized the time and place with which O'Hara is associated: New York City in the early 1960s. Adapt and expand this poem to a one-act play, with appropriate costumes and music, giving speaking roles to Turner and the "you" that the poet addresses.

- Read the poem "Fame is a Bee," by nineteenth-century American poet Emily Dickinson. Organize a debate with one side arguing that

the point of O'Hara's poem is the same point Dickinson is making, and one arguing that the two poets have different perspectives on the subject. Let your teacher decide which side has presented the best argument.

- O'Hara was associated with painters (Jackson Pollock and Willem de Kooning, among others) throughout his professional life. Search the Internet for two or three paintings that you think capture the mood of this poem, and write an explanation for each, saying what it tells about and how it reflects the poem.

- Watch some movies that starred Lana Turner. Splice together a sequence of scenes into a digital multimedia presentation that will help you explain to your class what O'Hara might have found so fascinating about her.

- This poem was noted in its day for its realistic approach to the feel of the New York City of O'Hara's time. Find a poem created by one of the young adults participating in the Urban Word NYC Teen Poetry Slam (http://www.urbanwordnyc.org/uwnyc) that you think best captures the same elements of the city that O'Hara's poem conveys. Read both poems to your class and give a detailed explanation about what makes the two alike in terms of both style and theme.

---

or drug abuse. A direct link is indicated, without being stated, between the way he has behaved and Lana Turner's collapse.

Optimism

In this poem, O'Hara shows an optimistic point of view, but he does so with subtlety. He expresses his distress over Lana Turner's sudden illness, but he also indicates a belief that knowing about her fans' love for her might be a positive force for helping her recover. He shows some degree of optimism in his enthusiasm for going to meet

the person referred to, despite the obstacles that are holding him back.

The poem's most direct indicator of optimism lies in the different explanations of the weather. O'Hara rejects the other person's opinion that it is hail coming from the sky because, he says, hail would be more painful. It is not an enthusiastic embrace of the joy of life, but still, the poet's position shows that he is not inclined toward the negative interpretation. The weather is a nuisance, but the poem refrains from overemphasizing its importance. Whatever he is experiencing in this storm, he clearly believes, more than his friend believes, that it could be worse.

Hail falling from the stormy sky *(Sebastian Knight / Shutterstock.com)*

STYLE

Second Person

Often, poets will use the word *you* to give a poem a conversational feel. The other person's relation to the poet is usually implied by the details that are given. It might be a friend, a lover, or an intellectual sparring partner. A poem that seems to be spoken to another person has a sense of immediacy, as if readers are eavesdropping on a conversation in progress.

O'Hara's use of the second-person form of address is vague in this poem. From this one poem, readers cannot gain a clear sense of who that person is in the poet's life, but that is not important. Knowing that it is someone the poet is racing to see, someone who sees the snow as hail—worse than the way the poet sees it—tells readers enough.

There is, however, unevenness regarding where the second person is physically. In line 4, the other person is talking to the poet, advancing an opinion about whether it is snow or hail falling, but in lines 7 and 8, the poet is racing to meet someone to whom he refers in the second person. This slight inconsistency prevents readers from making this character an important part of the story, focusing their attention on what is happening to the poem's speaker instead.

Enjambment

Enjambment is the poetic practice of ending a line in an unexpected, even awkward place, instead of ending it at the close of a complete phrase. It serves to force readers to think about the poet's word usage, inviting them to question the choices that the poet has made. A good example of this technique in this poem is in the second line, which ends with the notice that something suddenly occurred but does not say what it was until the following line. Because this poem is not divided into stanzas, readers never know which thoughts will be complete and which will be pursued further. For instance, the idea that continues from line 14 to line 15 to line 16 does not carry on to line 17, but readers will not know that until they have read line 17.

O'Hara often draws attention to his use of enjambment by using the words *and* or *but* around line breaks. When he puts *and* at the end of a line, readers know that the thought will continue and are drawn forward. When he puts *and* at the start of the line (as in lines 4, 10, and 15) or *but* at the start of the line (as in lines 5 and 16), it gives the poem a sense that the poet is improvising or adding on ideas as he goes along.

HISTORICAL CONTEXT

New York School of Poets

In the 1950s, New York City became a leading international center for art. World War II caused chaos in western European nations, crippling the artist community that had thrived in Paris. As America became a dominant artistic culture after the war ended in 1945, American painting took on worldwide importance for the first time. New York was home to abstract expressionism, a movement that included painters such as Jackson Pollock and Willem de Kooning, who, among others, brought modern, kinetic, urbane sensibilities to their works.

The abstract expressionists living in New York became referred to, in an expression coined by one of their own, Robert Motherwell, as the "New York School." This tag was a playful reference to the previous artistic powerhouse, the "Paris School," which was itself a somewhat sarcastic name derived from the more serious historical groupings, such as the "School of Florence" and the "School of Venice." The artists of the New York School of painters frequently associated with other intellectuals who lived in the city. The writers who were in this cultural collective came to be known as the New York School of Poets.

Frank O'Hara is one of the writers whose name most frequently comes up in any discussion of the New York School of Poets. His work at the Museum of Modern Art drew an immediate connection between the poets and the painters working in the city at the time. Other poets from the New York School were influenced by the visual arts as well. John Ashbery, for instance, wrote art criticism for the Paris *Herald Tribune* and *Art News*. James Schuyler worked for the Museum of Modern Art with O'Hara. Barbara Guest, like the others, had works published frequently in *Art News*. Kenneth Koch, often associated with the group, did not have any immediate connection to the art world, but his association with

avant-garde theater made him a central figure in the city's arts scene.

The poetry produced by the writers of the New York School was, like its counterpart in painting, vibrant and urban. It took city life as its subject and steered away from the kind of pensive, inwardly directed poetry produced by the influential Black Mountain College group of poets who were writing at the same time. Humor and common language, with a basic but unstated sense of seriousness, were the main points of the poets grouped under the title New York School.

The New York School was short lived. After O'Hara's death in 1966, other poets associated with the group eventually drifted away from the city to take up residence in other parts of the country. Although it lasted less than ten years, the influence of these writers is still felt in the poetry world.

Lana Turner

Film legend Lana Turner was born Julia Jean Mildred Francis Turner in Wallace, Idaho, in 1920 or 1921. Her childhood was tumultuous: her parents separated, her father was murdered on his way home from a dice game, and Turner spent time in a foster home, where she was abused. Her mother eventually came and retrieved her and took her to Los Angeles.

Turner's start in films has become the standard legend of movie-star discovery. According to the story, she was sixteen and skipped her typing class at Hollywood High School. She was drinking a soda at Schwab's drugstore when her beauty was noticed by a show-business reporter, who referred her to an agent. After playing a few small roles, she was signed by MGM studios in 1938. The studio built her image and her career over the next few decades, making her a star in films like *Johnny Eager*, *The Postman Always Rings Twice*, and *The Bad and the Beautiful*.

Turner's personal life was never calm. She was married nine times to eight men, and her numerous other affairs were frequently covered in the newspapers. In 1958, she was involved in a major international scandal that almost ended her career. The man she was dating, Johnny Stompanato, was a known mobster with a violent, possessive nature. He threatened Turner in public on various occasions. During a violent argument at her house, Turner's fourteen-year-old daughter stabbed Stompanato to death with a kitchen knife to protect her mother. The incident was ruled a justifiable homicide, and the daughter was freed, but the publicity

COMPARE
&
CONTRAST

- **1962:** A person walking down the street might stumble across a newspaper that has important breaking news announced in its headline.

  Today: News alerts can be programmed, so that a person will be alerted to breaking news about any subject as soon as the story occurs if they sign up for updates on a portable electronic device.

- **1962:** O'Hara mocks popular obsession with the lives of celebrities and the ways in which fans think of their own lives as being affected by celebrities' troubles.

  Today: The culture of celebrity watching is in full bloom, with more magazine and television shows dedicated to the lives of celebrities than ever before.

- **1962:** California's reputation for even, temperate weather makes it possible for a New Yorker to fantasize about California as a place where it does not rain.

  Today: As the climate change has been reported in recent decades, there are more and more stories about flooding, wildfires, and even mud slides battering California.

- **1962:** The news of a celebrity like Lana Turner collapsing immediately makes a fan like O'Hara assume that there was some disgraceful behavior at a party involved.

  Today: Stories about drug and alcohol abuse are still common among celebrities. In the late 2000s, Brittany Murphy, Michael Jackson, Anna Nicole Smith, and Corey Haim join the list of those who die of prescription drug overdoses.

- **1962:** The public images of movie stars are controlled by the Hollywood studios, which can fire them for bad moral behavior.

  Today: Celebrities are responsible for their own public images, though they still tend to spend vast resources on public-relations teams, especially after embarrassing social behavior.

blitz surrounding her trial made the movie studio wary of Turner. By the time this poem was written in the 1960s, however, she was back with two hit movies, *Peyton Place* and *Imitation of Life*. As she aged, however, Turner's image as a glamorous movie star dwindled. She worked less, and in more obscure roles, until her death in 1995.

CRITICAL OVERVIEW

Frank O'Hara was very popular among the writers and artists with whom he associated, but he was not widely known beyond New York City. One reason for this is that he did not publish very often, with just five collections of poetry produced mostly by small presses. Still, his friends were fiercely loyal and wrote glowing reviews for him whenever they could. As his friend Kenneth Koch

notes about the long, eleven-part poem "Second Avenue" in *Partisan Review* in 1961, "I think O'Hara is the best writer about New York alive, perhaps the only good one; he succeeds in conveying the city's atmosphere not by writing directly about it but by writing about his emotions."

Critics who were not personally familiar with O'Hara still recognized and respected his poetic originality, seeing in his work a voice that others echoed but never managed to get just right. Gilbert Sorrentino provides an example of this perspective in his *Bookweek* review of *Lunch Poems*, the collection in which "Poem (Lana Turner Has Collapsed)" was originally published. To Sorrentino, O'Hara's poems.

> move in a world of wry elegance, of gesture, a world made up of a certain kind of strictly New York *joie de vivre*: slightly down at heels and rumpled, but with a kind of style always a step above the current "style."

Traffic busy and blurred *(Perov Stanislav | Shutterstock.com)*

After working so hard to characterize O'Hara's style, Sorrento identifies the poet's uniqueness, stating that "all in all, there is no one quite like Frank O'Hara, although the New York 'scene' has produced a number of little O'Haras in the past year or two."

O'Hara's reputation has remained strong since his death in 1966. Most critics recognize the aspects that are summed up in *Frank O'Hara* by Alan Feldman, who noted in 1979:

> O'Hara's critics are in general agreement that his importance is based on true originality, and that he has to be considered in his own right. But O'Hara is not only new, he is also good by the most basic (and most important) standard: his poems are touching and complex.

The other writers associated with the New York School freely admitted that he was the best writer among them, and critics agreed. As one of the few openly gay writers of his day, he provided a role model for young poets who would otherwise have remained closeted. New critical studies of his works are published every year, testifying to the fact that the poems that he made look casual or conversational bear more than meets the eye.

CRITICISM

David Kelly

Kelly is a college instructor of creative writing and literature. In the following essay, he discusses how a poem like "Poem (Lana Turner Has Collapsed)" helps establish O'Hara's appeal as an "everyman" across the social spectrum.

Frank O'Hara has enjoyed a solid reputation as a poet for the past half century. He was a talented writer, of course, but bookstore aisles are strewn with forgotten works by poets who were at least as talented. Part of O'Hara's appeal has to be the way that his readers continue to feel about him personally. To readers who are not deeply into reading or analyzing poetry, his poems come off as someone who is just talking. The feeling one gets from O'Hara's poetry is that he is just a regular guy.

It was quite an achievement for an openly gay man to achieve this level of comfort with such a wide audience in the homophobic early 1960s. O'Hara's sexual orientation may be less relevant today—it seems that the current political climate would be more inclined to reject him as an elitist: a museum curator and a New Yorker. Readers might be

WHAT DO I READ NEXT?

- O'Hara offers his personal reaction to the fate of another famous person, the jazz singer Billie Holiday, in his poem "The Day Lady Died," which competes with this poem as one of his most frequently reprinted works. It is available in *The Collected Poems of Frank O'Hara*, published in 1995.

- Lana Turner's turbulent personal life, which moved O'Hara so deeply, is explained in her own words in her 1982 autobiography *Lana: The Lady, the Legend and the Truth*.

- In 1959, O'Hara published "Personism: A Manifesto," a statement of his artistic theory, presented in his trademark semi-serious manner. It is available in the appendix of his *Selected Poems*, most recently reprinted in 2008.

- Randi Reisfeld and Marie Morreale have compiled dozens of anecdotes of stars talking to teens about what life is really like for them in *Got Issues Much? Celebrities Share Their Traumas and Triumphs*, published in 1999.

- John Keats touched upon a similar subject when he wrote his poem "On Fame" almost 150 years before O'Hara published. Keats's poem can be found in *The Complete Poems of John Keats*, published in 1994.

- The French Moroccan novelist Tahar Ben Jelloun wrote a poem lacking O'Hara's irony, a tribute to Louise Brooks, one of the most celebrated actresses of Hollywood's silent era. The poem, "The Touch of a Glance," is found in *Louise Brooks: Portrait of an Anti-Star*, edited by Roland Jaccard and published in 1986.

---

expected to steer clear of him, out of fearing poetry too deep, too mired in arcane connections derived from his artistic theories. There have been writers who do whatever they can to avoid the appearance of snobbish intellectualism, looking to the hard labor of their parents or their own student days to sing of a life that they and their readers seem to feel more "real" than a life of words. O'Hara was no poseur, though. His work managed and still manages to create a connection with readers across economic and educational spectra just by being charming. He bonds with readers through directness and simplicity, without pretending that he was any greater or less than he really was.

This dedication to simplicity shows itself across all of O'Hara's poetry. One fine example is one of his most popular works, a poem that he simply called, like many others, "Poem," though it is generally referred to by its first line ("Lana Turner Has Collapsed"). There is really nothing to the poem but a portrait of the author walking down the street, finding out from an errant glance at a newspaper a bit of the day's show-business gossip. O'Hara does not lead readers away from the moment into a meditation on what Lana Turner's life, or its endangerment, means to him. He does not talk about his life at all. He focuses on the event and does not badger his readers to come around to thinking of things as he does.

The persona O'Hara adapts in the poem is that of an average man battling a commonplace foe: the weather, which decides to turn ugly as he trudges, or rather trots, along on his business. The language of the poem is nothing fancy. The whole thing plays out as one long, rambling sentence, which O'Hara accomplishes by stringing one idea after another with *and* or *but* and by ignoring the rules of punctuation that an English professor or an academic poet might obsess over. By comparison, another poet, such as a Beat poet, from the generation just before O'Hara's, might ignore the rules of punctuation as well, but do so with more audacity, making words and phrases jump out from the text, leaving readers, after finishing the poem, wondering what just barreled past them. O'Hara instead keeps everything on a calm, even level, assuring readers that nothing terribly remarkable is happening.

There is, of course, no good reason for a poet to maintain a mien of ordinariness unless readers can feel that something extraordinary is about to come rolling around the bend. In this case, the author's mundane life is shaken by the news that Lana Turner, a star he evidently reveres, has done something vague, only referred to as collapsing. Few readers today would be familiar with Turner's work, but most realize, or are told in footnotes accompanying reprints of the poem, that she was an actress. That in itself is enough. Readers do not need to know what impressed O'Hara about her or where she was in her career at that point. All they need to know to make sense of this poem is that O'Hara had a case of hero worship.

Iconic Hollywood sign *(Cary Kalscheuer | Shutterstock.com)*

Being starstruck is a trait of a common person. A poet might seem to be something of a celebrity to a reader, but not when they stand together, looking up at a real star of the silver screen.

The character O'Hara plays in this poem is starstruck to the extreme, someone who cannot even believe it would rain or snow where Lana Turner lives. He blurts out the news of her awful collapse twice, once with such incredulity that it can only be rendered on the page in capital letters. Skeptical readers, however, will not fall so easily for his awestruck attitude and will focus on why, if he is so concerned about her, he shows so little curiosity about her. He tries to understand what has happened, but only in terms of his own life, turning straight to his own past raucous party behavior, assuming that what is wrong with Lana Turner must be what is wrong with him, sometimes, when he has behaved disgracefully. This might be a winking acknowledgment of the behavior for which Lana Turner was known, a background so familiar that O'Hara could count on his audience in the 1960s to catch the reference with no further explanation; but the poem still works to this day because it conveys an egotism that contradicts the wide-eyed fan that O'Hara pretends to be. He is a common enough man to care about a celebrity he will never know, the poem says, but it questions how much a person really *can* care about a stranger, a media figure— perhaps not very much at all.

O'Hara is hardly being insincere when he gasps over Turner's health in some places but forgets her in others. He is giving celebrity worship realistic perspective. With language that is a little clumsy, in a poem that rambles on about nothing much more major than the weather, from a point of view that can only imagine someone else's troubles if they have the same source as his own, he manages to capture the timeless relationship between stars and their fans. The concerns of the very famous are important to average people, the poem says, but only once in a while, and only for fleeting moments. This is not a deep insight, but it strikes home with its readers because it is true.

This core truth shows what has kept Frank O'Hara relevant to readers whose lives are nothing like his. In the Lana Turner poem, he makes no pretense about speaking for anyone but himself. Like the best of poems throughout all time, this one is able to win its audience over by acting as if the audience does not exist. Readers do not come away from a Frank O'Hara poem feeling that human nature is any better or any worse than they thought when they started with the first line, but they do come away with a good feeling because life—his life, as well as their own—is what it is.

Source: David Kelly, Critical Essay on "Poem (Lana Turner Has Collapsed)," in *Poetry for Students*, Gale, Cengage Learning, 2011.

John Lowney

In the following excerpt, Lowney explores O'Hara's utilization of parody, appropriation, and allusion in his poetry and addresses his treatment of the "issue of cultural memory in postwar America."

In "Personism: A Manifesto," Frank O'Hara writes that "Personism" was "founded by me after lunch with LeRoi Jones on August 27, 1959, a day in which I was in love with someone" (*Collected Poems*). In accentuating the moment in which this "movement" was "founded and which nobody knows about," this manifesto / "diary" mocks the pretentiousness of vanguardist polemics. Similarly, "Poem Read at Joan Mitchell's," O'Hara's celebration of Jane Freilicher's impending marriage to Joe Hazan, playfully inscribes his poetic stance within the "vanguard," as "it's" signifies not only the poem's occasion but the act of celebration itself. Like "Personism," "Poem Read at Joan Mitchell's" dramatizes a moment of emotional urgency: the fear of losing his close friendship with Jane Freilicher informs O'Hara's subtle satire of the institution of marriage. Yet like so much of his poetry, this "occasional poem" self-consciously reflects on its own place in the "tradition of the new." The description of the marriage combines economic and aesthetic terms, situating this poetic act within the cultural politics of representing the "vanguard"; an "original" act, as the intensifier "so" implies, is original only insofar as it is mediated by definitions of the "new." The proper name describing this "original" marriage, "WilliamCarlosWilliamsian," epitomizes this recognition, for Williams's name represents a site of contention in the 1950s "poetry wars," not only for his literary reputation but for the meaning of American modernism. While Williams was variously invoked as a predecessor for the "new American poetry," the academic writing of him into the modernist canon was blunting the critical edge of his early "vanguard" poetics. This "WilliamCarlosWilliamsian" marriage marks both O'Hara's affiliation with Williams's poetics and the objectification of his name as the commodity, "vanguard" writer. The parodic tone of this gesture furthermore suggests O'Hara's critique of the masculinist, Americanist stance associated with Williams's postwar protégés. Whether in mock manifesto or mock epithalamion, such references to modern literary history—although seemingly offhand—challenge claims like Helen Vendler's influential overview of O'Hara that "the will *not* to impute significance has scarcely been stronger in lyric poetry." Instead O'Hara's modulations of vanguardist rhetoric frequently foreground not only the politics of literary reputation but also

> O'HARA'S STATEMENTS ON THE SOCIAL FUNCTIONS OF ART ARE DIFFUSE AND SOMETIMES CONTRADICTORY, BUT HIS OCCASIONAL WRITINGS ON HIS CONTEMPORARIES, IN BOTH THE LITERARY AND VISUAL ARTS, EXPRESS A MORE COMPLEX CONSIDERATION OF THE HISTORICAL DIFFERENCE OF THE AVANT-GARDE IN POSTWAR AMERICAN CULTURE THAN IS GENERALLY ACKNOWLEDGED."

his own position within conflicting constructions of modernism. In the following pages I will examine how the intertextual devices of parody, appropriation, and allusion operate in O'Hara's revision of modernism, especially of the modernist lyric, to show how his "post-anti-esthetic" poetics of the quotidian addresses the issue of cultural memory in postwar America.

The majority of O'Hara's academic readers have concurred with Vendler that his poetry levels the "significant" with the mundane, thus rejecting traditional modes of poetic transcendence. His best-known poems, the occasional poems he called his "'I do this I do that' poems" (*Collected Poems*), are most frequently cited to exemplify his interest in the "ordinary incident" instead of the "important public" event (Perloff 147). Vendler attributes O'Hara's refusal to "impute significance" to his effort "to make the personal the poetic," thus severing the personal from the ideological. Other critics have explained O'Hara's evasion of symbolist correspondences by demonstrating his radical transformation of lyric subjectivity. In his reading of O'Hara's revisionary "poetics of immanence," Charles Altieri stresses the anxiety informing O'Hara's play of surfaces, his landscape without depth, without underlying significance. In emphasizing the ever-changing experience of temporal process in O'Hara's poetry, James E. B. Breslin similarly concludes that experience in his poetry is "absorbed with a kind of evenly suspended attention that does not permit discrimination, emphasis, or even interpretation." Even those analyses that situate O'Hara's poetics in socioeconomic terms, such as Charles Molesworth's summation that his poetry represents the "highest product of commodity-market capitalism," or in the oppositional politics of gay language practices (Boone), base their claims on the leveling process effected especially by his paratactic syntax. I would like to concentrate on one question this leveling process raises, that of O'Hara's postmodernist representation of modern literary and cultural history. None of O'Hara's readers fully account for his intertextual evocations of the vanguardist stance whose critical edge he seeks to retain yet whose critical mode appears inadequate for addressing postwar American historical conditions. The tone of crisis so prevalent in O'Hara's poetry is informed by an acute sensitivity to the oppressive mechanisms that an ideology which represses difference can deploy. And this tone evokes the more general threat of nuclear annihilation, a threat which paradoxically levels distinctions between kinds of experience while heightening awareness of the ephemerality of the quotidian. O'Hara's poetry demonstrates that the progressivist faith in technology and technique that animates Williams's vanguardist dictum to "make it new" can no longer be asserted unproblematically.

If formulations of postmodernism tend to dispute how postmodernist texts reflect or subvert the social effects of postwar capitalism, they generally agree that postmodernist and modernist aesthetics can be differentiated by their positions toward the past. Fredric Jameson has argued that postmodernism's "commitment to surface and the *superficial*" signifies a retreat from the "protopolitical vocation and the terrorist stance of the older modernism" (Foreword xviii). In distinguishing pastiche from parody, Jameson further argues that postmodernist art thematizes the failure of the modernist project ("Postmodernism and Consumer Society"). Given the eclipse of conditions for modernist stylistic innovation—that is, of individualism and of any linguistic norm with which to contrast styles—postmodernist imitation lacks any satirical impulse. Instead of parody, pastiche is thus the only possible mode for responding to the past: "All that is left is to imitate dead styles, to speak through the masks and through the voices of the styles in the imaginary museum. But this means that contemporary or postmodernist art is going to be about art itself in a new kind of way; even more, it means that one of its essential messages will involve the necessary failure of art and the aesthetic, the failure of the new, the imprisonment in the past." Jameson's formulation accurately describes the play of allusion and quotation on the textual surface of a writer like

O'Hara. O'Hara's writing, however, represents less an "imprisonment in the past" than the recognition that history is accessible only through its representations. If O'Hara's multivalent texts suggest that style is not freely expressed but is written through cultural codes, they also reveal that history is not a given that is immediately accessible by allusion but rather must be always constructed. Furthermore, Jameson's totalizing formulation of postmodernism as a cultural dominant, following Ernest Mandel's socioeconomic periodization, obscures how postmodernist practices often retain the vanguardist oppositional impulse while rejecting the formalist notion of textual autonomy, as Andreas Huyssen and Linda Hutcheon have argued. Huyssen's analysis of postwar American cultural politics is especially germane for analyzing the poetry of the New York school. He underlines the importance of the reception and institutionalization of modernism—in the academy, as well as in the "burgeoning museum, gallery, concert, record and paperback culture"—for defining the adversarial stance of 1960s postmodernism: "It was this specific radicalism of the avantgarde, directed against the institutionalization of high art as a discourse of hegemony and a machinery of meaning, that recommended itself as a source of energy and inspiration to the American postmodernists of the 1960's.... The irony in all of this is that the first time the U.S. had something resembling an 'institution art' in the emphatic European sense, it was modernism itself, the kind of art whose purpose had always been to resist institutionalization." From his prominent position within "institution art," that is, within the New York art-publishing and museum world, O'Hara in his poetry actually invokes a dialogical relation between past traditions and the present more analogous to Charles Jencks's examples of postmodernist architecture and Hutcheon's examples of "historiographic metafiction" than to clearly politically marked postmodernist practices. Jencks argues that postmodernist architecture subverts modernist aestheticism through a process of "double coding," an interplay of modernist technique with allusion to popular traditions to communicate both with "experts" and a more general public audience. In O'Hara's case, if the "experts," literary critics and historians, concentrate primarily on the narrative surface of his poetry, it is because his process of double coding challenges this dichotomy of experts and public. Many of his most obscurely autobiographical texts also participate in the general project of rewriting modern literary history. While his poetry appeals to a general audience through its recognizable narrative structures, it challenges "experts" to become conversant with the details of his life, especially within the New York art world and the gay community, as well as with modern literary history. In stressing the moment and site of enunciation, and frequently the specific receiver as well as the sender of the poetic text, O'Hara subverts the expertise of literary critics while enhancing the value of "local" knowledge.

An early O'Hara poem which cogently, although obliquely, evokes the postwar crisis of historical memory that Jameson associates with the postmodern is "Memorial Day 1950." This "pastiche" of modernist styles critically interrogates the concept of the "vanguard," anticipating O'Hara's more specific, more explicit practice and explanation of intertextuality in his later lyric poetry and criticism. Marjorie Perloff cites this poem, written during O'Hara's final year at Harvard, as a breakthrough which adumbrates his later distinctive poetic achievement, the fusion of the surrealist "dialectic of polarized images" with Williams's colloquialism. Yet this poem not only replicates the vanguardist techniques of the artists it names, it enacts an interrogation of the subtexts relating modernism and modernity. From the poem's title—specifying a moment of reflection at the midpoint of the twentieth century—until its enigmatic yet apocalyptic conclusion, "Memorial Day 1950" fuses and confuses personal memory with codified historical memory, personal desire with textual knowledge, imagination with recollection. The title memorializes not only the moment of reflection but the moments reflected on, from the reflection on the war dead designated by the official holiday to the poet's reflection on his biological and literary "parents." In what seem like random associations between fractured literary fragments and recollections of childhood trauma, the poem explores the structures of feeling linking aesthetic vanguardism with military vanguardism. While mocking the self-aggrandizing posture of both the aesthetic manifesto and the bildungsroman, the poem conveys a version of modern literary history that acknowledges the rhetorical appeal of vanguardist utopianism while questioning the corresponding impulse to destroy past accomplishments. In parodying modernist texts, it mocks its own destructive impulse. In leaving the poet's attitude toward his modernist predecessors ambivalent, "Memorial Day 1950" implicates its readers in a questioning of how aesthetic forms represent modes of interpreting history.

The semantic instability of "Memorial Day 1950" begins with its cryptic opening sentence:

Picasso made me tough and quick, and the world;
just as in a minute plane trees are knocked down
outside my window by a crew of creators.
(*Collected Poems*)

The comma which separates "and the world" from the initial clause is especially puzzling, as it raises questions concerning both the production and the reception of complex artistic texts. What is the status of "made" in this clause? Do we locate the semantic stress on the act of making, the "made" text, or the audience "made... tough and quick" by the text? Did Picasso make "me... and the world," thus implying the poet's total identification with Picasso's made world? Or is he maintaining some distance from Picasso while affirming the effects of his painting? Such interpretive questions are specific to complex artistic texts, but they also foreground the interpreter's historical difference. To consider Picasso in 1950 calls into question the relation of cubist aesthetics to modern warfare posited by such commentaries as Gertrude Stein's: "I very well remember at the beginning of the war being with Picasso on the boulevard Raspail when the first camouflage truck passed. It was at night, we had heard of camouflage but we had not yet seen it and Picasso amazed looked at it and then cried out, yes it is we who made it, that is cubism." Furthermore, it is impossible to read "Picasso," perhaps *the* signifier for the international avant-garde, without acknowledging the diverse appropriations of his aesthetics and his name. As the poem's parody of Stein's syntax and diction suggests, the effect of Picasso's multiple technical revolutions on the poet's own development cannot be severed from the objectification of Picasso as a cultural icon. As the opening line of "Memorial Day 1950" dramatizes the semantic instability of vanguardist texts through its fractured syntax, the conclusion of this opening sentence, although an apparently straightforward statement, becomes more questionable in its equation of destruction and creation. The textualized trees, "in a minute plane" of the cubist surface, fuse with the "plane trees... outside my window." The mundane act of knocking down trees to "create" a new landscape, an act epitomizing bourgeois progressivism, evolves into the image of Picasso the ax wielder. In the understated tone of this first verse paragraph, the poem establishes a problematic affiliation of vanguardist manifesto rhetoric with the rhetoric of warfare: "to fight for the last ditch and heap / of rubbish" in response to Picasso asserts the value of the quotidian and the demotic for artistic texts, but only because the context of modern warfare animates our awareness of such value.

It could be argued that "Memorial Day 1950" is hardly surrealist at all, that the images of artistic production, warfare, and bourgeois family life follow an internal logic of violent rebellion that challenges the polarity of destruction and creation. The poem does not follow consistently logical rhetorical patterns, however. Its generative principle appears to arise from the exhaustion felt by the artist in the wake of the historical avant-garde, as the second verse paragraph implies:

> Through all that surgery I thought
> I had a lot to say, and named several last things
> Gertrude Stein hadn't had time for; but then
> the war was over, those things had survived
> and even when you're scared art is no dictionary.
> Max Ernst told us that.

This passage epitomizes the anxiety of the postmodernist poet that everything has been said, that formal innovation is no longer possible, and that the world wars have achieved the act of revolutionary destruction that vanguardist rhetoric called for. The postwar artist must then accept a role analogous to that of Alice B. Toklas, the "autobiographical" subject constructed by Stein, as the poet is "made" by Picasso. The remainder of the poem enacts this process of literary ventriloquism, as the names and words of Klee, Auden, Rimbaud, Pasternak, and Apollinaire, among others, comically reverberate through the fragments of battles the young poet has with his parents. In fusing vanguardist models of rebellion with the recollections of his own adolescent rebellion, O'Hara imparts an absurd sense of the quotidian to these artists whose earlier transformations of everyday life had earned them a monumental status by 1950. And in situating these fragmentary fusings of manifestos and family disputes in the bloodshed of modern warfare, O'Hara imparts an urgency to his poem's articulation of its own historical moment. "Memorial Day 1950" enacts a process of appropriation and distancing from O'Hara's modernist predecessors, as one of its buried narratives, the transformation of Picasso's "The Man with the Blue Guitar," epitomizes. At first the original "maker," Picasso is next invoked through his best-known commentary on wartime destruction: "Guernica hollered look out." Immediately following this, the poet figures himself as the artist in "tight blue pants," as he confronts

his disapproving parents. His parents are then generalized as the "older people" who "entered / my cheap hotel room and broke / my guitar and my can / of blue paint." The figure made by Picasso has now become the maker, the man with the "can / of blue paint," as well as the made, the man with the guitar. This image reappears in the poem's conclusion:

> Guitar strings hold up pictures. I don't need
> a piano to sing, and naming things is only the
>   intention
> to make things.

In distancing himself from the maker of "The Man with the Blue Guitar," O'Hara does not reject the technical accomplishments of Picasso, not to mention Wallace Stevens; rather, he rejects the definition of art that limits the object to its exchange value as a commodity. In figuring his own poetic stance as an improvisational act of holding up pictures with guitar strings, O'Hara portrays the postmodernist representation of the past as a mode of bricolage. "Memorial Day 1950" is indeed a pastiche of vanguardist rhetoric, yet its parodic play on modes of rebellion underscores the complex historicity of any aesthetic, including (and especially) that of its own.

O'Hara's statements on the social functions of art are diffuse and sometimes contradictory, but his occasional writings on his contemporaries, in both the literary and visual arts, express a more complex consideration of the historical difference of the avant-garde in postwar American culture than is generally acknowledged. In differentiating between the European notion of vanguardism and its American counterpart in "American Art and Non-American Art," O'Hara claims that European art treats the aesthetic and the political as equally important distinct categories, whereas American art combines the aesthetic with the political, thus resulting in its "metaphysical quality" (*Standing Still* 97). Yet this does not mean that art in America serves no social function. Citing Gregory Corso's poem "Bomb," he writes: "It is the character of the avant-garde to absorb and transform disparate qualities not normally associated with art, for the artist to take within him the violence and evil of his times and come out with something. . . . In this way society can bear and understand and finally appreciate the qualities of alien and even dangerous things." This description of the avant-garde's relation to "society" corresponds with O'Hara's understanding of how the vanguardist stance is internalized. In a 1965 interview with Edward Lucie-Smith, O'Hara generalizes that the avant-garde can no longer be defined by a political or socioeconomic condition of detachment or isolation, arguing that when artists such as Andy Warhol become celebrities, such a stance is absurd: "there's no reason to attack a culture that will allow it to happen, and even foster the impulse—and create it. Which is a *change*, you see, from the general idea of, that all avant-garde art has to be attacking the bourgeoisie" (*Standing Still*). As postwar American capitalism contains opposition to the extent that the marketplace even encourages it, the vanguardist impulse for innovation no longer plays such a viable critical role. What becomes most important, then, is how art positions itself within traditions of innovation and in doing so transforms our perception of past forms. O'Hara's monograph on Jackson Pollock is especially instructive for explaining this conception of intertextuality. . . .

Source: John Lowney, "The 'Post-Anti-Esthetic' Poetics of Frank O'Hara," in *Contemporary Literature*, Vol. 32, No. 2, Summer 1991, pp. 244–64.

Fred Moramarco

In the following excerpt, Moramarco depicts O'Hara's poetry as a manifestation of the "painterly esthetic of Abstract Expressionism."

It is in the poetry of New York poets like O'Hara and Ashbery that the painterly esthetic of Abstract Expressionism manifests itself in literary art. . . .

O'Hara's connection with the New York art scene dates from about 1950, when he first worked at the Museum of Modern Art and became acquainted with many of the most innovative painters in the New York area at the time. But I am concerned here less with the biographical relationships between O'Hara . . . and the New York painters than with the esthetic relationship between [his] poetry and the canvases of the New York School. The "casual insight" that O'Hara finds at the center of Jackson Pollock's achievement, for example, is a description as well of his own poetic style. Writing about Pollock, O'Hara finds.

> the ego totally absorbed in the work. By being "in" the specific painting, as he himself put it, he gave himself over to the cultural necessities which, in turn, freed him from the external encumbrances which surround art as an occasion of extreme cultural concern.

These external encumbrances are precisely what O'Hara liberates himself from in his own poetry. His is not a poetry of extreme cultural concern, but rather is one focused on the momentary and the transient, on the hundreds of minor details which make up all of our days. His poetry is concerned with movies he has seen, friends he has visited, stores he has shopped at, birthdays he has celebrated, meals he has eaten. The "action" of O'Hara's life is in his poetry in the same way that Pollock's creative life is directly captured in his paintings.

So many of O'Hara's poems are playful, "casually insightful" celebrations of the esthetic autonomy of the creative act. The last stanza of "Autobiographia Literaria" (the serious, Coleridge-inspired title, of course, totally at odds with the spirit of the poem) specifically celebrates this esthetic ego involvement:

> And here I am, the
> center of all beauty!
> writing these poems!
> Imagine!

The wonder here is a mock-wonder—whimsical rather than Whitmanic—but it is aimed at calling our attention to the "action" of making the poem. Here, as elsewhere in O'Hara's work, the mock-heroic posturing is only superficially satirical. Underlying the casual chronicles of everyday events in his work is a deep commitment to the transformative qualities of poetry—its ability to open our eyes, sharpen our perceptions, involve us more totally with the world around us. O'Hara's whimsy is, if I may be permitted an oxymoron, a serious whimsy. . . .

[O'Hara's work] has apparent affinities with Pop-Art: in poems like the one beginning "Lana Turner has collapsed" or the delightful poem called "the Lay of the Romance of the Associations" in which the Fifth and Park Avenue Associations in New York attempt to get together, only to be frustrated because "that bourgeois Madison Avenue continues to obstruct our free intercourse with each other." But the sense of playfulness and social satire O'Hara's poems share with Pop-Art seems to me less substantial than the "action" involvement of the writer within the poem and the relationship of that literary idea to the painterly esthetic of Abstract Expressionism. . . .

One gets the . . . sense of what I would like to call the "casual" total involvement in O'Hara's work in this statement by William Baziotes, the well-known painter of the New York School: "I work on many canvases at once. In the morning I line them up against the wall of my studio. Some speak; some do not. They are mirrors. They tell me what I am like at the moment." The last two sentences are pure O'Hara; the mimetic function of art is limited to an imitation of the artist's immediate sensibility—"what I am like at the moment"—not an external or objective scene or series of events, or enduring and universal human values.

The achievement of O'Hara and the Abstract Expressionists shows us that transient matters can be dealt with in an enduring way. The art of the moment does not always have to be propagandistic and tied to rapidly changing social issues. When the moment-to-moment reality of the individual becomes the focus, the art becomes made up of the very stuff of life itself. Art has always been preoccupied with the universal, these artists seem to be telling us, but life continues to serve up a steady diet of particulars. It is as a careful chronicler of those particulars that O'Hara has made his mark on literary history. . . .

"Poem for a Painter" makes specific O'Hara's painterly sympathies and his inclination to view the art of painting as more able to capture fleeting emotional moments than poetry. In lines reminiscent of Hart Crane, he writes, "The ice of your imagination lends / an anchor to the endless sea of pain." The painterly imagination is frozen; the event captured on the canvas is its own enduring record. O'Hara wrote a great deal about painters in his poetry as well as his prose, and there can be no question, I think, that he attempted to consolidate the achievement of Abstract Expressionism in literary art. . . .

Source: Fred Moramarco, "John Ashbery and Frank O'Hara: The Painterly Poets," in *Journal of Modern Literature*, Vol. 5, No. 3, September 1976, pp. 436–62.

SOURCES

Feldman, Alan, *Frank O'Hara*, Twayne Publishers, 1979, p. 158.

Koch, Kenneth, Review of "Second Avenue," in *Partisan Review*; reprinted as "From 'Poetry Chronicles,'" in *Frank O'Hara: To Be True to a City*, edited by Jim Elledge, University of Michigan Press, 1990, p. 9.

O'Hara, Frank, "Poem (Lana Turner Has Collapsed)," in *Digressions on Some Poems by Frank O'Hara*, by Joe LeSueur, Farrar, Straus and Giroux, 2003, p. 264.

Sorrentino, Gilbert, Review of *Lunch Poems*, in *Bookweek*; reprinted in *Frank O'Hara: To Be True to a City*, edited by Jim Elledge, University of Michigan Press, 1990, pp. 15–16.

"Turner, Lana," in *Lana Turner Home Page*, http://www.lanaturner.org/lana-turner-biography (accessed November 16, 2010).

Ward, Jeff, "Introduction: The New York School of Poets," in *Statues of Liberty: The New York School of Poets*, 2nd ed., Palgrave, 2001, pp. 1–4.

FURTHER READING

Blasing, Mutlu Konuk, "Frank O'Hara: 'How Am I to Become a Legend?'" in *Politics and Form in Postmodern Poetry*, Cambridge University Press, 1995, pp. 30–66.
  This book devotes long sections to postmodern poets, including James Merrill and Elizabeth Bishop. In the section about O'Hara, Blasing provides a look at the broader social significance of the poetry.

Dyer, Richard, "Judy Garland and Gay Men," in *Heavenly Bodies: Film Stars and Society*, Macmillan Educational, 1986, pp. 137–91.
  Garland was an even greater icon than Turner in gay male culture throughout the 1960s, for similar reasons. Dyer's analysis of the appeal of Judy Garland can offer some background about what made Lana Turner special to O'Hara and his audience.

Gooch, Brad, *City Poet: The Life and Times of Frank O'Hara*, Alfred A. Knopf, 1993.
  This massive, extensively researched work is considered the definitive biography of O'Hara.

LeSueur, Joe, *Digressions on Some Poems by Frank O'Hara*, Farrar, Straus and Giroux, 2003.
  LeSueur, who lived with O'Hara for ten years, recounts his memories about the circumstances surrounding the writing and publication of some poems, including this one.

Shaw, Lytle, *Frank O'Hara: The Poetics of Coterie*, University of Iowa Press, 2006.
  Shaw's book focuses on O'Hara's close friendships with other writers and painters and how these associations affected his work.

Silverberg, Mark, *The New York School Poets and the Neo-Avant-Garde: Between Radical Art and Radical Chic*, Ashgate Press, 2010.
  Silverberg's book provides context for the literary movement with which O'Hara is most often associated, showing its place in history and particularly the contemporary world of poetry.

Stevens, Wallace, "Relations between Poetry and Painting," *The Necessary Angel: Essays on Reality and the Imagination*, Vintage Press, 1965, pp. 157–92.
  Stevens, one of the most revered American poets of the twentieth century, delivered this address at the Metropolitan Museum of Art in 1951. It is considered to be a prime influence on O'Hara's artistic theories.

SUGGESTED SEARCH TERMS

Frank O'Hara

Frank O'Hara AND Lana Turner

New York School of Poetry

Lana Turner AND gay culture

Frank O'Hara AND celebrity

city poetry

1960s poetry

current events AND poetry

poetry AND popular culture

Lana Turner AND celebrity gossip

Pride

DAHLIA RAVIKOVITCH
1969

"Pride" is a poem by the Israeli poet Dahlia Ravikovitch. It was first published in Hebrew in her collection *The Third Book* in 1969. The poem was translated into English and is available in Ravikovitch's *The Window: New and Selected Poems*, translated and edited by Chana Bloch and Ariel Bloch (1989), and, in a slightly different translation, in *Hovering at a Low Altitude: The Collected Poetry of Dahlia Ravikovitch*, translated by Chana Bloch and Chana Kronfeld (2009). "Pride" is written in free verse and explores by analogy the quality of pride in human life. The poem describes how over time even rocks will crack, and the process takes place in surprising fashion, as it does in people when pride is eventually cast away. Although Ravikovitch's work is not well known to English-speaking readers, she was for decades one of Israel's most popular and acclaimed poets. Her sudden death in 2005 made headlines in the nation's newspapers. "Pride" is an accessible introduction to her work and is a good example of the poetic voice she cultivated over the years.

AUTHOR BIOGRAPHY

Ravikovitch was born on November 17, 1936, in Ramat Gan, Palestine. This was before the creation of the modern state of Israel in 1948, and

Cracked rocks *(Max Baumann / Shutterstock.com)*

Palestine was under British rule. Ravikovitch's father, Levi, was a Jewish-Russian engineer who emigrated to Palestine from China in the early 1930s. Her mother, Michal, was a teacher. In 1942, when Ravikovitch was six, her father was killed after being run over by a car. Following this tragedy, her mother moved to Kibbutz Geva with her daughter and twin sons. Ravikovitch was unhappy in this environment, and at the age of thirteen, she left for Haifa, where she lived with the first of a number of foster families.

In high school in Haifa, Ravikovitch discovered her love of literature, and she was mentored by her teacher Baruch Kurzweil. She published her first poetry when she was eighteen and serving in the Israeli Army Signal Corps. She also married at eighteen, but the marriage ended after only three months.

Ravikovitch entered the Hebrew University in Jerusalem, studying English literature and Hebrew linguistics. She was awarded a fellowship for study at Oxford University in England. Her first collection of poetry, *The Love of an Orange*, written in Hebrew, was published in

1959 and immediately established her as an important new voice in what was known in Israel as the post-1948 Statehood Generation.

From 1959 to 1963, Ravikovitch worked as a high-school teacher in Tel Aviv and later as a journalist writing about theater and television. Her second volume of poetry, *Hard Winter* (1964) further established her reputation, as did *The Third Book*, published in 1969, in which the poem "Pride" appears. After *Deep Calleth* (1976), a volume of her poetry was published in English for the first time, as *Dress of Fire* (1978), she gained many new readers worldwide. In 1978, with Haim Kalire, with whom she lived for thirteen years, she gave birth to a son, Ido.

Up to this point, Ravikovitch's poetry had focused mostly on the personal, but during the 1980s, following the Israeli invasion of Lebanon in 1982, she dealt also with political issues. She became an outspoken supporter of rights for the Palestinians and a member of the Israeli peace movement. The fruits of this greater political awareness appeared in her books *True Love* (1987) and *Mother and Child* (1992). By this time Ravikovitch was a much-loved and admired figure in Israel, gaining the status of a celebrity. *The Window: New and Selected Poems* (1989) was another selection of her poems translated into English. It was in this volume that "Pride" appeared for the first time in English. In the 1990s, Ravikovitch published *The Complete Poems So Far* (1995) and *Half an Hour Before the Monsoon* (1998).

During her career, Ravikovitch also published three collections of short stories, *Death in the Family* (1976), *Willie Mandela's Soccer Team* (1997), and *Come and Gone* (2005). She published eight books of children's verse, as well as many translations of children's books and English-language poetry, including the works of T. S. Eliot, W. B. Yeats, and Edgar Allan Poe.

Ravikovitch won many awards, including the Bialik Prize in 1997 and the Israel Prize in 1998, the highest national award in Israel. Her poetry has been translated into twenty-three languages.

Ravikovitch died suddenly on August 21, 2005, in Tel Aviv, Israel. Many believed that she committed suicide since she had spent time in psychiatric hospitals and had several episodes of depression during her life. However, suicide as the cause of death was never established beyond doubt. Her collection *Many Waters: Poems, 1995–2005* was published posthumously in 2006.

POEM TEXT

Even rocks crack, I tell you,
and not on account of age.
For years they lie on their backs
in the cold and the heat,
so many years,   5
it almost creates the impression of calm.
They don't move, so the cracks can hide.
A kind of pride.
Years pass over them as they wait.
Whoever is going to shatter them   10
hasn't yet come.
And so the moss flourishes, the seaweed is cast
   about,
the sea bursts out and slides back,
and it seems the rocks are perfectly still.
Till a little seal comes to rub against them,   15
comes and goes.
And suddenly the stone has an open wound.
I told you, when rocks crack, it happens by
   surprise.
Not to mention people.

POEM SUMMARY

Lines 1–7

In its English translation, "Pride" is a free-verse poem consisting of nineteen lines of varying length. It is written in the form of a direct address by a first-person speaker to her readers. This is apparent from the first line, in which the speaker makes clear she is going to give out a piece of wisdom that is on the surface about rocks, although rocks throughout the poem are metaphors for people. She announces in line 1 that rocks, even though they are very hard substances, will eventually develop cracks. This will not be simply because they are old, line 2 states. In lines 3 and 4, the rocks are presented as being like living creatures that lie supine, whatever the weather, in all seasons, for a very long time. It might seem to an observer, line 6 states, that the rocks are calm and untroubled (again, the rocks are discussed as if they were living beings). Nothing moves, so if there are any cracks in the rocks, they are not noticeable.

Lines 8–14

In line 8, the speaker expresses the idea that the qualities of rocks she has presented in the first seven lines mean that rocks can be seen as possessing pride. It is as if they are confident that they will never change, as if they are masters of their environment.

Lines 9 to 14 elaborate on the seeming invincibility of the rocks. Years go by, and nothing appears to happen to them, although lines 10 and 11 make clear that such a situation will not endure forever. Lines 12 and 13 describe some of the things that happen to rocks, all in terms of natural phenomena. Moss grows on them, seaweed is swept back and forth over them as the tides of the sea wash in and then retreat. Still, line 14 proclaims, the rocks seem to endure everything without changing.

Lines 15–19

In line 15, something unexpected happens. The rocks have endured, seemingly for time immemorial, without any apparent change. Then a seal rubs up against them, and suddenly (or so it seems) the rock is changed—opened up, it would appear, and in such a way that suggests a wound. Something has happened to affect its apparently unchangeable, invincible nature.

In line 18, the poet reminds the reader of what she said in the first line of the poem in order to point out that she has now demonstrated the truth of what she said at the beginning. What is emphasized is the surprising nature of the event she has described.

In the final line, she makes explicit the implicit metaphor that has been operating throughout—the pride of rocks is a metaphor for the quality of pride in people—by stating that people change too, in just such a surprising manner.

THEMES

Pride

The word pride has two main meanings, one positive and the other negative. If a person is proud of his achievements in life, or proud of his children, for example, this is taken as a virtue. It conveys the person's sense of dignity or worth; it is related to self-esteem and self-respect. The second meaning of the word pride indicates that a person has an exaggerated or unrealistic opinion of himself. He may be conceited, for example, and show arrogant and haughty behavior. It is pride in this negative sense that is intended in this poem. Indeed, in Christianity, pride is considered to be one of the seven deadly sins, and sometimes the worst of them all. It is the opposite of humility. A person is guilty of pride when he exalts himself above others. He may think himself more important than others, for example, or morally superior. In the religious sense, pride is related to taking too much credit oneself for one's qualities or behaviors rather than acknowledging that all goodness flows only by the grace of God. Ravikovitch is a Jewish rather than a Christian poet, but scriptures that are common to both traditions and known to Christians as the Old Testament have plenty of references to the sin of pride. The book of Proverbs, for example, contains the following admonitions: "Pride goes before destruction, and a haughty spirit before a fall" (16:18) and "A man's pride will bring him low, but he who is lowly in spirit will obtain honor" (29:23).

What is emphasized in the poem is a particular aspect of pride, or an attitude that flows from being too proud: a refusal to bend or change, no matter what happens. This is said of rocks, but the poet has people in mind as well. It implies a kind of stubbornness, the belief that one is not affected by external events, that one is not part of a wider whole and can go on remaining just as one is for as long as one likes. The point of the poem is that such a belief is erroneous because wider forces play upon the individual at all times. Many of these may appear to have no effect at all, but in reality they do, because eventually something happens to cause change even in that which appears impervious to change (a prideful or stubborn person, for example). The poem suggests that these direct agents of change can be very surprising, not at all what one might have expected. It suggests that life cannot be controlled quite in the way that the proud might prefer. Even pride, in the long run, is vulnerable and can be broken.

Change

In order to illustrate the theme that even the most prideful person will eventually come up against something that will put a dent in his or her pride, the poet employs the notion of geological change over a long period of time. Geology, the study of the history of the structure of the earth, is very different from psychology or sociology, the studies of how people behave individually or in groups, but the poet finds some commonality in them. Geology deals with vast stretches of time; there are two allusions in the poem to the age of rocks, and the passage of many years is also mentioned three times. In the physical structure of the earth, change shows up only very gradually; everything can look the same for millennia, but nonetheless a process of geological evolution is going on. In that sense, appearances are deceptive. Nothing remains the same forever; even the hardest of substances is eventually subject to visible change. The poem implies that change is latent within the rock, even when that change cannot be directly observed. In exactly the same way, change comes to people, even to those who most stubbornly resist it. The poem thus presents an optimistic theme. It implies that even in situations that might appear hopeless—dealing with a stubborn or prideful person or society, perhaps—change will come if one is patient, and it may come from an unexpected source.

TOPICS FOR FURTHER STUDY

- Research the latest news on Israeli-Palestinian relations by searching Google News (using search terms such as "Israeli-Palestinian conflict"). Write an entry on your blog site in which you express your reaction to the latest news. Consider what in your view should or could be done to advance the peace process.

- Write a poem in which you take a process in nature and apply it to human life. In "Pride," for example, rocks eventually crack, and there is a lesson in this for people, too. In nature also, flowers bloom and wither, while clouds gather and pass. It is not difficult to think of hundreds of examples. As you write your poem, try to use personification, as Ravikovitch does in "Pride." (Personification is the description of inanimate objects in terms that would normally be used only of people.) Using personification effectively can make your poem more powerful and subtle than it might otherwise be.

- Read *The Enemy Has a Face*, by Gloria D. Miklowitz (2003), a young-adult novel about a fourteen-year-old Israeli student in Los Angeles who at first dislikes Palestinians. But when her brother goes missing, one of her Palestinian classmates befriends her, and she is forced to rethink her attitude toward Palestinians. After reading the novel, write a short essay in which you describe the theme of the novel and then relate it to Ravikovitch's poem "Pride." Does the novel shed any light on the poem, or vice versa?

- Organize a class debate about the Israeli-Palestinian conflict. There should be two groups: one that argues for the Palestinian cause and the other that makes the case for the Israelis. Whatever side you choose to be on, you will need to get clear in your mind the main elements in this long-running conflict. Why do the two sides find it so difficult to come to an agreement? What does each side want? Have each side create an online bookmarking site to collect resources to use when formulating evidence for the debate.

STYLE

Free Verse

The poem is written in free verse. Free verse does not follow traditional forms of rhyme or meter. The poet is free to invent his or her own structure, following no rules, guided only by what the poet believes to be the best way of expressing the intended subject or theme. This poem does not employ rhyme at all; its most noticeable stylistic feature, which marks much free verse, is a variation in line length. There are long lines containing up to eleven or twelve syllables (lines 12 and 18), and several short lines of between three and five syllables (such as lines 5, 8, 11, 16, and 19). The purpose of the differing line lengths is to give variety to the poem. Another way of providing variety in a long line is through the caesura, a pause within the line. The poet uses commas to create caesuras in lines 1, 7, 12, and 18.

Six of the nineteen lines consist of a single sentence, ending with a period; such lines are said to be end-stopped. This means that the end of the line coincides with the end of a clause. The meaning is self-contained within the line. In end-stopped lines, there is no push for the reader to go on to the next line to get the meaning. End-stopped lines can also end with commas.

Personification

Personification is a figure of speech in which an inanimate object or abstract idea is presented as if it were alive and acted like a person, with human feelings and sensibilities. In "Pride," rocks are

Moss on stones (*R. Jegosyn / Shutterstock.com*)

personified; they appear as conscious actors. They lie on their backs and have the capacity to wait. They also feel pride. In reality a rock has neither front nor back, cannot lie down on its back (as if it could make a conscious choice to do so), and cannot "wait" for anything, since waiting for something implies consciousness, the ability to envision something happening in the future, for which one is waiting. Nor can a rock possess a quality such as pride. Humans can do and feel these things, but rocks cannot—except when the poet personifies them, making them seem alive.

Metaphor

A metaphor is a figure of speech in which descriptive words that apply to one object or thing are extended to another object. On the surface, the second object may seem very different from the first, but by means of the metaphor, a similarity or even equality between the two is created. Sometimes the subject of the comparison is described as the tenor of the metaphor, and the object that carries the comparison is the vehicle. In this poem, the vehicle is rocks; the

tenor is people. In other words, qualities that apply to rocks are also being extended to people. The metaphor is implied throughout the poem by the personification of rocks; they are presented as doing things and possessing qualities that rocks do not possess literally. The metaphor is made explicit in the final line, when people are mentioned directly for the first time. The metaphor creates the impression the poet wants: rocks are like people; people are like rocks.

HISTORICAL CONTEXT

Israeli Poetry in the 1950s and 1960s

Not long after the creation of the State of Israel in 1948, a new generation of poets changed the direction of Israeli poetry. They reacted against those who had been the dominant figures in Hebrew poetry during the 1930s and 1940s. These established poets included Avraham Schlonsky (1900–1973), Nathan Alterman (1910–1970), Leah Goldberg (1911–1970), and Uri Zvi Greenberg (1894–1981). These poets, all born in Germany

COMPARE & CONTRAST

- **1960s:** In 1967, in the Six-Day War, Israel defeats Egypt, Syria, and Jordan, capturing territory from all three Arab countries. The United Nations Security Council passes a resolution calling for Israeli withdrawal and a peace settlement.

  Today: Israel is at peace with Egypt (since 1979) and Jordan (since 1994). No peace agreement exists with Syria, however. Despite decades of intermittent peace efforts, the two nations remain hostile toward each other.

- **1960s:** The Palestine Liberation Organization (PLO) is founded in 1964. Its purpose is to destroy Israel. In 1969, Yasser Arafat becomes PLO leader. The PLO continues a guerrilla war against Israel and also makes terrorist attacks on civilians in pursuit of its goals.

  Today: The PLO is recognized internationally as the legitimate representative of the Palestinian people. The PLO rejects violence and terrorism and recognized Israel's right to exist in 1993 but is still considered by most experts to be a key player in terrorism against Israel.

- **1960s:** Palestinians who were displaced following the creation of Israel in 1948 and the Six-Day War in 1967 live in refugee camps in the West Bank and the Gaza Strip, as well as in Jordan, Syria, Lebanon, and Iraq.

  Today: Efforts to resolve the Israeli-Palestinian conflict center around the "two-state" solution, which aims to establish an independent Palestinian state in the West Bank and the Gaza Strip. Brokered by the United States, direct talks between the Israelis and Palestinians begin in September 2010.

---

or eastern Europe, introduced modernist themes and techniques into Hebrew literature.

The new poets who emerged in the 1950s were known as the Statehood Generation, those who had come of age after the creation of the State of Israel. These young poets felt the need for a different type of poetry. According to Hamutal Tsamir in his essay "Jewish-Israeli Poetry, Dahlia Ravikovitch, and the Gender of Representation," the young poets viewed the work of Alterman, Schlonsky, and Goldberg in particular as placing too much emphasis on elaborate poetic techniques and on collective rather than personal experience. Furthermore, Tsamir states,

> The dominant symbolist poetics... with its musical rhythms, rich metaphors, high-flown language, pathos, and glorification of heroism and death—were seen... as impersonal and as obscuring the individual experience. In order to express the specific life experience of the individual person, the Statehood Generation poets favored free verse and internal rhyme, plain language, a prosaic and subdued tone, and a focus on the daily lives of ordinary people.

In his article "The 1960s: The New Israelis," Mordechai Bar-On makes a similar point about this change in terms of the wider Israeli culture. He notes that for most of the 1950s, "Israeli culture was dominated by the spirit and traditions... of patriotism, nation building, of heroism and shared struggle." However, by the end of the decade there was a significant cultural shift:

> [A] new wave appeared, a wave of poets, songwriters, authors and critics who deliberately broke with the previous generation and announced a change in approach. They thought the old generation was too collectivist, too nationalistic. The young artists were influenced by the new wave that was sweeping through Europe and the West, focusing on the individual, on freedom and self-expression.

Prominent figures in the poets of the Statehood Generation, in addition to Ravikovitch, were Natan Zach (sometimes spelled Nathan

Seal on the beach *(Petrova Maria | Shutterstock.com)*

Zakh), David Avidan, Yehuda Amichai, Moshe Dor, Aryeh Sivan, Binyamin Hrushovsky, and Israel Pinkas. By the late 1950s, they had become the dominant voices in Israeli poetry. According to Tsamir, it was Zach who was their most important spokesman. Zach was born in Berlin, Germany, in 1930 and immigrated at the age of six with his parents to what was then Palestine. He published his first collection of poetry in 1955 and several more in the 1960s. He also wrote an influential essay, published in 1966, in which he outlined fifteen major characteristics of the new movement in Israeli poetry. Tsamir describes this as "a programmatic manifesto of the Statehood Generation and, moreover, a demonstration of their power as the new arbiters of taste."

Despite Zach's prominence, however, it was Amichai who went on to become the most noted of the Statehood Generation poets. He was born in Germany in 1924 and immigrated to Palestine with his family in 1935. He fought in the Arab-Israeli War of 1948 and published his first collection of poetry in 1955. Amichai was also a novelist. In the 1960s, with the translation of his work into English, he began to acquire an international reputation. His *Selected Poetry* was published in English in 1968, and his novel *Not of This Time, Not of This Place*, published in Hebrew in 1963, was translated into English and published in the United States also in 1968.

Israel in the 1950s and 1960s

The modern nation-state of Israel was born during the time that Ravikovitch was growing up. The creation of Israel in 1948 was immediately followed by an Arab invasion, and during the war, twelve-year-old Ravikovitch wrote an idealistic poem about how in the future, the nation of Israel would not pursue a course of violence or war.

During the 1950s, immigration produced a sharp rise in the population of Israel. Immigrants consisted mainly of Holocaust survivors and Jews from Arab countries. The population of Israel in 1958 was more than double what it had been in 1948. Tel Aviv, where Ravikovitch lived, underwent enormous growth during the 1950s and 1960s.

However, also during this period, Israel, a small state surrounded by enemies that wished to destroy it, was involved in two wars. In the Sinai War in 1956, Israel joined forces with Britain and France following Egypt's closure of the Suez Canal to Israeli shipping and subsequent nationalization of the canal. The joint military campaign to retake the canal was initially successful, but by March 1957, pressure from the United States and the Soviet Union forced the Israelis, the British, and the French to withdraw.

In June 1967, the Six-Day War was fought, in which the Arab nations of Egypt, Syria, and Jordan were quickly defeated by Israel. Israel captured East Jerusalem and the West Bank (of the River Jordan) from Jordan; the Gaza Strip and Sinai Peninsula from Egypt; and the Golan Heights from Syria. In November 1967, the United Nations Security Council passed resolutions calling for Israel to withdraw from the territories it occupied as a result of the war in exchange for a peace that would be accepted by all parties in the conflict. The issue of the Israeli-occupied territories became a vital question for the remainder of the decade and into the 1970s and beyond.

The fate of the Palestinians and their descendants who had been made refugees as a result of the Arab-Israeli War of 1948 also became a major issue at this time. The Palestine Liberation Organization was founded in 1964. Since the Six-Day War, most of the Palestinians have lived in the occupied West Bank and Gaza Strip.

CRITICAL OVERVIEW

Reviews of Ravikovitch's work that have appeared in English have been universally positive. Matthew Rothschild, reviewing *Hovering at a Low Altitude* in *Progressive* magazine, states that Ravikovitch is "a poet of tremendous range and formal control" and that she "can dazzle you with a romantic poem and shake you with a political insight." Lurie Margot, reviewing the same volume in *New Criterion*, comments on "the extraordinary stylistic control that lets her poems hum their messages like tuning forks."

In an obituary of Ravikovitch published in the London *Guardian*, Lawrence Joffe observes that "Ravikovitch's poems seem disarmingly simple, yet swarm with multiple meanings." Joffe also states,

Subversive wit and a yearning for liberty and justice inform much of Ravikovitch's writing. Her earlier work is full of puns, Biblical references and playful allusions to Greek mythology, faraway palaces and kings. In "Pride" she transposes human emotions on to an inanimate object, a rock that survives eons, only to crumble when rubbed by a little seal.

For translators Chana Bloch and Chana Kronfeld, in their introduction to *Hovering at a Low Altitude*, Ravikovitch's poetry is primarily about "power and powerlessness"; she presents "the devastating consequences of unequal power relations for the individual and for society, the self in a state of crisis refracting the state of the nation."

CRITICISM

Bryan Aubrey

Aubrey holds a PhD in English. In the following essay, he discusses "Pride" in terms of Ravikovitch's work as a whole and also in terms of the Israeli-Palestinian conflict.

In Israel, Dahlia Ravikovitch was for decades one of the most popular and well-loved poets in the nation, honored not only for her poetry but also for her work in the cause of peace and justice, including advocating for the rights of the Palestinians. In "The Bell Jar Shatters: the Political Poetry of Dahlia Ravikovitch," an article by Chana Bloch and Chana Kronfeld that appeared in *Tikkun* shortly after Ravikovitch's death, the authors wrote, "Adapting the terms used in the poem, all conflicts, even those involving liberal doses of pride, eventually end, because something comes along, often something quite unpredictable, that alters the rigidity of the status quo."

No other Hebrew poet, with the exception of the late Yehuda Amichai, was so universally embraced by Israelis, whatever their political convictions. Ravikovitch's poems, like Amichai's, were integrated into all facets of Israeli public life—set to music and adapted in theatrical productions, experimental films, dance performances, and art exhibits.

However, at the time of her death, though Ravikovitch's work had been known beyond the borders of Israel for many years, English-speaking students of poetry who did not read Hebrew had access to only a fairly small part of her work, mostly confined to the poems contained in *The*

WHAT DO I READ NEXT?

- *Poets on the Edge: An Anthology of Contemporary Hebrew Poetry*, compiled and translated by Tsipi Keller (2008), is a selection in English from the work of twenty-seven contemporary Israeli poets. Some poems are translated into English for the first time. The collection as a whole conveys the vibrancy and variety of poetry in Israel today. Poets represented, in addition to Ravikovitch, include Yehuda Amichai, David Avidan, Maya Bejerano, T. Carmi, Raquel Chalfi, Mordechai Geldman, Tamir Greenberg, Sharron Hass, Irit Katzir, Tsipi Keller, Amir Or, Dan Pagis, Hava Pinhas-Cohen, Ruth Ramot, Asher Reich, Yona Wollach, Meir Wieseltier, Natan Zach, and Nurit Zarhi.

- Yehuda Amichai is an Israeli poet with an international reputation. His work has been translated into thirty languages, and he is generally considered to be Israel's finest poet. *The Selected Poetry of Yehuda Amichai*, translated by Chana Bloch and Stephen Mitchell (revised and expanded edition, 1996), is an ideal introduction to the range and quality of his work.

- *A Brief History of Israel* (2008), by Bernard Reich, is a book for young adults that describes the history of the modern state of Israel. Reich begins by telling the story of the Jewish people from biblical times to the establishment of the State of Israel in 1948. He then discusses Israeli history over seven main time periods: early development (1948–1967), the Six-Day War and the Yom Kippur War (1967–1975), peace with Egypt (1975–1979), the Palestinian Intifada (1979–1990), the Persian Gulf War and the Middle East peace process (1990–1996), the governments of Benjamin Netanyahu and Ehud Barak (1996–2000), and the al-Aqsa Intifada (2000 to the present). The book includes a chronology and forty-eight photographs and is an excellent introduction to a complex and difficult topic.

- *Poets for Palestine* (2008), compiled by Remi Kanazi, is a collection of poetry and art devoted to Palestine. It includes a range of poets, from contemporary Palestinian voices to the work of more established poets. Authors represented include Mahmoud Darwish, Amiri Baraka, Naomi Shihab Nye, Melissa Tuckey, Ghassan Zaqtan, Remi Kanazi, Dima Hilal, Sholeh Wolpe, Ibtisam Barakat, Philip Metres, Venus Khoury-Ghata, Kathy Engel, Laila Halaby, Junichi P. Semitsu, J. A. Miller, Marian Haddad, Fady Joudah, Marilyn Hacker, Alicia Ostriker, and Annemarie Jacir.

- *Israeli Poetry: A Contemporary Anthology* (1988), edited by Warren Bargad and Stanley F. Chyet, includes selections from forty years of Israeli poetry. The eleven poets represented are Amir Gilboa, Abba Kovner, Haim Gouri, Yehuda Amichai, Dan Pagis, Natan Zach, David Avidan, Dahlia Ravikovitch, Ory Bernstein, Meir Wieseltier, and Yona Wollach. Succinct introductions to each poet put their work in perspective.

- *Understanding the Palestinian-Israeli Conflict: A Primer* (2007), by Phyllis Bennis, is appropriate for anyone who wants to understand the basic issues involved in the long-running conflict between the Israelis and the Palestinians. Bennis, who is an acknowledged authority on the region, explains such important basics as who the Palestinian people are, what the occupied territories are, U.S. policy in the region, and the goals of each party to the conflict. She also discusses such issues as the roles of the United Nations, Europe, and the Arab world.

- *With an Iron Pen: Twenty Years of Hebrew Protest Poetry* (2009) edited by Tal Nitzan and Rachel Tzvia Back, is an anthology of Israeli poets and their response to the ongoing conflicts in the region. The forty-two poets represented, including Ravikovitch, protest against the injustices of war and oppression. In particular, they highlight the suffering of the Palestinians in the West Bank.

IT IS NOT DIFFICULT TO SEE THE ISRAELI-
PALESTINIAN ISSUE, WHICH AROUSED
RAVIKOVITCH'S PASSIONATE INTEREST, AS A
SITUATION IN WHICH A LOT OF ROCKS HAVE TO
BE CRACKED—UNBENDING POSITIONS MODIFIED—
BEFORE ANY PROGRESS CAN BE MADE."

Window: New and Selected Poems, published in 1989. It was only with the publication of *Hovering at a Low Altitude: The Collected Poetry of Dahlia Ravikovitch* in 2009 that the full range of her work became accessible. This book contains about three times as many poems as the earlier edition and allows the reader to see the evolution of Ravikovitch's poetic style. As the translators Bloch and Kronfeld point out, Ravikovitch's early poetry, in the volumes *The Love of an Orange* (1959) and *Hard Winter* (1964), observes traditional poetic forms—apparent even in the translations—but by *The Third Book* (1969), in which "Pride" appears, she had developed a much freer style and a more colloquial kind of language.

This style is quite noticeable in "Pride," with its varied line lengths and quiet, conversational tone. The key image, of the baby seal, is also a striking one, since it is this small, innocent animal—not the cold, not the heat, not the sea—that eventually puts a crack into the rock. This is why it is a surprise. There is a paradox here, also. The immobility of rocks, their apparent immunity to change, suggests the hardness and inflexibility in a person that often accompanies the quality of pride. But the pride of the rock (or the person) is eventually broken or cracked not by some apparently greater or mightier force but by a seemingly lesser one—something that appears on the surface to be weak. Ravikovitch is not the first writer to come up with this rather attractive idea. It can be found for example, albeit with a more conventional image, in the ancient Chinese text known as the *Tao Te Ching*. This text, which is a guide to good living and good government, states, "In the world there is nothing more submissive and weak than

water. Yet for attacking that which is hard and strong nothing can surpass it.... And the submissive overcomes the hard."

So it is, or very nearly so, in "Pride." The poem suggests that everything will yield at some point, even the hardest substance (or person), and when the passage of time has done its work of preparation, almost anything can accomplish the task, even, in the case of a rock, a baby seal. The poet leaves the equivalent in the human world up to the reader's imagination but seems to give the assurance that even the most prideful state of mind in a person will eventually crack and, perhaps, dissolve into something else.

Another arresting image in the poem occurs in line 17. One does not normally think of stones or rocks as things that are capable of being wounded or of carrying a wound. Rocks may crack, but it is people who get wounded. The image is one of several that clearly show the poet's metaphoric intention. The image is interesting from a psychological point of view because it suggests that when an unyielding pride is forced finally to give way, the vulnerability, the hidden hurt, of the person is revealed. It suggests that stubborn pride is in fact a mask for something else, for emotional pain, perhaps. When a crack appears in the pride, the pain is revealed, so it is hardly surprising that people tend to resist anything that might lead to the revelation of the real face behind the mask.

The exploration of the real that lies behind the surface appearances of things is the task of many a poet, and Ravikovitch is no exception. Commentators sometimes observe that her early work, including the poems in *The Third Book*, concentrate mainly on the personal rather than the social and political aspects of life. Some of the poems in *The Third Book* seem to confirm this, including the playful, self-deprecating "Portrait" and the exploration in "A Private Opinion" of whether pain has any value. (It does not, according to the speaker.) However, the description of her work as personal seems far too narrow to convey the great variety of subjects and themes that Ravikovitch explores, even at this fairly early stage of her career. Indeed, her translators comment in their introduction to *Hovering at a Low Altitude* that her poetry "has always had a political dimension." One has only to look at the poem that appears immediately before "Pride" to confirm this. It is called "In Chad and Cameroon," and it presents two contrasting

Rocks near the sea (*zahradales | Shutterstock.com*)

images. Chad and Cameroon are African nations that are former colonies of France. The images contrast the easy life of the Europeans who live there—even if they are discontented with it—with a group of passing lepers, no doubt indigenous to the area. If the poem is somewhat oblique, it nonetheless has all the ingredients of a critique of imperialism. Many of Ravikovitch's later poems have a much sharper and more direct political slant. These include "Get Out of Beirut," a protest against the Israeli invasion of Lebanon in 1982; "Lullaby," about the plight of the Palestinians in the refugee camps in the West Bank and the Gaza Strip; and "The Captors Require a Song," which has a similar theme.

Given the fact that all commentators on Ravikovitch's work remark on the political dimension to her work, and because the hints of such a dimension can be found in *The Third Book*, it is tempting for the reader new to Ravikovitch to see "Pride" in this light too, even if that may not have been Ravikovitch's overt intention when she wrote the poem. But any observer of the continuing conflict between Israel and the Palestinians—the failure over a period of more than forty years, dating from the Six-Day War, to find a just solution—might well think that pride, and "Pride," might have some connection with this unfortunate situation. The Israeli-Palestinian conflict is one of the most intractable conflicts in the world; no one under the age of fifty who follows world events can remember a time when this conflict, and its associated diplomatic maneuvering, the seemingly never-ending, never-producing "Middle East peace process," was not part of the political vocabulary of the times. It might not be irrelevant to point out that in many conflicts between people—both individuals and nations—pride or stubbornness, which tend to go hand in hand, play a role. In disputes involving nations, neither side wants to back down from its declared position, which is often rigidly defined as defending what is "ours," for to do so would involve the humiliation of losing face. So rigid positions are taken up that militate against the compromises necessary for any negotiations in which people have strong disagreements to succeed. It is not difficult to see the Israeli-Palestinian issue, which aroused Ravikovitch's passionate interest, as a situation in which a lot of rocks have to be cracked—unbending positions modified—before any progress can be made. Adapting the terms used in the poem, all conflicts, even those involving liberal doses of pride, eventually end, because something comes along, often something quite unpredictable, that alters the rigidity of the status quo. Those who campaign, as Ravikovitch did, for peace and justice have long been left to reflect that, as in line 9 of the poem, the time for the old rigidities to crack has not yet come. Writing "Pride" in 1969, just two years after the Six-Day War, Ravikovitch could not have guessed how, more than forty years later, her poem would carry such resonance for the troubled situation in her native land.

Source: Bryan Aubrey, Critical Essay on "Pride," in *Poetry for Students*, Gale, Cengage Learning, 2011.

Yair Mazor

In the following essay, Mazor calls Ravikovitch's The Window: New and Selected Poems *a good representative collection.*

The Window offers a good representative collection of poems by Dahlia Ravikovitch (b. 1936), undoubtedly the most prominent female figure in modern Israeli poetry (see *WLT* 58:3, pp. 354–59). The poems are taken from five earlier volumes and are arranged according to chronological order: "The Love of an Orange" (1959), "A Hard Winter" (1964), "The Third Book" (1969), "Deep Calleth unto Deep" (1976), and "Real Love" (1986).

Most of the poems in focus seem plausibly to represent prevailing tendencies in Ravikovitch's poetics. A female narrator dominates the poems' rhetorical layer while portraying herself as a deprived, deserted, and even chastised woman trapped and exploited by a hostile, humiliating society of notably male characteristics. The soft, sometimes childlike tone adopted by the narrator fortifies her iconic stance as a shy, weak woman, a Cinderella besieged by an oppressive, subjugating reality. In light of this, the pining for distant, enchanting, even spellbinding realms in many of the poems is cogently reasoned: the narrator seeks to free herself from her castigating deprivation and to extricate herself from her

deteriorating misery. Hence also the many references to different kinds of birds, to flying, to hovering: these function as metonyms for the narrator's desire to leave behind her the admonishing dominions in which she is painfully anchored.

The opening of "The Marionette" radiates Ravikovitch's very poetic essence: "To be a marionette / in a gray, darling, dawn." A sense of deprivation is interwoven here with a sense of a shrouded, distant enchantment. The fact that some of Ravikovitch's recent poems report the agony resulting from war echoes her everlasting inclination to touch the cry in the dark. Robert Alter's foreword is informative and sensitive, and the Blochs' translation successfully preserves the original verbal tone.

Source: Yair Mazor, Review of *The Window: New and Selected Poems*, in *World Literature Today*, Vol. 64, No. 2, Spring 1990, p. 357.

Karen Alkalay-Gut

In the following excerpt, Alkalay-Gut explains why there has been little Hebrew poetry written by Jewish women.

Despite a constant state of war for forty years, before 1982 Hebrew poetry had almost no examples of political poems or poems about war by women. There are a number of reasons for this selective silence, and certainly there was a precedent in history for the exclusion of women in the essential use of the Hebrew language. Hebrew had been used only in prayer for many years and was a scholars' language, the property of religious men, and most women had little actual knowledge of it until the twentieth century. Although Jewish women may have been literate in other languages, there were no encouragements to possess more than a rudimentary ritual knowledge of the prayers in Hebrew. When the dream of a Jewish homeland was revitalized in the late nineteenth century, however, the women who helped bring Hebrew to modern times by writing poetry found appreciative audiences. Because Hebrew was a language consciously resurrected for daily use, it needed all the help it could get from the world of literature, and the competition for publication and honors between men and women writers that characterized the literature of the United States was entirely absent from the Hebrew literary scene. Anyone who wrote in Hebrew was encouraged, a hero of the cause, and the work of

> THE SILENCE WAS BROKEN, DESPITE THE
> FEARS OF THE DANGER OF SPEAKING OUT, AND
> THE REASONS WERE NOT BASED ON MISGIVINGS
> ABOUT PHYSICAL DANGER, NOT ON MATERNAL
> FEARS AND NEEDS FOR PROTECTION, BUT THE
> MORAL JUSTIFICATION OF THIS RISK."

women was welcomed by publishers eager for a variety of voices.

The socialist basis of the society emphasized the equality of women, and these ideals were put into practice in the fields, in the hospitals, and on the building sites. Nevertheless, when women wrote, they restricted their subjects to selected matters and described only their new and long-anticipated landscape, their love of the country, and their emotions. They did not touch the one central subject that pervaded the poetry of male writers: the necessity of military defense and the tragic loss of life.

Poetry by men concerning war until 1982 was concerned not with its justification but with the fact of the existence of war, and the poets of the first generation of the Israeli state, known as the "Palmach Generation" (the name for the army before 1948), wrote about the horrors and tragedies of battle as terrible inevitabilities. Wars were viewed as defensive, vital to the very existence of Israel and the Jewish people, and admittedly dangerous to the moral fiber of society. A typical poem is "Guard Me, My God" by S. Shalom, which begins: "Guard me, God, from hating my fellow man / Guard me from remembering what he did to me in my youth." Another example of poetry by men on this subject is Amir Gilboa's "Isaac," a wrenching contemporization of Abraham's obligation to sacrifice his only son, as Israel felt it was forced to sacrifice its young men to battle.

> In the morning the sun strolled in the woods
> with me and father,
> my right hand in his left,
>
> A knife flashed from between the trees like lightning.
> and I shrink from my eyes' terror before the blooded
> leaves.

> Father, father, come rush to save Isaac
> so no one will be missing from the meal at noon.
>
> It is I who am slaughtered, my son.
> Already my blood is on the leaves.
> And father's voice was stilled,
> his face pale
>
> I wanted to scream, writhing against belief
> and tearing open my eyes
> I awoke.
>
> And my right hand was drained of blood.

The sense of personal involvement in inter-related political, spiritual, and military issues—and the authority to comment on these issues—is extremely apparent.

Rachel Blaustein (1890–1931), with a degree in agronomy, worked the fields and tended the animals, yet her poem "To My Country," written in the twenties, was the perfect example of the way women viewed their role in the literary world. The poem begins, "I didn't sing of thee, my country, / Nor laud thy name / With acts of heroism / In myriads of battles! / Only a tree—my hands planted / On the quiet Jordan shores. / Only a path—my feet wore / to the fields," and continues with an apology for the poverty of her gift of poems to her motherland. Her poetry constitutes only a partial involvement in the country, only a poor substitute for the complete involvement from which she was excluded as a woman.

The poems of "Rachel," as she is known, were concerned with the individual in a spiritual environment, relating to the land of her dreams, and her dreams within that land. "To My Country" and other poems by her have been set to music and are played regularly on the radio, as are the poems of the freedom fighter Hana Senesh. Best known by Senesh is "Walking to Caesarea": "My God, My God / May it never end: / The sand and the sea / Whisper of water / The flash of sky / The prayers of man." Senesh, who was captured when she parachuted into enemy territory during World War II, then tortured and killed, emphasizes the hope for a more spiritual world and a better future. In 1940 she wrote "In the Fires of War," in which she searches the battlefield with her flashlight for a human face. In other poems she emphasizes the power of the individual to institute major changes in the world. "Blessed Be the Match" praises the "match" which, though extinguished, ignites a flame in the hearts of mankind and extols the honorable hearts that know when self-sacrifice is necessary.

This voice from the dead affirming the value of life and the necessity for involvement in it has been a consolation for many, and the poems of Hana Senesh, although considered less than significant poetically, remain standard fare for memorial days and other public occasions. The affirmation of the significance of life, moreover, has continued to be a major subject for women. "Each Man Has a Name" by Zelda Mishovsky (1914–84), a long list of the characteristics that individualize each human being, is a poem particularly valuable in a time of military crisis.

> Each man has a name
> given him by God
> and by his father and mother
> each man has a name
> given him by his stature and his smile
> and given him by his clothes
> each man has a name
> given him by the hills
> and given him by his walls
> each man has a name
> given him by his fate
> and given him by his friends
> each man has a name
> given him by his sins
> and given him by his yearnings
> each man has a name
> given him by his enemies
> and given him by his love
> each man has a name
> given him by his celebrations
> and given him by his work
> each man has a name
> given him by his seasons
> and given him by his blindness
> each man has a name
> given him by the sea
> and given him
> by his death.

Because the poem emphasizes, in a way perhaps never intended, the value of significant death, it is read often at military funeral services, and the effect of poems like this one—read over the grave of an eighteen-year-old soldier—on a constantly grief-stricken society cannot be underestimated.

Whatever their roles were in real life, in poetry the role of women in war was initially to support, to comfort, and to inspire. An important aspect of this affirmation of the significance of existence and the necessity for individual efforts to enable social change has been an optimism about future peace. War was only a temporary situation, and there was always anticipation of better times. Speaking to a woman, Leah Goldberg (1911–70) wrote during the war in 1948: "You will go in the field. Alone. Unscorched by the heat of fires / On roads that once bristled with horror and blood. / And with integrity you will be once again humble and acquiescent / As of the grasses, as one of mankind." The suggestion here is that not only war but also the heroic role—even of woman—was only temporary and that the role of woman would revert to its natural "humble and acquiescent" position once peace could be achieved.

Because the military situation seemed quieter in the late fifties and early sixties, poetry in Israel followed the precedent of American and British literature and became confessional. As if obeying Leah Goldberg's declaration, the women poets seemed to become "humble and acquiescent." Turning from the concept of "public" poetry, poetry written consciously to become part of a nation's literary heritage with an eye always on universally shared emotions, the poets of the 1960s wrote about themselves. The subjects were the same ones then popular in American poetry by women: loneliness, identity, the impossibility of love. Typical was the poetry of Dahlia Ravikovitch (b. 1936), who wrote of herself, her isolation, and her pain as a woman. Her "Mechanical Doll," describing an apparent recovery after a nervous breakdown and a return to the empty existence of a woman, has been standard reading for high-school students since it was written.

> And that night I was a mechanical doll
> and I turned right and left, to all sides
> and I fell on my face and broke to bits,
> and they tried to put me together with skillful hands
>
> And then I went back to being a correct doll
> and all my manners were studied and compliant.
> But by then I was a different kind of doll
> like a wounded twig hanging by a tendril.
>
> And then I went to dance at a ball,
> but they left me in the company of cats and dogs
> even though all my steps were measured and patterned.
>
> And I had golden hair and I had blue eyes
> and I had a dress the color of the flowers in the garden
> and I had a straw hat decorated with a cherry.

The message in this poem—of the necessity for a public façade, the inability of the sensitive person to function in an uncaring, unreal society, the irrelevance and even danger of the real individual to society—struck a note of recognition in many readers, as did poems like "Time Caught in a Net," in which the narrator describes herself as "one of those little girls / who sail around the whole world in one night / and come to the land of Cathay / and Madagascar, // and who smash plates and cups / from so much love, / so much love, / so much love." This image of the passive-aggressive woman caught in a double bind is so similar to that of the American woman of this period that there are times when the poetry of Ravikovitch and that of Anne Sexton or Sylvia Plath seem almost interchangeable.

The fact that there *were* so few differences between the self-perceptions of American and Israeli women would not have been surprising had Ravikovitch been living on a peaceful street in the suburbs of Boston or Devon, but Israel was only temporarily at rest, in the eye of the storm. The Six-Day War of 1967 was followed by the surprise attack on all the nation's many borders during Yom Kippur of 1973. No one was more than a few miles from any of these borders; war in Israel physically involves every individual, and in 1973 not only was there the very real immediate danger of personal annihilation but also fear and uncertainty about loved ones at the front. Thousands of young men and fathers were killed immediately, and many more met their deaths in the months following that attack. Wives, sisters, friends, and mothers divided their time between the radio and the television, spinning the dials for more news. Still, no matter how much their lives were taken up with the unavoidable problems of communications, supplies, fear, blackouts, et cetera, there seemed to be no specific poetic reaction. To live so entirely in a specific experience, and to avoid it so completely, is a truly amazing achievement and begs further inquiry.

Dahlia Ravikovitch and Yona Wollach (1945–86) were the dominant women poets of this generation. Living in antithetical situations, these two very different women may be viewed as paralleling the Plath/Sexton duo: Ravikovitch controlled, intellectual, and interested in children; Wollach flamboyant, self-involved, hungering aloud for love. For Wollach, the military situation was reflected only in her choice of language in discussing her own situation. The terms of war, of contemporary religious and political conflicts, were employed as metaphors for personal relationships. "Feelings" is a typical example.

> Our feelings are hostages—
> We exchange them
> With each other
> Mine for yours
> Yours for mine
> We give and take
> What for what
> Two hostages
> For your love
> Two hostages
> For a kiss
> Ten hostages
> For your honesty
> A plot of land
> For your last thought
> A jet plane
> For silence
> Release from follow-up
> For your laughter
> A bundle of money
> For understanding

Though there is here, as in other poems by Wollach, a clear causal connection between the failure of individual relationships and the principles of communication embedded in the military uncertainty, the concern is with the couple and not the society.

Why has there been so little overt concern by women poets with the war that has constantly been threatening the existence of Israel since its generation? In the poems of Lisa Fliegel, an American immigrant, the major distinction between women and men in Israeli society is vocalized: "Those born here wear cradle to grave uniforms / these are the conditions that unite them—war and the valley of death." Men, who from the age of eighteen until their forties are at the command of their country, who lay their lives on the line for over twenty years, are viewed as having more authority to deal with the subject of war than do women, who only remain behind the front lines and wait. On Memorial Day Fliegel describes herself as standing "apart because a woman can't really know— / she doesn't fight." Because they feel they have no right to speak of a war in which they cannot physically risk themselves, she notes, many women avoid the topic of war and concentrate on their own problems.

The reasons for keeping women behind the front lines are complex, dynamic, and beyond the scope of this discussion. The result, however, has been that women in the army since the War of Independence in 1948 have in general played a diminishing role. This tendency has been reversed in the past three years, partly because of increasing technology, which makes physical strength less significant, and partly because the long-term mobilization necessitated by the war in Lebanon has made woman-power more important. If alterations in the concept of gender roles have also been a factor in these changes, they are not apparent or measurable, but they do correspond with greater political and military involvement and criticism.

There were other reasons for silence than lack of the authority of military involvement. How could one discuss a war in which one's family was actively engaged? The possibility of endangering the life or the morale of a loved one was too great. For women standing on the sidelines to suggest to their men that the battles they were fighting were better not fought was to increase the chances that the men would be killed. The role of the woman in society was one of unquestioning support, and consequently the potentially significant voice in poetry was silenced.

The political female poet who maintained popular recognition during this time and remained popular through the Begin administration was the lyricist Nomi Shemer, whose gentle militarism was in line with the established concept of a woman's role and the accepted politics of the government. In one of her most popular songs, "On the Honey and the Thorn," she warns that God combines the bitter (defense) with the sweet (peace) for the sake of "our baby daughter." The acceptability of Shemer is clearly linked to her fulfillment of perceived roles and attitudes.

The general political consensus until the election of Menachem Begin in 1977 helped contribute to the relative military silence of women. Women felt no need to interfere in a situation about which there seemed to be almost no alternative and which the men in charge appeared to be handling competently. There was no discussion of the basic issue of war in the poetry by men either, but with the dissolution of a general consensus and the rise of a more militaristic party which seemed to encourage obvious prevarication both to government leaders and to the public, general discussion became necessary.

The situation grew extreme when the war in Lebanon began in 1982. Although initially viewed by the general population as a possibly justifiable preemptive strike, the operation soon began to be perceived as a full-scale war, one led by potentially irresponsible leaders. Having condemned Nazi war criminals because the excuse of following orders can constitute no justification for immoral acts, Israeli society could not justify itself by blaming the leaders. It was up to the individual to keep informed of all the vagaries and implications, to take a proportional share of the responsibility and the blame, and to do whatever possible to rectify the situation.

My own situation was illustrative. Two months before Israel's invasion of Lebanon I was attending an academic conference in Austria. One of my colleagues was from the University of Beirut, and the questions we asked each other brought forth my first tentative political poems when the war broke out two months later.

To One in Beirut

Not a day goes by without my thinking of you . . .
as in a clandestine affair I am reminded
by the newspapers, the sounds in the air,
that you are there, and I in Tel Aviv.

Today brings a letter, postmarked Princeton,
sent through Jounieh to Larnaca on its way here.
You are well, as of the sixteenth of July, 1982,
and today is the 30th. Last night
on the news, we were still pounding the city.

As long as we kept from politics, we were friends
strolling together down the sea road in an Austrian
   town,
shocking the guide with our nationalities
and talking Pound, sex, divorce, food, wine.

How our lives would be fine
now, if that was all there was
to talk of. But where we live
we speak only of death and think
of somewhere else.

The helplessness of the individual in a political situation was part of the issue. The other part could be seen in "Friend and Foe," written a few days earlier: "Skyhawks fly over my city / on their way to bomb yours. / We are awakened by the noise / and I fall asleep restlessly / dreaming of you and your daughters." My Lebanese friend had reminded me that "If anything happens to my girls, / I hold you personally responsible." And in the poem I found myself answering: "Friend! My husband is in civil defense / and my sons are too small for the army. You / have daughters and are old and alcoholic. / We can't fight this war. / But both of us are in it / and responsible."

Responsibility was a central issue. Not only was this war the first considered avoidable and nondefensive; it was the only war in which decisions concerning its progress continued to be made for an extended period of time. The military action, although initially perceived as defensive (to stop the Katyushas, fired from PLO bases in Lebanon, from killing Israeli citizens), was becoming an offensive war. The basic values embedded in the original conception of Israel—of love of peace, of war only as self-defense, of society as a place of protection for the innocents—were now becoming fogged, and it seemed time for an acknowledgment of this fact. Even if some aspects of the war were considered necessary, a traditional acknowledgment of shame and regret was equally necessary.

I was not the only one. An unprecedented movement, "Mothers against Silence," urging the government to consider the significance of the lives of their sons in all political and military decisions, was a major sign that something had changed in the attitude of women toward war. Simultaneously, political poems by women began to appear in literary journals and newspapers. Riva Rubin, who had come to Israel from South Africa years before to escape the immorality of apartheid, now found her two sons in Lebanon. The elder was a medic, the younger a tank driver. Both of them seemed so young, so helpless. They should have been protected, but like Sarah in the story of Isaac, mothers backed out of the picture when it came time for the sacrifice.

Rubin's poems traced a growing aggressiveness in her personality that was reinforced by her maternal concerns. Some reflect the defensive maternal instinct. Just before the war she protested the endangered situation of children living in border towns: "Night Fears // Boogeyman, Goblin, / Sandman, Troll, / Babayaga / Tokolosh / KATYUSHA." The Katyusha rockets had become incorporated into the terrors of childhood, but these fears, random and faceless as any fairy-tale monster, were real. The alternatives were equally terrifying: it was against these rockets that her sons were being sent to fight, and in fighting the nightmares of children they too had entered the world of nightmare,

where the concepts of villain and hero were often interchangeable.

> Hero
>
> Let me sing a song of love on this mountain peak till they find me
>
> (The colours of thousands
> of universes imploding
> to softness) blackly
>
> Black (my throat my lips)
> burned away
> (Silver
> the cold) fills me
> black (the stars soft
> their tips) black
> as my stagnant tears
>
> (I warm myself)
> on the cooling turret (clinging)
> with my charred arms
>
> I will require large points of reference now my vision is shattered

It was on the more popular level, however, that poetry by women really struck home. At a demonstration outside the Parliament building one of the organizers read the following poem by "an anonymous mother":

> Being the mother of a soldier in Lebanon,
> Is to tremble each time you hear the helicopter's roar,
> And to jump each time the phone rings,
> and to freeze with shock at each knock on the door.
> Our boys do not complain: only their eyes speak . . .
> their bodies are not tired, and they have strength,
> But in their hearts there are questions and their souls know no rest.
> Forgive us, our sons, that, this once,
> We presume to break our silence and shout aloud.

The silence was broken, despite the fears of the danger of speaking out, and the reasons were not based on misgivings about physical danger, not on maternal fears and needs for protection, but the moral justification of this risk.

The moral crisis came when the Christian Lebanese Army massacred women and children in the Palestinian camps of Sabra and Shatila, and Israeli soldiers, guarding the camps, refrained from intervention. The Israeli public was outraged, not only because of the terrible murder of women and children, but also because of the morally equivocal position of the soldiers. Dahlia Ravikovitch published two poems in the most popular literary journal, *Moznaim*. Both poems take their stand on the war on the basis of the simple humanity Ravikovitch felt was being lost in the rhetoric of politicians. "A Baby Can't Be Killed Twice," for example, pairs the young Israeli soldiers with the children they did not allow to escape from the massacre.

> "Back to camp, march!" the soldier ordered
> the shrieking women of Sabra and Shatila.
> He had his orders to fulfill.
> And the children were already lying in the puddles of sewage,
> mouths gaping,
> calm.
>
> No one will hurt them.
> A baby can't be killed twice.
>
> . . .
>
> Our sweet soldiers—
> they asked nothing for themselves.
> How strong their wish
> to come home in peace.

The effect of Ravikovitch's subsequent public appearances at antiwar rallies, where she was interviewed for the evening news and quoted in the daily papers, can only begin to be measured if one imagines Sylvia Plath at a sit-in. If someone who has been the emblem of self-involvement could now conceive it her duty to protest the war, who could remain silent?

These poets were widely discussed, their poetry published in newspapers and newsstand magazines and debated in panels at the university. They have been anthologized, published in book form, and—most significantly—read and talked about. Other voices also began to be heard, some more stridently than others, and all of them—in a country that thrives on controversy—welcomed by magazines, weekly literary supplements of daily newspapers, and feminist journals. Maya Bejerano, whose intellectual poetry, influenced by Eliot and Stevens, has been concerned with the role of women, took on the subjects of Lebanon and the destruction of the country. The "good fence," the open border between Israel and Lebanon, considered in 1980 a great step forward in Israel because it indicated improved relations between the two countries, was reconsidered by Bejerano three years later: "Child's play makes it possible to understand the 'Good Fence.' / The high railing is the good fence to children on the balcony / Who know that it is possible to fly off it, and do not fly, / See the distance and covet it, / for hours look through its bars as their desire grows." . . .

Source: Karen Alkalay-Gut, "Poetry by Women in Israel and the War in Lebanon," in *World Literature Today*, Vol. 63, No. 1, Winter 1989, pp. 19–25.

SOURCES

Bar-On, Mordechai, "The 1960s: The New Israelis," in *Jewish Daily Forward*, May 1, 2008, http://www.forward.com/articles/13283/ (accessed September 1, 2010).

Bloch, Chana, and Chana Kronfeld, "The Bell Jar Shatters: The Political Poetry of Dahlia Ravikovitch," in *Tikkun*, Vol. 20, No. 6, November/December 2005, p. 63.

———, Introduction to *Hovering at a Low Altitude: The Collected Poetry of Dahlia Ravikovitch*, W. W. Norton, 2009, pp. 19, 28.

"Book of Proverbs," in *The Holy Bible*, Revised Standard Version, Oxford University Press, 1952, pp. 692, 706.

Joffe, Lawrence, "Dahlia Ravikovitch," in *Guardian* (London, England), August 30, 2005, http://www.guardian.co.uk/news/2005/aug/30/guardianobituaries.israel/ (accessed September 2, 2010).

Lao Tzu, *Tao Te Ching*, translated by D. C. Lau, Penguin, 1972, p. 140.

Margot, Lurie, Review of *Hovering at a Low Altitude: The Collected Poetry of Dahlia Ravikovitch*, in *New Criterion*, Vol. 28, No. 1, September 2009, p. 73.

"Poets from Israel," in *Israel-Poetry International Web site*, http://israel.poetryinternationalweb.org/piw_cms/cms/cms_module/index.php?obj_id = 12 (accessed September 4, 2010).

Ravikovitch, Dahlia, "Pride," in *Hovering at a Low Altitude: The Collected Poetry of Dahlia Ravikovitch*, translated by Chana Bloch and Chana Kronfeld, W. W. Norton, 2009, p. 131.

Rothschild, Matthew, "Poets of Tragedy," in *Progressive*, Vol. 74, No. 7, July 2010.

"Timeline of Israeli-Palestinian History and the Arab-Israeli Conflict," in *Mideast Web*, http://www.mideastweb.org/timeline.htm (accessed September 5, 2010).

Tsamir, Hamutal, "Jewish-Israeli Poetry, Dahlia Ravikovitch, and the Gender of Representation," in *Jewish Social Studies*, Vol. 14, No. 3, 2008, p. 85.

FURTHER READING

Badran, Margot, and Miriam Cooke, eds., *Opening the Gates: An Anthology of Arab Feminist Writing*, 2nd ed., Indiana University Press, 2004.
      This is a wide-ranging anthology of poetry, fiction, essays, pamphlets, and speeches by Arab feminist writers. Over fifty different pieces are included.

Dyson, Michael Eric, *Pride: The Seven Deadly Sins*, Oxford University Press, 2006.

> Dyson examines pride in all its facets, with many references to popular culture and current social and political issues.

Katz, Lisa, "Dahlia Ravikovitch: *Hovering at a Low Altitude: The Collected Poetry of Dahlia Ravikovitch*," in *Bridges: A Jewish Feminist Journal*, Vol. 14, No. 2, 2009, pp. 135–39.

> Katz reviews Ravikovitch's poetry and discusses some of the challenges involved in translating poetry from Hebrew to English. Katz concludes that the translations by Bloch and Kronfeld succeed in preserving Ravikovitch's tone and voice.

Powers, Janet M., *Blossoms on the Olive Tree: Israeli and Palestinian Women Working for Peace*, Praeger, 2006.

> This is a collection of stories and essays in which Powers describes the work being done for peace by Israeli and Palestinian women. Powers is an American scholar who made several trips to Israel and the occupied territories from 2002 to 2005, during which she met many of the women who work to create the organizational structures for peace in their troubled region.

SUGGESTED SEARCH TERMS

Dahlia Ravikovitch

Dahlia Ravikovitch AND Pride

Hovering at a Low Altitude AND Ravikovitch

personification

Israel AND Ravikovitch

Palestine AND Ravikovitch

seven deadly sins

Six-Day War AND Israel

Israeli-Palestinian conflict

West Bank AND Gaza Strip

Ravikovitch AND Hebrew literature

Stanza LXXXIII

GERTRUDE STEIN

1956

In 1932, Gertrude Stein wrote an extensive poetic sequence called *Stanzas in Meditation*. The eighty-three-stanza work was not published as a whole until 1956, after Stein's death. The final stanza, identified only by stanza number like all the other stanzas in the series, is reflective of Stein's experimental aims concerning the poetic form, language and meaning, and abstraction. "Stanza LXXXIII" is almost completely devoid of visual imagery, and the language Stein uses is suggestive of multiple layers of meaning and seems to insist upon its own lack of ability to convey intention or significance. Stein combines this careful selection of language with an infrequent usage of punctuation, along with line breaks that seem to cut off streams of thought midway through their expression. Such elements work together to lend the stanza a hazy, indistinct quality. The brief verse includes suggestions of coming and going, of doors opening and closing, implying that the stanza series as a whole, while coming to an end, initiates a new phase for the reader and the writer. The overall effect of Stein's wordplay and stream-of-consciousness style underscores themes Stein develops elsewhere in the larger poetic sequence. In particular, Stein meditates on the purpose and effect of language and poetic expression, allowing her internal, philosophical explorations a voice.

Originally published by Yale University Press in 1956, *Stanzas in Meditation*, the sequence that includes "Stanza LXXXIII," is available in a 1998

Gertrude Stein (*AP Images*)

collection by the Library of America. This collection, *Stein: Writings, 1932–1946*, includes poetry, lectures, essays, and short fiction and was edited by Catharine R. Stimpson and Harriet Chessman.

AUTHOR BIOGRAPHY

Stein was born on February 3, 1874, in Allegheny, Pennsylvania, as the youngest of the five children of Amelia Keyser and Daniel Stein. Stein's birth was preceded by the arrival of two other siblings who died during their infancy. A year after Stein's birth, her family moved to Europe, first to Vienna, Austria, and then to Passy, France, in 1878. Under the care of a Hungarian governess and a Czech tutor, Stein learned several languages as a child, speaking French and German before she spoke English. In 1880, the Steins returned to the United States, settling in California. Stein lost her mother to cancer in 1888, and her father died in 1891.

Beginning in 1893, Stein studied at the Harvard Annex, to become Radcliffe College in 1894, following in her brother Leo's footsteps after he left for Harvard. Stein studied psychology and

graduated in 1898. She entered Johns Hopkins University in 1897 in pursuit of a career in psychology but relinquished this plan and instead traveled abroad with her brother. In 1903, Stein settled into a new life in Paris. She quickly became immersed in the vibrant literary and artistic scene there and devoted herself to writing. Stein and her brother Leo began to hold salons (meetings of cultural notables) in which they showcased the work of a number of artists, becoming friends with Henri Matisse and Pablo Picasso. In 1905 and 1906, Stein began work on a series of novellas, *Three Lives*, which was published in 1909. In 1907, Stein was introduced to the woman who would become her companion and partner for the rest of her life, Alice B. Toklas. The pair traveled together to England in 1913, seeking publishers for Stein's work. After a period abroad, they returned to France, where Stein continued to write essays and poetry. In 1925, her novel *The Making of Americans* was finally published. Stein, with Toklas, traveled to the United States in 1934 for a lecture tour.

The two returned to Europe in 1937, where Stein's literary activities continued. At the onset of World War II in 1939, Stein and Toklas retrieved personal items from their home in Paris and took up residence in a town in the south of France, Bilignin, although they had been advised by American officials to leave the country because of their Jewish ancestry. Stein published the novel *Ida* in 1941, amidst the upheavals of war. She and Toklas lived on meager rations and were forced to move to Culoz in 1943 after a dispute with their landlord. Italian and German officers and soldiers took over their home in 1944, but the town of Culoz was later liberated by the French Resistance. After the war, Stein was treated as a celebrity by American soldiers; she subsequently toured U.S. Army bases in Germany. In 1946, Stein was diagnosed with stomach cancer. She pursued surgery as a course of action against the disease, despite being advised by her physicians that she was too weak to tolerate an invasive operation. Stein died on July 27, 1946, in Paris, never having regained consciousness following the surgery.

POEM SUMMARY

"Stanza LXXXIII" is a fourteen-line poem. While Stein does punctuate the ends of many of the lines of poetry with periods, there are no instances of internal punctuation, such as commas. In the first line, the lack of commas forces the reader to question the intent of the speaker's sentiment. Depending on where the reader pauses in the course of the line, the meaning shifts, although the relationship of the words in the sentence to one another is such that the meaning remains unclear regardless of where the reader might insert a pause or an internal question. At first, the speaker appears to be wondering about the purpose of her existence. The next phrase in the sentence introduces the concept of doubt. This sense of doubt may be applied to the speaker's questioning the nature of her existence. Alternatively, it may apply to the next portion of the sentence, concerned with the role of reason. The speaker may also be suggesting that this central issue of doubt and uncertainty applies to the ideas both that precede and follow it.

In the second sentence, Stein lists a series of words without commas. The line is a string of four verbs; the first verb is repeated and then followed by three additional verbs that rhyme with each other but not with the first two words. The verbs appear to have little relation to one another, except in the repetition of sounds. Essentially, the meaning of the line, if the meaning of each word is related, would be "stay stay suggest rest selected." Without a subject, the verbs, as verbs, do not carry the connotation of action. They possibly could be regarded as a command to the reader, but such a reading of the line is complicated by the fact that the last verb is technically in the past tense. Alternatively, they may be regarded in terms of the sound patterns they produce, evoking a sense of a mantra or chant.

The next three lines form one sentence and, more than the other lines in the poem, convey images and employ more-traditional sentence structure. In the third line of the poem, the speaker describes the way she calls out—the reader does not know to whom she calls—that her door is open, that is, perhaps, unlocked. She observes in the next line that the individuals to whom she has called may opt to not enter. In the fifth line, Stein speaks of hurrying to close something, presumably the previously mentioned door, if lines 4 and 5 are read as a single clause. Thus, if the door is not opened, no one can hurry to shut it. One may interpret the word *close* in another sense here, in that it may refer to an end, such as the end of the poem.

In lines 6–10, each line comprises one sentence. In line 6, the speaker uses a third-person-plural pronoun that has no clear antecedent, providing the reader with no context for the rest of the statement, which concerns the speaker taking possession of the group in question. It is possible that this statement is connected to the series of statements that has preceded it, in which an open door goes unused by a group also referred to by a third-person-plural pronoun. Line 7 offers a more conventional sentence format in which the speaker states explicitly that everyone knows that she has made a choice. What this choice is, however, is not explained, not in this line nor in the next. In lines 8 and 9, the speaker uses the word *therefore* four times, using substantial line space within the poem on the same word, a word that derives its value based on what has come before and what will come after. The first instances of the word, in lines 6 and 8, lacking the final *e*, may have subtly different connotations. The word is typically used to suggest that as a consequence of a certain event or condition, something else will happen, yet previous sets of circumstances have not been clearly identified. The future event that typically follows such a statement is a promise, an expectation; this future event is also not elaborated upon. The tenth line would be the natural place in the poem to discover what it was the speaker was offering after her series of therefores, yet she states only that she insists upon not missing something. Again, the ultimate meaning of this statement is not explored further.

In the poem's final four lines, the speaker once again employs conventional sentence structure involving nouns and verbs, insisting in line 11 that when she arrives, she will be well received. Again she states, in line 12, that she is in fact coming. Line 13 is a similar recapitulation; the speaker states that she arrives having already arrived. The repetition involved in these lines underscores the circular nature of the speaker's intent throughout the poem; the reader is referred forward and backward repeatedly in a search for reference points. In these last lines, the repeated emphasis on arrival and on previous arrivals creates the same effect of perpetual motion, into the future and back to the past. The fourteenth and final line of the poem is the simple statement that the stanza series as a whole is now concluded.

TOPICS FOR FURTHER STUDY

- Stein's "Stanza LXXXIII" is the final poem in a long poetic sequence, *Stanzas in Meditation*. Peruse the entire series, read some of the other stanzas from various sections of the sequence, and select two stanzas to compare with "Stanza LXXXIII." What characteristics do the stanzas have in common? How do they differ? Does Stein treat the role of language within the sequence in a manner similar to that which she employs in "Stanza LXXXIII"? Write an analysis in which you compare and contrast the stanzas. Can you form any conclusions based on Stein's overall style in the sequence as a whole based on your analysis of these three stanzas? Why or why not?

- Stein's experimental approach to language in her work mirrored to some degree the abstraction and experimentation of the artwork of Stein's friend Pablo Picasso. Using print and online sources, study the characteristics of Picasso's style. How did he represent landscapes, people, or objects? What were his approaches to line and color? After investigating the particulars of Picasso's style, create a work of art in which you attempt to emulate his style. Be prepared to share your work with the class and to discuss the elements of your work in which you attempted to emulate Picasso's style.

- As women of Jewish descent, both Stein and Toklas undertook enormous risk by staying in German-occupied France during World War II. The 2005 young-adult novel *The Book Thief*, by Markus Zusak, explores this period in European history in the story of a young German girl during World War II. Although Liesel, the girl at the center of the novel, is not Jewish, she nevertheless becomes aware of and experiences the horrors of the war and witnesses the atrocities suffered by Jewish people during the war. With a group, read Zusak's novel. What is unique about the narration of this novel? Did your understanding of the war change at all after you read the book? How did Liesel's story shape your understanding of the German experience of the war? Despite the grim nature of the subject matter of the novel, does the author present any elements of hopefulness in the novel? How does the author's treatment of the power of words compare with Stein's treatment of language in "Stanza LXXXIII"? Create an online blog in which your group's book discussion can take place. Share your thoughts on these questions and any other opinions you have about the novel.

- The Harlem Renaissance was a poetry movement among African American poets that occurred in the 1920s and 1930s, roughly the same time period as the modernist movement's emerging and taking hold in Europe. The 1996 young-adult anthology *Shimmy, Shimmy, Shimmy, Like My Sister Kate: Looking at the Harlem Renaissance through Poetry*, edited by Nikki Giovanni, explores the poetry of this movement. Read selections from this volume. Who were some of the key figures of this movement? What themes do you notice recurring in poems by different authors? Using this volume as a starting point, research the Harlem Renaissance and create a digital multimedia presentation on the history of the movement. Provide examples of the art, music, and literature of the time. As you conduct your research, consider whether the poetry of the Harlem Renaissance shared any traits in common with the literature of the modernist movement.

THEMES

Language and Languages

In "Stanza LXXXIII," Stein explores the notion of language itself, questioning its utility as a means of conveying meaning and significance. Using a literary mode of expression—the poem, which relies on language to express the poet's intention—Stein forces the reader to explore the variations of meanings attached to the words she employs. The meanings of words shift based on their context within a line in particular and within the poem in general. Within the poem, the contextual meaning is rarely clear. The lack of punctuation, the repetition of words and sounds, the lack of visual imagery, and the word choice in the poem all contribute to the sense of indistinct context in which the language of the poem may be understood. Language itself seems, at a number of points in the poem, so full of variation in meaning that it could also be regarded as devoid of meaning. In this way, Stein's "Stanza LXXXIII" is consistent with much of Stein's body of work. As Meredith Yearsley states in the *Dictionary of Literary Biography*, Stein's body of work "amounts to a systematic investigation of the formal elements of language (parts of speech, syntax, phonetics, morphemics, etymology, punctuation) and of literature (narrative, poetry, prose, drama, and genre itself.)" In the first line of the poem, for example, there is no internal punctuation within the line; there is only an ending period. Depending on where the reader elects to pause within the reading of the line, the meanings of the phrases embedded in the line shift. Such possibilities for variance occur in most of the other lines in the poem as well, leading the reader to wonder whether Stein is celebrating the possibilities in language or meditating on the imprecise nature of language and the futility of employing language to convey one's thoughts and feelings.

Time

Inherent in "Stanza LXXXIII" is a temporal element, largely embedded in the poem in Stein's use of verb tense. Throughout the poem, Stein uses a mixture of present, past, and future verb tenses, exploring the speaker's role in various moments in time. In the present and future tenses, the verb choices are particularly centered on states of being, although a few action verbs are used. By employing a speaker who contemplates the nature of and reasons for existence, who calls out to others, who offers thoughts and opinions, Stein creates a sense of stasis. The speaker appears as an unmoving focal point of the poem, calling, thinking, postulating, predicting. In this way, Stein prolongs the moment of the present, creating the sense that like all activity, time has stopped within this sphere from which the speaker operates. The imagery of the open door also highlights the nature of possibilities inherent in the present moment. The speaker refers to the door as being open, possibly in the sense of unlocked, rather than ajar, for the individuals to whom the speaker calls are spoken of in terms of their possible refusal to open the door and enter. Nevertheless, the essence of the possibility remains; the speaker exists in a state of readiness for the future, for the opening of the door and for what that might entail. Near the poem's conclusion, Stein uses one of the few past-tense verbs in the poem, stating that her arrival has already been preceded by her previous arrival; yet she insists that currently, she is coming. The notion of arrival exists in these closing lines of the poem in past, present, and future states. The circularity of this concept of time underscores the notion of the present as always happening, or rather, of the speaker's sense of the persistence of the present. In this way, Stein's exploration of time mirrors her exploration of the nature of language, in that both time and language are depicted as rife with possibility. Likewise, just as language is so full of possible meaning it appears to be meaningless, so too is time depicted as so full of possibility that the speaker appears inert, devoid of action or progress.

STYLE

Free Verse

"Stanza LXXXIII" mimics a structured poem in many ways. The poem appears to have a rhyme scheme, at least for the opening lines, intermittently within the poem, and at the conclusion. However, the poem lacks sufficient structure in terms of meter (the pattern of unaccented and accented syllables within a line of poetry) and rhyme to be considered anything but free verse. Free-verse poetry is poetry that lacks metrical structure and a regular pattern of end rhyme sustained throughout the poem. (End rhymes are rhyming words at the ends of lines of poetry, as opposed to internal and initial rhymes, which appear within and at the beginnings of lines,

Woman lost in her thoughts *(Karuka | Shutterstock.com)*

respectively.) Stein's poem employs the use of end rhyme sporadically, which lends the poem the feel of more traditional, structured verse. Upon further study of the poem, however, the reader becomes aware that despite the sporadic rhyme pattern, the poem is experimental in its use of language. By employing the appearance of structured verse in a free-verse poem that questions the meaning of language, Stein explores the boundaries of poetic form.

Repetition and Internal Rhyme

"Stanza LXXXIII," like many free-verse poems, makes use of repetition and internal rhyme in order to shape the poem and the reader's response to the poem. A number of lines in the poem contain a repeated word. Also, instead of using end rhymes, Stein in some case repeats the

same word at the end of two or more lines, achieving an effect similar to rhyme in terms of the poem's sound. The repetition of a word can serve a variety of purposes. It may emphasize meaning, demonstrating the way the poet insists on the significance of the word. When used in combination with rhyming words, a repeated word can also have the effect of a chant. That is, the word can, in effect, lose its meaning through repetition. In this way, Stein's use of repetition mirrors her thematic approach to the notion of language as potentially meaningless.

In many of the lines in the poem, Stein uses rhyming words within the confines of a single line, as internal rhyme. In the absence of rhythm established through the use of meter, the poem gains a rhythmic effect through the poet's use of internal rhyme. The frequency with which this element appears in "Stanza LXXXIII" under-scores the detailed choreography of the poem, giving the work a structure that can sometimes seem absent from a free-verse poem.

First-Person Speaker

In this poem, Stein additionally employs a first-person speaker, a voice referring to itself as "I." This voice may be regarded either as Stein herself or a narrator created for the purposes of the poem. The speaker in this poem is a self-conscious, philosophical individual. Through the use of the first-person speaker, Stein explores the relationship between the poet and the poem and that between the poet and the reading audience. She twice refers to a third-person group. In doing so, Stein forces the reader to consider his or her own role in the poem, evaluating his or her participation in the group of others to which the speaker refers.

HISTORICAL CONTEXT

Interwar Europe

In Europe during the time period between World War I and World War II, a general pervasive feeling of anxiety and horror existed. Devastated economies struggled to recover, and the 1930s saw widespread global economic depression. Throughout Europe, in the years following World War I, countries suffered as they attempted to rebuild their cities and their economies. Unemployment and poverty were rampant for many years. In eastern Europe, geopolitical boundaries were redrawn after the dismantling of the Austro-Hungarian Empire at the close of World War I. A new Soviet Union was emerging in the wake of a revolution that coincided with the closing war years, as the czarist government was overthrown and Stalin rose to power. Under Stalin's influence, Communism was transforming the nations that bordered the former Russia, as Stalin sought to protect the nation from attack from the west. Despite these hardships, or perhaps inspired by them, a thriving art community had begun to develop in Paris, and literary and artistic modernism was shaping the cultural world. Before a new optimism or a true recovery could fully take hold, however, Hitler rose to power in Germany and sought to regain territories lost to Germany after World War I. Hitler's aggression began with occupation of the

Rhineland in 1935. After Hitler's 1939 invasion of Poland, World War II began.

Late Modernism in Paris in the 1930s

Stein's poetic sequence *Stanzas in Mediation* was written in 1932. During this time, Stein was living and working in Paris, France. Paris in the 1930s was commonly regarded as the literary and artistic epicenter of the world. Stein did much to cultivate this notion, drawing into her circle up-and-coming artists and writers. Befriending Henri Matisse, Pablo Picasso, and Marcel Duchamp, to name a few, Stein participated in the salon culture of the era and hosted gatherings to display the work of her artist friends. New movements in the art world focused on new evolutions in the modernism of the post–World War I era. After World War I, modernist painters began to explore new modes of expression divorced from traditional, realistic models. These ideas developed throughout the next decade, and iterations of earlier developments were, by the 1930s, referred to as examples of late modernism. Artistic movements during the modernist and late modernist period shared the rejection of traditional, realistic modes of the pre–World War I era. Expressionism focused on hazy images seemingly inspired by memory, while cubism explored lines, angles, and colors over realistic representations of landscapes or people. Surrealism was immersed in the realm of the unconscious mind as revealed by dreams and depicted scenes featuring outlandish perspectives, distortions, and often-disturbing, cartoon-like images.

Literary modernism paralleled events in the art world. In the years between the two world wars, a number of writers began to experiment with language and genre. Some employed stream-of-consciousness narration in their works. New modes of expression were explored here, just as in the art world, and poets experimented with visual imagery and form, while novelists investigated avenues of nonlinear narration. Just as in the art world, modernist writers focused on the mind and expression, rather than on the literal, real, external world. T. S. Eliot, Ezra Pound, Gertrude Stein, Marcel Proust, and James Joyce were among the most prominent modernist writers.

As an American woman abroad establishing her own literary reputation, Stein served as a wellspring of advice for a number of American

COMPARE
&
CONTRAST

- **1930s:** Modernist literature experiments with form and genre, rejecting traditional modes of the past. Stream-of-consciousness writing is explored in poetry and fiction. Writers also employ narrative elements that achieve a sense of abstraction. Prominent modernist writers include Stein, T. S. Eliot, James Joyce, Marcel Proust, and Ford Madox Ford.

  1950s: Modernism remains a relevant approach to art and literature and has become increasingly respected. Through this decade, a transition begins to occur from modernism to postmodernism. Postmodernism reflects uncertainty regarding the modernist search for meaning and rejects the modernist explorations of emotions and the unconscious mind as sources of inspiration and understanding.

  Today: Having flourished in the 1960s and 1970s, postmodernism remains a part of twenty-first-century literature, although the contemporary literary landscape is just as likely to feature works characterized by realist or modernist influences. Richard Powers, Joanna Scott, and David Foster Wallace are contemporary authors whose work has been described as late postmodernist.

- **1930s:** Europe during this time remains in the period of depression that followed the devastation and economic trauma wrought by World War I. Postwar unemployment and poverty are common. From the Great Depression in the United States to widespread economic recessions across Europe, the global economy struggles to regain its footing.

  1950s: The global economy begins to recover after the end of World War II. The United States emerges from the war as a powerful and still-wealthy nation and, unlike its European counterparts, has little rebuilding to do; aside from the Japanese attack on Pearl Harbor, the war took place on foreign soil. The United States is therefore able to help its European allies rebuild and in this way contributes to the global economic recovery.

Today: Comparisons between the economic depression of the 1930s and the global recession of the early twenty-first century abound. As David Leonhardt of the *New York Times* states in 2010, "The world's rich countries are now conducting a dangerous experiment. They are repeating an economic policy out of the 1930s—starting to cut spending and raise taxes before a recovery is assured—and hoping today's situation is different enough to assure a different outcome."

- **1930s:** Modernism in art explores new techniques and aims, looking to individual perceptions, emotions, and the unconscious mind as revealed in dreams for inspiration. Cubism, surrealism, and abstract impressionism are examples of this new mode of expression, in which the internal realities of the mind are favored over external realities. Pablo Picasso, Henri Matisse, and Salvador Dalí are artists whose work exemplifies modernist aims.

  1950s: Late modernist artwork develops along similar lines as the earlier years of the movement. René Magritte and Jackson Pollock are artists who feature prominently in the late modernist art world.

  Today: New movements in the art world in the twenty-first century develop out of postmodernism's rejection of the notion that art could be defined at all. Performance art and installation art (art that is three-dimensional or specific to the site where the work is installed) are examples of art that questions the boundaries of artistic representation. "Steampunk" is another twenty-first century art form, in which objects from the past, as from the Victorian era, are combined with new elements to suggest an as-yet-unrealized future. The Heidelberg Project, a work by installation artist Tyree Guyton in Detroit, Michigan, is an example of twenty-first-century installation art.

Silhouette of woman reaching out (debra hughes / Shutterstock.com)

expatriate (living in a foreign land) writers in Paris, including Ernest Hemingway and F. Scott Fitzgerald. This large community of expatriate American writers came to be known as the "Lost Generation," a term coined by Stein. As Donald Pizer points out in *American Expatriate Writing and the Paris Moment*, the writing of American expatriates in Paris at this time is often "implicitly critical of specific features of American life even while obliquely celebrating other aspects of it." Pizer maintains that to American writers, Paris represented a sense of freedom of expression and a "nourishment for the spirit" that they could not find in America. Not all of the American writers in Paris at this time could be classed with experimental, modernist writers like Stein, Eliot, and Pound. Fitzgerald and Hemingway both took more traditional narrative approaches to their work, yet thematically, these writers incorporated modernist ideas into their work, exploring in depth the notions of loneliness, isolation, and disaffectedness or disillusionment.

CRITICAL OVERVIEW

According to Logan Esdale in the 2005 volume *A Companion to Twentieth-Century American Poetry*, Stein's contemporary reception was mixed. Esdale cites reviews by other authors,

including T. S. Eliot and Samuel Beckett, that indicate both an understanding of what Stein was attempting to do with her experiments with language and also a lack of appreciation for the effort. Esdale quotes Eliot as stating that Stein's work, in 1927, was neither "amusing" nor "interesting." Nevertheless, Eliot seem to have responded on some level to "its rhythms."

Catharine R. Stimpson and Harriet Chessman, the editors of *Stein: Writings, 1932–1946*, note in the chronology that as early as 1909, Stein was receiving favorable reactions, in this case to *Three Lives* (1909). Furthermore, Stimpson and Chessman point out that in the mid-1930s, Stein was traveling throughout the United States on a lecture tour, which indicates her popularity at the time.

Assessments of *Stanzas in Meditation* typically focus on the work's experiments with language. Jack Kimball, in a 1998 essay for *Time-Sense*, an online journal dedicated to Stein's work, prefaces his discussion of *Stanzas in Meditation* by noting that "Stein's use of language to break down convention is, of course, perplexing, deliberately so." In a review of a new edition of Stein's works for the *New York Times*, Richard Howard describes Stein's writing in works such as *Stanzas in Meditation* as "rare and difficult (and moving)." He further characterizes *Stanzas in Meditation* as Stein's "best poetry." In a 1957 review of *Stanzas in Meditation* in *Poetry* magazine, John Ashbery describes the poetry in *Stanzas*: "Like people, Miss Stein's lines are comforting or annoying or brilliant or tedious. Like people, they sometimes make no sense and sometimes make perfect sense."

CRITICISM

Catherine Dominic

Dominic is a novelist, freelance writer, and editor. In the following essay, she investigates Stein's appropriation of the sonnet form in "Stanza LXXXIII," the final stanza in the poetic sequence Stanzas in Meditation. *She argues that within the sonnet form, Stein explores the potential both of language and of consciousness as it is depicted in the moment that the poem describes.*

Gertrude Stein was known to have an avid interest in genre, and in many of her works she challenges the conventions of the form within which she is working. As Franziska Gygax

WHAT DO I READ NEXT?

- Originally published privately in 1914, Stein's *Tender Buttons* is a collection of experimental pieces; the works are sometimes regarded as prose poems. The writings reveal Stein's early interest in language, meaning, and genre. The work is often recommended for young-adult audiences. A 2007 edition of the work is available.

- Stein's *The Making of Americans* is a lengthy novel exploring three generations of one family. Like many of her works, this novel tests the boundaries of its form. After being published in serial form in the magazine *Transatlantic Review*, through the efforts of Ford Madox Ford and Hemingway, the work as a whole was published in 1925 and then in an abridged version in 1934. A modern, unabridged version was published in 1995.

- Rubén Darío was a Nicaraguan poet who became identified as the forerunner of the Hispanic modernist movement, with his works predating the surge in European modernism experienced during the years just prior to World War I. His *Songs of Life and Hope*, originally published in 1905, is available in a 2004 bilingual edition.

- *Flygirl*, a 2009 young-adult novel written by Sherri L. Smith, tells the story of a young African American woman who, during World War II, attempts to pass as a white woman in order to become a pilot and fly noncombat missions in the war. Students interested in Stein's personal life will find a parallel between this story and the Stein's participation as a driver in World War I. Stein, who lived through both world wars, learned to drive in order to participate in the war effort by delivering supplies to French hospitals during World War I.

- Rebecca Beasley's *Theorists of Modern Poetry: T. S. Eliot, T. E. Hulme, Ezra Pound* (2007) explores the philosophical, social, and literary theories behind the writings of three major modernist poets.

- Ernest Hemingway's *A Moveable Feast* is a memoir of his years in Paris as a young writer trying to get published. In this work, he discusses a number of American expatriate writers living in Paris at that time, including Stein. Originally published in 1964, after Hemingway's death, the work is now available in a 1996 edition.

observes in *Gender and Genre in Gertrude Stein*, "it seems she intended her works to be read with certain generic expectations in mind, be it only to have them undermined." Gygax continues, "most of the expectations related to a specific genre are never met in her works." For instance, Stein challenged the conventions of the dramatic form by writing plays without characters. Additionally, Stein wrote *The Autobiography of Alice B. Toklas* (1933), approaching the work not as an ordinary biography of Toklas but proclaiming it to be an autobiography. In her poetry, Stein was known to experiment with language and form as well, and she does so extensively in

the poetic sequence *Stanzas in Meditation*. The final stanza of the sequence, "Stanza LXXXIII" is not only a conclusion to the sequence as a whole but also a rich and complex poem in its own right. In 'Stanza LXXXIII,' Stein incorporates several structures of the sonnet form; the work might be described as a free-verse sonnet. By utilizing conventions of this particular poetic form, Stein draws attention to the form only to question and challenge its parameters, as she has done elsewhere in her work.

Stein's use of the sonnet form, primarily in the work *Patriarchal Poetry*, has been studied by critics such as Margaret Dickie in *Stein, Bishop &*

IN 'STANZA LXXXIII,' STEIN INCORPORATES SEVERAL STRUCTURES OF THE SONNET FORM; THE WORK MAY BE DESCRIBED AS A FREE-VERSE SONNET. BY UTILIZING CONVENTIONS OF THIS PARTICULAR POETIC FORM, STEIN DRAWS ATTENTION TO THE FORM ONLY TO QUESTION AND CHALLENGE ITS PARAMETERS, AS SHE HAS DONE ELSEWHERE IN HER WORK."

Rich: Lyrics of Love, War & Place. In the sonnets in *Patriarchal Poetry*, Stein draws attention to the form as an example of patriarchal poetry. To Stein, the sonnet form in particular was regarded as a poetic structure dominated by the male perspective. As Dickie points out, Stein uses the phrase "patriarchal poetry" apparently "to mimic and deflate that poetry," but her use of the form demonstrates an ambivalence as well. Stein appropriates the sonnet form, writing paradoxically from a feminist perspective, but also uses the language of the sonnet, as her male predecessors did, to praise a lover.

"Stanza LXXXIII" stands out as another example of Stein's experiment with the sonnet structure. Stein composed the poem as fourteen lines, the traditional number of lines in any sonnet. Furthermore, while the poem does not duplicate the precise structure of traditional sonnets, such as the forms developed by William Shakespeare and Edmund Spenser, Stein's poem closes with a rhymed couplet. Shakespearean sonnets are roughly divided into three quatrains, that is, three four-line units, in which each quatrain is characterized by a particular rhyme scheme. Spenserian sonnets are similarly divided into three quatrains and a couplet but feature a different rhyme scheme in the quatrains, in which the quatrains are more intimately linked to one another than in a Shakespearean sonnet. Stein's poem initially suggests a similar structuring, but the poem does not utilize either of these rhyme schemes throughout the entirety of the poem. Rather, Stein dabbles in end rhyme and repetition and additionally incorporates internal

rhyme. In "Stanza LXXXIII," the end rhyme of the first two lines is repeated in the second quatrain, unifying those lines structurally and thereby suggesting the linguistic and thematic relationship among the lines of the quatrains. In the third quatrain, there is no end-rhyme feature, but Stein makes heavy use of internal rhyme in this section, linking lines 9 and 10 to one another, as well as lines 11 and 12 to one another, through the use of internal rhyme.

Shakespeare and Spenser used the structure and rhyme schemes of the sonnet forms they developed to show the connectedness of ideas within the poem and to establish a particular rhythm; Stein links ideas in this way as well. Stein's ideas, however, pertain to words and meaning, to existence and intention, rather than to intimate relationships between individuals. Unlike Shakespeare and Spenser, whose sonnets are devoted to romantic themes, the relationships Stein explores are those that exist between words as symbols and meaning as what an individual perceives. She further links this relationship to the notion of personal consciousness in a given moment and to the idea of potential within that state of existence. In the opening lines of "Stanza LXXXIII," Stein appears to question the purpose of existence and the nature of self-doubt. However, in the absence of punctuation, the lines threaten the reader's tenuous grasp on this possible meaning. Stein's repeated use throughout the poem of the end rhyme utilized in the first two lines of the poem forces the reader to look back, to question the meaning that has been derived, and to possibly identify variations in meaning with each subsequent reading. The reader's understanding of the poem shifts moment by moment, and yet Stein's persistent use of present-tense, state-of-being verbs insists on the perception that the poem occurs within one prolonged moment of time, as if it is a single instance of one's consciousness. Existing also in this moment is an understanding of the speaker's intention; Stein uses future tenses in the third quatrain of the poem. Despite the willingness to move forward, evidenced by the repeated use of the word *will*, no action occurs, thereby reinforcing the sensation that the poem describes the activity of the consciousness within a single given moment.

The perception that the poem occurs within a particular moment of consciousness is underscored in the repetition of the notion of arrival in the final lines of the poem. The speaker discusses how she will be welcome when she arrives and then states that in fact she is in the act of coming. A sense of stasis, of prolonged inactivity in a single moment, is again achieved when the speaker stresses that she arrives having already come. This philosophical exploration of consciousness, of being, reflects what Meredith Yearsley observes in the *Dictionary of Literary Biography*. Yearsley discusses the way Stein explored a concept she referred to as "entity—the memory-free mode of consciousness that occurs in the act of doing anything, when the individual cannot be conscious of his identity." In "Stanza LXXXIII," Stein seems to be writing from such a state of awareness, when one considers the language used and the stream-of-consciousness style employed.

Stein makes another challenge to the usual sonnet form through her spare use of imagery in "Stanza LXXXIII." In traditional sonnets, such as those by Shakespeare and Spenser, a wealth of imagery, often relating to the natural world, is employed; but Stein does not reflect on stars, tempests, summer days, or flowers, as did her male predecessors in their love poems. Rather, Stein employs one single image in her poem: the door. A utilitarian object, made by an individual for a specific purpose, the door in Stein's poem functions as a symbol of opportunity. An unlocked door is mentioned, although, despite the invitation inherent in its status as open, the door remains closed. The static moment continues to exist, unchanged, without intrusion, suspended within its state of potentiality.

Readers can only speculate upon Stein's intentions in appropriating some of the conventions of this form, such as the use of end and internal rhyme and the fourteen-line structure. Some critics have argued that for Stein to employ the form in a way so distinct from the sonnet's origins suggests that she reclaims it for her own gender-specific (feminist) purposes. She does not use the sonnet as a platform for extolling the virtues of love or a lover but rather to focus on one's personal consciousness. One could argue that the contrast of these two perspectives serves as Stein's commentary on the male use of the sonnet form. Despite Stein's reputation as a feminist, however, her use of the sonnet form may also be read not simply as a reappropriation of a traditionally male or patriarchal poetic form. Rather, it may be viewed as

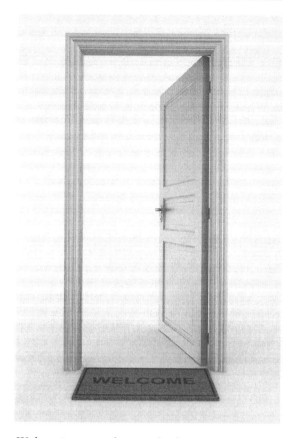

Welcoming open door to the future (zentilia / *Shutterstock.com*)

another extension of her experimental approach to poetry. She playfully employs a poetic form traditionally used to extoll the virtues of love, woo a lover, pine for a lover, or praise a lover, to instead meditate. In the final stanza in *Stanzas on Meditation*, Stein trains her consciousness on a single moment and contemplates the use and meaning of language within the confines of a word, a phrase, a line, or a sonnet. Conversely, she uses the multiplicity and potential of language to explore a state of consciousness that exists as both static identity and potential identity. As is typical with Stein's work, the essential meaning of the work shifts based on one's perspective, like an optical illusion, forcing the reader to question whether, in "Stanza LXXXIII," language is used to explore consciousness or consciousness is used to explore language.

Source: Catherine Dominic, Critical Essay on "Stanza LXXXIII," in *Poetry for Students*, Gale, Cengage Learning, 2011.

Jean Mills

In the following excerpt, Mills suggests that Stanzas in Meditation is a surrender and literary transformation initiated by private issues with Stein's muse, Alice B. Toklas.

Gertrude Stein once wrote, referring to Alice B. Toklas, that she is "the air of here and there," but I would suggest that the "heir" space Toklas occupies during the composition of *Stanzas in Meditation* is confined to a single one of Gertrude Stein's lungs, perhaps the right. The other houses Stein's mantra, with all of mantra's deepest associations to consciousness and its Sanskrit origin *manyate*, meaning "he thinks," which is for Stein, "I write." For *Stanzas in Meditation* is both a solemnization of and surrender to the Word, to Love, to Alice B. Toklas, as muse-turned-harpy, but also to the demon paradox of language to both affirm and deny Stein's left lung, words.

During an extraordinarily prolific period between the summer and fall of 1932, Gertrude Stein wrote *Stanzas in Meditation* at night as she simultaneously wrote *The Autobiography of Alice B. Toklas* by day. Stein's critics and biographers often point to *The Autobiography* as a turning point in Stein's writing career and the fame conferred upon Stein as a result of its publication in the *Atlantic Monthly* from May–August 1933 as the reason for a dramatic shift in Stein's literary perspective. However, if we accept *Stanzas in Meditation* as "half of a paired work," or as Stein writes "her autobiography one of two," though one which has been largely ignored in stark contrast to its renowned companion, then we must also consider any shift in Stein's writing and perspective in terms of *The Autobiography*'s bastard twin—*Stanzas in Meditation*, which is to a certain extent Stein's debut as scolded poetic bad boy. An analysis of Stein's long poem, as well as the historical context in which it was written, completes the picture of the influence of audience on Stein's literary sea-change by adding with emphasis Alice B. Toklas, as transfigured addressee, to the equation. I further suggest Stein's career be considered in terms of pre- and post-*Stanzas in Meditation* as opposed to pre- and post-*Autobiography* as is usually the case, or, at the very least, as a pairing of the two with *Stanzas in Meditation* receiving its due with top-billing as *Stanzas* is the more significant text

in terms of Stein's literary transformation. It is one of the underlying subversions of this essay to privilege Stein's prodigal but, in my opinion, more radiant son, *Stanzas in Meditation*, in an attempt to close the textual gap between the twins and end our readerly estrangement from Stein's deserving testimonial, a kind of haunted credo from her consciousness, on writing and love, and a plea to publishers that any succeeding editions of *The Autobiography* be rejoined by *Stanzas in Meditation*.

Therefore, I would say that before *Stanzas in Meditation*, Stein's work, whether using the trope of "inside / outside," one's "bottom nature," or the determinism of words to denote versus connote the self, reveals a confidence in the ability of language to articulate identity. Stein scholar Ulla E. Dydo, for example, makes the distinction between Stein "the modernist innovator" and Stein "the personality" when she made her selections for *A Stein Reader*, choosing from Stein's earlier works "written 'from inside'" as opposed to "her late public works written 'from outside' in conventional English." As Stein's early work attests, before *Stanzas*, Stein is dominatrix, gatekeeper, and warden of the I(Eye). Before *Stanzas*, we have a cheerful, confident, and playful Stein, the unknown underground sound machine, dropping science with a verbal agility that gestures generously towards a future hip-hop nation. But she is, significantly, playing for an audience of one—essentially herself and Toklas, the lover and the loved, but separate and intact, as one, the happy muse. Before *Stanzas*, we are as readers in the capable hands of the instructor, who challenges us to indict our own imaginations as well as our cognition and understanding of words and their meanings. As Margo Jefferson noted in her tribute to Gertrude Stein in *PEN-Presents*: Gertrude Stein "opens up the vernacular" with a "talking/listening, palpable rhythm" that changes the way we read. In one of Stein's "antimimetic" portraits, "Guillaume Apollinaire," for example, we have what Ulla Dydo calls both "a bilingual eye [. . . and] ear lesson" from Stein as master:

> Give known or pin ware.
> Fancy teethe, gas strips.
> Elbow elect, sour stout pore, pore caesar,
>   pour state at.
> Leave eye lessons I. Leave I. Lessons. I.
>   Leave I lessons, I.

At this stage in her career, Stein is in command of the "eye lessons," playing on the sound and visual representation of words on the page, taking risks with language that indicate a profound confidence in the ability of words, even letters, fractals, in essence, the infinitesimal atoms in the grand-scale patterns of speech, to both convey, in the broadest sense of "transmit," and purvey, in the narrowest sense of "supply as a matter of business"—Stein's business—I write. Or as in "Article" we have Stein as (I would say transgendered) dominatrix, "the best demander" who commands "best do it best and most [...] The best and the best" and finishes with "The suck and the suck and that in the suck. The suck."

After *Stanzas in Meditation*, however, Stein becomes hostage of the I(Eye), but not only because of her newly found public audience and lionization in the American press with the success of *Autobiography*, the reason most frequently declared as evidence of Stein's "crisis with identity," but also in terms of her private audience, Alice B. Toklas, the one, both the lover and the loved, without whom Gertrude Stein cannot survive. The influence of fame on Gertrude Stein's identity and work, an influence which continues to commodify her today, is well documented. Ashton explores the '70s and early '80s *L=A=N=G=U=A=G=E* journal's embrace of Stein and the desire to associate her with a postmodernist poetics of indeterminacy. Ashton asks, and I agree, "Why should [Stein's] insistence on the irreducible materiality of language go along with an insistence on its indeterminacy [...]?" Ashton is indeed referring to what I would characterize as an early Stein, pre-*Stanzas*, principle that reference equals denotation, "reference is what names are, not merely what they do," but applies the concept to what I would consider a post-*Stanzas* text, *Four in America*, which she finishes in 1933. *Four in America*, Stein's study of proper names, George Washington, Ulysses S. Grant, Wilbur Wright, and Henry James, reveals a much more self-conscious Stein pointedly trying to reclaim her identity, and any analysis of that text requires consideration as part of a post-*Stanzas* Steinian world. As Kirk Curnutt notes, after the success of *Autobiography*, Stein "questioned her freedom to pursue abstruse literary experiments without concern for reader's expectations." In the conventional narrative prose of *Everybody's Autobiography*, throughout which Alice Toklas is notably

absent, Stein questions identity. Upon her return to France, after experiencing *la gloire* during her enormously successful lectures in America tour 1934–1935, she writes, "Settled down in Bilignin, I became worried about identity and remembered the Mother Goose, I am I because my little dog knows me and I was not sure but that that only proved the dog was he and not that I was I." But despite the Steinian departure into reader-friendly prose, she is mocked by critics who try to write Steinese reviews and refer to her as an indecipherable sphinx. And the other works she published following *The Autobiography*, like *Geographical History*, *Lectures in America*, and *Narration* were "less accessible works" and read, according to Curnutt by "baffled" critics as a "veiled assertion of artistic autonomy." The editors at *Vanity Fair* try to "heterosexualize" her work as they too parody her literary identity in order to sell subscriptions to the magazine. Stein's literary output during this period is a post-*Stanzas* Stein trying to right her balance after the double blow of both the private scrutiny of her soul and the public commodification of her work.

This agonizing, prolonged journey back to self is set in motion by *Stanzas in Meditation* and comes during its composition in early spring 1932. While Stein was writing *Stanzas*, Alice discovered another manuscript, which she had never seen before called *Q.E.D.*, a novel based on an affair Gertrude had had with a family friend, May Bookstaver [Knoblauch], "a young graduate of Bryn Mawr (where Stein had friends) whom Stein saw in Baltimore and New York from 1901–1903." Even though the affair took place before Stein had met Toklas, Toklas felt betrayed and threatened to leave the relationship. It is in the midst of the potential disintegration of their marriage that Stein makes concessions to Toklas who had earlier urged Stein to write a "money maker" in reader-friendly prose. As Stein writes *The Autobiography of Alice B. Toklas*, she also writes her "other autobiography" *Stanzas in Meditation* in a style much more commonly associated with Stein, "abstract."

The timing of Toklas' discovery of *Q.E.D.*, according to Stein biographer Linda Wagner-Martin, occurred during the first week of May 1932, when "Gertrude unearthed her first (lost) novella and showed it to Alice and Louis Bromfield," which would place Toklas' rage at the beginning of *Stanzas'* composition. Ulla Dydo's invaluable research on Stein's manuscripts confirms this chronology. She writes that Stein refers to the tension created by *Q.E.D.*'s discovery "within two days after arrival in Bilignin in the first week of May 1932" in a piece called "Here. Actualities." But Dydo seems to contradict herself in the later *A Stein Reader* where she writes that "The stanzas were complete by late July 1932 and typed by Alice Toklas. However, in late summer Toklas read the manuscript of Stein's first novel *Q.E.D.*" Did Toklas read the manuscript of *Q.E.D.* in "early spring" before Stein wrote *Stanzas*, or "late summer" after *Stanzas* was typed? Toklas' angry reaction, however, is not in dispute. The "late summer" reading must be an oversight on Dydo's part, because the text of *Stanzas in Meditation* favors the notion of a Toklas reading of *Q.E.D.* during the early stages of the writing of *Stanzas* in early spring, and points to an aggrieved Toklas presence which has knowledge afore-hand of Stein's perceived "transgressions." In her analysis of *Stanzas in Meditation*, though asking us to view the poem as "pure" Stein and "her most abstract and disembodied work" about which I disagree, Dydo admits "Plainly Gertrude Stein and Alice Toklas are quarreling."

In *The Autobiography of Alice B. Toklas*, Stein's most "concrete, referential work," Toklas' presence is undeniable, despite the ultimate foregrounding of Gertrude Stein's voice. But Alice both inscribes and interrupts the text in *Stanzas in Meditation* not only in terms of Stein's awareness of an angry Toklas as audience, but also in terms of Toklas' physical, historical mark upon the page. The original manuscript of *Stanzas in Meditation* at Yale's Beinecke Library shows a relentless and vigorous elision of "mays" (for May Bookstaver) in deep, dark pencil lead throughout both the handwritten manuscript and typescript drafts. These are substituted with "cans" instead. Ulla Dydo writes that these revisions are in Stein's hand, but at Toklas' insistence and "no doubt initiated by Toklas." But there are other instances that were written by Toklas, herself. As Wagner-Martin points out in Favored Stranger:

> [...] in the manuscripts of the 1932 *Stanzas in Meditation* and *The Autobiography of Alice B. Toklas*, Alice began writing for herself. For instance, refrains like these appear in her handwriting, "Where they are alike a like and alike forget it" and "aroused by suspicion—Everything

away and aroused by suspicion." There is also a longer addition in her writing about possible "arrangements," necessary now because of the way "the wind can blow does blow," until truth is "suddenly recognized. A question and answer. Where did it come from." [...] The dynamic of the women's familiar dialogue was being seriously tested.

While I understand that the replaced "cans" must be, according to Dydo, in Stein's handwriting, how are we to determine whether the penciled crossing out of "mays" is the work of a betrayed, "paranoid" Toklas or a resentful but compliant Stein? When I viewed the manuscripts myself in January 2003, albeit with an inexperienced eye, and obviously in error, I took the "cans" to be in Toklas' handwriting as well as at other points in the text where phrases and words were changed as Wagner-Martin attests, because the handwriting seemed to have a decidedly different slant from Gertrude's distinctive, and flowing script. Whether Toklas made the changes herself (according to Wagner-Martin) or Stein on Toklas' insistence (according to Dydo), Toklas' position as muse, separate but intact, and Steinian audience of one is transformed and corrupted as is the Steinian response in text, which is significantly spun in a different direction as a result. And from this point on Stein's writing I(Eye) is changed from perceiver to perceived.

Stanzas in Meditation then becomes Stein's night-passage through language, but also marks the beginning of the dismantling of the Steinian self, as she writes what I would characterize as "nearly a block," and anticipates a complete cessation to her writing on the other side. Stein's historical writing block coincides with the publication and overnight success of the more popular twin, *The Autobiography of Alice B. Toklas*, but needs also to be considered in terms of *Stanzas'* neglect by the public, as well as Alice's slow burn inscribed on each page during *Stanzas'* composition. Despite the time lapse between the writing of *Stanzas* and *The Autobiography* and Stein's subsequent writer's block with the publication of *Autobiography* (May–August 1933), the Stein-Toklas relationship remains unsteady even after *Stanzas in Meditation* is complete and continues to be challenged as the couple begin Stein's lecture tour in America a year later between 1934–1935. The ongoing and considerable difficulties in the relationship, in addition to public fame, add dimension to our understanding of Stein's block and flight from her literary principles, as being a result of scrutiny by her private audience as well.

If we are to read then *The Autobiography of Alice B. Toklas* as "I obey" with its uncharacteristic adherence to conventional narrative prose, then *Stanzas in Meditation* can be read as "I confess," but also as a text rife with the anxiety of the impossibility of language to articulate feeling, in the midst of the historical tension and desperation Stein felt at the potential death of her marriage. Stein writes, "Once now I will tell all which they tell lightly. / How were we when we met," and "what I wish to say is this," as she repeatedly confesses or asks permission to tell, but to be allowed to do so in her own words, and in her own style. Ulla Dydo, however, counsels us not to read *Stanzas* "as concealed pieces of autobiography."

While it is impossible to do so with any degree of accuracy, it is also equally impossible not to read the text without acknowledging the past, as Dydo herself does in her earlier article "*Stanzas in Meditation*: The Other Autobiography." Being informed by historical context, without being overwhelmed by it, does not preclude a reading of *Stanzas* as Dydo insists they "must be read" as "word constructions." Nor does it change the fact that in *Stanzas* we are deep inside Stein's consciousness and in the milieu of Stein's mantra "I write." However, there is an undeniable desperation and a building of anxiety in the text, which suggests, regardless of history, that Stein is cowering before her mantra instead of wielding it or experiencing it as she does in her earlier work. Stein who once wrote that "every word I am ever using in writing has for me very existing being" is uncertain of that claim in *Stanzas in Meditation*, and it is difficult to dismiss a betrayed and enraged Toklas, when she is implicated in nearly every line. Susan M. Schultz writes that *Stanzas in Meditation* is "a work that eschews the muse [. . . and] invites us to forget Toklas" but gives no evidence of this amnesia in the text. To my mind, Toklas is never more present in a Stein text than in *Stanzas in Meditation* and Stein can no more forget Toklas than she can forget how to breathe. In fact, the more Stein tries to breathe on her own, with a single lung, through words, the more anxious she becomes. Are we to imagine that Stein is addressing a "word construction" but not Toklas, or no one at all, when she

beckons "Come hither. Neither / Aimless and with a pointedly rested displeasure" or when she writes "Often make it be believed that they marry / It is not only that there was no doubt" or with the exquisite "Out from the whole wide world I chose thee"? And to whom is she asking "Tell me darling tell me true / Am I all the world to you" if not Toklas?

In a characteristic display of grandiosity, a post-*Stanzas* Gertrude Stein once proclaimed "think of Shakespeare and think of me" (*The Geographical History of America*), and in terms of *Stanzas in Meditation* I believe the analogy to be apt. In addition to the "Come hither"'s, "thee"'s and other Elizabethan-type echoes in the poem, *Stanzas* has striking parallels to Shakespeare's sonnet CXVI "Let me not to the marriage of true minds admit impediments . . . ," his meditation on writing and love and the paradoxical power of words to both express and deny love. Both "Let me not . . . " and *Stanzas in Meditation* can be read as (subversive) wedding poems. In "Let me not to the marriage of true minds . . . ," which in a queer reading is a sonnet written by a man to a man, Shakespeare collages from the traditional Christian wedding ceremony and solemnization of vows, the "impediment" to their union. In the case of *Stanzas*, Stein, who has been married to Toklas as husband to wife for twenty-five years at this writing, is seeking a reaffirmation of vows when she writes:

> They do not think not only only
> But always with prefer
> And therefor I like what is mine
> For which not only willing but willingly
> Because which it matters.
> They find it one in union.
> In union there is strength.
> (*SM*)

Stein's posture at this early point in the sequence, Part II, Stanza VII, in addition to an air of solemnization, resonates with a Nietzschean logic that suggests "I want you to love me willingly, 'always with prefer,' but I also want to construct a world in which I am your only logical choice, 'And therefor I like what is mine.'" As Dydo has shown, the dropped "e" at the end of 'therefor' echoes the five "therefor's" in the final stanza of the sequence, and points out Stein's desire for Toklas to be "there for" her as well as her wish to be "there for" Alice and that they "therefore" should stay together. Her composure at this early point in the sequence, however, is violently breached in Stein's declarative "This is what I say / A poem is torn in two." With the rupture, the anxiety in the text increases as she writes "Now I recount how I felt when I dwelt on it," but she cannot sustain the telling, because in her next breath she writes "I now I do not know what I feel." Stein is progressively being taken away from her mantra "I think / I write" into unfamiliar territory, "feelings":

> What do I think when I feel.
> I feel I feel they feel they feel which they feel
> And so borrowed or closed they will they will win
> How can any one know the difference between worry and win.

Gertrude seems to be fighting a losing battle and decidedly on the side of "worry" as opposed to "win" when she writes "Who is winning why the answer of course is she is." Alice's presence shadows the text as the speaker's words cope with tension and struggle on a battleground dictated by the victor. Perhaps Gertrude "will not be often betrayed by delayed / Not often" but sometimes she will be delayed and forced to confess, and perhaps this is one of those times. Though an admonished Stein begins hopefully with a potential chance to undo and repair, when she writes:

> And so it is a better chance to come
> With which they know theirs to undo
> Getting it better more than once alike
> For which fortune favors me,
> (*SM*)

she also considers that her luck may have run out because "Four leaf clovers make a Sunday / And that is gone." But the language of the battlefield is set in motion, and Stein seems prepared to admit that she has fallen a bit short of Caesar as her "We learned we must we saw we conquered most" edits the Caesarian boast, "veni, vidi, vici."

. . . Reading *Stanzas* as a request for a reaffirmation of vows, one would think that Stein would end with the love line: "I can I wish I do love none but you." But she instead writes five more stanzas and ends with sex, as if in a last-ditch effort to retain her earlier Steinian self, as [. . .], hot daddy, and Steinian sex machine:

> I will be well welcome when I come.
> Because I am coming.
> Certainly I come having come.
> These stanzas are done.

But this final sensual gesture is coupled with a reiteration of her uncertainty and inability to say exactly what she wants to say. She repeats, "I

wish once more to say that I know the difference between two" before the quintessential polite Stein says "Thank you for hurrying through." Stein's final stanza, however, like the couplet in Shakespeare's sonnet which reads "If this be error and upon me proved / I never writ nor no man ever loved," reveals the paradox of language to both affirm and deny her love. She begins with a hopeful affirmation of love through language, a promise that Stein will stay open, open legs, open ass, open arms, open heart, open door, until she is forgiven, redeemed, let in. She writes:

> Why am I if I am uncertain reasons may inclose.
> Remain remain propose repose chose.
> I call carelessly that the door is open
> Which if they may refuse to open
> No one can rush to close.
> Let them be mine therefor.
> (*SM*)

Like Shakespeare offering his poem as proof of the existence of true love, Stein offers her *Stanzas*:

> Everybody knows that I chose.
> Therefor if therefore before I close.
> I will therefore offer therefore I offer this.
> Which if I refuse to miss may be miss is mine.

Stein is offering Alice "this," both her love and her mantra "I write" in hopes that if she doesn't "miss" the "miss is mine."

Stanzas in Meditation, then, is an act of reverse fetishization, wherein eroticism replaces object instead of the other way around, as Toklas progressively replaces the air in both of Gertrude Stein's lungs. Rather than a "pure," "disembodied," "abstract" Stein, *Stanzas*, by the historical end of its composition, becomes a seepage of "heir" space and like *The Autobiography of Alice B. Toklas*, if not a complete departure, then a slipping away of Stein. Despite her attempts to save both her loves, Toklas and her writing I(Eye), Stein does indeed seem to be aware of what lies ahead, the proverbial "writing on the wall," when she writes:

> To know and feel and may be tell
> Is all very well if no one stealing past
> Is stealing me for me.
> Oh why oh why may they count most
> If most and best is all
> Of course it is all or all at all
> Most and best met from there to here
> And this is what I change.

Stein's literary transformation from "inside" to "outside" self is initiated not by the hostage lens, the public scrutiny of fame with the publication of *The Autobiography* (for by then it is clear it's too late and she actually experiences a complete block), but brought on by the private scrutiny of her transfigured muse, Alice B. Toklas, in the early spring of 1932. *Stanzas in Meditation* marks the literary portal through which Stein passes and irretrievably alters her mantra from "I write" to "I love," a transmogrification of consciousness, which ultimately, one could argue, leads both lovers bodily to their single grave (in the cemetery for the rich and famous, Pere-Lachaise, in Paris). . . .

Source: Jean Mills, "Gertrude on the Block: Writing, Love, and Fame in *Stanzas in Meditation*," in *Philological Quarterly*, Vol. 83, No. 2, Spring 2004, pp. 197–210.

Publishers Weekly

In the following review, the critic suggests the lengths to which Stein will go with words.

Stein's *Stanzas in Meditation*, published previously in only a very limited edition, is a monumental and rather terrifying word machine. By contrast to the chattiness of the popular *Autobiography of Alice B. Toklas*, with which it is contemporaneous, the poem is representative of Stein's work at its most mind-boggling and austere. The book's five parts, 162 stanzas, and 225 pages do not meditate on anything in particular; instead they construct and explore basic linguistic structures within the mental space of meditation. Meditation is a state of mind in which nothing has to happen, but anything and everything could; Stein's poem is accordingly general in concern and conditional in articulation, occupied throughout with such considerations as "Should it be well done or should it be well done / Or can they be very likely or not at all / Not only known but well known." The tone of the poem is flat, reminiscent of logical exercises, sentences from primers and travelers' phrase books, and nursery rhymes; the words are mostly monosyllabic. In one sense, the relentlessly repetitive yet always slightly shifted use of a number of basic terms draws one's attention to the surface of the poem and hedevils any effort to go beyond it. But the mechanically proliferating stanzas involve a depth of desperation: "Let me see let me go let me be not only determined."

This poem is a fascinating if exhausting performance. The unbearable lengths to which Stein will go with words figure an impossible desire to leave words behind for good—to think and feel simply, for once—and this human predicament makes her experimentalism of abiding interest.

Source: Review of *Stanzas in Meditation*, in *Publishers Weekly*, Vol. 241, No. 44, October 31, 1994, pp. 53–54.

Susan M. Schultz

In the following excerpt, Schultz discusses Stein's ruminations on her writing career in Stanzas in Meditation *and her autobiographical prose works.*

> I often think how celebrated I am.
> It is difficult not to think how celebrated I am.
> And if I think how celebrated I am
> They know who know that I am new
> That is I knew I know how celebrated I am
> And after all it astonishes even me.
> All this is to be for me.

Gertrude Stein defies the attempts we make at describing her career historically; the antihistorical historian par excellence, Stein wrote two autobiographies in 1932 alone. The first purports to be history, albeit the history of another's life; *The Autobiography of Alice B. Toklas* is one of Stein's most ostensibly accessible works. The second, *Stanzas in Meditation*, records the process of telling rather than offering us the tale itself. But the very accessibility of the Toklas autobiography tends to obscure its central sleight of hand, as well as its left hook at literary tradition, for Stein not only writes as her own muse—Alice B. Toklas—but she has Toklas perform a service quite different from that of the traditional muse. Conventionally, the muse has been at once the power behind the text and the text's best audience. But Stein's muse does not so much inspire as advertise her work; her muse promotes the text as a literary, not a spiritual, agent. Even more radically, the work that Stein has Toklas advertise is not the work that she finds herself "writing"; instead, it is the kind of experimental work that we find in *Stanzas in Meditation*, work that eschews the muse. Toklas, then, invites us to forget Toklas, just as Stein invites us to become one with Stein. The central subject of the second autobiography, like the first, is the question of audience: for whom is Stein writing, herself or someone else? To what extent can she become her own audience? To what extent does the equation of the artist with her audience obviate or exacerbate the modern artist's problem with audience? She poses these questions in both works, although her strategies are more radical in *Stanzas in Meditation*.

> STEIN'S TRIUMPH IN *STANZAS*—HOWEVER
> UNEVEN—IS TO SHOW TO WHAT EXTENT THAT
> RELATIONSHIP DEFINES THE WRITER, EVEN WHEN
> SHE TRIES TO WRITE WITHOUT EITHER A MUSE OR
> AN AUDIENCE."

This doubling of concerns is only appropriate for an author as concerned with repetition and difference as Stein. Creation is for Stein tantamount to repetition since, lacking a muse apart from herself, Stein (at least figuratively) lacks a subject or an audience. Language becomes poetry, in Stein's experimental work, not because it names the world, but precisely because it refuses to do so, over and again. Surprisingly perhaps, Stein's poetics are radical for their very formalism; the text insists on its separateness from its possible subjects, not on its union with them. But Stein's formalism is not that of the New Critics; rather it seems closer to the self-reflexive formalism of her contemporary, Laura Riding, and to the unacknowledged formalism of contemporary language poets. Both Riding and the language poets write poems whose primary subject is the material—the language—that creates them. Stein's long poem *Stanzas in Meditation* resists closure only insofar as it resists a muse outside of itself. Stein seeks to find something internal to poetry itself on which to authorize her text. In a poem whose title *sounds* Romantic, Stein deconstructs the Romantic landscape and moves toward a purely linguistic one, which cannot be described because it is a landscape of words, not a place.

This problem is as sexual as it is linguistic. Stein's repetitions bespeak the impossibility of ever actually saying the same thing twice—she is the Heraclitus of modern writers. But they also testify to her ambivalence about the sameness that her repetitions seem to assert. The sameness that Stein desires with her audience is metaphorically like the lesbian union she shared with Toklas. She parodies the homosexual nature of that union of like with like in her conflation of herself with Toklas in the *Autobiography*. She parodies that intimacy again in the first

sentence of *Everybody's Autobiography*, published in 1937—"Alice B. Toklas did hers and now anybody will do theirs"—in which she—anybody, everybody—becomes one with all audiences, not just with Toklas. To write everybody's autobiography is both to deny the difference between writer and reader and to assert control over the reader's reception of the text.

. . . Stein is, if anything, less obscure about her position in *Stanzas*, where she chides herself for wishing too desperately for an audience. The very circularity of the passage that follows, in which she listens to herself think about the problem of audience, insures that the work matters because it is hers, but is hers only insofar as it examines its relation to its audience. *Stanzas* is so long, then, because it forms a loop. From Stanza VII of Part II:

> When they were not only laden with best wishes
> But indeed not inclined for them to be careless
> Might they be often more than ever especially
> Made to be thought carelessly a vacation
> That they will like this less.
> Let me listen to me and not to them
> Can I be very well and happy
> Can I be whichever they can thrive
> Or just can they not.
> They do not think not only only
> But always with prefer
> And therefore I like what is mine
> For which not only willing but willingly
> Because which it matters.

But this is to jump ahead of things; Stein sets up several questions from the beginning of this 150-odd page poem. Richard Bridgman is right to identify the "they"s so often-referred to (twenty-four times in Stanza I alone) as a reference to Stein's audience. That Stein's particular audience is Toklas also seems evident in the passage that follows.

> They like it as well as they ever did
> But it is very often just by the time
> That they are able to separate
> In which case in effect they could
> Not only be very often present perfectly
> In each way which ever they chose.
> All of this never matters in authority
> But this which they need as they are alike
> Or in an especial case they will fulfill
> Not only what they have at their instigation
> Made for it as a decision in its entirety

Stein's particular anxiety is revealed in the line, "All of this never matters in authority"; if she, as writer, wielded authority over her audience, in other words, none of this would be a problem. That she does not in this instance do so is because

"they are alike," as she and Toklas are alike in the
Autobiograhy. As she writes in Stanza XIII of Part
IV, "This is an autobiography in two instances."
The two instances, of course, may refer to the two
autobiographies she was writing at the time, or to
the two people whose autobiographies she was
writing as one. And the problem, it seems, has to
do not so much with the audience's particular likes
or dislikes, but with its attendant separation from
the writer: "But it is very often just by the time /
That they are able to separate."

Stein's anxiety is heightened by the threat
she feels from her audience; it threatens to con-
trol her, and she has to plead with herself to
ignore the audience outside her, and instead to
heed the one within.

> It is always what they will out loud
> Can they like me oh can they like me.
> No one can know who can like me...
> Let me listen to me and not to them
> Can I be very well and happy
> Can I be whichever they can thrive
> Or just can they not.
> They do not think not only only
> But always with prefer
> And therefore I like what is mine
> For which not only willing but willingly
> Because which it matters.

The last line ends her thought ambiguously;
whether she likes her work because it matters, or
whether it matters because she likes it, is not
clear. The making of "material" is obviously
important to Stein—an enormously prolific
writer—as a sign that matter matters. And, by
extension, her material will insure that she, the
mother of the text, will also matter.

> It is for this that they come there and stay.
> Should it be well done or should it be well done
> Or can they be very likely or not at all
> Not only known but well known.
> I often think I would like this for that
> Or not as likely
> Not only this they do
> But for which not for which for which
> This they do.
> Should it be mine as pause it is mine
> That should be satisfying

The concluding "should" clause seems to
confirm Stein's inability to find her work satisfy-
ing on its own terms; work "well done" ought to
insure the result of its being "well known." One
final example (and there are dozens more)
should complete the picture of a writer who
cared so desperately not to care what her audi-
ence thought of her.

> I have been worried I will be worried again
> And if again is again is it
> Not to be interested in how they think
> Oh yes not to be interested in how they think
> Oh oh yes not to be interested in how they think.

The only means which Stein finds to persuade
her audience is to incorporate or to absorb it into
herself, as she claims to do in Stanza XIV of Part
II, playing on an ambiguity in the word *absorb*:

> It is not only early that they make no mistake
> A nightingale and a robin.
> Or rather that which can which
> Can which he which they can choose which
> They know or not like that
> They make this be once or not alike
> Not by this time only when they like
> To have been very much absorbed.
> And so they find it so
> And so they are
> There
> There which is not only here but here as well as
> there.
> They like whatever I like.

The obsessive use of "they" gives way arbitra-
rily to a use of "it" in Stanza II of Part I, separated
only by enjambment from the first stanza. The
problem unraveled in this stanza is that the sepa-
ration between writer and audience—one not per-
mitted in *The Autobiography of Alice B. Toklas*—
causes strife. They (here, most likely, Toklas her-
self) do not always like what they read, or worse
yet, they are not always interested in it.

> They could have pleasure as they change
> Or leave it all for it as they can be
> Not only left to them as restless
> For which it is not only left and left alone
> They will stop it as they like
> Because they call it further mutinously

Stein snipes further at her audience: Toklas
passes on her work, she more than implies,
because it is named after her. As I have already
suggested, the intimate connection between Stein
and her muse has sexual overtones. The "they"s
seem first to be Stein and Toklas, who are "always
alike," and then to be the audience beyond them:
"For which they will not like what there is." Prob-
ably Stein's conflation of inside and outside here
(including the phrase "mind do they come," which
suggests both a mental and a sexual process)
reflects on her own ambivalence about a cou-
pling—and a writing—that she knows is consid-
ered "strange." The word "like," then, is rife with
meaning; it signifies "likeness," as in a simile, and
also denotes affection: one likes what one is like.
"Or however not a difference between like and

liked." Sexuality redeems what has been unlike, and unlikeable, in what preceded this passage:

> As they will willingly pass when they are restless
> Just as they like it called for them
> All who have been left in their sense
> All should boisterous make it an attachment
> For which they will not like what there is
> More than enough and they can be thought
> Always alike and mind do they come
> Or should they care which it would be strange.

Yet Stein must force this likeness, too, as she does in Part IV, where she talks most explicitly about the dual autobiography she is embarked upon, and conflates herself with Toklas more overtly than she does in *The Autobiography of Alice B. Toklas* (with the exception of that book's remarkable last paragraph). Stein first parrots the Toklas of the *Autobiography* in her assertions that Stein is a genius:

> She knew that she could know
> That a genius was a genius
> Because just so she could know
> She did know three or so
> So she says and what she says
> No one can deny or try
> What if she says.

This simply rephrases Toklas's claim in the first chapter of the *Autobiography* that "I may say that only three times in my life have I met a genius and each time a bell within me rang and I was not mistaken, and I may say in each case it was before there was any general recognition of the quality of genius in them." In the poem, Stein blithely adds that no one will know which autobiography of the two this is. Then farther into the stanza she baldly announces her absorption of Toklas into herself: "She will be me when this you see." And, even more strongly:

> I would have liked to be the only one
> One is one.
> If I am would I have liked to be the only one.
> Yes just this.
> If I am one I would have liked to be the only one
> Which I am.

The author so uncomfortable with mere "likeness" for the gaps that it leaves between lovers, or between the writer and her audience, closes that gap by declaring oneness with her muse. Her assertion is not without its violence; to declare that "all this is to be for me," as she does at the end of the stanza, is to deny the reader the liberty of interpretation. Interpretation, of course, depends upon just those gaps and holes in the text that Stein proclaims nonexistent, filled. She requires opacity

precisely so that she can possess her text. That she also wished to "possess" Toklas is clear in her description of her as a "prostitute" in many journal entries early in their relationship.

...Her language steadily loses mimetic value as the poem continues; in Stanza LXVI of Part V, she deliberately conflates a "plain" with plainness. It is here that language becomes the landscape rather than a means of describing it. (I am reminded of Beckett's conflation of the self with the landscape on which his speaker rests in "Lessness.")

> Once in a while as they did not go again
> They felt that it would be plain
> A plain would be a plain
> And in between
> There would be that would be plain
> And in between
> There would be that would be plain
> That there would be as plain
> It would be as it would be plain
> Plain it is and it is a plain
> And addition to as plain
> Plainly not only not a plain
> But well a plain.
> A plain is a mountain not made round
> And so a plain is a plain as found

And yet, at the end of this poem about a poet's renunciation of audience, Stein ushers her muse back in, and her language once again becomes instrumental; one cannot but think that her invitation to the muse, and to an audience, comes too late.

> No what I wish to say is this.
> Fifty percent of the roses should be cut
> The rest should bloom upon their branch...
> Because because there is very little wind here
> Enough of rain sometimes too much
> But even so it is a pleasure that whether
> Will they remain or will they go even so.

And, apparently to Toklas: "I can I wish I do love none but you." The final stanza is worthy of the inconclusive conclusion to Whitman's "Song of Myself" and announces Stein's presence in the poetic world, much as his "Preface" to *Leaves of Grass* had some seventy years previously.

> I call carelessly that the door is open
> Which if they can refuse to open
> No one can rush to close.
> Let them be mine therefor.
> Everybody knows that I chose.
> Therefor if therefor before I close.
> I will therefore offer therefor I offer this.
> Which if I refuse to miss can be miss is mine.

I will be well welcome when I come.
Because I am coming.
Certainly I come having come.
These stanzas are done.

Stein's final choice seems a conservative one; she writes, finally, for a muse, and in so doing her poetry becomes more lyrical, more Romantic—especially in its obvious bow to Whitman. Yet this conclusion seems less earned than imposed, as if in the turning of Stein's mind toward and then away from her audience, she merely happened upon these conciliatory lines.

Stein's final bow to the audience raises the question of the troubled relation between her desire to find an audience and the obscurity that would seem to deny her such an audience. I would suggest that Stein *uses* such obscurity as an important card in her long career of self-advertisement. The self-effacement of *Stanzas* covers up what is actually the opposite impulse (just as Stein becomes at once everybody and nobody in *Everybody's Autobiography*). The writer who proclaims over and again that she is "the only one," and that she is one of the three great geniuses of the century, displays that genius in works so obscure that even devoted readers of *The Autobiography of Alice B. Toklas* or *Everybody's Autobiography* might turn away from them. The unreadable text is less a text, in the usual sense, than an icon—less an act of communication than of bravado. A work such as *Stanzas in Meditation* becomes a commodity through which Stein can buy the label of genius, and become famous less for what she writes than for the fact that she writes so obscurely. That she recognized the sometimes humorous connection between autobiography and publicity is clear from a passage in *Everybody's Autobiography*: "But now well now how can you dream about a personality when it is always being created for you by a publicity, how can you believe what you make up when publicity makes them up to be so much realer than you can dream. And so autobiography is written which is in a way a way to say that publicity is right, they are as the public see them Well yes."

Stanzas in Meditation forces us to reconsider Stein's use of the word "autobiography," as well as our own. For how can a writer who believes (at least in this poem) in the utter separation of the text from the world write an autobiography, or several autobiographies? What does it mean to tell one's story only "for oneself and strangers," to paraphrase Stein in the opening to *The Making of Americans*? Where are we to find Stein—in *The*

Autobiography of Alice B. Toklas, in *Stanzas in Meditation*, or in *Everybody's Autobiography*? Perhaps the lesson that Stein teaches us is that the autobiographer makes and remakes herself out of her perceived relationship with her audience. Stein's triumph in *Stanzas*—however uneven—is to show to what extent that relationship defines the writer, even when she tries to write without either a muse or an audience.

Source: Susan M. Schultz, "Gertrude Stein's Self-Advertisement," in *Raritan*, Vol. 12, No. 2, Fall 1992, pp. 71–87.

SOURCES

Abney, Lisa, "Gertrude Stein," in *American Women Writers, 1900–1945: A Bio-Bibliographical Critical Sourcebook*, edited by Laurie Champion and Emmanuel Sampeth Nelson, Greenwood Press, 2000, pp. 318–27.

Ashbery, John, "The Impossible," in *Poetry*, July 1957, pp. 250–54, http://writing.upenn.edu/~afilreis/88/stein-per-ashbery.html (accessed October 12, 2010).

Dickie, Margaret, Introduction to *Stein, Bishop & Rich: Lyrics of Love, War & Place*, University of North Carolina Press, 1997, pp. 1–17.

Esdale, Logan, "Gertrude Stein," in *A Companion to Twentieth-Century American Poetry*, edited by Burt Kimmelman, Facts on File, 2005, pp. 474–76.

Gygax, Franziska, "Introduction: Gendered Genre," in *Gender and Genre in Gertrude Stein*, Greenwood Press, 1998, pp. 1–12.

Howard, Richard, "There Is a Lot of Here Here," in *New York Times*, May 13, 1998, http://www.nytimes.com/books/98/05/03/reviews/980503.03howardt.html (accessed October 12, 2010).

Jones, Geoffrey, "Restoring a Global Economy, 1950–1980," in *Harvard Business School's Working Knowledge*, August 22, 2005, http://hbswk.hbs.edu/item/4961.html (accessed October 12, 2010).

Kenney, Robert V., "France: Culture, Politics, and Society, 1895–1939," in *Encyclopedia of Modernism*, edited by Paul Poplawski, Greenwood Press, 2003, pp. 134–50.

Kimball, Jack, "Gertrude Stein and the Natural World," in *Time-Sense: An Electronic Quarterly on the Art of Gertrude Stein*, 1998, http://www.tenderbuttons.com/gsonline/timesense/1_1kimball.html (accessed October 12, 2010).

Leonhardt, David, "Governments Move to Cut Spending, in 1930s Echo," in *New York Times*, June 29, 2010, http://www.nytimes.com/2010/06/30/business/economy/30leonhardt.html (accessed October 12, 2010).

Martel, Gordon, ed., "Introduction: Europe in Agony, 1900–1945," in *A Companion to Europe, 1900–1945*, Blackwell, 2006, pp. xxi–xxx.

Pizer, Donald, "Epilogue," in *American Expatriate Writing and the Paris Moment: Modernism and Place*, Louisiana State University Press, 1996, pp. 141–49.

Stein, Gertrude, "Stanza LXXXIII," in *Stein: Writings, 1932–1946*, edited by Catharine R. Stimpson and Harriet Chessman, Library of America, 1998, p. 145.

Stimpson, Catharine R., and Harriet Chessman, eds., "Chronology," in *Stein: Writings, 1932–1946*, Library of America, 1998, pp. 827–37.

Wheale, Nigel, "Modernism's Aftermath," in *The Postmodern Arts: An Introductory Reader*, Routledge, 1995, pp. 30–32.

Yearsley, Meredith, "Gertrude Stein," in *Dictionary of Literary Biography*, Vol. 54, *American Poets: 1880–1945, Third Series*, edited by Peter Quatermain, Gale Research, 1987, pp. 428–63.

FURTHER READING

Harrison, Charles, *Modernism*, Cambridge University Press, 1997.

Harrison provides a survey of the artistic movements that fall under the larger umbrella of modernism, detailing the particulars of each approach, such as cubism, fauvism, and abstract expressionism. Numerous reprints of significant works aid the student's understanding of various techniques.

Keliner, Bruce, ed., *A Gertrude Stein Companion: Content with Example*, Greenwood Press, 1998.

Keliner provides a collection of essays from various scholars on Stein and her work. The essays range from detailed analyses of particular works to overviews of Stein's place within the context of literary tradition.

Monk, Craig, *Writing the Lost Generation: Expatriate Autobiography and American Modernism*, University of Iowa Press, 2008.

Monk focuses on the autobiographical writings of several key figures associated with the group of American modernist writers living in Paris in the 1920s and 1930s. Stein and Hemingway are among the more prominent writers whose autobiographies Monk explores, although the critic offers a broad approach and studies the works of lesser-known authors as well.

Overy, R. J., *The Inter-War Crisis, 1919–1939*, 2nd ed., Pearson Education, 2007.

Originally published in 1994, Overy's assessment of the years between the two world wars explores the social, political, and economic issues at work in Europe, focusing on the conflicts that gradually escalated and contributed to the onset of World War II.

Stein, Gertrude, *Picasso*, Dover, 1984.

Stein's memoir of Picasso, originally published in 1912, explores her relationship with the artist and comments on his work and his role within the art community of Paris during this time period.

SUGGESTED SEARCH TERMS

Gertrude Stein AND Stanzas in Meditation

Gertrude Stein AND poetry

Gertrude Stein AND modernism

Gertrude Stein AND Paris

Gertrude Stein AND Lost Generation

Gertrude Stein AND Picasso

Gertrude Stein AND Alice B. Toklas

Gertrude Stein AND World War II

Gertrude Stein AND fiction

Gertrude Stein AND American expatriates

Still I Rise

MAYA ANGELOU

1978

"Still I Rise," by Maya Angelou, is a courageous and inspiring poem written about the emerging prominence of African Americans during the nation's civil rights movement. It channels the expression of the free spirit of all African Americans through the voice of one woman who speaks of overcoming the hardships of the beginnings of the race in America. The poem responds to black ancestors' embittered cries with an indomitable exclamation that African Americans will rise above all inequities and flourish as a people. It remains Angelou's favorite poem and theme amidst a great oeuvre of books, plays, and poetry; she often includes a dramatic reading in personal appearances. "Still I Rise" was published in Angelou's poem collection titled *And Still I Rise* in 1978, two years after her musical dramatic production *And Still I Rise* was produced. It can also be found in *The Complete Collected Poems of Maya Angelou*, published by Random House in 1994.

Angelou's voice rings loudly with hope and determination. She has recounted that all her work is about survival, and she encourages all to look for the positive things in life, especially in times of adversity. While her poems remind readers of past tragedies and injustices, overall they are a testimony to the power of striving to survive in life with dignity and grace. "Still I Rise" is an excellent example offering just that.

Maya Angelou (Getty Images)

AUTHOR BIOGRAPHY

Angelou was born Marguerite Ann Johnson on April 4, 1928, in St. Louis, Missouri, the second child of Bailey Johnson, Sr., and Vivian Baxter Johnson. When she was three years old, her parents divorced, and she traveled by rail, along with her brother, Bailey, Jr., to live with their paternal grandmother, Annie Henderson, in Stamps, Arkansas. She and Bailey called her "Momma," and aptly so, as she provided what little stability the children would have in her world of work, duty, and religion. Bailey started calling his sister "Maya" as short for "my-a sister."

In 1935, Bailey, Sr., swept the children away to leave them with their mother in St. Louis. Tragically, the environment was unstable, and Maya was raped by her mother's boyfriend, a Mr. Freeman. At the trial, she was too frightened to testify against him, and he was subsequently released; but "justice" was served in the streets, as the innocent girl's uncles beat Mr. Freeman to death. Maya, however, equated his death with her disclosing of his name and felt acutely guilty. She stopped talking as a consequence, which her mother interpreted as impudence. The children were sent back to live in Stamps with Henderson, who enlisted the aid of Mrs. Flowers, the community's intellectual, to help draw the still-mute Maya out of her shell. Mrs. Flowers introduced Maya to poetry, telling her that it must be read aloud to be loved. Maya began speaking again as she recited poetry to herself, and she developed a love of literature and learning. Her voice now resounds continually through her volumes of verse and prose; the stories of her childhood can be found in her first autobiography, *I Know Why the Caged Bird Sings* (1969).

In 1940, Johnson graduated with honors from Lafayette County Training School in Stamps and then moved to California to live with her mother and her new paramour, Daddy Clidell. Johnson attended night classes in drama and dance at the California Labor School and became the first black female trolley-car conductor. She graduated from Mission High School in San Francisco in 1945, and through an unplanned pregnancy, her son Clyde was born the same year. She married Tosh Angelos in 1949, but they divorced in 1952. Later that year she won a scholarship to study dance, and she began a career as a performer, touring with the U.S. State Department's sponsorship of the African American opera *Porgy and Bess* through 1954 and 1955. She adapted her name to Maya Angelou (a variant of Angelos) when she became a performer. In 1957, she appeared in the off-Broadway play *Calypso Heatwave* as a featured singer and dancer. She performed until 1961, when she traveled with a new love, a South African named Vusumzi Make, to London and Africa. The relationship fell apart, though, as he disapproved of her working for a newspaper in Cairo, and she continued alone to Ghana, where she worked as the assistant director of music and drama at the University of Ghana, as well as at the Ghanaian Broadcasting Corporation and the *Ghanaian Times*. She was asked by Malcolm X to return to the United States and help with his campaign, but he was assassinated shortly after her arrival.

In 1966, back in California, Angelou continued to write and perform, including writing and producing a ten-part program for the Public Broadcasting Service (PBS) on African traditions in American life, *Black, Blues, Black*, which aired in 1968. In 1970, *I Know Why the Caged Bird Sings* was nominated for the National Book Award. In 1971, a collection of poems, *Just Give Me a Cool Drink of Water 'fore I Diiie* became a Pulitzer nominee. From there, more poetry, musicals, films, books, and screenplays filled Angelou's life, and she became beloved by Americans. She was presented with the *Ladies' Home Journal* Woman of the Year in Communications award in 1976, was dubbed one of *USA Today's* Fifty Black Role Models in 1989, and has received a multitude of other awards, including over twenty-five honorary doctorate degrees. Her documentary on African American women in the arts received the Golden Eagle Award from PBS. Women in Communications, Inc., gave her the Matrix Award for Books in 1983. She held a pioneering role in the Screen Directors Guild and was elected to the board of trustees of the American Film Institute. President Gerald Ford appointed her to the Bicentennial Commission, and President Jimmy Carter gave her a position on the Commission for the International Year of the Woman. She was given a Fulbright Scholarship to tour with an international commission to Ghana in 1986. She received the Candace Award in 1990 and the Horatio Alger Award in 1992. A crowning achievement in her life was being selected by President William J. Clinton to write a poem and deliver it at his inauguration in 1993. "On the Pulse of Morning" was delivered with grace and humor in a spirit of hope and unity.

POEM SUMMARY

Stanza 1

Lies about and misrepresentations of the treatment of the narrator—an autobiographical voice that stands not just for Angelou, or an anonymous black woman narrator, but for all African Americans—are addressed softly. The *you* of the poem may thus refer to a white (or nonblack) oppressor or perhaps to the white race more broadly. More degradations ground the narrator into the dust, which swirls up with the solemn promise of resilience. The dark beginnings of the poem are registered as a starting place from which to rise.

Stanza 2

The narrator asks poignant questions inferring that her attitude may be disturbing, as she is not dragged down by the weight of prejudice and injustice. She wants to know if anyone is annoyed that she walks with the self-satisfaction of a wealthy oil tycoon. Does she appear to be putting on airs? Is

MEDIA ADAPTATIONS

- The *Maya Angelou Poetry Collection* contains more than one hundred unabridged poems performed in dramatic readings by Angelou. She selected her favorite poems spanning a lifetime of hardship and raising awareness of prejudice against African American success, recognition, and wisdom. This audio CD is available through Random House Audio and was published in October 2001.

- The collection *And Still I Rise: A Selection of Poems Read by the Author* contains the title selection "Still I Rise." It also contains other powerful poems of her earlier career about the hardships of her past as a poor African American girl in 1960s Arkansas. It was produced in August 2001 by Random House Audio Voices.

- *Poetry Speaks Who I Am: Poems of Discovery, Inspiration, Independence and Everything Else* includes a CD containing 108 poems by classic and contemporary authors that speak to issues that teens face. "Still I Rise" is read by Angelou as an inspiration to African American teens and others who experience racial prejudice. It was published by Sourcebooks Jabberwocky in March 2010.

- *And Still I Rise*, a powerful film by Ngozi Onwurah inspired by Angelou's collection of poems *And Still I Rise*, which includes the poem "Still I Rise," uses images from popular culture to show how mass media misrepresent the beauty and sexuality of black women. It was produced in 1993 by Women Make Movies and is available in 16mm, VHS, and DVD.

she arrogant? Does it make anyone want to "put her in her place," so to speak? It seems evident that the answers do not matter to the author: the questions are rhetorical and more like statements of her courage and protest.

Stanza 3

The narrator assumes her place of dignity among the highest things of nature: the suns and the moons. And like them, as reliably as they rise, and with as much inspiration as hopes bursting into the air like a dancer, she will rise, too. Having been a professional dancer herself, Angelou knows the sense of dancing gleefully, on what she has called feet that were too big.

Stanza 4

More questions, which are now more direct, spatter this stanza. Was it hoped that the narrator could be perceived as beaten, shamed, afraid to look into the eyes of her so-called betters? Was it thought her demeanor should be woeful, downtrodden, fatigued, and weepy? The assumed and unequivocal answers to these questions on the part of the other would be shamefaced assents. But the narrator only mildly protests with her thought-provoking questions; there is no chanting or ranting to be found here.

Stanza 5

The next question is similarly direct. Whether the *you* is white people as a whole or just the masters of the plantations and the like, it is assumed that they will be made ill at ease by the arrogance of the narrator. Does it irk you, she asks on behalf of her race, that I am laughing about my newly found wealth of independence and self-importance? She suspects that the answer again is "yes" and humorously hopes to teach a lesson.

Stanza 6

This stanza is like a declaration, a promise, and even almost a dare. No matter what you do to me, the black everywoman narrator asserts, I will rise. The weapons to be employed by the antagonist are words, cutting eyes, and hatefulness. But I, says the narrator, will not be killed; I will rise anyway. As long as there is air to breathe, I will speak again. These words fall in line with the message of Dr. Martin Luther King, Jr., with whom she worked closely before his assassination.

Stanza 7

This stanza is probably the most controversial one of the poem. It challenges black female stereotypes, typically drawing on or encompassing images of a slave girl, a sexual victim, a "Mammy," a spiritual leader, a physical healer, and/or a pillar of wisdom and of home, hearth, and sustenance. This stanza breaks those molds and fashions the narrator into a siren, a seductive, sensuous woman. Her beauty is powerful, and she is as desirable and luminous as fine diamonds.

Stanza 8

The narrator here begins to solidify the truth in the continuity of her message. The past is painful, and history is shameful. Let it be set aside. The narrator will rise, leaping high as the giant swells of a big, black ocean. A new image of the black woman is on the rise, and it is coming in with the new tide. It is certain, it is inevitable, it will wash away the past. This vision was and remains quite prophetic, and it becomes more true every day.

Stanza 9

It is a hopeful new day; the terrors and fears of the past nights fade away. The narrator rises by virtue of the great sacrifices of the slaves and wounds of the ancestors. She gives homage to the past and to those who have suffered as well as to those looking hopefully to the future. She is the epitome of the dreams and indomitable spirits of the past, to rise again, and again, and again. She not only assures society that her rising will happen but further implores everyone to let it come about with grace, unity, mutual respect, and positivity.

THEMES

African American Pride

African American pride is a theme that encompasses the struggles, the courage, the culture, and the contributions of African Americans in the face of many difficulties. It is a celebration of recognition of the victories of overcoming prejudice, winning the fight for equal rights, and glorifying the intrinsic qualities and strengths that make the race invaluable as a complement to all peoples. It is a testament to the strong sense of community that has remained intact among African Americans and to their implacable sense of self-worth. Angelou has stated, as quoted by Lyman Hagen in *Heart of a Woman, Mind of a Writer, and Soul of a Poet: A Critical Analysis of the Writings of Maya Angelou*, that "Still I Rise" represents the "indomitable spirit of the black people." This is a burning spirit that four hundred years of oppression have been unable to extinguish. The poem infers that the race will not only endure but will rise above all. In Angelou's exuberant metaphors, they are the owners of oil wells, gold mines, and exquisite physical and inner beauty. They are represented as a wide, leaping ocean, strong and invincible. Their bodies alone are as if adorned with jewels, and they dance with exultation. The narrator's voice soars with pride as she proclaims that they

TOPICS FOR FURTHER STUDY

- Write a poem from an autobiographical point of view using the same style and theme as "Still I Rise." In place of Angelou's descriptions of the hardships she and her people have endured and the way she rises above them, write about an event or issue that has been difficult in your life. Include a repeating phrase in your poem that is representative of your struggle through the event or issue. Recite the poem to your class.

- Present a dramatic interpretation of "Still I Rise" using a mode such as mime or dance. One student with good vocal interpretive skills should recite the poem, focusing on the expression of the words, and let the mood be expressed by the physical interpretation by the mime/dancer. Be careful to interpret the tone justly; for instance, while joy and celebration are applicable, humor is inappropriate.

- Write a short story that depicts the themes of injustice and prejudice. The story may include people of any race who have suffered hardship from another race or group of people. Maintain the attitude of Angelou, which is not angry or retaliatory, concentrating on how the injured party is able to overcome the circumstances through endurance, positivity, creativity, and courage.

- Create a digital slide show that depicts the story of "Still I Rise" while the words are recited. Free downloads of Angelou performing the poem are available online.

- Write a song that reflects the subject and mood of "Still I Rise." Perform it for the class, or record it and play it for the class. If you play an instrument, accompany yourself. You may make the song instrumental only, but ensure that it still represents the mood changes in the poem.

- Use your artistic skills to create a piece of artwork inspired by the poem. Use watercolor, oil, or whatever medium you desire, as applied to a canvas. Be prepared to have your work displayed in a prominent place.

- Write an essay about the person you consider to be the most inspirational African American. Back up your opinions with facts about the person's accomplishments, deeds, and courage. Post your essay to the class blog site and invite debate on the merits of your choice.

- Read the lyrics to the song "I've Got a Right to Sing the Blues," composed by Harold Arlen and with lyrics by Ted Koehler, released by Warner Bros. in 1932. It has been performed by famous black artists such as Billie Holliday, Ella Fitzgerald, and Louis Armstrong. Write an essay comparing the song with the poem "Still I Rise." Possible issues to discuss include style, mood, tempo, activism versus complacency, celebration versus sadness, sassiness versus submission, and self-confidence versus victimization.

- Read *Becoming Billie Holliday* by Carole Weatherford, published in 2008. The young-adult book is a fictionalized verse memoir by Holliday, written in the first person, containing over one hundred poems that speak to her life and trials as a black woman in the spotlight. Select one of the poems from this volume that has a similar theme to "Still I Rise," and do extra research on Holliday and Angelou using online and print resources. Describe the similarities in the struggles both women faced in a white-dominated world. What were regrettable choices made by both? How did they triumph over their struggles and rise above them? Compare the two poems as to style, rhythm, tone, theme, and voice. Create a multimedia presentation that illustrates your comparisons and contains both the words and voices of the two women.

will not be bound to the chains and sorrows of the past. They will continue to rise, she proclaims, in spite of any adversity, and because of their trials, they will become even stronger. In "Still I Rise," Angelou has accomplished a remarkable thing, in that she speaks to blacks and whites together and separately in a voice that can be heard by both.

Racism

Injustice arises from ignorance of or disbelief in the concept—enshrined in the founding documents of the United States—that all people are born equal, regardless of race. Disenfranchisement, mistreatment, and prejudice against a race ultimately result in social, political, and economic hardship perpetrated against those people. Virtually every form of injustice has been endured by African Americans. Prejudice, hatred, slavery, torture, murder, and rape lead the long list of injustices that have been condemned by many brave voices like Angelou's. "Still I Rise" conveys the spectacular weight of the hardships that African Americans have had to overcome. Although the overall theme of the poem is one of determination to prevail, injustice is presented throughout to bring reality and a sense of history. But this is not considered to be a militant poem. It simply tells the truth, and lightly at that, about the plight of African Americans. Misconceptions and lies are alluded to, such as common early myths that they were of lesser intelligence, had no souls, or were not even human. The poem determines to dispel such myths, but with a positive tone, with a jubilant and cheerful taunting. It leaves little room for woes, sorrows, and tears of suffering.

Determination

Determination is the quality of having a strong degree of self-control to achieve the things that one deems important. Angelou has been lauded as one of the most determined, devoted, and courageous black women in the twentieth century. She continues to maintain that status in the early twenty-first century as a woman in her eighties, still determined to use her voice as long as it lasts to speak to the worldwide audience she has gained. By the time the narrator finishes the poem "Still I Rise," she has stated that she will rise nearly a dozen times. It is paramount to see the everywoman narrator as proud, beautiful, and responsible despite the ugliness of racism. Developing a positive posture in the midst of unfair stereotyping must be enabled. The narrator demands that whites step back and try to be objective about their preconceived ideas. Willing things to change works, when

courage and determination are applied. Determining to press on day after day is the essence of survival.

African American History

Angelou's narrator invokes the origins of the African American race when she alludes to the shabby huts the slaves were lodged in upon arrival in North America. She refers to that history as a time of pain and shame for her people. She notes that some may twist the horror of that history into lies, or forget it or pretend it never happened. Some may just walk right over that history, and her people, grinding them into the ground. She asks white listeners if they want to keep her downtrodden: do things have to remain as they were in the past? Is it time for change, or do whites want blacks to always sing the blues and be sorrowful and oppressed? Is a frown all she will be entitled to, and must she wear her tears every day?

Self-Confidence

One of Angelou's main themes in "Still I Rise" is to say, "I like me." Her self-confidence abounds as she imagines herself strutting around like an Arabian princess who owns all the oil in the world. She compares her determination to succeed to the likelihood of the sun rising in the morning. She describes herself as a bit arrogant because she acts like she owns the largest gold mine in Africa. She depicts herself as a diva whose legs are as if adorned with diamonds. All of this may seem over the top, but it is intentionally done in juxtaposition to the images that have been borne by or projected onto black women before her. Angelou wants to tell her sisters that it is appropriate to laugh, dance, and love themselves, and most importantly to believe in themselves.

Resilience

Line 4 of stanza 1 informs the reader that the poem is about resilience. It is a rephrasing of the famous civil rights movement motto of Martin Luther King (with whom she worked): "We shall overcome." There is a note of defiance when she asks about her right to appear sassy. The inference is that if it is insulting, that response is unwarranted, but if it is simply surprising, she is pleased.

The first line of stanza 5 is much the same. Is she haughty because she is black, self-confident, and happy and has a great deal of self-esteem? Her attempts to be shocking are peppered with humor, while the tones of resistance and defiance are defused but deliberate. True resistance is evident in stanza 6 when Angelou accuses the (white)

Oil wells pumping *(Chepko Danil Vitalevich /*
Shutterstock.com)

reader of being hostile and violent. This stanza takes on the most defiant tone in the poem, evoking anger and a resolve to overcome.

STYLE

Representative Voice
Angelou says that the narrator in "Still I Rise" is feminine, and she speaks not only for herself but for her gender and her entire race. Thus, in the tradition of black writers speaking for the race, she can speak of the injustices done to the slaves of the past as if they were done to her. She can speak for African Americans of the future as if she will rise for them. She can be militant at times but always covers this sense with a soothing balm of reconciliation.

Repetition
The incremental repetition of the title phrase serves to build the poem from whisper to climactic shout. Angelou often recites this poem aloud because of the effect this technique has in inspiring the listener. It is reminiscent of a song, or a sermon, where the message is repeated with increasing fervor, to stir the hearts of listeners.

Rhyme
Rhyme is present in "Still I Rise," as used to link lines 2 and 4 of the first seven stanzas and in couplet form in the final two stanzas. Jive talk and internal rhyme have been popular in black culture, from familiar folklore to rap music; Angelou also uses rhyme for humor in her light poetry. The rhymes in "Still I Rise" seem to enhance the dramatic tone of the poem. Perhaps the fact that she is a singer helps her hear and compose verse in rhyme.

Rhythm
The theatrical in Angelou comes out in her rhythms. She says that before she writes a poem, she always starts with finding a rhythm. Hagen, in *Heart of a Woman, Mind of a Writer, and Soul of a Poet*, quotes Angelou in an interview with Bill Moyers:

> Quite often there are allusions made in black American writing, there are rhythms set in the writing and counter-rhythms that mean a great deal to blacks. A white American can come in and he will hear, he will understand hopefully, the gist. And that's what one is talking about. The other, is sort of "in" talk.

The "in" talk is the sort of rhythm and sound that, as she suggests, perhaps only African Americans can appreciate. The use of vernacular is applied to complement the rhythm to make the poetry unique and entertaining to people of all cultures. Although a knowledge of black slang is useful to understanding many of her phrasings, this poem encompasses universal themes, ordinary occurrences, and fundamental concepts, bringing the piece together for the enjoyment of all.

Spiritual Sound
"Still I Rise" sounds like a sermon by Martin Luther King or a spiritual song like "We Shall Not Be Moved" or "We Shall Overcome." Hagen states, "The lines remind us of the black spiritual 'Rise and Shine' as well as other religious hymns that express hope." The poem seems to call for a boost in volume through the stanzas; as the narrator rises, so will the volume and intensity of the sound. The poem is rousing and inspirational, bringing home Angelou's themes of survival and determination.

COMPARE
&
CONTRAST

- **1978:** African Americans hold the same civil rights as white Americans after the passage of the Civil Rights Act and Voting Rights Act of the 1960s, but enforcement is still not complete across all parts of the nation.

  Today: Great strides have been made concerning prejudice and overt racism, but law-enforcement officers are still regularly accused of racial profiling.

- **1978:** African Americans legally have equal access to education, but equality of education is not always achieved. Proportionally, fewer African Americans attend college than whites. The federal courts still must force busing to

desegregate primary and secondary schools in some districts.

  Today: African American enrollment in college has increased dramatically, but an alarming trend is emerging: close to 40 percent of inner-city African American males drop out of high school.

- **1978:** African American median income is approximately 60 percent of that of white Americans, at 8,000 dollars compared to just over 13,000 dollars, respectively.

  Today: The income gap has narrowed between African Americans and white Americans, but African Americans still earn just 72 percent of the median income of white Americans.

HISTORICAL CONTEXT

Civil Rights Movement

Angelou began her writing career in the midst of one of the greatest upheavals of social change in U.S. history. American society, though based on freedom and democracy, had always been dominated by white males. During the 1960s, the civil rights movement reached its pinnacle. Many organizations were formed to publicize the surge for racial equality. Angelou had married the civil rights activist Vusumzi Make and moved to Cairo and then Ghana, where a thriving group of African American expatriates had moved. She met the radical civil rights activist Malcolm X during one of his visits to Ghana and corresponded with him frequently after he returned to the United States. Their discussions of the civil rights movement in America were highly conceptual, and she remained a faithful friend as his views changed from radical stances into a more mature vision for the cause. After divorcing the abusive Make, Angelou returned to the United States in 1964 in order to help Malcolm X start his new Organization of Afro-American Unity. Just days after her arrival, Malcolm X was assassinated. His cause

died with him, and Angelou began to align herself closely with Dr. Martin Luther King, Jr.

The Southern Christian Leadership Conference (SCLC), led by African American clergy, and the Student Nonviolent Coordinating Committee (SNCC) took a peaceful approach to civil rights. King asked Angelou to be the northern coordinator for the SCLC. Freedom rides and sit-ins were staged where segregation prohibited access, such as on buses and in restaurants. At the March on Washington of 1963, more than two hundred thousand demonstrators heard King, by now the most prominent voice in America for civil rights, give his "I Have a Dream" speech. Soon after, in 1964, Congress passed the Civil Rights Act, which secured for African Americans an end to various forms of legal discrimination. The Voting Rights Act followed in 1965, finally guaranteeing African Americans the right to vote in the United States. The federal affirmative-action program—taking into account race and gender when hiring or in school admissions to counter the historical effects of discrimination—also began in earnest in 1965.

By the late 1960s, louder voices, impatient with the drawn-out process of moving African Americans into mainstream society, came forward into the fray. SNCC, now led by the radical Stokely Carmichael, coined the phrase "Black Power" and condoned violence, if necessary to achieve social and legal justice and economic equality. King's assassination at a motel in Memphis, Tennessee, in 1968, occurred on Angelou's birthday, as she busied herself with party preparations. She was devastated. His assassination set off rioting in many major cities, creating further tears in the racial fabric of society. In Detroit, police were diligent in quashing the uprising when violent riots left forty-three dead and caused forty-five million dollars in property damage.

Much work was left to be done, and Maya Angelou continued the fight in her own way. Publishing over sixty works, including books, plays, screenplays, essays and children's books, Angelou has won the hearts of Americans of all colors. She has been on the lecture circuit since the 1990s, inspiring audiences worldwide with her message of inclusion and peace.

The Feminist Movement

With the publication of *The Feminine Mystique* by Betty Friedan in 1963, a feminist movement was launched in the United States. It challenged the long-standing idea that women should find fulfillment only through child rearing and homemaking. Friedan also presided over the development of the National Organization for Women (NOW) until the 1970s. The Equal Rights Amendment was proposed by Congress in 1972 but failed to gain the ratification of three-fourths of the states. By 1981, Friedan was still promoting the ideas of women, redefining the family and bringing men into the realm of child care; she also supported equal rights for women at work and flexible work schedules.

But at times there has seemed to be a disconnect between the realities of white feminism and of African American feminism. According to Angelou, the African American family was almost always held together entirely by the woman. *I Know Why the Caged Bird Sings* (1969) became a great inspiration to black feminists, especially since the experiences of black women have been so different from those of white women. The poem "Still I Rise" is written specifically with a feminine voice. It gives praise to the black woman's courage, identity, and self-worth. It recognizes the pain and hardships she has had to overcome and her emergence as a force to be reckoned with. Among Angelou's other poems, "Phenomenal Woman" is the black woman's feminist outcry. Angelou proclaims that being a woman is not about being pretty and that women are beautiful because

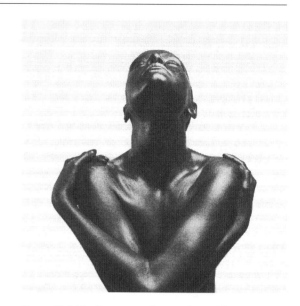

Beautiful black woman loving herself (*Mayer George Vladimirovich | Shutterstock.com*)

they are strong, capable, proud, and independent. "Weekend Glory" is a humorous guidebook to living a successful life as a single black woman. Therein Angelou expounds on the blessing of work (even if it is not the highest paying), staying out of debt, going to church, going dancing, and being thankful for being a woman of color. She calls out posers and those who pretend to be rich, buying fancy cars and houses they cannot afford. She says such people should watch her on Saturday night and thus learn how to live a glorious and simple life. "Our Grandmothers" is one of Angelou's most beloved poems, recalling stories of slave women and their children who hid from slave owners when the children became old enough to be sold. The poet chronicles the stories of black women over the centuries and the tears that followed the heartbreaks in their lives. From tortured slave to poverty-stricken pregnant woman at the abortion clinic, the poem is both heartrending and triumphant, as the black grandmother becomes the angel to watch over the new generations of strong, independent black women.

CRITICAL OVERVIEW

"Still I Rise" is a poem that celebrates black women, inspiring hope while challenging the stereotypical roles assigned to them throughout American history. Sandra Cookson reviewed *The*

Complete Collected Poems of Maya Angelou in *World Literature Today* and reports that Angelou "prefers strong, straightforward rhyme to free verse." Scriptural language, the exhortation of the pulpit, and the rhythm of rap music are all used in her poetry. While the voice of "Still I Rise" is definitively female, the poem speaks to all blacks as well as whites, as she invokes the horrors of the travesties endured by the slaves of the past. According to Cookson, Angelou speaks harshly to whites. She asks poignant questions of them and challenges their tolerance of a black woman who is sassy, exuberant, proud, and sexy. She calls upon them to examine their prejudices while at the same time using humor to de-escalate the challenge. Amidst the cries of pain and bitterness, she propounds the ability to overcome it all and embrace life. Cookson describes the poem as "celebratory." She says that Angelou's poems are at their best when southern slang is employed along with a streetwise type of dialogue. She notes the use of rhythm in the poem, which Angelou recognizes as the starting point for the conception of her poetry; she leans heavily on the musical rhythms of blues, jazz, and rap. Cookson also points out the use of religious language and the vehicle of poetry as a pulpit. And while Angelou may use her pulpit to heap guilt upon whites, she can quickly turn her message to secular matters, such as sexual attraction. Cookson notes that "Still I Rise" is "a poem about the survival of black women despite every kind of humiliation" and every prohibition that has been forced upon them since the days of slavery. She calls the rhetoric "in-your-face" in stanza after stanza, until the powerful climax in which Angelou exults joy.

In reviewing Angelou's first three autobiographies in *Feminist Review*, Ingrid Pollard declares that "Maya Angelou hopes her influence will be to 'encourage courage,'" which she does by talking, writing, and persisting as an African American woman in complete control of her life. She *is* the woman in "Still I Rise." She challenges not only blacks but whites as well, in that she encourages both races to have the courage to do what they know is right in their heart.

Lyman B. Hagen, in *Heart of a Woman, Mind of a Writer, and Soul of a Poet: A Critical Analysis of the Writings of Maya Angelou*, reveals that Angelou categorizes "Still I Rise" as a poem of mild protest, although newspaper reviews yet categorized it as quite radical in 1978. According to Hagen, the more militant poems appear in the second half of Angelou's first volume of poetry, a

section titled "Just Before the World Ends." In reviewing "Still I Rise," Hagen praises the poet, stating, "Angelou expresses unshakable faith that one will overcome; one will triumph; one will Rise!"

"Still I Rise" deserves much greater attention from critics. In "'Older Sisters Are Very Sobering Things': Contemporary Women Poets and the Female Affiliation Complex," Jane Dowson asks, "Are there adequate critical works on Maya Angelou...to keep the record straight?" She answers the question by asserting that more reviews of contemporary women writers are vital to fuller understanding. "Still I Rise" is a poem that deserves literary praise as well as significant sociological recognition in American culture as a beacon toward equality for all.

CRITICISM

Cynthia Gower Betts
Betts is a novelist, playwright, and freelance writer. In the following essay, she suggests that the African American woman depicted in "Still I Rise" is a model for women in regard to self-esteem, body image, and beauty.

Many women in modern society base a great deal of their self-worth on their appearance. Throughout American history, acceptance of the white Euro-American standard of beauty has prevailed. The standard is one that is difficult and sometimes impossible for African American women to achieve, such that it has had a devastating effect on psychic and emotional development in the lives of many. Societal adherence to this unrealistic standard only serves to widen the gap between white women and those of color.

Maya Angelou seeks to dispel the lies told by our forefathers concerning the appearance and worth of African women from the days they arrived on the shores of the continent. Many, including Thomas Jefferson, were culpable in denigrating the black race as ugly, deformed, and ignorant. Since that tragic time, African American women have been given constant reminders that they do not measure up because of their hair, skin color, or body shape. Farah Jasmine Griffin explains in "Textual Healing: Claiming Black Women's Bodies, the Erotic and Resistance in Contemporary Novels of Slavery" that "the manner in which black women writers address this legacy of the ugly black body begs the attention

WHAT
DO I READ
NEXT?

- *Phenomenal Woman: Four Poems Celebrating Women* was written by Angelou and published in 1995. This small collection celebrates the spirit of the African American woman—her beauty, inner strength, and self-image. It includes four poems that she said she wrote specifically for women: "Phenomenal Woman," "Still I Rise," "Weekend Glory," and "Our Grandmothers."

- *Poetry for Young People: Maya Angelou* is a collection of twenty-five of Angelou's best poems for teens. It was published in 2007 and afforded her the honor of being the first living poet to be included in Sterling's "Poetry for Young People" series.

- *Free My Mind: Anthology of Black and Asian Poetry* is a collaboration by Judith Elkin and C. G. Duncan that was published in 1990. This anthology of multiracial poetry from around the world is targeted toward young-adult readers.

- *The Firefly Letters: A Suffragette's Journey to Cuba* is a tale of oppressed women, from those of privileged backgrounds to enslaved women, told in free-verse narrative. Elena is a teenage slave who is captured in the Congo, sold by her own father, and sent to work in Cuba. The work was written by Margarita Engle and published in 2010.

- *Mare's War* (2009), written by Tanita S. Davis, is the story of a road trip by fifteen-year-old Octavia and seventeen-year-old Tanis with their grandmother over the border of California to the states of the Deep South. The teens begin the trip begrudgingly but end up fascinated and awed by the stories of their grandmother, who grew up as a maid in a prejudiced society, and the courage and resilience she gained. This selection is the Coretta Scott King Awards' Author Honor Book for 2010.

- *Freedom's Children: Young Civil Rights Activists Tell Their Own Stories* is a book containing the stories of southern African Americans whose childhoods were embroiled in the years of the civil rights movement and the tragic repercussions they endured as a result. It was compiled by Ellen S. Levine in 1993.

- In her novel *Their Eyes Were Watching God* (1937), Zora Neale Hurston offers a portrait of a dreamy young woman who grows up in the South and evolves personally throughout her life and three marriages.

- Harriet Beecher Stowe's *Uncle Tom's Cabin* (1852), which depicts the tragic antebellum circumstances of African Americans, proved revelational in bringing the horrors of slavery to sheltered northern audiences.

---

of black feminist critics." Angelou dares to defy that legacy in "Still I Rise" by saying that she is confident, self-sufficient, beautiful, and sexy. She shines with the exquisiteness of diamonds, and her carefree dance suggests that she is rich with gold and oil.

Angelou has described herself physically as too tall and too large, with large thighs and big feet. She wore a natural Afro, which was fashionable in 1978, a time marked by many Afrocentric protest campaigns, embodied in the "Black is Beautiful" slogan. Nothing about Angelou's appearance kept

her from shining as an entertainer, singer, dancer, director, and actor, as well as writer. She started as a singer and dancer in a group called Blue Calypso. She traveled abroad in the cast of *Porgy and Bess*, written and produced by DuBose Heyward and George and Ira Gershwin. She agreed to appear in *Roots*, a television miniseries based on the novel by Alex Haley, in exchange for directing two scenes. Her beauty seemed to rise above those big feet in a magnificent way.

But Angelou learned firsthand the injustices and prejudices that came with growing up as a poor black child in the South. And she knew the stories of how slave women used bacon grease and other oils to straighten their hair to appear more "white." These were desperate acts for survival. She speaks of the slave women who were ground into the dirt in her verse; they were the ones who were blacker, with kinky hair and broad noses. The fairer-skinned, wavy-haired slaves with more European features were allowed to escape the fields and work in the houses. Prejudices against "blacker"-looking women are chronicled in Toni Morrison's books, like *The Bluest Eye*, and in the stories told by Oprah Winfrey about growing up as a darker-skinned child.

African American women have felt such offenses keenly for decades. It was as if they were erased from the television picture and the movie screen until brave men and women began to speak out during the civil rights movement. The climate for change was right, and the younger white generation began their own revolution for change in the 1960s and 1970s. More African American women began to appear on television, and commercials for African American hair products began to appear on television.

However, in the process of assimilation, black women began to try to look whiter and to achieve greater success. Diahann Carroll became the first black beauty to play a nonstereotypical role on television in the show *Julia*, which ran until 1971. The door was open, and through it walked beauties like Pam Grier, Vanessa Williams, Whitney Houston, Tyra Banks, Naomi Campbell, Oprah Winfrey, Queen Latifah, and Beyoncé Knowles. One problem remains: most of these women are half white. Oprah Winfrey has no white ancestors in her lineage, and when she was told, she was greatly relieved. Jennifer Hudson of *Dreamgirls* fame, who is also half white, was told as a contestant on *American Idol* that she was too fat to be an "American Idol." Sadly (or is it?), she is now sporting a size six and appearing in weight-loss commercials. Since obesity carries health risks with it, she fortunately escapes the "sell-out" list. The Afrocentrist movement is quick to recognize a sell-out and has been promoting a campaign echoing the themes of greats like Booker T. Washington and Malcolm X, who said it was shameful for black women to appear white. Currently the movement has had a great deal of success, with more African American women sporting natural hairstyles and promoting the products on Target ads.

Recently a new video appeared on *Sesame Street* titled, "I Like My Hair." It features a young African American girl sporting a natural Afro and singing about why she loves her hair and all the ways she can make it pretty. She sings gleefully that she can wear it with a bow or a clip, and it looks great in cornrows. *Sesame Street* has been teaching children about self-respect and tolerance for decades, and this video is a wonderful tool for teaching young girls of color to learn to love their hair. It was written by an African American father after watching his daughter longingly stroke the long blonde hair of her Barbie doll. The video has elicited a great deal of attention and praise from Afrocentric Web sites, blogs, and tweets. The responses from the black community have been overwhelming, with moms responding with a resounding "Thank you!" and African American women of all ages wishing someone had taught them that their hair was beautiful when they were young. Trying to attain "white" hair had been one of their struggles over the years, provoking the use of relaxants, oils, and straighteners to make their hair acceptable. Mattel has released an African American Barbie with a broader nose and larger lips, with long hair in braids, but it has met with mixed reviews, being criticized because it comes with a hair-straightening tool. A similar doll was quickly removed from the market after its release, in a tie-in with the cookie brand, as an "Oreo" doll; Mattel was obviously oblivious to the common racial slur associated with the term. *Sesame Street* should be applauded for adding the "I Like My Hair" video to their repertoire. With a mainstream audience worldwide, it challenges the norms and sets the stage for the next generation of black women to truly like themselves inside and out. More media and venues that target all races should incorporate these themes, to help undo the damage of our forefathers and, perhaps unwittingly, ourselves.

Is assimilation the answer? Is Afrocentricity the answer? Perhaps Maya Angelou has the answer for this as well. She stresses creativity, imagination, and courage in the face of lack of money, position, or perceived beauty. She proclaims that positivity, resourcefulness, and self-respect are strong barriers against prejudicial norms. To "rise above," to her, means looking at the way people are more alike than unlike. She describes herself as not necessarily pretty and far from being the size of a model. But one gets the feeling that even at eighty years old, she

Woman enjoying the sunrise (*Dudarev Mikhail / Shutterstock.com*)

feels pretty. She has an aura of pride and expectancy when she walks into a room, the light dancing in her eyes. She walks gracefully and joyously, with a smile glistening on her lips. Her beauty is in her soul, her self-love, and her exuberant spirit.

Source: Cynthia Gower Betts, Critical Essay on "Still I Rise," in *Poetry for Students*, Gale, Cengage Learning, 2011.

Lyman B. Hagen

In the following excerpt, Hagen presents an anatomy of Angelou's poetry and its subject matter.

Of Maya Angelou's six published volumes of poetry, the first four have been collected into one Bantam paperback volume, titled *Maya Angelou: Poems* (1986). Her early practice was to alternate a prose publication with a poetry volume, and a fifth "collection" follows her fifth autobiography. Unlike the four previous volumes of poetry, this fifth work titled *Now Sheba Sings the Song* (1987), adds a new dimension. Here fifteen or so short poems are responses to sketches of African-American women done by artist Tom Feelings, whom Angelou has known for many years. The combined talents of these two are highly complementary and the results are particularly appealing. A sixth volume, *I Shall Not Be Moved* (1990), contains new love poems and praise poems. A four poem inspirational collection has been available under the title *Phenomenal Woman*. These four are previously published poems.

Angelou's poems are a continuum of mood and emotion. They go from the excitement of love to outrage over racial injustice, from the pride of blackness and African heritage to suffered slurs. Angelou follows Countee Cullen's literary perspective that black authors have the prerogative to "do, write, create what we will, our only concern being that we do it well and with all the power in us." Angelou indeed speaks out in many ways and with the best of words she can summon.

Angelou's poetry is generally brief, in the tradition of Langston Hughes who believed that a poem should be short—the shorter the better. Forty percent of the 135 poems in the Bantam edition are 15 lines or less. Of this forty percent, fifteen poems contain three stanzas, twelve have two stanzas, and eleven poems are unstructured. These eleven seem rather forced and rhetorical. Another dozen poems contain between eleven and fifteen lines each. The remainder of her 135 collected poems range from 30 to 50 lines. Angelou never indulges in lengthy narrative poems. She chooses words frugally. The length of line in her poems is also short. Most lines of her three-stanza poems are trimeter; others, particularly those in the unstructured poems, are from two to four syllables long. Some critics do cite her poetry as "oversimplistic or slight because of the short lines, easy diction, and heavy dependence on rhythm and rhyme in her poetry." But Angelou herself has frequently commented on the difficulty of reducing complex thoughts and ideas to a poetic format. She says she begins with many pages of words on her yellow legal pad and works long and hard at distilling them.

Total poetic meaning stresses both emotional content and rhythmical elements. If the emotional content can be considered the bricks of the poem, the rhythm would be the mortar that binds. Angelou is a natural builder of poetry for she not only has a keen sensitivity to feeling, but also a marvelous sense of rhythm. Her musical awareness is so strong that she claims she *hears* music in ordinary, everyday circumstances. A rhythmical awareness has been reinforced by four important influences on her: first, her many readings of the lyrical King James Bible; second, acknowledged reading of traditional white writers such as Edgar Allan Poe, William Thackeray, and particularly William Shakespeare; and of prominent black writers such as Paul Laurence Dunbar, Langston Hughes, James Weldon Johnson, Countee Cullen, and of W. E. B. DuBois' "Litany at Atlanta." A third strong influence grew out of her participation in the rhythmical shouting and singing in African-American church services with their emotional spirituals; and the strong, moving sermons preached in those churches, whose tones she absorbed into her being. The fourth shaping force derives from childhood chants, songs and rhyme games long familiar in folklore.

With her keen sense of feeling, it is natural for Angelou, when she decides to compose a poem, first to find the rhythm of a subject, however mundane that subject may be. This approach is outlined in an interview with Arthur Thomas as Angelou explains the lengthy procedure she follows to produce a poem:

> When I write a poem I try to find a rhythm. First, if I wanted to write a poem about today.... I would write everything I know about today.

> Then I find the rhythm. Everything in the universe, Art, has rhythm. The sun rises and sets. The moon rises and sets. The tides come, they go out. Everything moves in rhythm. Tangentially, I would like to say that when people say of black people, "You have rhythm," it is not an insult....

> It means that you are close to the universe.... I will find that maybe the rhythm changes.... This rhythm is slow and simple, and then maybe it's faster, more complex; and then there's the audience, and then—it's marvelous! Exciting!

> *Then* I start to work on the poem, and I will *pull* and *push* it and *kick* it and *kiss* it, *hug* it, everything. Until finally it reflects what this day has been.

> It costs me. It might take me three months to write that poem. And it might end up being six lines.

Angelou has often spoken about this painful process of distilling her thoughts and the flow of her words. She mentions that 15 pages of notes

might end up producing four lines of poetry. She has explained that the effort involved encompasses a discipline that is very difficult. But she finds the results rewarding and is still attracted to this means of expression.

A few of her poems seem pretentious with somewhat forced language, but most of her poetry has the spritely diction of the vernacular and the dialectical. It is with this language mode that she is most successful. She has no objection to using dialect, as long as it does not denigrate. She admires the dialect poems of Paul Laurence Dunbar because of "the sweetness of them." The high regard for this kind of poetry might have astonished Dunbar. He was dismayed that his vernacular poems were more appreciated than his romantic and cultured ones.

Of the poetry Angelou has published, only a few poems first appeared in journals or literary reviews, the usual path to publication for poets. Her work finds its way immediately into books. R. B. Stepto waspishly observes that Angelou's slight poems "cannot but make lesser-known talents grieve all the more about how this thin stuff finds its way to the rosters of a major New York house while their stronger, more inventive lines seem to be relegated to the low-budget (or no-budget) journals and presses." Angelou's 'thin stuff' is not so thin if read with an eye to inner meaning. Her deliberate distillations are effective. They are written for people, not other poets. Some of the poems in her first volume, *Just Give Me a Cool Drink of Water 'fore I Diiie*, were originally published as songs. The volume includes many of the lyrics from her 1969 recording of "The Poetry of Maya Angelou" for GWP Records. Most of her other poetry could easily be set to music. It is purposely lyrical. It is designed to elicit stirring emotional responses. Much of it is meant to show fun with the familiar.

There has been little critical attention given to Angelou's poetry beyond the usual book reviews. A scattering of negative responses have greeted each book of poetry. Ellen Lippman writes that "... Angelou is more adept at prose than verse." Janet Blundell agrees: "This *Shaker, Why Don't You Sing?* poetry is no match for Angelou's prose writings." A third reviewer, J. A. Avant, judges that "... this *Just Give Me a Cool Drink of Water* isn't accomplished, not by any means..." But he concedes that "... some readers are going to love it." And S. M. Gilbert suggests publishers have exploited Angelou. Gilbert comments that her second poetry book, *Oh, Pray My Wings Are Gonna Fit Well* "... is such a painfully untalented collection of poems that I can't think of any reason other than the Maya myth for it to be in print; it's impossible indeed." It is not unusual to capitalize on a successful author's name. A new book by a currently popular writer generally guarantees at least minimum sales with minimum promotion. But Angelou had been writing poetry long before her prose ventures and has considered herself basically a poet. These negative reviewers have failed to look beyond the apparent simplistic lines to discover the power of their message. Angelou tries to reach readers not attuned to soaring poetics but comfortable with sparse exchanges.

Contrary to the negative criticism, positive comments have also appeared. The reviewer in *Choice* magazine finds that Angelou's work is "... craftsmanlike and powerful (though not great poetry)." Chad Walsh says the work in *Just Give Me* is "... a moving blend of lyricism and harsh social observation." The reviewer of *Shake, Why Don't You Sing?* in *Publishers Weekly* says, her "poems speak with delicacy and depth of feeling." Robert Loomis, Angelou's long-time editor at Random House, supports her with his well-taken remarks:

> I've always believed that those who have reservations about Angelou's poetry simply don't understand what she's doing. She is very strongly in a certain tradition of Black American poetry, and when I hear her read or declaim the works of other Black American poets, I can see very clearly what her heritage is and what her inspiration is. Furthermore, Maya is not writing the sort of poetry that most of us grew up in school admiring. What she is writing is poetry that is very definitely in what I would call the oral tradition. That is, what she writes can be read aloud and even acted. When her words are spoken, they are extremely effective and moving. They always sound just right.

Although few critics have found great merit in her poetry, Angelou has acquired a dedicated audience. Her work seems to have a special appeal to college students. At her public readings, a generally balanced cross-section, male and female, black and white, is in attendance. She delights and enchants the entire group with her timing and her powerful delivery. Some admirers of her poetry have been so impressed with its rhymes, rhythms, and content that they themselves have been encouraged to write. Many poets manque have sent Angelou their unsolicited creations. Quite a few of these can be found

stored with her collected papers at the Wake Forest University library. Angelou encourages young people to express themselves openly and seeks to inspire them.

The titles of Angelou's first four books of poems are attention getters. They are catchy black vernacular expressions. Her first volume, *Just Give Me a Cool Drink of Water* (1971), refers to Angelou's belief that "we as individuals ... are still so innocent that we think if we asked our murderer just before he puts the final wrench upon the throat, 'Would you please give me a cool drink of water?' and he would do so. That's innocence. It's lovely."

Angelou covers a wide range of subject matter. In Angelou's writings, poetry or prose, she holds to tradition and makes a special effort to dispel false impressions about African Americans, but does not use this as her sole motivation.

Angelou's poetry belongs in the category of "light" verse. Her poems are entertainments derived from personal experiences and fall into one of two broad subject areas. First, she writes about everyday considerations—the telephone, aging, insomnia—topics that are totally neutral. Second, she writes with deep feeling about a variety of racial themes and concerns.

"The Telephone," for example, exemplifies her universally identifiable reflections on an ordinary subject. She admits in verse that she is dependent on it. Its importance to her daily life is notable by a contrast to its periods of silence.

But she can't stand the quietude long, nor the isolation implied, and so she impatiently demands that the phone ring. This demand follows three structured stanzas: the first physically describes the telephone; the second, its active effect on people's lives; and the third, the effect of its silence. In the second stanza, she emphasizes the familiar and the feminine by employing a metaphor of sewing, tatting, crocheting, hemming, and darning. The intrinsic themes of black and blue and week-end loneliness are often found in popular blues songs.

Another light general rumination is "On Reaching Forty." In somewhat stuffy language Angelou regrets the passage of time and expresses tongue-in-cheek admiration for those departing this world early and by this bestows upon the poem an unexpected conclusion. She is saddened by the passing of youthful milestones. The years forward will weigh even more heavily.

Inasmuch as Angelou is an accomplished cook, it is not surprising to find that she addresses the appreciation of traditional foods. In "The Health-Food Diner" exotic, faddish health food items are rejected in favor of standard fare such as red meat. In alternating tetrameter and trimeter quatrains, Angelou concludes each stanza with a food preference. Her reader finds life must be sustained by solid values, not notional influences.

Angelou not only has a keen ear for dialogue and dialect, but she also evidences a keen psychological understanding of an adolescent girl's romantic concerns and possessiveness. The speaker in "No Loser, No Weeper" expresses in the vernacular a universal sentiment. Again Angelou carefully structures her poem. In each stanza, the speaker notes how her reaction to losing something, beginning with childish items and advancing to that of major worth: in the first stanza, a dime; then a doll; then a watch; but especially in the last stanza when she truly hates to lose her boy friend.

The same subject matter—the loss of a boy friend—is expressed in "Poor Girl." The speaker is a teenager who addresses a fickle fellow playing the field. She's afraid there will be another disappointed girl in a long line of disappointed girls, just like her. One girl, she says, will believe the lies but can't be forewarned because of a possible misunderstanding. Eventually the truth will be realized and awareness will set in.

Angelou is a realist. She knows that a married man who sees other women usually returns home to his wife in spite of the attraction and charm of the Other Woman. The speaker in "They Went Home" is aware that she plays a loser's role. While the sentiment is psychologically sound, the lines are prosaic, reflecting the pitiful state of the abandoned.

Sometimes Angelou uses contrasting pairs in her poetry. For example, in "Phenomenal Woman," considered a personal theme-poem, she asserts the special qualities of a particular woman. The woman described is easily matched to the author herself. Angelou is an imposing woman—at least six feet tall. She has a strong personality and a compelling presence as defined in the poem. One can accept the autobiographical details in this poem or extend the reading to infer that all women have qualities that attract attention. Angelou's dramatic presentation of this poem always pleases her audience and is frequently the highlight of her programs.

Angelou pairs this poem with "Men." The speaker is a woman whose experience has taught her the games men play. In this she uses a raw egg metaphor to contrast fragile femininity with dominant masculinity, but the female speaker has perhaps learned to be cautious.

Other contrasting poetic pairs are "America" and "Africa"; "Communication I" and "Communication II"; and "The Thirteens (Black and White)".

In *Gather Together in My Name*, Angelou describes being shown a room full of dope addicts and the impact this picture had on her. In both "A Letter to an Aspiring Junkie" and in "Junkie Monkey Reel" she details the dangerous consequences of using drugs. In both poems the slave master of today is drugs, and the junkie is tied to the habit as if he were the monkey attached to the street vendor's strap. Both poems contain particularly disturbing images.

Angelou uses every opportunity to build African-American pride and in "Ain't That Bad?" she praises black culture, mores, customs, and leaders. Its short lines, its repetition of imperatives, and its repetition of the title help constitute a chant, which categorizes it as a "shouting poem."

In black West African English (Sierra Leone) *i gud baad* means "it's very good." Thus "bad" as used extensively in this poem carries a favorable connotation, meaning to be "very good, extremely good." This meaning has been incorporated into everyday black vernacular and therefore is commonly understood. The last word in the last line of the poem sustains the positive connotations and provides a closure.

As detailed in an earlier chapter, a number of children's activities and responses have been handed down through the years in all cultures and are considered folk materials and light entertainments. This wealth of rhyming folklore, so important in Angelou's childhood, provides an indigenous and unconscious source of much of the style and the flow of both her poetry and prose. It dictates the structure of much of her poetry.

Angelou's second group of meditations is concerned with racial subjects and themes. This group allies poetry with morality by continuing the themes of protest and survival found in her autobiographies. These poems are not excessively polemical; they voice only mild protest.

In this category is Angelou's favorite poem and theme, "Still I Rise," the same title as that of a play she wrote in 1976. The title, Angelou says, refers "to the indomitable spirit of the black people." She often quotes this poem in interviews and includes it in public readings. The poem follows Angelou's customary fashion of incremental repetition, and catalogues injustices.

In spite of adversity, dire conditions and circumstances; in spite of racial epithets, scorn, and hostility, Angelou expresses unshakable faith that one will overcome; one will triumph; one will Rise! The lines remind us of the black spiritual "Rise and Shine" as well as other religious hymns that express hope: "Oh, rise and shine, and give God the glory, glory! / Rise and shine, and give God the glory, glory!" In "Our Grandmothers" Angelou voices a similar sentiment contained in another dearly loved spiritual: "Like a tree, down by the riverside, I shall not be moved."

The "I" in "Still I Rise" is designated female by Angelou herself as she numbers this poem as one of the four about women in *Phenomenal Woman*. She speaks not only for herself but also for her gender and race. This extension of self occurs in Angelou's autobiographies and protest poetry. It is in keeping with a traditional practice of black writers to personalize their common racial experiences. Moreover, Angelou implies that the black race will not just endure, but that in the words of Sondra O'Neale, "will triumph with a will of collective consciousness that Western experience cannot extinguish." Angelou's most militant poems are contained in the second section of her first volume of poetry, "Just Before the World Ends." They have "more bite—the anguished and often sardonic expression of a black in a white dominated world," Chad Walsh observes. In her moving address "To a Freedom Fighter," Angelou again as a spokesperson for all blacks acknowledges a debt owed to those who fought earlier civil rights battles. They did more than survive; they endured all indignities for the maintenance of their race....

Source: Lyman B. Hagen, "Poetry: Something about Everything," in *Heart of a Woman, Mind of a Writer, and Soul of a Poet: A Critical Analysis of the Writings of Maya Angelou*, University Press of America, 1997, pp. 118–36.

Sandra Cookson

In the following review, Cookson praises Angelou's use of black-speech rhythms, inflections, and patterns in her poetry.

Maya Angelou's five volumes of poems are here collected, reset in a handsome typeface, and produced in a collector's first edition. As a sort of companion volume, her publisher, Random House, has brought out a separate, pocket-size volume of "four poems celebrating women," entitled *Phenomenal Woman* (after the title poem). It too is handsomely designed; the publisher no doubt hopes to capitalize on the wider recognition of the poet, following her reading of her poem "On the Pulse of Morning" at the inauguration of President Clinton in 1993.

Angelou's poems celebrate black people, men and women; at the same time, they bear witness to the trials of black people in this country. Implicitly or directly, whites are called to account, yet Angelou's poetry, steeped though it is in the languages and cultures of black America, does not exclude whites. Quite the reverse: the poems are generous in their directness, in the humor Angelou finds alongside her outrage and pain, in their robust embrace of life. They are truly "celebratory."

Though Angelou's repertory is wide, she is at her best when working in the rhythms and highly inflected speech patterns of black Southern dialect, or being street-wise hip. She prefers strong, straightforward rhyme to free verse. The musical currents of blues and jazz, the rhythm of rap songs, and the language of the Bible mingle in her poems. The rhetoric of the pulpit is here too, though Angelou sometimes turns it to secular purposes. "Still I Rise," a poem about the survival of black women despite every kind of humiliation, deploys most of these forces, as it celebrates black women while simultaneously challenging the stereotypes to which America has subjected them since the days of slavery. "Does my sassiness upset you?" "Does my haughtiness offend you?" "Does my sexiness upset you?" the poet demands in an in-your-face tone through successive stanzas, leading to the poem's inspirational conclusion. The penultimate stanza is especially strong: "Out of the huts of history's shame / I rise / Up from a past that's rooted in pain / I rise / I'm a black ocean, leaping and wide, / Welling and swelling I bear in the tide."

Angelou is master of several poetic idioms, and her voices are many. From the admonitory "Letter to an Aspiring Junkie" ("Let me hip you to the streets, / Jim, / Ain't nothing happening") to the simple prayer of a black man giving thanks for another day on earth ("Thank You, Lord"), she provides her readers direct access to her poems.

> I was once a sinner man,
> Living unsaved and wild,
> Taking my chances in a dangerous world,
> Putting my soul on trial.
> Because of Your mercy,
> Falling down on me like rain,
> Because of Your mercy,
> When I die I'll live again,
> Let me humbly say,
> Thank You for this day.
> I want to thank You.

Maya Angelou does not stint and she does not spare the often painful details of her people. Still, she somehow gives hope.

Source: Sandra Cookson, Review of *The Complete Collected Poems of Maya Angelou* and *Phenomenal Woman: Four Poems Celebrating Women,* in *World Literature Today,* Vol. 69, No. 4, Autumn 1995, p. 800.

SOURCES

Angelou, Maya, "Still I Rise," in *The Complete Collected Poems of Maya Angelou,* Random House, 1994, pp. 163–64.

Cookson, Sandra, Review of *The Complete Collected Poems of Maya Angelou* and *Phenomenal Woman: Four Poems Celebrating Women,* in *World Literature Today,* Vol. 69, No. 4, Autumn 1995, p. 800.

Dowson, Jane, "'Older Sisters Are Very Sobering Things': Contemporary Women Poets and the Female Affiliation Complex," in *Feminist Review,* No. 62, Summer 1999, pp. 6–20.

Fox-Genovese, Elizabeth, "Myth and History: Discourse of Origins in Zora Neale Hurston and Maya Angelou," in *Black American Literature Forum,* Vol. 24, No. 2, Summer 1990, pp. 224, 229, 232–33.

Griffin, Farah Jasmine, "Textual Healing: Claiming Black Women's Bodies, the Erotic and Resistance in Contemporary Novels of Slavery," in *Callalou,* Vol. 19, No. 2, 1996, pp. 520–24.

Hagen, Lyman B., *Heart of a Woman, Mind of a Writer, and Soul of a Poet: A Critical Analysis of the Writings of Maya Angelou,* University Press of America, 1997, pp. 60, 111, 123–34, 159, 161–63.

Harris, Trudier, "This Disease Called Strength: Some Observations on the Compensating Construction of Black Female Character," in *Literature and Medicine,* Vol. 14, No. 1, 1995, pp. 109–11, 114–16.

Milner, D., "20 Years Then and Now—1970 to 1990," in *Black Collegian,* Vol. 21, No. 3, January/February 1991, pp. 1–2, 4–5.

Neubauer, Carol E., "An Interview with Maya Angelou," in *Massachusetts Review,* Vol. 28, No. 2, Summer 1987, pp. 286–88.

Pollard, Ingrid, Review of *I Know Why the Caged Bird Sings, Gather Together in My Name,* and *Singin' and Swingin' and Gettin' Merry Like Christmas,* in *Feminist Review,* No. 17, Autumn 1984, pp. 116–17.

FURTHER READING

Angelou, Maya, *The Heart of a Woman,* Bantam, 1997.
> This volume, first published in 1981, is the fourth in the series of Angelou's autobiographies. It chronicles the years when she began writing and was an activist in New York. She recalls the African American celebrities she came to know, the days of working for the Reverend Martin Luther King, Jr., and becoming the director of the Southern Christian Leadership Conference's New York office.

Angelou, Maya, *I Know Why the Caged Bird Sings,* Ballantine Books, 2009.
> This is the first of five autobiographies written by Angelou throughout her life. It begins with her life in Stamps, Arkansas, with her grandmother from age three. It recounts years of displacement and disappointment, a tragic occurrence, and gaining independence at long last.

Angelou, Maya, *I Shall Not Be Moved: Poems,* Random House, 1990.
> The poems included in this volume speak of racial injustice in painful and moving statements about the strength of African Americans in the face of prejudice and hardship.

Angelou, Maya, *Wouldn't Take Nothing for My Journey Now,* Random House, 1993.
> Angelou's love of humanity shines in these prosaic essays on themes of love, friendship, morality, tolerance, and understanding.

Lupton, Mary Jane, *Maya Angelou: A Critical Companion,* Greenwood Press, 1998.
> This volume is an excellent literary introduction and critique of Angelou's five autobiographies and a very helpful reference for students.

Pettit, Jayne, *Maya Angelou: Journey of the Heart,* Puffin, 1998.
> This is a short, readable biography aimed at young adults. It is helpful as a read along with *I Know Why the Caged Bird Sings* and contains clearly written chapter notes.

SUGGESTED SEARCH TERMS

Maya Angelou

African American poetry

Still I Rise AND Maya Angelou

civil rights movement

Maya Angelou AND African American literature

Maya Angelou AND feminism

Maya Angelou AND poetry

Maya Angelou AND autobiography

Maya Angelou AND civil rights

A Storm in the Mountains

ALEXANDER SOLZHENITSYN

1964

Best known for his depiction of life inside
Soviet labor camps, Nobel Prize-winning
author Alexander Solzhenitsyn also authored
a number of prose poems. In these brief, lyrical
pieces, Solzhenitsyn explores such themes as
life in rural Russian villages and the beauty of
nature. "A Storm in the Mountains" focuses on
the natural world, specifically a rugged moun-
tain landscape in the throes of a storm. In the
poem, an unnamed narrator and his compan-
ions find themselves caught in a mountain pass
during a fierce thunderstorm. Solzhenitsyn
vividly describes the progress of the storm
and the reactions of its awestruck human wit-
nesses. The poem illustrates the power and the
beauty of nature, and it underscores the desire
of man to feel a sense of unity with nature. In
the structure and language of the piece, Solzhe-
nitsyn depicts the storm and the reaction of the
narrator and his companions almost as a con-
versation, an interplay between nature and
humanity.

"A Storm in the Mountains" was originally
published in 1964 in Russian in the journal
Grani, along with a number of other short
pieces, under the title *Krokhotki* (a title that
refers to the brevity of the stories). "A Storm
in the Mountains" was later translated into
English by Michael Glenny and published by
Bodley Head in 1971 in the collection *Stories
and Prose Poems*.

Alexander Solzhenitsyn (*AP Images*)

AUTHOR BIOGRAPHY

Solzhenitsyn was born in Kislovodsk, Russia, on December 11, 1918, at the close of the Russian Revolution. As czarist Russia fell, Russia became known as the Russian Soviet Federative Socialist Republic (R.S.F.S.R.). Solzhenitsyn's mother was widowed just prior to his birth. His father, Isaakiy Solzhenitsyn, was a young army officer who died in a hunting accident. Raised by his mother and an aunt, Solzhenitsyn grew up during the Russian Civil War, a power struggle waged between the Bolsheviks who had overthrown the czar and those who opposed Communist rule. As a young man, Solzhenitsyn studied mathematics at Rostov State University and took correspondence courses from the Moscow Institute of Philosophy, Literature, and History. While studying at Rostov, Solzhenitsyn met and married a fellow student, Natalia Reshetovskaya, in 1940. They would later divorce in 1952, remarry in 1957, and divorce again in 1972.

Solzhenitsyn served as a commander in the Red Army during World War II. Later writings reveal that during this period in his life, Solzhenitsyn began to doubt aspects of Soviet rule. In 1945, under the dictatorship of Joseph Stalin, Solzhenitsyn was accused of anti-Soviet propaganda and arrested after writing letters in which he questioned Stalin's policies and power. Sentenced to eight years in a labor camp, Solzhenitsyn served his term in several different camps. While serving in Ekibastuz in Kazakhstan, Solzhenitsyn had a tumor removed, although the cancer that was slowly spreading through his body went undiagnosed. In 1953, having served his eight years, Solzhenitsyn was next sent into exile in Kok-Terek in Kazakhstan. After receiving medical treatment in 1954, Solzhenitsyn experienced a remission of his cancer. During this period in his life, he abandoned Marxism and turned to Christianity. Throughout his years in prison and exile, Solzhenitsyn wrote prolifically, although works from this period were not published until decades later.

Following Stalin's death in 1953, Nikita Khrushchev rose to power in the Soviet Union, and Solzhenitsyn and countless other political prisoners were freed and exonerated. In 1962, Solzhenitsyn's novel *One Day in the Life of Ivan Denisovich* was published. The work details the horrors of the Soviet prison-camp system. The work was lauded in the West, even while many marveled that Solzhenitsyn went unpunished for speaking out against the state in this manner. Khrushchev welcomed the step away from Stalinism that was reflected in the uncensored publication of Solzhenitsyn's novel. After Khrushchev's fall from power in 1964, however, such criticism of the ruling party would no longer be tolerated under Leonid Brezhnev. With the help of others, Solzhenitsyn kept hidden from the secret police the manuscript for a novel even more damning than *Ivan Denisovich*. This three-volume work, *The Gulag Archipelago*, was written during the years 1958 through 1967. After being awarded the Nobel Prize in Literature in 1970, Solzhenitsyn saw *The Gulag Archipelago* published in the West in 1973. It was privately circulated in the Soviet Union until 1989, when it would finally be published. Also in 1973, Solzhenitsyn married Natalia Svetlova, with whom he had three sons. The Soviet secret police, the KGB, eventually found a portion of *The Gulag Archipelago* manuscript. In 1974, Solzhenitsyn was arrested and deported to Frankfurt, West Germany. Stripped of his Soviet citizenship, Solzhenitsyn came to live in Germany, Switzerland, and the United States. In 1990, the Soviet Union restored Solzhenitsyn's Soviet citizenship. After the dissolution of the Soviet Union, Solzhenitsyn returned in 1994 to what was now Russia once again. At the age of eighty-nine, Solzhenitsyn died of heart failure on August 3, 2008, near Moscow.

POEM SUMMARY

Paragraph 1

As a prose poem, Solzhenitsyn's "A Storm in the Mountains" is divided into paragraphs, rather than the traditional stanzas often used to divide poems. In the first paragraph, a first-person-plural narrator is introduced; that is, the narrator is a member of a group and refers to the group as *we*. The members of the group find themselves at the base of a mountain pass during the night as a storm approaches. Tents are abandoned as the members of the party run toward sturdier shelter, although the narrator does not explicitly state how or where the party takes cover. Additionally, it is only through the title of the poem that the reader is made aware of what is actually coming upon the group in the night, for the storm is only referred to by the pronoun "it" in this first paragraph of the poem.

Paragraph 2

In the second paragraph, the narrator reiterates how the darkness of the night obliterates any indication of the mountainous landscape. As lightning flashes, two enormous mountain peaks are illuminated. The pine trees appear to tower over the members of the group at a supernatural height. In the light of the lightning strike, the narrator indicates that the group is able to feel once again as though they are on solid ground. But when the blackness of night returns, the members of the group feel as though they are unmoored in the chaotic darkness.

Paragraph 3

The landscape takes on a surreal aspect to the narrator's eyes in the third paragraph of the prose poem. When the lightning illuminates the landscape, it appears in a variety of colors. The mountains and trees suddenly appear in their natural places once again, despite the incredible nature of their immense size. As darkness returns,

the narrator observes that it is hardly believable that the pines and mountains even existed, so completely has the night erased them.

Paragraph 4

Up to this point, the narrator has regarded the storm only in terms of its visual display, but now, in the fourth paragraph, the sound of the storm is the center of the narrator's discussion. The thunder fills the gorges between the mountains with its particular voice. Turning once again to the ever-present lightning, the narrator uses a biblical term to liken the storm's flashes to the arrows of God's holy army. Using this analogy, the narrator describes the way the mountain peaks are attacked as the force of the lightning showers down upon the rocks. The lightning is also described as a force that is almost alive.

Paragraph 5

In the final paragraph, the narrator claims with wonder that the group has forgotten to fear the storm, including the power of the lightning and the deafening thunder. The narrator compares the presence of the members of the group in the thick of the storm to the presence of water droplets in the ocean, which would not fear a hurricane but might desire to become a part of this enormous force. Describing the singular insignificance of each member of the group, the narrator asserts that they have recognized their role as a part of something much greater than each individual person. They now view themselves, at least for this moment, as part of the world of nature and as witness to its creation.

THEMES

Nature

In "A Storm in the Mountains," Solzhenitsyn explores the power of nature as well as the related theme of the connection of humankind to nature. The focus of the poem is largely on the interplay between the weather and the natural features of the mountainside, including the peaks, the pine trees, the gorges, and the response of the narrator and his companions to both the storm and the mountainous landscape. While the narrator and his companions seek shelter and observe the storm as it approaches over a ridge of mountains, the world is black. The physical landscape is

TOPICS FOR FURTHER STUDY

- Solzhenitsyn's "A Storm in the Mountains" was written and published during the transition in power in the Soviet Union from Khrushchev to Brezhnev. Using print and online sources, research this period in Soviet history. What was the nature of Khrushchev's ousting? Was it a violent or peaceful transition of power? Which individuals or groups supported each leader? What happened to Khrushchev after he left office? Write a report or prepare an oral presentation for your class.

- Prose poetry uses some elements of poetry and incorporates these into a brief prose piece, with the result being a hybrid work benefiting from both "parent" genres. Flash fiction is similar in that it abbreviates the short-story format; it is typically defined as a complete story written with fewer than a thousand words. Given this restriction, works of flash fiction must employ language as succinct and imagery as efficient as is typically used in poetry. Read some works of flash fiction, such as those found on the site *Flash Fiction Online* (http://www.flashfictiononline.com). Write your own work of flash fiction, publishing it on a Web page that you have created. Consider carefully your subject matter, language, and imagery. Invite your classmates to review your work on the Web page.

- Growing up under Stalin's regime and witnessing several changes of power in the Soviet Union, Solzhenitsyn experienced many deprivations during his life under Communist rule, including punishment and incarceration in a labor camp for questioning this form of government. In Moying Li's memoir, *Snow Falling in Spring: Coming of Age in China during the Cultural Revolution*, the author reveals the way her life changed during the Cultural Revolu-

tion, when Mao Zedong, the chairman of the Communist Party in China, instituted violent, sweeping, and oppressive measures designed to secure the stability of Communism in China. The Cultural Revolution began in 1966, and in many ways the oppression experienced in China was mirrored in the Soviet Union of this time. With a group, read Moying Li's memoir, which was written for a young-adult audience. What was life like for young people during the Cultural Revolution, according to this account? How did their lives change during the Revolution? What was important to the author during that time, and how did she personally change during the span of the Cultural Revolution? Create an online blog in which members of your group can ask and answer questions such as these and discuss reactions to the book.

- The Beat poetry movement of the 1960s experimented with existing forms of poetic expression and explored new forms. Examine works such as the 1995 anthology of Beat poetry geared toward a young-adult audience, *Beat Voices: An Anthology of Beat Poetry*, edited by David Kherdian. Identify Beat poets who employed the prose-poetry form. Compare such works to the prose poetry of Solzhenitsyn in the 1971 translation of a selection of his work, *Stories and Prose Poems*. Do Beat poets such as Russell Edson and Bob Kaufman explore natural themes, as Solzhenitsyn does? What subject matter do they explore? How do the physical forms of the Beat prose poems compare with those of Solzhenitsyn's prose poetry? Keeping such considerations in mind, write a formal analysis in which you detail the similarities and differences in the Beat prose poems and those of Solzhenitsyn.

Trees in the dark forest *(andreiuc88 | Shutterstock.com)*

obliterated by the darkness of night. When lightning flashes, the peaks and trees are revealed. Without this illumination, the narrator and the members of the group feel disoriented, as if the structure of their world has been dismantled. Outside the known confines of their tents, and huddled against the onslaught of the storm, the narrator and his companions perceive the natural world in a new and overwhelming way. Only when the world is illuminated by lightning does the group feel reassured, viewing the trees and mountains once again in their proper place, in their proper proportions to one another. The very existence of the mountains and trees is questioned in the darkness, so penetratingly powerful is the blackness of night during the storm. The sound of the thunder adds to the sense of the limitless power of nature perceived by the group. Flashes of lightning are now regarded in terms of biblical proportions. The conversation between storm and landscape continues as the thunder is heard throughout the gorge. In each paragraph of

the prose poem, not only does Solzhenitsyn depict the storm in terms of its relation to the landscape, but he also incorporates the reaction of the narrator and his companions to the storm and to the mountainous landscape. The storm is initially observed as heading over the ridge and straight for the party. The group loses its footing in the darkness but gains it again as lightning flashes. They hear the thunder, and in the final paragraph they contemplate their insignificance within the universe while remaining thankful that they have a role within this vast and powerful world of nature.

Spirituality

In two distinct ways, the narrator draws attention to the religious and spiritual significance of the mountain storm. In the penultimate paragraph, the narrator compares the flashes of lightning to arrows belonging to Sabaoth. According to James F. Driscoll in a description of the term *Sabaoth* in the 1912 *Catholic Encyclopedia*, it refers to God's title as "Lord of Hosts," where the "hosts" are meant to represent either the armies of Israel or heavenly angels. There is both a violence and a spiritual reverence, then, in describing the lightning in this manner, as sacred weaponry. Additionally, Solzhenitsyn devotes the full final paragraph to the response of the narrator and his companions to the storm. The narrator describes the fears of the group as forgotten, somehow assuaged. He now compares the people in the storm to drops of water in an ocean, which do not fear a hurricane but are rather incorporated into it. With great respect, the narrator observes the insignificance of the group when considered within the larger context of the world, and he insists on the gratefulness of the group in being a part of the natural world. Significantly, the narrator describes the storm as an act of creation, a characterization that draws attention to the enormous sense of reverence the narrator and his companions feel for the storm.

STYLE

Prose Poetry

Prose poetry is a type of poetry in which traditional poetic conventions such as repetition, rhyme, and symbolism are employed, but within a prose structure. This means that the poet uses sentences and paragraphs, rather than lines and stanzas, as the backbone of the poem. In many ways, it may be seen as an exploration of the boundaries of both genres. The prose poem format complements the subject matter of "A Storm in the Mountains." In this work, the poet capitalizes on the structural elements to convey a particular moment that, in the consciousness of the members of the group, seemingly unfolds in a slow and gradual fashion. The use of prose draws out this brief event into a narrative that focuses on the progression of the emotional responses of the group members to the mountainous landscape and to the storm. At the same time, the particular language and imagery Solzhenitsyn uses maintains the poetic effect of the piece, as when the images of darkness and light are used to reflect the group's alternating sense of fear and reassurance, or when natural elements are described in supernatural terms in order to amplify the impact of these elements and to

highlight the human response to the mountainside during the storm.

First-Person-Plural Narration

The event described in "A Storm in the Mountains" is narrated by a first-person-plural narrator, an uncommon perspective in both poetry and prose. A first-person-plural narrator is a member of a group, and the personal pronoun used is *we*. In the poem, the identity of the group is unspecified. This naturally leads to questions that the poet opts not to answer. The reader is uncertain about the nature of the business of the group in the mountains. The group of travelers is large enough to have more than one tent, but beyond that no other clues are given about the nature of the group. Given the spiritual nature of the poem's closing, it may be argued that the experience of the group as a whole is more significant than the individual histories or responses of the group's members. Such a reading underscores the poet's emphasis on the emotional and spiritual impact of the storm on the group. The use of the first-person-plural narrator highlights the poem's insistence on the importance of recognizing personal insignificance and of asserting one's role as a part of the natural world.

HISTORICAL CONTEXT

The Soviet Union in the 1960s

The Soviet Union underwent several key changes of leadership in Solzhenitsyn's lifetime. Stalin's regime, under which Solzhenitsyn lived for many years, was unremittingly harsh. In the years after World War II, Stalin sought to protect his Soviet borders by cultivating a bloc of Communist states on the eastern border of the Soviet Union, using the Soviet secret police to assist local Communists in Albania, Romania, Poland, Czechoslovakia, Hungary, and East Germany in bringing about compliance with Soviet ideals. Many of these regions were attempting to rebuild economies devastated by World War II, and they sought to advance by emulating Soviet industrial efficiencies. Stalin was known for using tactics such as torture and imprisonment in forced labor camps to maintain his control over Soviet citizens. It was under Stalin's rule that Solzhenitsyn served time in a labor camp.

COMPARE
&
CONTRAST

- **1960s:** Poets in the Soviet Union and abroad experiment with the form of prose poetry. In the Soviet Union, practitioners of this form include Solzhenitsyn and Venedict Yerofeyev. American prose poets include Russell Edson and Bob Kaufman. Mexican author Octavio Paz also publishes prose poetry during this time.

  Today: Prose poetry is less popular than it was in the 1960s but remains an avenue of poetic expression explored by poets such as the Yugoslavian writer Charles Simic and the Uruguayan poet Eduardo Galeano. Until his death 2008, Chicano poet Luis Omar Salinas also published in this genre.

- **1960s:** This turbulent time in Soviet politics brings the ousting of Nikita Khrushchev, who attempted to rid Soviet Communism of its harshest Stalinist elements. After Khrushchev is removed from power in 1964, Leonid Brezhnev becomes the new Soviet leader, taking the role of the first secretary of the Communist Party. Brezhnev bankrupts the Soviet economy in an attempt to transform the Soviet Union's military and industrial capabilities.

  Today: Following the dissolution of the Soviet Union in 1991, Russia and other former Soviet states achieved independence. In 2010, Russia is defined as a federation; it is made up of regions that have some autonomy, but the country as a whole is governed by a president and a parliament. Russia, under the governance of President Dmitry Medvedev and Premier Vladimir Putin, allows a number of political parties the right to be represented by candidates in the election of officials in 2010.

- **1960s:** In the 1960s, some works of literature that are critical of the Soviet Union, or at least its harshest Stalinist elements, are allowed to be published, such as Solzhenitsyn's *One Day in the Life of Ivan Denisovich* (1962). Other works that openly question the value and efficacy of the Soviet Union's Marxist-Leninist socialist principles are forbidden, including the novella *Lyubimov* (ca. 1962) by Andrei Sinyavsky and the novella *Govorit Moskva* (1961) by Yuli Daniel.

  Today: Twenty-first-century Russian literature is often focused on looking back to Russia's Soviet history. Works such as the 2002 collection *Sonechka: A Novella and Stories*, by Ludmila Ulitskaya, and the 2009 Russian Booker Prize–winning novel *A Time of Women*, by Yelena Chizhova, depict the deprivations and challenges of life under Soviet rule.

After Stalin's death in 1953, Nikita Khrushchev rose to power and sought to de-Stalinize Soviet socialism. Ronald Gigor Suny observes in *The Structure of Soviet History: Essays and Documents* that the external face of the Soviet government changed, but the internal authoritarian structures remained in place. The years of Khrushchev's reign, states Suny, "can be seen as a period of gradual, hesitant reform within the contours of an authoritarian regime, with short lurches forward and long, slow retrenchments." Suny highlights the reforms to the Stalinist protocol made by his successors, discussing the release of prisoners and noting the new hesitancy in using the police to demonstrate the power of the state unnecessarily. Furthermore, the new leadership attempted to bring about a higher standard of living and a greater openness in the arts. It was under Khrushchev's rule that Solzhenitsyn's novel *One Day in the Life of Ivan Denisovich*, which criticizes the Soviet labor-camp system, was allowed to be published.

In 1964, however, Khrushchev was ousted, forced from office by a coalition led by Leonid Brezhnev. The same year, Solzhenitsyn's prose

Lightning storm in the mountains *(James "BO" Insogna | Shutterstock.com)*

poem "A Storm in the Mountains" was published abroad, along with a number of other prose poems. Under Brezhnev, the more liberal policies of Khrushchev were immediately curtailed. The new leader denounced Khrushchev's more liberal agenda and developed a policy known as the Brezhnev Doctrine, which asserted that the Soviet government had the right to intervene in the affairs of its Soviet states if the Communist agenda was threatened. Brezhnev used this doctrine to justify the Soviet invasion of Czechoslovakia in 1968. Throughout the years of his rule, he continued to expand and modernize the Soviet military and the industrial infrastructure of the Soviet Union.

Soviet Literature in the 1960s

In the 1960s, Soviet literature reflected the political climate. Khrushchev's loosening of Stalin's grip on the Soviet people resulted in the publication of works of literature that critiqued harsh, Stalinesque Soviet policy. At the same time, the Soviet Union still venerated the socialist and communist ideals of Karl Marx and Vladimir

Lenin. There was a limit to the criticism the state would tolerate. *One Day in the Life of Ivan Denisovich*, published in 1962, highlighted the cruelty of Stalin's regime; it was deemed acceptable for publication. Solzhenitsyn published a collection of short stories a year after his novel, but he was turned away by Soviet publishers thereafter. Solzhenitsyn secretively sought publication abroad, as did writers such as Boris Pasternak, whose *Doctor Zhivago* was published in 1957 in the West after being turned down by Soviet publishers who feared reprisal from the state; the work was severely critical of Marxist-Leninist philosophy. During the 1960s, two other Soviet writers attracted attention first from international literary audiences and critics, and then from the Soviet secret police, the KGB. Andrei Sinyavsky and Yuli Daniel secretly submitted novels, stories, and essays to a Western contact who saw to their publication abroad. As Harry T. Moore and Albert Parry explain in *Twentieth-Century Russian Literature*, "These Western editions were smuggled into the Soviet Union and circulated secretly but widely." In 1965, Sinyavsky and Daniel were arrested, tried, and convicted of anti-Soviet agitation. Both subsequently served time in labor camps, described by Moore and Parry as "concentration-camp imprisonment" and "slave camp." The punishment received by Sinyavsky and Daniel served as an example to writers who might be tempted to speak out against Soviet policies.

CRITICAL OVERVIEW

Much of the criticism of Solzhenitsyn's work has been focused on his overtly political writings, whereas his prose poetry has received far less critical attention. In 1962, Solzhenitsyn published the work that made him famous, *One Day in the Life of Ivan Denisovich*, with the approval of Khrushchev, who saw in the work a denunciation of the same elements of Stalinism that Khrushchev himself was striving to siphon from Soviet politics and government. N. J. Anning points out in *Russian Literary Attitudes from Pushkin to Solzhenitsyn* that Khrushchev regarded the work as "valuable anti-Stalin propaganda." Anning also observes that Solzhenitsyn's novel was highly praised in the Soviet Union and went on to receive worldwide attention. Despite the work's obvious indictment of Stalinism, it also served a broader purpose, according to critics such as Robert Porter, a contributor to the 1998 *Reference Guide to Russian Literature*. Porter notes that many critics saw the labor camps in the novel as representative of Soviet society in general, and he also observes that the work is "subversive in its quiet dismissal of materialist philosophy." After Khrushchev was removed from power in 1964, Solzhenitsyn found it impossible to sell his manuscripts to Soviet publishing houses, and as Anning states, he began to be harassed by the Soviet secret police. Nevertheless, Solzhenitsyn managed to get his works published abroad, and internationally he continued to gain attention, both as a literary figure and as a political target of the Soviet government.

While Solzhenitsyn's literary reputation is based on his fiction, his poetry and short fiction have not received the same level of attention or acclaim. In 1971, Richard Locke reviewed Solzhenitsyn's *Stories and Prose Poems*, translated by Michael Glenny, for the *New York Times*. This publication presented the first English translations of many of the works included in the volume. Locke, in his assessment, finds that the poems in the volume "lack intensity and grace," are overly sentimental or very nearly so, and employ symbolism that is "too obvious." Locke concludes that even the best of Solzhenitsyn's stories and poems in this volume "never approach the literary stature of his novels." Edward E. Ericson, Jr., in a 2004 essay for *Dictionary of Literary Biography*, discusses the poems that Solzhenitsyn published in the journal *Grani* in 1964 and which later appeared in English translation in *Stories and Prose Poems*. Ericson praises the "rhythmic structure" of these poems and explains that in general they "move from a single episode or observation to a broad philosophical insight." Additionally, Ericson observes that in these poems, Solzhenitsyn demonstrates such values as "joy in the beauty of nature" and a "recognition of the life force at all levels." In *Russian Literature since the Revolution*, Edward James Brown states that in poems such as "A Storm in the Mountains," Solzhenitsyn explores "the wonder of creation itself." Adrian Wanner, in *Russian Minimalism: From the Prose Poem to the Anti-Story*, asserts that the prose poems in this 1964 cycle "are an attempt to re-spiritualize contemporary secularized reality."

CRITICISM

Catherine Dominic

Dominic is a novelist and a freelance writer and editor. In the following essay, she explores the language and imagery in Solzhenitsyn's "A Storm in the Mountains," demonstrating the way the poet deconstructs traditional forms of expression in order to illustrate the possibilities of emotional and spiritual transformation that the natural world invites.

In terms of critical attention, "A Storm in the Mountains" is typically only referred to, if mentioned directly at all, within the context of the selection of prose poems published in 1964 in the journal *Grani*. It is usually described in the briefest of terms, within the space of a sentence, as reflective of Solzhenitsyn's glorification of nature. While it appears to be a poem concerned with one simple theme, nature's power, "A Storm in the Mountains" nonetheless is imbued with details of imagery and expression that lend a sense of wonder to the poem and furthermore underscore the poet's deeply spiritual sentiment.

WHAT DO I READ NEXT?

- Solzhenitsyn's *One Day in the Life of Ivan Denisovich* is one of his best-known works. Originally published in 1962, the novel is available in a 2005 edition. It is a short book but a powerful look inside the Soviet prison camps in Siberia.

- *The Solzhenitsyn Reader: New and Essential Writings, 1947–2005*, edited by Edward Ericson, Jr., and Daniel J. Mahoney, gathers Solzhenitsyn's significant speeches and essays along with many of his later writings, including numerous short stories and poems. The collection was published in 2006.

- *Eagle or Sun*, by Mexican poet Octavio Paz, is a series of prose poems originally published in 1951 in Spanish and in English in the 1960s. The book explores Mexican life and culture and investigates the possibilities of language and imagery within the prose-poem form. The work is available in a 1976 edition.

- *The Road of Bones*, by Anne Fine, is a young-adult novel concerned with growing up under an oppressive Soviet Socialist regime. The novel was published in 2008.

- *A History of the Soviet Union from the Beginning to the End*, by Peter Kenez, provides a detailed exploration of Soviet politics, economy, and culture. The second edition of the work was published in 2006.

- *Doctor Zhivago* was written by a contemporary of Solzhenitsyn's, Boris Pasternak. As with many of Solzhenitsyn's writings, Soviet publication of the work was suppressed until many years after it had been published in the West. The novel takes place during the early years of the Soviet Union under Stalin. Originally published in 1957 after a manuscript was smuggled out of the Soviet Union, *Doctor Zhivago* is available in a 2010 edition.

> WHILE IT APPEARS TO BE A POEM CONCERNED WITH ONE SIMPLE THEME, NATURE'S POWER, 'A STORM IN THE MOUNTAINS' NONETHELESS IS IMBUED WITH DETAILS OF IMAGERY AND EXPRESSION THAT LEND A SENSE OF WONDER TO THE POEM AND FURTHERMORE UNDERSCORE THE POET'S DEEPLY SPIRITUAL SENTIMENT."

The poem is straightforward in many ways, but it nonetheless possess intricacies that elevate it from the realm of simplicity.

Solzhenitsyn's poem is filled with stark contrasts. Details that seem unreal to the narrator are often used to underscore the wonder and amazement the narrator perceives when these seemingly impossible or otherworldly elements are in fact very real aspects of the natural world. Distortions and oppositions are marveled at and then praised as examples of a truly wondrous reality. One of the poem's most obvious contrasts is that between darkness and light. As is typical of such imagery, darkness is associated in the poem with a sense of the unknown, and with it comes fear and confusion. Light in Solzhenitsyn's poem is associated with revelation and understanding, not uncommon uses for this type of imagery. However, what makes Solzhenitsyn's appropriation of this imagery unique and fascinating is that the light that brings a sense of revelation is generated by a force typically associated with destruction: lightning. Viewing lightning as an enlightening force highlights a theme that builds throughout the poem through the final paragraph. Within this framework of the opposition between dark and light, other details and images are used that display similar inversions of expectations.

Initially, the campers on the mountainside are forced from their tents by the storm. Already, in this first paragraph, the poet does not follow expected narrative paths. As the storm approaches, the narrator and his company leave what appears to be shelter—the tents—in order to seek alternate shelter. Understandably, tents may not provide enough protection from severe wind, rain, and lightning associated with a powerful storm. Yet the reader is not led to the alternate shelter along with the group. The members of the company have fled their tents, but the poet does not make explicit where they have gone or what other, sturdier shelter they have found. The reader is, in a way, tripped twice. He or she is provided with an image of a group of people running from their tents but no knowledge of where they have gone. In the mind of the reader, the people are now scattered on the mountainside. Additionally, the narrator introduces himself as a member of a group by using the pronoun *we*. No explanation is offered as to the identity of the group. The mental picture the reader forms must remain hazy in this regard as well. Solzhenitsyn, through these details and carefully crafted omissions, leaves the reader feeling a sense of disorientation and confusion that mirrors what the narrator and his companions must feel as they stumble sleepily out into the darkness and the storm.

In the second paragraph, the intensity of the darkness is made plain. The blackness of night has blotted out the landscape completely. Yet when the lightning flashes, revealing the details of the surroundings once again to the narrator and his company, reality seems distorted. The narrator describes the pine trees as suddenly seeming as tall as the mountain peaks. Despite the skewed perceptions, however, the narrator is relieved to have the night lit, even in a distorted fashion by the lightning, as the light allows the group to feel as if their feet are once again planted on solid ground. In the darkness, the narrator explains, a sense of chaos reigns. By describing the sense that in the light, the members of the group feel gratefully anchored once again to the earth, the narrator underscores that in the darkness, they feel unmoored, loosed from their own sense of reality.

As the third paragraph opens, Solzhenitsyn continues to employ details that highlight the distortions of the group's perceptions. In the flashes of lightning, the mountains and pine trees seem to leap into their proper positions once again, inspiring a sense of amazement at their terrific size in the members of the narrator's group. When darkness returns, in the absence of lightning, these natural features of the landscape are described as having vanished. Furthermore,

the narrator finds it hard to believe that the trees and mountains even existed. The darkness is so powerful it threatens to obliterate the group's sense of known reality.

Thunder appears in the fourth paragraph of the prose poem, shrouding the sound of the rivers. Lightning is now described in a new way, as the arrows of God showering the mountain peaks, spraying the rocks. The narrator goes on to observe the way the lightning is similar to a living being in the way it splinters across the face of the rock. Again, Solzhenitsyn uses language and imagery that challenge the reader's expectations. Lightning is now compared to a weapon (arrows), but it does not destroy, at least not in this poem. It splits into snaking streams, showering the rocks, but the narrator does not observe or comment on any actual damage done to the landscape. When the lightning is further compared to something living, the language used suggests otherwise. The lightning fractures into shards, according to the narrator's observations, and would seem by this description to be more like something solid and inanimate, like glass, rather than the living thing to which the narrator compares the lightning. Expectations are once again thwarted, reality once again distorted.

In the final paragraph of the prose poem, the narrator focuses intently on the reaction of the members of the group to the storm, and in particular the lightning. The fear the individuals would normally have had of the lightning has been forgotten, and the narrator explains why. He and his companions have realized, at least in this moment, their place in the world of nature. They possess no individual significance but are part of something greater. In the narrator's comparison, the members of the group are like drops of ocean water in the midst of a hurricane, individually insignificant but part of this enormous, powerful surge of energy that is the storm. The narrator goes on to characterize the natural world as one that is being created in this moment the group is experiencing, in the storm. The image of the storm and the lightning, like that of the hurricane, summons the notion of destruction. Yet throughout the poem, nothing is destroyed. The lightning fails to strike and burn, the winds of the storm do no harm. In fact, the narrator regards the event as essentially a process of creation.

Solzhenitsyn turns standard language and imagery inside out in the course of "A Storm in the Mountains." A typically violent and destructive

Mountain stream *(windmoon | Shutterstock.com)*

image—lightning—is appropriated in a new way, used now to emphasize the benign properties most often associated with light. The effect of this technique is to emphasize a sense of spiritual interaction with nature in which the expected, normal, traditional responses are transformed. Having stripped away the traditional, often fearful reactions of man to the powerful forces of nature, Solzhenitsyn emphasizes the shift in perception that has occurred in the narrator and in his companions. The members of the group, having viewed the storm as a vibrant, creative process, shed their fears and are open to responding with a spiritual sense of awe and connection to the natural world.

Source: Catherine Dominic, Critical Essay on "A Storm in the Mountains," in *Poetry for Students*, Gale, Cengage Learning, 2011.

SOURCES

"Aleksander Solzhenitsyn," in *Tudorancea Bulletin: English Edition*, July 18, 2010, http://www.tititudorancea.com/z/ biography_of_aleksandr_solzhenitsyn.htm (accessed October 5, 2010).

Anning, N. J., "Solzhenitsyn," in *Russian Literary Attitudes from Pushkin to Solzhenitsyn*, edited by Richard Freeborn, Macmillan, 1976, pp. 120–40.

Brown, Edward James, "The Surface Channel, I: The Village," in *Russian Literature since the Revolution*, Harvard University Press, 1982, pp. 292–312.

Driscoll, James F., "Sabaoth," in *The Catholic Encyclopedia*, Vol. 13, Robert Appleton, 1912, http://www.newadvent.org/cathen/13286a.htm (accessed October 4, 2010).

Ericson, Edward E., Jr., "Aleksandr Solzhenitsyn," in *Dictionary of Literary Biography*, Vol. 302, *Russian Prose Writers after World War II*, edited by Christine Rydel, Thomson Gale, 2004, pp. 324–55.

Kreis, Steven, "Leonid Brezhnev, 1906–1982," in *The History Guide: Lectures on Twentieth Century Europe*, May 13, 2004, http://www.historyguide.org/europe/ brezhnev.html (accessed October 5, 2010).

Locke, Richard, "Solzhenitsyn's Short Fiction," in *New York Times*, July 16, 1971, http://www.nytimes.com/ books/98/03/01/home/solz-short.html (accessed October 8, 2010).

Moore, Harry T., and Albert Parry, "The Forbidden Ones," in *Twentieth-Century Russian Literature*, Southern Illinois University Press, 1974, pp. 124–46.

"Nikita Khrushchev," in *PBS: Biography*, 1999, http://www.pbs.org/redfiles/bios/all_bio_nikita_khrushchev.htm (accessed October 5, 2010).

"Political Parties and Movements," in *Russia Profile.org: Unwrapping the Mystery inside the Enigma*, http://www.russiaprofile.org/resources/political/index.wbp (accessed October 5, 2010).

Porter, Robert, "*One Day in the Life of Ivan Denisovich*," in *Reference Guide to Russian Literature*, edited by Neil Cornwell and Nicole Christian, Fitzroy Dearborn, 1998, pp. 774–75.

"Russia," in *CIA: World Factbook*, https://www.cia.gov/library/publications/the-world-factbook/geos/rs.html (accessed October 5, 2010).

Solzhenitsyn, Alexander, "A Storm in the Mountains," in *Stories and Prose Poems*, translated by Michael Glenny, Bodley Head, 1971, pp. 238–39.

"Stalin, the Nazis and the West," in *PBS: World War II; Behind Closed Doors*, http://www.pbs.org/behindclosed doors/ (accessed October 5, 2010).

Suny, Ronald Grigor, "From Autocracy to Oligarchy," in *The Structure of Soviet History: Essays and Documents*, Oxford University Press, 2003, pp. 329–30.

Wanner, Adrian, "Epilogue," in *Russian Minimalism: From the Prose Poem to the Anti-Story*, Northwestern University Press, 2003, pp. 148–52.

FURTHER READING

McDowell, Gary L., and F. Daniel Rzicznek, *The Rose Metal Press Field Guide to Prose Poetry: Contemporary Poets in Discussion and Practice*, Rose Metal Press, 2010.

McDowell and Rzicznek's collection features prose poems and explanatory essays about this unique form. The anthology focuses on modern examples of the prose poem genre.

Pipes, Richard, *Communism: A History*, Modern Library, 2001.

Pipes examines Communism and all its variations—Marxism, Leninism, Stalinism—and explores the way these philosophies have been utilized and exploited by various governments.

Rzhevsky, Nicholas, *An Anthology of Russian Literature from Earliest Writings to Modern Fiction: Introduction to a Culture*, M. E. Sharpe, 1996.

Rzhevsky offers a chronological anthology of Russian literature from a variety of authors, from early anonymous writers to well-known authors writing during the Soviet period.

Scammell, Michael, *Solzhenitsyn: A Biography*, W. W. Norton, 1984.

Scammell's highly acclaimed biography of Solzhenitsyn details the author's life and explores the critical and political responses to his many writings.

SUGGESTED SEARCH TERMS

Solzhenitsyn AND Storm in the Mountains

Solzhenitsyn AND prose poetry

Solzhenitsyn AND Russian literature

Solzhenitsyn AND Brezhnev

Solzhenitsyn AND nature poetry

Solzhenitsyn AND imprisonment

Solzhenitsyn AND spirituality

Solzhenitsyn AND exile

Solzhenitsyn AND Nobel Prize

Solzhenitsyn AND Khrushchev

Two Bodies

OCTAVIO PAZ

1943

"Dos cuerpos," translated as "Two Bodies," is a poem by the Mexican political essayist and poet Octavio Paz. The poem was originally published in Paz's 1949 collection *Libertad bajo palabra* (Freedom under Oath, or Freedom through Word). *Libertad bajo palabra* gathers together Paz's poetry from 1933 to 1949 and is divided into six sections, called books. Interestingly, Paz did not divide this collection chronologically. Instead, he divided the poems according to the themes they represented and the styles they used. Therefore, although "Two Bodies" was written in 1943 while Paz was living briefly in the United States, it is included in the book "Condicion de nube" (Condition of Clouds), a section of *Libertad bajo palabra* that deals primarily with Paz's life before he arrived in the United States. Paz extensively revised the collection five times, editing and rearranging the poems in the collection. Though many of these poems underwent drastic changes, "Two Bodies" remained untouched and stayed in "Condition of Clouds" in each revision. Paz wrote "Two Bodies" as an experiment in metaphor early in his career under the influence of the surrealist movement, during which he wanted to emphasize the importance and isolation of each individual person in relation to the surrounding world. "Two Bodies" stands as an example of how the modernist tradition in the arts emerged in Mexico during the twentieth century.

Octavio Paz *(AP Images)*

AUTHOR BIOGRAPHY

Paz was born in Mexico City, Mexico, on March 31, 1914, four years into the Mexican Revolution. His father, Octavio Paz Solórzano, was a journalist and lawyer who was actively involved in politics as an ardent supporter of Mexican revolutionary Emilio Zapata, and he was absent for most of Paz's life. Paz was raised by his mother, his aunt, and his paternal grandfather in the village of Mixcoac, outside Mexico City. As a child, Paz was exposed to a wide variety of literature through his grandfather and gained a solid training in Western classics, as well as rich exposure to Mexican authors through the nineteenth century.

The first half of the twentieth century was a time of drastic social change in Mexico and throughout the world. Paz traveled widely and published consistently. He published his first collection of poetry, *Luna silvestre*, in 1933. In 1935, he went to Yucatan, Mexico, to work at a peasant school. In 1937, he traveled to Spain to participate in the Second International Congress of Anti-Fascist Writers and show solidarity with the ideals of the revolutionaries there. While in Europe, Paz traveled to Paris and met with several leading intellectuals and artists who exposed him to surrealism, an artistic and philosophical movement that focused on psychology as opposed to rationalism. He returned to Mexico in 1938 and helped to found a literary journal called *Taller* (which means "Workshop"), in which he published many of his poems and firmly established his place as a modernist poet.

In 1943, Paz traveled to the University of California, Berkeley, on a Guggenheim Fellowship. It

was then that he began to experiment in the modernist style and wrote "Two Bodies." He entered the Mexican diplomatic corps, and in 1945 he went to Paris, where he wrote *The Labyrinth of Solitude*, a prose study of Mexican identity. In Paris, Paz met André Breton, a French writer who pioneered surrealism. From Paris, Paz traveled to India, Japan, and Switzerland. Finally, in 1954, he returned to Mexico City. He went back to Paris the following year, and in 1962, he returned to India as the Mexican ambassador. Paz stayed in India until 1968, collaborating with young poets there and gaining an appreciation for Eastern philosophy and cultures. He resigned his diplomatic post that year in protest after the Tlatelolco massacre in Mexico during the Olympic Games, which resulted in the deaths of dozens of students and civilian protesters at the hands of the government. During his time in the diplomatic service, Paz wrote and published a vast number of poems and critical essays.

Paz founded another literary magazine, *Plural*, in 1970, the same year he began lecturing at Harvard University as the holder of the Charles Eliot Norton professorship. The Mexican government closed *Plural* in 1975, so Paz founded *Vuelta* (which means "Return"), and he edited it until his death from cancer in 1998.

In addition to the prestigious Guggenheim Fellowship and the professorship at Harvard, Paz was awarded the Jerusalem Prize in 1977, an honorary doctorate from Harvard in 1980, the Neustadt Prize in 1982, and the Nobel Prize for Literature in 1990.

POEM TEXT

Two bodies face to face
are at times two waves
and night is an ocean.

Two bodies face to face
are at times two stones   5
and night a desert.

Two bodies face to face
are at times two roots
laced into night.

Two bodies face to face   10
are at times two knives
and night strikes sparks.

Two bodies face to face
are two stars falling
in an empty sky.   15

POEM SUMMARY

The poem examines the relationship between two beings. The metaphor could be two lovers, but it could also refer to something larger, such as the individual and society or the speaker and the reader. It could very well mean all of these. The poem contrasts the two entities against the larger scheme of existence, or the universe. The poem contains many metaphors comparing the two beings with waves, stones, roots, knives, and stars. It is composed of five stanzas of three lines each. The first line is the same for each stanza; it sets up the metaphor, letting the reader know that the poem concerns two bodies that will be compared to something else. The last line of the first four stanzas includes a reference to night. Stanzas 1, 2, and 4 compare the night to an ocean, a desert, and sparks, respectively. Stanza 5 replaces the reference to night with one to the sky, thus implying yet another, larger metaphor between the sky and the night. Therefore, each stanza contains at least two metaphors, and the stanzas together create a third metaphor when the poem is studied as a whole.

Stanza 1

The first stanza compares the two bodies to waves and the night to the ocean. Waves move together, one propelling the next to crash on the shore and then retreat again to the sea. Individual waves are very small when compared with the vastness of the ocean, yet they are always present and in motion. Further, the speaker says that the two bodies are only waves at times, not all the time. Thus, they sometimes move together and help each other, but sometimes they do not. The night, however, is always an ocean. Therefore, the reader might determine that the two things to which the speaker is referring are always floating somewhere in a vast space, perhaps the universe, but only sometimes are they together in that space.

Stanza 2

The second stanza uses the metaphor of stones for the two bodies and compares the night to a desert. Stones are solid and immovable, and the presence of one stone does not necessarily affect the other stone. The two bodies in this stanza are separate and individual. A desert is another vast place, but unlike the ocean, it is not full of life and hidden depths; it is harsh and barren. The night, then, which the reader has already determined (in the first stanza) might represent the world or the

universe at large, can be dry and without life. By making the form of the stanzas so much alike, the speaker has added another layer of metaphor to the poem. The bodies in this stanza are compared to stones, and the stones are implicitly compared to the waves in the first stanza; similarly, the night is compared to a desert, while the desert is implicitly compared to the ocean from the previous stanza. This suggests that both the two individuals and the world or universe can sometimes be more than one thing. In fact, they can be contradictory. Once again, the speaker says that only at times are the individuals, the two bodies, stones. Only sometimes do they stand alone.

Stanza 3

In the third stanza, the speaker compares the two bodies to roots of a plant or tree. They are growing, and it is through them that the tree is nourished. They supply the plant with life. In this stanza, the speaker does not compare the night directly to anything else. Instead, it is said that the roots are laced together in the night. It could mean that the roots grow together when it is night, but it could also mean that they are, in fact, roots *of* the night. This suggests a metaphor comparing the night and the tree from which the two bodies are both growing and, in turn, helping to grow. Each stanza adds another layer of metaphor. This stanza compares the two bodies to roots, while it also compares the roots to stones and waves. The night is compared to a tree, while it also brings back comparison with the ocean and the desert.

Stanza 4

For the first time, in the fourth stanza, the bodies are compared not to something natural but to something made by humans. The bodies are knives, sharp tools made specifically to cut things. This suggests that the two bodies have the capability to hurt each other and that this ability is something that is forged by humans rather than by nature. The night here is compared, in Spanish, to *relámpago*. This can be translated as either *lightning* or *sparks*. When knives are forged, the heat and pressure used cause sparks. In this case, the speaker is not saying that the night is filled with the sparks from the knives; rather, the night *is* the spark. Thus, the violence and heat from the knives turn the night (which the reader knows is a metaphor for the world or universe) into sparks, into what results from the knives. This suggests that the speaker is trying to show how the interactions of one person with another can affect the world. In this stanza, it is not the bodies that are controlled by the night or that are subjects of the night. They are, in fact, controlling the night. The metaphor here of the bodies being part of something larger and subject to some larger force has been reversed, and the reader understands that not only does the world affect the individual, but individuals also affect the world through conflict with one another.

Stanza 5

The fifth and final stanza breaks the pattern of the first four stanzas a little. The last line does not mention night; instead, it references a sky (something else vast and mysterious) that is empty. The two bodies are stars falling in or through the sky. The reader would think that, therefore, the sky should not be empty; it should at least have the two stars in it. However, the speaker says there is nothing there, indicating that the falling stars have already burned themselves out and disappeared. The stars—bodies—are transitory. The sky will always be there, but the stars are fleeting. The bodies are merely two small points of light that pass through the eternity of the sky, which, by examining the metaphors earlier in the poem,

the reader understands is the world or the universe. Individuals come and go, but the universe will always be here.

THEMES

Alienation

Alienation is the act or process of becoming strange to something or someone, such as society, nature, another person or persons, or oneself. Philosophers and scholars sometimes use this term in relation to the self, that is, self-alienation, in which a person becomes alien to himself or herself through his or her own actions, whether intentional or unintentional. The term has also been applied both to individuals and to society as a whole, single entity. Alienation from God is a theme in literature and poetry that can be seen across the centuries. However, in modernist literature, alienation from God is often portrayed as a result of a loss of traditional societal values. Some philosophers theorize that a period of alienation is necessary to the process of understanding oneself in relation to the "Other"— whether it be a larger concept such as those discussed above or simply another person. The impact of alienation theory reaches beyond literature and the arts to politics and economics, and the idea plays a large part in the tenets of Socialism, which holds that capitalist societies isolate the individual and set people against each other in the search for material wealth. The theory is also greatly influenced by the philosophy of existentialism. "Two Bodies" explores the role of the individual as contrasted to that of society. Alienation from the collective is a prevalent theme in much of Paz's work. He examines the disconnect between the individual and the world.

Existentialism

Existentialism holds that individuals form their own identity and discover personal meanings for existence through interaction with the world. Existentialism discourages obeying convention. Instead, the individual is encouraged to face the notion that a person is responsible for forming his or her own place in the world by confronting harsh truths rather than simply living life according to a preconceived role. Existentialists believe that a person should face things that inspire fear or dread, such as death or the unknown. Humans have choices in life, and the nature of their existence is determined by the choices they make.

TOPICS FOR FURTHER STUDY

- Research the techniques that surrealist poets and artists used to produce their works, then pick two or three of these techniques and adapt them to twenty-first-century technology. For example, create a poem with automatic writing or one that exemplifies echo writing with a classmate using a chat board or a Web log. Experiment with surrealist painting using a computer paint program. Accompany your project with an explanation of the technique you chose to study, how you used it with modern technology, and how your finished product represents the concepts of surrealism.

- Choose three short stories, poems, or novel excerpts written in Mexico in the last twenty years. Research current events in Mexico and the effect they are having on the literature of Mexico today. What parallels can you draw? Is the literature a reflection of or reaction to the social climate of Mexico? What ethnic influences can you pick out from the text? Identify three key events or conflicts in current events and their effects on your selected piece or pieces of literature, and write a one-page explanation of your conclusions for each one. Be sure to provide supporting evidence from the literature.

- Read *Death of Artemio Cruz*, by Carlos Fuentes. How do the events of the novel result in a picture of Mexican identity? What parallels can you draw between the struggles of Artemio Cruz and those of Mexican artists in the twentieth century? Write a paper on what the novel shows you about life and identity in Mexico.

- The results of modernist thinking are all around. Make a list of common examples of modernism in the real world. Be sure to include the fields of architecture, design, advertising, and film, as well as visual and literary arts. Along with two classmates, compile your observations on a Web page, and write a blog that focuses on explaining how each is an example of modernism. Invite discussion and comments.

- Read the young-adult novel *Mexican Whiteboy*, by Matt de la Peña, an examination of the alienation felt by a Mexican American teenager named Danny Lopez. Compare the themes of social alienation felt by Danny with those expressed by Paz. Write your own free-verse poem that expresses the cultural disconnect the protagonist of the novel feels.

Every action represents a choice. As Jean-Paul Sartre said, "I can always choose, but I must know that if I do not choose, that is still a choice." Therefore, the theory focuses on actual experience. Modern existentialists tend to believe that the individual human is completely alone in the world, and thus atheism is a prevalent belief in the philosophy, though some existentialists, such as Søren Kierkegaard, argue in favor of the existence of a God.

Existentialism also had a great impact on politics in the twentieth century. Because bureaucracy and the pursuit of wealth were seen by many existentialists to create preconceived roles for the individual according to social status, the pursuit of a purely individual experience is greatly obstructed in capitalism. Many existentialists favored some form of Socialism instead. Sartre, Simone de Beauvoir, and Albert Camus are among the most influential existential philosophers and writers. Paz's "Two Bodies" illustrates that the universe and the world have an effect on the individual, but also that the individual has profound effects on the universe in return. Each person is left to decide his or her own role in the greater scheme of society.

Cultural Conflict

The mid-twentieth century was a time of great change in the world. Its multiple conflicts—two world wars and many social uprisings around the globe—led to rearrangements of world power, alliances, and political doctrines. On a social level, the

Two bodies face to face (bezikus / Shutterstock.com)

Mexico is in such close proximity to the United States that it holds a special place in the global order. Though the society of the United States is one of the most affluent in history, much of Mexico was and is impoverished. The modern United States is free of domestic conflict and has an established and stable form of democratic government, whereas Mexican politics have seemed on the verge of violence for decades. Therefore, not only do Mexicans have to address the same issues of cultural conflict as the rest of the world because of the rapidly changing era of the twentieth century, but they are also faced with additional cultural conflicts from within. This theme of searching for identity in a changing society and uncertain culture resonates through much of Paz's poetry and many of his essays, including "Two Bodies."

STYLE

Metaphor

Metaphor is a figure of speech and an important technique in poetry and literature. In a metaphor, one thing or idea is compared to another thing or idea, which points out the common characteristics between the two. For example, "a heart of stone" compares the heart to a stone, implying that it is hard and unfeeling. The first thing or idea (what is being referred to) is called the *tenor*, and the phrase or word that is used to refer to it is called the *vehicle*. In the earlier example, "heart" is the tenor, and "stone" is the vehicle. When the word "like" or "as" is included (his heart is *like* a stone), then the convention is called a simile, not a metaphor. Metaphors are implied comparisons; similes are directly stated comparisons. Metaphors engage the reader of the poem by forcing an examination of the common characteristics between the tenor and the vehicle. If a speaker says, "I'm no angel," the reader must think of the things that are typically associated with angels in order to figure out what the speaker is not—good, pure, or kind. Metaphors may involve nouns, verbs ("my head is spinning"), or adjectives ("his empty mind"). "Two Bodies" is composed of multiple layers of metaphor. The key terms—bodies and night—are compared with something different in each stanza. In addition, the stanzas themselves are compared, through their very similar forms, to one another. Finally, the poem as a whole is a metaphor for the use of language and form within poetry itself.

established rules of society rapidly changed to place successful businesspeople and the wealthy above the previous upper class of people born into their station, such as aristocrats. The individual became prized over the collective; that is, people began to realize that they could make their own choices about their individual lives rather than adhering to previous notions of societal norms, and individual accomplishment became the biggest mark of success. For example, organized religion greatly decreased as an influence in many societies.

Mexico suffered an even more intense identity crisis than most of the world. The revolution early in the twentieth century left Mexico with many questions as to what constituted a Mexican identity. Unlike the United States, which early on accepted the idea of a "melting pot," in which people from all over the world could become American, Mexico had never resolved the conflict between Spanish Europeans and indigenous cultures, and the Mexican Revolution threw questions of class and nationality to the forefront of almost everything within the nation. In addition,

Free Verse

Free-verse poetry has no set meter or rhyme scheme. However, this does not necessarily mean that it is without form. Often, the poem contains a pattern in spoken sounds (assonance or consonance), visual form (the way the poem looks on the page), or poetic devices (such as metaphor or simile). In other words, free verse does not mean complete inattention to form, but rather a deliberate decision on the part of the poet to refrain from traditional forms of poetry (such as the sonnet or villanelle). Paz often wrote that poetry must have some form; to deliberately abandon all form is, in fact, to adhere to a convention, the very thing that the surrealists and other experimental writers were trying not to do. Paz believed that freedom of expression lay in the way poets chose to utilize language and form. Though his poems often have no rhyme scheme or meter, they do have form. "Two Bodies," for example, repeats the first line of each stanza and takes advantage of repeated images to keep a certain order within the poem.

Modernism

Modernism is the general name for the experimental trends in the early part of the twentieth century. Its most important feature is that it was a reaction to the reason and realism of nineteenth-century and Enlightenment traditions in literature. Experimentation in form and style are key elements of modernism, which attempted to reconcile literature and the arts with modern times, or modernity. Concepts that writers explored included technology, science, the individual in society, capitalism versus communism, and the changing role of religion. Modernist artists viewed their work as a revolution against established ideals and created new "rules" for literature and poetry, oftentimes resulting in what seemed like no rules at all.

In modernism, the individual is understood to both affect and be affected by culture, society, and the larger world. Paz extensively explored this notion in his essays and poetry, and this examination is one of the key themes of "Two Bodies." The interaction between the individual and something larger—God, humanity, social constructs—results in a change in both. Individualism, therefore, is the focal point of most modernist poetry and literature, along with a deep skepticism regarding any traditional authority structures such as government or religion.

The discoveries by Sigmund Freud in the realm of psychoanalysis contributed greatly to the formation of the modernist movement by giving new ways to view the workings of an individual's mind, especially in regards to concepts such as dream theory and the subconscious. For the first time, people looked more deeply into their personalities, habits, and the effect that their environment had on them. Modernism was also characterized by crossovers between written and visual art. For example, in her poems, Gertrude Stein attempted to transform the cubist ideology of artists such as Pablo Picasso into written words. Conversely, painters such as René Magritte experimented with the application of modernist philosophy into visual art.

Though modernism hit its peak in the first half of the twentieth century, the effect it had on the arts was huge. It changed the way that poets and writers, for example, viewed the purpose of literature and the rules to which it should or should not adhere. Techniques such as free verse and stream of consciousness are still employed today.

Surrealism

Surrealism was a cultural and artistic movement that began in the 1920s and lasted until the mid- to late 1940s. The surrealist philosophy held that the rational thought that led into the disastrous period of World War I should be replaced by a focus on the subconscious. It was greatly influenced by Freud's studies on dreams and the subconscious. In literature, a practice called "automatic writing" became popular. This technique called for the elimination of conscious thought between the creation of the idea and the words on the page. Juxtaposition (that is, placing things next to each other) of ideas not typically associated with one another was another key aspect of surrealism. Surrealists believed that this type of thinking would bring about social change and the success of middle-class and working-class revolutions. Emphasis was also placed on the subtext of images rather than definitive and formal language. Though surrealism was initially a literary movement, it quickly grew to include a thriving visual arts movement as well. Paz was greatly influenced by surrealist philosophy, though he denounced several of its tenets, including the assertion that poetry should be completely without form. Surrealist overtones can be seen in the way Paz's poetry delves into the hidden parts of an individual and the human experience within the universe.

COMPARE
&
CONTRAST

- **1940s:** World War II advances modern warfare to a global level and sets the stage for the cold war between the United States and the Soviet Union, the two world superpowers.

  Today: Long-standing conflicts between the countries in the Middle East escalate, causing tensions between the region and Western nations. Once more, the United States emerges as a global leader in conflict resolution.

- **1940s:** Mexican immigrants and Mexican Americans are regarded as socially inferior minorities and subject to much of the same discrimination and segregation that African Americans endured before the civil rights movement.

  Today: Mexican Americans are the fastest-growing population in the United States, and Mexican immigration is one of the most controversial topics debated in politics.

- **1940s:** Intellectuals and politicians engage in heated debates about economic systems such as capitalism and Socialism, and some countries in Europe become totalitarian states, in which the central government exercises complete control over all aspects of the lives of its citizenry.

  Today: The American model of democracy is practiced by over 120 of the world's governments and in all of Europe. Capitalism is still regarded as the most effective economic system and is practiced on every continent.

HISTORICAL CONTEXT

The Mexican Revolution

Mexico's president Porfirio Díaz had been in power for over thirty years by the time elections were scheduled to be held on November 20, 1910. His rule was characterized by overwhelming favors granted to rich landowners and exploitation of the peasants who worked the land. Díaz had his chief challenger, Francisco Madero, imprisoned, and Díaz declared himself the winner of the elections. This was the breaking point for a Mexico already in social turmoil, and it served as the start to a ten-year revolution.

Madero and fellow revolutionaries, among them Emiliano Zapata, successfully drove Díaz to exile in 1911. However, Madero was less concerned with bringing about social and economic reform than he had claimed to be. In November 1911, Zapata issued the Plan de Ayala, which put the focus of the revolution back on agrarian reform and denounced Madero. Madero's own general, Victoriano Huerta, imprisoned Madero, executed him, and seized the presidency.

The revolutionaries denounced Huerta and overthrew him in July 1914, installing Venustiano Carranza as president. Soon, differences between Carranza and the other rebels emerged again, and each leader developed his own faction and army. Violent and pronounced infighting continued between factions until about 1920.

The chaos that resulted from the Mexican Revolution left most of the country distrustful of government and somewhat lost within changing societal roles. "Two Bodies," along with much of Paz's work, examines the role of the individual within the upheaval of modern society. It explores the human condition as contrasted against the backdrop of violence and confusing social roles of not only Mexico but the world as a whole.

The Spanish Civil War

In 1931, the Spanish monarchy was replaced by a democratically elected government dedicated to major social reforms. The new government was largely middle class and promoted policies that attacked the traditional privileged structure of Spanish society. This attack on established authority (such as the Catholic Church, the military, and

Roots laced into night *(andreiuc68 | Shutterstock.com)*

the aristocracy) alienated these formerly privileged groups, and an inability to produce social change resulted in the loss of support from the reformists.

In 1936, the opponents of the government formed the Nationalists and began an armed conflict against the supporters of reform, the Republicans. The Nationalist army was commanded by General Francisco Franco and aided by Adolf Hitler of Germany and the fascist Nazi party, which supplied Franco with military equipment and supplies. Republican sympathizers from France, England, and the United States journeyed to Spain to join the Republican army, though none of these countries officially recognized the rebels. Desperate for supplies, the Republicans sought and gained the aid of the Soviet Union, which created high tensions between the Communist and non-Communist members of the Republican army. Franco defeated the Republicans decisively by January 1939, and his new government was officially recognized internationally soon after.

Paz sympathized with the revolutionaries and was an ardent advocate for their cause. He was devastated and disillusioned when they failed

to prevail. The failure of the rest of the world to recognize the change the revolutionaries were trying to effect and to help them make the changes that would have kept the tyrannical Franco from rule caused a loss of faith in the ability of nations as a whole to bring about social change. Instead, Paz turned to the idea that the only real change that was possible was individual change. Only by changing oneself could one hope to have an impact on the world. "Two Bodies" contrasts the individual against the world and universe at large, emphasizing the role that the individual plays within the greater picture.

CRITICAL OVERVIEW

"Two Bodies" was originally published under the Spanish title "Dos cuerpos" in Paz's 1949 collection *Libertad bajo palabra* (Freedom under Oath, or Freedom through Word). Paz's position was that the freedom to use language consciously is part of the point of poetry and the deliberate arrangement of words themselves. This differs from the automatic writing of the surrealists, who claimed that there should be no conscious censorship of the words between the idea and the poem. The title informs the reader that Paz is attempting to fuse the concept of liberty with that of words. He wants to explore freedom of language while still remaining engaged in the form and structure of the poem.

"Two Bodies" is in the section of *Libertad bajo palabra* called "Condicion de nube" (Condition of Clouds). This section is composed of poems written after Paz left Mexico for the United States on his Guggenheim Fellowship. In *Understanding Octavio Paz*, Jose Quiroga states: "*Condicion de nube* speaks of change arrested into form." The era of Paz's poetry beginning with his visit to the United States showed a deliberate shift away from the overtly lyrical and idealistic poetry of the earlier, self-isolated and political Paz. The work Paz produced in this period focuses on the individual rather than society and explores the notion that poetry is a means to use language to explore the self. Dorothy Clotelle Clarke, in her review of *Libertad bajo palabra: Obra poética (1935–1958)* in *Books Abroad* says that Paz "gropes through his immediate surroundings for the meaning of his own existence."

Some critics believed Paz to be "pessimistically agnostic" and overly negative, as Donato Internoscia states in his review of *Libertad bajo palabra* in *Books Abroad*. However, even Internoscia finds Paz's poetry to be "rich in unexpected metaphors and poetic overtones." It is the combination of the search for identity and the exploration of language that makes the collection such a success. Manuel Durán writes in his review of *Poemas (1935–1975)* in *World Literature Today* that Paz's poetry.

> is a combination of luminous imagery, condensed sentence structure that gives strength and agility to the text, and existential quests trying to overcome loneliness and anguish by a thrust which is purely human and yet as ambitious as that of the mystics of the past.

Most critics agree that *Libertad bajo palabra* must be studied as a constantly changing work and that the extensive revisions that each subsequent edition underwent must be factored into a study of the work as a whole. As Enrico Mario Santi says in his introduction to the fifth edition of the collection, Paz's revision and changing of the work as a whole forms a metaphor for the relationship of the poet and poetry to life as a whole. Paz's main theme, therefore, of poetry representing change within the individual, is expressed through his revision process.

CRITICISM

Kristy Blackmon

Blackmon holds a bachelor's degree in English from Southern Methodist University. In the following essay, she considers Paz's use of metaphor to explore existential themes in his poetry.

In his lecture upon winning the Nobel Prize for Literature in 1990, Octavio Paz spoke of the alienation the individual feels in modern society, saying that it.

> is born at the very moment of our birth: as we are wrenched from the Whole we fall into an alien land. . . . All our ventures and exploits, all our acts and dreams, are bridges designed to overcome the separation and reunite us with the world and our fellow-beings.

For Paz, poetry was a nearly ideal vehicle for this process. He used words as tools to examine the human condition and to try and form connections with the world around him. His poetry is existential; it examines the nature of human existence. Paz's poetry challenges the reader to find individual meanings within the words and within the world.

"Two Bodies" is a poem in Paz's collection *Libertad bajo palabra* (Freedom through Word) in the book section titled "Bajo tu clara sombra" (Under Your Clear Shadow). This book is further divided into six sections, the last of which, "Condicion de nube" (Condition of Clouds), contains "Two Bodies." The collection has never been published in English, so it is difficult for the English-speaking reader to comprehend the long and detailed process of the revision and publication of the subsequent editions of this book. It was published in five editions from 1949 to 1988. In each edition, Paz reordered the poems; he revised individual poems, adding or subtracting text where he chose, and included or excluded different texts from each revision. In addition, the poems themselves are not arranged in chronological order. According to Jose Quiroga in *Understanding Octavio Paz*, Paz instead ordered the poems according to "affinities of theme, color, rhythm, beat or atmosphere," as stated in an advertisement for the 1960 collection. A study of each edition, therefore, must take into account those that came before it in order for one to fully grasp the evolution of Paz as a poet.

For this reason, it is difficult to examine a single poem out of *Libertad bajo palabra* in light only of the time in which it was written, though

WHAT DO I READ NEXT?

- *Multicultural Writers since 1945: An A–Z Guide*, edited by Alba Amoia and Bettina L. Knapp in 2004, contains biographical and critical short essays on 102 different authors. It examines postcolonial multicultural literature and how literature developed around the world.

- André Breton's 1924 *Manifestoes of Surrealism* is an important work on surrealism, its ideals, its goals, and its definitions. It is considered to be the ultimate work on the surrealist movement and the basis for all future criticism on the period. It is available in a 1969 edition.

- *The Mangy Parrot*, by José Joaquin Fernández de Lizardi, is often reported to be the first Latin American novel. Published in 1830, the novel is hailed for its criticism of the ruling Spanish class and the conflict between the Europeans and the indigenous people in postcolonial Mexico. Combining Lizardi's journalistic background with an innate understanding of Mexican culture, the novel is an acclaimed account of a pivotal moment in Mexican history. An abridged edition was published in 2005.

- More biography than criticism, Nick Caistor's 2007 volume *Octavio Paz* examines the life of Paz. Caistor emphasizes Paz's personal life over a study of his poetics.

- Rodolpho "Corky" Gonzales has collected many of his speeches and writings advocating the rights of the Chicano people in his 2001 *Message to Aztlan: Selected Writings.* Included is his famous poem "Yo soy Joaquin," which traces the history of Mexico from the Aztecs to the present day.

- *The Collected Poems of Octavio Paz: 1957–1987* collects work written after the author's move to India and shows the influence that the East had on his philosophy and work. It continues through his return to Mexico and subsequent travels, reflecting three decades of change in the world of a cosmopolitan Mexican poet. A bilingual edition was published in 1991.

- Paz's early career is chronicled and collected in *Libertad bajo palabra* in the last revised edition of 1988. It contains poems from the early 1930s to the mid-1950s, from Paz's years in Mexico, through his involvement in the Spanish Civil War, and through his travels to the United States and Paris. Revised extensively with each edition, this volume is an ever-changing work, and each publication serves as further testament to Paz's continued development as a poet and social critic.

- Teresa Pijoan's *La cuentista* (1994) is a bilingual collection of Hispanic stories for young adults preserved by oral tradition, called *cuentos*. The stories examine how generations pass down history and folklore while keeping traditional values alive in their culture.

---

this essay focuses mainly on Paz's literary development and influences in the mid-1940s, when "Two Bodies" was created. If the critic looks at the evolution and refinement of Paz's poetic philosophy throughout his career, a much more comprehensive understanding can be gained. Paz wrote the poem during his two-year stay in the United States, when he traveled around the country on a Guggenheim Fellowship. This was an important step in his artistic growth. Paz grew up in a Mexico shadowed by a long and devastating revolution, and his early career was greatly influenced by the ideals held by the rebels in the Spanish Civil War. However, by the time he embarked on his travels in the United States, he was disillusioned with politics. The Spanish revolutionaries had been crushed, his own country was still corrupted by officials and the rich, and ideologies such as socialism and communism, which had once seemed so promising, were proving to be less than ideal in reality. In 1943, when Paz wrote "Two Bodies," World War II was in full swing. Paz was no longer

METAPHOR CAUSES TENSION BETWEEN
WHAT THE READER KNOWS AND WHAT THE POET
IS PRESENTING AS KNOWLEDGE."

a starry-eyed revolutionary who believed that it was possible for society to be changed through revolt. He was a poet in confusing times trying to find a way to express his alienation through language, that is, to find individual freedom through words. Jason Wilson, in his biography of Paz, quotes him as saying in his literary journal *Taller*, "Poetry is innocence, but the poet is not innocent.... With poetry the poet recovers his innocence." Paz believed that poetry was the purest way to examine the self and that it was only through an understanding of self that any real change could take place or any peace could be had. Revolution, then, was not to be effected by means of war. True revolution had to happen first within the individual, and Paz believed that poetry should be used to that end.

The first half of the twentieth century is generally held to be the modernist period. Modernists rejected the prevailing views of nineteenth-century Enlightenment philosophy. The world had changed drastically and quickly. The first part of the twentieth century saw the absolute horror of modern warfare in World War I and bloody revolutions around the globe, as well as a worldwide economic depression. At the same time, technology, urbanization and capitalism were replacing traditional roles of religion and established social structures as ways by which people identified themselves. Fewer people attended church, more lived in the impersonal cities, and there came a sense of not knowing one's place in the order of things. Traditional, restrictive forms were abandoned in many areas of the arts, including poetry. Many avant-garde movements—artistic movements that experimented with new forms and techniques—arose during the modernist period. One such movement was surrealism. Though Paz never completely adopted surrealist theories, he was greatly influenced by surrealist philosophy. According to the surrealists, individuals should try to reach beyond the conventional, "real" world around them. They should explore their subconscious minds in the tradition

of Sigmund Freud's psychoanalysis in order to discover their place within the world and their relationship to society at large. "Man is going nowhere if it is not to find himself," Paz wrote in *Mexico en la cultura* in 1960 (quoted by Jason Wilson). "The great conquest," he continued, "is not of outer space but of inner."

Paz was inspired to believe that a change in the individual was the first, necessary step to changing the world. The individual must recognize even the most hidden parts of himself in order to truly understand life. Much of Paz's poetry is devoted to this theme: the discovery of what philosophers often call the "Other." The Other is, in its simplest definition, what the first is not. All human characteristics can be defined by their Others: man is man only because he is not woman (man's Other); an individual is not an entire society; a Mexican is not a Canadian. It is the dynamic between the two things, the difference between them and the way they interact, that causes conflict. Paz used poetry to try and resolve inner conflict by examining aspects of the Other in life. He believed that only after we have addressed the inner conflict can we possibly be prepared to honestly and effectively address conflict on a bigger stage. This is to say not that this conflict must be or can be resolved, only that it be studied and confronted. As Quiroga writes in *Understanding Octavio Paz*, "The exchange between self and other becomes an eternal dialectical interplay." (A dialectic is an exchange or formal argument in which two opposing perspectives, thesis and antithesis, interact and produce a synthesis that transcends the two.) Such a conversation should never be terminated.

The purpose of poetry in this process of examination is to hold up a mirror of sorts to both the reader and the poet, providing some distance from which they can study themselves. Thus, "Two Bodies" explores several dualities at one time: the individual and the universe; man and woman; reader and speaker; and even the poet and the speaker, since Paz is using the vehicle of his poem to explore all of these conflicts within himself. Paz's theme, then, is a conversation, or dialectic, between a self and its Other that hopefully results in some sort of change in the self and then the world. In *From Art to Politics: Octavio Paz and the Pursuit of Freedom*, Yvon Grenier writes that Paz's poetry is "a dialectical process through which the world is constantly transformed by actions deriving from the belief that the world is 'made,' and can always be criticized and improved." Since Paz used poetry to change himself, his readers, and his environment positively, poetry itself became a means of revolution to him. This concept is the core of what many understand as modernity or modernism.

However, Paz did not subscribe fully to surrealist thought. He criticized the surrealists' dogged belief in freedom from form. By refusing to engage in any sort of formal way of arranging words, Paz believed, poets actually restrict themselves to writing *only* without form. Freedom of language should mean the freedom to write within form as well as out of it, as Quiroga explains. Literary conventions are useful things for the poet. In "Two Bodies," the convention Paz utilizes most extensively is metaphor. Metaphor is one of the most prevalent figures of speech. It compares one idea or thing to another in order to draw connections between the two and create new ideas. The poem is a series of metaphors that build upon one another with each stanza. The five stanzas compare the two bodies to waves, stones, roots, knives, and stars. In addition, stanzas 1, 2, and 4 contain metaphors for night: ocean, desert, and sparks. Stanza 3 references night but does not make an explicit comparison to something else. Stanza 5 does not mention night at all but instead speaks of the sky. The uniformity of all five stanzas invites comparison between them. Thus, the waves in stanza 1 (the first metaphor for the two beings) are compared to the stones in stanza 2 (the second metaphor for the two beings). Each stanza adds another layer to the larger metaphor of the poem: that two bodies are both everything and nothing in the vastness of the universe. Who or what the two bodies are is never explicitly stated. Instead, the reader must develop an individual opinion. Paz deliberately leaves the meaning unclear. Paz's use of metaphor forces the reader to take the language apart and interpret it. It is only through this process that the reader can understand the poem and, through it, the reader's own relationship to Paz: freedom through words.

In a sense, this thought process could be characterized as surrealism, even if the form of the poem goes against surrealist ideas. The critic Rachel Phillips writes in *The Poetic Modes of Octavio Paz* that from metaphor, something new arises. The two ideas or things being compared are no longer only what the language specifically defines them as, but they also become something else by virtue of the comparison. The reader develops new connections between concepts and, through

Two rocks in the desert (*Dudarev Mikhail / Shutterstock.com*)

imagery, new ideas about perception. Metaphor causes tension between what the reader knows and what the poet is presenting as knowledge. The reader knows that the night, for example, is not literally a desert. However, because Paz placed the two concepts—night and desert—next to each other, the reader is forced to develop another, new idea: that of the night/ desert, that is, something that has the characteristics of both. In this way, metaphor accomplishes exactly what the surrealists wanted: it transforms reality. "Poetry," Paz wrote in *Taller*, "the best poetry, is a conduct: it expresses itself in acts. It is an image come to life."

Source: Kristy Blackmon, Critical Essay on "Two Bodies," in *Poetry for Students*, Gale, Cengage Learning, 2011.

Edward Hirsch

In the following essay, Hirsch offers an overview of theme and use of language in Paz's poetry.

Octavio Paz practiced poetry like a secret religion. He dwelt in its mysteries, he invoked its sacraments, he read its entrails, he inscribed its revelations. Writing was for him a primordial act, and he stared down at the blank page like an abyss until it sent him reeling over the brink of language. The poems he brought back are filled with ancient wonder and strangeness, hermetic

HERE IS A POETRY THAT SEEKS TO RETURN
US—TO RESTORE US—TO THE TOTALITY OF BEING.
IT IS A LIVING POETRY THAT LEAPS OVER TIME
AND DELIVERS INSCRIPTIONS OF TIMELESSNESS,
TIME WITHOUT LIMIT OR MEASURE, THE
EMPTINESS AND PLENITUDE OF A MOMENT
'FOREVER ARRIVING.'"

wisdom, a dizzying sense of the sacred. They are
magically—sometimes violently—uprooted from
silence. They are drawn from a deep well. Here is
his three-line poem "Escritura" ("Writing"): "Yo
dibujo estas letras / como el día dibuja sus imáge-
nes / y sopla sobre ellas y no vuelve":

> I draw these letters
> as the day draws its images
> and blows over them
> and does not
> return

Paz started writing poems as a teenager and
never let up until the end of his life. Lyric poetry
was for him a core activity, at the root of being,
and for nearly seventy years he was driven by
invisible demons to try to connect to himself and
to others through the sensuality—the rhythmic
fervor—of words. Inspiration was for him not a
static entity, but a forward thrust, an aspiration,
the act of "going beyond ourselves to the encoun-
ter of ourselves." Paz wrote poetry with a sharp
awareness of being oneself and, simultaneously,
someone or something else. He called this "the
other voice." He experienced the merging of voices
as a submersion, a type of flooding. "We still keep
alive the sensation of some minutes so full they
were time overflowing, a high tide that broke the
dikes of temporal succession," he writes in *The
Bow and the Lyre*, a sustained defense of poetry
Shelley himself might have cherished. "For the
poem is a means of access to pure time, an immer-
sion in the original waters of existence." He also
defined the poetic experience as "an opening up of
the wellsprings of being. An instant and never. An
instant and forever."

Paz was—and in his work he remains—a
seeker, and the quest for a moment to abolish linear

or successive time is one of the driving forces of his
aesthetic, a defining feature of his pilgrimage. Poetry
is a wayward siren song calling him to a perpetual
present, to an erotic consecration of instants, and to
a superabundance of time and being. "Poetry is in
love with the instant and seeks to relive it in the
poem, thus separating it from sequential time and
turning it into a fixed present," he says in his Nobel
lecture, "In Search of the Present."

The fixed present, the endless instant, the
eternal moment—the experience is for Paz some-
thing to be attained, like reality, like being itself.
"Door of being, dawn and wake me," he prays
near the conclusion of his circular masterpiece
"Sunstone":

> allow me to see the face of this day,
> allow me to see the face of this night,
> all communicates, all is transformed,
> arch of blood, bridge of the pulse,
> take me to the other side of this night,
> where I am you, we are us,
> the kingdom where pronouns are intertwined,
> door of being: open your being
> and wake, learn to be . . .

If you can get to the present, there are presen-
ces, Paz suggests, and he trusts poetry's capacity to
deliver those presences through images incarnated
in words, through words flowing in rhythm. "The
instant dissolves in the succession of other nameless
instants. In order to *save it* we must *convert it* into a
rhythm," he writes in *Alternating Current*, where he
also defines rhythm as "the reincarnation of the
instant." Rhythm serves the poet as a means of
access—a reliable guide—to originary or pure time.

Paz needed lyric poetry as a primary mode of
crossing, of rendering the self diaphanous, of
becoming "a wind that stops / turns on itself and
is gone" ("The Face and the Wind"). The words
themselves become a way of seeking others that
also links him back to the spaces opening up
inside himself. "Between now and now, / between
I am and you are, / the word *bridge*," he declares
in his short poem "The Bridge":

> Entering it
> you enter yourself:
> the world connects
> and closes like a ring.

Language becomes a form of practical magic
as the word becomes a bridge, a juncture, a span
of connection. "Everything is a door / everything a
bridge," he proclaims in "Sleepless Night." Words
are transfiguring and have a threshold power.
They are portals to the other side. "Words are
bridges," he writes in a refrain that reverberates

through his poetic cantata, "Letter of Testimony." They are a form of a linkage, a way of reaching out, reaching across, that is also a means of reaching in:

> Let yourself be carried by these words
> toward yourself.
> ("Letter of Testimony")

The words become the only way for him of attaining himself, attaining a truer identity than social identity—a shadowy, psychic truth, a mode of being. "I'm not finished with myself yet," he declares in his prose poem "The Besieged." "I am the shadow my words cast," he concludes in "A Draft of Shadows." It's as if he doesn't have that real self, that hidden or shadow identity without the word, the syllable, the poetic act. The word *bridge*, the wordbridge, becomes the site of a poetic crossing into true being. As he puts it in "Pillars":

> Between the end and the beginning
> a moment without time,
> a delicate arch of blood,
> a bridge over the void.

I'm struck by how many of Paz's poems seem to unfold and take place in liminal spaces, in pauses and intervals, odd crossings, interrupted movements. He is poetically empowered not just by bridging, but also by moments when bridges go up, by disconnection. He finds a poetic space opening up in gaps and ruptures ("Poetry is the crack / the space / between one word and another," he announces in "Letter to León Felipe"), in the transitional realm of the betwixt and the between. Think of the slippage in his well-known poem dedicated to the linguist Roman Jakobson, "Between What I See and What I Say . . .":

> Between what I see and what I say,
> between what I say and what I keep silent,
> between what I keep silent and what I dream,
> between what I dream and what I forget:
> poetry.

Paz takes up the essential ambiguity—the elusive clarity—of such marginal or liminal moments in his poem "Interval":

> Instantaneous architectures
> hanging over a pause,
> apparitions neither named
> nor thought, wind-forms,
> insubstantial as time,
> and, like time, dissolved.
> Made of time, they are not time;
> they are the cleft, the interstice,
> the brief vertigo of *between*
> where the diaphanous flower opens:

> high on its stalk of a reflection
> it vanishes as it turns.
> Never touched, the clarities
> seen with eyes closed:
> the transparent birth
> and the crystalline fall
> in the instant of this instant
> that forever is still here.
> Outside the window, the desolate
> rooftops and the hurrying clouds.
> The day goes out, the city
> lights up, remote and near.
> Weightless hour. I breathe
> the moment, empty and eternal.

Paz is trying to nail down the cleft and interstice, the fissure in temporal process, the brilliant weightlessness of what Wordsworth calls "those fleeting moods / Of shadowy exultation."

It seems crucial to Paz to keep affirming that the real self is achieved in such intervals, luminous moments, fluid states. These states are utterly essential: they are perceptions of reality, modes of transparency. Moreover, it's as if we all exist most fully in these spacious intervals, these widening gaps and eternal pauses, which are perceived as a true condition of the world itself. What seems like a struggle attained in bridging over the self in some lyrics becomes a canny reconnaissance about the world in others. Such a perception seems to inhere in the poem "Between Going and Staying":

> Between going and staying the day wavers,
> in love with its own transparency.
> The circular afternoon is now a bay
> where the world in stillness rocks.
> All is visible and all elusive,
> all is near and can't be touched.
> Paper, book, pencil, glass,
> rest in the shade of their names.
> Time throbbing in my temples repeats
> the same unchanging syllable of blood.
> The light turns the indifferent wall
> into a ghostly theater of reflections.
> I find myself in the middle of an eye,
> watching myself in its blank stare.
> The moment scatters. Motionless,
> I stay and go: I am a pause.

The lyric exploration is for Paz always epiphanic, always precarious. Such key or luminous moments (it is "Within a Moment: A Pulsation of the Artery," Blake writes, "When the Poets Work is Done") are by definition sudden, unexpected, revelatory, unconscious. They are dangerous breakthrough experiences. Such "Moments of Being" (the phrase is Virginia Woolf's) are also transitory and difficult to pin down. They usurp the social realm and create their own sense of eternity. They also create ruptures in ordinary experience, pockets of emptiness, holes in time. They defy time-bound narratives. Think, for example, of the playful, paradoxical, quasi-philosophical way that Paz traces the struggle between temporal process and the atemporal instant in "Into the Matter":

> it's not time now
> now it's now
> now it's time to get rid of time
> now it's not time
> it's time and not now
> time eats the now

Paz structures and arranges his poems in such a way—in a non-narrative manner—to create disjunctions that deliver how epiphanies derange and rupture chronological time. I'm thinking of the spatial arrangements in his poems, the length of his lines and minimal use of punctuation, the associative drift of his surrealist attention, the sonorousness of his Spanish, his trust in circularities ("Sunstone") and white spaces ("Blanco"), in presences that defy narrative closure. They are structured for immediacy, to approach and hold a moment. And they try to create a space in which "the present is motionless" ("Wind from All Compass Points"). Like Joseph Cornell boxes, they become "monuments to every moment" and "cages for infinity" ("Objects and Apparitions").

Paz was a restless innovator, and he was continually seeking forms that would create a house for being, consecrating a stillness. That stillness was something he desperately sought, something he spiritually needed, and as a result he was willing, even eager, to cross thresholds and risk an annihilation he could embody in poems. At times he seems cut off from the moment itself, lost in a dire, chaotic, threatening form of inner exile. His lyric access produces a kind of terror. I suspect that's why so many of his poems are filled with shadowy tunnels and traps, elemental passageways, vertiginous heights. They move through endless "corridors terraces stairways" ("A Wind from All Compass Points"). "I crossed through arches and over bridges," he writes at a key moment in "Coming and Going": "I was alive, in search of life." But the restless search for life also becomes, paradoxically, a search for death. "The sun of the high plains eats my remains," he concludes: "I was alive and went in search of death." Life and death are held together in a single weightless moment beyond time.

Paz's poems are filled with moments of bewildering quest, with a lost searching. He could at times "engrave vertigo" ("Tomb"). He vacillates between isolation and connection, solitude and communion, doubt and rapture. He had an uncanny feeling for the inner spaces that keep opening up in poetry and his poems can induce a kind of mental slippage and dizziness, a sense of travelling down interminable corridors. "I follow my raving, rooms, streets, / I grope my way through corridors of time, / I climb and descend its stairs, I touch / its walls and do not move," he writes in "Sunstone":

> I search without finding, I write alone,
> there's no one here, and the day falls,
> the year falls, I fall with the moment,
> I fall to the depths, invisible path
> over mirrors repeating my shattered image,
> I walk through the days, the trampled moments,
> I walk through all the thoughts of my shadow,
> I walk through my shadow in search of a moment.

What made Paz such a deep initiate of connection was the psychic truth that so much of his poetry was elaborated out of a radical sense of human estrangement and exile, a feeling of unreality. He considered the experience of being born "a wound that never heals"—it is "a fall into an alien land"—and he sought through poetry to reunite with others, a way back toward the maternal Other. "I am living / at the center / of a wound still fresh," he writes in "Dawn." Always he was seeking to heal a human cleft, an irreparable sense of division, a fissure in being. He universalized the experience ("The consciousness of being separate is a constant feature of our spiritual history," he said), but it was a generalization experienced on his pulse, in his own body, which is why it motivated, both consciously and unconsciously, so much of his poetic production.

The same lyric practice that gives us moments of annihilation also gives us moments of ecstatic union, fusion with the glorious Other. They salvage and deliver back to us the enormous moment when we glimpse "the unity that we lost" and recall "the forgotten astonishment of being alive" ("Sunstone"). Paz had a skeptical intelligence, but he was never really a cerebral poet, as has often been suggested. Rather, his poems are driven by a sometimes anguished, sometimes joyous eroticism. Most of his poems seem shadowed by the obscure absence or presence of the beloved. When the beloved is absent from the poem he feels acutely cut off from nature and from himself, delivered back to his own estranging desires, and to the linear flow of time. But when the beloved visits the poem he feels the overflowing circularity of time, the dance of being, the affirmation of an eternal moment. Poetry becomes a means of attainment, the reconciliation of opposites, a way of participating in an abundant universe. It becomes a form of creative love that moves beyond the duality of subject and object, annulling the temporal world, offering up the mysteries of carnation. Here the moment widens into eternity:

> all is transformed, all is sacred,
> every room is the center of the world
> it's still the first night, and the first day,
> the world is born when two people kiss,

And:

> the two took off their clothes and kissed
> because two bodies, naked and entwined,
> leap over time, they are invulnerable,
> nothing can touch them, they return to the
> source,
> there is no you, no I, no tomorrow,
> no yesterday, no names, the truth of two
> in a single body, a single soul,
> oh total being . . .
> ("Sunstone")

"Being is eroticism," Paz affirms. In his splendid book on love and eroticism, *The Double Flame*, he explicitly links the erotic act and the poetic act through the agency of imagination. "Imagination turns sex into ceremony and rite, language into rhythm and metaphor," he writes. "The poetic image is an embrace of opposite realities, and rhyme a copulation of sounds; poetry eroticizes language and the world, because the operation is erotic to begin with." I am moved by Paz's suggestion that love, like poetry, "is a victory over time, a glimpse of the other side, of the there that is here, where nothing changes and everything that is, truly is."

Paz's poetry of attainment fulfills the Sufi or mystical maxim, "The Beloved and I are One." He defines—he defends—the creative moment when two people merge and thereby protect their share of the eternal, our ration of paradise.

> To
> love:
> to open the forbidden door,
> the passageway
> that takes us to the other side of time.
> The moment:
> the opposite of death,
> our fragile eternity.
> ("Letter of Testimony")

"The poet endeavors to make the world sacred," Octavio Paz declared (*The Siren and the Seashell*), and in his restless search for the present, the contemporaneous, he never lost sight of poetry's irrational power and sacred mystery, its archaic roots, its spiritual audacity. "Poetry is knowledge, salvation, power, abandonment," he declares at the outset of *The Bow and the Lyre*. He treated lyric poetry as a revolutionary emotional activity, a spiritual exercise, a means of interior liberation, a quest for transfiguration. His poems inscribe a quest and an attainment as they hold together what he calls "life and death in a single instant of incandescence." Here is a poetry that seeks to return us— to restore us—to the totality of being. It is a living poetry that leaps over time and delivers inscriptions of timelessness, time without limit or measure, the emptiness and plenitude of a moment "forever arriving."

Source: Edward Hirsch, "Octavio Paz: In Search of a Moment," in *American Poetry Review*, Vol. 29, No. 2, March/April 2000, pp. 49–51.

John Zubizarreta

In the following excerpt, Zubizarreta explores thematic and aesthetic similarities among Paz and poets Wallace Stevens and Rubén Darío.

. . . The self-conscious use of metaphor as a function of language that helps the poet chisel away at an experience in order to arrive at its clear meaning is a quality that pervades Stevens's poetry as well as the modern Latin American poets'. Darío's "Caracol," 'The Seashell,' for example, is similar to Stevens's "Anecdote of the Jar" in that both poems focus on a single object that becomes the vehicle for a statement about the function of metaphor in poetry. "Caracol" begins with the declarative statement, "En la playa he encontrado un caracol de oro / macizo y recamado de las perlas más finas"; 'I found a golden seashell on the beach. / It is massive, and embroidered with the finest pearls' (*Cantos* 130; *Selected* 86). Stevens's poem begins, "I placed a jar in Tennessee, / And round it was, upon a hill" (*Palm* 46). Quickly, however, both poems move to a level of metaphor that illustrates how the figurative use of language defines and orders our perceptions and conceptions of the world. In Darío, the shell recalls the sacred yet sensual beauty of the mythical Europa upon her heavenly bull: "Europa le ha tocado con sus manos divinas / cuando cruzó las ondas sobre el celeste toro"; 'Europa touched it with her sacred hands / as she rode the waves astride the celestial bull.' Like Jason's dream and the Argonauts' quest, the myth represents man's imaginative response to the inscrutable and seductive beauty of the sea. The poet is carried through various metaphoric experiences of the sea until in the last line he returns to the self-conscious awareness that the shell's "forma . . . de un corazón," 'shape of a heart,' is the vehicle for his reveries: desire, myth, memory, and poetic invention are interwoven. In Stevens, the jar is also the starting point for a meditation on how "the slovenly wilderness" rises up to the jar and is reflected in it. The difference between the image of the wilderness on the jar and the wilderness itself is like the difference between the actual, untamed sea and its image in Darío's poem and the ancient myths. It is a matter of how metaphor shapes and defines for the mind the reality that would otherwise be chaos. Without the jar, the wilderness simply "sprawled around," giving only "bird or bush"; without the shell, only a hint of waves, tide, and wind remains: "y oigo un rumor de olas y un incógnito acento / y un profundo oleaje y un misterioso viento"; 'and I hear a murmur of waves and an unknown voice / and a vast tide-swell and a mysterious wind.' In the transformation of nature into poetry—into metaphor—the phenomenal world gains meaning.

To underline the importance of eccentric metaphor in Stevens and in his Latin American counterparts, we may also compare Paz's "Dos cuerpos," 'Two Bodies,' to Stevens's "Metaphors of a Magnifico." The poems are similar not only in the thematic concern with the process of metaphor but in technique. Both poems exhibit the "transparency and density" of which Paz speaks in his estimation of Stevens in *Children of the Mire* (135). In "Dos cuerpos," the speaker presents five metaphoric representations of two people face to face. Each stanza begins, "Dos cuerpos frente a frente," 'Two bodies face to face,' and each is linked by common grammatical patterns and images of two, helping to unify the poem but also to give it an unusual analogical structure:

> Two bodies face to face
> are at times two waves
> and night is an ocean.
> Two bodies face to face
> are at times two stones
> and night a desert.
> Two bodies face to face
> are at times two roots
> laced into night.
> Two bodies face to face
> are at times two knives

and night strikes sparks.
Two bodies face to face
are two stars falling
in an empty sky.

Paz's struggle to capture an essential meaning through successive metaphors finds its parallel in Stevens's poem, in which the image of "[t]wenty men crossing a bridge / Into a village" undergoes a variety of perceptual changes while the poet fights for the "meaning" that "will not declare itself" (*Palm*). The first few lines show how Stevens, like Paz, considers a series of propositions about a single view:

> Twenty men crossing a bridge,
> Into a village,
> Are twenty men crossing twenty bridges,
> Into twenty villages,
> Or one man
> Crossing a single bridge into a village.
> This is old song
> That will not declare itself . . .

Source: John Zubizarreta, "Darío, Stevens, and Paz: The Modernist Connection," in *South Atlantic Review*, Vol. 56, No. 1, January 1991, pp. 47–60.

Manuel Duran

In the following essay, Duran profiles Paz and examines his contribution to world literature.

A welcome surprise, a pleasant surprise: this is how most readers and critics have received the news of the awarding of the 1990 Nobel Prize in Literature to Octavio Paz. The element of surprise was due mostly to the fact that no one, or almost no one, thought that a Nobel could be accorded to a Hispanic writer so soon after the 1989 selection of the Spanish novelist Camilo Jose Cela. After all, this is not the way—or so we surmised—the Swedish Academy thinks and acts: after an award to a representative of a certain cultural or linguistic area, attention is displaced to another area. We expected the prize to go to a writer from Asia, Africa, Eastern Europe, anywhere else in the world. Moreover, Paz had been bypassed so often, he was such an obvious candidate yet had been ignored for such a long time, that we were beginning to imagine a dark plot, a mysterious conspiracy that had managed to sabotage his candidacy in the past and would continue to do so in the future.

Paz himself had no inkling that the prize would go to him until the very last minute. I remember clearly having dinner with him, together with a group of professors and graduate students at Silliman College (one of the colleges that are part of Yale University) the night before the award was announced. Someone—tactlessly, I thought—mentioned the Nobel Prize and asked him what were his chances of winning it. He answered briefly that he did not think he would ever get it, adding that he never thought about the prize any more, then changing the conversation to another subject. I must conclude that either he is an excellent actor, which I doubt, or else he was as much in the dark about the impending announcement as was everybody else in that room.

The obvious fact is that for many years Paz's poetic voice has been a major contribution to world literature, his many-faceted talent a force to be reckoned with on several continents. He comes closer than anyone else I can think of to being the ideal candidate for a distinction such as the Nobel Prize, and the list of the literary awards and honors he has received is a long one: among many others the Jerusalem Prize, the Cervantes Prize, and the Neustadt Prize—this last one considered by many the antechamber of the Nobel Prize, since so many of its recipients, candidates, and jurors have gone on to receive the Swedish Academy's accolade.

Perhaps the first question that we must ask, therefore, is not why Paz has been awarded the prize, but why it has taken so long. This question is essentially fruitless, however, as it can only be answered by an insider, by a member of the Swedish Academy, and these gentlemen seldom talk about their deliberations and the motives that lead them to their choices. Let us ask ourselves instead what is the place in world literature of Paz as a writer, what impact he has had so far, and what we can expect of him in the future.

The core of Paz's output, his compelling vocation, has always been, from the very beginning, poetry. If we want to start with the barest of definitions, one limited to a minimum of words, we have to state that Paz is a Mexican poet. After that we should add: Paz is a great Mexican poet whose poetry transcends the barriers of nationalism and can be effective even outside his language area, since it deals with feelings, intuitions, ideas, and sensations that can be called truly universal. Born in a Mexico that had become, after the turmoil of the 1910 revolution, inward-looking and often suspicious of foreign ideas, Paz has managed to open the windows of Mexican culture to all influences: he is at home in the Orient, in Western Europe, in the United States, not to mention countries such as Spain and Argentina, which are essentially part

of his cultural and linguistic area. He is the very opposite of the chauvinistic Mexican intellectual caricatured by Carlos Fuentes, who recommended to his friends only Mexican authors, avoiding all foreign influences, for "those who read Proust, prostitute themselves."

Some of the most important titles in Paz's vast production are deeply rooted in the Mexican experience, the Mexican psyche, and Mexican history. A book such as *The Labyrinth of Solitude*, for instance, could not have been written by anyone outside the mainstream of Mexican culture. In it Paz defines values, outlines a collective experience, explores the conscious and unconscious mind of his country. A book as easy to read as it is difficult to classify, *Labyrinth* approaches the Mexican present through insights into the past, carried out with the skills of an anthropologist, a historian, a poet, a visionary: Paz speaks to us with many voices, for he realizes that a difficult subject has to be tackled from many sides. The circular patterns of ancient Mexican culture are present in Paz's long poem "Sun Stone"; the baroque tensions and beauty of colonial Mexico are an integral part of his book on Sor Juana Ines de la Cruz, *The Traps of Faith*. Contemporary Mexico is the subject of innumerable poems by Paz, yet often the conclusions of his books, whether long poems or volumes of essays, allow him to express something that connects Mexican experience and culture to a more general pattern. His exploration of Mexican existential values is illuminating in and by itself and also as a path toward a wider understanding, a more general approach. No real understanding can be achieved when we start with generalities, Paz seems to be saying, and at the same time the concrete experience is properly lived and examined, it can become the transcendent path toward a universal horizon.

Paz is therefore, as I have stated more than once, a poet-philosopher, a philosophical poet. As Anna Balakian points out, he "belongs to the new breed of humans, more numerous each day, who are freeing themselves of ethnic myopia and walking the earth as inhabitants of the planet, regardless of national origin or political preferences."

This polarity, provincial-universal, could be illustrated by a tree, with deep roots in the Mexican soil and branches, flowers, fruits, and leaves spreading out in all directions. Without in any way diminishing Paz's merit, we may point out that there is always an element of luck to every success story. Part of Paz's new poetic vision can be attributed to the fact that he was born at the right time: 1914, a fateful year that saw the beginning of World War I and the dramatic highlight of the Mexican Revolution, with the ragged armies of Villa, Zapata, and Obregon marching toward Mexico City. It was a very good year for the literary and artistic avant-garde: the guns of August in Europe, like Villa's and Zapata's cavalry charges in Mexico, were about to shake to its foundations the establishment that had dominated Western culture during most of the nineteenth century and the first years of the twentieth. The Mexican Revolution plays the same role as World War I in the cultural field: in both cases it cannot be said the upheaval creates a new system of values, and it is possible to find important forerunners of the new avant-garde styles before the beginning of the bloody years; yet the changes in dynasties and political regimes, the rise of minorities to power, and, above all, the failure of the system of values prevalent before 1914 make it possible for the avant-garde to spread inexorably and displace the old styles, the entrenched sensitivities that had been prevalent in many instances since the early nineteenth century. Paz was born in the year when true modernity in literature and the arts began for most of the Western world.

A sense of openness to the world, of old structures crumbling away and affording a glimpse of a wider horizon, is part of Paz's childhood remembrance. Paz has said about himself:

> As a boy I lived in a place called Mixcoac, near the capital. We lived in a large house with a garden. Our family had been impoverished by the revolution and the civil war. Our house, full of antique furniture, books, and other objects, was gradually crumbling to bits. As rooms collapsed we moved the furniture into another. I remember that for a long time I lived in a spacious room with part of one of the walls missing. Some magnificent screens protected me inadequately from wind and rain. A creeper invaded my room.... A premonition of that surrealist exhibition where there was a bed lying in a swamp.

If there is a message I see in most of Paz's writings, it is that man is both a wide-eyed receiver of messages reaching him from all directions and a giver of messages and a ruler through his language and his mind. If the German philosopher Ernst Cassirer defined man as the animal who can create language and myths, we can also state that it is language, myths, and poetry that have created man.

Man is a speaking, mythmaking, poetry-writing animal. A vast shuttle is at work, back and forth, between our mind, the inner recesses of our minds, and the world around us, including the remote galaxies far beyond our telescopes. Paz knows by instinct what the German philosophers of the romantic era, Fichte, Schelling, Hegel, found out through a lifetime of reasoning, and what in our century Martin Buber has restated: there is no "I" without a "Thou," no individuality without an otherness; we are all a plurality without giving up our individual selves. (*Plural* is the title Paz decreed for the magazine he founded in Mexico after his return from India.) As Paz put it in his acceptance speech at the Neustadt Prize presentation ceremony in 1982:

> In esthetic terms, Plurality is a richness of voices, accents, manners, ideas and visions; in moral terms, Plurality signifies tolerance of diversity, renunciation of dogmatism and recognition of the unique and singular value of each work and every personality. Plurality is Universality, and Universality is the acknowledging of the admirable diversity of man and his works.... To acknowledge the variety of visions and sensibilities is to preserve the richness of life and thus to ensure its continuity.

Plurality means also tolerance, acceptance of other viewpoints, freedom to make statements that others may accept or reject. Only in a society committed to freedom and democracy can plurality flourish, and with it our best chance to reach fuller integration with the vast world around us, to influence it and be influenced by it. Language is at the center of a vast movement, language that expresses our mind and expands it, language as a tool that allows us to delve into ourselves and into the world around us, language as a mirror that shows us our own face, language as a shuttle that goes back and forth, weaving reality, weaving the whole world around us, as a vast cocoon, as a cradle that may bring forth other worlds. Being and Becoming are the two sides of the coin, both real, each influencing the other. The shuttle again goes back and forth in Paz's most ambitious philosophical poem, "Blanco."

> The spirit
> Is an invention of the body
> The body
> An invention of the world
> The world
> An invention of the spirit

Lines pregnant with meaning, part of a long poem that has few parallels in contemporary literature. The shuttle in its huge unstoppable movement, back and forth, creating worlds and erasing them, mixing and blurring what we thought permanent, has become a symbol of our history and our destiny. Hope and fear are intermingled. We are part of history, part of being, also part of the destruction and death of history and of becoming. Everything depends on another aspect of being coming to the rescue, inventing our reality, so that we in turn can invent a reality that will sustain our creator and, by doing so, save ourselves from utter collapse; yet our anguish is not warranted, since as part of the shuttle we are also part of the circle of being and creation—and destruction—part of the never-ending process and, as such, truly immortal.

The preceding paragraph is not necessarily the only reading of Paz's lines; his poem can well be interpreted in other different ways. What I mean by my reading is simply that Paz is a true philosophical poet, that his visions are deep and sustaining, that his gift is a special one, a gift few other poets possess. How many philosophical poets can we find in the traditional Western canon? Dante certainly, also Lucretius, Shakespeare, Quevedo, Calderon, Milton, Donne, T. S. Eliot, and a few others. Not many. Coleridge, Keats, Novalis among them. The hallmark of the philosophical poet is always that he is not alone, even when he thinks he is. He is constantly urged by an inner demon to go forth and explore, to find his place, his role, in the cosmos—not only for himself but for all of us.

Of course Paz is not only a philosophical poet. His voice can be intimate, occasionally ironic. His love poems are erotic and refined. Moreover, the importance of Paz as a literary theoretician and critic has grown constantly during the last decades, and some of his titles (*The Bow and the Lyre* comes to mind) have become indispensable. His public persona is also much in evidence of late, with frequent appearances on Mexican television, his founding and organizing of magazines (*Plural, Vuelta*), and his contribution to newspapers with articles and notes dealing with current events. If we are to compare Paz's total impact with that of other famous poets, we might say that he is as much a philosophical poet as T. S. Eliot was, but he is more intimate, more erotic, warmer than Eliot. We might add that he has become as much of a public poet and writer as Victor Hugo was in the nineteenth century, although Paz's style is less grandiloquent than Hugo's; Paz never overacts.

In any case, Paz's place in the literary canon of our century is secure: I would like to point out in conclusion that occasionally the Nobel Prize calls attention to an unknown writer and may be helpful, for a while, to the writer's influence, whereas at other times, when judiciously given to a deserving writer, it helps restore credibility in the value and importance of the prize itself. The Nobel Prize awarded to Paz belongs to the latter category: since it was so obviously deserved by the recipient, it has helped renew our confidence in the award-giving process, and therefore we should congratulate not only Paz but most especially the members of the jury who made such a wise choice.

Source: Manuel Duran, "Octavio Paz: Nobel Laureate in Literature, 1990," in *World Literature Today*, Vol. 65, No. 1, Winter 1991, pp. 5–8.

Grace Schulman

In the following excerpt, Schulman examines Paz's poetics and explains that in Paz's view "the poet does not speak the language of society but turns away from it, gaining strength in exile."

Octavio Paz is a living incarnation of those tensions in modern poetry between human commitment and aesthetic concern, a dialectic that is fundamental to the art of all nations. And his poetics is important, for it places the poet at the heart of modern life, singing his solitary song in company with the massed voices of human solitude. In his view, the poet does not speak the language of society but turns away from it, gaining strength in exile.

In our time poets, pressed to a keen awareness of human misery, have worked toward an austere art. At an extreme, poets who are acutely conscious of modern horror have subordinated the music of poetry to argument and sacrificed the personal vision that informs their art. Since around 1925, a reaction against individuality, as well as against rhetorical devices, has grown more severe with each generation. Often it appears as if the greater an artist's revulsion from destruction, the stronger is his reluctance to indulge his personal perceptions.

In fact, the Renaissance concept of the individual has dwindled in that modern poetry of which Hopkins, Whitman and Baudelaire were progenitors.... And after around 1945, consciousness of brutality became so acute, especially in European writers, that poetry of the person, however divided, was considered an impossible indulgence. The poet who reports the world in crisis writes of inner fragmentation as well as outward disaster, and often retreats into silence under the pressure of that disruption.

Despite his acquaintance with suffering, however, Octavio Paz has a vision of personal integrity. He maintains that the artist, rebuffed by a community that would substitute technological priorities for spiritual growth, transcends those social limitations and ransoms his dying world. What is more, Paz believes that political crisis nourishes great literature, although the people may not be aware of a poet's genius at the time he is writing. And that is natural, for poetry, with its plurality of meanings, seldom is read for what the words convey: the works of St. John of the Cross, for example, were read originally for their exemplary value, rather than for their beauty.

Even in times of crisis, Octavio Paz asserts, poetry lives on the deepest levels of being, while ideology constitutes superficial layers of consciousness. His faith in the power of language to reveal truth makes him affirm that poetry renews daily life and creates meaning in the present. Just as Confucius was said to have called for the reform of language when asked what he would do to administer his country, Paz believes that the poet who is committed to his art rebuilds empires.

Unending emphasis is laid by Octavio Paz on the poet's power to resuscitate a lifeless world. Paz feels that the poet finds a sacred knowledge by confronting his deepest feelings in the practice of his art. In that encounter, he perceives unity in a universe that had appeared fragmented.... By seizing the truth revealed to him in the present moment, he knows that all faces are one face and centuries are confined to an instant.

Between the collectivist leanings of his youth and the spiritual vision of his later years, the poet's life followed a dialectic pattern that is, curiously, analogous to the lives or poetic roles of other Western writers. At an extreme, Baudelaire wavered between aristocratic and revolutionary positions, while Rilke shifted continually between the personae of nobleman and outcast. In the case of Octavio Paz, various political and literary influences molded his thought.... [He] withdrew from political activity at the time of the Munich pact.... [He] met [surrealist artists]... and discovered in his own response to surrealism a liberating vitality that recalled his attractions to Blake, Novalis and Hölderlin. For, according to the tenets of surrealism, the poet's imagination, cleansed in the fire of the creative act, had the sacred power to rescue the contemporary world.

For all his divagation, these works of the nineteen-fifties and sixties read like the testimony of a man who has witnessed the destruction of all images and then found in the resurrection of those images a creative, sustaining force. In *Alternating Current*, a collection of short essays, and in *The Bow and the Lyre*, a treatise on aesthetics, Paz describes a poetic universe that transcends a world he knows well. Vacillating between patriotism and rebellion, wavering between political activity and artistic solitude, Paz found in pure art the preserving strength of our world. It was as though he had found stars at the bottom of hell.

If Paz envisions an art that goes beyond contraries, he allows that it normally moves between two poles which he calls the magical and the revolutionary. In *The Bow and the Lyre*, he says that the magical extreme consists of a desire to return to the natural world, "to sink forever into animal innocence or to free oneself from the weight of history." The revolutionary endeavor, on the other hand, requires a recovery of the alienated consciousness. And although his poetry is alive with a constant dialectical tension between the magical and the revolutionary aims, the impulse that commands his art is the drive to surpass those poles.

The poetics of Octavio Paz is built on his belief in pure time, to which the poet has access. Where calendar time, the rhythm that governs daily life, attaches an end to days and years, mythical time creates life: "The mythical date arrives if a series of circumstances combine to reproduce the event." Paz writes in *The Bow and the Lyre*.

By the process of rhythmic repetition, the poem invokes the myth that returns to begin a new cycle. Octavio Paz believes that language, like the universe, is generated by rhythms that manage separation and union, harmony and discord. That double rhythm is the scaffolding of most cultures, he says: just as the ancient Chinese saw the universe as the cyclical combination of Yin and Yang that form the Tao, the Greeks conceived the cosmos as a struggle and fusion of opposites. And his conjecture recalls that modern poetry is heir to William Blake's union of antinomies in *The Marriage of Heaven and Hell*, as well as to the truth of his assertion: "Without Contraries is no progression."

Although he had embraced contraries from the beginning of his writing career, [as] Mexican

Ambassador to India [he] found in Tantric thought and in Hindu religious life dualities that enforced his conviction that history turns on reciprocal rhythms. In *Alternating Current*, he writes that the Hindu gods, creators or destroyers according to their name and region, manifest contradiction. "Duality," he says, "a basic feature of Tantrism, permeates all of Hindu religious life: male and female, pure and impure, left and right.... In Eastern thought, these opposites can co-exist; in Western philosophy, they disappear for the worst reasons: far from being resolved into a higher synthesis, they cancel each other out, due to a gradual deterioration of values."

In fact, the title, *Alternating Current*, refers to those opposites the poet contains either in joy or in anguish: language and silence, solitude and communion, fall and resurrection. The image, of an electric flow that reverses its direction at regular intervals, suggests the galvanic excitement that oscillating rhythms can generate in art.

"Another art is dawning," Paz declares, and predicts that poetry's departure from the linear time of modern progress will be even more radical than the change that two centuries ago altered the Christian notion of a motionless eternity. The art he foresees will be based on a concept of time that recurs, as in ritual, and on a present that incorporates the past and future. Paz writes that the new poetry was inaugurated by Apollinaire, who juxtaposed different spaces within a single poem, and by Eliot and Pound, who used texts from other times and languages in their works. Paz calls the rising poetry an "art of conjugation"; he sees the artist as one who exists in a state of blessed confusion, for he holds in his mind other eras, languages and continents.

Paz assumes that the modern "ritual" of hallucinogenic drugs implies a severe criticism of our world's linear time. When people use drugs, he speculates, they perceive the wholeness of life and death, the unity of men and women. Their sensibilities altered, they see the absence of frontiers between people and nations. But Paz feels that the drug experience—like meditation, fasting and ascetic discipline—is a false road to the spiritual oneness that poetry provides. He maintains that the total surrender required by Buddhism and Tantrism is only analogous to the dedication poetry demands. For the poet actually creates new life, making the day begin again and compressing all time into an instant.

The structure of *Alternating Current* supports its argument that completeness depends upon the rhythmic assertion of contradictory realities. The essays of its framework—prose poems, really—shine like revelations. His blazing prose, though, dwindles in the English translation, and the periodic structure, however integrated with the theme, is not the clearest setting for his luminous ideas.

The Bow and the Lyre, on the other hand, his most comprehensive discourse on poetic theory, is a book to be grateful for....

In that book, Paz writes that rhythm and imagery reveal the world's unity. While rhythm is an alternating current that moves language and the universe, imagery, which also oscillates between contraries, reconciles disparate meanings without suppressing any. (St. John's "silent music" combines antithetical things as does the tragic heroine, Antigone, who is torn between divine piety and human law.) Like rhythm, imagery comes from primordial time: if rhythm generates new cycles, imagery closes the gap between name and object that was unknown to primitive man.

Because of the unity they provide, the poet has access to a primordial sensibility in which opposites are one, a state reminiscent of Freud's description of the unconscious as a place where antithetical things appear to be the same. This state, though fundamental to art, horrifies Western man. The truth we learn from Paz is that in magical moments—when we see light strike water or watch rock-hollows suck sea—we know that life and death are a totality, not a dilemma.

Nor does he feel languages are separable. All languages, he believes, have in common the split between words and the things they signify. If language itself is a translation, then the gap between languages is far less compelling than the distance between names and objects.

Early Poems covers the period of surrealist influence; *Configurations*, enclosing the work of the late nineteen-fifties and sixties, is the title given to Paz's innovative work. In *Configurations*, a name signifying the form produced by the relative disposition of parts, meanings emerge from explosive phrases that correspond to a universe that we see in an alternating current, as a whole and as bits of a whole. As novel as this may sound, however, the power of his art lies in his vibrant marriage of opposites—sound and silence, attraction and repulsion—in methods as traditional as Blake's fusion of heaven and hell, or Dante's union of light and dark. And although Paz's images of opposition may flow from the alternating rhythms of separation and union he found in the cultures of the world, they suggest very strongly the antinomies found in all great poetry. But then, the most original poetry always tends to draw its newness from conventional means.

It must be said at once that, ironically, inaccuracies of translation are even more apparent in a poetry that transcends language barriers.

These are, however, important books. The poetry is at once of Mexico and of the world, moving beyond nations to reach the inner lives of people everywhere. That universality is what the surrealists hoped to achieve when they diminished the role of author and called for the intervention of the unconscious in poetic creation. Paz is a characteristic Mexican. He draws on a rich Aztec heritage and on his American Indian ancestry. If his mind is disciplined by European poetic forms, he envisions the vast empty areas of space that are central to poets born in the Americas.

Like Whitman, Paz uses the self as metaphor to permit discoveries on a deep psychic level, and to merge with others. Just as Whitman creates in *Leaves of Grass* an observer who identifies with every leaf, star and atom, Paz constructs a speaker who sees nature as an organic part of the soul: "I go forward slowly and I people the night with stars, with speech, with the breathing of distant water waiting for me where the dawn appears."

For Paz, poetry is an alchemy whose agents of transmutation are fire and water. . . .

In fact, the dominating image of his poetry is the mystic oxymoron of burned water

The poetry of Octavio Paz is an urgent matter because it insists on the wholeness of life, love, and nations, a unity that only art can reveal. And if I have always known that poetry lives on the deepest levels of the world's being, the voice of Octavio Paz commands me to admit the rightness of this knowledge. For Paz sees the world burning, and knows with visionary clarity that opposites are resolved in a place beyond contraries, in a moment of pure vision: in that place, there are no frontiers between men and women, life and death. If his poetry incarnates the mind's journey toward insight, his voyage is my voyage, his passion my passion . . .

Source: Grace Schulman, "Man of Two Worlds," in *Hudson Review*, Vol. 27, No. 3, Autumn 1974, pp. 381–96.

SOURCES

Clarke, Dorothy Clotelle, Review of *Libertad bajo palabra: Obra poética (1935–1958)*, in *Books Abroad*, Vol. 36, No. 2, Spring 1962, p. 185.

Durán, Manuel, Review of *Poemas (1935–1975)*, in *World Literature Today*, Vol. 54, No. 3, Summer 1980, pp. 409–10.

"Electoral Democracies (123), 2007," in *Freedom House*, http://www.freedomhouse.org/template.cfm?page=368&year=2007 (accessed November 8, 2010).

Gray, John, *Enlightenment's Wake: Politics and Culture at the Close of the Modern Age*, Routledge, 1955.

Grenier, Yvon, *From Art to Politics: Octavio Paz and the Pursuit of Freedom*, Rowan and Littlefield, 2001, p. 79.

Internoscia, Donato, Review of *Libertad bajo palabra: Obra poética (1935–1958)*, in *Books Abroad*, Vol. 25, No. 2, Spring 1951, p. 160.

Paz, Octavio, *Libertad bajo palabra: Obra poética (1935–1958)*, edited by Enrico Mario Santi, Catedra, 1988.

———, "Nobel Lecture," in *The Official Website of the Nobel Prize*, http://nobelprize.org/nobel_prizes/literature/laureates/1990/paz-lecture-e.html (accessed August 12, 2010).

———, "Respuesta y algo mas," in *Mexico en la cultura*, February 1960, p. 7.

———, "Two Bodies," in *Early Poems: 1935–1955*, translated by Muriel Rukeyser et al., Indiana University Press, 1973, p. 11.

Phillips, Rachel, *The Poetic Modes of Octavio Paz*, Oxford University Press, 1972, p. 69.

Quiroga, Jose, *Understanding Octavio Paz*, University of South Carolina Press, 1999, pp. 10, 13, 15.

Wilson, Jason, *Octavio Paz*, Twayne Publishers, 1986, pp. 2, 4, 20.

FURTHER READING

Foster, David William, ed., *Mexican Literature: A History*, University of Texas Press, 1994.
This selection of essays examines the evolution of Mexican literature from pre-Columbian times to the twentieth century. It contains an informative section on Paz.

Neruda, Pablo, *The Essential Neruda: Selected Poems*, edited by Mark Eisner, City Lights Books, 2004.
The Chilean Neruda, like Paz, is considered one of Latin America's greatest modern poets. This collection of fifty of Neruda's poems draws from his entire body of work.

Paz, Octavio, *Children of the Mire: Modern Poetry from Romanticism to the Avant-Garde*, Harvard University

Press, 1974.

This famous and critically acclaimed work by Paz examines what it means to be a "modern" poet in modern times. Paz examines modern movements in the context of time as a whole.

Paz, Octavio, ed., *Mexican Poetry: An Anthology*, translated by Samuel Beckett, Grove Press, 1985.

Paz presents thirty-five Mexican poets from 1521 to 1910 and describes their historical and literary significance. This work is a wonderful glimpse into the way Paz viewed the legacy of poetry in Mexico and what he appreciated in the poets who came before him.

Wilson, Jason, *Octavio Paz, a Study of His Poetics*, Cambridge University Press, 1979.

Wilson examines Paz's poetry and his unique take on the surrealist philosophy of André Breton. Though Paz used surrealism as an inspiration for much of his work, he differs in important ways from established surrealist thought.

SUGGESTED SEARCH TERMS

Octavio Paz

Two Bodies

Dos cuerpos

Libertad bajo palabra

Octavio Paz AND surrealism

Octavio Paz AND modernism

Two Bodies AND metaphor

alienation in literature

poetry AND Octavio Paz

Mexican Revolution AND culture

Octavio Paz AND Mexican literature

The Weary Blues

LANGSTON HUGHES

1925

The publication of "The Weary Blues" in 1925 was the centerpiece of one of the most successful publicity stunts in literary history, one that elevated its author, Langston Hughes, to fame as a leading African American writer. Hughes thought of himself as a poet, but like most modern poets, found that he had to write in other formats to support himself, and so he was also a short-story writer, novelist, essayist, and newspaper columnist. Hughes is generally ranked among the greatest African American writers of the first half of the twentieth century; he is slightly older than the novelists Ralph Ellison and Richard Wright, who are the best comparisons for his literary achievement. Hughes is a figure of the Harlem Renaissance, the flourishing of black artistic achievement centered in the Harlem neighborhood of New York City during the 1920s. Hughes was widely traveled, and his aesthetic and political views were informed by the wider perspective of an international black community embracing Paris, Africa, and the Caribbean. "The Weary Blues" was written at the beginning of Hughes's career. It brought him popularity in the black community as a leading poet and representative voice, as well as in the American scene at large, popularity that had him using his summer breaks from college for national book tours.

Langston Hughes *(The Library of Congress)*

AUTHOR BIOGRAPHY

James Langston Hughes usually stated that he was born on February 1, 1902, in Joplin, Missouri, but with no birth certificate, he was not completely certain. This uncertainty can stand, perhaps, as a symbol of the marginal nature of the world he was born into, a world in which African Americans were treated as something less than full citizens because of the segregation and discrimination written into the legal codes and accepted in society. Hughes's mother, Carrie, came from an upper level of the African American community. (Her uncle, for instance, was a congressman during Reconstruction, an American diplomat, and eventually the president of Virginia State University.) She ran away from home, though, dreaming of a career on Broadway. This career did not materialize, and she eventually married James Hughes, who worked as a Pullman porter (an attendant on the sleeping coaches of trains), a prestigious job in the black community. Carrie eventually worked as a schoolteacher, so the family should have had a comfortable middle-class life. However, Hughes's father could not stand the daily wounds to his pride that life in the United States meant for a black man, so he

moved to Mexico City. His wife did not follow, and by the time Langston was six years old, his parents were separated.

Growing up in Kansas and Ohio, Hughes did not face the extreme discrimination experienced by blacks living in the South, but he felt all the more keenly the unfair treatment he did experience. (He particularly felt the sting when his white schoolmates praised him for his rhythm, a stereotype about blacks.) In 1920, as soon as he graduated from high school, Hughes went to visit his father. Crossing the Mississippi River by train at St. Louis, Missouri, Hughes wrote "The Negro Speaks of Rivers," which is often regarded as his best poem. In the next year, he began publishing poetry regularly, but only in publications such as the *Crisis*, aimed at a black readership. Wealthy black patrons recognized his talent and paid his way to attend Columbia University for a year, but Hughes was too restless for college. He decided to see the world as a sailor, but by some misunderstanding, he spent several months on a crew tending mothballed transport ships halfway up the Hudson River. It was while he was working in 1923 or 1924 that he wrote the first draft of "The Weary Blues." After a more rewarding period of service that took him to Africa and Europe, Hughes moved to Washington, DC, to live with his mother; there, he worked as a busboy at a hotel restaurant. He happened to see that Vachel Lindsay, one of the most prominent white poets of the era, was staying at the hotel, and quietly slipped him three of his poems, including "The Weary Blues." The next day, Hughes read of himself in the newspaper as a great black poet found working as a busboy. This was hardly a "discovery," since Hughes was already a well-published poet, but is a measure of the distance that separated the white and black worlds. The poem was published in 1925 in *Opportunity*. With Lindsay's help, Hughes began to publish in mainstream publications such as *Vanity Fair*. He almost immediately got a book contract, which resulted in his first poetry collection, published as *The Weary Blues* in 1926. When more patrons in the black community paid for Hughes to complete college at the all-black Lincoln University, he found himself in the unique position of having to spend his undergraduate summers on book tours.

Hughes continued to be a successful writer for the rest of his life, producing new poems, short stories, plays, opera libretti, children's literature, and essays. The larger part of his audience was white readers. He also taught at the university level occasionally. He was a leader of the Harlem Renaissance in the 1920s and 1930s and lived the rest of his adult life in Harlem. He died on May 22, 1967, of complications following surgery.

POEM SUMMARY

Lines 1–18

"The Weary Blues" consists of a narrative spoken by an anonymous narrator in which are embedded two fragments of a song performed by a bluesman that the speaker hears (lines 19–22 and 25–30). The poem begins with a recollection of hearing the bluesman sing and play. In the first sentence, the performer is identified as African American using the term Negro, a term now outdated but still current when this poem was written. The word is capitalized, lending it a special dignity. The music is described with technical terms that would signal, especially to a white audience, that he is performing traditional black music. Since ragtime had become popular a generation before, syncopation (irregular musical rhythm) was associated with black music. Hughes evokes terms characteristic of black performance that would later pass into popular white culture. Crooning, originally a term referring to birds' song, was applied to black singing as a metaphor for a particular style long before it was taken up by white performers such as Bing Crosby. Similarly, Hughes anticipates the coining of the phrase "rock and roll." Hughes uses poetic techniques such as alliteration and assonance (the repetition of sounds) to suggest the musicality he evokes with the poem.

The events of the poem take place on Lenox Avenue, doubtless at one of the many jazz clubs that thrived there during the Harlem Renaissance of the 1920s. The structure of the poem now begins to suggest the structure of the blues, with the repetition of whole lines. Although the individual lines of the poems all stay within traditional metrical forms, the poem was considered innovative for its time for techniques such as this repetition, as well as the apparently arbitrary lengths of the lines. Although the performer is seated at a piano bench as he plays and sings, he is moving in a way that suggests dancing, and that kind of motion, as much as any musical form, is suggested by Hughes's metrical choices.

MEDIA ADAPTATIONS

- Langston Hughes recites "The Weary Blues" as the third selection on the audio CD *The Voice of Langston Hughes*, released by Smithsonian Folkways in 1995. It is also available as an MP3 download at Amazon.com.

The narrator contrasts the bluesman's black skin with the white keys of the piano. The piano, of course, has black keys too, so this suggests a more fundamental identification between musician and music. The melancholy feeling that will soon pour forth in the bluesman's song is already to be heard in his piano playing.

The eleventh line of the poem is an interjection that breaks out of the voice of the poem thus far, invoking the spirit of the blues itself. It suggests the call-and-response format used in many black churches and among southern field laborers. It is an invocation to the power of those black traditions, and at the same time a cry of despair before the sadness of life. The blues itself is a music of sadness and loss.

Lines 12 and 13 are often taken as comic, but they may also be read as serious. Although the bluesman is sitting in a precarious position, he is playing music that is ragged in the sense of being syncopated, like ragtime. Moreover, he is portrayed as a virtuoso. An idiom holds that an outstanding track-and-field athlete would be "a running fool," that is, devoted to running beyond all reason, and the same term is applied to the bluesman's musicianship here.

Lines 16 and 17 are further interjections about the blues. Experience of the blues, they suggest, however painful it may be, is not without rewards, because it is living, and not to experience them would be not living. The source of the blues, the narrator insists, is the interior mental and spiritual condition of American blacks, who have lived under one form of oppression or another for centuries.

Hughes now introduces the first quotation of the blues song, describing the bluesman and his voice. He is again identified as a Negro, and the words that apply to him might just as well apply to all African Americans, weighed down with long suffering and a vast depth of sadness. The performer and his music are again strongly identified, suggesting an identity between the black experience and the blues.

Lines 19–22

The poem now switches to the first snippet of the bluesman's song. He expresses the idea that he is completely isolated. He is determined not to let his loneliness get him down, but to get the better of his difficult circumstances. It seems as though he wants to turn from self-pity to self-reliance. Hughes's characters are often representatives of the black race, and in this sense, the bluesman is facing up to the difficulties imposed on blacks in a segregated America.

Lines 23 and 24

The next two lines divide the two quotations of the bluesman's song from each other. This could also have been accomplished by inserting a blank line, so these lines must communicate some important aspect of the poem or else Hughes would not have included them. They report the bluesman's actions in between singing the two stanzas, realistically describing the actions of tapping his foot and playing the piano. However, the lines are filled with repeated words and an emphasis on repeated action that seems figurative, as if the repetition of action reflects the lives of black Americans, lived over and over again in oppression.

Lines 25–30

Now the bluesman's tune is quite changed. Earlier, he had resolved to set aside his sadness, but in these lines he seems overwhelmed by it. The theme of repetition is continued by repeating two couplets with only slight variation, a device typical of, for example, the biblical Psalms, but supplanted in genuine blues songs by groups of three repeated lines. Hughes is drawing on spiritual traditions from within the black community other than the blues. The bluesman is worn down to the point where happiness seems impossible to him and he longs for death.

Lines 31–35

Finally, the narrator continues to listen to the bluesman's performance, perhaps until dawn.

The narrator does not describe his own actions following the end of the performance, but rather those of the bluesman. He goes to bed but cannot stop contemplating the melancholy subject of his song. At last, though, he sleeps like a dead man. Although that is a common metaphor for a particularly sound sleep, there is an intimate connection between death and sleep in the poetic tradition, and the closing of the poem suggests that the bluesman is finally worn down by his cares and surrenders to death.

THEMES

Black Culture

"The Weary Blues" is a celebration of distinctive black culture through its music. However, it is even more a lament for the state of black culture in the America of the 1920s. Even in the North, blacks faced fairly strict segregation and had to exist apart from mainstream culture, in prescribed areas of large urban cities (later called ghettos after the neighborhood that Jews were restricted to in medieval Venice). Thus, blacks had to create a shadow world, with their own businesses and institutions that were allowed only limited interaction with the surrounding white society. Black artists and intellectuals were equally isolated. One of the great distinctions of Hughes's career was his breakthrough to popularity in the white world. Although Hughes had published several poems over a number of years in national magazines, when Vachel Lindsay "discovered" him, Hughes was treated as a completely unknown young poet because of the isolation of the two worlds.

Hughes eventually found his solution to the artistic problems posed by segregation in the movement known as *negritude*. Hughes encountered this movement in Paris, where it was centered among the black expatriate community from the French colonies, but it became widespread among black intellectuals throughout the world, especially in Africa and the Caribbean. Its main idea was that blacks ought to make their own culture for themselves, without reference to the white communities that simultaneously surrounded and rejected them. Negritude did not reject Western culture, since its followers realized it was not possible and not even desirable to break out of the Western civilization that had conditioned their own experiences. The goal was to create a black culture that, if it had to be separate, would not be inferior. The term

TOPICS FOR FURTHER STUDY

- Many Western intellectuals during the 1930s became enchanted by the promise of freedom and equality offered by the Soviet Union, before the brutal, oppressive character of Stalin's regime became clear. Hughes lived in Uzbekistan as a guest of the Soviet Union in 1932–1933. One project he undertook there was to oversee the publication of a volume of his poetry (including "The Weary Blues") in the Uzbek language. This included five poems that he wrote specially and whose English originals have been lost, so they exist only in Uzbek and in English translations made by others. If you know a second language, try translating a few lines of "The Weary Blues." Make side notes as to the difficulties of maintaining meaning and style while translating. Turn in your translation to your foreign language teacher to check for accuracy.

- In 1955, Hughes published an introduction to jazz (which is related to the blues) for young people called *The First Book of Jazz*. Read the book and look for ideas that might help you interpret "The Weary Blues." Then, write a brief paper discussing connections between the two works.

- One notable feature of the Harlem Renaissance was the intersection of high culture, such as poetry, and popular culture, such as jazz. How might the segregation imposed on black culture have influenced this? How was jazz treated and received in white American or even European culture? The reception of black cultural material by outsiders tended to produce a simplified or stereotypical image of black culture. Hughes, is, of course, a member of the black community, but any poet is in some respects an outsider to and a commentator on his own culture. Examine how Hughes uses jazz in his poetry—what it represents and in what contexts it appears—and compare it to how jazz was discussed in mainstream newspapers or magazines of the time. How similar are the treatments? Are there meaningful differences? What might be their source? Write a paper discussing these issues.

- An Internet search for videos using the term "blues" or "blues music" returns thousands of examples of blues music from all eras. How do some of these songs treat the same themes Hughes addressed in "The Weary Blues"? How do some seem to suggest entirely other interpretations of the blues? Choose several of the songs from different eras and create a digital multimedia presentation that discusses the common themes of blues music throughout its history. Show this presentation to your class and explain what you found.

- What music is important in your life? Write a poem in the style of Hughes that illustrates its aesthetic and philosophical impact on you. Post your poem to your blog or social networking site and ask your classmates to comment on it.

---

negritude means "blackness," and Hughes himself coined the slogan "The negro is beautiful," which in time became the 1960s saying "Black is beautiful," as the idea percolated through popular culture. Although the international negritude movement eventually took its tone from the Harlem Renaissance, Hughes was its chief ambassador back to that environment. Hughes longed for freedom and equality as much as anyone else, but he realized it was not coming in his lifetime and

consequently felt that blacks ought to make the most of their sheltered, limited cultural existence. "The Weary Blues," however, is an early work, filled more with passion than reflection. It presents a vision of black culture as being ultimately doomed by its oppression.

Music

The blues is a form of music that first developed within the black community of the Deep South, about 1900. It was at this early date generally performed by individuals in part as an expression of deeply felt personal sadness, but always by professional or semiprofessional musicians as dance music or as entertainment in black bars and clubs ("juke joints," as they were called). The musical form is indebted to the music of spirituals performed, usually, by the whole congregation of black churches, as well as to songs sung in the fields to regulate the physical activities of planting and harvesting. Although the African origin of this music is hotly disputed and often loudly insisted upon, no research has ever linked any aspect of the music to African roots, unlike many forms of music in the black cultures of the Caribbean, which have obvious and well-established African connections. The blues seems to be entirely the invention of the African American community, derived from the Protestant hymn tradition adapted from white culture.

Hughes latched onto the blues because by the 1920s it was recognized by both blacks and whites as emblematic of black culture and because it expressed the deep melancholy that pervades his poem. Thus, the blues and spirituals descend from the same church music, and for Hughes the blues is able to express spiritual meaning. However, as Stephen C. Tracy points out in the essay "Langston Hughes: Poetry, Blues, and Gospel," which appears in the collection *Langston Hughes: The Man, His Art, and His Continuing Influence*, such a view would not find easy acceptance in the conventional black culture of the time, desperately trying to become bourgeois:

> The fact that Hughes could throw one arm around spirituals and gospel music and the other around the blues simultaneously would seem remarkable, even blasphemous, in some circles, primarily Christian ones where the blues might be dubbed 'the devil's music.'

For Hughes, however, they were one and the same thing, a spiritual expression of the inner life of black humanity. As he wrote in his autobiography *The Big Sea*,

> Like the waves of the sea coming one after another, always one after another, like the earth moving around the sun, night, day—night, day—night, day—forever, so is the undertow of black music with its rhythm that never betrays you, its strength like the heat of the human heart, its humor, and its rooted power.

This music, this emotion, is *The Big Sea* of Hughes's autobiography. It is the weary blues.

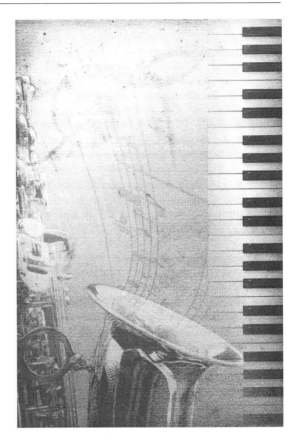

Old blues music instruments (Benjamin Haas / Shutterstock.com)

STYLE

Meter

"The Weary Blues" can be approached as two different parts in terms of its metrics: the narrative voice of the poem and the quotations from the bluesman. The frame seems, like much traditional poetry in English, loosely written in iambic pentameter; even the shorter lines, which have fewer than five feet, are still iambic. A foot in poetry is a set of stressed or unstressed syllables, and those sets are given special names depending on their pattern. An iamb is an unstressed followed by a stressed syllable, although English allows pretty free substitution of other feet such as trochees (stressed unstressed) and spondees (stressed stressed). Here, many of the longer lines should perhaps be read rather as tetrameter, or four feet per line, with some of the feet containing three (or even four) syllables, one stressed and two (or three) unstressed. In the opening lines particularly, Hughes uses various feet to achieve some rather spectacular metrical fireworks of the kind so favored by, for example, Edgar Allan Poe and, not coincidentally, Vachel Lindsay (Hughes's first white patron). In fact, it is difficult to read the opening lines of "The Weary Blues" and not have Poe's poem "The Bells" called to mind.

Syncope is a device whereby the unstressed syllable of a word has to be elided (skipped over or condensed) to make the word fit the meter, for example, *over* becoming *o'er*. Although Hughes mentions musical syncopation in the first line, the poetic device of syncope is not actually used within the poem until the speech of the bluesman (note that eliding the *f* from *of* in line 8 mimics speech, but it does not alter the syllable count and is not syncope). There, however, the poetic syncopation is quite regular, occurring in all the contracted forms for *am not*, *cannot*, and *going to* that echo ordinary speech. There is another example of syncopation in the bluesman's first line, where a vowel that begins a word has to be elided after a word ending in a vowel. Syncopation as a poetic device is as old as Western poetry and occurs in the oldest Greek verse. Here, Hughes is suggesting the meter of blues music. However, he does not use many of the most obvious poetic markers of blues songs, such as an *aaa* rhyme scheme.

Black Dialect

The narrative voice of "The Weary Blues" speaks in standard English. The anonymous bluesman whose song is twice quoted in the poem speaks in dialect. Dialectical speech is not a mistaken form of some privileged, correct speech. One must imagine the development of language as akin to the branching of a genealogical tree, with a single source (Old English) giving rise to more and more descendants in each succeeding generation. It is not possible, on philological (language study) grounds, to privilege one of the descendant dialects over the other as being correct. It is, however, possible to attempt to privilege a single dialect of a language on political grounds, as had been done by the nineteenth century in all of the centralized European states, so that, for example, French is the dialect of Paris, Italian is the dialect of Florence, and English is the dialect of Oxfordshire. Mass education and, in the twentieth century, mass media help to enforce the favored dialect. Various English dialects continued to exist in the United States, since settlers in a specific location in the New World usually came from a certain particular area of the old. In the United States, the normalizing forces of education and

the media tend to enforce a rather bland average of English dialects. The dialect spoken by many African Americans originated in the American South and is not very different from the speech of white southerners, which descends from the dialect of England's West Country. Contrary to popular wisdom, this form of English does not contain very many African elements (though a small number of words are of West African origin).

The effect of giving the two speakers in "The Weary Blues" differing dialects is exotic, something that black and white readers alike in the 1920s thought black poetry ought to be. The dialectical elements are not very pronounced, since Hughes intends the piece to be intelligible to speakers of standard English like himself. The only repeated element is the dropping of the final *g* from the present participles (words ending in *ing*), which almost everyone does in informal speech. More interesting is what Hughes does to the vowel sound in the form he writes in place of the standard *going*. This form collapses the distinct *o* and *i* into a diphthong far more resonant than its standard counterpart, which Hughes presents with a *w*, though really, no ordinary English letter can quite record the sound as it is heard from many southerners, black and white. *Ain't* is a standard form in English speech and is exiled only from the most artificially perfect and formal dialects. Similarly, the double negative, in almost all English speech, serves the same function as in other European languages, to intensify the negative, and it is overly fussy to insist that they cancel each other out to become a positive. The presentation of the bluesman's dialect is light and subtle, but it left Hughes's audience in no doubt that black dialect was being invoked.

The word *blue* as it is used in "blues music," denoting sadness, goes back to medieval usage in English. It is a metaphor based on the livid color of corpses, with the color of pale skin in death standing for sadness and melancholy.

HISTORICAL CONTEXT

Harlem Renaissance

Whether Hughes was principally inspired by music he heard in Harlem or elsewhere, he chose to place this poem on Lenox Avenue in Harlem. The Harlem Renaissance was a rebirth of black

COMPARE
&
CONTRAST

- **1920s:** Music in live performance has to be made entirely by the performers on stage and is not amplified.

  Today: Live performance, especially of popular music, is usually supported to some degree by recorded music, and it is almost invariably heard over loudspeakers.

- **1920s:** The Harlem neighborhood of New York City is at its peak of cultural productivity.

  Today: After a long cultural and economic decline, Harlem is a neighborhood in transition again.

- **1920s:** The blues is a culturally vital art form growing in popularity throughout the world.

Today: As a musical form, the blues is known only to a small group of performers and fans of the genre. However, it has left its mark on the culture as an expression of African American identity and as a style of music and lyrics.

- **1920s:** Racial discrimination and segregation are both commonplace and enforced by law, especially in the South.

  Today: While racial discrimination and segregation still exist, they are now prohibited by law and are diminishing, especially with the rise of black media figures and politicians, such as Oprah Winfrey and Barack Obama.

---

cultural expression through a diverse community of artists who lived in the New York neighborhood of Harlem in the 1920s. At the time it was called the "New Negro" movement, and Hughes became its leading voice. The cultural brilliance of the Harlem Renaissance blazed up from the prosperity of the 1920s and died out with the Great Depression of the 1930s. An entirely new black literature came out of the Harlem experience from a new generation of black authors, including Hughes, Zora Neale Hurston, and Countee Cullen, to name only the most notable. They kept to traditional forms of Western literature, such as novels, dramas, and formally structured poetry. The key to their success was gaining the acceptance of white publishers and a reading audience that was primarily white, but to whom they could speak in their black voices. Their economic viability depended upon their white audience. The black artists of the Harlem Renaissance have been called to task for using Western forms and embracing Western tradition rather than creating a new art that took a stand against Western culture and its racism. Such an innovation, however, could not have succeeded against Western influence; the authors would have failed to make

sales and find readers. The possibility of escape from Western tradition—what has been called Orientalism—is itself an inherently Western fantasy. The artists and writers who made the Harlem Renaissance were Americans, working in the Western tradition, and if they had chosen to take over and use African cultural elements, they would not have been able to do so with much authenticity.

Black popular entertainers had performed for white audiences throughout much of the nineteenth century in the form of the minstrel show, which included black and white performers (both dressed and made-up as racist caricatures of blacks). In the early twentieth century, black forms of music such as jazz and the blues became popular with white audiences when nightclubs and dance halls came into existence. Eventually, it became possible for black performers to perform for white audiences in these venues. Hughes's own mother tried and failed to become such a performer. Many black performers achieved the highest level of fame and commercial success, including orchestra leaders such as Duke Ellington, soloists such as Louis Armstrong, and dancers such as Josephine Baker.

The dull pallor of an old gas light (*Samuel Haas | Shutterstock.com*)

Although the performances of these black celebrities entailed nothing that was not firmly grounded in Western tradition, they were lauded by white critics and audiences as authentic in part because of the primitive, even animalistic character of their art. It was no coincidence that black art rose to prominence especially after the trauma of World War I, which sent Western civilization scrambling for relief in anything that seemed non-Western or even anti-Western. Black performance became, as termed in Edward Said's *Orientalism*, a fantasy of everything that was non-Western, made safe for consumption by a Western audience. Harlem nightclubs became the meeting point between white and black, because blacks were not generally allowed to perform outside Harlem. The audiences at establishments such as the Cotton Club were all white. The dancer Josephine Baker left the United States after she tried to buy a drink at the bar of the same club where she was a headline performer but was refused entry by the bouncers. However, black intellectuals such as Hughes were let into the Cotton Club because white audiences found them both safe and interesting. The Harlem Renaissance made many black intellectuals and performers famous in American culture, but at the cost of being reduced to an exotic Other. Some, such as Baker and Hurston, embraced that identity. One of the dichotomies that Hughes is getting at in "The Weary Blues" is the white enthusiasm for the Harlem Renaissance and black performers despite the continuing white rejection of blacks as a people.

Hughes had a special attachment to Harlem, no doubt owing to his own experience in what had been achieved there in the 1920s. Other black intellectuals and celebrities, such as Richard Wright (a novelist who vies with Hughes as the greatest writer of the Harlem Renaissance) and Baker, moved to France as soon as they practically could to be free of the racism inherent in the American culture of that time. (Baker, ironically, had to live under the Nazi occupation.) But Hughes stayed in Harlem until his death in 1967, long enough to see its decline into one of the poorest, most crime-ridden neighborhoods in America.

CRITICAL OVERVIEW

There is some controversy over the inspiration of "The Weary Blues" because of Hughes's lack of clarity on the subject. Stephen C. Tracy, in "Langston Hughes: Poetry, Blues, and Gospel—Somewhere to Stand," repeats an often-asserted statement: "[Hughes] recalled the first time he heard the blues in Kansas City on the appropriately named Independence Avenue, which provided him with material for his 'The Weary Blues.'" This seems to be the majority opinion among Hughes scholars, but it arose from a basic confusion in Hughes's autobiography, *The Big Sea*. He indeed says of the bluesman's song that it was "the first blues verse I'd ever heard way back in Lawrence, Kansas, when I was a kid." In a 1964 interview for a Kansas City newspaper, quoted by Tracy, Hughes changed his story so that he heard the inspirational song in Kansas City on Independence Avenue. In the poem itself, though, Hughes claims to have heard the song on Lenox Avenue in Harlem, a detail that seems to be confirmed as autobiographical elsewhere in *The Big Sea*: "That winter I wrote a poem called 'The Weary Blues,' about a piano player I heard in Harlem." It is conceivable, of course, that while the Harlem piano player may have inspired the poem, Hughes elected to use the lyrics he had heard long before.

Among more recent work on "The Weary Blues," Edward E. Waldron, in the *Negro American Literature Forum* for 1971, derives the themes of loneliness, despair, and frustration that predominate in Hughes's work as a whole from the blues, as exemplified in the blues song embedded in "The Weary Blues." David Chinitz, in the 1996 issue of *Callaloo*, points out that the traditional structure of Hughes's early poems, especially his insistence on closure (Hughes wrestled with "The Weary Blues" for months to find just the right ending) stand in contrast to the relatively amorphous (free-form) structure of traditional blues, which often uses a lack of closure to create irony. While "The Weary Blues" seems assured of a prominent place among Hughes's works and in their scholarly reception, Karen Jackson Ford, in a Hughes anthology edited by Harold Bloom, argues that this poem and others of his most discussed works, such as "The Negro Speaks of Rivers," ought to be de-emphasized in favor of the poetry that Hughes composed for the mouth of his character Jesse B. Simple, a black Everyman about whom Hughes wrote in his syndicated newspaper column for many years. While most critics dismiss these works as satire, Ford sees them as a more authentic black voice.

CRITICISM

Rita M. Brown
Brown is an English professor. In the following essay, Brown explores Hughes's use of the blues as a symbol of the black experience of oppression in America.

All of Langston Hughes's writings can be read as an expression on some level of the black experience in America, and that inevitably means the experience of suffering and oppression. Each work may be more or less urgent, more or less defeated or triumphant in its reaction, but the same theme underlies it. Each work finds a new symbol or a new tone or a new means of expression to relate the same idea. Hughes's work draws its strength from being a single monument. Each poem is like a ruined piece of that monument that tells the whole story by encapsulating the whole in a microcosm.

In "The Weary Blues," Hughes uses the blues itself as songful lament for the black experience in America, and at the same time, he uses the bluesman as an Everyman to stand for the black community. Music is a constant in the poem that

WHAT DO I READ NEXT?

- *Langston Hughes in the Hispanic World and Haiti* (1977), edited by Edward J. Mullen, presents Hughes's writings about Latin America and Spain and his translations from the Spanish, together with a bibliography of the translations of his own works into Spanish and several essays (some in Spanish) on Hughes's mutual exchange of influence with Spanish-language literature, emphasizing his role as a multicultural author.

- The *Encyclopedia of the Harlem Renaissance*, published in 2004 and edited by Cary D. Wintz and Paul Finkelman, covers the entire cultural spectrum of Hughes's environment but concentrates on the graphic and performing arts.

- Throughout his career, Hughes wrote for children and young adults and was often active in primary and secondary education. *The Dream Keeper and Other Poems* (1922) was the first of his many books for school-age audiences.

- Alice Walker's *Langston Hughes: American Poet* (2001) is one of many biographies of Hughes intended for young adults.

- Hans A. Ostrom's *Langston Hughes Encyclopedia* (2002) concentrates on Hughes's verse, containing an entry on each of his more than eight hundred published poems.

- Steven C. Tracy's *Langston Hughes and the Blues* (1988) integrates popular black music into the world of the Harlem Renaissance.

- Countee Cullen's *The Black Christ and Other Poems*, originally published in 1929, collects the early work of a close friend and colleague of Hughes who was another prominent poet of the Harlem Renaissance.

draws the two elements together. Hughes names elements of music such as syncopation and crooning and constantly imitates the effects of music in the rhythm and repetition of his language. The

> HUGHES SUGGESTS THAT THE BLACK COMMUNITY WILL BE PULLED BETWEEN THE TWO POLES OF THE BLUESMAN'S TWO VERSES FOR AS LONG AS IT IS OPPRESSED UNDER THE WEIGHT OF THE WEARY BLUES."

whole poem is tied together by the mournful assonance of the letter *o* like the mouths of so many singers crying out in pain. The long *u* in the word *blues* itself stands in complement like a blue note. The music, therefore, is not just any music, but the blues. The blues, as a black expression of American folk music, as an expression of suffering and loss, is ideally suited to bear the history of oppression under which blacks have groaned in America from slavery until the legal racism that still prevailed in Hughes's time. By using the blues, Hughes and his bluesman are able to keep their black identity but also to speak in an idiom increasingly accepted among the dominant white culture.

The blues is a music of sorrow and loss, as experienced by individuals. Most often the thing that was lost is described in melancholy detail. However, Hughes does not do that in this poem. The blues is expressed in the weariness that falls like a shadow over the whole poem and is expressed again in the song of the bluesman. The source of the sadness, though, is never stated. That sorrow comes from the very nature of the existence of the poet who sings the poem and the bluesman who sings the blues. The blues, Hughes says, comes from the black soul. It wells up from the heart and mind, from the deepest reaches of the self. It is a bone weariness that defines the black experience, conditioned by its history of oppression. Hughes does not need to spell it out because he knows it—feels it—the bluesman knows it, and the audience, black and white, knows it. No American can help but know it. If Hughes had spelled out the cause of the black man's blues, the entire tone of the work would have been altered. It would have become strident, and, not coincidently, unpublishable in a white magazine. In a genuine blues song, what has been lost might be romantic love, a loss for which there is no remedy. What has been lost in "The Weary Blues" is justice, and there is a remedy for that, but not one that, in 1925, anyone was prepared to undertake. The public and legal rejection of racism had to wait another generation or two.

However, "The Weary Blues" is after all about more than music. Casual readers in 1925 were enchanted by the poem as a piece of exotic black culture set down in their living rooms that they could read by the fire. A closer reading of the poem, though, shows that it makes more specific prescriptions about the state and nature of black culture. Unexpectedly, the part spoken by the poet or narrator of the poem sets the musical framework. The song of the bluesman, in contrast, along with the brief narrative about him at the end, comes much closer to a political or social meaning.

The bluesman stands for every black American because every black American groaned under the same oppression and felt the same weary blues. The two verses of his song make a stark contrast with each other. In the first verse (lines 19–22), the bluesman has been abandoned and is alone in the world. This is surely a cause of trouble to him, but the bluesman resolves that if he is left to himself, then he will rely upon himself and use his own inner resources to chase away the blues and restore his equilibrium and happiness. This is more than a hint of practical action. In fact, the easiest way to read these lines is in relation to the aesthetic philosophy of negritude embraced by Hughes. This movement among blacks in France and the French colonial empire was in part inspired by the artistic ferment of the Harlem Renaissance that was already brewing in the early 1920s and that acted as an international example. It taught that because white culture generally turned its back on blacks, blacks must make their own way, relying only on themselves, just as the bluesman at first determines to do. Blacks must look to establish their own cultural and aesthetic goals and reach them by themselves. If whites appreciate black art, that is fine, but blacks should not pander to white taste. To paraphrase a segregationist slogan, if blacks were forced to be separate, they would not settle for anything less than being equal. Although the negritude in the bluesman's song comes about in reaction to segregation and discrimination, it is nevertheless optimistic. The troubles that black culture faces can be met and overcome by the resilience of the black character and black creativity.

Between the bluesman's two verses fall two lines spoken by the narrative voice that carries the poem. They describe him playing the piano between the two parts of his song, stomping his foot on the floor in time to the music. Everything about the two lines builds a picture of repetition. The repetition is necessary in performing music, surely, but it must indicate much more, considering the effect that the pause has on the bluesman's second verse. Given the premise that the poem deals with the sorrow and loss of all of black history in America and with the grinding weariness brought about by centuries of racism, it does not seem too much to suggest that the repetition in these lines can be read like the passage of time covered over by the curtain falling between two acts of a play, the repetition of oppression suffered again and again in each generation. If that is the meaning these lines are meant to convey, they could have done so more strongly, but Hughes was a poet who took the long view, and we have his own testimony that he struggled with the resolution of the poem, perhaps beginning here.

In any case, the second verse of the bluesman's song (lines 25–30) is entirely different in tone from the first. Now all talk of self-reliance and determined action to bring back his own happiness is ended. The bluesman has finally succumbed and sees no hope of happiness, no recovery from loss. The weary blues have worn him down. Rather than go on hopelessly, he wishes that he could die. If his self-confidence before came from negritude, his spiritual collapse too must represent something that Hughes encountered in the black world. The world of blues musicians was by and large an underclass, made up of men who had been broken by personal loss. For a young man like Hughes, they could act as a portal to a world of crime, poverty, and hopelessness from which his middle-class background had largely shielded him. This is the world that, for instance, the young Malcolm X inhabited and recounts in his autobiography. This is a different paradigm of the black experience, one that is hopeless in and of itself. Hughes suggests that the black community will be pulled between the two poles of the bluesman's two verses for as long as it is oppressed under the weight of the weary blues.

After the conclusion of the bluesman's second verse, the whole character of the poem changes. The first half is devoted to the narrator as an audience member watching the bluesman's performance,

Langston Hughes on U.S. postage stamps from 1934 (casinozack | Shutterstock.com)

and it is told realistically, if expressively, from that limited perspective. There, the narrator quotes and describes the bluesman's song in detail. Now, however, the narrative voice follows the bluesman where an audience member could not go; into his soul, maybe. The bluesman plays until dawn, but dawn is never mentioned; rather, he plays until the cosmic lights of the moon and stars are extinguished. This begins to suggest, ever so slightly, apocalyptic imagery from the Bible, where the end of the world is presaged by the fall of the stars from heaven. It is perhaps a metaphor of cosmic extinction, a symbol for the death of a man or the death of a race. The bluesman goes to bed, but he cannot sleep because he cannot shake the weary blues out of his mind. Finally he does sleep, but he sleeps like a dead man. There can be no question but that this sleep represents death. This is a common metaphor in the Western tradition. In the Bible, for instance, when the kings of Israel die, they are said to sleep with their fathers. Sleep and death are brothers, according to the Greek poet Hesiod. The only rest that the bluesman, or the black race he stands for,

can find in this world of oppression is in death. Hughes the poet wants to be optimistic, wants to believe he can work to make the future better, but he sees all around him the evidence that he cannot. That is the conflict that he expresses in "The Weary Blues."

Source: Rita M. Brown, Critical Essay on "The Weary Blues," in *Poetry for Students*, Gale, Cengage Learning, 2011.

Shane Vogel

In the following excerpt, Vogel reflects on Hughes's poems and their relationship to the social atmosphere of the times.

... In framing the debate around the verifiability of Hughes's sexuality, Rampersad and his critics ask questions of an archive that it cannot answer. Indeed, it is precisely a "strict regard for the rules of evidence" that Hughes resists. As scholars at the intersection of queer studies and performance studies have demonstrated, the textual and material logic of the institutional archive often fails to document—and sometimes

> THOUGH THESE POEMS HAVE BEEN GIVEN
> LESS ATTENTION, THEY ARE A NECESSARY
> ACCOMPANIMENT TO HIS BLUES POEMS, A MUSICAL
> SECOND LINE THAT INSCRIBES THE SPACE AND TIME
> OF HARLEM'S PERFORMANCE WITH A QUEERNESS
> THAT IS BOTH CONTAINED WITHIN AND EXCEEDS
> BLUES MUSIC AS SUCH."

actively participates in the erasure of minoritarian histories, such as those of queer African Americans. Hughes's first two published collections of verse, *The Weary Blues* (1926) and *Fine Clothes to the Jew* (1927), respond to these archival conditions. Both are populated with spaces, figures, values, and social relationships at odds with the normalizing impulses of racial uplift. I argue here that these lyric explorations of Harlem's cabaret performances and sexual nightlife were one strategy by which Hughes evaded the terms of an archival imperative toward empiricism and positivist legibility, while still recording the criminal and sexual spaces of the early twentieth century. In these volumes, we will see, Hughes turns to the lyric form to construct what Ann Cvetkovich calls an "archive of feeling." Archives of feeling attend to the textual traces of affect and experience as well as to "the practices that surround their production and reception." They thus direct us toward modes of documentation that sometimes stand in a queer (that is, oblique and askew) relationship to official archives, imagining other ways to preserve and read that which positivist historiography fails to admit (as my mobilization in what follows of newspapers, special collections of libraries, and, yes, Rampersad's biography will attest). At other times, such alternative archives index precisely that which cannot be preserved, those affective states and experiences that both intentionally and unintentionally elude historic inscription.

Hughes's 1920s poetry archives spaces and temporalities that seek to escape empirical confirmation and refuse identificatory foreclosure. His poetry thus forces the question: When is the literary not only an object to be historicized, but also itself a

repository of historical counterknowledge? My focus here will be on Hughes's lyric archive of the specific spatio-temporal manipulations that emerge from the sexual and musical underworlds of the early twentieth century: closing time (as a temporal event) and afterhours (as a temporal register). It is in the sometimes prohibited, sometimes tolerated time and space of afterhours that the rhythms and ethics of Harlem nightlife developed. Hughes's poems trace the temporal profile of such spaces, offering an elusive counterevidence to the city's bureaucratic repositories of knowledge (including police reports, arrest records, and investigative statements). *The Weary Blues* and *Fine Clothes to the Jew* demonstrate, against the normalizing logic of official archives, Elizabeth Freeman's claim that "various queer social practices, especially those involving enjoyable bodily sensations, produce form(s) of time consciousness, even historical consciousness, that can intervene upon the material damage done in the name of [historical] development." In locating the queer and transient space of the afterhours club within its specific temporal profile—that is, an illegal temporality that is made possible by and exceeds the regulatory administration of the modern city—Hughes poetically inscribes a queer time consciousness that is impossible to archive under the official regimes of documentation and verification. The queer time and space of the afterhours club, in other words, is archived in the line of the poem, if not at the library at Yale.

...Operating between the gaps of established nightclubs, afterhours clubs shaped an expressive musical tradition as well as constituted modern subject positions. Such clubs offered many black musicians a crucially supportive environment, both economically and socially. In Harlem's afterhours clubs, musicians could find a place to get a start in a new city, hear about new work, and develop an expressive culture. These networks contributed to a subterranean opportunity for the dissemination of information and the cultivation of social networks. Cotton Club bandleader Cab Calloway described the spread of jazz through the underworld institution of the afterhours club: "Singers, pianists, drummers, horn players, guitarists—we all hustled around the clubs for a drink when we were up against it. That was the way jazz spread in America, not through the big concert halls, not through the big fancy clubs like the Cotton Club and Connie's Inn, but through small cafes and gambling houses and speakeasies, where we could hustle up a drink in exchange for a little of our souls." The movement Calloway describes is not simply one of geography, linking large and small cities through musical pathways, but also one of subjective expansion, in which the exchange of musical production for the sociability and recreation offered in semipublic drinking establishments is a negotiation of one's selfhood. Hughes's cabaret poems, as we will see, take up this time and space of afterhours that is central to queer and African-American historical and imaginative geographies.

The central role of musicians and performers in the afterhours economy suggests that the queer temporality of such spaces is also informed by musical time. Like the time signature on a piece of sheet music, a distinct tempo governs the social compositions of the afterhours club, even when there is no band in the room. Far from a temporal free-for-all, afterhours structures a countertemporality that unwinds the reified clock of rationalized time and marks time instead by musical sets and the flows of musical time. Willie "the Lion" Smith, Harlem's renowned stride pianist, calls this tempo of a place its "vibration," the totality of the rhythms, gestures, beats, moods, and movements, the precisely perceptible quiver of the air, that marks the aura of any collectivity or scene. These vibrations are produced and managed by sound and performance. Duke Ellington elaborates the ways that these vibrations are felt in, around, and through the body and establish their own autonomous temporal flows. Descending into the Capitol Palace, an afterhours basement speakeasy, to hear Smith play, Ellington described the vibrations of the room: "A square-type fellow might say, 'This joint is jumping,' but to those who had become acclimatized—the tempo was the lope—actually everything and everybody seemed to be doing whatever they were doing in the tempo the Lion's group was laying down. The walls and furniture seemed to lean understandably—one of the strangest and greatest sensations I ever had. The waiters served in that tempo, everybody who had to walk in, out, or around the place walked with a beat." The tempo of the performance and the time signature of afterhours establish the beats and values of such spaces, governing the pulse that organizes such (musical, social) improvisations. In Hughes's poetic world, for example, a blues time signature marks the social and historical matrix by which Hughes records the queer relations and subjects in the afterhours club. The unique time-signature of an afterhours club—its uncommon time—is one way in which we can understand the confusion, discombobulation, and ineffable ache that often underlies what is invariably characterized as a sense of "return" to the rhythms and beats of normal and normalizing time and space.

... Those of us who do queer Harlem Renaissance studies secretly wish Hughes had written "Cafe: 3 A.M." for *The Weary Blues*, rather than for his 1951 collection, *Montage of a Dream Deferred*. "Cafe: 3 A.M." is the only poem in his oeuvre where Hughes explicitly references the terminology of homosexual deviance ("degenerates," "fairies," and "Lesbians"), and the poem's thematic interest in indeterminate and uncertain identity resonates with the vice policing of the Progressive Era and its pre-closet closet sexual epistemologies. In fact, though the poem was published in the 1950s, there is nothing to suggest that it does not take place in the 1920s, looking back to a time when sexual group identifications allowed for a greater movement of desire. It is, in many ways, a poem out of time, harkening back on the eve of a sexually and politically conservative decade to an earlier moment.

We can find the genealogical traces of "Cafe: 3 A.M." in Hughes's Harlem Renaissance poetry collections, *The Weary Blues* and *Fine Clothes to the Jew*. Even while his early poems like "The Negro Speaks of Rivers" (1921) and "I, Too, Sing America" (1925) earned him recognition and opportunity from uplift guardians of the Harlem Renaissance, Hughes's commitment from early in his career to the musical and sexual underworlds of Harlem's nightlife and his valorization of the black folk as something other than a mass to be elevated often made it a challenge to assimilate his work into the cultural uplift endeavors of the black middle-class. *The Weary Blues* and *Fine Clothes to the Jew* are commonly noted for Hughes's choice of subject matter, his use of vernacular language, his invocation of the space of performance, and his formal experimentation with the structure and rhythm of the blues. Robert Hale identifies *Fine Clothes to the Jew* in particular as both culturally and aesthetically revolutionary, in that it "embodies a shift in the subject and style of poetry" that constituted the literary norm at the time, and Rampersad suggests that with this volume, Hughes is "deliberately defining poetic tradition according to the standards of a group often seen as sub-poetic—the black masses." In poems like "Cabaret Girl," "Red Silk Stockings," "Young Prostitute," "Nude Young Dancer," and "Jazzonia," his revolutionary redefinition of the poetic tradition sketched both the pleasurable possibilities and exploitative relations of the underworld and gave poetic attention to men and, more often, women who stood outside the sexual norms and standards of racial uplift. Black artists and intellectuals of the Harlem Renaissance generally promoted Hughes's poetry, though many critics were wary of his turn to imagery that too-easily substantiated dominant racial images of sexual excess and nightlife existence. *Fine Clothes to the Jew*, for that reason, gave rise to some of the most personal and virulent critical denunciations leveled against Hughes by his contemporaries.

In *The Weary Blues* and *Fine Clothes to the Jew*, Hughes draws from the rhythms, sounds, improvisations, and intimacies of the blues and urban nightlife performance to map the spatio-temporal experience of afterhours. As Stephen Tracy and Brent Edwards have shown, Hughes's use of musical rhythm and blues cadence not only records and documents the scene of black performance but marks and ensures future performances. Tracy's meticulous notation of these blues poems, including diagrams of basic chord changes and time signatures onto Hughes's verse, supports the notion that with them Hughes seeks to perform, rather than simply describe, the time and place of the blues song. Hughes's blues poem, Edwards argues, not only "suggests a transcription" of the blues, but at the same time also "suggests the graphic particularities of a musical score: a writing that precedes and structures a performance rather than follows and records it."

These blues poems share the page with a number of free verse poems that similarly evoke the time, space, and performance of Harlem's nightlife. Though these poems have been given less attention, they are a necessary accompaniment to his blues poems, a musical second line that inscribes the space and time of Harlem's performance with a queerness that is both contained within and exceeds blues music as such. Hughes's attention to the temporal profile and time consciousness—the vibrations—of afterhours is one place where we can locate this queerness, not only in his reorganization of respectable time and his critique of the reification of normative temporal orders, but also in his poetry's relationship to history, the archive, and documentation. The specificities of time and place are central to understanding these poems. In titles like "Lenox Avenue: Midnight," "Midnight Dancer," "Harlem Night Song," "To Midnight Nan at Leroy's," and

> SURELY THE MAIN REASON THAT READERS HESITATE TO HEAR OR SEE HUGHES IN THESE POEMS IS THAT 'THE VARIOUS BLUES PERSONAE' CROSS GENDER POSITIONS AND, IN CONVENTIONAL BLUES FASHION, ADDRESS OR MOURN AN ABSENT, OFTEN MALE LOVER."

"The Cat and the Saxophone (2 A.M.)," Hughes locates the lyric scene in the spatial and temporal coordinates of Harlem's nightlife and indexes people and events that consciously seek to evade archival legibility. . . .

Source: Shane Vogel, "Closing Time: Langston Hughes and the Queer Poetics of Harlem Nightlife," in *Criticism*, Vol. 48, No. 3, Summer 2006, pp. 397–425.

Martin Joseph Ponce
In the following excerpt, Ponce analyzes the language and structure of Hughes's blues poems.

. . . This returns us to the question of who speaks in Hughes's blues poems. It is worth rehearsing the shift in poetics registered from "The Weary Blues" to the unframed blues poems in order to clarify what is at stake in reading the latter. "The Weary Blues" deploys two voices: a narrator's voice describes the context of a blues performance he heard in the past, while the blues singer's song is quoted in the poem. Those voices, marked by differences in diction, quotation marks, and indentions, already begin to invade one another by the third line.

> Droning a drowsy syncopated tune,
> Rocking back and forth to a mellow croon,
> I heard a Negro play.
> Down on Lenox Avenue the other night
> By the pale dull pallor of an old gas light
> He did a lazy sway . . .
> He did a lazy sway . . .
> To the tune o' those Weary Blues.

The "I" and the "he" are potentially conflated through the syntax of the dangling modifier. Supposedly, it is not the narrating "I" who drones a syncopated tune or rocks to a mellow croon, but "he," the "Negro" bluesman. A similar operation occurs later in the poem, just before the blues singer's song is inserted:

In a deep song voice with a melancholy tone
I heard that Negro sing, that old piano moan—
"Ain't got nobody in all this world,
Ain't got nobody but ma self.
I's gwine to quit ma frownin'
And put ma troubles on the shelf."

In spite of the typographic and linguistic demarcations (the bluesman's voice rendered in dialect) that divide the two voices, the syntactic confusions, line repetition, rhyme schemes, and rhythmic cadences indicate the narrator's tentative identification with the blues singer.

In the blues poems in *Fine Clothes to the Jew*, by contrast, Hughes drops the framing apparatus that kept the two voices in "The Weary Blues" at least mostly distinct. In the process, he dissolves the formal and linguistic distance between himself and the culture that has produced the blues. The "I's" of the persona and the bluesman become inextricable from one another. It is this self-projection into the poem that reveals Hughes's identification with black working-class culture. Rather than hover around the edges of the blues performance, the "I" of the unframed blues poem is thrown into the space of the blues and addresses us from "inside" that space ("Hey!"). Eschewing the predominant view of poetics advocated by New Negro theorists—what Paul Allan Anderson terms a linear, progressive "folk to formal" narrative of black cultural modernity (167–68)—Hughes no longer positions himself "straddling the discursive gap between literary and 'folk' culture" but resolutely crosses that gap, leaping into the blues while leaving the reader no other perspective in which to seek refuge (Ramazani, 144). These voices hit the reader with a force that the "brown man's fist" in "Beale Street Love" seems to allegorize, forcing one to reckon with them without any mediating assistance from an external narrator (*FC*). One must either accept the affect that these poems evoke, the form in which the experiences are cast, and the culture from which they spring and simultaneously articulate, or deny all three any legitimacy. The form of these poems, in short, "compells recognition" of "the black folk . . . as human" through a relentless insistence on the vernacular "art of the black folk" (DuBois, 297). But as implied by the embattled politics of representation with which the New Negro movement wrestled, the outcome of such a reckoning is far from foreordained.

In noting the formal shift from "The Weary Blues" to the later blues poems, most readers automatically, naturally, assume that the voices represented in the latter are analogous to the bluesman's in the former, not the poet's. Hartmut Grandel suggests of "The Weary Blues" that "through his imaginative involvement the speaker has been transformed, he has become a blues singer himself" (124). But critics balk at carrying through that logic, sidestepping the possibility that Hughes positions himself as the "blues singer" of the later blues poems. Explicating these formal differences, Ramazani claims, "No longer the intrusive amanuensis of 'The Weary Blues' . . . the poet discards the frame and vanishes behind the various blues personae" (148). But does he actually vanish? Did Hughes, to give voice to black working-class culture, have to silence his own?

Hughes lends support to this idea in *The Big Sea* when he states that the poems in *Fine Clothes to the Jew* are "more impersonal" than those in his first book. Indeed, in contrast to all those "I's" falling down the left side of the page in "Proem" ("I am a Negro," "I've been a slave," "I've been a singer," etc.), which frames *The Weary Blues*, the "I" of *Fine Clothes to the Jew* surfaces inconspicuously. Not until the second line of "Hey!" does an "I" appear, and even there, rather than begin the line, it is embedded in the middle, pressed up against a contraction, unstressed and glided over: "Sun's a settin', / This is what I'm gonna sing." "A Note on Blues" makes no reference to the poet himself, and in that respect it diverges greatly, for example, from Johnson's elaborate preface to *God's Trombones* (also 1927), which, running to some eleven pages, combines personal narrative, social history, and an explanation of poetics. Hughes's compressed description of the blues, by contrast, is registered in the passive voice: the poems that bookend *Fine Clothes to the Jew* "are written after the manner of the Negro folk-songs known as Blues." It is as if Hughes were relinquishing or suppressing his own poetic agency.

Surely the main reason that readers hesitate to hear or see Hughes in these poems is that "the various blues personae" cross gender positions and, in conventional blues fashion, address or mourn an absent, often male lover. Implicitly or explicitly presuming that the "I" solely represents the position of the blues speaker, some commentators place the blues poem in the genre of dramatic monologue. In effect, this reading effaces Hughes's presence from the poem. Steven C. Tracy elaborates on this issue:

Hughes attempted to present a variety of the subjects dealt with in the blues, and in order to do that it was necessary to speak in voices other than his own. Hughes told Nat Hentoff that much of his poetry "is in the form of a kind of dramatic monologue," indicating that there are speakers other than Hughes who are expressing themselves and characterizing themselves as they speak, not only through their language but by their choice of the blues as the vehicle of expression. This dramatic dialogue technique is obvious, for example, in the poems that have female speakers. Of Hughes's blues poems which have speakers whose sex is identifiable from external evidence (i.e., pronouns, references to the opposite sex, presumed heterosexuality, and placement in sections of books with sexual indicators like "Blues for Men" or "Mammy Songs" in *Shakespeare in Harlem*), about one-quarter have women speakers; just a slightly greater fraction use men as speakers.

Leaving aside the unexplained "dramatic dialogue," *Fine Clothes to the Jew* is not divided into sections labeled "Blues for Men," "Blues for Ladies," or "Mammy Songs" as *Shakespeare in Harlem* (1942) is. More to the point, can one so confidently make recourse to "presumed heterosexuality"? Is it so "obvious" that Hughes does not identify with his "female speakers"?

Conceiving the blues poems as dramatic monologues helps account for the wide array of gender-crossing speakers in *Fine Clothes to the Jew*, since the form, broadly defined, refers to "a poem in the first person spoken by, or almost entirely by, someone who is indicated not to be the poet." Signals that the speaker is not the poet include the title (Tennyson's "Ulysses" [1842], Browning's "Andrea del Sarto" [1855], Eliot's "Love Song of J. Alfred Prufrock" [1917], or, closer to Hughes's own sensibility, the 244 character titles presented in Edgar Lee Masters's *Spoon River Anthology* [1915]), the construction of a specific time and place often removed from the poet's and the reader's "plane of reality" (Sinfield, 23), and the implicit presence of a "silent auditor" (typified in Browning's "My Last Duchess") who exerts an influence on the movement of the speaker's speech. Of the seventeen blues poems in *Fine Clothes to the Jew*, only four have titles corresponding to the speaker (and they are not reserved solely for female speakers: "Bad Man," "Po' Boy Blues," "Gal's Cry for a Dying Lover," and "Young Gal's Blues"). The other titles either are thematic ("Hard Luck") or refer to the character who is sung about ("Gypsy Man"). Neither does Hughes develop a concrete setting for his

blues speakers; the poems' power comes in part from the directness of the utterances.

Most important, discussions of the form have shown that "speakers of the dramatic monologue are not totally autonomous: we always hear the poet's voice through theirs." The most relevant way that the poet's voice is heard, for my purposes, is through the distinction between the fiction of speech and the conventions of poetry. As Loy D. Martin explains, "Dramatic monologues call attention to the fact that language within their domain seems to operate both at a level that is consciously 'poetic' in some traditional sense and at a separate syntactic, semantic, or merely 'message' level"; these two levels reveal "a doubleness or bifurcation of the text." This splitting is most apparent when poetic devices such as rhymed couplets violate the realism of the speaker's colloquial speech.

The idea that in the dramatic monologue there is an "inherent dichotomy between the voice of the poem's speaker and that of the poet, who is inevitably present" can be productively recontextualized to shed light on the dynamics of the blues poems and Hughes's presence in them (Howe, 8). Whereas in many Victorian instances "the voice of the poem's speaker" is derived from historical or mythological sources or simply fabricated out of thin air, in Hughes's blues poems it stems from contemporary black vernacular expressivity. Thus the notion that "classical epic and lyric forms... have their origins in song, while the dramatic monologue emphatically represents speech" needs to be modified when applied to Hughes's blues poems, since they do have their origins in song. Pursuing queer resonances in his work, Anne Borden characterizes Hughes as "a Black man who heard the voices of many... within and without himself." Of course, he not only heard those voices but wrote them into poetry. The suggestion that those voices emerge from "within and without himself" points us back to the question of how the blues poems relate to the vernacular blues....

Source: Martin Joseph Ponce, "Langston Hughes's Queer Blues," in *Modern Language Quarterly*, Vol. 66, No. 4, December 2005, pp. 505–37.

David Chinitz

In the following excerpt, Chinitz credits Hughes with having invented blues poetry.

... Langston Hughes was the first writer to grapple with the inherent difficulties of blues poetry, and he succeeded—not always, but

> THERE ARE IDIOMATIC *IMAGES* IN HUGHES AS WELL: THE KNIFE THAT AVENGES INFIDELITY, THE RIVER THAT IS THE LETHAL LAST RESORT OF THE UNHAPPY, THE RAILROAD THAT BOTH PROFFERS ESCAPE AND THREATENS DESERTION."

often—in producing poems that manage to capture the quality of genuine blues in performance while remaining effective as poems. This essay will show how in inventing blues poetry Hughes solved the two closely related problems I have sketched: first, how to write blues lyrics in such a way that they work on the printed page, and second, how to exploit the blues form poetically without losing all sense of authenticity.

I

It is sometimes useful to define "blues poetry" in the broadest possible terms, as Onwuchckwa Jemie does, for example, in his introduction to Hughes's work: "The blues poem...is one that, regardless of form, utilizes the themes, motifs, language, and imagery common to popular blues literature." Such a definition usefully stresses how pervasively the blues influence Hughes's art; in fact, Jemie is quite willing to classify much of Hughes's *prose* as blues poetry. For the purposes of this essay, however, I am considering the category of blues poetry to include those lyrics that make use of blues imagery, formulae and rhythms, as well as a stanza that is at least closely related to the normative blues form. This reasonably narrow definition makes systematic analysis of Hughes's blues poems fruitful, for within this class of poems a certain consistency of technique can be identified.

Blues use a number of stanzaic forms, but the three-line "AAB" stanza is so ubiquitous as to have become the standard from which all others are seen as deviating. This form is generated by a single line which is first repeated, often with minor impromptu variations, and then rhymed in a line that elaborates on or answers it:

My gal's got legs, yes, legs like a kangaroo.
My gal's got legs, legs like a kangaroo.
If you don't watch out she'll hop all over you.
(qtd. in Hughes and Bontemps 395)

The second and third lines are often referred to as the *repeat line* and the *response line*. (In Hughes's poetry, each line is halved so that the stanza is rendered in six lines rather than three; lines 3–4, in this case, function together as repeat lines and lines 5–6 as response lines.) In performance the blues stanza generates dramatic suspense as the audience anticipates the satisfying closure of rhyme and sense in the response line; this suspense gives the singer or lyricist opportunities for irony, surprise, humor, understatement and other effects. The repeat line heightens the suspense by delaying the resolution.

Hughes was attracted to the blues particularly by what the music represented to him: an expression of the resilience and tragedy of the African-American lower class. To some extent Hughes romanticized this social group, with which he always identified but to which he himself never really belonged. What Hughes called "just plain folks" are, in his portraiture, never merely "plain": they are sensitive, passionate, and frequently wise, drawing unconvoluted wisdom from their very lack of sophistication. Most significantly, Hughes's black proletariat is endowed with an inexhaustible energy that veils and relieves its suffering. It is this quality that is expressed with particular clarity in both jazz and the blues:

For sad as Blues may be, there's almost always something humorous about them—even if it's the kind of humor that laughs to keep from crying.
("Songs")

Hughes's explanation for this coincidence of opposing emotions was straightforward: the disenfranchisement of the African-American masses and the various frustrations it engendered demanded indirect outlets supplied by the subculture. The blues were "sad songs" because they manifested the "hopeless weariness" of an oppressed people; they were "gay songs because you had to be gay or die" (*Big Sea*). Hughes sought to catch this "blues spirit"—this compensatory expression of conflicting emotions—in his poetry, in part by imitating the blues themselves.

There are as many blues styles as there are regions and periods of blues activity. The one distinction of real importance for Hughes, however, separates the genres often referred to as "folk blues" and "classic blues"—a classification that points to differences in performer (indigenous talents or touring professionals), in patronage (local community or mass audience), in style (traditional or polished), in creation (improvised or composed) and in transmission (oral or written). Classic blues are comparatively self-conscious, structurally complex, and carefully packaged, a stage sophistication of the original folk product. Popularized by great singers like Ma Rainey, Bessie Smith and Ida Cox, the "vaudeville blues," as they are also called, won over many of the early blues admirers among the intelligentsia. Folklorists, however, including Zora Neale Hurston and Sterling Brown, have often rejected the classic blues as mercenary and inauthentic. Hughes did not share in this condemnation; on the contrary, as Steven Tracy has shown, when Hughes discusses the blues with any specificity, he seems almost always to have the classic blues in mind. Though Hughes was intimately familiar with the folk blues, as a northern urbanite his access to the music flowed naturally through commercial channels. Ever catholic in his tastes, he evidently thought of classic blues singers as products of the same folk culture and did not object to their merging of blues with popular song.

That Hughes writes his best blues poetry when he tries least to imitate the folk blues is a critical commonplace. So seen, Hughes is too self-conscious, too determined to romanticize the African-American proletariat, too intent on reproducing what he takes to be the quaint humor and naive simplicity of the folk blues to write successfully in that vein. Tracy argues that in extending the blues into another art form, Hughes actually identifies with the professional blues composer, through whose influence his own blues are "limited in expression" ("Tune" 73). Like the commercial songwriter, Hughes is determined to write lyrics more like the blues than the blues themselves.

This critical consensus needs to be challenged, for Hughes's blues poems—including his best in the genre—are in fact considerably closer stylistically to the folk blues than to the deliberately cultivated classic blues. It is true that Hughes emphasizes his own reading of the blues, using the form to reinforce a particular construction of the African-American character. But he conveys his perceptions as a folk artist should: through an accumulation of details over the entire span of his blues oeuvre, rather than by overloading each poem with quaintness and naivete. The differences between Hughes's lyrics and the folk blues are better explained by the exigencies of writing blues for the printed page than by an identification on Hughes's part with the commercial lyricist. And these differences are not

inevitably to Hughes's disadvantage: they are just differences.

Hughes's "Young Gal's Blues" will serve to illustrate the relationship between his poetry and the folk blues:

> I'm gonna walk to de graveyard
> 'Hind ma friend Miss Cora Lee.
> I'm gonna walk to de graveyard
> 'Hind ma friend Miss Cora Lee.
> Cause when I'm dead some
> Body'll have to walk behind me.
> I'm goin' to de po' house
> To see ma old Aunt Clew.
> Goin' to de po' house
> To see ma old Aunt Clew.
> When I'm old an' ugly
> I'll want to see somebody, too.
> De po' house is lonely
> An' de grave is cold.
> O, de po' house is lonely,
> De graveyard grave is cold.
> But I'd rather be dead than
> To be ugly an' old.
> When love is gone what
> Can a young gal do?
> When love is gone, O,
> What can a young gal do?
> Keep on a-lovin' me, daddy,
> Cause I don't want to be blue.

Arnold Rampersad has observed that virtually all of the poems in *Fine Clothes to the Jew*, the 1927 collection in which Hughes essentially originated blues poetry, fall deliberately within the "range of utterance of common black folk" (141). This surely applies to "Young Gal's Blues," in which Hughes avoids the conventionally "poetic" language and ideas that the subjects of death, aging and love sometimes elicit in his ordinary lyric poetry. But how folkish is the voice we hear in this poem? Spellings like *po'* and *de* point up the speaker's dialectical pronunciation, yet her grammar is standard. Her stanzas cohere, too, with a logic that would be remarkable in an improvised folk composition, where the verses generally relate to each other not through a rational progression but through a consistency of mood, music and theme. But Hughes is aware of this discrepancy. Had he wished to write a neat, polished poem, he could have ended "Young Gal's Blues" with the third stanza, which resolves the opposition set up by its predecessors with a satisfying finality. Instead, Hughes sacrifices what would have been a most un-folkish tidiness by having the girl step outside the apparent parameters of the poem to elaborate on her fear of loneliness. The structural superfluity of the fourth stanza, in other words, is functional.

One of the challenges facing the blues poet is the portrayal of character in the absence of a performer. Working on his small canvas, Hughes brings his "young gal" to life in a few brush strokes. These include her charitable activities in the opening stanzas and her pretended explanation for them—"pretended" because Cora Lee and Aunt Clew have put her in mind of her own future, and not, of course, vice versa. The intrusive frankness of the phrase "old an' ugly" in a verse that describes the girl's kindness to her aunt, the decisive conclusion of the third stanza, and the struggle against melancholy in the last all contribute to a quick and effective delineation of the girl's character and frame of mind. Her turns of thought are fresh and sometimes surprising, but their development is well controlled by the poet. Without calling undue attention to the poet's craft, for instance, the first two stanzas delicately create the dilemma that is resolved in the third. The girl seems to be depicting two similar situations when she is actually setting up an opposition between contrasting evils. Yet the inverted chronological sequence—death in the first stanza, old age in the second—implies that the speaker is not sketching a narrative of her future; she does not expect to grow old and die, but to choose one fate or the other. Hughes thus maintains the illusion of an inconsequential folk-blues logic, while the structural grammar of the poem takes the place of the performing personality that a blues audience normally has before it.

To see what Hughes's blues poetry might have been like if he had truly adopted the vaudeville blues as his model, one need only contrast "Young Gal's Blues" with the "Golden Brown Blues," a lyric Hughes wrote for composer W. C. Handy:

Dusky eyes tantalize,
Hair just like Moses';
Finger tips, sugar lips
Sweet as red roses.
Ma Beale street Mamma some charmer,
Ma sweet Golden Brown.

Watch your man—understand?
All the men's ravin'.
Better see 'mediately
That he's behavin'.
Man in the moon in a swoon
Fell for this Golden Brown.
(Handy 91)

Hughes might well have invoked the sharp distinction he made between his *poetry* and his

verse in the case of this commercial-style blues (*Big Sea* 53). The continual internal rhyme is alien to the folk blues, which, as improvisations, tend to eschew complex prosody. The images and allusions are, likewise, uncharacteristic of the traditional blues, as is the diction, which is conspicuously remote from the common "range of utterance." The restraint of "Young Gal's Blues" is obvious in comparison. Even when, after the quoted introductory verses, "Golden Brown Blues" modulates into standard AAB form, the lyrics remain slicker than Hughes's blues poems ever get, though by no means better as poetry:

Ashes to ashes, ashes to ashes,
Dust to dust, right down to dust.
Ashes to ashes, ashes to ashes,
Dust to dust, right down to dust.
Golden Brown done got him,
An' I'm bound to rust.

Yet this song was written only a year after the publication of the brilliant blues poems in *Fine Clothes to the Jew* (Rampersad 160). Clearly Hughes could write vaudeville blues when he chose to, and just as clearly his poetic efforts were in another direction. If he considered the blues poet a relative of the classic blues composer, they remained distant cousins.

II

... But Hughes's unclosed endings serve a further purpose: they tend to run his blues poems together, building them into a larger mechanism. Hughes's natural attraction to closure is demonstrated by the neatly recapitulative endings of many of the lyrics in *The Weary Blues*; by the time he wrote the impressive blues poetry of *Fine Clothes to the Jew*, he seems to have learned the value of *avoiding* closure. Understanding the dialogical flow of the blues poems into each other is important as a corrective to the charge that Hughes strove too hard to make his blues poems "generally representative" of an idealized African-American commonfolk (Tracy, "Tune" 79). Each poem's lack of finality suggests that it be read *not* as conclusive or representative, but as one piece in a montage portrait of the African-American proletariat. Hughes would later develop this principle still further in *Montage of a Dream Deferred*, where the poems are explicitly worked into a sequence.

Like many other genres of folk song, the blues use formulaic phrases and images freely. Phrases like "Going down the road," "I had a dream last night," and "I'm laughing to keep from crying" are an important part of the blues idiom and accordingly find their way into Hughes's blues poems. There are idiomatic *images* in Hughes as well: the knife that avenges infidelity, the river that is the lethal last resort of the unhappy, the railroad that both proffers escape and threatens desertion. But Hughes frequently gives these traditional elements a new twist, turning them to his own purposes. . . .

Source: David Chinitz, "Literacy and Authenticity: The Blues Poems of Langston Hughes," in *Callaloo*, Vol. 19, No. 1, Winter 1996, pp. 177–92.

Ruth A. Banes

In the following excerpt, Banes reviews Steven C. Tracey's view that Hughes's variant poetic forms parallel a variety of blues performances and that his themes reflect urban blues lyrics.

. . . Paradoxically, we learn more about blues from poetry, literature and academic research than from the autobiography of a bluesman. Steven C. Tracy's *Langston Hughes & the Blues* offers the best and most comprehensive view of blues research available. Chapter two, "Defining the Blues," presents a detailed historiography of blues scholarship, still emphasizing that the complexity as well as the emotional and cultural depth of blues will intimidate those "trying to reduce it to a pithy phrase" (60). Anthropologists, ethno-musicologists, literary critics, and historians have asked and debated contradictory questions: to what extent does the blues reflect African culture? Does a literary treatment of blues necessarily romanticize folk culture? Has commercialization destroyed the authenticity of blues? Should one dismiss the criticism of the black bourgeoisie? Does blues create a false consciousness?

Basing his conclusions upon previous scholarship, Tracy asserts that there is a demonstrated parallel between the African griot (a community leader, mystic and trickster) and the bluesman, and that African influences can be discerned in the musical structure and performance of blues, including blue notes, flattened thirds and sevenths, and diatonic, heptatonic and pentatonic scales. However, it is important to remember that blues borrow from European music as well. Blues origins are in work songs or field hollers, but the first blues were probably sung in the 1890s and represent an adaptation of older instrumental and vocal techniques (which responded to one kind of oppressive system) to a new kind of music, one that addressed the unique problems posed by the new oppressive

system and provided an appropriate way of expressing these problems. (75)

Blues themes are various and complex, reflecting a wide range of experience, and dealing, as Tracy points out, especially with male-female relations but with a good deal more as well: work, raising children, hunger, politics, war, automobiles, various kinds of sexuality, dancing, good times—even trips into outer space—and most of the gaps in between. (86)

Blues forms are equally complex, but the AAB form is prevalent. Lyrics are not logical but associative, relating a series of thoughts or events. Blues are cathartic for both performer and audience, affirming African-American, rejecting white culture, protesting oppression in its variant forms in "social status, situation, life-style, and social institutions," and asserts an individual's "ability to overcome inequities and extend his power" (102).

Unlike most scholars who have analyzed blues, Tracy does not [dis]miss "vaudeville" or "classic" blues as unauthentic simply because of the music's urban origins or commercialization. As a blues performer and former disc jockey for blues radio in Cincinnati, he is well acquainted with the music and thus willing to recognize that it changes: "the vaudeville influence diversified the blues tradition, sometimes sweetening it, sometimes making it maudlin or stilted, and occasionally complementing it, providing varied stanzaic patterns that were departures from the traditional stanzas" (171–172). Because of his familiarity with blues music, Tracy is able to detail blues forms, rhythms and themes in Hughes's poetry, showing parallels between musical and poetic structure and providing examples of blues songs which resemble specific poems. Whether or not one can read music, Tracy's explanations of *AAA, AAB, ABB* and *ABC* forms are as clear and easily understandable as his chord progressions and poetic notation.

Tracy's main point is that Hughes's variant poetic forms parallel a variety of blues performances, emphasizing the diversity of blues, and that his themes reflect urban blues lyrics which may be "harshly realistic, unabashedly lascivious, euphemistically suggestive, unadorned or highly decorated, naive and sweet, sentimental, and sometimes fantastical, depending upon who wrote and performed them" (182). Perhaps because of the possibility of censorship, Hughes avoided the blatant sexuality of blues, discarding in his poetry the countless rough metaphors for intercourse and genitalia, as well as references to homosexuality, drugs or alcohol—also frequent subjects of blues songs. However, many of Hughes's poetic themes do parallel the music: superstition and bad luck, suicide, violence and death. Most significantly, Hughes condemns racial prejudice as well as social stratification by skin shade. His humor makes use of slapstick, sarcasm, hyperbole and understatement—"a kind of humor that laughs to keep from crying" (183). He shows how despair, hunger, joblessness and poverty linked together create an unending series of pressures and disadvantages which distort and limit individual lives. A blue mood resists oppression with a hope for escape, symbolized by a train, a river, a trip North or a sunrise. Through a unique combination of hope and despair, the blues poem or song becomes "a type of therapy, a way of working out difficulties and a way of facing, not evading, the problem at hand" (192).

Most memorable for me are Tracy's readings of Hughes's boogie poems, which comprise an intricate series of interwoven improvisations over a set boogie-woogie rhythm...words, imagery, moods, and themes...constructing a complex interrelationship between music, the musical instrument, the performance, and a set or attitudes exemplified by them. (225).

Hughes describes "the boogie-woogie rumble of a dream deferred" (227), a situation which elicits the black solidarity and strength heard in the driving rhythm of a wild music. Hughes knew best the music of the city: Kansas City, Chicago, New York and Washington. From this urban folk music, which was, and continues to be, disparaged among middle-class blacks, Hughes perceived sensitive and diverse responses to racism. In his words,

> "....the alternating despair and hope of the blues, the tears and laughter, are like the eternal roiling of the waves under the alternating light and darkness of time, and the indomitable spirit of the human heart beats through it all, accepting it as it comes, sometimes despairing but never giving up ....the despair articulated is in the service of the hope expressed either in words or in the black musical performance itself." (116)

After 1930, Hughes's poetry increasingly expressed the socio-political protest only implied in boogie-woogie, sometimes directly advocating revolution as a solution for blues. Tracy shows

how the poem "Backlash Blues" resembles Bessie Smith's song "Poor Man Blues," since both angrily protest a system which forces poverty upon black people; Hughes, however, is more radical in his overt call for black rage and revolt....

Source: Ruth A. Banes, "Relentlessly Writing the Weary Song: Blues Legacies in Literature," in *Canadian Review of American Studies*, Vol. 21, No. 1, 1990, pp. 57–71.

SOURCES

Chinitz, David, "Literacy and Authenticity: The Blues Poems of Langston Hughes," in *Callaloo*, Vol. 19, No. 1, 1996, pp. 177–92.

Ford, Karen Jackson, "Do Right to Write Right: Langston Hughes's Aesthetics of Simplicity," in *Langston Hughes*, edited by Harold Bloom, Infobase Publishing, 2002, pp. 101–22.

Hughes, Langston, *The Collected Works of Langston Hughes*, Vol. 13, *Autobiography: The Big Sea*, edited by Joseph McLaren, University of Missouri Press, 2002.

————, "The Twenties: Harlem and Its Negritude," *African Forum*, Vol. 1, 1966, pp. 11–20; reprinted in *The Collected Works of Langston Hughes*, Vol. 9, *Essays on Art, Race, Politics, and World Affairs*, edited by Christopher C. De Santis, University of Missouri Press, 2002, pp. 465–74.

————, "The Weary Blues," in *The New Oxford Book of American Verse*, edited by Richard Ellmann, Oxford University Press, 1976, pp. 692–93.

Hutchinson, George, *The Harlem Renaissance in Black and White*, Belknap, 1997.

Johnson, Patricia A., and Walter C. Farrell, "How Langston Hughes Used the Blues," in *MELUS*, Vol. 6, No. 1, 1979, pp. 55–63.

Said, Edward W., *Orientalism*, Pantheon, 1978.

Tracy, Stephen C., "Langston Hughes: Poetry, Blues, and Gospel—Somewhere to Stand," in *Langston Hughes: The Man, His Art, and His Continuing Influence*, edited by C. James Trotman, Garland, 1995, pp. 51–61.

Waldron, Edward E., "The Blues Poetry of Langston Hughes," in *Negro American Literature Forum*, Vol. 5, No. 4, 1971, pp. 140–49.

X, Malcolm, with Alex Haley, *The Autobiography of Malcolm X*, Ballantine, 1999.

FURTHER READING

Haugen, Brenda, *Langston Hughes: The Voice of Harlem*, Compass Point Books, 2006.
    Haugen's comprehensive biography of Hughes is aimed at a young-adult audience.

Hughes, Langston, *The Collected Works of Langston Hughes*, University of Missouri Press, 2001–2011.

This series is the standard source for all of Hughes's writings and runs to sixteen volumes as of 2011.

Hughes, Langston, *I Wonder as I Wander*, Rinehart, 1956.

This second volume of Hughes's autobiography focuses on his travels overseas during the 1930s.

Smith, Katherine Capshaw, ed., *Children's Literature of the Harlem Renaissance*, Indiana University Press, 2004.

The essays in this anthology explain the children's literature produced by black authors in light of the black experience in America. In particular, it considers the aesthetic qualities of Hughes's children's literature written in collaboration with Arna Bontemps.

SUGGESTED SEARCH TERMS

Langston Hughes

Harlem Renaissance

Langston Hughes AND Weary Blues

African American poetry

negritude

Edgar Allan Poe AND The Bells

jazz AND literature

ragtime

jazz AND Harlem

Vachel Lindsay

music AND Langston Hughes

The World Is Too Much with Us

"The World Is Too Much with Us" is a sonnet by English romantic poet William Wordsworth. It was first published in Wordsworth's *Poems in Two Volumes* in 1807, although the poem was written several years before that, probably in 1803 or 1804 but possibly as early as 1802. Wordsworth had only started writing sonnets in May 1802. Before that he had not cared for the form, but hearing his sister Dorothy read aloud to him some sonnets by John Milton, England's great seventeenth-century poet, he was inspired to write a flurry of sonnets himself. He then made extensive use of the sonnet form throughout his poetic career.

The year in which "The World Is Too Much with Us" was published marks the end of what is sometimes referred to as Wordsworth's "great decade"; it was the time during which he wrote almost all his great works. This sonnet expresses some of Wordsworth's typical themes: a concern with nature and how nature is perceived by the human mind; the need to develop the faculty of imagination; and the lament for a lost, visionary way of perceiving the world.

"The World Is Too Much with Us" is available in almost any collection of Wordsworth's poetry as well as in anthologies of works of the romantic period. It can be found, for example, in *Selected Poetry of William Wordsworth* (2002), edited by Mark van Doren.

WILLIAM WORDSWORTH

1807

William Wordsworth (*The Library of Congress*)

AUTHOR BIOGRAPHY

Usually regarded as England's finest poet since John Milton in the seventeenth century, William Wordsworth was born in Cockermouth, Cumberland, in the English Lake District, on April 7, 1770. Wordsworth grew up absorbing the natural beauty of the Lake District, which was later to provide inspiration for his poetry. He had three brothers and one sister. His mother died when he was eight, and his father, John Wordsworth, died when William was thirteen, leaving him an orphan. When he was nine, he attended Hawkshead Grammar School, about twenty-five miles south of Cockermouth, and remained there until 1787. In that year he moved south to attend St. John's College, Cambridge. He had little interest in his studies, although he did manage to graduate in 1791. After this he spent a year in France, where he enthusiastically embraced the ideals of the French Revolution, which had broken out two years earlier.

Wordsworth published his first poetry collection, *Descriptive Sketches*, in 1793. The poems were written about a trip he had made in 1790 to the Swiss Alps. Two years later, when Wordsworth was living in Racedown, Dorset, in southwestern England, he met Samuel Taylor Coleridge

(1772–1834). Coleridge was also a poet, and the two men soon became close friends.

In 1797, Wordsworth and his sister Dorothy, with whom he was very close, moved to Somerset so they could see more of Coleridge. In 1798, Wordsworth and Coleridge published *Lyrical Ballads*, one of the most important works of English romanticism. Most of the poems were by Wordsworth, but four were written by Coleridge. In 1800, Wordsworth wrote a preface to a second edition of *Lyrical Ballads*, in which he explained the poetic principles that inspired his work.

Wordsworth, his sister, and Coleridge traveled in Germany during 1798 and 1799, and on their return, the Wordsworths moved back to the Lake District, living in Grasmere. Coleridge went to live in nearby Keswick. In 1802, Wordsworth married Mary Hutchinson, whom he had known since he was a child. They had five children, two of whom died in infancy.

In 1807, Wordsworth published *Poems in Two Volumes*, which included "The World Is Too Much with Us" as well as one of his greatest poems, "Ode: Intimations of Immortality from Recollections in Early Childhood." Several years later, Wordsworth had a major quarrel with Coleridge; it took nearly twenty years for them to reconcile.

In 1813, Wordsworth moved to Rydal, England, a few miles from Grasmere, and became a government employee. His official title was distributor of stamps for Westmoreland, and the job provided him with financial security. He continued to write and publish poetry, including in *The Excursion* in 1814, although almost all his best work was now behind him. This decline in poetic quality made no difference to his public reputation, however. He had become a famous poet and was to remain so for the rest of his long life. In 1843, Wordsworth was appointed England's poet laureate.

Wordsworth died at his home in Rydal on April 23, 1850. What is usually regarded as his greatest work, an epic, autobiographical poem titled *The Prelude*, was published posthumously, in 1850.

POEM TEXT

> The world is too much with us; late and soon,
> Getting and spending, we lay waste our
>   powers:

Little we see in Nature that is ours;
We have given our hearts away, a sordid boon!
This Sea that bares her bosom to the moon;   5
The winds that will be howling at all hours,
And are up-gathered now like sleeping flowers;
For this, for everything, we are out of tune;
It moves us not.—Great God! I'd rather be
A Pagan suckled in a creed outworn;   10
So might I, standing on this pleasant lea,
Have glimpses that would make me less
    forlorn;
Have sight of Proteus rising from the sea;
Or hear old Triton blow his wreathèd horn.

POEM SUMMARY

Lines 1–4

Lines 1 and 2 of "The World Is Too Much with Us" set out the basic argument the poet wishes to make. Subsequent lines will elaborate on this basic premise. When he mentions the world in the first line, the poet is referring to the world of material goods—things people like to buy. He suggests that people spend too much time acquiring these kinds of material goods; they spend too much time being consumers of whatever products are sold in the marketplace. In other words, the poet makes a complaint against the materialism of the culture.

In the second part of line 1, he states that this situation has been going on for some time and is likely to continue in the future. The result of such activity is stated at the end of line 2: although people may acquire material wealth, they pay a price because the focus on acquiring material things diminishes another, far more important aspect of life.

In lines 3 and 4, the poet explains a little more of what he means. In their rush to acquire material things, people have lost their connection with nature. In doing so, they have lost something of vital importance, something that is essential to their humanity. The poet claims that what has been gained is not worth the loss.

Lines 5–8

In these lines the poet gives examples of what he is talking about when he says that people have lost their connection with nature. He mentions the sea and the winds: the sea under moonlight and the fierceness of the winds. Line 7 means that the winds as the poet writes are quiet, as if they are asleep.

In line 8, the poet states that people are out of touch with these phenomena in nature, and with all other aspects of nature as well. An entire connection has been lost.

Lines 9–14

Continuing the thought he has been developing, the poet states that nothing in nature makes any impression on people any more. He implies that people barely notice it, and it leaves them unmoved. In the second part of line 9, he begins his vehement protest against such a state of affairs and goes on to describe the kind of vision he would prefer to have when he looks at nature. He would sooner, as he explains in line 10, go back to living in a pre-Christian, pagan world, one that has long since been left behind. He would like to do this because it would allow him to see nature in a different way from the way modern people do. He imagines that then he would be able, from the pleasant meadow where he stands now, to look out at the sea and see the ancient pagan gods. This would make him happier, he says. In the last two lines he

TOPICS FOR FURTHER STUDY

- Read Wordsworth's sonnet "Composed upon Westminster Bridge, September 3, 1802." Write an essay in which you compare it to "The World Is Too Much with Us." How are the sonnets similar and how do they differ in theme and mood?

- Write a sonnet on any topic, following the Shakespearean rather than the Petrarchan sonnet form. You can get assistance for this project by reading the instructions contained in the article "Writing a Sonnet," available at the Dummies.com Web site maintained by Wiley Publishing: http://www.dummies.com/how-to/content/writing-a-sonnet.html.

- Wordsworth's sister Dorothy is famous for the journals she kept that describe many walking expeditions she and Wordsworth undertook in the Lake District. Sometimes Wordsworth drew on Dorothy's descriptions to write his poems. Take a trip out in nature and take a notebook with you. At some point, sit down and record your impressions of the scene in front of you or something that you encountered earlier in the walk. Record your feelings too, as you sit in nature. Does being in nature make you feel different from how you feel on, say, a normal school day? If so, why do you think this should be? Upload your notebook entries to your blog site so others can share them and comment on their feelings as well.

- If possible, consult *Poetry for Young People: William Wordsworth* (2003), edited by Alan Liu, and illustrated by James Muir. It contains twenty of Wordsworth's poems, each accompanied by a full-page illustration. In a small group, take turns reading a poem aloud and leading a discussion about it with the group. How effective are the illustrations in bringing out the meaning of the poems? If this edition is not available, choose poems from whatever edition you have. Note how reading the poem aloud often makes the meaning easier to understand.

---

mentions two such gods in ancient Greek mythology: Proteus, who was able to assume a variety of shapes, and Triton, who was often shown blowing on a conch shell to calm the waters. Both gods were associated with the sea.

THEMES

Nature

The major theme in "The World Is Too Much with Us" is a longing for the human connection with nature that the poet believes has been lost in the materialism of modern culture. He was writing during the Industrial Revolution, when more and more people in England were living in crowded urban conditions, cut off from nature and the English countryside where former generations had lived. The poet may also be referring to the perpetual busyness of many people's lives; they are rushing around, yesterday, today, and tomorrow, on whatever small tasks fill up their lives without understanding how their lives as humans connect to the deeper life that is nature. Whatever is gained in the accumulation of possessions or the filling up of one's time with trivial pursuits results also in a much deeper loss: the loss of a sense of organic connection to the universe, the feeling that humans belong to nature. Failure to experience that means that people give their hearts away. In this poem, heart refers to the thing that is closest to the kernel of life, that nourishes life in its largest sense. Just as the physical heart pumps blood through the veins of the body, so the heart as envisioned by the poet is the vital element in life that connects humans to nature. The poet says that the heart has been given away in a fruitless

Signs of the Industrial Revolution (*Dmitry Naumov / Shutterstock.com*)

bargain: the vitality of real life has been traded for something small and petty. The things of the world have closed in on people and made them small also, cut off from the vastness of nature, as represented in the expansive images in the poem of sea and wind. This means that nothing in human life is quite right any more; people's lives are like a musical instrument that is out of tune.

Alienation

In this lyric poem the poet expresses his own feelings in addition to offering generalizations about human life. The complaint he makes, that humans have lost their sense of wonder about nature, applies also to him. The tone of the poem suggests frustration and regret that the kind of feeling the poet wants and declares to be desirable is unobtainable to him. In this sense, the speaker in the poem can be said to be in an alienated state of mind. Alienation means being estranged, disconnected, separate, or indifferent to that which formerly was held in affection.

Isolation replaces a feeling of belonging. As applied in the poem, alienation means that the poet is no longer able to respond to nature the way that, one presumes, he formerly did. Line 3 first expresses this sense of alienation; what was formerly perceived as being a part of oneself, or as belonging to oneself, is no longer understood in that way. Nature has been disowned, and people, including the poet, are the poorer for it. The poet's sense of alienation finds its strongest expression in lines 8 and 9. In the first part of line 8, there is repetition for emphasis, expressing the poet's frustration; line 9 expresses the flatness of the poet's state of mind, generalized to include everyone: people are unmoved by what formerly delighted them or filled them with awe and wonder. Line 9 invokes God in another expression of frustration or disgust at the state of mind the poet has been identifying. Line 12 also expresses the poet's sad and lonely state of mind, cut off from something that is essential to his well-being.

Mythology

Wordsworth employs mythology in the last five lines of the poem as a way of expressing the change he would like to see in human perception when applied to nature. The point of evoking ancient Greek gods such as Triton and Proteus is to convey that there may be a different way of seeing nature. He suggests that to someone who in ancient days believed in the pantheon of gods—even though such a worldview has long since been superseded—nature was an awesome reality, populated by gods whose actions could affect humans. For the pagan, and for the would-be pagan who is the speaker of the poem, nature is alive with conscious beings or forces that are called gods. This way of seeing nature, the poet says, is an antidote to the deadness of modern perception, in which consciousness is experienced only in the individual human self, not as something that pervades animate and inanimate nature alike. He uses these gods of classical mythology as a way of personifying natural forces or powers; he wants to make those powers more arresting or immediate to the human observer, to jolt people out of their dullness when they look at nature.

STYLE

Sonnet

"The World Is Too Much with Us" is a sonnet. A sonnet is easily recognized because it consists of fourteen lines and follows a standard rhyme scheme. There are, however, different types of sonnet—the Shakespearean, Spenserian, and Petrarchan (or Italian) sonnets—which have different structures and rhyme scheme. This is a Petrarchan sonnet, named after the medieval Italian poet Petrarch (1304–1374) who first used the form. It divides into two sections. The first is called the octave because it consists of the first eight lines. It is followed by the sestet—the concluding six lines. The argument or problem is put forward in the octave, and the response or solution is contained in the sestet. In this poem, the complaint that people have favored a materialistic way of life and have therefore lost their living connection to nature is elaborated in the octave. In the sestet, the thought turns: the poet both expresses his frustration at the current state of things and suggests that it would be better to go back to classical times to see nature the way the ancient Greeks did.

The rhyme scheme for the Petrarchan sonnet is as follows: in the octave, line 1 rhymes with line 4, and line 2 rhymes with line 3. This is repeated in the second quatrain (four lines): line 5 rhymes with line 8, and line 6 with line 7. Here, the same rhyming syllables are used in both quatrains. In the sestet, line 9 rhymes with line 11 and line 13; line 10 rhymes with line 12 and line 14. The overall scheme, then, is *abbaabba cdcdcd*.

The sonnet was a popular form in English literature in the Renaissance. William Shakespeare wrote over 150 sonnets. In the seventeenth century, the master of the sonnet in English was John Milton. The form fell into disuse during the eighteenth century, but was revived by the English romantic poets, who excelled in writing lyric forms that allowed the expression of personal feelings. Wordsworth wrote over five hundred sonnets, and John Keats (1795–1821) and Samuel Taylor Coleridge also used the form.

Meter

The meter of the poem is iambic pentameter. An iamb is a poetic foot consisting of two syllables, the first unstressed and the second stressed. It is the most common foot in English poetry. Pentameter is a line that consists of five metrical feet. Line 14 is the best example in the poem of a completely regular iambic pentameter line.

In this poem, the poet makes a number of variations in the basic iambic rhythm for emphasis and to avoid monotony. In line 2, for example, he substitutes a trochee for an iamb in the first foot. A trochee is the opposite of an iamb, consisting of a stressed syllable followed by an unstressed syllable. The inversion of the first foot in this manner is the most common form of metrical variation in iambic pentameter. It occurs again in line 3.

The poet also uses a spondee at a key point in the poem. A spondee is a foot in which both syllables are stressed. The third foot of line 9 is a spondee. The variation in meter makes this exclamation stand out strongly against the metrical base that the reader expects to hear. Fittingly, it comes at the beginning of the sestet, as an expression of frustration before the poet explains in the remaining lines how he would rather see nature.

In line 8 there is an extra syllable, making eleven in all, one more than an iambic pentameter calls for. The extra syllable is included in the second-to-last foot and is unstressed. Line 7 might be read as containing an extra unstressed syllable at the end. This is known as a feminine ending. Normally, a line consisting of iambic feet ends with a stressed syllable. Here, line 7's final word can be read as a single syllable to fit the metric and rhyme scheme.

Figurative Language

The poem contains an example of the simile. A simile is a comparison of one thing to another that brings out the similarity between them. The two things may not seem to be alike on the surface, but the simile shows them in such a way as to reveal a previously unnoticed similarity. The simile is contained in line 7, comparing wind and flowers.

There is a metaphor in line 10. A metaphor is a figure of speech in which one object or idea is described in terms of something else in such a way that suggests their identity, not just their similarity. In line 10, the outmoded creed is presented as a mother nursing her child. The two components of the metaphor thus share the same qualities.

The poem also has an example of personification. Personification is the presentation of an abstraction or inanimate thing as if it were a person. This occurs in line 5 in connection with the sea. The purpose of this personification is to emphasize that the sea has an intimate connection with other aspects of nature (such as the moon) that humans should emulate.

HISTORICAL CONTEXT

The English Romantic Movement

The romantic movement in English literature began in the last decade of the eighteenth century. This was when Wordsworth and his friend Samuel Taylor Coleridge began publishing their poems. William Blake (1757–1827) also published during this period, and his *Songs of Innocence* was published even earlier, in 1789.

Romanticism, which was also a literary movement in France and Germany, was a reaction to the eighteenth-century neoclassical period. That period valued qualities such as order, reason, rules, decorum (what is appropriate for a given subject), and elaborate poetic diction. Individualism and imagination were not valued highly, nor was the expression of emotion. The favorite poetic form of the neoclassicists was the heroic couplet. Romanticism, however, represented a sweeping change in which almost everything the neoclassicists valued was rejected.

The most important theoretical document of early romanticism was the preface to Wordsworth and Coleridge's *Lyrical Ballads*, published in 1798. In the preface, Wordsworth explained his poetic practice. He rejected the formal poetic diction of neoclassicism in favor of a simpler language, closer to that used by real people. He favored simplicity over artful complexity and chose as his subject matter humble country people and everyday incidents that affected their emotions. He wanted to reveal how people felt in such situations. Unlike the eighteenth-century poets, Wordsworth thought that social outcasts, such as a retarded boy, a convict, a beggar, and others, were suitable subjects for poetry. Whereas the neoclassicists had valued reason and logic, Wordsworth declared that the origin of poetry lay in the feelings of the poet. When the poet writes, he recollects in a calm way the powerful emotions he felt at the time of the incident he is recalling.

Wordsworth's emphasis on subjectivity, the feelings and emotions of the poet as he contemplates his subject, became one of the hallmarks of English romanticism. In their poetry, the romantics preferred to listen to the heart rather than the head because they believed that the heart allowed them to access a deeper level of truth than was available to the rational mind. The romantics therefore valued personal, individual experience rather than knowledge passed down by tradition. Since this was a radical break with existing practice, the romantics can be regarded as innovators, experimenting with new forms of thought and expression. Because of their emphasis on the inner rather than the outer world, they excelled at the lyric poem, in which they explored their personal feelings. Outstanding examples of the romantic lyric poem include Wordsworth's "Lines Composed a Few Miles above Tintern Abbey" and Coleridge's "Frost at Midnight." The second generation of English romantic poets, which included John Keats (1795–1821), Percy Bysshe Shelley (1792–1822), and Lord Byron (1788–1824), also excelled at the lyric poem. Examples include Keats's "Ode to a Nightingale" and Shelley's "Ode to the West Wind."

The romantics also opened up other areas of human experience as subjects for poetry. Impatient with the limitations of reason, they explored the significance of dreams and the supernatural. Coleridge and Blake in particular delved into esoteric systems of thought, hoping to find the key to

COMPARE
&
CONTRAST

- **Early 1800s:** The sonnet form becomes popular with English poets after a century of neglect. Wordsworth, Coleridge, Keats, Charles Lamb (1775–1834), Leigh Hunt (1784–1859), William Lisle Bowles (1762–1850), John Clare (1793–1864), and George Darley (1795–1846) all publish sonnets in the early 1800s.

  Today: Most poets prefer to write in free verse rather than in traditional forms such as the sonnet. However, a number of contemporary poets write sonnets. These include Northern Irish poets Seamus Heaney and Paul Muldoon. American poets Marilyn Hacker, J. D. McClatchy, X. J. Kennedy, and Brad Leithauser and British poet Carol Ann Duffy are also fond of the sonnet form of verse.

- **Early 1800s:** Wordsworth lives in the Lake District, a rural area in northwest England that has many lakes and mountains. It is here that he writes almost all of his great poetry. Wordsworth spends many hours walking in the Lake District, and in 1810 he publishes his *Guide to the Lakes*. The term "the Lake School" is invented to describe Wordsworth and his fellow poets Coleridge and Robert Southey (1774–1843), who also live in the Lake District.

  Today: The Lake District is a national park and is a magnet for tourists. Dove Cottage,

  the house in Grasmere in which Wordsworth lived when he wrote "The World Is Too Much with Us," is open to the public and draws thousands of visitors every year.

- **Early 1800s:** Europe is at war. From 1803 to 1815 an imperialistic France under Napoleon is opposed by Britain and its allies, including, at different times, Prussia, Austria-Hungary, Russia, and Spain. Wordsworth visits France in 1802 during a truce in a conflict that goes back to 1793. Wordsworth admired France during the early years of the French Revolution, in the early 1790s, before the Reign of Terror, but now he supports his own country, writing a number of sonnets defending liberty, which he associates with the English cause.

  Today: Europe is at peace. France and England are allies, both members of the European Union. For both countries, the days of building empires are over. However, both France and Britain have troops fighting in the U.S.-led war in Afghanistan. In 2010, France has 3,750 troops in Afghanistan, making it the fourth-biggest Western military contributor to the war in that country. Britain, with 10,000 troops, is the second-largest military presence in Afghanistan.

---

a more holistic understanding of life. Blake, Wordsworth, and Coleridge all valued childhood as an innocent, spontaneous state of being in which spiritual truth could be directly perceived. Wordsworth's "Ode: Intimations of Immortality from Recollections of Early Childhood" is a good example of this, as are Blake's *Songs of Innocence.*

Many of the romantics, including Wordsworth, Coleridge, Blake, and Shelley, searched for transcendental experience. Sensing the unity of all life, they wanted to go beyond all limitations

and experience the infinite. Wordsworth in particular experienced unusual modes of consciousness, especially when stimulated by being alone in nature. Many passages in Wordsworth's *The Prelude, or Growth of a Poet's Mind* (published in 1850), an epic poem about the development of his own mind and sensibilities, express this transcendental awareness. For Wordsworth and the other romantics, the agent of this new mode of perception was not reason but the imagination. The imagination was the faculty that should most

Busy world (Shebeko | Shutterstock.com)

be cultivated by the poet because it gave direct access to higher realms. This was quite different from the very limited role the imagination played in neoclassic poetic theory, in which it merely supplied embellishments to poetry that originated in the rational intellect. Because of the importance they ascribed to the imagination, the romantics held a very high view of the role of poetry and the poet: the poet was like a seer, a visionary, who had access to wisdom and truth.

Many of the romantics held strong opinions about social and political issues and were usually on the side of liberty and reform. Wordsworth and Blake were early supporters of the French Revolution, which broke out in 1789. They thought it would produce a new era of freedom and justice. Later, when the revolution betrayed its ideals, both poets reexamined their attitudes toward it. Byron and Shelley were strong supporters of liberty in a time of political repression, and Byron actively supported the cause of Greek independence from Turkey. Wordsworth, however, became conservative in middle age and took up reactionary political positions, as did the poet Robert Southey, a friend of Wordsworth and Coleridge who was better known in his own day as a poet than he is today.

The romantic movement in England was relatively brief. It is usually considered to have ended in 1832. By that time all the major poets were dead, except for Wordsworth, whose best years were long behind him, and Coleridge, who would live only another two years. The year 1832 was also the year Sir Walter Scott (1771–1832) died. Although his poetry is little read now, Scott in his day was one of the most popular poets.

CRITICAL OVERVIEW

The popularity of Wordsworth's "The World Is Too Much with Us" cannot be doubted since it appears not only in almost all selected editions of Wordsworth's poetry but also in many anthologies. Literary critics have not found a great deal to say about it, however, and it has usually been discussed, if at all, along with Wordsworth's other sonnets. Opinions of Wordsworth's achievement as a sonneteer vary greatly. A number of critics from the mid-twentieth century, including the influential F. R. Leavis, did not regard the sonnets highly, but others, including Russell Noyes in *William Wordsworth*, argued that some of Wordsworth's finest work was in the sonnet form. Noyes notes that "The World Is Too Much with Us" "has the same mood" as Wordsworth's sonnets of 1802 "that lament the unworthiness of the times." Noyes identifies this mood as one of "agitated passion." David B. Pirie also comments directly on the poem. In *William Wordsworth: The Poetry of Grandeur and of Tenderness*, he writes of the poem in the context of how the innocence of childhood is lost in the growth to maturity: "In a fine sonnet, Wordsworth voices the inane slogans of maturity with which we exhaust our capacity for feeling by babbling to each other." This renders people unable to "hear the larger harmony, whose unharassed sense of time embraces 'all hours' and whose relationships have the unstinting openness of the sea baring itself to the sky."

CRITICISM

Bryan Aubrey

Aubrey holds a PhD in English. In the following essay, he discusses "The World Is Too Much with Us" in terms of remarks made by Wordsworth in his Preface to Lyrical Ballads *about the times in which he lived.*

WHAT DO I READ NEXT?

- *The Prelude* is Wordsworth's great epic poem that tells the story of the growth of his own mind. He produced the first, short version of this poem in 1799 and continued revising it on and off for the rest of his life. It was finally published in 1850, shortly after his death. Many readers over the years have found the first two books of this long poem the most accessible and enjoyable. They tell of Wordsworth's childhood and youth growing up in the Lake District as he recalls many long summer days spent exploring nature and enjoying his own deep connection to it. The poem is available as *The Prelude: The Four Texts (1789, 1799, 1805, 1850)*, edited by Jonathan Wordsworth (1995).

- Wendell Berry is a contemporary American poet, novelist, essayist, and environmentalist who has explored in a considerable body of work the connections between humans and nature. Like Wordsworth, he is intensely aware of the calming spirit that nature brings to human life, and in his poetry he describes many such moments from his own experience. *The Selected Poems of Wendell Berry* (1999) provides a representative selection of his work.

- *Winter Poems along the Rio Grande* (2004), by Jimmy Santiago Baca, is a highly praised volume by a Mexican American poet. In thirty-nine poems Baca explores among other topics his own life and dreams; he is firmly grounded in the American Southwest, which he describes in careful and appreciative detail. His poetic voice has been compared to that of Walt Whitman, and his love of nature will appeal to anyone who appreciates the same quality in Wordsworth.

- Juliet Barker's *Wordsworth: A Life* (2006) is the most recent biography of the poet. Reviewers praise Barker's meticulous scholarship, which does not get in the way of her ability to present a readable and enjoyable narrative. The biography is notable for Barker's refusal to present Wordsworth's mid-life abandonment of his earlier radical beliefs in a negative light. She argues that his responsibilities as a family man left him little choice but to accept a government position.

- *A Treasury of Poetry for Young People: Emily Dickinson, Robert Frost, Henry Wadsworth Longfellow, Edgar Allan Poe, Carl Sandberg, Walt Whitman* (2008), edited by Frances Schoonmaker, Gary D. Schmidt, Jonathan Levin, and Brod Bagert, is a poetry anthology compiled with young readers in mind. The book is illustrated, and there are biographies of each poet, as well as definitions of difficult words and a literary commentary.

- Wordsworth's friend Samuel Taylor Coleridge was a great poet in his own right, as well as a literary critic whose lectures on Shakespeare and views on Wordsworth's poetry are still read today. As a poet, his finest achievements include "The Rime of the Ancient Mariner," which was one of his contributions to *Lyrical Ballads* (1798), "Kubla Khan," "The Eolian Harp" and "Frost at Midnight." Coleridge may have written far fewer great poems than Wordsworth, and his poetic gift flamed out while he was still a young man, but his contribution to English romantic literature is immense. His work can be found in *Samuel Taylor Coleridge: The Complete Poems* (1997), edited by William Keach.

Wordsworth was a poet of visionary possibility; he treasured those moments in nature when he was gifted with a special sort of sight that enabled him to see into the essence of things and sense the unity of all life. Many of his greatest poems, such as "Tintern Abbey" and *The Prelude*, express this vision. However, if Wordsworth was the poet of infinite possibility, he was also a poet of loss

"THERE IS MORE THAN A WHIFF HERE OF
THE DISGUST WITH WHICH THE LIFELONG
COUNTRYMAN VIEWS LIFE IN THE CITY, SO
DIFFERENT FROM WHAT HE IS USED TO."

who looked back at the past with a sense of regret. If he often paid tribute to his peak experiences in nature when he was young, he also mourned the fact that they no longer occurred. Both these elements of possibility and loss appear in "The World Is Too Much with Us," although not quite in the terms in which Wordsworth usually presents them.

It is clear in this sonnet that if Wordsworth is lamenting a personal loss of vision—the ability to experience a deep connection between himself and nature—he is also lamenting the times in general. There is a malaise, the poet says, throughout English society. The sonnet was written sometime between 1802 and 1804, but Wordsworth had addressed this point earlier, in his preface to *Lyrical Ballads*, published in the second edition of that work in 1800. In the preface, which is one of the major documents in English romanticism, Wordsworth argues that one of the main purposes of a poet is to excite the mind "without the application of gross and violent stimulants." He knows this is possible but says that in the current state of society it is difficult because an array of forces have combined "to blunt the discriminating powers of the mind, and unfitting it for all voluntary exertion to reduce it to a state of almost savage torpor." This is exactly the passive, weak state of mind that Wordsworth complains about in "The World Is Too Much with Us." In the preface he identifies the causes of this degradation of human sensibilities as.

> the great national events which are daily taking place, and the increasing accumulation of men in cities where the uniformity of their occupations produces a craving for extraordinary incident which the rapid communication of intelligence hourly gratifies.

Wordsworth is referring first to England's war with France, which began in 1793. After a short

peace in 1802 the war resumed in 1803, so it was likely in progress when he wrote the sonnet. The second element Wordsworth identifies is a result of the Industrial Revolution, which produced a massive drift of population from the countryside to the cities. This was particularly apparent in northern counties such as Lancashire—south of the Lake District, where Wordsworth lived, but not that far away from the area he knew and loved. Lancashire had been thinly populated in 1700, but by the end of the eighteenth century, over fifteen thousand new workers a year were arriving there, since the numerous cotton factories in the county were always in need of new hands. The division of labor in the factories meant that men, women, and children worked for long hours performing repetitive, mind-numbing tasks, slaves to the requirements of the machines. The industrial worker, without any roots in the town in which he now lived in overcrowded conditions, formed part of a social dislocation that affected the whole of England during this time. As Derek Jarrett explains in *Britain, 1688–1815*, "By the end of the eighteenth century every social unit in the country, from the smallest rural parish to the largest factory community, bore witness to the passing of the settled society of the past."

Wordsworth pictured the factory worker, bored by his daily routine, seeking out any sort of stimulation that would temporarily divert him from the depressing reality of his life. By "communication of intelligence" Wordsworth is referring to the growth of daily newspapers in England at this time. For example, in 1777, there was just one daily newspaper in London, but by 1813, stimulated by the need to convey information about the Napoleonic Wars, there were thirty-four. To these main causes of what Wordsworth saw as the dispiriting state of affairs in England, he added another that necessarily followed from what he had already identified: a decline in the quality of literature—Gothic novels out to supply quick thrills, "sickly and stupid" German melodramas on the stage, and "idle and extravagant stories in verse." It is clear from his tone that he is immensely irritated (just as he is in the sonnet) by these trends in English culture at the time, which he describes as a "degrading thirst after outrageous stimulation." There is more than a whiff here of the disgust with which the lifelong countryman views life in the city, so different from what he is used to. Wordsworth made a number of visits to London, England's biggest city, so he knew something of what he was talking about. However, Wordsworth does not see the situation as entirely hopeless. In the preface, he goes on to console himself with the optimistic belief that better times will come, because the true nature of man will eventually reassert itself. He writes that he believes in "certain inherent and indestructible qualities of the human mind, and likewise of certain powers in the great and permanent objects that act upon it, which are equally inherent and indestructible."

Here, in essence, in these passages from the preface to *Lyrical Ballads*, is the argument in prose that Wordsworth would present just a few years later in "The World Is Too Much with Us." People have diminished themselves, wasting their powers and gifts on objects unworthy of their attention. They are no longer in touch with their own true selves, and this also alienates them from a deep communion with nature. The real spirit of life has become deadened and atrophied. People are capable of so much more.

There is one important difference however. In the preface, Wordsworth is confident that the situation can be reversed and that it is his job as a poet to accomplish this. That is the task of the poet. But in "The World Is Too Much with Us" he no longer seems to possess that confidence. Whereas in the preface, he stands apart, the superior spirit who can hoist men up out of the sorry condition they have fallen into, in the sonnet, he includes himself in their number. By his use of the first person, both plural ("we") and later singular ("I"), he indicates that he is no better off than the common run of men. He too has lost those powers that enable people to live in the way that they were designed to do, and the poem is therefore filled with a tone of regret and frustration; the poet is hoping against hope, one feels, that he can regain at least a smidgeon of what in the preface he so boldly asserts to be the "inherent and indestructible qualities of the human mind," but he is none too certain that he can.

In this respect, it is no coincidence that Wordsworth wrote "The World Is Too Much with Us" at roughly the same time as the great "Ode: Intimations of Immortality," which he began in 1802 and finished in 1804. The theme of that poem is vanished vision. He writes that when he was younger, he saw nature in an exalted way; everything he looked at was bathed in a glorious light, and it was as if he lived in a kind of heaven. But now he is older (he is in his early to mid-thirties, actually), and that vision has gone; he no longer sees nature the way he

formerly did, and this causes him distress. He also believes that the exalted vision will never return. The tone of regret in the ode is not dissimilar to that of "The World Is Too Much with Us," although resignation has replaced anger and frustration.

Another difference between ode and sonnet is in the terms Wordsworth uses. Wordsworth usually speaks about higher vision, whether won or lost, in terms of the power of his own mind, its infinite capacity. He does not usually invoke a god or gods because in a sense his own mind, in interaction with nature, is his god. In its expanded state, it constitutes his experience of the divine. It is something of a surprise, then, to find in "The World Is Too Much with Us" that superimposed on the kind of landscape and seascape that would be familiar to readers of *The Prelude*, or "Tintern Abbey" or other lyric poems by Wordsworth, are the ancient Greek gods Proteus and Triton. Other examples can be found in Wordsworth's later poetry in which the ancient gods are given their place, but it is still not his usual practice, and certainly not at this period in his career. Its very unusualness for him perhaps gives a clue to the rather desperate state of mind the poet seems to have slipped into: his own, personal creed having failed him, he looks to another, more distant, out-of-date one to come to the rescue.

While the experienced reader of Wordsworth will note details such as this, perhaps readers who come to Wordsworth for the first time, in the second decade of the twenty-first century, may wonder if a poet so removed in time from our own has anything to say that is relevant to their own lives. One might ask such readers to glance back at the passage in the preface to *Lyrical Ballads*, quoted above alluding to the increase in the number of newspapers available that lure people into feeling the need to constantly get updated on what is happening in the wider world. Now fast-forward two hundred years to today's Information Age, with its 24/7 news cycles and its panoply of digital computing and communication technology to which no one seems immune; millions of people find they have an almost obsessive need to stay connected electronically all the time in one form or another. Some social analysts have worried that this constant immersion in the virtual rather than the "real" world may have negative consequences in terms of reducing people's attention spans and their capacity for reflective thought. It is really not a great leap from Wordsworth's concern about the "craving for extraordinary incident," stimulated at least in part by the proliferation of newspapers, which have the effect of "blunt[ing] the discriminating powers of the mind," to the arguments sometimes put forward today about the possible hazards of this multitasking digital age. Interesting in this light is an article by Matt Richtel titled "Outdoors and Out of Reach, Studying the Brain," that appeared in the *New York Times* in August 2010. Richtel reports on an experiment conducted by five neuroscientists that Wordsworth might well have approved of. The five men left their digital devices behind and spent a week hiking, rafting, and camping in a remote area of Utah. Interested in how the constant use of modern communication technology alters the way people think and act, they wanted to know whether a brief sojourn in nature would offer insight into issues such as attention, memory, and learning. They were aware of a University of Michigan study that showed it is easier for people to learn after they have taken a walk in the woods rather than on a city street. The conclusions the researchers reached would not have surprised Wordsworth (or anyone, come to that). Not only did time seem to slow down as they immersed themselves in nature, but one of the researchers commented that in nature,

> Our senses change. They kind of recalibrate—you notice sounds, like these crickets chirping; you hear the river, the sounds, the smells, you become more connected to the physical environment, the earth, rather than the artificial environment.

This is exactly Wordsworth's point, of course—exactly what, in the preface to *Lyrical Ballads* and in "The World Is Too Much with Us," he tries to explain about power given away and power gained, about connections with nature lost and regained. If our modern-day researchers did not exactly see Proteus and Triton rising from the waters, they certainly made Wordsworth's point for him.

Source: Bryan Aubrey, Critical Essay on "The World Is Too Much with Us," in *Poetry for Students*, Gale, Cengage Learning, 2011.

Review of English Studies

In this excerpt, it is argued that Wordsworth's poetry implies a return to myth to understand nineteenth-century existence.

Wordsworth refers to Greek gods Proteus and Triton (*Ackab Photography | Shutterstock.com*)

'The world is too much with us' is perhaps the most arresting of Wordsworth's sonnets, but also one that is particularly open to misunderstanding. It does not seem to belong very obviously with other poems composed around the same time. How are we to interpret the climactic outburst of the poet which breaks obliquely across his measured indictment of 'getting and spending' and the imaginative sterility and alienation that result from it?

> Great God! I'd rather be A Pagan suckled in a creed outworn; So might I, standing on this pleasant lea, Have glimpses that would make me less forlorn; Have sight of Proteus rising from the sea; Or hear old Triton blow his wreathed horn.

Wordsworth is saying, presumably, that superstition is preferable to worldliness or apathy if it preserves the life of the imagination and our sense of nature as a living presence with purposes akin to our own. The poet is not commending paganism at the expense of Christianity, but contrasting its

" JUST BECAUSE IN 'THE WORLD IS TOO MUCH
WITH US' THE PAGAN CREED IS 'OUTWORN' BUT NOT
'EXPLODED,' IT STILL RETAINS ITS IMAGINATIVE
FORCE AND APPEAL WHICH CAN BE REVIVED BY THE
POET'S VISIONARY POWER."

'poetry' with the deadly materialism of modern living which is out of tune with nature's 'powers' and nullifies our own. We can accept paganism as 'outworn,' while admitting that it can still be a source of imaginative energy and power—as Hazlitt found it: … as we shape towers, and men and armed steeds, out of the broken clouds that glitter in the distant horizon, so, throned, above the ruins of the ancient world, Jupiter still nods sublime on the top of blue Olympus… the sea gods ride upon the sounding waves, the long procession of heroes and demi-gods passes in endless review before us, and still we … 'have sight of Proteus coming from the sea, / And hear old Triton blow his wreathed horn.' But there is nothing in the first eight lines of the sonnet to prepare the reader for the startling paradox with which it closes. The irruption of deities from the Ancient World into what is apparently a contemporary English landscape is disconcerting, even surreal; and though Wordsworth is echoing Spenser and Milton, the 'feeling' of these lines is very different from theirs. In fact, there is nothing quite like it in his poetry up to 1803, the most likely date of the sonnet.

Hitherto, he had banished the pagan gods entirely from his poetic universe. Poetry that aspired to the 'Truth that cherishes our daily life' no longer had any place for such polite fictions which, as Locke had remarked long before, were 'more like the inventions of wit and adornments of poetry, than the serious persuasions of the wise and sober.' Could the classical gods ever again be anything more than personifications or figures of speech? The day seemed long gone by when they might be thought to embody in allegorical form the spiritual energies or 'powers' underlying the appearances of nature, which Wordsworth aspired to celebrate as 'an inmate of this active universe' and 'even as an agent of the one great Mind.' The Virgilian animism he clung to as a child, which

survived into the poetry of 'Nutting' and the earliest versions of *The Prelude*, was, for him, a better guide to the living processes of nature than the old anthropomorphic cults. The English Bible spoke of analogous 'powers' having control or influence in creation, and Shakespeare in *The Tempest* attributed to them the retribution that fell on Alonzo and his companions for their treachery to Prospero:

> for which foul deed The powers, delaying, not forgetting, have Incens'd the seas and shores, yea all the creatures, Against your peace.

A universe of active 'powers,' pagan or Christian, was not incompatible with the forces of Newtonian physics, and even with Godwin's law of Necessity, and could thus be accepted as a poetic embodiment of both ancient and modern experience. It was for the poet to convey his own emotional responses to nature, not a body of doctrines. Wordsworth may have had this in mind in his letter of c. 1804 about education in which he recommended, along with the study of fairy tales, romances, and histories, 'such parts of natural history relating to the powers and appearances of the earth and elements' as would together constitute 'a magazine of form and feeling.'

When therefore, developing beyond the crude vision of the energies of nature in *Descriptive Sketches*, he came to celebrate in *Lyrical Ballads* and the earlier books of *The Prelude* the interaction between his own imaginative powers and 'the blessed power, that rolls / About, below, above,' he had no need of mythological intermediaries to embody the spirit of nature that also dwells in the mind of man. It was the same 'active Principle' which subsists In all things, in all natures; in the stars Of azure heaven, the unenduring clouds, In flower and tree, in every pebbly stone That paves the brooks, the stationary rocks, The moving waters, and the invisible air. Whate'er exists hath properties that spread Beyond itself, communicating good… Spirit that knows no insulated spot, No chasm, no solitude; from link to link It circulates, the Soul of all the worlds.

These lines from the climax of *The Excursion* (1814), composed in 1798, echo *Tintern Abbey* and the anima mundi of *Aeneid VI*, circling back towards the Virgilian influences from which Wordsworth set out, and forward to the 'Powers' that continue to haunt his later poetry, for example in the second sonnet of the *Ecclesiastical*

Sketches, and in 'At Sea off the Isle of Man,' from the *Itinerary Poems* of 1833. As late as the Preface of 1815 he was arguing that 'the anthropomorphitism of the Pagan religion' subjected the minds of the poets of the Ancient World too much to 'the bondage of definite form.' In spite of these reservations, however, the pagan gods stage something of a come-back in his poetry from 1803 onwards, as we have seen in 'The world is too much with us.' There is, for example, the moving evocation of classical pastoral in *The Prelude* Book VIII, written in the knowledge that Coleridge was actually enjoying the Italian landscapes which Wordsworth could conjure up only in imagination:

> Smooth life had herdsman, and his snow-white herd To triumphs and to sacrificial rites Devoted, on the inviolable stream Of rich Clitumnus; and the goat-herd lived As calmly, underneath the pleasant brows Of cool Lucretilis, where the pipe was heard Of Pan, Invisible God, thrilling the rocks With tutelary music, from all harm The fold protecting.

'Great Pan himself' also appears at the climax of the sonnet 'Composed by the Side of Grasmere Lake' (1807) as an image of the tranquillity of nature spread out under the vault of heaven beneath the planetary powers of Jove, Venus, and Mars. Pan, or 'the universal frame of things,' was 'a noble fable,' according to Bacon, who assigned the deepest significance to classical myth, 'and big almost to bursting with the secrets and mysteries of Nature.' Wordsworth would also recall Milton's description of the early creation:

> Universal Pan, Knit with the Graces, and the Hours in dance, Led on th' eternal Spring.

But pagan mythology returns to Wordsworth's poetry with the most sustained splendour in the evocation of the ancient religions in Book IV of *The Excursion*, which is part of the Wanderer's message of hope to the Solitary as he emerges from the wilderness of Enlightenment scepticism and from his disappointment at the failure of the French Revolution. The passage was deeply engaging to all the poet's early admirers, who credited him with the restoration of their spiritual and imaginative well-being, and it will be examined in more detail below. Thereafter, as if with renewed confidence in the appropriateness of myth, Wordsworth occasionally returned to the pagan gods: in the 'Ode, 1814,' for example, the ode 'On the Power of Sound,' and in a late poem, 'Love Lies Bleeding,' which, with its companion-piece, offers an original of the Venus and Adonis myth. What had made

him more favourably disposed to what he had at first so firmly rejected?

Towards the end of his life, in a Fenwick Note (1842) attached somewhat arbitrarily to the little-known 'Ode to Lycoris' (1817), one of the least interesting of his mythological poems, Wordsworth belatedly went some way towards providing an explanation. It constitutes his sole pronouncement on classical mythology. Recalling his love of the Greek and Roman poets in childhood ('Classical literature affected me by its own beauty'), and the prestige of classical culture at the Renaissance, he recognizes the objections of modern readers 'who think mythology and classical allusion too far-fetched and therefore more or less unnatural and affected'; but while voicing his own reservations on the subject, he finally comes down on the side of allowing it a place in modern poetry:

> No doubt the hackneyed and lifeless use into which mythology fell towards the close of the seventeenth century, and which continued through the eighteenth, disgusted the general reader with all allusion to it in modern verse; and though, in deference to this disgust, and also in a measure participating in it, I abstained in my earlier writings from all introduction of pagan fable—surely, even in its humble form, it may ally itself with real sentiment …

What had convinced him that, while pagan divinities in modern poetry often amounted to little more than poetic devices or grotesque fancies that had lost all reality and naturalness, they were not necessarily so, and could still on occasion embody permanent truth and feeling? What had prompted him to think again about the living power of myth?

The revival of poetic interest in the pagan gods of antiquity is usually traced back to Schiller's 'Die Gotter Griechenlands,' published in Wieland's *Teutscher Merkur* in 1788. As has often been pointed out, the poem marked a turning-point in European feeling about the pagan religions. The ancient Greek gods, according to Schiller, represent an ideal of harmonious beauty and power which has vanished from the world, to be replaced by an outlook on life in which sense and spirit are at odds with each other, so that disenchantment and alienation set in. But there is no evidence that Wordsworth was at any time influenced by this poem, or even knew it. Coleridge, on the other hand, may have read it, and it possibly coloured his lines about the ancient gods in his translation of Schiller's *Piccolomini* which

Wordsworth certainly knew and remembered, as they were completed under his own roof at Dove Cottage in spring 1800. The burden of Coleridge's lament is that the old gods, once the familiar friends of man, have forsaken the earth for the 'starry world' above, where (according to the medieval view) they have become remote astrological influences. The lines won the praise of Sir Walter Scott for 'the feelings so exquisitely expressed by a modern poet':

> The intelligible forms of ancient poets, The fair humanities of old religion, The Power, the Beauty, and the Majesty, That had their haunts in dale, or piny mountain, Or forest by slow stream, or pebbly spring, Or chasms and wat'ry depths; all these have vanished. They live no longer in the faith of reason! But still the heart doth need a language, still Doth the old instinct bring back the old names . . . .

Coleridge's wistful elegy for the passing of the old divinities is, however, unlikely to have stimulated Wordsworth's experiments with classical fable. In spite of his apparent nostalgia for the old order, Coleridge categorically pronounced pagan myth to be 'exploded,' and much preferred Hebrew and Christian poetry. As a committed Christian, he could hardly do otherwise. Coleridge wrote to William Sotheby in 1802:

> It must occur to every Reader that the Greeks in their religious poems address always the Numina Loci, the Genii, the Dryads, the Naiads, &c &c—All natural Objects were dead—mere hollow Statues—but there was a Godkin or Goddessling included in each—In the Hebrew Poetry you find nothing of this poor Stuff—as poor in genuine Imagination as it is mean in Intellect . . . .

In a more buoyant mood he might have had some sympathy for Elizabeth Barrett Browning's celebration, much later, of the triumph of Christianity:

> Earth outgrows the mythic fancies Sung beside her in her youth; And those debonaire romances Sound but dull beside the truth. Phoebus' chariot course is run! Look up, poets, to the sun! Pan, Pan is dead.

Wordsworth's emphasis, on the other hand, is quite different. Just because in 'The world is too much with us' the pagan creed is 'outworn' but not 'exploded,' it still retains its imaginative force and appeal which can be revived by the poet's visionary power. There is a sense in which it remains a permanent part of man's imaginative inheritance, a folk memory that is never entirely superseded. Like the pagan temples, it lingered on

in the imagination long after the old religion had given way to the new. Wordsworth's delight in 'the universal Pan' and the other tutelary powers seems in fact to owe little or nothing either to Schiller or to Coleridge, and another source must be found for the new feeling about the pagan gods which enters his poetry around 1803 and reaches full development in *The Excursion*. A likely source can be found, I suggest, in Boccaccio's Latin treatise *Genealogia Deorum Gentilium*. It is now clear for the first time that the Wordsworths and Coleridge were reading this work together in Italian in 1803 to help Coleridge improve his knowledge of the language before his departure for Malta early the following year. What is more, Coleridge's copy of *Genealogia degli Dei Pagani* (Venetia, 1588) remained in Wordsworth's library for many years, being listed in the manuscript catalogue of his books compiled in 1829; and it was not returned to Derwent Coleridge until after Coleridge's death. Wordsworth had known Boccaccio's *Decameron* much earlier, at Racedown in 1795, but he probably learnt first of Boccaccio's scholarly endeavours as a humanist from Gibbon, who in his account of the early Italian Renaissance described the *Genealogia* as 'a work, in that age, of stupendous erudition,' which the author had 'ostentatiously sprinkled with Greek characters and passages, to excite the wonder and applause of his more ignorant readers.' It is highly unlikely that Wordsworth would have accepted, without further enquiry, such a dismissive valuation of an author whose shaping influence was writ large on English poetry from Chaucer onwards. Neither would Coleridge, who later on was planning a complete edition of Boccaccio's scholarly works, have done so. The *Genealogia Deorum Gentilium*, a kind of encyclopaedia of classical myth, was one of several treatises which Boccaccio contributed in his later years to the revival of learning pioneered by his friend Petrarch. A vast range of classical reading is summarized in fifteen Books under nearly 700 headings, each dealing with a particular figure in ancient mythology. Wordsworth would have found Proteus and Triton discussed under divinities of the ocean in Book VII. The myths are allegorized to give, where possible, a moral, and even a Christian sense above their literal or historical meaning, according to a tradition of interpretation going back to classical and patristic times and handed on to the Renaissance, where it received definitive formulation in Bacon's *De Sapientia Veterum* and in the Preface to Sir John

Harington's translation of Ariosto's *Orlando Fur-ioso* (1591), a work well known to Wordsworth:

The ancient Poets haue indeed wrapped as it were in their writings diuers and sundry meaning, which they call the sences or mysteries thereof. First of all for the litterall sence (as it were the vtmost barke or ryne) they set downe in manner of an historie, the acts and notable exploits of some persons worthy memorie; then in the same fiction, as a second rine and somewhat more fine, as it were nearer to the pith and marrow, they place the Morall sence, profitable for the actiue life of man, approuing vertuous actions and condemning the contrarie. Manie times also vnder the selfsame words they comprehend some true vndestanding of natural Philosophie, or sometimes of politike gouernement, and now and then of diuinitie: and these same sences that comprehend so excellent knowledge we call the Allegorie.

Source: "Wordsworth, Boccaccio, and the Pagan Gods of Antiquity," in *Review of English Studies*, Vol. 45, No. 177, February 1994, pp. 26–41.

SOURCES

Dabundo, Laura, ed., *Encyclopedia of Romanticism: Culture in Britain, 1780s–1830s*, Garland Publishing, 1992, p. 300.

Drury, Ian, "France Risks Diplomatic Row after Snubbing Obama's Call to Send More Troops to Afghanistan," in *Mail Online*, January 26, 2010, http://www.dailymail.co.uk/news/worldnews/article-1246165/France-refuses-send-soldiers-Afghanistan–Germany-vows-increase-troops-850.html (accessed August 24, 2010).

Jarrett, Derek, *Britain, 1688–1815*, reprint, Longman, 1970, p. 339.

Noyes, Russell, *William Wordsworth*, Twayne Publishers, 1971, pp. 128–29.

Pirie, David B., *William Wordsworth: The Poetry of Grandeur and of Tenderness*, Methuen, 1982, p. 156.

Richtel, Matt, "Outdoors and Out of Reach, Studying the Brain," in *New York Times*, August 15, 2010.

Wordsworth, William, "The World Is Too Much with Us," in *Wordsworth: Poems*, Knopf, 1995, p. 143.

———, Preface to *Lyrical Ballads*, edited by R. L. Brett and A. R. Jones, reprint, Methuen, 1975, pp. 248–50.

FURTHER READING

Heath, Duncan, and Judy Boreham, *Introducing Romanticism*, edited by Richard Appignanesi, Totem Books, 2001.
This is an introduction to the romantic movement in literature, art, and music. The authors focus on the leading figures in romanticism in Britain, France, Germany, the United States, Italy, and Russia.

Mason, Emma, *The Cambridge Introduction to William Wordsworth*, Cambridge University Press, 2010.
This is an excellent introduction to Wordsworth's poetry. It covers all of Wordsworth's major poems as well as some of the lesser-known ones. Mason also gives a valuable history of the reception of Wordsworth's poetry from Victorian times to contemporary approaches. There is an annotated bibliography.

Robinson, Daniel, *William Wordsworth's Poetry*, Continuum, 2010.
This is a reader's guide to Wordsworth's poetry, suitable for undergraduate students. It includes an account of Wordsworth's poetic career and explains the various literary, philosophical, and political contexts for his work.

Wolf, Norbert, *Romanticism*, Taschen, 2007.
This is a brief, well-illustrated guide to romanticism in art. Artists discussed include George Bingham, William Blake, Thomas Cole, John Constable, Peter von Cornelius, Jean-Baptiste Camille Corot, Eugene Delacroix, Caspar David Friedrich, Henry Fuseli, Jean Auguste Dominique Ingres, Friedrich Overbeck, Franz Pforr, Pierre-Paul Prudhon, Ludwig Richter, Philipp Otto Runge, Carl Spitzweg, and William Turner.

SUGGESTED SEARCH TERMS

The World Is Too Much with Us

The World Is Too Much with Us AND Wordsworth

William Wordsworth

sonnet AND Wordsworth

Petrarchan sonnet

English romanticism

English romantic movement

lyrical ballads

Lake District

Industrial Revolution

Glossary of Literary Terms

A

Abstract: Used as a noun, the term refers to a short summary or outline of a longer work. As an adjective applied to writing or literary works, abstract refers to words or phrases that name things not knowable through the five senses.

Accent: The emphasis or stress placed on a syllable in poetry. Traditional poetry commonly uses patterns of accented and unaccented syllables (known as feet) that create distinct rhythms. Much modern poetry uses less formal arrangements that create a sense of freedom and spontaneity.

Aestheticism: A literary and artistic movement of the nineteenth century. Followers of the movement believed that art should not be mixed with social, political, or moral teaching. The statement "art for art's sake" is a good summary of aestheticism. The movement had its roots in France, but it gained widespread importance in England in the last half of the nineteenth century, where it helped change the Victorian practice of including moral lessons in literature.

Affective Fallacy: An error in judging the merits or faults of a work of literature. The "error" results from stressing the importance of the work's effect upon the reader—that is, how it makes a reader "feel" emotionally, what it does as a literary work—instead of stressing its inner qualities as a created object, or what it "is."

Age of Johnson: The period in English literature between 1750 and 1798, named after the most prominent literary figure of the age, Samuel Johnson. Works written during this time are noted for their emphasis on "sensibility," or emotional quality. These works formed a transition between the rational works of the Age of Reason, or Neoclassical period, and the emphasis on individual feelings and responses of the Romantic period.

Age of Reason: See *Neoclassicism*

Age of Sensibility: See *Age of Johnson*

Agrarians: A group of Southern American writers of the 1930s and 1940s who fostered an economic and cultural program for the South based on agriculture, in opposition to the industrial society of the North. The term can refer to any group that promotes the value of farm life and agricultural society.

Alexandrine Meter: See *Meter*

Allegory: A narrative technique in which characters representing things or abstract ideas are used to convey a message or teach a lesson. Allegory is typically used to teach moral, ethical, or religious lessons but is sometimes used for satiric or political purposes.

Alliteration: A poetic device where the first consonant sounds or any vowel sounds in words or syllables are repeated.

Allusion: A reference to a familiar literary or historical person or event, used to make an idea more easily understood.

Amerind Literature: The writing and oral traditions of Native Americans. Native American literature was originally passed on by word of mouth, so it consisted largely of stories and events that were easily memorized. Amerind prose is often rhythmic like poetry because it was recited to the beat of a ceremonial drum.

Analogy: A comparison of two things made to explain something unfamiliar through its similarities to something familiar, or to prove one point based on the acceptedness of another. Similes and metaphors are types of analogies.

Anapest: See *Foot*

Angry Young Men: A group of British writers of the 1950s whose work expressed bitterness and disillusionment with society. Common to their work is an anti-hero who rebels against a corrupt social order and strives for personal integrity.

Anthropomorphism: The presentation of animals or objects in human shape or with human characteristics. The term is derived from the Greek word for "human form."

Antimasque: See *Masque*

Antithesis: The antithesis of something is its direct opposite. In literature, the use of antithesis as a figure of speech results in two statements that show a contrast through the balancing of two opposite ideas. Technically, it is the second portion of the statement that is defined as the "antithesis"; the first portion is the "thesis."

Apocrypha: Writings tentatively attributed to an author but not proven or universally accepted to be their works. The term was originally applied to certain books of the Bible that were not considered inspired and so were not included in the "sacred canon."

Apollonian and Dionysian: The two impulses believed to guide authors of dramatic tragedy. The Apollonian impulse is named after Apollo, the Greek god of light and beauty and the symbol of intellectual order. The Dionysian impulse is named after Dionysus, the Greek god of wine and the symbol of the unrestrained forces of nature. The Apollonian impulse is to create a rational, harmonious world, while the Dionysian is to express the irrational forces of personality.

Apostrophe: A statement, question, or request addressed to an inanimate object or concept or to a nonexistent or absent person.

Archetype: The word archetype is commonly used to describe an original pattern or model from which all other things of the same kind are made. This term was introduced to literary criticism from the psychology of Carl Jung. It expresses Jung's theory that behind every person's "unconscious," or repressed memories of the past, lies the "collective unconscious" of the human race: memories of the countless typical experiences of our ancestors. These memories are said to prompt illogical associations that trigger powerful emotions in the reader. Often, the emotional process is primitive, even primordial. Archetypes are the literary images that grow out of the "collective unconscious." They appear in literature as incidents and plots that repeat basic patterns of life. They may also appear as stereotyped characters.

Argument: The argument of a work is the author's subject matter or principal idea.

Art for Art's Sake: See *Aestheticism*

Assonance: The repetition of similar vowel sounds in poetry.

Audience: The people for whom a piece of literature is written. Authors usually write with a certain audience in mind, for example, children, members of a religious or ethnic group, or colleagues in a professional field. The term "audience" also applies to the people who gather to see or hear any performance, including plays, poetry readings, speeches, and concerts.

Automatic Writing: Writing carried out without a preconceived plan in an effort to capture every random thought. Authors who engage in automatic writing typically do not revise their work, preferring instead to preserve the revealed truth and beauty of spontaneous expression.

Avant-garde: A French term meaning "vanguard." It is used in literary criticism to describe new writing that rejects traditional approaches to literature in favor of innovations in style or content.

B

Ballad: A short poem that tells a simple story and has a repeated refrain. Ballads were originally intended to be sung. Early ballads, known as folk ballads, were passed down through generations, so their authors are often unknown. Later ballads composed by known authors are called literary ballads.

Baroque: A term used in literary criticism to describe literature that is complex or ornate in style or diction. Baroque works typically express tension, anxiety, and violent emotion. The term "Baroque Age" designates a period in Western European literature beginning in the late sixteenth century and ending about one hundred years later. Works of this period often mirror the qualities of works more generally associated with the label "baroque" and sometimes feature elaborate conceits.

Baroque Age: See *Baroque*

Baroque Period: See *Baroque*

Beat Generation: See *Beat Movement*

Beat Movement: A period featuring a group of American poets and novelists of the 1950s and 1960s—including Jack Kerouac, Allen Ginsberg, Gregory Corso, William S. Burroughs, and Lawrence Ferlinghetti—who rejected established social and literary values. Using such techniques as stream of consciousness writing and jazz-influenced free verse and focusing on unusual or abnormal states of mind—generated by religious ecstasy or the use of drugs—the Beat writers aimed to create works that were unconventional in both form and subject matter.

Beat Poets: See *Beat Movement*

Beats, The: See *Beat Movement*

Belles-lettres: A French term meaning "fine letters" or "beautiful writing." It is often used as a synonym for literature, typically referring to imaginative and artistic rather than scientific or expository writing. Current usage sometimes restricts the meaning to light or humorous writing and appreciative essays about literature.

Black Aesthetic Movement: A period of artistic and literary development among African Americans in the 1960s and early 1970s. This was the first major African-American artistic movement since the Harlem Renaissance and was closely paralleled by the civil rights and black power movements. The black aesthetic writers attempted to produce works of art that would be meaningful to the black masses. Key figures in black aesthetics included one of its founders, poet and playwright Amiri Baraka, formerly known as LeRoi Jones; poet and essayist Haki R. Madhubuti, formerly Don L. Lee; poet and playwright Sonia Sanchez; and dramatist Ed Bullins.

Black Arts Movement: See *Black Aesthetic Movement*

Black Comedy: See *Black Humor*

Black Humor: Writing that places grotesque elements side by side with humorous ones in an attempt to shock the reader, forcing him or her to laugh at the horrifying reality of a disordered world.

Black Mountain School: Black Mountain College and three of its instructors—Robert Creeley, Robert Duncan, and Charles Olson—were all influential in projective verse, so poets working in projective verse are now referred as members of the Black Mountain school.

Blank Verse: Loosely, any unrhymed poetry, but more generally, unrhymed iambic pentameter verse (composed of lines of five two-syllable feet with the first syllable accented, the second unaccented). Blank verse has been used by poets since the Renaissance for its flexibility and its graceful, dignified tone.

Bloomsbury Group: A group of English writers, artists, and intellectuals who held informal artistic and philosophical discussions in Bloomsbury, a district of London, from around 1907 to the early 1930s. The Bloomsbury Group held no uniform philosophical beliefs but did commonly express an aversion to moral prudery and a desire for greater social tolerance.

Bon Mot: A French term meaning "good word." A *bon mot* is a witty remark or clever observation.

Breath Verse: See *Projective Verse*

Burlesque: Any literary work that uses exaggeration to make its subject appear ridiculous, either by treating a trivial subject with profound seriousness or by treating a dignified subject frivolously. The word "burlesque" may also be used as an adjective, as in "burlesque show," to mean "striptease act."

C

Cadence: The natural rhythm of language caused by the alternation of accented and unaccented syllables. Much modern poetry—notably free verse—deliberately manipulates cadence to create complex rhythmic effects.

Caesura: A pause in a line of poetry, usually occurring near the middle. It typically corresponds to a break in the natural rhythm or sense of the line but is sometimes shifted to create special meanings or rhythmic effects.

Canzone: A short Italian or Provencal lyric poem, commonly about love and often set to music. The *canzone* has no set form but typically contains five or six stanzas made up of seven to twenty lines of eleven syllables each. A shorter, five- to ten-line "envoy," or concluding stanza, completes the poem.

Carpe Diem: A Latin term meaning "seize the day." This is a traditional theme of poetry, especially lyrics. A *carpe diem* poem advises the reader or the person it addresses to live for today and enjoy the pleasures of the moment.

Catharsis: The release or purging of unwanted emotions—specifically fear and pity—brought about by exposure to art. The term was first used by the Greek philosopher Aristotle in his *Poetics* to refer to the desired effect of tragedy on spectators.

Celtic Renaissance: A period of Irish literary and cultural history at the end of the nineteenth century. Followers of the movement aimed to create a romantic vision of Celtic myth and legend. The most significant works of the Celtic Renaissance typically present a dreamy, unreal world, usually in reaction against the reality of contemporary problems.

Celtic Twilight: See *Celtic Renaissance*

Character: Broadly speaking, a person in a literary work. The actions of characters are what constitute the plot of a story, novel, or poem. There are numerous types of characters, ranging from simple, stereotypical figures to intricate, multifaceted ones. In the techniques of anthropomorphism and personification, animals—and even places or things—can assume aspects of character. "Characterization" is the process by which an author creates vivid, believable characters in a work of art. This may be done in a variety of ways, including (1) direct description of the character by the narrator; (2) the direct presentation of the speech, thoughts, or actions of the character; and (3) the responses of other characters to the character. The term "character" also refers to a form originated by the ancient Greek writer Theophrastus that later became popular in the seventeenth and eighteenth centuries. It is a short essay or sketch of a person who prominently displays a specific attribute or quality, such as miserliness or ambition.

Characterization: See *Character*

Classical: In its strictest definition in literary criticism, classicism refers to works of ancient Greek or Roman literature. The term may also be used to describe a literary work of recognized importance (a "classic") from any time period or literature that exhibits the traits of classicism.

Classicism: A term used in literary criticism to describe critical doctrines that have their roots in ancient Greek and Roman literature, philosophy, and art. Works associated with classicism typically exhibit restraint on the part of the author, unity of design and purpose, clarity, simplicity, logical organization, and respect for tradition.

Colloquialism: A word, phrase, or form of pronunciation that is acceptable in casual conversation but not in formal, written communication. It is considered more acceptable than slang.

Complaint: A lyric poem, popular in the Renaissance, in which the speaker expresses sorrow about his or her condition. Typically, the speaker's sadness is caused by an unresponsive lover, but some complaints cite other sources of unhappiness, such as poverty or fate.

Conceit: A clever and fanciful metaphor, usually expressed through elaborate and extended comparison, that presents a striking parallel between two seemingly dissimilar things—for example, elaborately comparing a beautiful woman to an object like a garden or the sun. The conceit was a popular device throughout the Elizabethan Age and Baroque Age and was the principal technique of the seventeenth-century English metaphysical poets. This usage of the word conceit is unrelated to the best-known definition of conceit as an arrogant attitude or behavior.

Concrete: Concrete is the opposite of abstract, and refers to a thing that actually exists or a description that allows the reader to experience an object or concept with the senses.

Concrete Poetry: Poetry in which visual elements play a large part in the poetic effect. Punctuation marks, letters, or words are arranged on a page to form a visual design: a cross, for example, or a bumblebee.

Confessional Poetry: A form of poetry in which the poet reveals very personal, intimate, sometimes shocking information about himself or herself.

Connotation: The impression that a word gives beyond its defined meaning. Connotations may be universally understood or may be significant only to a certain group.

Consonance: Consonance occurs in poetry when words appearing at the ends of two or more verses have similar final consonant sounds but have final vowel sounds that differ, as with "stuff" and "off."

Convention: Any widely accepted literary device, style, or form.

Corrido: A Mexican ballad.

Couplet: Two lines of poetry with the same rhyme and meter, often expressing a complete and self-contained thought.

Criticism: The systematic study and evaluation of literary works, usually based on a specific method or set of principles. An important part of literary studies since ancient times, the practice of criticism has given rise to numerous theories, methods, and "schools," sometimes producing conflicting, even contradictory, interpretations of literature in general as well as of individual works. Even such basic issues as what constitutes a poem or a novel have been the subject of much criticism over the centuries.

D

Dactyl: See *Foot*

Dadaism: A protest movement in art and literature founded by Tristan Tzara in 1916. Followers of the movement expressed their outrage at the destruction brought about by World War I by revolting against numerous forms of social convention. The Dadaists presented works marked by calculated madness and flamboyant nonsense. They stressed total freedom of expression, commonly through primitive displays of

emotion and illogical, often senseless, poetry. The movement ended shortly after the war, when it was replaced by surrealism.

Decadent: See *Decadents*

Decadents: The followers of a nineteenth-century literary movement that had its beginnings in French aestheticism. Decadent literature displays a fascination with perverse and morbid states; a search for novelty and sensation—the "new thrill"; a preoccupation with mysticism; and a belief in the senselessness of human existence. The movement is closely associated with the doctrine Art for Art's Sake. The term "decadence" is sometimes used to denote a decline in the quality of art or literature following a period of greatness.

Deconstruction: A method of literary criticism developed by Jacques Derrida and characterized by multiple conflicting interpretations of a given work. Deconstructionists consider the impact of the language of a work and suggest that the true meaning of the work is not necessarily the meaning that the author intended.

Deduction: The process of reaching a conclusion through reasoning from general premises to a specific premise.

Denotation: The definition of a word, apart from the impressions or feelings it creates in the reader.

Diction: The selection and arrangement of words in a literary work. Either or both may vary depending on the desired effect. There are four general types of diction: "formal," used in scholarly or lofty writing; "informal," used in relaxed but educated conversation; "colloquial," used in everyday speech; and "slang," containing newly coined words and other terms not accepted in formal usage.

Didactic: A term used to describe works of literature that aim to teach some moral, religious, political, or practical lesson. Although didactic elements are often found in artistically pleasing works, the term "didactic" usually refers to literature in which the message is more important than the form. The term may also be used to criticize a work that the critic finds "overly didactic," that is, heavy-handed in its delivery of a lesson.

Dimeter: See *Meter*

Dionysian: See *Apollonian and Dionysian*

Discordia concours: A Latin phrase meaning "discord in harmony." The term was coined by the eighteenth-century English writer Samuel Johnson to describe "a combination of dissimilar images or discovery of occult resemblances in things apparently unlike." Johnson created the expression by reversing a phrase by the Latin poet Horace.

Dissonance: A combination of harsh or jarring sounds, especially in poetry. Although such combinations may be accidental, poets sometimes intentionally make them to achieve particular effects. Dissonance is also sometimes used to refer to close but not identical rhymes. When this is the case, the word functions as a synonym for consonance.

Double Entendre: A corruption of a French phrase meaning "double meaning." The term is used to indicate a word or phrase that is deliberately ambiguous, especially when one of the meanings is risque or improper.

Draft: Any preliminary version of a written work. An author may write dozens of drafts which are revised to form the final work, or he or she may write only one, with few or no revisions.

Dramatic Monologue: See *Monologue*

Dramatic Poetry: Any lyric work that employs elements of drama such as dialogue, conflict, or characterization, but excluding works that are intended for stage presentation.

Dream Allegory: See *Dream Vision*

Dream Vision: A literary convention, chiefly of the Middle Ages. In a dream vision a story is presented as a literal dream of the narrator. This device was commonly used to teach moral and religious lessons.

E

Eclogue: In classical literature, a poem featuring rural themes and structured as a dialogue among shepherds. Eclogues often took specific poetic forms, such as elegies or love poems. Some were written as the soliloquy of a shepherd. In later centuries, "eclogue" came to refer to any poem that was in the pastoral tradition or that had a dialogue or monologue structure.

Edwardian: Describes cultural conventions identified with the period of the reign of Edward VII of England (1901-1910). Writers of the Edwardian Age typically displayed a strong reaction against the propriety and conservatism of the Victorian Age. Their work often exhibits distrust of authority in religion, politics, and art and expresses strong doubts about the soundness of conventional values.

Edwardian Age: See *Edwardian*

Electra Complex: A daughter's amorous obsession with her father.

Elegy: A lyric poem that laments the death of a person or the eventual death of all people. In a conventional elegy, set in a classical world, the poet and subject are spoken of as shepherds. In modern criticism, the word elegy is often used to refer to a poem that is melancholy or mournfully contemplative.

Elizabethan Age: A period of great economic growth, religious controversy, and nationalism closely associated with the reign of Elizabeth I of England (1558-1603). The Elizabethan Age is considered a part of the general renaissance—that is, the flowering of arts and literature—that took place in Europe during the fourteenth through sixteenth centuries. The era is considered the golden age of English literature. The most important dramas in English and a great deal of lyric poetry were produced during this period, and modern English criticism began around this time.

Empathy: A sense of shared experience, including emotional and physical feelings, with someone or something other than oneself. Empathy is often used to describe the response of a reader to a literary character.

English Sonnet: See *Sonnet*

Enjambment: The running over of the sense and structure of a line of verse or a couplet into the following verse or couplet.

Enlightenment, The: An eighteenth-century philosophical movement. It began in France but had a wide impact throughout Europe and America. Thinkers of the Enlightenment valued reason and believed that both the individual and society could achieve a state of perfection. Corresponding to this essentially humanist vision was a resistance to religious authority.

Epic: A long narrative poem about the adventures of a hero of great historic or legendary importance. The setting is vast and the action is often given cosmic significance through the intervention of supernatural forces such as gods, angels, or demons. Epics are typically written in a classical style of grand simplicity with elaborate metaphors and allusions that enhance the symbolic importance of a hero's adventures.

Epic Simile: See *Homeric Simile*

Epigram: A saying that makes the speaker's point quickly and concisely.

Epilogue: A concluding statement or section of a literary work. In dramas, particularly those of the seventeenth and eighteenth centuries, the epilogue is a closing speech, often in verse, delivered by an actor at the end of a play and spoken directly to the audience.

Epiphany: A sudden revelation of truth inspired by a seemingly trivial incident.

Epitaph: An inscription on a tomb or tombstone, or a verse written on the occasion of a person's death. Epitaphs may be serious or humorous.

Epithalamion: A song or poem written to honor and commemorate a marriage ceremony.

Epithalamium: See *Epithalamion*

Epithet: A word or phrase, often disparaging or abusive, that expresses a character trait of someone or something.

Erziehungsroman: See *Bildungsroman*

Essay: A prose composition with a focused subject of discussion. The term was coined by Michel de Montaigne to describe his 1580 collection of brief, informal reflections on himself and on various topics relating to human nature. An essay can also be a long, systematic discourse.

Existentialism: A predominantly twentieth-century philosophy concerned with the nature and perception of human existence. There are two major strains of existentialist thought: atheistic and Christian. Followers of atheistic existentialism believe that the individual is alone in a godless universe and that the basic human condition is one of suffering and loneliness. Nevertheless, because there are no fixed values, individuals can create their own characters—indeed, they can shape themselves—through the exercise of free will. The atheistic strain culminates in and is popularly associated with the works of Jean-Paul Sartre. The Christian existentialists, on the other hand, believe that only in God may people find freedom from life's anguish. The two strains hold certain beliefs in common: that existence cannot be fully understood or described through empirical effort; that anguish is a universal element of life; that individuals must bear responsibility for their actions; and that there is no common standard of behavior or perception for religious and ethical matters.

Expatriates: See *Expatriatism*

Expatriatism: The practice of leaving one's country to live for an extended period in another country.

Exposition: Writing intended to explain the nature of an idea, thing, or theme. Expository writing is often combined with description, narration, or argument. In dramatic writing, the exposition is the introductory material which presents the characters, setting, and tone of the play.

Expressionism: An indistinct literary term, originally used to describe an early twentieth-century school of German painting. The term applies to almost any mode of unconventional, highly subjective writing that distorts reality in some way.

Extended Monologue: See *Monologue*

F

Feet: See *Foot*

Feminine Rhyme: See *Rhyme*

Fiction: Any story that is the product of imagination rather than a documentation of fact. Characters and events in such narratives may be based in real life but their ultimate form and configuration is a creation of the author.

Figurative Language: A technique in writing in which the author temporarily interrupts the order, construction, or meaning of the writing for a particular effect. This interruption takes the form of one or more figures of speech such as hyperbole, irony, or simile. Figurative language is the opposite of literal language, in which every word is truthful, accurate, and free of exaggeration or embellishment.

Figures of Speech: Writing that differs from customary conventions for construction, meaning, order, or significance for the purpose of a special meaning or effect. There are two major types of figures of speech: rhetorical figures, which do not make changes in the meaning of the words, and tropes, which do.

Fin de siecle: A French term meaning "end of the century." The term is used to denote the last decade of the nineteenth century, a transition period when writers and other artists abandoned old conventions and looked for new techniques and objectives.

First Person: See *Point of View*

Folk Ballad: See *Ballad*

Folklore: Traditions and myths preserved in a culture or group of people. Typically, these are passed on by word of mouth in various forms—such as legends, songs, and proverbs—or preserved in customs and ceremonies. This term was first used by W. J. Thoms in 1846.

Folktale: A story originating in oral tradition. Folktales fall into a variety of categories, including legends, ghost stories, fairy tales, fables, and anecdotes based on historical figures and events.

Foot: The smallest unit of rhythm in a line of poetry. In English-language poetry, a foot is typically one accented syllable combined with one or two unaccented syllables.

Form: The pattern or construction of a work which identifies its genre and distinguishes it from other genres.

Formalism: In literary criticism, the belief that literature should follow prescribed rules of construction, such as those that govern the sonnet form.

Fourteener Meter: See *Meter*

Free Verse: Poetry that lacks regular metrical and rhyme patterns but that tries to capture the cadences of everyday speech. The form allows a poet to exploit a variety of rhythmical effects within a single poem.

Futurism: A flamboyant literary and artistic movement that developed in France, Italy, and Russia from 1908 through the 1920s. Futurist theater and poetry abandoned traditional literary forms. In their place, followers of the movement attempted to achieve total freedom of expression through bizarre imagery and deformed or newly invented words. The Futurists were self-consciously modern artists who attempted to incorporate the appearances and sounds of modern life into their work.

G

Genre: A category of literary work. In critical theory, genre may refer to both the content of a given work—tragedy, comedy, pastoral—and to its form, such as poetry, novel, or drama.

Genteel Tradition: A term coined by critic George Santayana to describe the literary practice of certain late nineteenth-century American writers, especially New Englanders. Followers of the Genteel Tradition emphasized conventionality in social, religious, moral, and literary standards.

Georgian Age: See *Georgian Poets*

Georgian Period: See *Georgian Poets*

Georgian Poets: A loose grouping of English poets during the years 1912-1922. The Georgians reacted against certain literary schools and practices, especially Victorian wordiness, turn-of-the-century aestheticism, and contemporary urban realism. In their place, the Georgians embraced the nineteenth-century poetic practices of William Wordsworth and the other Lake Poets.

Georgic: A poem about farming and the farmer's way of life, named from Virgil's *Georgics*.

Gilded Age: A period in American history during the 1870s characterized by political corruption and materialism. A number of important novels of social and political criticism were written during this time.

Gothic: See *Gothicism*

Gothicism: In literary criticism, works characterized by a taste for the medieval or morbidly attractive. A gothic novel prominently features elements of horror, the supernatural, gloom, and violence: clanking chains, terror, charnel houses, ghosts, medieval castles, and mysteriously slamming doors. The term "gothic novel" is also applied to novels that lack elements of the traditional Gothic setting but that create a similar atmosphere of terror or dread.

Graveyard School: A group of eighteenth-century English poets who wrote long, picturesque meditations on death. Their works were designed to cause the reader to ponder immortality.

Great Chain of Being: The belief that all things and creatures in nature are organized in a hierarchy from inanimate objects at the bottom to God at the top. This system of belief was popular in the seventeenth and eighteenth centuries.

Grotesque: In literary criticism, the subject matter of a work or a style of expression characterized by exaggeration, deformity, freakishness, and disorder. The grotesque often includes an element of comic absurdity.

H

Haiku: The shortest form of Japanese poetry, constructed in three lines of five, seven, and five syllables respectively. The message of a *haiku* poem usually centers on some aspect of spirituality and provokes an emotional response in the reader.

Half Rhyme: See *Consonance*

Harlem Renaissance: The Harlem Renaissance of the 1920s is generally considered the first significant movement of black writers and artists in the United States. During this period, new and established black writers published more fiction and poetry than ever before, the first influential black literary journals were established, and black authors and artists received their first widespread recognition and serious critical appraisal. Among the major writers associated with this period are Claude McKay, Jean Toomer, Countee Cullen, Langston Hughes, Arna Bontemps, Nella Larsen, and Zora Neale Hurston.

Hellenism: Imitation of ancient Greek thought or styles. Also, an approach to life that focuses on the growth and development of the intellect. "Hellenism" is sometimes used to refer to the belief that reason can be applied to examine all human experience.

Heptameter: See *Meter*

Hero/Heroine: The principal sympathetic character (male or female) in a literary work. Heroes and heroines typically exhibit admirable traits: idealism, courage, and integrity, for example.

Heroic Couplet: A rhyming couplet written in iambic pentameter (a verse with five iambic feet).

Heroic Line: The meter and length of a line of verse in epic or heroic poetry. This varies by language and time period.

Heroine: See *Hero/Heroine*

Hexameter: See *Meter*

Historical Criticism: The study of a work based on its impact on the world of the time period in which it was written.

Hokku: See *Haiku*

Holocaust: See *Holocaust Literature*

Holocaust Literature: Literature influenced by or written about the Holocaust of World War II. Such literature includes true stories of survival in concentration camps, escape, and life after the war, as well as fictional works and poetry.

Homeric Simile: An elaborate, detailed comparison written as a simile many lines in length.

Horatian Satire: See *Satire*

Humanism: A philosophy that places faith in the dignity of humankind and rejects the medieval perception of the individual as a weak, fallen creature. "Humanists" typically believe in the perfectibility of human nature and view reason and education as the means to that end.

Humors: Mentions of the humors refer to the ancient Greek theory that a person's health and personality were determined by the balance of four basic fluids in the body: blood, phlegm, yellow bile, and black bile. A dominance of any fluid would cause extremes in behavior. An excess of blood created a sanguine person who was joyful, aggressive, and passionate; a phlegmatic person was shy, fearful, and sluggish; too much yellow bile led to a choleric temperament characterized by impatience, anger, bitterness, and stubbornness; and excessive black bile created melancholy, a state of laziness, gluttony, and lack of motivation.

Humours: See *Humors*

Hyperbole: In literary criticism, deliberate exaggeration used to achieve an effect.

I

Iamb: See *Foot*

Idiom: A word construction or verbal expression closely associated with a given language.

Image: A concrete representation of an object or sensory experience. Typically, such a representation helps evoke the feelings associated with the object or experience itself. Images are either "literal" or "figurative." Literal images are especially concrete and involve little or no extension of the obvious meaning of the words used to express them. Figurative images do not follow the literal meaning of the words exactly. Images in literature are usually visual, but the term "image" can also refer to the representation of any sensory experience.

Imagery: The array of images in a literary work. Also, figurative language.

Imagism: An English and American poetry movement that flourished between 1908 and 1917. The Imagists used precise, clearly presented images in their works. They also used common, everyday speech and aimed for conciseness, concrete imagery, and the creation of new rhythms.

In medias res: A Latin term meaning "in the middle of things." It refers to the technique of beginning a story at its midpoint and then using various flashback devices to reveal previous action.

Induction: The process of reaching a conclusion by reasoning from specific premises to form a general premise. Also, an introductory portion of a work of literature, especially a play.

Intentional Fallacy: The belief that judgments of a literary work based solely on an author's stated or implied intentions are false and misleading. Critics who believe in the concept of the intentional fallacy typically argue that the work itself is sufficient matter for interpretation, even though they may concede that an author's statement of purpose can be useful.

Interior Monologue: A narrative technique in which characters' thoughts are revealed in a way that appears to be uncontrolled by the author. The interior monologue typically aims to reveal the inner self of a character. It portrays emotional experiences as they occur at both a conscious and unconscious level. Images are often used to represent sensations or emotions.

Internal Rhyme: Rhyme that occurs within a single line of verse.

Irish Literary Renaissance: A late nineteenth- and early twentieth-century movement in Irish literature. Members of the movement aimed to reduce the influence of British culture in Ireland and create an Irish national literature.

Irony: In literary criticism, the effect of language in which the intended meaning is the opposite of what is stated.

Italian Sonnet: See *Sonnet*

J

Jacobean Age: The period of the reign of James I of England (1603-1625). The early literature of this period reflected the worldview of the Elizabethan Age, but a darker, more cynical attitude steadily grew in the art and literature of the Jacobean Age. This was an important time for English drama and poetry.

Jargon: Language that is used or understood only by a select group of people. Jargon may refer to terminology used in a certain profession, such as computer jargon, or it may refer to any nonsensical language that is not understood by most people.

Journalism: Writing intended for publication in a newspaper or magazine, or for broadcast on a radio or television program featuring news, sports, entertainment, or other timely material.

K

Knickerbocker Group: A somewhat indistinct group of New York writers of the first half of the nineteenth century. Members of the group were linked only by location and a common theme: New York life.

Kunstlerroman: See *Bildungsroman*

L

Lais: See *Lay*

Lake Poets: See *Lake School*

Lake School: These poets all lived in the Lake District of England at the turn of the nineteenth century. As a group, they followed no single "school" of thought or literary practice, although their works were uniformly disparaged by the *Edinburgh Review*.

Lay: A song or simple narrative poem. The form originated in medieval France. Early French *lais* were often based on the Celtic legends and other tales sung by Breton minstrels—thus the name of the "Breton lay." In fourteenth-century England, the term "lay" was used to describe short narratives written in imitation of the Breton lays.

Leitmotiv: See *Motif*

Literal Language: An author uses literal language when he or she writes without exaggerating or embellishing the subject matter and without any tools of figurative language.

Literary Ballad: See *Ballad*

Literature: Literature is broadly defined as any written or spoken material, but the term most often refers to creative works.

Lost Generation: A term first used by Gertrude Stein to describe the post-World War I generation of American writers: men and women haunted by a sense of betrayal and emptiness brought about by the destructiveness of the war.

Lyric Poetry: A poem expressing the subjective feelings and personal emotions of the poet. Such poetry is melodic, since it was originally accompanied by a lyre in recitals. Most Western poetry in the twentieth century may be classified as lyrical.

M

Mannerism: Exaggerated, artificial adherence to a literary manner or style. Also, a popular style of the visual arts of late sixteenth-century Europe that was marked by elongation of the human form and by intentional spatial distortion. Literary works that are self-consciously high-toned and artistic are often said to be "mannered."

Masculine Rhyme: See *Rhyme*

Measure: The foot, verse, or time sequence used in a literary work, especially a poem. Measure is often used somewhat incorrectly as a synonym for meter.

Metaphor: A figure of speech that expresses an idea through the image of another object. Metaphors suggest the essence of the first object by identifying it with certain qualities of the second object.

Metaphysical Conceit: See *Conceit*

Metaphysical Poetry: The body of poetry produced by a group of seventeenth-century English writers called the "Metaphysical Poets." The group includes John Donne and Andrew Marvell. The Metaphysical Poets made use of everyday speech, intellectual analysis, and unique imagery. They aimed to portray the ordinary conflicts and contradictions of life. Their poems often took the form of an argument, and many of them emphasize physical and religious love as well as the fleeting nature of life. Elaborate conceits are typical in metaphysical poetry.

Metaphysical Poets: See *Metaphysical Poetry*

Meter: In literary criticism, the repetition of sound patterns that creates a rhythm in poetry. The patterns are based on the number of syllables and the presence and absence of accents. The unit of rhythm in a line is called a foot. Types of meter are classified according to the number of feet in a line. These are the standard English lines: Monometer, one foot; Dimeter, two feet; Trimeter, three feet; Tetrameter, four feet; Pentameter, five feet; Hexameter, six feet (also called the Alexandrine); Heptameter, seven feet (also called the "Fourteener" when the feet are iambic).

Modernism: Modern literary practices. Also, the principles of a literary school that lasted from roughly the beginning of the twentieth century until the end of World War II. Modernism is defined by its rejection of the literary conventions of the nineteenth century and by its opposition to conventional morality, taste, traditions, and economic values.

Monologue: A composition, written or oral, by a single individual. More specifically, a speech given by a single individual in a drama or other public entertainment. It has no set length, although it is usually several or more lines long.

Monometer: See *Meter*

Mood: The prevailing emotions of a work or of the author in his or her creation of the work. The mood of a work is not always what might be expected based on its subject matter.

Motif: A theme, character type, image, metaphor, or other verbal element that recurs throughout a single work of literature or occurs in a number of different works over a period of time.

Motiv: See *Motif*

Muckrakers: An early twentieth-century group of American writers. Typically, their works exposed the wrongdoings of big business and government in the United States.

Muses: Nine Greek mythological goddesses, the daughters of Zeus and Mnemosyne (Memory). Each muse patronized a specific area of the liberal arts and sciences. Calliope presided over epic poetry, Clio over history, Erato over love poetry, Euterpe over music or lyric poetry, Melpomene over tragedy, Polyhymnia over hymns to the gods, Terpsichore over dance, Thalia over comedy, and Urania over astronomy. Poets and writers traditionally made appeals to the Muses for inspiration in their work.

Myth: An anonymous tale emerging from the traditional beliefs of a culture or social unit. Myths use supernatural explanations for natural phenomena. They may also explain cosmic issues like creation and death. Collections of myths, known as mythologies, are common to all cultures and nations, but the best-known myths belong to the Norse, Roman, and Greek mythologies.

N

Narration: The telling of a series of events, real or invented. A narration may be either a simple narrative, in which the events are recounted chronologically, or a narrative with a plot, in which the account is given in a style reflecting the author's artistic concept of the story. Narration is sometimes used as a synonym for "storyline."

Narrative: A verse or prose accounting of an event or sequence of events, real or invented. The term is also used as an adjective in the sense "method of narration." For example, in literary criticism, the expression "narrative technique" usually refers to the way the author structures and presents his or her story.

Narrative Poetry: A nondramatic poem in which the author tells a story. Such poems may be of any length or level of complexity.

Narrator: The teller of a story. The narrator may be the author or a character in the story through whom the author speaks.

Naturalism: A literary movement of the late nineteenth and early twentieth centuries. The movement's major theorist, French novelist Emile Zola, envisioned a type of fiction that would examine human life with the objectivity of scientific inquiry. The Naturalists typically viewed human beings as either the products of "biological determinism," ruled by hereditary instincts and engaged in an endless struggle for survival, or as the products of "socioeconomic determinism," ruled by social and economic forces beyond their control. In their works, the Naturalists generally ignored the highest levels of society and focused on degradation: poverty, alcoholism, prostitution, insanity, and disease.

Negritude: A literary movement based on the concept of a shared cultural bond on the part of black Africans, wherever they may be in the world. It traces its origins to the former French colonies of Africa and the Caribbean. Negritude poets, novelists, and essayists generally stress four points in their writings: One, black alienation from traditional African culture can lead to feelings of inferiority. Two, European colonialism and Western education should be resisted. Three, black Africans should seek to affirm and define their own identity. Four, African culture can and should be reclaimed. Many Negritude writers also claim that blacks can make unique contributions to the world, based on a heightened appreciation of nature, rhythm, and human emotions—aspects of life they say are not so highly valued in the materialistic and rationalistic West.

Negro Renaissance: See *Harlem Renaissance*

Neoclassical Period: See *Neoclassicism*

Neoclassicism: In literary criticism, this term refers to the revival of the attitudes and styles of expression of classical literature. It is generally used to describe a period in European history beginning in the late seventeenth century and lasting until about 1800. In its purest form, Neoclassicism marked a return to order, proportion, restraint, logic, accuracy, and decorum. In England, where Neoclassicism perhaps was most popular, it reflected the influence of seventeenth-century French writers, especially dramatists. Neoclassical writers typically reacted against the intensity and enthusiasm of the Renaissance period. They wrote works that appealed to the intellect, using elevated language and classical literary forms such as satire and the ode. Neoclassical works were often governed by the classical goal of instruction.

Neoclassicists: See *Neoclassicism*

New Criticism: A movement in literary criticism, dating from the late 1920s, that stressed close textual analysis in the interpretation of works of literature. The New Critics saw little merit in historical and biographical analysis. Rather, they aimed to examine the text alone, free from the question of how external events— biographical or otherwise—may have helped shape it.

New Journalism: A type of writing in which the journalist presents factual information in a form usually used in fiction. New journalism emphasizes description, narration, and character development to bring readers closer to the human element of the story, and is often used in personality profiles and in-depth feature articles. It is not compatible with "straight" or "hard" newswriting, which is generally composed in a brief, fact-based style.

New Journalists: See *New Journalism*

New Negro Movement: See *Harlem Renaissance*

Noble Savage: The idea that primitive man is noble and good but becomes evil and corrupted as he becomes civilized. The concept of the noble savage originated in the Renaissance period but is more closely identified with such later writers as Jean-Jacques Rousseau and Aphra Behn.

O

Objective Correlative: An outward set of objects, a situation, or a chain of events corresponding to an inward experience and evoking this experience in the reader. The term frequently appears in modern criticism in discussions of authors' intended effects on the emotional responses of readers.

Objectivity: A quality in writing characterized by the absence of the author's opinion or feeling about the subject matter. Objectivity is an important factor in criticism.

Occasional Verse: poetry written on the occasion of a significant historical or personal event. *Vers de societe* is sometimes called occasional verse although it is of a less serious nature.

Octave: A poem or stanza composed of eight lines. The term octave most often represents the first eight lines of a Petrarchan sonnet.

Ode: Name given to an extended lyric poem characterized by exalted emotion and dignified style. An ode usually concerns a single, serious theme. Most odes, but not all, are addressed to an object or individual. Odes are distinguished from other lyric poetic forms by their complex rhythmic and stanzaic patterns.

Oedipus Complex: A son's amorous obsession with his mother. The phrase is derived from the story of the ancient Theban hero Oedipus, who unknowingly killed his father and married his mother.

Omniscience: See *Point of View*

Onomatopoeia: The use of words whose sounds express or suggest their meaning. In its simplest sense, onomatopoeia may be represented by words that mimic the sounds they denote such as "hiss" or "meow." At a more subtle level, the pattern and rhythm of sounds and rhymes of a line or poem may be onomatopoeic.

Oral Tradition: See *Oral Transmission*

Oral Transmission: A process by which songs, ballads, folklore, and other material are transmitted by word of mouth. The tradition of oral transmission predates the written record systems of literate society. Oral transmission preserves material sometimes over generations, although often with variations. Memory plays a large part in the recitation and preservation of orally transmitted material.

Ottava Rima: An eight-line stanza of poetry composed in iambic pentameter (a five-foot line in which each foot consists of an unaccented syllable followed by an accented syllable), following the abababcc rhyme scheme.

Oxymoron: A phrase combining two contradictory terms. Oxymorons may be intentional or unintentional.

P

Pantheism: The idea that all things are both a manifestation or revelation of God and a part of God at the same time. Pantheism was a common attitude in the early societies of Egypt, India, and Greece—the term derives from the Greek *pan* meaning "all" and *theos* meaning "deity." It later became a significant part of the Christian faith.

Parable: A story intended to teach a moral lesson or answer an ethical question.

Paradox: A statement that appears illogical or contradictory at first, but may actually point to an underlying truth.

Parallelism: A method of comparison of two ideas in which each is developed in the same grammatical structure.

Parnassianism: A mid nineteenth-century movement in French literature. Followers of the movement stressed adherence to well-defined artistic forms as a reaction against the often chaotic expression of the artist's ego that dominated the work of the Romantics. The Parnassians also rejected the moral, ethical, and social themes exhibited in the works of French Romantics such as

Victor Hugo. The aesthetic doctrines of the Parnassians strongly influenced the later symbolist and decadent movements.

Parody: In literary criticism, this term refers to an imitation of a serious literary work or the signature style of a particular author in a ridiculous manner. A typical parody adopts the style of the original and applies it to an inappropriate subject for humorous effect. Parody is a form of satire and could be considered the literary equivalent of a caricature or cartoon.

Pastoral: A term derived from the Latin word "pastor," meaning shepherd. A pastoral is a literary composition on a rural theme. The conventions of the pastoral were originated by the third-century Greek poet Theocritus, who wrote about the experiences, love affairs, and pastimes of Sicilian shepherds. In a pastoral, characters and language of a courtly nature are often placed in a simple setting. The term pastoral is also used to classify dramas, elegies, and lyrics that exhibit the use of country settings and shepherd characters.

Pathetic Fallacy: A term coined by English critic John Ruskin to identify writing that falsely endows nonhuman things with human intentions and feelings, such as "angry clouds" and "sad trees."

Pen Name: See *Pseudonym*

Pentameter: See *Meter*

Persona: A Latin term meaning "mask." *Personae* are the characters in a fictional work of literature. The *persona* generally functions as a mask through which the author tells a story in a voice other than his or her own. A *persona* is usually either a character in a story who acts as a narrator or an "implied author," a voice created by the author to act as the narrator for himself or herself.

Personae: See *Persona*

Personal Point of View: See *Point of View*

Personification: A figure of speech that gives human qualities to abstract ideas, animals, and inanimate objects.

Petrarchan Sonnet: See *Sonnet*

Phenomenology: A method of literary criticism based on the belief that things have no existence outside of human consciousness or awareness. Proponents of this theory believe that art is a process that takes place in the

mind of the observer as he or she contemplates an object rather than a quality of the object itself.

Plagiarism: Claiming another person's written material as one's own. Plagiarism can take the form of direct, word-for-word copying or the theft of the substance or idea of the work.

Platonic Criticism: A form of criticism that stresses an artistic work's usefulness as an agent of social engineering rather than any quality or value of the work itself.

Platonism: The embracing of the doctrines of the philosopher Plato, popular among the poets of the Renaissance and the Romantic period. Platonism is more flexible than Aristotelian Criticism and places more emphasis on the supernatural and unknown aspects of life.

Plot: In literary criticism, this term refers to the pattern of events in a narrative or drama. In its simplest sense, the plot guides the author in composing the work and helps the reader follow the work. Typically, plots exhibit causality and unity and have a beginning, a middle, and an end. Sometimes, however, a plot may consist of a series of disconnected events, in which case it is known as an "episodic plot."

Poem: In its broadest sense, a composition utilizing rhyme, meter, concrete detail, and expressive language to create a literary experience with emotional and aesthetic appeal.

Poet: An author who writes poetry or verse. The term is also used to refer to an artist or writer who has an exceptional gift for expression, imagination, and energy in the making of art in any form.

Poete maudit: A term derived from Paul Verlaine's *Les poetes maudits* (*The Accursed Poets*), a collection of essays on the French symbolist writers Stephane Mallarme, Arthur Rimbaud, and Tristan Corbiere. In the sense intended by Verlaine, the poet is "accursed" for choosing to explore extremes of human experience outside of middle-class society.

Poetic Fallacy: See *Pathetic Fallacy*

Poetic Justice: An outcome in a literary work, not necessarily a poem, in which the good are rewarded and the evil are punished, especially in ways that particularly fit their virtues or crimes.

Poetic License: Distortions of fact and literary convention made by a writer—not always a poet—for the sake of the effect gained. Poetic license is closely related to the concept of "artistic freedom."

Poetics: This term has two closely related meanings. It denotes (1) an aesthetic theory in literary criticism about the essence of poetry or (2) rules prescribing the proper methods, content, style, or diction of poetry. The term poetics may also refer to theories about literature in general, not just poetry.

Poetry: In its broadest sense, writing that aims to present ideas and evoke an emotional experience in the reader through the use of meter, imagery, connotative and concrete words, and a carefully constructed structure based on rhythmic patterns. Poetry typically relies on words and expressions that have several layers of meaning. It also makes use of the effects of regular rhythm on the ear and may make a strong appeal to the senses through the use of imagery.

Point of View: The narrative perspective from which a literary work is presented to the reader. There are four traditional points of view. The "third person omniscient" gives the reader a "godlike" perspective, unrestricted by time or place, from which to see actions and look into the minds of characters. This allows the author to comment openly on characters and events in the work. The "third person" point of view presents the events of the story from outside of any single character's perception, much like the omniscient point of view, but the reader must understand the action as it takes place and without any special insight into characters' minds or motivations. The "first person" or "personal" point of view relates events as they are perceived by a single character. The main character "tells" the story and may offer opinions about the action and characters which differ from those of the author. Much less common than omniscient, third person, and first person is the "second person" point of view, wherein the author tells the story as if it is happening to the reader.

Polemic: A work in which the author takes a stand on a controversial subject, such as abortion or religion. Such works are often extremely argumentative or provocative.

Pornography: Writing intended to provoke feelings of lust in the reader. Such works are often condemned by critics and teachers, but those which can be shown to have literary value are viewed less harshly.

Post-Aesthetic Movement: An artistic response made by African Americans to the black aesthetic movement of the 1960s and early '70s. Writers since that time have adopted a somewhat different tone in their work, with less emphasis placed on the disparity between black and white in the United States. In the words of post-aesthetic authors such as Toni Morrison, John Edgar Wideman, and Kristin Hunter, African Americans are portrayed as looking inward for answers to their own questions, rather than always looking to the outside world.

Postmodernism: Writing from the 1960s forward characterized by experimentation and continuing to apply some of the fundamentals of modernism, which included existentialism and alienation. Postmodernists have gone a step further in the rejection of tradition begun with the modernists by also rejecting traditional forms, preferring the anti-novel over the novel and the anti-hero over the hero.

Pre-Raphaelites: A circle of writers and artists in mid nineteenth-century England. Valuing the pre-Renaissance artistic qualities of religious symbolism, lavish pictorialism, and natural sensuousness, the Pre-Raphaelites cultivated a sense of mystery and melancholy that influenced later writers associated with the Symbolist and Decadent movements.

Primitivism: The belief that primitive peoples were nobler and less flawed than civilized peoples because they had not been subjected to the tainting influence of society.

Projective Verse: A form of free verse in which the poet's breathing pattern determines the lines of the poem. Poets who advocate projective verse are against all formal structures in writing, including meter and form.

Prologue: An introductory section of a literary work. It often contains information establishing the situation of the characters or presents information about the setting, time period, or action. In drama, the prologue is spoken by a chorus or by one of the principal characters.

Prose: A literary medium that attempts to mirror the language of everyday speech. It is distinguished from poetry by its use of unmetered, unrhymed language consisting of logically related sentences. Prose is usually grouped into paragraphs that form a cohesive whole such as an essay or a novel.

Prosopopoeia: See *Personification*

Protagonist: The central character of a story who serves as a focus for its themes and incidents and as the principal rationale for its development. The protagonist is sometimes referred to in discussions of modern literature as the hero or anti-hero.

Proverb: A brief, sage saying that expresses a truth about life in a striking manner.

Pseudonym: A name assumed by a writer, most often intended to prevent his or her identification as the author of a work. Two or more authors may work together under one pseudonym, or an author may use a different name for each genre he or she publishes in. Some publishing companies maintain "house pseudonyms," under which any number of authors may write installations in a series. Some authors also choose a pseudonym over their real names the way an actor may use a stage name.

Pun: A play on words that have similar sounds but different meanings.

Pure Poetry: poetry written without instructional intent or moral purpose that aims only to please a reader by its imagery or musical flow. The term pure poetry is used as the antonym of the term "didacticism."

Q

Quatrain: A four-line stanza of a poem or an entire poem consisting of four lines.

R

Realism: A nineteenth-century European literary movement that sought to portray familiar characters, situations, and settings in a realistic manner. This was done primarily by using an objective narrative point of view and through the buildup of accurate detail. The standard for success of any realistic work depends on how faithfully it transfers common experience into fictional forms. The realistic method may be altered or extended, as in stream of consciousness writing, to record highly subjective experience.

Refrain: A phrase repeated at intervals throughout a poem. A refrain may appear at the end

of each stanza or at less regular intervals. It may be altered slightly at each appearance.

Renaissance: The period in European history that marked the end of the Middle Ages. It began in Italy in the late fourteenth century. In broad terms, it is usually seen as spanning the fourteenth, fifteenth, and sixteenth centuries, although it did not reach Great Britain, for example, until the 1480s or so. The Renaissance saw an awakening in almost every sphere of human activity, especially science, philosophy, and the arts. The period is best defined by the emergence of a general philosophy that emphasized the importance of the intellect, the individual, and world affairs. It contrasts strongly with the medieval worldview, characterized by the dominant concerns of faith, the social collective, and spiritual salvation.

Repartee: Conversation featuring snappy retorts and witticisms.

Restoration: See *Restoration Age*

Restoration Age: A period in English literature beginning with the crowning of Charles II in 1660 and running to about 1700. The era, which was characterized by a reaction against Puritanism, was the first great age of the comedy of manners. The finest literature of the era is typically witty and urbane, and often lewd.

Rhetoric: In literary criticism, this term denotes the art of ethical persuasion. In its strictest sense, rhetoric adheres to various principles developed since classical times for arranging facts and ideas in a clear, persuasive, appealing manner. The term is also used to refer to effective prose in general and theories of or methods for composing effective prose.

Rhetorical Question: A question intended to provoke thought, but not an expressed answer, in the reader. It is most commonly used in oratory and other persuasive genres.

Rhyme: When used as a noun in literary criticism, this term generally refers to a poem in which words sound identical or very similar and appear in parallel positions in two or more lines. Rhymes are classified into different types according to where they fall in a line or stanza or according to the degree of similarity they exhibit in their spellings and sounds. Some major types of rhyme are "masculine" rhyme, "feminine" rhyme, and "triple" rhyme.

In a masculine rhyme, the rhyming sound falls in a single accented syllable, as with "heat" and "eat." Feminine rhyme is a rhyme of two syllables, one stressed and one unstressed, as with "merry" and "tarry." Triple rhyme matches the sound of the accented syllable and the two unaccented syllables that follow: "narrative" and "declarative."

Rhyme Royal: A stanza of seven lines composed in iambic pentameter and rhymed *ababbcc*. The name is said to be a tribute to King James I of Scotland, who made much use of the form in his poetry.

Rhyme Scheme: See *Rhyme*

Rhythm: A regular pattern of sound, time intervals, or events occurring in writing, most often and most discernably in poetry. Regular, reliable rhythm is known to be soothing to humans, while interrupted, unpredictable, or rapidly changing rhythm is disturbing. These effects are known to authors, who use them to produce a desired reaction in the reader.

Rococo: A style of European architecture that flourished in the eighteenth century, especially in France. The most notable features of *rococo* are its extensive use of ornamentation and its themes of lightness, gaiety, and intimacy. In literary criticism, the term is often used disparagingly to refer to a decadent or over-ornamental style.

Romance: A broad term, usually denoting a narrative with exotic, exaggerated, often idealized characters, scenes, and themes.

Romantic Age: See *Romanticism*

Romanticism: This term has two widely accepted meanings. In historical criticism, it refers to a European intellectual and artistic movement of the late eighteenth and early nineteenth centuries that sought greater freedom of personal expression than that allowed by the strict rules of literary form and logic of the eighteenth-century neoclassicists. The Romantics preferred emotional and imaginative expression to rational analysis. They considered the individual to be at the center of all experience and so placed him or her at the center of their art. The Romantics believed that the creative imagination reveals nobler truths—unique feelings and attitudes—than those that could be discovered by logic or by scientific examination. Both the natural world and the state of childhood were important sources for revelations

of "eternal truths." "Romanticism" is also used as a general term to refer to a type of sensibility found in all periods of literary history and usually considered to be in opposition to the principles of classicism. In this sense, Romanticism signifies any work or philosophy in which the exotic or dreamlike figure strongly, or that is devoted to individualistic expression, self-analysis, or a pursuit of a higher realm of knowledge than can be discovered by human reason.

Romantics: See *Romanticism*

Russian Symbolism: A Russian poetic movement, derived from French symbolism, that flourished between 1894 and 1910. While some Russian Symbolists continued in the French tradition, stressing aestheticism and the importance of suggestion above didactic intent, others saw their craft as a form of mystical worship, and themselves as mediators between the supernatural and the mundane.

S

Satire: A work that uses ridicule, humor, and wit to criticize and provoke change in human nature and institutions. There are two major types of satire: "formal" or "direct" satire speaks directly to the reader or to a character in the work; "indirect" satire relies upon the ridiculous behavior of its characters to make its point. Formal satire is further divided into two manners: the "Horatian," which ridicules gently, and the "Juvenalian," which derides its subjects harshly and bitterly.

Scansion: The analysis or "scanning" of a poem to determine its meter and often its rhyme scheme. The most common system of scansion uses accents (slanted lines drawn above syllables) to show stressed syllables, breves (curved lines drawn above syllables) to show unstressed syllables, and vertical lines to separate each foot.

Second Person: See *Point of View*

Semiotics: The study of how literary forms and conventions affect the meaning of language.

Sestet: Any six-line poem or stanza.

Setting: The time, place, and culture in which the action of a narrative takes place. The elements of setting may include geographic location, characters' physical and mental environments, prevailing cultural attitudes, or the historical time in which the action takes place.

Shakespearean Sonnet: See *Sonnet*

Signifying Monkey: A popular trickster figure in black folklore, with hundreds of tales about this character documented since the 19th century.

Simile: A comparison, usually using "like" or "as," of two essentially dissimilar things, as in "coffee as cold as ice" or "He sounded like a broken record."

Slang: A type of informal verbal communication that is generally unacceptable for formal writing. Slang words and phrases are often colorful exaggerations used to emphasize the speaker's point; they may also be shortened versions of an often-used word or phrase.

Slant Rhyme: See *Consonance*

Slave Narrative: Autobiographical accounts of American slave life as told by escaped slaves. These works first appeared during the abolition movement of the 1830s through the 1850s.

Social Realism: See *Socialist Realism*

Socialist Realism: The Socialist Realism school of literary theory was proposed by Maxim Gorky and established as a dogma by the first Soviet Congress of Writers. It demanded adherence to a communist worldview in works of literature. Its doctrines required an objective viewpoint comprehensible to the working classes and themes of social struggle featuring strong proletarian heroes.

Soliloquy: A monologue in a drama used to give the audience information and to develop the speaker's character. It is typically a projection of the speaker's innermost thoughts. Usually delivered while the speaker is alone on stage, a soliloquy is intended to present an illusion of unspoken reflection.

Sonnet: A fourteen-line poem, usually composed in iambic pentameter, employing one of several rhyme schemes. There are three major types of sonnets, upon which all other variations of the form are based: the "Petrarchan" or "Italian" sonnet, the "Shakespearean" or "English" sonnet, and the "Spenserian" sonnet. A Petrarchan sonnet consists of an octave rhymed *abbaabba* and a "sestet" rhymed either *cdecde, cdccdc,* or *cdedce.* The octave poses a question or problem, relates a narrative, or puts forth a proposition; the sestet presents a solution to the problem, comments upon the narrative, or applies the proposition put forth in the octave. The Shakespearean sonnet is divided into three quatrains and a couplet rhymed *abab cdcd efef gg.* The couplet provides an epigrammatic comment on the narrative or problem put forth in the quatrains. The Spenserian sonnet uses three quatrains and a couplet like the Shakespearean, but links their three rhyme schemes in this way: *abab bcbc cdcd ee.* The Spenserian sonnet develops its theme in two parts like the Petrarchan, its final six lines resolving a problem, analyzing a narrative, or applying a proposition put forth in its first eight lines.

Spenserian Sonnet: See *Sonnet*

Spenserian Stanza: A nine-line stanza having eight verses in iambic pentameter, its ninth verse in iambic hexameter, and the rhyme scheme ababbcbcc.

Spondee: In poetry meter, a foot consisting of two long or stressed syllables occurring together. This form is quite rare in English verse, and is usually composed of two monosyllabic words.

Sprung Rhythm: Versification using a specific number of accented syllables per line but disregarding the number of unaccented syllables that fall in each line, producing an irregular rhythm in the poem.

Stanza: A subdivision of a poem consisting of lines grouped together, often in recurring patterns of rhyme, line length, and meter. Stanzas may also serve as units of thought in a poem much like paragraphs in prose.

Stereotype: A stereotype was originally the name for a duplication made during the printing process; this led to its modern definition as a person or thing that is (or is assumed to be) the same as all others of its type.

Stream of Consciousness: A narrative technique for rendering the inward experience of a character. This technique is designed to give the impression of an ever-changing series of thoughts, emotions, images, and memories in the spontaneous and seemingly illogical order that they occur in life.

Structuralism: A twentieth-century movement in literary criticism that examines how literary texts arrive at their meanings, rather than the meanings themselves. There are two major types of structuralist analysis: one examines the way patterns of linguistic structures unify a specific text and emphasize certain elements of that text, and the other interprets the way literary forms and conventions affect the meaning of language itself.

Structure: The form taken by a piece of literature. The structure may be made obvious for ease of understanding, as in nonfiction works, or may obscured for artistic purposes, as in some poetry or seemingly "unstructured" prose.

Sturm und Drang: A German term meaning "storm and stress." It refers to a German literary movement of the 1770s and 1780s that reacted against the order and rationalism of the enlightenment, focusing instead on the intense experience of extraordinary individuals.

Style: A writer's distinctive manner of arranging words to suit his or her ideas and purpose in writing. The unique imprint of the author's personality upon his or her writing, style is the product of an author's way of arranging ideas and his or her use of diction, different sentence structures, rhythm, figures of speech, rhetorical principles, and other elements of composition.

Subject: The person, event, or theme at the center of a work of literature. A work may have one or more subjects of each type, with shorter works tending to have fewer and longer works tending to have more.

Subjectivity: Writing that expresses the author's personal feelings about his subject, and which may or may not include factual information about the subject.

Surrealism: A term introduced to criticism by Guillaume Apollinaire and later adopted by Andre Breton. It refers to a French literary and artistic movement founded in the 1920s. The Surrealists sought to express unconscious thoughts and feelings in their works. The best-known technique used for achieving this aim was automatic writing—transcriptions of spontaneous outpourings from the unconscious. The Surrealists proposed to unify the contrary levels of conscious and unconscious, dream and reality, objectivity and subjectivity into a new level of "super-realism."

Suspense: A literary device in which the author maintains the audience's attention through the buildup of events, the outcome of which will soon be revealed.

Syllogism: A method of presenting a logical argument. In its most basic form, the syllogism consists of a major premise, a minor premise, and a conclusion.

Symbol: Something that suggests or stands for something else without losing its original identity. In literature, symbols combine their literal meaning with the suggestion of an abstract concept. Literary symbols are of two types: those that carry complex associations of meaning no matter what their contexts, and those that derive their suggestive meaning from their functions in specific literary works.

Symbolism: This term has two widely accepted meanings. In historical criticism, it denotes an early modernist literary movement initiated in France during the nineteenth century that reacted against the prevailing standards of realism. Writers in this movement aimed to evoke, indirectly and symbolically, an order of being beyond the material world of the five senses. Poetic expression of personal emotion figured strongly in the movement, typically by means of a private set of symbols uniquely identifiable with the individual poet. The principal aim of the Symbolists was to express in words the highly complex feelings that grew out of everyday contact with the world. In a broader sense, the term "symbolism" refers to the use of one object to represent another.

Symbolist: See *Symbolism*

Symbolist Movement: See *Symbolism*

Sympathetic Fallacy: See *Affective Fallacy*

T

Tanka: A form of Japanese poetry similar to *haiku*. A *tanka* is five lines long, with the lines containing five, seven, five, seven, and seven syllables respectively.

Terza Rima: A three-line stanza form in poetry in which the rhymes are made on the last word of each line in the following manner: the first and third lines of the first stanza, then the second line of the first stanza and the first and third lines of the second stanza, and so on with the middle line of any stanza rhyming with the first and third lines of the following stanza.

Tetrameter: See *Meter*

Textual Criticism: A branch of literary criticism that seeks to establish the authoritative text of a literary work. Textual critics typically compare all known manuscripts or printings of a single work in order to assess the meanings of differences and revisions. This procedure allows them to arrive at a definitive version that (supposedly) corresponds to the author's original intention.

Theme: The main point of a work of literature. The term is used interchangeably with thesis.

Thesis: A thesis is both an essay and the point argued in the essay. Thesis novels and thesis plays share the quality of containing a thesis which is supported through the action of the story.

Third Person: See *Point of View*

Tone: The author's attitude toward his or her audience may be deduced from the tone of the work. A formal tone may create distance or convey politeness, while an informal tone may encourage a friendly, intimate, or intrusive feeling in the reader. The author's attitude toward his or her subject matter may also be deduced from the tone of the words he or she uses in discussing it.

Tragedy: A drama in prose or poetry about a noble, courageous hero of excellent character who, because of some tragic character flaw or *hamartia*, brings ruin upon him- or herself. Tragedy treats its subjects in a dignified and serious manner, using poetic language to help evoke pity and fear and bring about catharsis, a purging of these emotions. The tragic form was practiced extensively by the ancient Greeks. In the Middle Ages, when classical works were virtually unknown, tragedy came to denote any works about the fall of persons from exalted to low conditions due to any reason: fate, vice, weakness, etc. According to the classical definition of tragedy, such works present the "pathetic"—that which evokes pity—rather than the tragic. The classical form of tragedy was revived in the sixteenth century; it flourished especially on the Elizabethan stage. In modern times, dramatists have attempted to adapt the form to the needs of modern society by drawing their heroes from the ranks of ordinary men and women and defining the nobility of these heroes in terms of spirit rather than exalted social standing.

Tragic Flaw: In a tragedy, the quality within the hero or heroine which leads to his or her downfall.

Transcendentalism: An American philosophical and religious movement, based in New England from around 1835 until the Civil War. Transcendentalism was a form of American romanticism that had its roots abroad in the works of Thomas Carlyle, Samuel Coleridge, and Johann Wolfgang von Goethe. The Transcendentalists stressed the importance of intuition and subjective experience in communication with God. They rejected religious dogma and texts in favor of mysticism and scientific naturalism. They pursued truths that lie beyond the "colorless" realms perceived by reason and the senses and were active social reformers in public education, women's rights, and the abolition of slavery.

Trickster: A character or figure common in Native American and African literature who uses his ingenuity to defeat enemies and escape difficult situations. Tricksters are most often animals, such as the spider, hare, or coyote, although they may take the form of humans as well.

Trimeter: See *Meter*

Triple Rhyme: See *Rhyme*

Trochee: See *Foot*

U

Understatement: See *Irony*

Unities: Strict rules of dramatic structure, formulated by Italian and French critics of the Renaissance and based loosely on the principles of drama discussed by Aristotle in his *Poetics*. Foremost among these rules were the three unities of action, time, and place that compelled a dramatist to: (1) construct a single plot with a beginning, middle, and end that details the causal relationships of action and character; (2) restrict the action to the events of a single day; and (3) limit the scene to a single place or city. The unities were observed faithfully by continental European writers until the Romantic Age, but they were never regularly observed in English drama. Modern dramatists are typically more concerned with a unity of impression or emotional effect than with any of the classical unities.

Urban Realism: A branch of realist writing that attempts to accurately reflect the often harsh facts of modern urban existence.

Utopia: A fictional perfect place, such as "paradise" or "heaven."

Utopian: See *Utopia*

Utopianism: See *Utopia*

V

Verisimilitude: Literally, the appearance of truth. In literary criticism, the term refers to aspects of a work of literature that seem true to the reader.

Vers de societe: See *Occasional Verse*

Vers libre: See *Free Verse*

Verse: A line of metered language, a line of a poem, or any work written in verse.

Versification: The writing of verse. Versification may also refer to the meter, rhyme, and other mechanical components of a poem.

Victorian: Refers broadly to the reign of Queen Victoria of England (1837-1901) and to anything with qualities typical of that era. For example, the qualities of smug narrowmindedness, bourgeois materialism, faith in social progress, and priggish morality are often considered Victorian. This stereotype is contradicted by such dramatic intellectual developments as the theories of Charles Darwin, Karl Marx, and Sigmund Freud (which stirred strong debates in England) and the critical attitudes of serious Victorian writers like Charles Dickens and George Eliot. In literature, the Victorian Period was the great age of the English novel, and the latter part of the era saw the rise of movements such as decadence and symbolism.

Victorian Age: See *Victorian*

Victorian Period: See *Victorian*

W

Weltanschauung: A German term referring to a person's worldview or philosophy.

Weltschmerz: A German term meaning "world pain." It describes a sense of anguish about the nature of existence, usually associated with a melancholy, pessimistic attitude.

Z

Zarzuela: A type of Spanish operetta.

Zeitgeist: A German term meaning "spirit of the time." It refers to the moral and intellectual trends of a given era.

Cumulative
Author/Title Index

Carruth, Hayden
I, I, I: V26
Carson, Anne
New Rule: V18
Carson, Ciaran
The War Correspondent: V26
Carver, Raymond
The Cobweb: V17
Casey at the Bat (Thayer): V5
Castillo, Ana
While I Was Gone a War Began: V21
Cavafy, C. P.
Ithaka: V19
Cavalry Crossing a Ford (Whitman):
V13
Celan, Paul
Late and Deep: V21
The Centaur (Swenson): V30
Cervantes, Lorna Dee
Freeway 280: V30
The Chambered Nautilus (Holmes):
V24
Chang, Diana
Most Satisfied by Snow: V37
The Charge of the Light Brigade
(Tennyson): V1
Chaucer, Geoffrey
The Canterbury Tales: V14
Chicago (Sandburg): V3
Ch'ien, T'ao
*I Built My Hut beside a Traveled
Road:* V36
Childe Harold's Pilgrimage (Byron):
V35
Childhood (Rilke): V19
Chin, Marilyn
How I Got That Name: V28
Chocolates (Simpson): V11
Chorale (Young): V25
Christ Climbed Down (Ferlinghetti):
V28
The Cinnamon Peeler (Ondaatje): V19
Cisneros, Sandra
*Once Again I Prove the Theory of
Relativity:* V19
The City Limits (Ammons): V19
Clampitt, Amy
Iola, Kansas: V27
Classic Ballroom Dances (Simic): V33
Clifton, Lucille
Climbing: V14
homage to my hips: V29
Miss Rosie: V1
Climbing (Clifton): V14
The Cobweb (Carver): V17
Coleridge, Samuel Taylor
Kubla Khan: V5
The Rime of the Ancient Mariner:
V4
Colibrí (Espada): V16
Collins, Billy
The Afterlife: V18

Come with Me (Bly): V6
The Constellation Orion (Kooser): V8
Concord Hymn (Emerson): V4
The Conquerors (McGinley): V13
Conscientious Objector (Millay): V34
The Continuous Life (Strand): V18
Conversation with a Stone
(Szymborska): V27
Cool Tombs (Sandburg): V6
Cooper, Jane
Rent: V25
The Cossacks (Pastan): V25
The Country Without a Post Office
(Shahid Ali): V18
Courage (Sexton): V14
The Courage That My Mother Had
(Millay): V3
Crane, Stephen
War Is Kind: V9
The Creation (Johnson): V1
Creeley, Robert
Fading Light: V21
The Cremation of Sam McGee
(Service): V10
The Crime Was in Granada
(Machado): V23
Cruz, Victor Hernandez
Business: V16
Cullen, Countee
Any Human to Another: V3
cummings, e. e.
anyone lived in a pretty how town:
V30
i was sitting in mcsorley's: V13
l(a: V1
*maggie and milly and molly and
may:* V12
old age sticks: V3
since feeling is first: V34
*somewhere i have never
travelled,gladly beyond:* V19
Curse (Bidart): V26
*The Czar's Last Christmas Letter. A
Barn in the Urals* (Dubie): V12

D

Daddy (Plath): V28
Dao, Bei
All: V38
The Darkling Thrush (Hardy): V18
Darwin in 1881 (Schnackenberg): V13
Daughter-Mother-Maya-Seeta
(Vazirani): V25
Dawe, Bruce
Drifters: V10
Daylights (Warren): V13
The Dead (Mitchell): V35
Dear Reader (Tate): V10
The Death of the Ball Turret Gunner
(Jarrell): V2

The Death of the Hired Man (Frost):
V4
Death Sentences (Lazić): V22
A Description of the Morning (Swift):
V37
Deep Woods (Nemerov): V14
Dennis, Carl
The God Who Loves You: V20
The Destruction of Sennacherib
(Byron): V1
Dickey, James
The Heaven of Animals: V6
The Hospital Window: V11
Dickinson, Emily
*Because I Could Not Stop for
Death:* V2
The Bustle in a House: V10
"Hope" Is the Thing with Feathers:
V3
I Died for Beauty: V28
I felt a Funeral, in my Brain: V13
*I Heard a Fly Buzz—When I
Died—:* V5
I'm Nobody! Who Are You?: V35
Much Madness Is Divinest Sense:
V16
*My Life Closed Twice Before Its
Close:* V8
A Narrow Fellow in the Grass: V11
The Soul Selects Her Own Society:
V1
Success Is Counted Sweetest: V32
There's a Certain Slant of Light:
V6
This Is My Letter to the World: V4
Digging (Heaney): V5
Divakaruni, Chitra Banerjee
My Mother Combs My Hair: V34
Diving into the Wreck (Rich): V29
Dobyns, Stephen
It's like This: V23
*Do Not Go Gentle into that Good
Night* (Thomas): V1
Donne, John
Holy Sonnet 10: V2
Song: V35
*A Valediction: Forbidding
Mourning:* V11
Doty, Mark
The Wings: V28
Dove, Rita
Geometry: V15
Grape Sherbet: V37
This Life: V1
Dover Beach (Arnold): V2
Dream Song 29 (Berryman): V27
Dream Variations (Hughes): V15
Drifters (Dawe): V10
A Drink of Water (Heaney): V8
Drinking Alone Beneath the Moon
(Po): V20

Cumulative
Nationality/Ethnicity Index

Cumulative Nationality/Ethnicity Index

Chilean

Jacobsen, Josephine
  Fiddler Crab: V23
Layton, Irving
  A Tall Man Executes a Jig: V12
McCrae, John
  In Flanders Fields: V5
Nowlan, Alden
  *For Jean Vincent D'abbadie, Baron
    St.-Castin:* V12
Ondaatje, Michael
  The Cinnamon Peeler: V19
  To a Sad Daughter: V8
Purdy, Al
  Lament for the Dorsets: V5
  Wilderness Gothic: V12
Service, Robert W.
  The Cremation of Sam McGee:
    V10
Strand, Mark
  Eating Poetry: V9

Chilean

Mistral, Gabriela
  Fear: V37
Neruda, Pablo
  Fully Empowered: V33
  The Heights of Macchu Picchu:
    V28
  Sonnet LXXXIX: V35
  Tonight I Can Write: V11

Chinese

Ch'ien, T'ao
  *I Built My Hut beside a Traveled
    Road:* V36
Chin, Marilyn
  How I Got That Name: V28
Dao, Bei
  All: V38
Fu, Tu
  Jade Flower Palace: V32
Po, Li
  Drinking Alone Beneath the Moon:
    V20

Egyptian

Cavafy, C. P.
  Ithaka: V19

English

Alleyn, Ellen
  A Birthday: V10
Arnold, Matthew
  Dover Beach: V2
Auden, W. H.
  As I Walked Out One Evening: V4
  Funeral Blues: V10
  Musée des Beaux Arts: V1
  September 1, 1939: V27
  The Unknown Citizen: V3

Blake, William
  The Fly: V34
  The Lamb: V12
  A Poison Tree: V24
  The Tyger: V2
Bradstreet, Anne
  To My Dear and Loving Husband:
    V6
  *Upon the Burning of Our House,
    July 10th, 1666:* V33
Brontë, Emily
  Old Stoic: V33
Brooke, Rupert
  The Soldier: V7
Browning, Elizabeth Barrett
  Aurora Leigh: V23
  Sonnet XXIX: V16
  Sonnet 43: V2
Browning, Robert
  My Last Duchess: V1
  Porphyria's Lover: V15
Byron, Lord
  Childe Harold's Pilgrimage: V35
  The Destruction of Sennacherib:
    V1
  She Walks in Beauty: V14
  When We Two Parted: V29
Carroll, Lewis
  Jabberwocky: V11
  The Walrus and the Carpenter:
    V30
Chaucer, Geoffrey
  The Canterbury Tales: V14
Coleridge, Samuel Taylor
  Kubla Khan: V5
  The Rime of the Ancient Mariner:
    V4
Donne, John
  Holy Sonnet 10: V2
  Song: V35
  *A Valediction: Forbidding
    Mourning:* V11
  The Waste Land: V20
Eliot, T. S.
  The Hollow Men: V33
  Journey of the Magi: V7
  *The Love Song of J. Alfred
    Prufrock:* V1
Fenton, James
  The Milkfish Gatherers: V11
Finch, Anne
  A Nocturnal Reverie: V30
Gray, Thomas
  *Elegy Written in a Country
    Churchyard:* V9
Gunn, Thom
  The Missing: V9
Hardy, Thomas
  *Ah, Are You Digging on My
    Grave?:* V4
  The Darkling Thrush: V18
  The Man He Killed: V3

Herbert, George
  Virtue: V25
Herrick, Robert
  The Night Piece: To Julia: V29
  *To the Virgins, to Make Much of
    Time:* V13
Hopkins, Gerard Manley
  Pied Beauty: V26
Housman, A. E.
  To an Athlete Dying Young: V7
  When I Was One-and-Twenty: V4
Hughes, Ted
  Hawk Roosting: V4
  The Horses: V32
  Perfect Light: V19
Jonson, Ben
  On My First Son: V33
  Song: To Celia: V23
Keats, John
  La Belle Dame sans Merci: V17
  *Bright Star! Would I Were
    Steadfast as Thou Art:* V9
  Ode on a Grecian Urn: V1
  Ode to a Nightingale: V3
  *On the Grasshopper and the
    Cricket:* V32
  To Autumn: V36
  *When I Have Fears that I May
    Cease to Be:* V2
Kipling, Rudyard
  If: V22
Larkin, Philip
  An Arundel Tomb: V12
  High Windows: V3
  Toads: V4
Lawrence, D. H.
  Piano: V6
Levertov, Denise
  The Blue Rim of Memory: V17
  In the Land of Shinar: V7
  A Tree Telling of Orpheus: V31
Lovelace, Richard
  To Althea, From Prison: V34
  To Lucasta, Going to the Wars: V32
Loy, Mina
  Moreover, the Moon: V20
Marlowe, Christopher
  *The Passionate Shepherd to His
    Love:* V22
Marvell, Andrew
  To His Coy Mistress: V5
Masefield, John
  Cargoes: V5
Maxwell, Glyn
  The Nerve: V23
Milton, John
  [On His Blindness] Sonnet 16: V3
  *On His Having Arrived at the Age
    of Twenty-Three:* V17
  When I Consider (Sonnet XIX): V37
Noyes, Alfred
  The Highwayman: V4

Subject/Theme Index

Harlem Renaissance
  The Weary Blues: 275, 277, 281–284, 289–290
Helplessness
  Pride: 191–192
Homoeroticism
  Fragment 16: 69–73
Homosexuality
  Poem (Lana Turner Has Collapsed): 157
Hope
  All: 18
  Still I Rise: 218, 221
  The Weary Blues: 297
Hopelessness
  Fable for When There's No Way Out: 43, 49
  The Guitar: 86
  The Weary Blues: 293
Human nature
  Invitation to the Voyage: 99
Humanity
  Pride: 192–193
Humor
  Still I Rise: 227
  The Weary Blues: 297
Husband-wife relationships
  Letter to My Wife: 115
  Marriage: 147–151

I

Identity
  Pride: 189
  Stanza LXXXIII: 207
Imagery (Literature)
  All: 15–16, 27–28
  Fable for When There's No Way Out: 43, 48, 54
  400-Meter Freestyle: 6–7
  The Guitar: 81, 86, 88
  Letter to My Wife: 118, 125
  Marriage: 141
  Stanza LXXXIII: 206
  A Storm in the Mountains: 242, 245–248
  Two Bodies: 272
  The Weary Blues: 287, 293, 296
  The World Is Too Much with Us: 303
Imagination
  All: 29
  Invitation to the Voyage: 96, 105–106
  Still I Rise: 229
  The World Is Too Much with Us: 299, 306–307, 311, 312, 314
Imprisonment
  Letter to My Wife: 113, 116–117, 126, 133
Independence
  Marriage: 141

Individual *vs.* society
  Two Bodies: 254–255, 261
Individualism
  All: 20, 28
  Invitation to the Voyage: 99
  Two Bodies: 270–271
Industrialization
  The World Is Too Much with Us: 309
Inequality
  Marriage: 142, 149, 152, 155
Injustice
  Marriage: 140
  Still I Rise: 223, 228–229, 234
Irony
  Fable for When There's No Way Out: 45, 56
  The Guitar: 90
  Marriage: 139–141
  Poem (Lana Turner Has Collapsed): 157
Isolation
  Pride: 189
  The World Is Too Much with Us: 303
Israeli culture
  Pride: 180–183, 187–193

J

Jazz
  The Weary Blues: 288–289
Joy
  All: 27, 28
  Still I Rise: 230

L

Language
  All: 18, 20, 27, 28, 31–32
  The Guitar: 86
  Letter to My Wife: 118–119
  Stanza LXXXIII: 195
Language and languages
  Stanza LXXXIII: 199, 206, 207–208, 210, 213, 215
  Still I Rise: 231, 234–235
  A Storm in the Mountains: 242, 247–248
  Two Bodies: 255, 259, 261–264, 266–267, 269, 270, 272
  The Weary Blues: 281, 285, 291
Life and death
  Fable for When There's No Way Out: 55, 56–57
Light and darkness
  A Storm in the Mountains: 242, 246, 247–248
Loneliness
  Pride: 189
  The World Is Too Much with Us: 303
Loss
  The Guitar: 92
  The Weary Blues: 277, 285–286

Love
  All: 18, 28, 33–34
  Fable for When There's No Way Out: 53–55, 57
  Fragment 16: 60
  The Guitar: 89
  Invitation to the Voyage: 98, 104–105
  Letter to My Wife: 115, 116, 124
  Marriage: 140, 142
  Stanza LXXXIII: 211
Lower class
  The Weary Blues: 293
Lust
  Fragment 16: 64–65
Lyric poetry
  Fragment 16: 65–66, 73
  The Guitar: 77
  Invitation to the Voyage: 94

M

Madness
  Fragment 16: 60
Marriage
  Fragment 16: 73
  Marriage: 138–143, 147–151, 153, 154
Materialism
  The World Is Too Much with Us: 301
Meaninglessness
  The Guitar: 77, 81, 86
Meditation
  Stanza LXXXIII: 212
Melancholy
  The Weary Blues: 278, 825
Memory
  Poem (Lana Turner Has Collapsed): 170
Metaphors
  All: 17, 21–22
  Fable for When There's No Way Out: 54, 55
  The Guitar: 75, 81, 88, 89
  Invitation to the Voyage: 105
  Letter to My Wife: 118
  Marriage: 154
  Pride: 178, 180
  Still I Rise: 221
  Two Bodies: 250, 252–253, 255, 262, 266–267, 273
  The Weary Blues: 297
  The World Is Too Much with Us: 305
Mexican culture
  Two Bodies: 268–269
Mexican history
  Two Bodies: 257
Militarism
  Fragment 16: 63, 66, 67–68
Mind and body
  Fable for When There's No Way Out: 43

Misery
    Marriage: 141
Modern life
    *Poem (Lana Turner Has
        Collapsed):* 160
Modernism (Literature)
    *Fable for When There's No Way
        Out:* 41, 46–47
    Letter to My Wife: 128–134
    Marriage: 138
    *Poem (Lana Turner Has
        Collapsed):* 168–172
    Stanza LXXXIII: 201, 203
    Two Bodies: 250, 256, 261–262
Music
    The Guitar: 75, 77, 78, 80, 81–82,
        84–87
    Still I Rise: 227
    The Weary Blues: 277, 279–280,
        284–290, 296–297
Mythology
    The Guitar: 88, 90
    The World Is Too Much with Us:
        302, 304, 311–314

N

Narrative poetry
    *Fable for When There's No Way
        Out:* 45
Nature
    *Fable for When There's No Way
        Out:* 47, 48, 53
    The Guitar: 77, 88, 89, 91–92
    Invitation to the Voyage: 98
    A Storm in the Mountains: 237,
        239, 241, 245–248
    The World Is Too Much with Us:
        299, 302–304, 308–312
Nihilism
    The Guitar: 78, 80, 81

O

Obscurity. *See* Vagueness
Obsession
    *Poem (Lana Turner Has
        Collapsed):* 160, 167
Omission
    All: 29
    400-Meter Freestyle: 10–13
Oneness. *See* Unity
Opportunity. *See* Possibility
Opposites
    All: 27, 36–38
    *Fable for When There's No Way
        Out:* 41, 44, 48, 50–51, 56
    Invitation to the Voyage: 98
    Marriage: 154, 155
    A Storm in the Mountains:
        246
    Two Bodies: 271, 272–273

Oppression (Politics)
    All: 27
    Still I Rise: 220
    The Weary Blues: 277, 278, 286,
        287, 293, 297
Optimism
    All: 18
    Letter to My Wife: 116
    *Poem (Lana Turner Has
        Collapsed):* 161
    Still I Rise: 218, 221
Order
    Invitation to the Voyage: 97
Orientalism
    Invitation to the Voyage: 102,
        108
Otherness
    *Fable for When There's No Way
        Out:* 55
    Two Bodies: 253, 265

P

Pacifism
    Pride: 193
Pain
    All: 18
    The Guitar: 86–87, 92
    Invitation to the Voyage: 109
    Pride: 185, 189
    The Weary Blues: 285
Paradoxes
    All: 17–18, 25–29, 34–38
    *Fable for When There's No Way
        Out:* 51, 56, 57
    Invitation to the Voyage: 96
    Pride: 185
    Stanza LXXXIII: 207
Parody
    *Poem (Lana Turner Has
        Collapsed):* 168–172
Passion
    *Fable for When There's No Way
        Out:* 53
    Marriage: 140–141
Past
    All: 18
    *Poem (Lana Turner Has
        Collapsed):* 170
    Still I Rise: 221
Patriarchy
    Marriage: 138
Perception (Psychology)
    *The World Is Too Much with
        Us:* 299, 304, 306,
        309, 311
Perfection
    400-Meter Freestyle: 3
Personification
    Pride: 179–180
    The World Is Too Much with Us:
        305

Philosophy
    All: 36
    Stanza LXXXIII: 195
    Two Bodies: 269–270
Politics
    All: 23–24, 32–33
    Letter to My Wife: 125–128, 130
    Pride: 186–187, 191–192
    Two Bodies: 255
Popular culture
    *Poem (Lana Turner Has
        Collapsed):* 160
Possibility
    Stanza LXXXIII: 206
Potentiality. *See* Possibility
Poverty
    The Weary Blues: 297
Power (Philosophy)
    Marriage: 140, 142, 143, 152
Power (Physical). *See* Strength
Prejudice
    Still I Rise: 223, 227, 228–229
    The Weary Blues: 297
Pride
    Pride: 175, 178, 186–187
    Still I Rise: 221, 223, 230, 233
Prostitution
    Fragment 16: 71–72
Protest
    Still I Rise: 227
    The Weary Blues: 297
Psychoanalysis
    Invitation to the Voyage: 103–105
    Two Bodies: 256
Psychology
    Invitation to the Voyage: 94

Q

Questing
    *Fable for When There's No Way
        Out:* 54

R

Racism
    Still I Rise: 223, 227
    The Weary Blues: 285, 297
Rage. *See* Anger
Rationality
    *Fable for When There's No Way
        Out:* 44–45
Reality
    All: 25
Reason
    *Fable for When There's No Way
        Out:* 41, 44–45, 50, 52
    Stanza LXXXIII: 197
Reform
    All: 24
Repetition
    All: 18, 28
    400-Meter Freestyle: 7

The Guitar: 80–81, 86
Stanza LXXXIII: 197, 200–201,
   205–206, 212, 213
Still I Rise: 224, 234
The Weary Blues: 278, 285, 286,
   291
The World Is Too Much with Us:
   303
Resilience
   Still I Rise: 223–224, 227, 234
   The Weary Blues: 293
Respect
   Still I Rise: 221
Responsibility
   Pride: 192
Revelation
   A Storm in the Mountains: 246
Rhythm
   *Fable for When There's No Way
     Out:* 46, 51, 57
   400-Meter Freestyle: 7
   The Guitar: 86
   Still I Rise: 224, 227, 230–231, 234
   Two Bodies: 271–272
   The Weary Blues: 280–281, 285,
     290, 291
   The World Is Too Much with Us:
     304–305
Romanticism
   Invitation to the Voyage: 97–99
   The World Is Too Much with Us:
     305–307
Rural life
   A Storm in the Mountains: 237
Russian history
   A Storm in the Mountains:
     242–244

S

Sacrifice
   Still I Rise: 221
Sadness
   The Guitar: 86
   The Weary Blues: 277, 278
   The World Is Too Much with Us:
     303
Sarcasm
   Marriage: 140
Satire
   *Poem (Lana Turner Has
     Collapsed):* 168
Self confidence
   Still I Rise: 223
Self doubt
   Stanza LXXXIII: 205
Self image
   Still I Rise: 227–230
Self reliance
   The Weary Blues: 278
Self worth
   Still I Rise: 221, 227–230

Selfishness
   Marriage: 142, 143, 150, 153
Sensory perception
   All: 18
   A Storm in the Mountains: 247,
     248
Sensuality
   *Fable for When There's No Way
     Out:* 53
   Invitation to the Voyage: 105–108
Sex roles
   Fragment 16: 70–71
   Marriage: 138, 139
   Pride: 191
Sexuality
   Fragment 16: 69–73
   Stanza LXXXIII: 214–215
Similes
   400-Meter Freestyle: 7
   Letter to My Wife: 118
   The World Is Too Much with Us:
     305
Simplicity
   *Poem (Lana Turner Has
     Collapsed):* 166
Sincerity
   Invitation to the Voyage: 108
Skepticism
   Marriage: 153, 154
Social change
   Two Bodies: 255
Social commentary
   Marriage: 147–151, 155
Solitude
   The Guitar: 87
Sonnets
   Stanza LXXXIII: 204–206
   The World Is Too Much with Us:
     299, 304, 309, 310
Sorrow
   All: 17, 18, 27, 28
   The Guitar: 77, 91–92
   Invitation to the Voyage:
     109–111
   The Weary Blues: 285, 286
Sound
   All: 28
Spaces
   All: 28
   *Fable for When There's No Way
     Out:* 56
   400-Meter Freestyle: 12
Spanish history
   The Guitar: 82–83
   Two Bodies: 257–258
Spirituality
   A Storm in the Mountains:
     241–242, 245, 249
   Two Bodies: 272–273
Sports
   400-Meter Freestyle:
     3, 4, 8

Stereotypes (Psychology)
   Marriage: 150
   Still I Rise: 221
Stream of consciousness
   Stanza LXXXIII: 195
Strength
   400-Meter Freestyle: 3, 4–5
Struggle
   *Fable for When There's No Way
     Out:* 41, 43, 44, 49–50
Success
   *Fable for When There's No Way
     Out:* 44, 45
Suffering
   The Guitar: 75, 78, 80, 84, 86,
     88–90
   The Weary Blues: 278, 285,
     293
Suicide
   The Weary Blues: 297
Surprise
   Pride: 177–178
Surrealism
   A Storm in the Mountains: 239
   Two Bodies: 256, 262
Survival
   *Fable for When There's No Way
     Out:* 41, 45, 50
   Still I Rise: 218, 224
Symbolism
   Fragment 16: 63–64
   The Guitar: 78, 81, 90
   Invitation to the Voyage: 94, 96,
     100, 102, 103–105
   The Weary Blues: 284–287, 297

T

Taoism
   All: 37
Tension
   All: 20, 32, 34
   *Fable for When There's No Way
     Out:* 49–50
   400-Meter Freestyle: 7
   Two Bodies: 270, 271
Time
   Stanza LXXXIII: 199, 205
Tone
   400-Meter Freestyle: 6–7
   Pride: 185
Totalitarianism
   All: 18, 20, 25–27
Transformation
   The Weary Blues: 291
Translation
   All: 21–22, 38
   Letter to My Wife: 133–134
Triumph
   Still I Rise: 234
Truth
   All: 36

Turkish history
Letter to My Wife: 119–120

U

Uncertainty
Stanza LXXXIII: 197
Understanding
A Storm in the Mountains: 246
Unity
Still I Rise: 221
A Storm in the Mountains: 237
Two Bodies: 272–273
Universe
All: 28
Two Bodies: 252, 261, 262

V

Vagueness
All: 17, 18, 20, 29, 38
Stanza LXXXIII: 216
Values (philosophy)
Fragment 16: 73
Vanity
Marriage: 142, 150
Violence
Fragment 16: 60
Two Bodies: 253
The Weary Blues: 297
Virtue
Fragment 16: 67

Vulnerability
Pride: 185

W

Warrior-heroes
Fragment 16: 63–64
Wars
Fragment 16: 60, 63, 67–68
The Guitar: 82–83
Pride: 188
Two Bodies: 257
Women's rights
Marriage: 145
World War I, 1914-1918
Marriage: 145–146

Cumulative
Index of First Lines

My life closed twice before its close— (My Life Closed Twice Before Its Close) V8:127

My long two-pointed ladder's sticking through a tree (After Apple Picking) V32:3

My mistress' eyes are nothing like the sun (Sonnet 130) V1:247

My one and only! (Letter to My Wife) V38:114

My uncle in East Germany (The Exhibit) V9:107

N

Nature's first green is gold (Nothing Gold Can Stay) V3:203

No easy thing to bear, the weight of sweetness (The Weight of Sweetness) V11:230

No monument stands over Babii Yar. (Babii Yar) V29:38

Nobody heard him, the dead man (Not Waving but Drowning) V3:216

Not like a cypress, (Not like a Cypress) V24:135

Not like the brazen giant of Greek fame, (The New Colossus) V37:238

Not marble nor the gilded monuments (Sonnet 55) V5:246

Not the memorized phone numbers. (What Belongs to Us) V15:196

Now as I was young and easy under the apple boughs (Fern Hill) V3:92

Now as I watch the progress of the plague (The Missing) V9:158

Now hardly here and there a Hackney-Coach (A Description of the Morning) V37:48

Now I rest my head on the satyr's carved chest, (The Satyr's Heart) V22:187

Now one might catch it see it (Fading Light) V21:49

O

O Captain! my Captain, our fearful trip is done (O Captain! My Captain!) V2:146

O Lord our Lord, how excellent is thy name in all the earth! who hast set thy glory above the heavens (Psalm 8) V9:182

O my Luve's like a red, red rose (A Red, Red Rose) V8:152

O what can ail thee, knight-at-arms, (La Belle Dame sans Merci) V17:18

"O where ha' you been, Lord Randal, my son? (Lord Randal) V6:105

O wild West Wind, thou breath of Autumn's being (Ode to the West Wind) V2:163

Oh, but it is dirty! (Filling Station) V12:57

old age sticks (old age sticks) V3:246

On a shore washed by desolate waves, *he* stood, (The Bronze Horseman) V28:27

On either side the river lie (The Lady of Shalott) V15:95

On the seashore of endless worlds children meet. The infinite (60) V18:3

Once some people were visiting Chekhov (Chocolates) V11:17

Once upon a midnight dreary, while I pondered, weak and weary (The Raven) V1:200

One day I'll lift the telephone (Elegy for My Father, Who Is Not Dead) V14:154

One day I wrote her name upon the strand, (Sonnet 75) V32:215

One foot down, then hop! It's hot (Harlem Hopscotch) V2:93

one shoe on the roadway presents (A Piéd) V3:16

Our vision is our voice (An Anthem) V26:34

Out of the hills of Habersham, (Song of the Chattahoochee) V14:283

Out walking in the frozen swamp one gray day (The Wood-Pile) V6:251

Oysters we ate (Oysters) V4:91

P

Pentagon code (Smart and Final Iris) V15:183

Poised between going on and back, pulled (The Base Stealer) V12:30

Q

Quinquireme of Nineveh from distant Ophir (Cargoes) V5:44

Quite difficult, belief. (Chorale) V25:51

R

Recognition in the body (In Particular) V20:125

Red men embraced my body's whiteness (Birch Canoe) V5:31

Remember me when I am gone away (Remember) V14:255

Remember the sky you were born under, (Remember) V32:185

Riches I hold in light esteem, (Old Stoic) V33:143

S

Season of mists and mellow fruitfulness, (To Autumn) V36:295–296

Shall I compare thee to a Summer's day? (Sonnet 18) V2:222

She came every morning to draw water (A Drink of Water) V8:66

She reads, of course, what he's doing, shaking Nixon's hand, (The Women Who Loved Elvis All Their Lives) V28:273

She sang beyond the genius of the sea. (The Idea of Order at Key West) V13:164

She walks in beauty, like the night (She Walks in Beauty) V14:268

She was my grandfather's second wife. Coming late (My Grandmother's Plot in the Family Cemetery) V27:154

Side by side, their faces blurred, (An Arundel Tomb) V12:17

since feeling is first (since feeling is first) V34:172

Since the professional wars— (Midnight) V2:130

Since then, I work at night. (Ten Years after Your Deliberate Drowning) V21:240

S'io credesse che mia risposta fosse (The Love Song of J. Alfred Prufrock) V1:97

Sky black (Duration) V18:93

Sleepless as Prospero back in his bedroom (Darwin in 1881) V13:83

so much depends (The Red Wheelbarrow) V1:219

So the man spread his blanket on the field (A Tall Man Executes a Jig) V12:228

So the sky wounded you, jagged at the heart, (Daylights) V13:101

Softly, in the dark, a woman is singing to me (Piano) V6:145

Some say a host of cavalry, others of infantry, (Fragment 16) V38:62

Some say it's in the reptilian dance (The Greatest Grandeur) V18:119

Some say the world will end in fire (Fire and Ice) V7:57

Something there is that doesn't love a wall (Mending Wall) V5:231

The wind was a torrent of darkness among the gusty trees (The Highwayman) V4:66

The windows were open and the morning air was, by the smell of lilac and some darker flowering shrub, filled with the brown and chirping trills of birds. (Yet we insist that life is full of happy chance) V27:291

The world is too much with us, late and soon, (The World Is Too Much with Us) V38:300

There are blows in life, so hard … I just don't know! (The Black Heralds) V26:47

There are strange things done in the midnight sun (The Cremation of Sam McGee) V10:75

There have been rooms for such a short time (The Horizons of Rooms) V15:79

There is a hunger for order, (A Thirst Against) V20:205

There is a pleasure in the pathless woods (Childe Harold's Pilgrimage, Canto IV, stanzas 178–184) V35:46

There is no way not to be excited (Paradiso) V20:190–191

There is the one song everyone (Siren Song) V7:196

There will come soft rains and the smell of the ground, (There Will Come Soft Rains) V14:301

There you are, in all your innocence, (Perfect Light) V19:187

There's a Certain Slant of Light (There's a Certain Slant of Light) V6:211

There's no way out. (In the Suburbs) V14:201

These open years, the river (For Jennifer, 6, on the Teton) V17:86

These unprepossessing sunsets (Art Thou the Thing I Wanted) V25:2–3

They eat beans mostly, this old yellow pair (The Bean Eaters) V2:16

They said, "Wait." Well, I waited. (Alabama Centennial) V10:2

They say a child with two mouths is no good. (Pantoun for Chinese Women) V29:241

they were just meant as covers (My Mother Pieced Quilts) V12:169

This girlchild was: born as usual (Barbie Doll) V9:33

This is a litany of lost things, (The Litany) V24:101–102

This is my letter to the World (This Is My Letter to the World) V4:233

This is the Arsenal. From floor to ceiling, (The Arsenal at Springfield) V17:2

This is the black sea-brute bulling through wave-wrack (Leviathan) V5:203

This is the ship of pearl, which, poets feign, (The Chambered Nautilus) V24:52–53

This poem is concerned with language on a very plain level (Paradoxes and Oxymorons) V11:162

This tale is true, and mine. It tells (The Seafarer) V8:177

Thou still unravish'd bride of quietness (Ode on a Grecian Urn) V1:179

Three days Natasha'd been astray, (The Bridegroom) V34:26

Three times my life has opened. (Three Times My Life Has Opened) V16:213

Time in school drags along with so much worry, (Childhood) V19:29

to fold the clothes. No matter who lives (I Stop Writing the Poem) V16:58

To him who in the love of Nature holds (Thanatopsis) V30:232–233

To replay errors (Daughter-Mother-Maya-Seeta) V25:83

To weep unbidden, to wake (Practice) V23:240

Toni Morrison despises (The Toni Morrison Dreams) V22:202–203

Tonight I can write the saddest lines (Tonight I Can Write) V11:187

tonite, *thriller* was (Beware: Do Not Read This Poem) V6:3

Truth be told, I do not want to forget (Native Guard) V29:183

Turning and turning in the widening gyre (The Second Coming) V7:179

'Twas brillig, and the slithy toves (Jabberwocky) V11:91

'Twas mercy brought me from my pagan land, (On Being Brought from Africa to America) V29:223

Two bodies face to face (Two Bodies) V38:251

Two roads diverged in a yellow wood (The Road Not Taken) V2:195

Tyger! Tyger! burning bright (The Tyger) V2:263

wade (The Fish) V14:171

Wailing of a flute, a little drum (In Music) V35:105

Wanting to say things, (My Father's Song) V16:102

We are saying goodbye (Station) V21:226–227

We came from our own country in a red room (Originally) V25:146–147

We cannot know his legendary head (Archaic Torso of Apollo) V27:3

We could be here. This is the valley (Small Town with One Road) V7:207

We met the British in the dead of winter (Meeting the British) V7:138

We real cool. We (We Real Cool) V6:242

We tied branches to our helmets. (Camouflaging the Chimera) V37:21

Well, son, I'll tell you (Mother to Son) V3:178

What dire offense from amorous causes springs, (The Rape of the Lock) V12:202

What happens to a dream deferred? (Harlem) V1:63

What I expected was (What I expected) V36:313–314

What of the neighborhood homes awash (The Continuous Life) V18:51

What passing-bells for these who die as cattle? (Anthem for Doomed Youth) V37:3

What thoughts I have of you tonight, Walt Whitman, for I walked down the sidestreets under the trees with a headache self-conscious looking at the full moon (A Supermarket in California) V5:261

Whatever it is, it must have (American Poetry) V7:2

When Abraham Lincoln was shoveled into the tombs, he forgot the copperheads, and the assassin … in the dust, in the cool tombs (Cool Tombs) V6:45

When despair for the world grows in me (The Peace of Wild Things) V30:159

When he spoke of where he came from, (Grudnow) V32:73

When I consider how my light is spent ([On His Blindness] Sonnet 16) V3:262

Cumulative
Index of Last Lines

And I am Nicholas. (The Czar's Last Christmas Letter) V12:45

And I let the fish go. (The Fish) V31:44

And I was unaware. (The Darkling Thrush) V18:74

And in the suburbs Can't sat down and cried. (Kilroy) V14:213

And it's been years. (Anniversary) V15:3

and joy may come, and make its test of us. (One Is One) V24:158

And kept on drinking. (Miniver Cheevy) V35:127

And laid my hand upon thy mane— as I do here. (Childe Harold's Pilgrimage, Canto IV, stanzas 178–184) V35:47

and leaving essence to the inner eye. (Memory) V21:156

And life for me ain't been no crystal stair (Mother to Son) V3:179

And like a thunderbolt he falls (The Eagle) V11:30

And makes me end where I begun (A Valediction: Forbidding Mourning) V11:202

And 'midst the stars inscribe Belinda's name. (The Rape of the Lock) V12:209

And miles to go before I sleep (Stopping by Woods on a Snowy Evening) V1:272

and my father saying things. (My Father's Song) V16:102

And no birds sing. (La Belle Dame sans Merci) V17:18

And not waving but drowning (Not Waving but Drowning) V3:216

And oh, 'tis true, 'tis true (When I Was One-and-Twenty) V4:268

And reach for your scalping knife. (For Jean Vincent D'abbadie, Baron St.-Castin) V12:78

and retreating, always retreating, behind it (Brazil, January 1, 1502) V6:16

And School-Boys lag with Satchels in their Hands. (A Description of the Morning) V37:49

And settled upon his eyes in a black soot ("More Light! More Light!") V6:120

And shuts his eyes. (Darwin in 1881) V13: 84

and so cold (This Is Just to Say) V34:241

And so live ever—or else swoon to death (Bright Star! Would I Were Steadfast as Thou Art) V9:44

and strange and loud was the dingoes' cry (Drought Year) V8:78

and stride out. (Courage) V14:126

and sweat and fat and greed. (Anorexic) V12:3

And that has made all the difference (The Road Not Taken) V2:195

And the deep river ran on (As I Walked Out One Evening) V4:16

And the midnight message of Paul Revere (Paul Revere's Ride) V2:180

And the mome raths outgrabe (Jabberwocky) V11:91

And the Salvation Army singing God loves us.... (Hopeis a Tattered Flag) V12:120

And therewith ends my story. (The Bridegroom) V34:28

and these the last verses that I write for her (Tonight I Can Write) V11:187

and thickly wooded country; the moon. (The Art of the Novel) V23:29

And those roads in South Dakota that feel around in the darkness ... (Come with Me) V6:31

and to know she will stay in the field till you die? (Landscape with Tractor) V10:183

and two blankets embroidered with smallpox (Meeting the British) V7:138

and waving, shouting, *Welcome back.* (Elegy for My Father, Who Is Not Dead) V14:154

And—which is more—you'll be a Man, my son! (If) V22:54–55

and whose skin is made dusky by stars. (September) V23:258–259

And wild for to hold, though I seem tame.' (Whoso List to Hunt) V25:286

And would suffice (Fire and Ice) V7:57

And yet God has not said a word! (Porphyria's Lover) V15:151

and you spread un the thin halo of night mist. (Ways to Live) V16:229

and your dreams, my Telemachus, are blameless. (Odysseus to Telemachus) V35:147

And Zero at the Bone— (A Narrow Fellow in the Grass) V11:127

(answer with a tower of birds) (Duration) V18:93

Around us already perhaps future moons, suns and stars blaze in a fiery wreath. (But Perhaps God Needs the Longing) V20:41

aspired to become lighter than air (Blood Oranges) V13:34

As any She belied with false compare (Sonnet 130) V1:248

As ever in my great Task-Master's eye. (On His Having Arrived at the Age of Twenty-Three) V17:160

As far as Cho-fu-Sa (The River-Merchant's Wife: A Letter) V8:165

as it has disappeared. (The Wings) V28:244

As the contagion of those molten eyes (For An Assyrian Frieze) V9:120

As they lean over the beans in their rented back room that is full of beads and receipts and dolls and clothes, tobacco crumbs, vases and fringes (The Bean Eaters) V2:16

as we crossed the field, I told her. (The Centaur) V30:20

As what he loves may never like too much. (On My First Son) V33:166

at home in the fish's fallen heaven (Birch Canoe) V5:31

away, pedaling hard, rocket and pilot. (His Speed and Strength) V19:96

B

Back to the play of constant give and change (The Missing) V9:158

Beautiful & dangerous. (Slam, Dunk, & Hook) V30:176–177

Before it was quite unsheathed from reality (Hurt Hawks) V3:138

before we're even able to name them. (Station) V21:226–227

behind us and all our shining ambivalent love airborne there before us. (Our Side) V24:177

Black like me. (Dream Variations) V15:42

Bless me (Hunger in New York City) V4:79

bombs scandalizing the sanctity of night. (While I Was Gone a War Began) V21:253–254

But, baby, where are you?" (Ballad of Birmingham) V5:17

But be (Ars Poetica) V5:3

But for centuries we have longed for it. (Everything Is Plundered) V32:34

but it works every time (Siren Song) V7:196

but the truth is, it is, lost to us now. (The Forest) V22:36–37

But there is no joy in Mudville—mighty Casey has "Struck Out." (Casey at the Bat) V5:58

But we hold our course, and the wind is with us. (On Freedom's Ground) V12:187

by a beeswax candle pooling beside their dinnerware. (Portrait of a Couple at Century's End) V24:214–215

by good fortune (The Horizons of Rooms) V15:80

C

Calls through the valleys of Hall. (Song of the Chattahoochee) V14:284

chickens (The Red Wheelbarrow) V1:219

clear water dashes (Onomatopoeia) V6:133

Columbia. (Kindness) V24:84–85

come to life and burn? (Bidwell Ghost) V14:2

Comin' for to carry me home (Swing Low Sweet Chariot) V1:284

cool as from underground springs and pure enough to drink. (The Man-Moth) V27:135

crossed the water. (All It Takes) V23:15

D

Dare frame thy fearful symmetry? (The Tyger) V2:263

"Dead," was all he answered (The Death of the Hired Man) V4:44

deep in the deepest one, tributaries burn. (For Jennifer, 6, on the Teton) V17:86

Delicate, delicate, delicate, delicate—now! (The Base Stealer) V12:30

Die soon (We Real Cool) V6:242

Do what you are going to do, I will tell about it. (I go Back to May 1937) V17:113

down from the sky (Russian Letter) V26:181

Down in the flood of remembrance, I weep like a child for the past (Piano) V6:145

Downward to darkness, on extended wings. (Sunday Morning) V16:190

drinking all night in the kitchen. (The Dead) V35:69

Driving around, I will waste more time. (Driving to Town Late to Mail a Letter) V17:63

dry wells that fill so easily now (The Exhibit) V9:107

dust rises in many myriads of grains. (Not like a Cypress) V24:135

dusty as miners, into the restored volumes. (Bonnard's Garden) V25:33

E

endless worlds is the great meeting of children. (60) V18:3

Enjoy such liberty. (To Althea, From Prison) V34:255

Eternal, unchanging creator of earth. Amen (The Seafarer) V8:178

Eternity of your arms around my neck. (Death Sentences) V22:23

even as it vanishes—were not our life. (The Litany) V24:101–102

ever finds anything more of immortality. (Jade Flower Palace) V32:145

every branch traced with the ghost writing of snow. (The Afterlife) V18:39

F

fall upon us, the dwellers in shadow (In the Land of Shinar) V7:84

Fallen cold and dead (O Captain! My Captain!) V2:147

False, ere I come, to two, or three. (Song) V35:237

father. (Grape Sherbet) V37:110

filled, never. (The Greatest Grandeur) V18:119

Firewood, iron-ware, and cheap tin trays (Cargoes) V5:44

Fled is that music:—Do I wake or sleep? (Ode to a Nightingale) V3:229

For I'm sick at the heart, and I fain wad lie down." (Lord Randal) V6:105

For nothing now can ever come to any good. (Funeral Blues) V10:139

For the coming winter (Winter) V35:297

For the love of God they buried his cold corpse. (The Bronze Horseman) V28:31

For the world's more full of weeping than he can understand. (The Stolen Child) V34:217

forget me as fast as you can. (Last Request) V14:231

4:25:9 (400—Meter Freestyle) V38:3

from one kiss (A Rebirth) V21:193–194

G

garish for a while and burned. (One of the Smallest) V26:142

going where? Where? (Childhood) V19:29

H

Had anything been wrong, we should certainly have heard (The Unknown Citizen) V3:303

Had somewhere to get to and sailed calmly on (Musée des Beaux Arts) V1:148

half eaten by the moon. (Dear Reader) V10:85

hand over hungry hand. (Climbing) V14:113

Happen on a red tongue (Small Town with One Road) V7:207

hard as mine with another man? (An Attempt at Jealousy) V29:24

Has no more need of, and I have (The Courage that My Mother Had) V3:80

Has set me softly down beside you. The Poem is you (Paradoxes and Oxymorons) V11:162

Hath melted like snow in the glance of the Lord! (The Destruction of Sennacherib) V1:39

He rose the morrow morn (The Rime of the Ancient Mariner) V4:132

He says again, "Good fences make good neighbors." (Mending Wall) V5:232

He writes down something that he crosses out. (The Boy) V19:14

here; passion will save you. (Air for Mercury) V20:2–3

History theirs whose languages is the sun. (An Elementary School Classroom in a Slum) V23:88–89

How at my sheet goes the same crooked worm (The Force That Through the Green Fuse Drives the Flower) V8:101

How can I turn from Africa and live? (A Far Cry from Africa) V6:61

How sad then is even the marvelous! (An Africian Elegy) V13:4

I

I am a true Russian! (Babii Yar) V29:38

I am black. (The Song of the Smoke) V13:197

I am going to keep things like this (Hawk Roosting) V4:55

I am not brave at all (Strong Men, Riding Horses) V4:209

I could not see to see—(I Heard a Fly Buzz—When I Died—) V5:140

I cremated Sam McGee (The Cremation of Sam McGee) V10:76

I didn't want to put them down. (And What If I Spoke of Despair) V19:2

I have been one acquainted with the night. (Acquainted with the Night) V35:3

I have just come down from my father (The Hospital Window) V11:58

I hear it in the deep heart's core. (The Lake Isle of Innisfree) V15:121

I know why the caged bird sings! (Sympathy) V33:203

I lift my lamp beside the golden door!" (The New Colossus) V37:239

I never writ, nor no man ever loved (Sonnet 116) V3:288

I rest in the grace of the world, and am free. (The Peace of Wild Things) V30:159

I romp with joy in the bookish dark (Eating Poetry) V9:61

I see Mike's painting, called SARDINES (Why I Am Not a Painter) V8:259

I shall but love thee better after death (Sonnet 43) V2:236

I should be glad of another death (Journey of the Magi) V7:110

I stand up (Miss Rosie) V1:133

I stood there, fifteen (Fifteen) V2:78

I take it you are he? (Incident in a Rose Garden) V14:191

I, too, am America. (I, Too) V30:99

I turned aside and bowed my head and wept (The Tropics in New York) V4:255

I would like to tell, but lack the words. (I Built My Hut beside a Traveled Road) V36:119

If Winter comes, can Spring be far behind? (Ode to the West Wind) V2:163

I'll be gone from here. (The Cobweb) V17:51

I'll dig with it (Digging) V5:71

Imagine! (Autobiographia Literaria) V34:2

In a convulsive misery (The Milkfish Gatherers) V11:112

In an empty sky (Two Bodies) V38:251

In balance with this life, this death (An Irish Airman Foresees His Death) V1:76

in earth's gasp, ocean's yawn. (Lake) V23:158

In Flanders fields (In Flanders Fields) V5:155

In ghostlier demarcations, keener sounds. (The Idea of Order at Key West) V13:164

In hearts at peace, under an English heaven (The Soldier) V7:218

In her tomb by the side of the sea (Annabel Lee) V9:14

in the family of things. (Wild Geese) V15:208

in the grit gray light of day. (Daylights) V13:102

In the rear-view mirrors of the passing cars (The War Against the Trees) V11:216

In these Chicago avenues. (A Thirst Against) V20:205

in this bastion of culture. (To an Unknown Poet) V18:221

in your unsteady, opening hand. (What the Poets Could Have Been) V26:262

iness (l(a) V1:85

Into blossom (A Blessing) V7:24

Is Come, my love is come to me. (A Birthday) V10:34

is love—that's all. (Two Poems for T.) V20:218

is safe is what you said. (Practice) V23:240

is still warm (Lament for the Dorsets) V5:191

It asked a crumb—of Me ("Hope" Is the Thing with Feathers) V3:123

It had no mirrors. I no longer needed mirrors. (I, I, I) V26:97

It is our god. (Fiddler Crab) V23:111–112

it is the bell to awaken God that we've heard ringing. (The Garden Shukkei-en) V18:107

it over my face and mouth. (An Anthem) V26:34

It rains as I write this. Mad heart, be brave. (The Country Without a Post Office) V18:64

It takes life to love life. (Lucinda Matlock) V37:172

It was your resting place." (Ah, Are You Digging on My Grave?) V4:2

it's always ourselves we find in the sea (maggie & milly & molly & may) V12:150

its bright, unequivocal eye. (Having it Out with Melancholy) V17:99

It's the fall through wind lifting white leaves. (Rapture) V21:181

its youth. The sea grows old in it. (The Fish) V14:172

J

Judge tenderly—of Me (This Is My Letter to the World) V4:233

Just imagine it (Inventors) V7:97

K

kisses you (Grandmother) V34:95

L

Laughing the stormy, husky, brawling laughter of Youth, half-naked, sweating, proud to be Hog Butcher, Tool Maker, Stacker of Wheat, Player with Railroads and Freight Handler to the Nation (Chicago) V3:61

Learn to labor and to wait (A Psalm of Life) V7:165

Leashed in my throat (Midnight) V2:131

Leaving thine outgrown shell by life's un-resting sea (The Chambered Nautilus) V24:52–53

Let my people go (Go Down, Moses) V11:43

Let the water come. (America, America) V29:4

life, our life and its forgetting. (For a New Citizen of These United States) V15:55

Life to Victory (Always) V24:15

like a bird in the sky . . . (Ego-Tripping) V28:113

like a shadow or a friend. *Colombia.* (Kindness) V24:84–85

Like Stone—(The Soul Selects Her Own Society) V1:259

Little Lamb, God bless thee. (The Lamb) V12:135

Look'd up in perfect silence at the stars. (When I Heard the Learn'd Astronomer) V22:244

love (The Toni Morrison Dreams) V22:202–203

Loved I not Honour more. (To Lucasta, Going to the Wars) V32:291

Luck was rid of its clover. (Yet we insist that life is full of happy chance) V27:292

M

'Make a wish, Tom, make a wish.' (Drifters) V10: 98

make it seem to change (The Moon Glows the Same) V7:152

May be refined, and join the angelic train. (On Being Brought from Africa to America) V29:223

may your mercy be near. (Two Eclipses) V33:221

midnight-oiled in the metric laws? (A Farewell to English) V10:126

Monkey business (Business) V16:2

More dear, both for themselves and for thy sake! (Tintern Abbey) V2:250

More simple and more full of pride. (I Am Not One of Those Who Left the Land) V36:91

must always think good thoughts. (Letter to My Wife) V38:115

My foe outstretchd beneath the tree. (A Poison Tree) V24:195–196

My love shall in my verse ever live young (Sonnet 19) V9:211

My soul has grown deep like the rivers. (The Negro Speaks of Rivers) V10:198

My soul I'll pour into thee. (The Night Piece: To Julia) V29:206

N

never to waken in that world again (Starlight) V8:213

newness comes into the world (Daughter-Mother-Maya-Seeta) V25:83

Nirvana is here, nine times out of ten. (Spring-Watching Pavilion) V18:198

No, she's brushing a boy's hair (Facing It) V5:110

no—tell them *no*—(The Hiding Place) V10:153

Noble six hundred! (The Charge of the Light Brigade) V1:3

nobody,not even the rain,has such small hands (somewhere i have never travelled,gladly beyond) V19:265

Nor swim under the terrible eyes of prison ships. (The Drunken Boat) V28:84

Not a roof but a field of stars. (Rent) V25:164

not be seeing you, for you have no insurance. (The River Mumma Wants Out) V25:191

Not even the blisters. Look. (What Belongs to Us) V15:196

Not of itself, but thee. (Song: To Celia) V23:270–271

Not to mention people. (Pride) V38:177

Nothing, and is nowhere, and is endless (High Windows) V3:108

Nothing gold can stay (Nothing Gold Can Stay) V3:203

Now! (Alabama Centennial) V10:2

nursing the tough skin of figs (This Life) V1:293

O

O Death in Life, the days that are no more! (Tears, Idle Tears) V4:220

O Lord our Lord, how excellent is thy name in all the earth! (Psalm 8) V9:182

O Roger, Mackerel, Riley, Ned, Nellie, Chester, Lady Ghost (Names of Horses) V8:142

o, walk your body down, don't let it go it alone. (Walk Your Body Down) V26:219

Of all our joys, this must be the deepest. (Drinking Alone Beneath the Moon) V20:59–60

of blackberry-eating in late September. (Blackberry Eating) V35:24

of blood and ignorance. (Art Thou the Thing I Wanted) V25:2–3

of gentleness (To a Sad Daughter) V8:231

of love's austere and lonely offices? (Those Winter Sundays) V1:300

of peaches (The Weight of Sweetness) V11:230

Of the camellia (Falling Upon Earth) V2:64

Of the Creator. And he waits for the world to begin (Leviathan) V5:204

of our festivities (Fragment 2) V31:63

Of what is past, or passing, or to come (Sailing to Byzantium) V2:207

Of which the chronicles make no mention. (In Music) V35:105

Oh that was the garden of abundance, seeing you. (Seeing You) V24:244–245

Old Ryan, not yours (The Constellation Orion) V8:53

On rainy Monday nights of an eternal November. (Classic Ballroom Dances) V33:3

On the dark distant flurry (Angle of Geese) V2:2

on the frosty autumn air. (The Cossacks) V25:70

On the look of Death— (There's a Certain Slant of Light) V6:212

On the reef of Norman's Woe! (The Wreck of the Hesperus) V31:317

On your head like a crown (Any Human to Another) V3:2

One could do worse that be a swinger of birches. (Birches) V13:15

"Only the Lonely," trying his best to sound like Elvis. (The Women Who Loved Elvis All Their Lives) V28:274

or a loose seed. (Freeway 280) V30:62

Or does it explode? (Harlem) V1:63

Or hear old Triton blow his wreathed horn. (The World Is Too Much with Us) V38:301

Or help to half-a-crown." (The Man He Killed) V3:167

Or if I die. (The Fly) V34:70

Or just some human sleep. (After Apple Picking) V32:3

or last time, we look. (In Particular) V20:125

or last time, we look. (In Particular) V20:125

Or might not have lain dormant forever. (Mastectomy) V26:123

or nothing (Queen-Ann's-Lace) V6:179

Or pleasures, seldom reached, again pursued. (A Nocturnal Reverie) V30:119–120

Or the dazzling crystal. (What I Expected) V36:313–314

or the one red leaf the snow releases in March. (ThreeTimes My Life Has Opened) V16:213

ORANGE forever. (Ballad of Orange and Grape) V10:18

our every corpuscle become an elf. (Moreover, the Moon) V20:153

Our love shall live, and later life renew." (Sonnet 75) V32:215

outside. (it was New York and beautifully, snowing ... (i was sitting in mcsorley's) V13:152

owing old (old age sticks) V3:246

P

patient in mind remembers the time. (Fading Light) V21:49

Penelope, who really cried. (An Ancient Gesture) V31:3

Perhaps he will fall. (Wilderness Gothic) V12:242

Petals on a wet, black bough (In a Station of the Metro) V2:116

Plaiting a dark red love-knot into her long black hair (The Highwayman) V4:68

Powerless, I drown. (Maternity) V21:142–143

Práise him. (Pied Beauty) V26:161

Pro patria mori. (Dulce et Decorum Est) V10:110

R

Rage, rage against the dying of the light (Do Not Go Gentle into that Good Night) V1:51

Raise it again, man. We still believe what we hear. (The Singer's House) V17:206

Remember. (Remember) V32:185

Remember the Giver fading off the lip (A Drink of Water) V8:66

Ride me. (Witness) V26:285

rise & walk away like a panther. (Ode to a Drum) V20:172–173

Rises toward her day after day, like a terrible fish (Mirror) V1:116

S

Sans teeth, sans eyes, sans taste, sans everything. (Seven Ages of Man) V35:213

Shall be lifted—nevermore! (The Raven) V1:202

shall be lost. (All Shall Be Restored) V36:2

Shall you be overcome. (Conscientious Objector) V34:46

Shantih shantih shantih (The Waste Land) V20:248–252

share my shivering bed. (Chorale) V25:51

she'd miss me. (In Response to Executive Order 9066: All Americans of Japanese Descent Must Report to Relocation Centers) V32:129

Show an affirming flame. (September 1, 1939) V27:235

Shuddering with rain, coming down around me. (Omen) V22:107

Simply melted into the perfect light. (Perfect Light) V19:187

Singing of him what they could understand (Beowulf) V11:3

Singing with open mouths their strong melodious songs (I Hear America Singing) V3:152

Sister, one of those who never married. (My Grandmother's Plot in the Family Cemetery) V27:155

Sleep, fly, rest: even the sea dies! (Lament for Ignacio Sánchez Mejías) V31:128–30

slides by on grease (For the Union Dead) V7:67

Slouches towards Bethlehem to be born? (The Second Coming) V7:179

so like the smaller stars we rowed among. (The Lotus Flowers) V33:108

So long lives this, and this gives life to thee (Sonnet 18) V2:222

So prick my skin. (Pine) V23:223–224

so that everything can learn the reason for my song. (Sonnet LXXXIX) V35:260

Somebody loves us all. (Filling Station) V12:57

Speak through my words and my blood. (The Heights of Macchu Picchu) V28:141

spill darker kissmarks on that dark. (Ten Years after Your Deliberate Drowning) V21:240

Stand still, yet we will make him run (To His Coy Mistress) V5:277

startled into eternity (Four Mountain Wolves) V9:132

Still clinging to your shirt (My Papa's Waltz) V3:192

Stood up, coiled above his head, transforming all. (A Tall Man Executes a Jig) V12:229

strangers ask. *Originally?* And I hesitate. (Originally) V25:146–147

Surely goodness and mercy shall follow me all the days of my life: and I will dwell in the house of the Lord for ever (Psalm 23) V4:103

syllables of an old order. (A Grafted Tongue) V12:93

T

Take any streetful of people buying clothes and groceries, cheering a hero or throwing confetti and blowing tin horns ... tell me if the lovers are losers ... tell me if any get more than the lovers ... in the dust ... in the cool tombs (Cool Tombs) V6:46

Than from everything else life promised that you could do? (Paradiso) V20:190–191

Than that you should remember and be sad. (Remember) V14:255

that does not see you. You must change your life. (Archaic Torso of Apollo) V27:3

that might have been sweet in Grudnow. (Grudnow) V32:74

That then I scorn to change my state with Kings (Sonnet 29) V8:198

that there is more to know, that one day you will know it. (Knowledge) V25:113

That when we live no more, we may live ever (To My Dear and Loving Husband) V6:228

That's the word. (Black Zodiac) V10:47

The benediction of the air. (Snow-Bound) V36:248–254

the bigger it gets. (Smart and Final Iris) V15:183

The bosom of his Father and his God (Elegy Written in a Country Churchyard) V9:74

the bow toward torrents of *veyz mir.* (Three To's and an Oi) V24:264

The crime was in Granada, his Granada. (The Crime Was in Granada) V23:55–56

The dance is sure (Overture to a Dance of Locomotives) V11:143

The eyes turn topaz. (Hugh Selwyn Mauberley) V16:30

the flames? (Another Night in the Ruins) V26:13

The frolic architecture of the snow. (The Snow-Storm) V34:196

The garland briefer than a girl's (To an Athlete Dying Young) V7:230

The Grasshopper's among some grassy hills. (On the Grasshopper and the Cricket) V32:161

The guidon flags flutter gayly in the wind. (Cavalry Crossing a Ford) V13:50

The hands gripped hard on the desert (At the Bomb Testing Site) V8:3

The holy melodies of love arise. (The Arsenal at Springfield) V17:3

the knife at the throat, the death in the metronome (Music Lessons) V8:117

The Lady of Shalott." (The Lady of Shalott) V15:97

The lightning and the gale! (Old Ironsides) V9:172

The lone and level sands stretch far away. (Ozymandias) V27:173

the long, perfect loveliness of sow (Saint Francis and the Sow) V9:222

The Lord survives the rainbow of His will (The Quaker Graveyard in Nantucket) V6:159

The man I was when I was part of it (Beware of Ruins) V8:43

the quilts sing on (My Mother Pieced Quilts) V12:169

The red rose and the brier (Barbara Allan) V7:11

The self-same Power that brought me there brought you. (The Rhodora) V17:191

The shaft we raise to them and thee (Concord Hymn) V4:30

the skin of another, what I have made is a curse. (Curse) V26:75

The sky became a still and woven blue. (Merlin Enthralled) V16:73

The song of the Lorelei. (The Lorelei) V37:146

The spirit of this place (To a Child Running With Outstretched Arms in Canyon de Chelly) V11:173

The town again, trailing your legs and crying! (Wild Swans) V17:221

the unremitting space of your rebellion (Lost Sister) V5:217

The woman won (Oysters) V4:91

The world should listen then—as I am listening now. (To a Sky-Lark) V32:252

their dinnerware. (Portrait of a Couple at Century's End) V24:214–215

their guts or their brains? (Southbound on the Freeway) V16:158

Then chiefly lives. (Virtue) V25:263

There are blows in life, so hard ... I just don't know! (The Black Heralds) V26:47

There is the trap that catches noblest spirits, that caught— they say— God, when he walked on earth (Shine, Perishing Republic) V4:162

there was light (Vancouver Lights) V8:246

They also serve who only stand and wait." ([On His Blindness] Sonnet 16) V3:262

They also serve who only stand and wait." (When I Consider (Sonnet XIX)) V37:302

They are going to some point true and unproven. (Geometry) V15:68

They have not sown, and feed on bitter fruit. (A Black Man Talks of Reaping) V32:21

They rise, they walk again (The Heaven of Animals) V6:76

They say a child with two mouths is no good. (Pantoun for Chinese Women) V29:242

They think I lost. I think I won (Harlem Hopscotch) V2:93

They'd eaten every one." (The Walrus and the Carpenter) V30:258–259

This is my page for English B (Theme for English B) V6:194

This Love (In Memory of Radio) V9:145

Tho' it were ten thousand mile! (A Red, Red Rose) V8:152

Though I sang in my chains like the sea (Fern Hill) V3:92

Till human voices wake us, and we drown (The Love Song of J. Alfred Prufrock) V1:99

Till Love and Fame to nothingness do sink (When I Have Fears that I May Cease to Be) V2:295

Till the gossamer thread you fling catch somewhere, O my soul. (A Noiseless Patient Spider) V31:190–91

To an admiring Bog! (I'm Nobody! Who Are You?) V35:83

To be a queen! (Fear) V37:71

To every woman a happy ending (Barbie Doll) V9:33

to float in the space between. (The Idea of Ancestry) V36:138

to glow at midnight. (The Blue Rim of Memory) V17:39

to its owner or what horror has befallen the other shoe (A Piéd) V3:16

To live with thee and be thy love. (The Nymph's Reply to the Shepherd) V14:241

To mock the riddled corpses round Bapaume. ("Blighters") V28:3

To strengthen whilst one stands." (Goblin Market) V27:96

To strive, to seek, to find, and not to yield (Ulysses) V2:279

To the moaning and the groaning of the bells (The Bells) V3:47

To the temple, singing. (In the Suburbs) V14:201

To wound myself upon the sharp edges of the night? (The Taxi) V30:211–212

too. (Birdfoot's Grampa) V36:21

torn from a wedding brocade. (My Mother Combs My Hair) V34:133

Turned to that dirt from whence he sprung. (A Satirical Elegy on the Death of a Late Famous General) V27:216

U

Undeniable selves, into your days, and beyond. (The Continuous Life) V18:51

under each man's eyelid. (Camouflaging the Chimera) V37:21

unexpectedly. (Fragment 16) V38:62

until at last I lift you up and wrap you within me. (It's like This) V23:138–139

Until Eternity. (The Bustle in a House) V10:62

unusual conservation (Chocolates) V11:17

Uttering cries that are almost human (American Poetry) V7:2

W

War is kind (War Is Kind) V9:253

watching to see how it's done. (I Stop Writing the Poem) V16:58

water. (Poem in Which My Legs Are Accepted) V29:262

We are satisfied, if you are; but why did I die?" (Losses) V31:167–68

we tread upon, forgetting. Truth be told. (Native Guard) V29:185

Went home and put a bullet through his head (Richard Cory) V4:117

Were not the one dead, turned to their affairs. (Out, Out—) V10:213

Were toward Eternity— (Because I Could Not Stop for Death) V2:27

What will survive of us is love. (An Arundel Tomb) V12:18

When I died they washed me out of the turret with a hose (The Death of the Ball Turret Gunner) V2:41

When locked up, bear down. (Fable for When There's No Way Out) V38:43

when they untie them in the evening. (Early in the Morning) V17:75

when you are at a party. (Social Life) V19:251

When you have both (Toads) V4:244

Where deep in the night I hear a voice (Butcher Shop) V7:43

Where ignorant armies clash by night (Dover Beach) V2:52

Which Claus of Innsbruck cast in bronze for me! (My Last Duchess) V1:166

Which for all you know is the life you've chosen. (The God Who Loves You) V20:88

which is not going to go wasted on me which is why I'm telling you about it (Having a Coke with You) V12:106

which only looks like an *l*, and is silent. (Trompe l'Oeil) V22:216

whirring into her raw skin like stars (Uncoiling) V35:277

white ash amid funereal cypresses (Helen) V6:92

Who are you and what is your purpose? (The Mystery) V15:138

Why am I not as they? (Lineage) V31:145–46

Wi' the Scots lords at his feit (Sir Patrick Spens) V4:177

Will always be ready to bless the day (Morning Walk) V21:167

will be easy, my rancor less bitter ... (On the Threshold) V22:128

Will hear of as a god." (How we Heard the Name) V10:167

Wind, like the dodo's (Bedtime Story) V8:33

windowpanes. (View) V25:246–247

With courage to endure! (Old Stoic) V33:144

With gold unfading, WASHINGTON! be thine. (To His Excellency General Washington) V13:213

with my eyes closed. (We Live by What We See at Night) V13:240

With silence and tears. (When We Two Parted) V29:297

with the door closed. (Hanging Fire) V32:93

With the slow smokeless burning of decay (The Wood-Pile) V6:252

With what they had to go on. (The Conquerors) V13:67

Without cease or doubt sew the sweet sad earth. (The Satyr's Heart) V22:187

Would scarcely know that we were gone. (There Will Come Soft Rains) V14:301

Wrapped in a larger. (Words are the Diminution of All Things) V35:316

Y

Ye know on earth, and all ye need to know (Ode on a Grecian Urn) V1:180

Yea, beds for all who come. (Up-Hill) V34:280

You live in this, and dwell in lovers' eyes (Sonnet 55) V5:246

You may for ever tarry. (To the Virgins, to Make Much of Time) V13:226

you who raised me? (The Gold Lily) V5:127

You're all that I can call my own. (Woman Work) V33:289

you'll have understood by then what these Ithakas mean. (Ithaka) V19:114